ACHI 2018

The Eleventh International Conference on Advances in Computer-Human Interactions

March 25 – 29, 2018

Rome, Italy

ACHI 2018 Editors

Birgit Gersbeck-Schierholz, Leibniz Universität Hannover, Germany
Christian Wögerer, Profactor GmbH, Austria
Steffen Gerhard Schulz, Karlsruhe Institute of Technology /Institute for Applied Computer Science (IAI), Germany

Printed from e-media with permission by:

Curran Associates, Inc.
57 Morehouse Lane
Red Hook, NY 12571

Some format issues inherent in the e-media version may also appear in this print version.

Printed by Curran Associates, Inc. (2018)

International Academy, Research, and Industry Association (IARIA)
412 Derby Way
Wilmington, DE 19810

Phone: (408) 893-6407
Fax: (408) 527-6351

petre@iaria.org

Additional copies of this publication are available from:

Curran Associates, Inc.
57 Morehouse Lane
Red Hook, NY 12571 USA
Phone: 845-758-0400
Fax: 845-758-2633
Email: curran@proceedings.com
Web: www.proceedings.com

Table of Contents

Facilitating Robots at Home: A Framework for Understanding Robot Facilitation 1
Rebekka Soma, Vegard Donnem Soyseth, Magnus Soyland, and Trenton Schulz

Storytelling at School with a Robot Playmate 7
Patrizia Marti and Iolanda Iacono

This is Not You! Identity Crisis in the 21st Century 13
Andrea Gasparini

Translation of Sign Language Into Text Using Kinect for Windows v2 19
Preeti Amatya, Kateryna Sergieieva, and Gerrit Meixner

Basic Study for a New Analysis Method of Biological Signals to Evaluate in Human Walking 27
Tatsuo Hisaoka, Naoki Hashimoto, Yusuke Kobayashi, Masaya Hori, Mayu Maeda, Hiroaki Inoue, and Shunji Simizu

Fundamental Study for A Noise Reduction Method on Human Brain Activity Data of NIRS using AR Model 33
Toshiya Tsubota, Tomohiko Kuroiwa, Takuya Kiryu, Yu Kikuchi, Hiroaki Inoue, Fumikazu Miwakeichi, and Shunji Shimizu

BrainSnake: Exploring Mode of Interaction in a Cooperative Multi-brain BCI Game Based on Alpha Activity 39
Marc van Almkerk, Lena Brandl, Rui Li, Pietro Romeo, and Mannes Poel

Real-time Shape-based Sensory Substitution for Object Localization and Recognition 45
Hossein Pourghaemi, Torkan Gholamalizadeh, Ahmad Mhaish, Gokhan Ince, and Damien Jade Duff

Programming in Natural Language: Building Algorithms from Human Descriptions 51
Alexander Wachtel, Felix Eurich, and Walter F. Tichy

Usability Evaluation with Heuristics, Beyond Nielsen's List 60
Toni Granollers

What's Hot in Interaction Design? An International Survey of Practitioners' Views on Personas 66
Engie Bashir and Simon Attfield

Exploring the User Security Experience of Mobile Payment in China 75
Jiaxin Zhang and Yan Luximon

Cyber Security Awareness Training Provided by the Competence Developing Game GHOST 81
Johannes Alexander Konig and Martin R. Wolf

Proposal and Evaluation of Kinect-based Physical Training System for Special Needs Education 88
Hiroki Matsuda, Hidemi Yamachi, Fumihiro Kumeno, and Kotomi Shiota

Fiction Design of a 3D Tutor for and with School Children 94
Monica Landoni, Emiliana Murgia, Fabrizio Gramuglio, and Giorgio Mnafredi

The User-Focused Storybuilding Framework for Competence Developing Games 98
Johannes Alexander Konig, Veronika Volker, and Martin R. Wolf

TeamAR – Generic Interface for Cooperation Using Augmented Reality 107
Dawid Pacholczyk and Mariusz Trzaska

Real-Time Recognition of Human Postures for Human-Robot Interaction 114
Zuhair Zafar, Rahul Venugopal, and Karsten Berns

Smart Home Resource Management based on Multi-Agent System Modeling Combined with SVM Machine Learning for Prediction and Decision-Making 120
Kalthoum Zaouali, Mohamed Lassaad Ammari, Mhamed Tabka, Amine Choueib, and Ridha Bouallegue

Numerical Approach to Simulation of Nanoprinting Processes 128
Tatyana Kudryashova, Sergey Polyakov, and Vistoria Podryga

Workflow Representations for Human and Artificial Agent Collaborations 132
Christian Wogerer, Georg Weichhart, and Andreas Pichler

MMAssist_II- A Lighthouse Project for Industrial Assistance 136
Christian Wogerer, Matthias Plasch, Manfred Tscheligi, and Sebastian Egger_Lampl

Approaches to a Practical Implementation of Industry 4.0 141
Ahmed Elkaseer, Hazem Ali, Mahmoud Salama, and Steffen Scholz

How Can a User-Centered Design Bring Innovation in a Business Intelligence Platform? 147
Elodie Rival, Celine Mateev, and Nicolas Maranzana

How do User Experience Experts Organize Their Knowledge of User Experience Criteria? 153
Josefina Isabel Gil Urrutia, Eric Brangier, and Laurent Cessat

The Impact of Visual Aesthetic Quality on User Engagement during Gameplay 159
Uttam Kokil

Time Before Negative Emotions Occur While Waiting for a Reply in Text Messaging with Read Receipt Functionality 165
Shogo Kato, Yasuyuki Ozawa, and Yuuki Kato

Perceived Usefulness of Features of Stickers in Text Messaging: Effects of Gender and Text-Messaging Dependency 168
Yuuki Kato, Shogo Kato, and Yasuyuki Ozawa

Fear, Feedback, Familiarity… How are These Connected? – Can familiarity as a design concept applied to digital feedback reduce fear? 171
Diana Saplacan and Jo Herstad

A Study on Visualization of User Reviews 180
Eric Yang

Moving with Style: Classifying Human and Robot Movement at Home 188
Trenton Schulz, Jo Herstad, and Jim Torresen

Detection and Classification of RBCs and WBCs in Urine Analysis with Deep Network 194
Xingguo Zhang, Guoyue Chen, Kazuki Saruta, and Yuki Terata

Line-Drawing Presentation Strategies with an Active-Wheel Mouse 199
Yoshihiko Nomura, Yoshiaki Kashino, and Tokuhiro Sugiura

Depth Perception for Virtual Object Displayed in Optical See-Through HMD 204
Kazutake Uehira and Masahiro Suzuki

Classifying Daily Activities Regardless of Wearable Motion Sensor Orientation 206
Aras Yurtman and Billur Barshan

Extended Method to Alternate the Estimation of Global Purposes and Local Objectives in Multiple Human-Agent Interaction 212
Yoshimasa Ohmoto, Takashi Suyama, and Toyoaki Nishida

Picking Assistance System with MS-KINECT and Projection Mapping 218
Yuki Takehara, Yoshitoshi Murata, and Takamichi Yoshikawa

User Centered Design of a Knowledge Management System for Production Workers 224
Gianni Campatelli and Sandro Mehic

Activity Recognition With Multiple Wearable Sensors for Industrial Applications 229
Adrien Malaise, Pauline Maurice, Francis Colas, Francois Charpillet, and Serena Ivaldi

Orientation and Mobility Skills Consideration for Visually Impaired Persons Based on Brain Activity 235
Hiroaki Inoue, Masaya Hori, Kobayashi Takuya, Takuya Kiryu, Yoshikazu Seki, and Shunji Shimizu

ACHI 2018

Forward

The eleventh edition of The International Conference on Advances in Computer-Human Interactions (ACHI 2018) conference was held in Rome, Italy, March 25 - 29, 2018.

The conference on Advances in Computer-Human Interaction, ACHI 2018, was a result of a paradigm shift in the most recent achievements and future trends in human interactions with increasingly complex systems. Adaptive and knowledge-based user interfaces, universal accessibility, human-robot interaction, agent-driven human computer interaction, and sharable mobile devices are a few of these trends. ACHI 2018 brought also a suite of specific domain applications, such as gaming, social, medicine, education and engineering.

The event was very competitive in its selection process and very well perceived by the international scientific and industrial communities. As such, it is attracting excellent contributions and active participation from all over the world. We were very pleased to receive a large amount of top quality contributions.

The accepted papers covered a wide range of human-computer interaction related topics such as graphical user interfaces, input methods, training, recognition, and applications.
We believe that the ACHI 2018 contributions offered a large panel of solutions to key problems in all areas of human-computer interaction.

We take here the opportunity to warmly thank all the members of the ACHI 2018 technical program committee as well as the numerous reviewers. The creation of such a broad and high quality conference program would not have been possible without their involvement. We also kindly thank all the authors that dedicated much of their time and efforts to contribute to the ACHI 2018. We truly believe that thanks to all these efforts, the final conference program consists of top quality contributions.

This event could also not have been a reality without the support of many individuals, organizations and sponsors. In addition, we also gratefully thank the members of the ACHI 2018 organizing committee for their help in handling the logistics and for their work that is making this professional meeting a success.

We hope the ACHI 2018 was a successful international forum for the exchange of ideas and results between academia and industry and to promote further progress in the human-computer interaction field.

We also hope that Rome provided a pleasant environment during the conference and everyone saved some time for exploring this beautiful city.

ACHI 2018 Chairs

ACHI Steering Committee
Leslie Miller, Iowa State University - Ames, USA
Alma Leora Culén , University of Oslo, Norway
Hermann Kaindl, Vienna University of Technology, Austria
Uttam Kokil, Kennesaw State University Marietta, USA
Flaminia Luccio, University Ca' Foscari of Venice, Italy
Jaehyun Park, Incheon National University (INU), South Korea

ACHI Industry/Research Advisory Committee
Jacki O'Neill, Microsoft Research, India
Weizhi Meng, Institute for Infocomm Research (I2R), Singapore
Harald Milchrahm, Institute for Softwaretechnology - Technical University Graz, Austria
Steffen Scholz, Karlsruhe Institute of Technology (KIT), Germany
Ryo Ishii, NTT Corporation, Japan
Zahen Malla Osman, The National Center for Scientific Research (CNRS), France
Mohammed Korayem, Careerbuilder.com, USA

ACHI 2018

COMMITTEE

ACHI Steering Committee
Leslie Miller, Iowa State University - Ames, USA
Alma Leora Culén , University of Oslo, Norway
Hermann Kaindl, Vienna University of Technology, Austria
Uttam Kokil, Kennesaw State University Marietta, USA
Flaminia Luccio, University Ca' Foscari of Venice, Italy
Jaehyun Park, Incheon National University (INU), South Korea

ACHI Industry/Research Advisory Committee
Jacki O'Neill, Microsoft Research, India
Weizhi Meng, Institute for Infocomm Research (I2R), Singapore
Harald Milchrahm, Institute for Softwaretechnology - Technical University Graz, Austria
Steffen Scholz, Karlsruhe Institute of Technology (KIT), Germany
Ryo Ishii, NTT Corporation, Japan
Zahen Malla Osman, The National Center for Scientific Research (CNRS), France
Mohammed Korayem, Careerbuilder.com, USA

ACHI 2018 Technical Program Committee

Andrea F. Abate, University of Salerno, Italy
Majed Alshamari, King Faisal University, Saudi Arabia
Popi Anastasiou, Open University, UK
David Benyon, Edinburgh Napier University, UK
Tobias Blanke, King's College London, UK
Christos Bouras, University of Patras and Computer Technology Institute & Press «Diophantus», Greece
Christian Bourret, UPEM - Université Paris-Est Marne-la-Vallée, France
DanaKai Bradford, Australian eHealth Research Centre | Commonwealth Scientific and Industrial Research Organisation, Australia
Jan Broer, ifib - Institut für Informationsmanagement Bremen GmbH, Germany
Adrien Brunet, Karlsruhe Institute of Technology (KIT)/Institute for Applied Computer Science, Germany
Marcin Butlewski, Poznan University of Technology, Poland
Nan Cao, NYU Shanghai, China
Jacek Chmielewski, Poznan University of Economics, Poland
Andre Constantino da Silva, Federal Institute of São Paulo – IFSP, Brazil
Patricia Cornelio, University of Sussex, UK
David Costa, Universidade de Lisboa, Portugal
André Magno Costa de Araújo, Federal University of Pernambuco, Brazil
Antonio Diaz Tula, University of São Paulo, Brazil
Rolf Drechsler, University of Bremen/DFKI, Germany
Ahmed Elkaseer, Karlsruhe Institute of Technology (KIT)/Institute for Automation and Applied Informatics (IAI), Germany
Larbi Esmahi, Athabasca University, Canada
Sascha Fagel, KV Telematik GmbH, Germany

Peter Forbrig, University of Rostock, Germany
Somchart Fugkeaw, Mahidol University - Nakhonpathom, Thailand
Bernard Grabot, LGP-ENIT, France
Denis Gracanin, Virginia Tech, USA
Andrina Granić, University of Split, Croatia
Toni Granollers, University of Lleida, Spain
John Alexis Guerra Gómez, Los Andes University, Colombia / UC Berkeley, USA
Celmar Guimarães da Silva, University of Campinas, Brazil
Ido Guy, eBay, USA
Maki Habib, The American University in Cairo, Egypt
Till Halbach, Norwegian Computing Center, Oslo, Norway
Ibrahim A. Hameed, Norwegian University of Science and Technology (NTNU), Ålesund, Norway
Sung H. Han, POSTECH, South Korea
José R. Hilera, University of Alcalá, Spain
Olivier Hugues, MINES ParisTech - PSL Research University, France
Francisco Iniesto, Institute of Educational Technology - The Open University, UK
Jamshed Iqbal, University of Jeddah, Saudi Arabia
Gökhan İnce, Istanbul Technical University, Turkey
Ryo Ishii, NTT Corporation, Japan
Shahram Jalaliniya, Malmö University, Sweden
Suhas Govind Joshi, University of Oslo, Norway
Hanmin Jung, Korea Institute of Science & Technology Information, Korea
Katarzyna Kaczmarek, Systems Research Institute - Polish Academy of Sciences, Poland
Hermann Kaindl, Vienna University of Technology, Austria
Ahmed Kamel, Concordia College, Moorhead, USA
Mahmoud Kamel Mahmoud Abdalaziz, Digitex Corporation, Egypt / Fashion Libretto Corporation, Italy
Saras Karanam, Utrecht University, Netherlands
Ljilja (Lilia) Ruzic Kascak, Georgia Institute of Technology, USA
Jesuk Ko, Gwangju University, Korea
Uttam Kokil, Kennesaw State University Marietta, USA
Mohammed Korayem, Careerbuilder.com, USA
Nataliya Kosmyna, Inria Rennes, France
Yong Ming Kow, City University of Hong Kong, Hong Kong
Neha Kumar, Georgia Tech, USA
Jiyoung Kwahk, POSTECH, South Korea
Wen-Hsing Lai, National Kaohsiung First University of Science and Technology, Taiwan
Dagmawi Lemma, Addis Ababa University, Ethiopia
Alma Leora Culén , University of Oslo, Norway
Tsai-Yen Li, National Chengchi University, Taiwan
Wenjuan Li, City University of Hong Kong, Hong Kong
Flaminia Luccio, University Ca' Foscari of Venice, Italy
Sergio Luján Mora, University of Alicante, Spain
Ameersing Luximon, Hong Kong Polytechnic University, Hong Kong
Yan Luximon, The Hong Kong Polytechnic University, Hong Kong
Zahen Malla Osman, The National Center for Scientific Research (CNRS), France
Weizhi Meng, Technical University of Denmark, Denmark
Daniel R. Mestre, CNRS Institute of Movement Sciences - Mediterranean Virtual Reality Center, Marseilles, France

Harald Milchrahm, Institute for Softwaretechnology - Technical University Graz, Austria
Les Miller, Iowa State University, USA
Yasser F. O. Mohammad, Assiut University, Egypt / KDDI Laboratories, Japan
Nicholas H. Müller, University of Applied Sciences Würzburg-Schweinfurt, Germany
Jaime Muñoz-Arteaga, Universidad Autónoma de Aguascalientes, Mexico
Minoru Nakayama, Tokyo Institute of Technology, Japan
Roger Ng, Hong Kong Polytechnic University, Hong Kong
Jacki O'Neill, Microsoft Research, India
Rita Orji, Dalhousie University, Canada
Jaehyun Park, Incheon National University (INU), South Korea
Linda Pfeiffer, Chemnitz University of Technology, Germany
Marina Puyuelo, Universitat Politècnica de València, Spain
Didier Puzenat, LIRIS - University Lyon 2, France
Rafael Radkowski, Iowa State University, USA
Andreas Riener, University of Applied Sciences Ingolstadt, Germany
Antonio M. Rinaldi, Università degli Studi di Napoli Federico II - Napoli, Italy
Cuauhtémoc Rivera-Loaiza, Universidad Michoacana de San Nicolás de Hidalgo, Mexico
Covadonga Rodrigo San Juan, E.T.S.I. Informática - UNED, Spain
Paul Rosenthal, University of Rostock, Germany
Juan Rosso, University Grenoble Alpes | CNRS, France
Ljilja (Lilia) Ruzic Kascak, Georgia Institute of Technology, USA
Sandra Sanchez-Gordon, Escuela Politécnica Nacional, Ecuador
Antonio-Jose Sanchez-Salmeron, Universitat Politecnica de Valencia, Spain
Danielle Santos Alves, Universidade Federal de Pernambuco - UFPE, Brazil
Steffen Scholz, Karlsruhe Institute of Technology (KIT), Germany
Trenton W. Schulz, University of Oslo / Norsk Regnesentral, Norway
Preethi Srinivas, Indiana University Center for Aging Research | Regenstrief Institute Inc., USA
Cristian Stanciu, University Politehnica of Bucharest, Romania
Ana Tajadura-Jimenez, Universidad Carlos III, Spain / University College London, UK
Hilda Tellioglu, Vienna University of Technology, Austria
Azeemsha Thacham Poyil, University of Hertfordshire, UK
Tommaso Venturini, INRIA / Institut Rhônalpin des Systèmes Complexes, France
Guri B. Verne, University of Oslo, Norway
Connie Veugen, Vrije Universiteit Amsterdam, Netherlands
Michael L. Walters, University of Hertfordshire, UK
Alexander Wachtel, Karlsruhe Institute of Technology, Germany
Pamela Wisniewski, University of Central Florida, USA
Y. Wayne Wu, University of Illinois at Urbana-Champaign, USA
Anbang Xu, IBM Research - Almaden, USA
Bin Xu, Cornell University, USA
Anja Zeising, ifib - Research Institute at the University of Bremen, Germany
Xiaoyi Zhang, University of Washington, USA
Ye Zhu, Cleveland State University, USA

Copyright Information

Facilitating Robots at Home

A Framework for Understanding Robot Facilitation

Rebekka Soma, Vegard Dønnem Søyseth, Magnus Søyland, Trenton Schulz
Department of Informatics
University of Oslo
Oslo, Norway
e-mail: [rebsaurus|vegardds|magnusoy|trentonw]@ifi.uio.no

Abstract—**One of the primary characteristics of robots is the ability to move autonomously in the same space as humans. In what ways does movement influence the interaction between humans and robot? In this paper, we examine how work is changed by the deployment of service robots. Through a multiple case study, the phenomenon is investigated, both in an industrial and domestic context. Through analyzing our data, we propose a framework for understanding the change of tasks named the Robot Facilitation Framework.**

Keywords-robots; facilitating; tasks; work; domestic; human-robot interaction

I. INTRODUCTION

Robots have been used in factories, offices, and hospitals for several decades. They have been cleaning floors, transporting materials, keeping watch, and operating in dangerous environments to reduce general labor and costs [1][2]. The typical aim of introducing robots into workplaces is to increase productivity by automating work, which will decrease costs by reducing the amount of manual work [3]. But often the result is not so much a *reduction* of manual work as a *redistribution* of manual work. As robots are introduced into work environments, the way work is performed in that environment *changes*. For instance, Argote et al. [1] reported that the work of the operators in their study shifted from primarily manual lifting activities to cognitive monitoring activities. Recently, the addition of robots in Amazon warehouses changed the workers' days from being centered around lifting to keeping an eye on the robots [4].

Robots in the form of machines autonomously moving around in space started making their way into homes in the beginning of the 2000s with vacuum cleaning robots [5]. Household robots are qualitatively different from traditional household appliances. Tools for home maintenance and cleaning are often kept at specific locations in the home from where they cannot move by themselves. An inherent quality of something stationary is that you decide where it goes, and it stays where you place it. Conversely, the mobile nature of a domestic service robot as it autonomously navigates the home gives the robot an element of ubiquity and sharing a domestic space with them is not without problems [6].

Historically, the way humans perform work has always evolved, from the very first technological advances such as knives and spears, through wash buckets and steam engines, to present day laptops and kitchen appliances. However, one common factor with technological advances is certain tasks become *easier*, but work never really disappears [7]. The work itself only changes forms as new technologies are introduced into our lives. A new tool requires maintenance to keep working and creates room for other tasks by allowing higher speed and precision. A vacuum cleaning robot does not create a void of work where you once had the traditional vacuum cleaner; the work associated with keeping a clean house merely changes form—just as it did when the traditional vacuum cleaner replaced the wash bucket and mop.

Because the human-robot relationship is different from other human-computer relationships [8], we must develop a different understanding of other technologies. As a technology for keeping a clean house, the ubiquitous nature of the technological space of domestic robots overlaps with the entire physical and social space of the home. Much research has been done on understanding how we accept robots as a part of the household [8]–[11]. However, there is not much research that examines *how* space is shared; what are the changes in practices that will eventually lead to acceptance or rejection of the robot. In this paper, we introduce a framework for understanding how tasks and task distributions (practices) change as robots are introduced into an environment.

This paper's contribution is to introduce the *Robot Facilitation Framework* to classify stages of facilitation of robots. We introduce the framework and its components: *pre-*, *peri-*, and *post-facilitation* that are the result of our analysis of our case studies. We start by looking at related work (Section II). Then, we present our method and three case studies that helped form our framework (Section III). In Section IV, we present our framework and its components. In Section V, we apply the framework to the cases of robots being introduced into homes from the studies in Section II. We find that the Robot Facilitation Framework does not replace other frameworks in human-robot interaction, but provides a new way to understand use of robots. We also discuss the relationship between the different types of facilitation. In Section VI, we provide our conclusion and opportunities for future work.

II. RELATED WORK

There are a few long-term studies of service robots in domestic settings. These focus on how and why people accept robots into their homes over time and use different frameworks for doing so.

Forlizzi and DiSalvo [8] use an ecological approach for determining how mobile, autonomous robots might fit into the domestic space, and how they differ from traditional vacuum cleaners. "The difference of physicality, autonomy, and mobility calls for a re-thinking of the experience of technologies in the domestic environment" [9]. They emphasize that robots and household members should be able to adapt to each other.

Looking at the social experience people deveplop around the use of a product (*product ecology*), Forlizzi [12] shows how robots, like other technologies, become social products as they are accepted into the home. In a product ecology, the environment affects how the product is used, and in turn, the use of the product itself changes the users and the context as a result. The products in the ecology simultaneously shape roles, social norms, human behavior, and how other products are used. There are five dimensions to understand how a product influences the product ecology: *functionality*, *aesthetics*, *symbolism*, *sociality*, and *emotionality*. These can in combination or individually start a process of sense-making, linking the familiar to the unfamiliar [12].

Forlizzi's study [12] compared the adoption of a traditional vacuum cleaner and a robotic one and found that the robotic vacuum cleaner caused a change in the product ecologies in the household while the traditional did not. The Roomba had a substantial and lasting impact on people, activities, and the use of other cleaning products within the product ecology.

Inspired by Forlizzi's use of the product ecology, Sung, Guo, Grinter, and Christensen [8] developed the Domestic Robot Ecology (DRE). This framework provides a holistic view on long-term interactions with robots and thus people's long-term acceptance of them. It looks at how people's attitudes and interactions towards robots change over time, especially as the novelty of the robot wears off (*the novelty effect* [13]).

The DRE has several dimensions. First, there are four temporal steps householders experience during their robot acceptance: (1) *pre-adoption*, (2) *adoption*, (3) *adaption*, and (4) *use and retention*. Second, there are three roles for the robots during this time: (1) *a tool to complete tasks*, (2) *a mediator to incur changes in the environments*, and (3) *an actor to elicit social responses*. Sung et al. combined these and presented three key aspects for how robots interact within all the four temporal steps, taking on one of the three roles. These aspects are: (1) *physical and social space*, the platform where the interactions can take place; (2) *social actors*, the living members of the home, such as householders, guests, and pets; and (3) *tasks*, the activity the robot is designed to serve. Thus, five types of relationships can occur, where the robot can be *a tool* to perform tasks, *an agent* directly impacting the surrounding environment, *a mediator* that motivates people to make changes to the environment, *a mediator* that enhances the social relationships, or *an agent* that engages with people in social events. With all these dimensions, the DRE provides a holistic view of the relationships that robots shape in the home and how these change over time.

Fink, Bauwens, Kaplan, and Dillenbourg [10] used the DRE to understand long-term adoption and acceptance of Roomba robots in the home.

III. METHOD

The study is based on multiple case studies [14]. We used a set of qualitative inquiry sessions in the investigation of robot facilitation. Each case consists of observations or multiple interviews. Case 1 is the Automated Ground Vehicles (AGV) at the hospital (Section III.A). In this case, we interviewed an operating manager on two separate occasions. Case 2 is the investigation of lawnmower robots (Section III.B). For this case, we interviewed two different owners. Case 3 is an ongoing study with older adults who borrow vacuum cleaning robots (Section III.C). This case is based on observations. The interview questions were open-ended and different in each case. But the questions *between* the participants in a case are the same. The interviews and observations was analyzed by coding interview transcriptions described in detail in Søyseth and Søyland [15]. As this was qualitative data, so statistics are unavailable.

A. AGV at a Hospital

There are numerous examples of robots within industry and organizations, but they are often found in separate and enclosed areas where only authorized personnel have access [16]. However, our informant told us that multiple hospitals have employed AGVs for several years to do most of the heavy-lifting transport tasks and thus decrease the need for human porters. These robots operate in the same areas as the hospital staff and thereby create an arena for observing spatial encounters between robots and humans.

Since 2008, a major Norwegian hospital has used an AGV system consisting of 22 robots. The robots have been in service for nearly ten years. This allows us to disregard the possibility of a novelty effect commonly caused by robots; the staff would regard them as commonplace.

The AGV robots require building structure and infrastructure to accommodate them. They follow magnetic markers embedded in the floor throughout their operating areas and use strategically placed charging stations. These infrastructure requirements were part of the planning and building process of the hospital. The robots operate mostly in the hospital basement where there are no unattended patients. A patient can only encounter a robot when it takes an elevator up to one of the hospital departments. Even then, the robots venture only a few meters into the departments to deliver their goods at a dedicated delivery nook.

According to our informant, the hospital administration initially assumed that the robots could operate almost entirely without supervision, needing only occasional checks by an operator. However, the hospital staff soon realized this was a flawed assumption. "If you leave the screen for 10 to 20 minutes, there is a standstill somewhere," said our informant.

Furthermore, he explained how a single standstill quickly would result in cascading failure. This would eventually lead to a total stop of the system since the AGVs cannot pass each

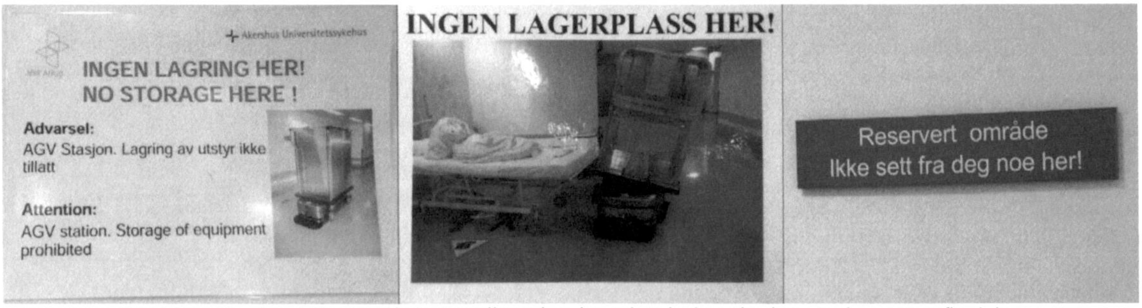

Figure 1: (*Left and center*) makeshift signs to tell people to leave the robot's nooks alone; (*right*) a more refined sign.

other. This highlights the importance of facilitating for seamless operation during the robot's working time.

Standstills can occur due to technical problems in the AGV themselves, but often it is "human error." Our informant described how the medical staff would leave all kinds of objects in the magnetic path or the delivery nooks of the robot. As the AGV has no way to make its way *around* obstacles, all obstacles are insurmountable. In these situations, the only solution is for an operator to find and remove the obstacle. To reduce the frequency of these standstills, signs had been put up throughout the hospital to inform people that the robots need a clear path to operate, reminding them not to leave anything in the hallways. Some of these signs look very professional and refined (Figure 1, right), while others have more of a makeshift look (Figure 1, left and center).

The maintenance and ongoing facilitation for the AGVs require three full-time employees. The employees' main task is ensuring the robots do not come to a standstill, working in shifts to always be present for robot monitoring. As mentioned above, the hospital had not expected the level of robot supervision required. The constant monitoring now carried out was not in the initial plan of the deployment strategy. Though the AGVs require a substantial amount of facilitation, their deployments give a net positive amount of work; they provide the same work as 15-25 full-time employees, based on between 400-500 assignments every day.

During the first two to three years of using the AGV within the hospital, three technicians from the AGV's manufacturer worked full-time on the implementation and configuration of the system, after which they considered the system stable enough for them to leave.

B. *Robotic Lawnmower*

In the case of the lawnmower robots, we interviewed two different individuals owning a lawnmower robot. Both robots were of the same brand and had the same functionality.

When the informants had set up the robot for their garden environments, the amount of setup work required help from family members. The preliminarily work of setting up the perimeter fence and programming amounted to between two to three days for each of the informants. This workload was *expected* by the users: They were informed in advance about what was needed to be done to set up the robots correctly.

However, both informants reported they needed to watch the robot during its working hours to make sure that it was not stuck somewhere. Moreover, they told us how they now kept their gardens clear of foreign objects, such as gardening tools, flowerpots and other decorations.

One informant had a diverse garden with steep hills, some steps making up a tiny stair, a sandpit from when her children were younger, some berry bushes, a flowerbed, an apple tree, and a large tree stump. Most of these obstacles created more work in facilitating the robot's work than she and her husband had anticipated. For instance, during late summer and early fall, apples fall from their apple tree, the fallen apples often caused the robot to stop altogether. Our informant reported picking apples off the lawn every morning to help the robot complete its job.

Furthermore, it was difficult for the robot to access all parts of the garden. In most of the accessible places, it would often get stuck. Our informant described an issue revolving around her robot's ability to get up the steep hill and the placement of the tree stump. The stump sat just at the top of the hill, right where the ground flattens out. To climb the hill, the robot needs momentum. The robot cannot see, and it can only detect obstacles by bumping into them. So, it can never plan its trajectory with these obstacles in consideration and simply moves in a randomized pattern. Thus, whenever it hit the tree stump, it would lose momentum and get stuck. This happened nearly every day and occurred more frequently on rainy days.

Since the robot getting stuck and disabling it from carrying out its task was inconvenient, the informant and her husband decided to remove the tree stump (Figure 2). She was uncertain whether she and her husband would have removed the stump if they did not have the robot: She found the stump charming, and had imagined placing flowerpots on it.

She had also contemplated removing the apple tree, but so far, she has not taken this measure as she has some regrets over removing the tree stump. Removing the apple tree, like removing the stump, is an irreversible action.

Figure 2: (*Left*) the tree stub being chopped up and removed, and (*right*) the robot going down the hill

C. Robotic Vacuum Cleaner

Setting up a robotic vacuum cleaner is a smaller job than setting up a robot lawnmower. Its navigational technology does not require a perimeter fence to move within the domestic environment. The process varies between brands and is a little more complicated if the user decides to use the smartphone application, but the only *required* set up by the user is placing the robot's docking station.

In our study, we provided a robotic vacuum cleaner to five older adult participants living independently in their own apartments. Most participants did not have wireless internet or a smartphone, and could thus not use the smartphone app, making set-up in their apartments easy.

While robotic vacuum cleaners can run without the supervision of human operators, most participants did not trust the robot to run while they were not home. They preferred to keep an eye on the robot during its operation time to prevent it from getting stuck or accessing unwanted areas.

IV. FINDINGS

We have seen how all the robots we have investigated altered existing tasks and added new ones for them to operate properly. Further, we saw that the tasks varied widely; from small alterations in the operational environment, through continuous tidying tasks, to substantial infrastructure modifications. We call all such tasks *facilitation*. After examining the tasks, we saw that the tasks begin to coalesce in some categories: *pre-facilitation*, tasks done before the robot can operate; *peri-facilitation,* tasks done while the robot is operating; and *post-facilitation*, larger tasks done after the robot has been deployed a while that reduce peri-facilitating tasks.

A. The Robot Facilitation Framework

The Robot Facilitation Framework helps designers understand *how work changes*. Its central idea is understanding how the introduction of robots change tasks and task distribution. The framework describes how we share space with a robot, rather than describing how we accept robots into our space. The framework has three components.

1) Pre-facilitation

The first kind of facilitation in our framework takes place right before the deployment of the robot. We call this *pre*-facilitation. The user makes the changes both necessary for the robot to start, as well as alterations they think will merit the robot's operations. Often, facilitation is required for starting the robot, such as the placement of a docking station and fence cable. Other changes to the environment are made because the user assumes the facilitation will accommodate the robot, for example, removing power cords to avoid tangling.

2) Peri-facilitation

However, the changes made in pre-facilitation are rarely sufficient. The technologies in today's robots require an uncluttered operating area, which is rarely found in domestic settings [17]. Consequently, to facilitate a smooth operation period for the robots, humans need to continuously tidy. We have discovered some required tasks might come as a surprise to the user and are not easy to anticipate such as picking up apples. As robots today cannot take care of and repair themselves, users also need to perform maintenance on the robot. Maintenance activities include changing the blade on the robotic lawnmower and changing the brushes of the robot vacuum cleaner, as well as larger maintenance tasks as done by technicians from the manufacturer that delivers robots in systems such as AGV found in the hospital.

We call this *peri*-facilitation because the tasks are required continuously during the robot's operational time. The bulk of time one used to spend doing the tasks now performed by the robot is replaced with smaller tasks requiring a few minutes every day. The tasks are performed by the user to make sure the robot operations run smoothly, such as removing clutter to prevent it from getting stuck, assisting it should it get stuck in or under something, and all time spent on robot maintenance. In other words, peri-facilitating tasks are a form of everyday maintenance.

3) Post-facilitation

As the users find recurring patterns for facilitation required during the robot's operations, they can decide to make bigger changes to their environment—such as removing a tree stump—as a way of reducing the need for peri-facilitation. We call this *post*-facilitation. A thorough understanding of how the robot operates in the specific domestic settings is required to make post-facilitation changes.

V. DISCUSSION

In Section II, we briefly presented a few long-term studies of service robots in domestic settings. These studies focused mainly on how and why people accept these robots into their homes over time. The product ecology and the Domestic Robot Ecology have their focus on *acceptance* of robot technology. Our framework is a supplement to other frameworks on understanding use of robots.

In this section, we compare the Robot Facilitation Framework to the Domestic Robot Ecology and product ecology. The Robot Facilitation Framework looks at how work changes with the introduction of a robot. The Domestic Robot Ecology and product ecology look at adoption and acceptance, but both possess elements that fit within the Robot Facilitation Framework. Finally, we discuss the interrelationship between the three categories of robot facilitation.

A. Robot Facilitation Framework in Other Cases

Sung et al. [8] describe robot acceptance as happening in four temporal phases. In the pre-adoption phase, the users form their expectation of the robot. Because the Roomba requires nothing but placing the docking station before it can start, users with high expectations of the robot perform little to no pre-facilitation. When little pre-facilitation has taken place, the robots could cause accidents. Whenever the Roomba caused accidents, the participants in their study made changes to the environment necessary to prevent the same accident from reoccurring: "Some of the actions included casual and temporary changes that they needed to repeat in each operation. Other changes were more permanent" [8] The more temporary changes were things like folding area rugs, blocking Roomba with objects, and picking up clutter. The changes considered more permanent included things like placing books under lamps to prevent Roomba from climbing it, or removing rug fringe to prevent it from getting stuck. These are good examples of both peri- and post-facilitation.

Forlizzi and DiSalvo [9] point out that the Roomba's need of a clutter-free environment caused some participants to engage in what they refer to as "pre-cleaning activities." By doing some pre-cleaning, the home environment was ready for Roomba to do the cleaning without supervision. They describe this as an "unusual dynamic between the product, the physical environment, and the participant" [9] where the participants must decide when they should intervene during the Roombas operational activities. Though there are few concrete examples described here, the problem area as described where the functionalities of the Roomba lead users to accommodate the robot's operations is the basis for peri-facilitation and key to understanding the processes around this type of facilitation.

Fink et al. [10] observed that their participants made changes to the environment that was encouraged by the robot. They also describe how participants spent different amounts of time on adjusting the space before turning Roomba on, and that some households had to solve further issues such as moving away delicate objects. In their study, participants expressed not wanting to let the Roomba work by itself at home while they were out, illustrating the need to be there and peri-facilitate should Roomba crash, get stuck, or other unforeseen peri-facilitating tasks. They further describe how participants, children especially, would assist the robot by collecting crumbs and placing them directly in front of the robot, or build walls out of obstacles.

Cesta, Cortellessa, Orlandini, and Tiberio [11] examined a telepresence robot in the home of an elderly couple over a year. The study had both pre-facilitation to prepare for the robot's arrival and peri-facilitation as the robot was in use. Since the study had a known end, there was no post-facilitation, but the suggestions from the couple about where the robot should be placed when charging indicate that post-facilitation would be needed for the robot to be used after the study.

B. Interrelationship between the types of facilitation

Setting boundaries for categories based on qualitative data is rarely clear-cut. When analyzing human-robot observations through the Robot Facilitation Framework, we find that some actions of facilitation are hard to place completely within one of the three categories. Should the three categories be considered as *types* of facilitation, *stages* of facilitation, or *phases* of facilitation?

In the following, we discuss the relationship between these categories, as illustrated in Figure 3. The solid arrows represent how the process of facilitating for a robot evolves. A pre-facilitation task would be finding a spot for the docking station, and setting it up. As the robot works, emptying out the robot's dust bin would be a peri-facilitating task. Upgrading the infrastructure to increase the usefulness of the robot is a post-facilitation task, which leads back to peri-facilitation as the robot works in the new environment.

However, some relations are more uncertain than others. These are marked by dashed arrows and question marks.

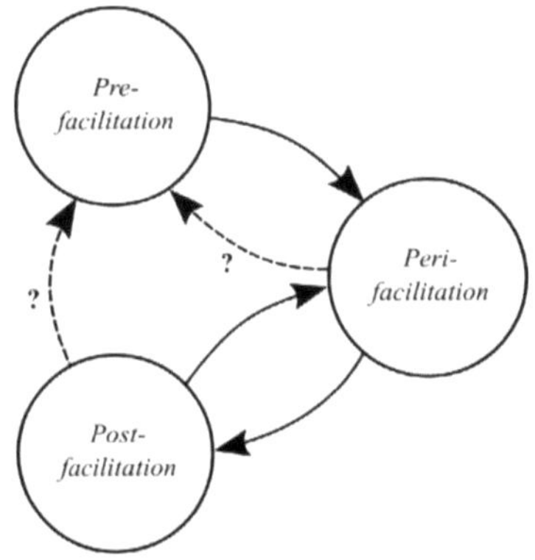

Figure 3: Interrelationship between the three facilitation categories

These uncertain relations raise questions such as "can one move from peri- and post-facilitation to pre-facilitation, or does pre-facilitation only happen once during the deployment of the service robot?" We need to decide what actions should be considered pre-facilitation. For instance, can pre-cleaning activities, as described by Forlizzi and DiSalvo [8] take place after the deployment of the robot, but not during its operational time? In the view of the Robot Facilitation Framework, should activities performed during the deployment period of the robot, but not when it is *currently active* be considered a *pre-* or a *peri-*facilitating task?

As we saw in the example of AGV, the infrastructure of the hospital tied to the deployment of the robots was planned during the construction of the hospital itself. Ozkil et al. [18] examined what was needed to implement service robots in a Danish hospital, a process which can be understood as pre-facilitation of robots.

This shows that pre-facilitation can be a huge process, starting already when planning a building, or it can be next to nothing should the user not feel the need to change anything in their domestic environment before they start the robot. Indeed, it seems that the extent of the pre-facilitation can vary greatly, and to some degree depend on the complexity of the environment it will be operating in, as well as its infrastructure. From our analysis, pre-facilitation sets the foundation for which new tasks arise as part of peri-facilitation when the robot is operationally active. Next, depending on how cumbersome the peri-facilitating tasks are, as well as their persistence and recurrence, will determine what measures will be taken to avoid these in the future. When changes are done to avoid certain peri-facilitating tasks, the users have post-facilitated their robot. What is unclear when it comes to the relationship between the stages, is whether the user after such a change finds themselves doing pre-facilitation again, or if they find themselves right back doing peri-facilitation.

Finally, how big is as post-facilitation change? Are only irreversible changes eligible post-facilitating actions, or can smaller one-time actions that could easily be reversed fit into this category? Irreversible changes include hiring full-time workers to look after the robot, removing a tree stump so the lawnmower can get up the hill, or replacing a floor lamp with a wall-mounted lamp so that vacuuming is easier. A reversible change would be placing a book under a lamp to prevent the robot from climbing it.

Tying all these questions together, we see that the answer to one of them will have consequences for the others. If placing books underneath a lamp is not post-facilitation because it is not irreversible, it must be either pre- or peri-facilitation. If peri-facilitation can only take place while the robot is running (except whenever the user is doing maintenance *on* the robot), then it must be pre-facilitation. However, if we define pre-facilitation as something that only takes place *before* the deployment, then it must be either post- or peri-facilitation after all. Is it important for the framework that post-facilitation actions are recognized as something big and irreversible? Similarly, is it important for the framework to recognize pre-facilitation actions as only taking place before the deployment of the robot?

VI. Conclusion and Future Work

Our study consisted of multiple case studies, considering human-robot interactions at a Norwegian hospital, in the gardens of two robotic lawnmower owners, and observations of elderly deploying robotic vacuum cleaner for one month. We found that work did not disappear, but that tasks were redistributed. We presented the Robot Facilitation Framework that divides facilitation into *pre-*, *peri-*, and *post-facilitation*. Using this framework, data collected from other studies can be understood in a different light, focusing on how work changes when robots are deployed. The categorization simplifies targeting challenges in the interaction between humans and robotic technologies. Moreover, it may also indicate specific design implications for what tasks should be put in which category. It also helps us to understand the amount of work that is included in introducing and keeping a robot in a location. This can help people to determine how best to introduce and use robots in new areas.

There is more that can be done with this framework. There is no precise answer to which activities belong to which categories. To make our categories and the relations between them more precise, we will carry out more studies of robots in use and analyze them. As a part of this, we will explore how facilitation relates to maintenance, performativity, and mediation, and how robot users experience to share their space with robots. This should make it easier for others to apply the framework in future scenarios where robots are introduced at work and at home.

Acknowledgments

This work is partly supported by the Research Council of Norway as a part of the Multimodal Elderly Care Systems (MECS) project, under grant agreement 247697. We would like to thank the participants in the MECS project, Professor Tone Bratteteig, Associated Professor Jo Herstad, and Postdoc Guri Verne for guidance in the design of the study, analysis, and discussion.

References

[1] L. Argote, P. S. Goodman, and D. Schkade, "The Human Side of Robotics: How Worker's React to a Robot," Carnegie Mellon University, Tepper School of Business, 1–1983, 1983.

[2] J. M. Evans, "HelpMate: an autonomous mobile robot courier for hospitals," 1994, vol. 3, pp. 1695–1700.

[3] S. Jeon and J. Lee, "Multi-robot multi-task allocation for hospital logistics," in *Advanced Communication Technology (ICACT), 2016 18th International Conference on*, 2016, pp. 339–341.

[4] N. Wingfield, "As Amazon Pushes Forward with Robots, Workers Find New Roles," *The New York Times*, 10-Sep-2017.

[5] L. Grossman, "Maid to Order," *Time.com*, 14-Sep-2002. [Online]. Available from: https://web.archive.org/web/20070714093510/http://www.time.com:80/time/roomba/. [Accessed: 02-Feb-2018].

[6] D. S. Syrdal, K. Dautenhahn, K. L. Koay, M. L. Walters, and W. C. Ho, "Sharing Spaces, Sharing Lives – The Impact of Robot Mobility on User Perception of a Home Companion Robot," in *Social Robotics*, 2013, pp. 321–330.

[7] S. Vikkelsø, "Subtle Redistribution of Work, Attention and Risks: Electronic Patient Records and Organisational Consequences," *Scand. J. Inf. Syst.*, vol. 17, no. 1, Jan. 2005.

[8] J.-Y. Sung, R. E. Grinter, and H. I. Christensen, "Domestic Robot Ecology," *Int. J. Soc. Robot.*, vol. 2, no. 4, pp. 417–429, Dec. 2010.

[9] J. Forlizzi and C. DiSalvo, "Service Robots in the Domestic Environment: A Study of the Roomba Vacuum in the Home," in *Proceedings of the 1st ACM SIGCHI/SIGART Conference on Human-robot Interaction*, New York, NY, USA, 2006, pp. 258–265.

[10] J. Fink, V. Bauwens, F. Kaplan, and P. Dillenbourg, "Living with a Vacuum Cleaning Robot: A 6-month Ethnographic Study," *Int. J. Soc. Robot.*, vol. 5, no. 3, pp. 389–408, Aug. 2013.

[11] A. Cesta, G. Cortellessa, A. Orlandini, and L. Tiberio, "Long-Term Evaluation of a Telepresence Robot for the Elderly: Methodology and Ecological Case Study," *Int. J. Soc. Robot.*, vol. 8, no. 3, pp. 421–441, Jan. 2016.

[12] J. Forlizzi, "How Robotic Products Become Social Products: An Ethnographic Study of Cleaning in the Home," in *Proceedings of the ACM/IEEE International Conference on Human-robot Interaction*, New York, NY, USA, 2007, pp. 129–136.

[13] J.-Y. Sung, H. I. Christensen, and R. Grinter, "Robots in the wild: Understanding long-term use," in *HRI '09 Proceedings of the 4th ACM/IEEE international conference on Human robot interaction*, New York, NY, USA, 2009, pp. 45–52.

[14] R. E. Stake, "Qualitative Case Studies," in *The Sage handbook of qualitative research, 3rd ed*, N. K. Denzin and Y. S. Lincoln, Eds. Thousand Oaks, CA: Sage Publications Ltd, 2005, pp. 443–466.

[15] V. D. Søyseth and M. Søyland, "'Hey, I'm walking here!' – An explorative study of spatial encounters between older adults and autonomous robots," 2017.

[16] International Organization for Standardization, "ISO 10218-1:2011 - Robots and robotic devices – Safety requirements for industrial robots – Part 1: Robots," *International Organization for Standardization*, Jul-2017. [Online]. Available from: https://www.iso.org/standard/51330.html. [Accessed: 02-Feb-2018].

[17] W. Edwards and R. Grinter, "At home with ubiquitous computing: Seven challenges," in *Ubicomp 2001: Ubiquitous Computing*, 2001, pp. 256–272.

[18] A. G. Ozkil, Z. Fan, S. Dawids, H. Aanes, J. K. Kristensen, and K. H. Christensen, "Service robots for hospitals: A case study of transportation tasks in a hospital," in *2009 IEEE International Conference on Automation and Logistics*, 2009, pp. 289–294.

Storytelling at School with a Robot Playmate

Patrizia Marti
Department of Social Political and Cognitive Science
University of Siena Siena, Italy
Department of Industrial Design
University of Technology Eindhoven, The Netherlands
e-mail: marti@unisi.it

Iolanda Iacono
Glitch Factory s.r.l.
Via E. Vezzosi, 15
Arezzo, Italy
e-mail: iolanda.iacono@glitchfatory.it

Abstract— **The paper illustrates an exploratory case study on the use of a toy robot at school to support storytelling in children with cognitive disabilities. Play is a key factor in children's development, yet disabled children are often prevented from playing because of their physical or cognitive impairments. Robot toys might represent a suitable means of favouring learning through play in inclusive activities at school. The robot used in this study is designed to support play scenarios addressing different educational goals for children with specific needs. This paper describes a storytelling scenario and the experiment conducted with the robot in a primary school over four weeks. The activity involved a group of students with typical development and a child with a learning delay due to a mild cognitive disability. The results of the study show that the performance of the child with learning delay improved in terms of memorization of the story elements, ability to focus attention and reduction of exuberant motility when she played with the robot. The results are supported by qualitative and quantitative evidence, as well as by the comments of the teacher who participated in the study.**

Keywords-Children; Robot; Play; Learning; Disability; Storytelling; Primary school.

I. INTRODUCTION

Play has a crucial role in a child's development. The International Classification of Functioning and Disabilities, version for Children and Youth (ICF-CY) [1] published by the World Health Organisation defines play as one of the most important aspects of a child's life to be considered when assessing children's quality of life. Through play, children experiment and learn about themselves and the environment around them. In childhood, skills related to moving, exchanging, experimenting and learning mainly develop through play [2].

Several studies demonstrated that the absence of play is detrimental to the development of a healthy child, leading to impairment in their learning potential. This causes isolation and a compromises social life [3].

Disabled children are often prevented from playing due to their cognitive or physical impairment.

In recent years, an increasing number of research studies have revealed the benefit of using robots as a playmate to support the development of different skills in children with special needs. Robots support engaging and rich interactions while exhibiting a repetitive and controllable behaviour. This stimulates the child with a disability to try out the activity several times without feeling unable or impaired.

However, in order to effectively use the robot and achieve educational objectives, it is important to design play scenarios suitable for the child with special needs.

In what follows, we first provide a literature review on robot-assisted play based on storytelling activities, later we present the robot and the experiment conducted at a primary school with a child with mild cognitive impairment and her peers. The case study provides a detailed description on how to use the robot to engage children with different abilities in playful activities based on storytelling. Furthermore, it provides the results obtained in terms of learning and understanding of the dynamics of a story, and the social interactions enabled by the robot.

The paper is structured as follows. In Section II we report a literature review on storytelling robots; in Section III we present IROMEC (Interactive RObotic Social MEdiator as Companions), the robotic platform used in the present study, in Sections V and IV we illustrate the methodology and the experimental study carried out with IROMEC in a primary school with a child with mild cognitive disability and her classmates, in Sections VI and VII we report and discuss the results of the study. We conclude this work in Section VIII.

II. STORYTELLING ROBOTS

Developing a narrative competence is for children the privileged and primary way to begin to be part of the culture [4]. Narrative is also a fundamental aspect of meaning construction, which is a negotiation activity that develops from early childhood through the whole human life [4].

Narrative has three main functions [5]:

- Cognitive: as a way to learn.
- Social: stories allow us to identify ourselves with a social and cultural group.
- Emotional: as a therapy.

Storytelling is key of children's development. Through it children learn to express themselves and make sense of the external world. They develop logical thinking, imagination and creativity, but also social skills.

Remembering and understanding a story, or using a proper language are all competences that develop more slowly in children with a cognitive disability [6][7].

However, researches in schools revealed that if properly stimulated, children with a cognitive disability may improve in understanding and remembering a story, as well as in meaning construction and communication [6].

Recently, robots and virtual agents have been designed to promote interaction and communication through storytelling in children's development [8]. Lizeberg et al. [9] found that students have better learning performances if the interaction takes place with a physical agent rather than with a virtual agent.

A recent survey conducted by Chen et al. [8] classified storytelling robots in three categories based on who is the user of the robot, what is the focus of the study, and what is the outcome of the study:

- Users: children with typical development [10] and children with disabilities [11];
- Focus of the study: robots used in the educational context as learning companions, educational material, and teaching assistants;
- Outcome of the study: prototype, learning environment, authoring environment, and pedagogy experience.

In the context of disability, the robots are used with different goals. Plaisant et al. [11] used a storytelling robot to stimulate children in carrying out the rehabilitation therapy. Probo robot was used to provide assistance during the therapy with autistic children [12]. NAO robot was used as story reader with expressive verbal and nonverbal behaviours [13].

Storytelling robots are also used with children with normal development. Fridin [14] designed Kindergarten Social Assistive Robotics (KindSAR) a social assistive technology for kindergarten educational staff which provides assistance to the staff by engaging the children in educational games.

III. ROBOT PLATFORM

IROMEC is a robotic platform that addresses play as a medium for disabled children's learning, development and enjoyment [15].

The body displays graphic interface elements related to different play scenarios on a 13 inch digital touchscreen. For example, the body screen can represent the features of an imaginary cartoon-like character, displaying digital fur that moves according to the direction of the platform's movement. When the robot stops, fur clumps appear that extend when it moves again. The head consists of an 8 inch digital screen that displays the robot's facial expressions.

The platform is composed of passive and interactive hardware modules and configurable interfaces to enable the creation of play scenarios adapted to fit the needs of children with different kinds of disabilities [16]. Furthermore, the platform permits creation of new games that can be implemented through the "play script".

"Play scripts" allow implementation of Graphical User Interfaces (GUIs) for different play scenarios, so that the robot can turn from an imaginary animal covered with fur into a creeping snake, an agile tiger or a quiet turtle (Figure 1). The robot can show facial expressions incorporating the mouth, nose, eyes and eyebrows, as well as different levels of expressiveness and emotional states. Smooth transitions are used to create a life-like impression.

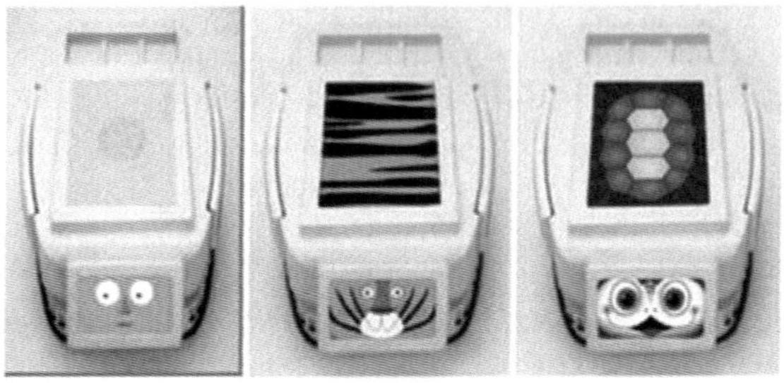

Figure 1. IROMEC imaginary animal-like character (left), IROMEC Tiger (centre), IROMEC Tortoise (right)

The interfaces are enriched by original sounds to structure and articulate the play experience. They have been designed in collaboration with experts, therapists and teachers to give the impression of a living entity without any specific human or animal connotations.

IV. CASE STUDY IN A PRIMARY SCHOOL

The study was conducted for about one month at "Giovanni Pascoli" elementary school in Siena, Italy.

The primary target of the study was an 8 year-old girl with a generalized cognitive delay associated with compromised ability to memorize, with limited verbal and communicative skills and motoric hyperactivity.

Her disorder was linked with difficulties in her life following removal from her family of origin at the age of 4. The early years of her life had been characterized by the presence of an environment providing little cognitive or affective stimulation.

The child's poor verbal skills had a negative impact on her ability to communicate and interact with the rest of the class. She was aware of this problem and felt frustrated by it. Her teacher considered integration into the class a priority goal.

The child had been included in the same curricular program as her classmates, with the addition of individualized activities with the support of a small group so that she would not be isolated.

In agreement with the special needs teacher, we decided to conduct the experimental sessions in a group, using the teaching model normally used in class, with three classmates involved in the study. The classmates' role was to facilitate the activity, promoting interaction, inclusion and the dynamics of play and learning.

The key goals of the study were:

- to improve the attention;
- to improve spontaneous verbalization and appropriate use of language;
- to improve narrative skills;
- to improve body awareness and coordination.

V. Methodology Case Study in a Primary School

The study was broken down into three sequential phases with the primary goal of ensuring understanding, learning and recall of the story *"The tortoise and the hare"* (Table 1).

TABLE I. EXPERIMENTAL PROCEDURE

PHASE I	**Reading the story** "The tortoise and the hare" in the classroom			
PHASE II	**First sub session:** learning and recalling of the story through use of images	**Second sub session:** learning and recalling the story with use of the robot	**Third sub session:** learning and recalling the story with the use of the robot	**Forth sub session:** learning and recalling the story through use of images
PHASE III	**Follow up** assessment of the acquired knowledge (learning, understanding and recalling) through a questionnaire			

The maximum duration of Phase II was about 20 minutes, as suggested by the teacher in view of the girl's difficulty focusing her attention for a longer period of time. The sessions using IROMEC had an average duration of about 18 minutes, while the sessions in which images were used as an aid lasted no longer than 12 minutes. The length of individual sessions depended on the child's behaviour and response. If she appeared bored or refused to participate in the game, she was not forced to do so; the session was interrupted.

A. *Experimental phases*

Phase I: Reading the story "The tortoise and the hare" in class

The teacher brings up the story of "The tortoise and the hare" and reads it in class.

"Once upon a time there was a hare who, boasting how he could run faster than anyone else, was forever teasing tortoise for its slowness. Then one day, the irate tortoise answered back: "Who do you think you are? even you can be beaten!.. Beaten in a race? By whom? Not you, surely! I bet, there's nobody in the world that can win against me, I'm so speedy. Now, why don't you try?...." The hare is so confident that it will win that it takes a nap midway through the course. But when the hare awakes, he finds that his competitor, crawling slowly but steadily, has arrived before him."

After the reading, the children are asked to tell the story together. The teacher pays special attention to the little girl in question in order to assess her comprehension and her ability to recall the story.

Phase II: Learning the story with the reinforcement of images and with the IROMEC

The second phase was divided into four sub-sessions characterized by use of pictures (in the first and fourth sessions) and introduction of the IROMEC (in the second and third sessions), each focusing on comprehension, learning and recall of the story.

The sessions were conducted twice a week over a two-week time span.

- *First session: analysis, comprehension and recall of the story.*

Images were used to aid comprehension of the story in this activity. The teacher used the pictures to guide the session and analyse the key character: the tortoise.

At the beginning of the session the teacher asked the little girl a series of questions to judge her ability to recall the story read in class. If she had difficulty, her classmates were asked to help. Then the teacher asked a series of questions about the tortoise that helped the children recall specific elements: Where does it live? What does it eat? How does it move? When does it hibernate?. The girl could answer the questions while looking at the pictures (Figure 2).

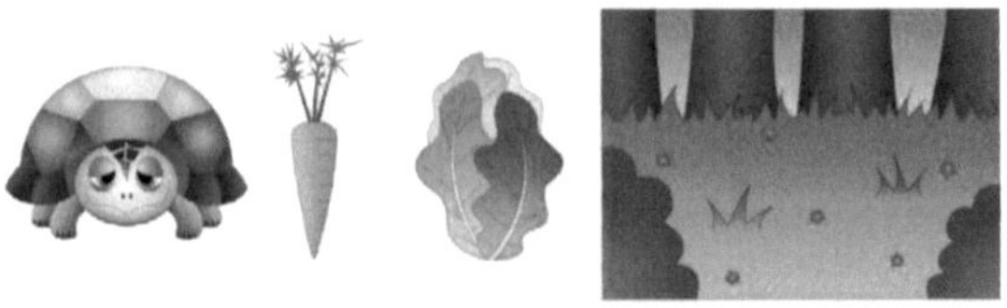

Figure 2. Images used to guide the session

- *Second session: learning the story with the robot.*

The interfaces used during the activity transformed the robot in the "tortoise" of the story (see Figure 1).

In this specific configuration, the robot was intended to look and behave like a tortoise. The robot's mobile configuration was used so that it could move about the classroom alone or with remote control. The robot's movement simulated that of the tortoise, with rather slow movements in follow-me mode. This is a coordination game that consists of playing with the robot, which follows the child. The other children can compete to attract the attention of the robot in order to be followed. The primary educational objectives of this scenario are related to energy and drive functions and to improve motivation to act and to feel in control. The scenario aims to develop the understanding of cause and effect connections, and to improve attention to mobility.

The teacher asked the girl the same series of questions as in the previous session conducted with the use of images: Where does the tortoise live? What does it eat? How does it move? When does it hibernate?

In this session the teacher asked the girl and her classmates to answer the questions while paying attention to the robot's behaviour and imitating it. In this session the children acted out the story in a way, playing the roles of the two characters and mimicking their behaviour.

- *Third session: learning and recalling the story with the robot*

The third session was identical to the second.

- *Fourth session: recalling the story with the use of images*

The fourth session was identical to the first.

Phase III: Follow-up

Follow-up was performed a week later. Questionnaires were given to assess the skills (learning, comprehension and recall) acquired by the girl in relation to the story.

During follow-up the teacher asked the child to recall what had been done during the other sessions, both in sessions with images and in sessions with IROMEC, in order to assess how described below:

- *Cognitive area*

Attention: the child's ability to pay attention to visual and spatial stimuli connected with the play activity, expressed in terms of time. This indicator is continuous.

Recall of verbal and visual content: the child's ability to recall verbal and visual content previously presented and use it to help answer questions. Recall also refers to content presented in previous sessions. This indicator is intended to assess the child's ability to retain long-term memory. It is a spot indicator.

- *Motorial area*

Exuberant motility unrelated to the activity: excessive motorial activity of the entire body unrelated to the game being played. This is a continuous indicator.

- *Communication area*

Spot naming of an object or action: the child's ability to verbally identify an object or action using precise, appropriate language. The indicator refers to spontaneous mentions, not repetition or completion of words pronounced by the teacher or by classmates. This is a spot indicator.

Spontaneous verbalization: the child's ability to clearly and comprehensibly spontaneously verbalize statements on the activity underway. The indicator does not include cases in which the statement is solicited by the teacher's questions or cases in which the spontaneous verbalization is unrelated to the context of the activity underway. It is a continuous indicator.

A written questionnaire was given to the children during the follow-up phase, and included multiple choice questions about the story and the character of the tortoise.

VI. RESULTS

A. Phase I: Reading the story "The tortoise and the hare" in class

Observation of Phase I in class session revealed that the child had difficulty paying attention to multiple stimuli, associated with difficulty in recalling concepts presented not long ago.

For example, when the teacher asked *"Do you know the story of the tortoise and the hare?"*, the child answered *"No"*, but at the end of the reading she picked up the book and said, *"I know this story, because I have the cartoon at home"*. The girl spontaneously began telling the story in very simple words:

"In the cartoon, there's a tortoise and... the other one... I don't remember... what it's called... and then they have a race and ... the other one... I can't remember what the other one's called....." and when the teacher prompted *"the hare"*, she seemed not to hear her but continued her story: *"Yes there was a hare and it ran very fast"*.

In response to the teacher's question, *"Who won the race, the hare or the tortoise?"* the child replied *"the hare"* without hesitation. Though the teacher pointed out that her answer was wrong, she continued to claim, *"In my cartoon it's the hare that wins"*.

The teacher had to remind her to pay attention repeatedly while reading the story. The girl gave the impression she was "hearing" and "seeing" what was happening around her, but not intentionally "listening" and "watching". Her attention seemed to be attracted primarily by the pictures in the book shown by the teacher, not by the story. She could not answer the questions asked of her without the teacher's help and the images. For example, in response to the teacher's question *"Is the hare fast or slow?"* the child hesitated and the teacher had to show her a picture of the two animals to elicit an answer.

The vocabulary she used was simple and very limited. The answers she gave often repeated the teacher's words.

During the reading, the child sat in a listening position with her arms crossed and resting on her desk, but did not seem to be at ease, and repeatedly moved her legs. She often picked up objects on the table during the reading, distracting herself.

B. Phase II: Learning the story "The tortoise and the hare" with the aid of images and with the IROMEC

The information obtained from video analysis of the sessions with the aid of images and with the IROMEC reveal the child's growing ability to pay attention visually (cognitive dimension) to the visual and spatial stimuli connected with the activity.

Visual attention was constant and prolonged in the sessions with the IROMEC, lasting almost the entire session, 18 minutes and 90 seconds out of 19 minutes and 10 seconds in the first session with the IROMEC and 18 minutes out of 18 minutes and 20 seconds in the second session. In both sessions, the child was only distracted from the activity underway for about 20 seconds during the first phase. In the sessions involving use of images, the duration of her visual attention in relation to the total duration of the session was significantly lower. The child was distracted from the game for extended periods of time, 3 minutes and 44 seconds in the first session and 4 minutes and 73 seconds in the last session. As noted above, the sessions involving use of images did not last as long as those involving use of the IROMEC, for the duration of the sessions was strictly dependent on the child's behaviour. The total duration of sessions involving use of images was 11 minutes and 20 seconds for the first session and 13 minutes and 40 seconds for the second. The Figure 3 shows the value in relation to total time, expressed in minutes and seconds, of the child's ability to pay visual attention to the visual and spatial stimuli presented.

These results are correlated with the results of exuberant movement indicator (motorial dimension), which tends to decrease during sessions conducted with the IROMEC and increase in sessions using images.

During sessions conducted with images, this indicator has a value of 3 minutes and 2 seconds, as compared to a total of 11 minutes and 20 seconds in the first session, and

7 minutes compared to a total of 13 minutes and 40 seconds in the second session. In sessions conducted with the IROMEC, her motorial activity was reduced to 0.67 minutes out of a total of 19 minutes and 10 seconds in the first session and 0.38 minutes out of a total duration of 18 minutes and 20 seconds in the second session.

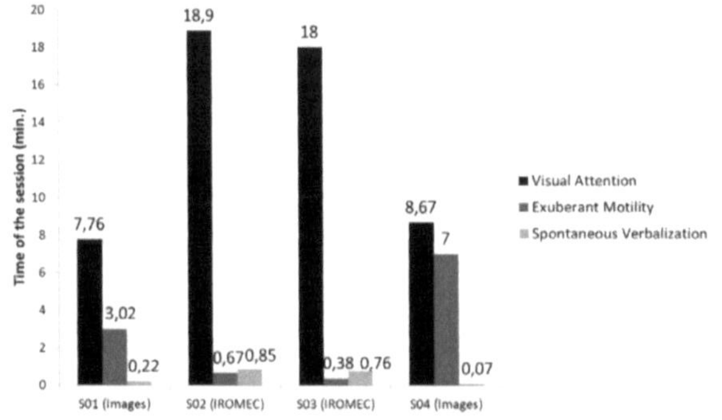

Figure 3. Results of: visual attention, exuberant motility and spontaneous verbalization

Her exuberant motility, which the teacher repeatedly had to contain in order to continue with the activity, translated into inappropriate behaviour, such as pretending to fall, rolling around, repeatedly tying her shoes or leaving the scene of the activity (Figure 4).

Figure 4. Session with the use of image

Spontaneous verbalization, as opposed to statements solicited by the teacher's questions but pertinent to the activity underway, did not exceed one minute in any of the sessions, as shown on the graph in Figure 3.

Spontaneous verbalization was lower in sessions involving use of images, in which the child participated verbally only when asked to do so by the teacher. In these sessions she made statements primarily linked with personal events and aspects unrelated to the activity underway, which distracted her from what was at hand. This form of communication is typical of her pathology and her experience, as noted by the teacher, who explained that the child used this technique in class to avoid tasks which were difficult for her to perform.

In the sessions involving use of the IROMEC, spontaneous verbalization was higher, though only by a few seconds; the child used precise terminology consistent with the context, interacted more frequently with the group and participated in the discussion, asking questions about the IROMEC and pertinent to the activity underway.

Her ability to recall verbal and visual content presented previously (cognitive dimension) improved significantly, from 12 items of content recalled after the first session with images to 21 items of content recalled in the first session with the IROMEC a figure which remained constant in the last session.

In sessions involving use of the IROMEC, the child demonstrated a greater ability to use different verbal content from that pronounced previously; she was, for instance, capable of using synonyms. This did not occur in the sessions conducted with images, where the teacher had to repeatedly prompt verbal content to complete an enunciation.

In the area of communication, the figures reveal that the child acquired a growing ability to name objects and actions narrated in the story with precision (Figure 5).

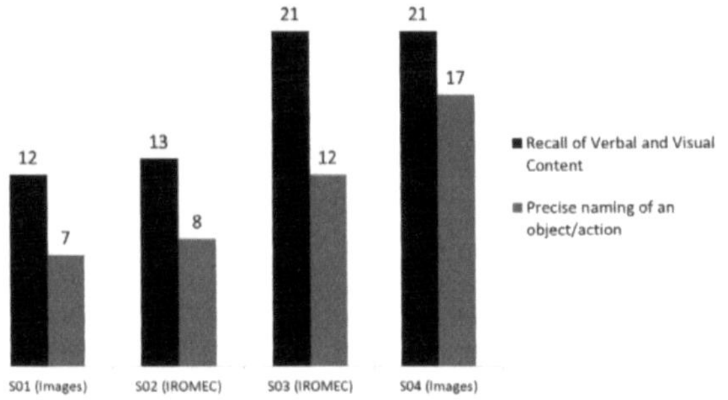

Figure 5. Results of: recall of verbal and visual content, precise naming of an object/action.

The figure reveals a progressive increase from 7 items of content named with precision in the first session to 17 items of content in the last session.

C. Phase III: Follow-up

A week after the end of the sessions, the child was asked to answer two different sets of questions, about the story and the characteristics of the tortoise.

The questionnaires were constructed according to instructions provided by the teacher, who regularly uses this type of test to assess acquisition of knowledge, normally after two lessons on a specific topic. As the teacher pointed out, in this kind of tests the child under observation almost always demonstrated difficulty filling in the questionnaire independently and needed help choosing the right answer.

In this study, the girl was able to fill in the questionnaires alone and answer the questions correctly without any help.

After the questionnaires had been filled in the teacher asked the children some questions about what they had done. The discussion revealed that the child had less difficulty recalling the content of sessions conducted with the IROMEC than sessions conducted with images. The girl specifically recalled activities involving motorial activities, such as imitating the slow movement of the robot representing the tortoise, and particularly the feedback on whether or not an activity had been performed correctly. This was made explicit in the child's words.

Teacher: *Now can you tell me what you liked most about all these things we did with the pictures and the little robot?*

Girl: *That the tortoise laughed that I was slow.*

VII. DISCUSSION

The data obtained from video analysis reveal that the sessions conducted with the IROMEC favoured the child's ability to pay attention and her learning and memorization of the story, decreasing the amount of behaviour inappropriate to the activity.

The results were discussed with the teacher, who expressed considerable satisfaction, particularly with the child's ability to remember the content between the two sessions conducted with the robot, as compared to the sessions with images. The teacher emphasised that involvement of the motorial sphere in addition to the cognitive sphere made a significant contribution to learning and memorization of the story.

The results of the study reveal that the child's ability to concentrate changed depending on the type of aid used (images/IROMEC). In sessions conducted with the IROMEC she was able to focus her attention constantly for a long time, focusing on the robot and on the feedback the IROMEC sent, while in the sessions with images her attention was attracted to her surroundings rather than focused on the activity underway.

An interesting aspect which emerged in sessions with the IROMEC as compared to sessions with images was the climate in the group, which was inclusive and social, revealing greater interest in the story.

VIII. CONCLUSIONS

The paper reports the outcomes of an exploratory study on the use of a toy robot at school to support storytelling in a girl with a mild cognitive disability. Results show that the robot promoted active participation and involvement on the part of the girl, reducing the inappropriate behaviour and exuberant motility which was normally present when doing schoolwork. Active involvement of the motorial sphere in the learning process facilitated learning of abstract concepts which are difficult to understand. The possibility of mimicking the behaviour of the characters of the story like the slowness of the tortoise and the speed of the hare with her body allowed the child to understand concepts which would otherwise have been difficult for her to learn.

IROMEC's presence promoted spontaneous verbalization and communication among the disabled child, the teacher and the other children. The child repeatedly asked the teacher questions about the robot's behaviour, such as *"What is it doing? Why is it turning around?"* referring to the robot turning around to face the children.

This interaction with the teacher had not occurred in the sessions conducted with images, where, to the contrary, there was practically no communication unless solicited by the teacher's questions.

ACKNOWLEDGMENT

The authors would like to thank the children and the teacher who participated to the study. We would also like to thank Sara Giosa for her help in designing the interfaces.

REFERENCES

[1] World Health Organization International classification of functioning, disability, and health: Children & youth version: ICF-CY. Geneva: World Health Organization. ISBN 9241545429, 2007.

[2] J. P. Piaget, Play, dreams, and imitation in childhood. Norton, New York, 1962.

[3] W. Winnicott, Playing and Reality. Penguin Books Ltd., Middlesex, 1971.

[4] J. S. Bruner, Acts of meaning. Harvard University Press, Cambridge MA, 1990.

[5] M. U. Bers, J. Cassell, "Interactive storytelling systems for children: using technology to explore language and identity". Journal of Interactive Learning Research, 9, pp. 183-215, 1998.

[6] R. Gersten, L. S. Fuchs, J. P. Williams, and S. Baker, "Teaching reading comprehension strategies to students with learning disabilities: A review of research". Review of Educational Research, 71, pp. 279-320, 2001.

[7] K. A. Kavale, J. H. Reese, "The character of learning disabilities: An Iowa profile". Learning Disability Quarterly, 15, pp.74–94, 1992.

[8] G. D. Chen, C. Y. Wang, "A survey on storytelling with robots", pp. 450-456, Springer, 2011.

[9] D. Leyzberg, S. Spaulding, M. Toneva, and B. Scassellati, "The physical presence of a robot tutor increases cognitive learning gains". In Proceedings of the 34th Annual Conference of the Cognitive Science Society. Austin,TX: Cognitive Science Society, 2012.

[10] K. Ryokai, M. Jongseon Lee, and J. M. Breitbart, "Children's storytelling and programming with robotic characters", In Proceedings of the seventh ACM conference on Creativity and cognition, October 26-30, 2009, Berkeley, California, USA, 2009.

[11] C. Plaisant, et al., "A storytelling robot for pediatric rehabilitation". In: Proceedings of the 4th ACM/SIGCAPH conference on assistive technologies (ASSETS'00), Washington, DC, USA, pp. 50–55, 2000.

[12] B. Vanderborght, et al., "Using the social robot Probo as a social story telling agent for children with ASD", Interaction Studies, 13, pp. 348-372, 2012.

[13] C. Pelachaud, R. Gelin, J. C. Martin, and Q. A. Le, "Expressive Gestures Displayed by a Humanoid Robot during a Storytelling Application", in Second International Symposium on New Frontiers in Human-Robot Interaction, United Kingdom, AISB 2010.

[14] M. Fridin, "Storytelling by a Kindergarten Social Assistive Robot: a tool for constructive learning in preschool education". Computers & Education, Vol. 70, pp. 53-64, 2014.

[15] R. J. Van den Heuvel, M. A. Lexis, R. M. Jansens, P. Marti, and L. P. De Witte, "Robots supporting play for children with physical disabilities: exploring the potential of IROMEC". Technol Disabil 29, pp. 109–120, 2017.

[16] P. Marti, "Bringing playfulness to disability". In: Proceedings of the 6th Nordic Conference on Human-Computer Interaction, (NordiCHI 2010) Reykjavik, Iceland, 17-20 October, 2010, pp. 851-856, 2010.

This Is Not You! Identity Crisis In the 21st Century

Andrea Alessandro Gasparini
Department of Informatics and
University of Oslo Library
University of Oslo
Oslo, Norway
Email: andreg@ifi.uio.no

Abstract **—Identity today has become a complex issue. An average user of the Internet has accounts for a number of services, and several traces of use are gathered by large companies. However, the same companies are using Artificial Intelligence in their services. This paper presents possible impacts the new wave of Artificial intelligence will have on users' understanding of their own identity if they approach services where this technology is active. Moreover, the effects of having an Artificial Intelligence-based service as a coach or advisor will be highlighted. A pragmatic stand will be applied to address the importance of the context in which the Artificial Intelligence will be used to understand the effects it may have on users' identity. As a case study, the paper presents the result of two design workshops where the goal was to prototype possible solutions and scenarios to support university students entering the academic life when Artificial Intelligence-based services are used.**

Keywords- Artificial intelligence; pragmatism; education; Design Thinking; service design.

I. INTRODUCTION

In the 21st century, the identity of humans has become an issue. Not only is it highly contextualized when technology is involved, but the way identity is used by technological platforms is becoming a problem for some users.

In the first place, identity is difficult to define, as it has many facets; it is highly sensible to many factors. For instance, for a person, the social context is important and is part of the task of defining their own identity [1]. Gender, age, music preferences, or religion are some of the various social categories persons may belong to, and are part of the act of defining themselves. A good example of modern social "tribe" offering an alternative identity to those otherwise defined by social norms, are skaters [2]. Another way for persons to define their own identity is the internal process of self-verification [3]. The two stands (context and internal processes) naturally influence each other [3]. Humans do search for ways of defining their own identity in several ways; some have a nomadic identity, and they easily adapt to different context, others have hidden identities that can emerge in specific contexts. Nevertheless, when a person interacts with a context, a continuous renegotiation and definition of the latter does occur [4]. This situated activity "*is conceived as an ongoing process of establishing, affirming, modifying, and sometimes destroying situated identities.*" [5] One such example is the indigenous cultures where, in many countries, their context is under constant redefinition and their identity under pressure.

Another significant aspect of the human identity is when technology has an active role in different contexts [4]. New technologies, like Augmented Reality (AR) or Virtual Reality (VR) act directly on the context, while the use of smartphones, iPads, smart-clocks and computer discloses all forms of activity and users' habits on the Internet.

In the 21st century, the identity of a person is under unprecedented scrutiny. Companies like Facebook, Google, Amazon, and Netflix use the data that users produce by gathering Big Data and then analyzing every aspect, so they can use it later to come with possible future use of their services. One can say they offer to us our own social navigation [6]. Examples are Amazon and Netflix, as they have recommendations for users to buy books or to see movies based on prior use. The user's voice in this context has been not well accepted, and is often overwhelmed by agreements with large companies which are very difficult to understand in the first place. An answer to this issue is the new European General Data Protection Regulation (GDPR) giving the user rights to decide how their own data is used by those companies [7]. One of the positive changes represents a quantum change for users, since "It must be as easy to withdraw consent as it is to give it." [7] However, during the last two years, an increased interest has been shown regarding Artificial Intelligence (AI). Some of the same companies not only are gathering Big Data on users, but they are also at the frontline of innovation in the field of AI. The dual role the AI can acquire is interesting as well. Firstly, it has access to a huge amount of data about its users and secondly, at the same time, it is able to understand the user in a unique way. This dual role needs further analysis. This paper presents possible effects and impacts the new wave of AI will have on users' understanding of their own identity when they approach services where this technology is active. Finally, the paper will look into how AI can abuse the necessary trust the user gives to a service.

The paper is organized as follows: Section one is the introduction; Section two is about the third wave in AI research; Section three presents Identity, Artificial Intelligence and pragmatism. The fourth section is a case study aiming to dismantle the interaction between AI and users in the context of student's academic life on campus.

The fifth section is a discussion. Finally, the sixth section presents the conclusion, which also includes future works.

II. The Third Wave of Artificial Intelligence

AI is not a new idea, as the approach used is to try to mimic human cognition [8]. Until now, three waves have occurred. The first during the 50s and 60s (cybernetics) originated from the seminal paper written by Alan Turing [9] and the famous Turing test; while the second wave can be pointed out to be in the 80s where the main discussion was around cyborgs, a hybrid of machine and organism, a creature of social reality, also used in fiction [10]. The third wave is now, as one of the elaborative advantages AI has is the access to more or less open large quantities of user's data (termed Big Data). In addition, as mentioned before, during the last few years this new wave of AI has been supported by large companies like Google, Amazon, Tesla, and IBM, where some of them are sharing the necessary technologies, like the TensorFlow open-source software library [11], to be used for programming AI. Machine learning, deep learning and neural network, define some of the approaches used, all aimed at knowledge architectures to perform analysis and predict possible outcome, and tasks, allowing AI to learn and therefore increase the possibility of a correct output. The results so far have the capability to overcome what humans can perform. For instance, IBM Watson [12] is able to read millions of medical journals in oncology and give doctors additional information about what and when to prescribe cures and medicaments. In Norway, companies and organizations are testing and implanting services offshore to predict service maintenance on oil platforms. In Sweden, a company has developed a small device that can monitor small variations in domestic power supply and tell users what is in use at home and how much energy each item uses [13]. The car manufacturer Tesla is already selling cars with ready-to-use self-driving hardware [14]. However, research on the effects that this new wave of AI may have on users when services are so clever, is still in its infancy. For instance, issues with ethics, norms and lack of regulation may have unpredicted effects on our society. For instance, Google's AI AlphaZero had to play in an aggressive way to win chess games against a common chess computer (Stockfish) [15]. The effects on a user when meeting an aggressive AI-based service are still being uncovered.

Another relevant change in this new wave of AI is the possibility to perform tests in vivo with functioning systems, and not only theorizing about this type of interaction between human and machine. For instance, during a series of matches of the game GO between a variant of the AlphaZero AI (AlphaGo) and a human [16], some strange forms of behaviors from both sides were observable. In the award-winning documentary about this series of matches [17] one can get a first glimpse of this new landscape of interaction. Among interesting observations to be made is the way programmers defined the behavior of AlphaGo on some occasions was "completely delusional". It is also remarkable how AlphaGo adapted and reacted to the way the human opponent played, defined by the programmers as creative. Finally, the sad reaction of the public and the press after the first game, when the human player lost, turned out to be surprising and unpredicted.

Therefore, several questions are timely to ask: Is it okay for an AI based service to become angry? Which identity has an intelligent AI? What are the factors provoking bias in an AI? And what is the right pedagogy to teach an AI? Who is programming the algorithm and how the system is trained may also produce bias. For instance, if the user data gathered is only from a specific context, the support given by the service can be erroneous.

For the user, a new endeavor is on the horizon, as AI based services are using all the gathered data users produces, and by analyzing every aspect they will present, in the near future, services tailored for them. Moreover the effects are unclear when the context is also under the influence of AI and therefore can be adapted accordingly. Next, we consider how services based on AI may influence the users. The paper will look into how pragmatism can be used to understand how the context, identity and AI influence one another.

III. Identity, Artificial Intelligence and Pragmatism

The paper presents pragmatism [18] as a framework to make sense of the context a user may find himself in when using a service based on AI. To start with, the notion of "inquiry" in pragmatism is a way to approach a not-defined situation (for example when approaching an AI-based identity) and try to change it in such a way that it is "thinkable". "Inquiry is the controlled or directed transformation of an indeterminate situation into one that is so determinate in its constituents distinctions and relations as to convert the elements of the original situation into a unified whole" [18, p. 108]. This passage is interesting, as it shows how a user may try to "redefine" an AI-based service by own parameters so it makes sense to him, i.e., make it thinkable. What fuels an inquiry for a human is then the necessity to react and perform thinking in a situation that is uncommon, out of place or difficult to understand (in our case making sense of the identity of an AI). However, pragmatism emphasizes the difference between thought and thinking. Thinking of sugar when looking at the snow falling in Norway is creative, however only a thought. Thinking consecutive thoughts like: snow, then snow on the road, then problems with traveling, then coming late to work, is a series of activity ending in an educated guess. Dewey writes about this line of thinking since humans *"consider the possibility and nature of the connection between the object seen and the object suggested"* [18]. A side effect of those subsequent thoughts is a learning effect, grounded in a reflective act. This learning activity is also relevant when making sense of a situation a person is involved in, for instance, in our case, when interacting with a brand new AI-based service. As pointed by [19], one's way of understanding a situation is based on prior experiences. However, since there are very few real situations where this can be tested, one can deduce a difficulty for users to acquire experience of interaction with an AI-based service, who may therefore be unprepared to tackle issues emerging from the interaction. A consequence for the user of this insecurity is an emerging relevance of the context where the activity is performed. In pragmatism the "situatedness" is a way to explain that persons, objects and phenomena are very contextually bounded, as they can only exist in a given situation. An effect of this is a quid pro quo between the context and its inhabitants: the situation cannot exist without the others, and vice versa.

Dewey presents an indeterminate situation as one not so stable and difficult to understand, in which the subjects, and the surroundings do not play together [18]. They are not aligned properly. An indeterminate situation, as described above, fits well to explain a possible situation a user could experience when approaching an AI-based service. This indeterminate situation is also under the effects of the continuous renegotiation and definition of the context done by the user [4]. Simultaneously this activity has an impact on the situated identity of the user. This process can support, modify or even destroy an identity [5], since context and internal processes of self-verification naturally influence each other [3].

A possible scenario could describe a user encountering an AI-based service so well informed about the user's needs and habits, able to exploit the user's weakness so the user cannot resist being pleased by the offer from the AI-supported service.

Pragmatism helps understand the construction of this specific context and why a person's identity is under pressure when approaching an AI-based service. The paper will now present the results of two workshops where the goal was to dismantle, using design methods, the interaction between an AI-based service and the users, in the context of students' academic life on campus.

IV. The Case

A. A design process informed by Design Thinking and Service Design

The University of Oslo Library received a grant from the Norwegian National Library early in 2017, to find out possible effects the use of Artificial Intelligence could have on services the library provided and how the user will accept using and interacting with this new type of services. Analysis has found out that AI-based technology will be relevant in academia and academic libraries over four to five years from now [20].

Opting for using an academic library constrained the type of users (e.g. students and researchers), and controlled the context. One of the goals of the project was to inform the process of developing and understanding AI-based services using a user-centered perspective and not the technology alone.

The theoretical foundation of the project stands on Design Thinking [21]. The goal of this approach is to support innovation where the output has the connotation of desirability, viability, feasibility. Each of these takes care of the user perspective, technical and business possibility. As design method for the two workshops presented in this paper, we opted for the use of Service Design [22], where the goal is to map out the whole journey of the user from the very start of using an AI-based service to the end and beyond (aftereffects). Each time a user is in contact with a service provider, it is possible to design, re-design or remove the contact points (touch-points). This design approach fits well with AI-based services, giving the opportunity to look into each touch-point.

The goal of the two workshops was to map out a user journey for a university student when approaching on campus an AI-based service for the first time. In the context of a university library, possible services to be worked with in the workshops could include, among others, help to find a spot to read peacefully, get help to find relevant literature or library courses, or to find out about other possibilities and services the university library could give the student.

The set-up of the workshop was one previously used by the author on several occasions [23]. The participants of the two workshops had different backgrounds, like researcher, IT-staff, directors of the library, and librarians, however all were from academia.

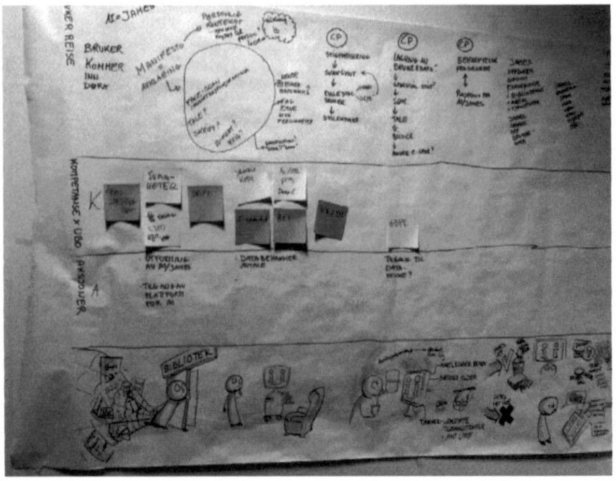

Figure 1. The photo shows the user journey for an AI-based service developed during the workshop. On top the actual user journey is mapped out. The second row describes the competence needed in the organization to complete each touch-points. The last row shows the activity needed to achieve the goal of the touch-point.

The first workshop, was a daylong activity, and used a design approach to sort out all aspects of AI in the context of a student's academic life on campus. Using Giga-mapping [24], as many perspectives as possible were addressed. The second phase of the workshop was rapid prototyping, where the outcome was several ideas of future services using AI. As mentioned, during this first workshop we used Service Design to describe how a journey for a student could be, and several of the ideas from the rapid prototyping act were used. The second workshop, a half day long, was used to enrich even more the user journey developed in the first workshop. The participants added new perspectives and issues, allowing for a redefinition of some of the touchpoints. For both workshops, the design act provoked several unexpected issues. Particularly interesting was the problem: the participants had to envision a future use of an AI-based service. Additionally, the lack of arenas where it could be possible to test and achieve more competence reinforced the effect. The final result of the two workshops was a user journey representing how a student approaching the service for the first time, acted. Each touch point (see Fig. 1 and redesigned excerpt Fig. 2) represented an interaction between the user and the AI-based service. The user journey highlights the need of in-depth analysis of each interaction. For instance, already at the very start of the journey, finalizing an agreement of data exchange is an obstacle for both. From one side, the service provider needs to gather relevant data, on the other side the user needs to decide to which degree it is necessary to accommodate the request to ensure the coaching is relevant. In the next phase, the AI-based service will ask for some type of identification, like ID-cards, or if allowed, to scan the face to recognize the identity of the person. The user journey (see Fig. 1 and redesigned excerpt Fig. 2) showed the possibility and necessity which the AI-based service has to gather as much as possible information about the context and the user, to be able to deliver the service. The context gives information about the place on campus, and possible services the user could get access to. In addition, there is a need to update the gathered data the AI-based services has, in case there are recent changes.

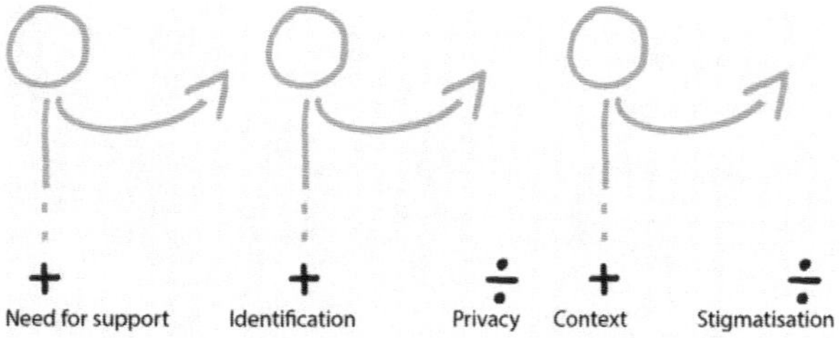

Figure 2. Redesigned excerpt of the user journey where the goal is to use an AI-based service. Privacy and stigmatization are critical points.

For instance, in the library it could be new books or, on campus, relevant information about upcoming presentations or seminars. After all, the main goal should be to communicate information as correctly as possible. However, to really help the users, the AI-service needs to gather information about them. Information about university courses the user is taking, and the curriculum needed, are all valuable information. In addition, information of possible disabilities, like dyslexia, is needed to avoid stigmatization, and to reconfigure the service to match the user's needs. Nevertheless, to really tune in the right type of help, additional user data should be monitored and saved for future use during the interaction. Examples of the latter are for instance, type of questions put and answers given, recording of interaction and video of activity performed in the physical space. Finally, the AI-based service should gather a lot of information online to construct a profile, so the service is tailored as well as possible.

The outcome of the workshops was a better understanding of the implications of the invasiveness that the user will be subject to, and the resulting effects. The user journey pointed out the exchange of data and communication as a Critical Point (see the touch point identification in Figure 2) since it is necessary for the service provider to have routines reflecting the local legislation (Privacy) and ensuring how the data will be used (for instance to avoid stigmatization). This information needs to be part of the agreement made at the beginning of the interaction. In conclusion, after the workshops it was possible to observe that the majority of the problems happened at the very start of the constructed user journey. Prevalent was the need to have empathy for user needs, tacit and otherwise, to avoid giving the user less priority.

B. *Issues with business-driven developing processes for Artifical Intelligence-based services*

The approach used in the presented case was a direct reaction from the overwhelming activity in business companies in Norway [25] aimed at reducing costs and increasing earnings using Artificial Intelligence, while the user perspectives in many cases seem to be absent. The author has participated in several conferences and workshops regarding the use of AI, and during a presentation in a major consultant company in Norway the user perspective was completely omitted from the development process. Using the Waterfall method to develop a service, they presented the following chain of activities:

Project plan for an AI-based service:

- Understand the business problem area
- Analytical approach to the problem area
- Gather large silo of curated data
- Use algorithms and modelling
- Evaluation of the algorithm
- Evaluation
- Real use
- Feedback

The user perspectives and his possibilities to inform the process are clearly very few.

V. Discussion

A. *Identity and Artificial Intelligence*

The identity of the user is under even greater pressure when approaching and using AI-based services. The results of the two presented workshops, and the observations from the documentary, support this view and raise questions as how users may react to this new type of technology. A method to discuss the necessary reflectivity a human needs to perform, named reflective thought, as a means to help define his identity, is pragmatism. As mentioned, one of the effects of the reflective act is learning. The problem is, as mentioned, what happens when the self-learning mechanism in the AI technology make its own predictions, supported by accessing Big Data, contextualized information, and simultaneously acts as a coach, in this case, a helping hand for students in an academic setting during studies?

This advantage may give unpredicted outcomes. What happens when the user starts learning from an AI-based service made to mimic humans? What if it is difficult to see the difference between a real interaction and one with an AI-based service? It may sound simplistic; however, one should remember special moments or occasions occurring during school. Some special events had a huge impact on how we perceive the context (school) and the willingness to learn later on. Therefore, when an AI-based service fits so perfectly with the user, when it is so well informed of the user's needs and habits and at the same time is able to exploit the user's weakness in a way the user cannot resist, the question to ask is: what kind of human identity will be the outcome of an interaction over a long period of time. The two workshops showed that the AI can perform this activity and the information required is not so difficult to gather, sometimes the users even give away that type of information regardless of privacy issues. The user's identity, especially in the context of education, needs to be protected when Artificial Intelligence is the driving force behind support systems. Young students, in the beginning of their academic life are eager for knowledge, and the faculty and other university staff need to advise prudence.

As earlier described, AI-based services can be aggressive in the way they try to solve problems [15], therefore unforeseen issues may arise when they can be critical and develop an opinion on their own. As the workshop showed, there is a potential to help students with their academic life by supporting research and study. AI-based services will probably be a game changer as new forms of interaction will develop new types of "hybrid selves" based on different aspects the persons interacting with the service have.

B. *Context and Artifical Intellingence*

With fresh and unexpected insights, an AI-based service may tune its identity and gain acceptance and legitimacy to interact with users. However, the context has also a role in defining the identity of the user. Section III explains how pragmatism helps understand the construction of a context since the "situatedness" explains why all the users, AI, and the context are contextually bounded, as they can only exist in a given situation. In addition, the "situatedness" is not stable and requires a continuous renegotiation by the user, which also affects his identity. In the documentary AlphaGo, this was present as both the player and the public were clearly sad about losing the game when the opponent was a non-human, and therefore required a redefinition of their own identity.

As pointed out by Dourish [4], so far there is some difficulty in designing well-functioning systems that take the context into account. Contextualized information, as mentioned, gives opportunities to gain an advantage. Context is also easy for an AI-based service to exploit, since users leave many traces when they are using search engines, email, and so on. For instance, the GPS, 4G and the Wi-Fi of the mobile phone monitors all the user's movement when moving from place to place, with added time stamps.

One of the results of the workshop has pointed out several touch-points relevant for the AI-based services to gather and adapt to the context, and in doing so support the user. For instance, to help users with disabilities, one needs to take into account physical issues when moving inside the library, and at the same time try to avoid any forms of stigmatization.

C. *This is not you!*

Finally the title, "This is not you!" has its own anecdotal story and deserves to be mentioned in this paper. As the author of this paper was in a University meeting in Spain, the story to be told unfolds at the airport while heading back to Norway. Unfortunately, the author had grown a large mustache and had gained some weight. Therefore, during check-in at the airport the author was denied a boarding card. The lady from the flight company at the counter desk, definitely did not believe the person in front of her was the right owner of the passport; "This is not you!" The reaction of the author was foremost surprise, since his identity is available everywhere, from the biometrics information in the passport, all the different physical cards, to all the accounts he has online in so many platforms and services. How could it be possible that his identity is so entangled?—Be so present and invisible at the same time? Showing other identity cards to the airline company did not help. After several checks by supervisors from the flight company and discussions, the author was finally allowed to travel. Being the first person of the entourage from the University participating at the meeting in Spain, it was a quite seldom experience, one difficult to forget. The critical point in this story was how the author experienced being mistaken for another person, and in addition one not desiderated. Considering this experience with an AI service the, outcome could be worse. If the system does not show judicial assessment, the only possibility the author had to react, was to reshape and redefine the identity.

VI. CONCLUSION

The paper presents indications about how to proceed when Artificial Intelligence, in the near future, will become a standard supporting system. The user's identity has shown, in the context of academic life, a need to be cared for when AI is the driving forces behind support systems. Young students, in the beginning of their academic life are eager for knowledge, and the faculty and other university staff need to advise wisely. The design process aiming to prepare users when encountering AI-based services may result in a tension about the embodiment of knowledge as it is able to gain opinions on its own using the user's data The offering of coaching and support will have an impact on the user's identity.

Unfortunately, several signs in the market show that new services are developed by ignoring the user's perspective, as the main goal is to maximize company profit. The paper has presented how difficult it is to be reflective and think in a "correct" way when approaching Artificial Intelligence-based systems and services. There are many companies outside academia who are interested in or are developing this type of platform, however, there is a lack of arena where this type of interaction and the effects can be monitored over a longer period of time. The paper supports an emerging necessity to make new legislations and new regulations to defend the users, while the creativity and the innovation emerging when using this new technology should not be constrained.

ACKNOWLEDGMENT

The author is indebted to all workshop's participants, and the University of Oslo Library for initiating the project. The National Library of Norway, in part, financed the project.

REFERENCES

[1] B. E. Ashforth and F. Mael, "Social identity theory and the organization," *Acad. Manage. Rev.*, vol. 14, no. 1, pp. 20–39, 1989.
[2] A. Gasparini, "Young and creative - A designerly approach to enhance interventions in the public space," presented at the ACHI 2016, The Ninth International Conference on Advances in Computer-Human Interactions, Venice, Italy, 2016, pp. 44–49.
[3] S. Stryker and P. J. Burke, "The past, present, and future of an identity theory," *Soc. Psychol. Q.*, vol. 63, no. 4, pp. 284–297, 2000.
[4] P. Dourish, "What we talk about when we talk about context," *Pers. Ubiquitous Comput*, vol. 8, no. 1, pp. 19–30, Feb. 2004.
[5] N. Alexander and M. G. Wiley, "Situated activity and identity formation," in *Social Psychology: Sociological Perspectives*, M. Rosenberg and R. T. Turner., Eds. New York: Basic Books.
[6] A. Dieberger, P. Dourish, K. Höök, P. Resnick, and A. Wexelblat, "Social navigation: Techniques for building more usable systems," *Interactions*, vol. 7, no. 6, pp. 36–45, Nov. 2000.
[7] EU GDPR, "EU GDPR," *EU GDPR Portal*. [Online]. Available: http://eugdpr.org/eugdpr.org.html. [Accessed: 03-Dec-2017].
[8] M. A. Shahin, "State-of-the-art review of some artificial intelligence applications in pile foundations," *Geosci. Front.*, vol. 7, no. 1, pp. 33–44, Jan. 2016.
[9] A. Turing, "Computing machinery and intelligence," *Mind*, vol. 59, no. 236, pp. 433–460, 1950.
[10] D. Haraway, "A manifesto for cyborgs: Science, technology and socialist feminism in the 1980s," *Social. Rev.*, vol. 80, p. 29, 1985.
[11] TensorFlow, "TensorFlow." [Online]. Available: https://www.tensorflow.org/. [Accessed: 18-Jan-2018].
[12] IBM Watson, "IBM Watson," *IBM Watson*, 2018. [Online]. Available: https://www.ibm.com/watson/. [Accessed: 15-Jan-2018].
[13] Watty, "Watty | A simple way to keep track of what goes on at home," *Watty*, 2018. [Online]. Available: https://watty.io/. [Accessed: 15-Jan-2018].
[14] Tesla, "Autopilot," 2018. [Online]. Available: https://www.tesla.com/autopilot. [Accessed: 16-Jan-2018].
[15] M. Klein (MikeKlein), "Google's AlphaZero destroys Stockfish in 100-game match," *Chess.com*. [Online]. Available: https://www.chess.com/news/view/google-s-alphazero-destroys-stockfish-in-100-game-match. [Accessed: 10-Dec-2017].
[16] D. Silver *et al.*, "Mastering the game of Go without human knowledge," *Nature*, vol. 550, no. 7676, p. 354, Oct. 2017.
[17] G. Kohs, "AlphaGo Movie," *AlphaGo Movie*, 2017. [Online]. Available: https://www.alphagomovie.com/. [Accessed: 18-Jan-2018].
[18] J. Dewey, *How We Think*. Mineola, N.Y: Dover Publ, 1997.
[19] P. Dalsgaard, "Pragmatism and design thinking," *Int. J. Des.*, vol. 8, no. 1, pp. 143–155, 2014.
[20] NMC, "NMC horizon report library edition," 2017.
[21] T. Brown, "Design Thinking," *Harward Bus. Rev.*, vol. 86, no. 6, pp. 84–92, 2008.
[22] A. Polaine, L. Løvlie, and B. Reason, *Service Design: From Insight to Implementation*. Brooklyn, N.Y.: Rosenfeld Media, 2013.
[23] A. Culén and A. Gasparini, "Find a book! Unpacking customer journeys at an academic library," in *ACHI 2014, The Seventh International Conference on Advances in Computer-Human Interactions*, 2014, pp. 89–95.
[24] B. Sevaldson, "GIGA-mapping: Visualisation for complexity and systems thinking in design," *Nordes*, vol. 0, no. 4, Mar. 2011.
[25] Nordic – AI, "Nordic AI Summit Norway - Oslo Innovation Week 2018." [Online]. Available: http://oiw.no/program/nordic-ai-summit-norway. [Accessed: 14-Dec-2017].

Translation of Sign Language Into Text Using Kinect for Windows v2

Preeti Amatya, Kateryna Sergieieva, Gerrit Meixner
UniTyLab
Heilbronn University
Heilbronn, Germany
emails: preetiamatya@gmail.com, kateryna.sergieieva@hs-heilbronn.de, gerrit.meixner@hs-heilbronn.de

Abstract—**This paper proposes methods to recognize and translate dynamic gestures of the German Sign Language (Deutsche Gebärdensprache, DGS) into text using Microsoft Kinect for Windows v2. Two approaches were used for the gesture recognition process: sequence matching using Dynamic Time Warping algorithm and a combination of Visual Gesture Builder along with Dynamic Time Warping. For benchmarking purposes, eleven DGS gestures, which were provided by an expert user from Germany, were taken as a sample dataset. The proposed methods were compared on the basis of computation cost and accuracy of these gestures. The computation time for Dynamic Time Warping increased steadily with increasing number of gestures in the dataset whereas in case of Visual Gesture Builder with Dynamic Time Warping, the computation time remained almost constant. However, the accuracy of Visual Gesture Builder with Dynamic Time Warping was only 20.42% whereas the accuracy of Dynamic Time Warping was 65.45%. On the basis of the results, we recommend Dynamic Time Warping algorithm for small datasets and Visual Gesture Builder with Dynamic Time Warping for large datasets.**

Keywords-Sign Language; Deutsche Gebärdensprache; DGS; German Sign Language; Dynamic Time Warping; Visual Gesture Builder.

I. INTRODUCTION

Sign language is a visual language [27] used by the deaf people around the world. According to the World Federation of the Deaf, there are about 70 million deaf people in the world who use sign language as their mother tongue [1]. It is often compared to spoken languages in terms of "modality difference" [19]. A spoken language is perceived auditorily whereas a sign language is perceived visually [19]. However, sign languages are not based upon the spoken languages [8]. Instead, it has its own grammar, syntax, semantics, and morphology [14][20], which makes it a highly structured language [17]. It is not a universal language [8] and it differs according to the deaf communities across the world. But, most of the sign languages are named after a country, for instance: in the USA – American Sign Language (ASL), in Germany – German Sign Language or Deutsche Gebärdensprache (DGS), in the UK – BSL (British Sign Language), in Poland – Polish Sign Language (PSL), etc. It involves the process of a gestural interaction where gestures consist of signs, which differ from each other by minor changes [3]. These changes include a change in handshape, motion, location, non-manual cues like facial expressions [3], lip movements, and head movements, which complicates the recognition process.

According to the Stokoe's notation, a sign in a sign language comprises of three different features, which are: place where it is made, the distinctive configuration of the hand or hands making it, the action of the hand or hands [28]. In terms of gestures, motion and configuration can be classified according to their positions, which may be static or dynamic. Harling classified the hand gestures into four categories, as follows [11]:

Static Hand Posture, Static Hand Location – SPSL:

1) SPSL includes the most of fingerspelling and numbers of a sign language, which does not involve hand motions. For instance, spelling 'A' in ASL (see Figure 1).

Figure 1. "A" fingerspelling in ASL [29]

2) Dynamic Hand Posture, Static Hand Location – DPSL: DPSL includes sign gestures, which do not have real meaning of a word. It can also be an acronym. For instance, spelling "OK" in ASL. To spell "OK" first "O" is spelled and then "K" (see Figure 2).

Figure 2. "OK" fingerspelling in ASL [29]

3) Static Hand Posture, Dynamic Hand Location – SPDL: SPDL includes gestures like "Thank you" in ASL (see Figure 3) where a hand posture is almost flat and location changes from touching the chin to in-front of and slightly below the chin.

Figure 3. "Thank you" gesture in ASL [21]

4) Dynamic Hand Posture, Dynamic Hand Location – DPDL: it includes gestures like "Hello" in ASL where the hand posture (like the position of thumb in "Hello") changes along with the location (See Figure 4).

Figure 4. "Hello" gesture in ASL [21]

Signing words of sign language using fingerspelling is a tedious task, and generally, deaf people do not prefer to use it as the main form of communication [24]. Also, most sign languages do not include fingerspelling but include gestures, which represent whole words [26].

This paper is based on the whole word representation of the German Sign Language (DGS) gestures, which are dynamic in nature, i.e., it involves some hand motions. Hence, SPDL and DPDL types of gestures were used for recognition using Microsoft Kinect for Windows v2 [6]. These gestures are used as input to the sign language translator application, which was built for this research. Gesture recognition is done on the basis of two approaches: using Dynamic Time Warping (DTW) algorithm (see Section 4.5) and Visual Gesture Builder (VGB) along with DTW (see Section 4.7). After a gesture is recognized, it is translated into text.

The rest of this paper is structured as follows: Section 2 describes related work done in the field of recognizing sign language. Section 3 describes the methodology used for the project. Section 4 explains the implementation of the approach in detail. Section 5 presents the performance benchmarks and evaluations of both variations of the application in terms of a central processing unit (CPU) cost and accuracy. The deductions made from the benchmarks and results, as well as further work, are discussed in Section 6.

II. Related Work

A lot of research has been done in the field of sign language recognition using various approaches. Oszust and Wysocki recognized isolated words of PSL on the basis of "features which include Kinect's skeletal image" and "features describing hands as skin colored regions" [18]. Cooper recognized sign language on the basis of linguistic subunits using Markov Models and Sequential Pattern Boosting based on openNI frameworks [3]. For learning appearance based on subunits (location, motion, hand arrangements), hand segmentation and the position of the face required a user needs to wear data gloves [3].

Starner recognized ASL sentences using single camera based on Hidden Markov Model (HMM) with word accuracy of 99.2% without modeling the fingers [26]. In his method, a user needs to wear distinct hand gloves [26]. Videos were captured at 5 frames per second with a 320x243 pixel resolution [26]. Fang and Gao proposed Transition Movement Model (TMM) for large vocabulary continuous sign language recognition [9]. The devices used for experimentation were Cybergloves and Pohelmus 3SPACE-position trackers [9]. Zhang, Zhou, and Li recognized sentences on the basis of Discrete HMM and DTW [30]. DTW was used for determining the end point of each sign [30].

Another widely used approach to gesture recognition is gesture classification with a help of machine learning techniques. Neural networks [23], support vector machine [25] or nearest neighbor [5] are often used for such purposes. Although, these methods show high accuracy level, they require not only determining the signing motion, but also design, fine-tuning and training of algorithmic model for classification.

In contrast to these approaches for sign language recognition, the methods used in this paper do not use hand segmentation approaches, and they do not use data gloves. Since our methods do not consider hand posture and focus on isolated words, only DTW algorithm was used for determining the signing motions performed by a user. The only constraint in DTW based approach is that a user has to stay in standstill positions to make a gesture, whereas VGB with DTW has no such constraints. The body joints tracking feature provided by Microsoft Kinect SDK 2.0 was used for sign language recognition, which does not require further color segmentation. Furthermore, we use VGB, which was released with Microsoft Kinect SDK 2.0 to recognize the start and end positions. Our training sets for start and end positions of a sign language is done by VGB application, which provides more custom features for our datasets. For instance: ignoring hands, ignoring lower body joints. Also, the VGB datasets can be experimented prior to recognition using VGB view to determine if the dataset is appropriate for sign language recognition. Finally, this paper also investigates the potential of DTW algorithm and VGB with DTW to recognize sign language gestures.

III. METHODOLOGY

To provide gesture recognition for DGS and its translation into the text, by means of DTW and VGB-with-DTW-based Translators, both learning machines have to be trained to perform this task. For these purposes, the system should be developed which cover data collection, which includes collecting data from the user, specifically filming videos with DGS gestures; data preprocessing, that has to transform video files into gesture dataset in a format acceptable for the translators; and translators training.

For the sample dataset, 11 DSG gestures were selected for recording. Video recording was decided to make with Microsoft Kinect for Windows v2 with SDK 2.0. It was chosen for this project because it can detect full body movements [6] using raw color frames and depth images. The sensors of Kinect include a color camera, a depth sensor, and IR (Infra-Red) emitter. The depth sensor and IR emitter of Kinect has a resolution of 512x424 pixels, and the camera has 1080p resolution [6]. It can capture frames at the rate of 30 FPS [6].

In this research Kinect ability for capturing body joints based on its depth images is used. The 2D body coordinates above the hip region are chosen because most sign language gestures include hand motions. For simplicity, hand postures and non–manual cues were not used for recognition.

Figure 5 shows the overall architecture of the sign language translator system.

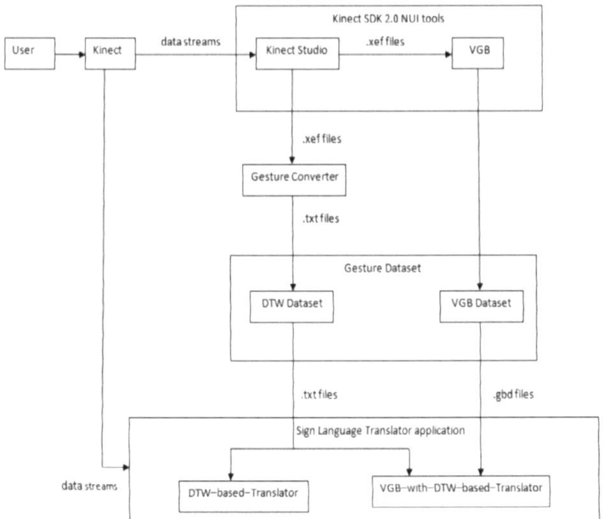

Figure 5. Overall System Architecture

An expert user is allowed to sign DGS gestures in front of the Microsoft Kinect for Windows v2. The Kinect captures the data streams from the user, and these data streams are recorded using Kinect Studio. The video files from the Kinect Studio (.xef files) are used for training datasets in VGB. These .xef files are processed using Gesture Converter, which returns DTW dataset (.txt files) after normalization (see Section 4.3). On the other hand, VGB datasets are created using the Visual Gesture Builder. After training VGB datasets, the generated .gbd files are used as a dataset in VGB-with-DTW-based Translator.

The .txt files from the DTW datasets are used in DTW-based Translator (see Section 4.5) as well as VGB-with-DTW-based Translator (see Section 4.7).

When a normal user signs a sign language gesture, the data streams are captured by sign language translator application (see Sections 4.5 and 4.7) and are translated into text (see Section 4.6).

IV. IMPLEMENTATION

4.1 Input Data

As mentioned before, input data for the system is data streams, which represents videos of gestures, filmed by Kinect Studio.

Kinect Studio is a recording tool, which can record 2D and 3D data captured by Kinect, along with the orientation of the body. Kinect studio records the data in a .xef file format. These files contain audio, video, depth information recorded by a user.

Recording clips with Kinect Studio was done by starting the Kinect service and user performing the gestures in front of Kinect. The Kinect records the videos in .xef format. These .xef files are used in VGB for training datasets.

4.2 Visual Gesture Builder

VGB is a tool, which was developed to recognize custom gestures using Kinect. VGB uses a data-driven solution for gesture recognition [8]. Gesture detection through VGB is done by training the gestures provided by users (content creation) rather than code writing [8]. The processes in VGB are described below in detail.

At first, VGB was used to tag the start and end positions of sign language gestures. A gesture in VGB is a posture in our context. A gesture in VGB was created with its custom features, which include "Body Side", "Gesture Type" and "Training Settings". A body side in VGB is differentiated into three categories, "Left", "Right" and "Any". "Any"-body side was chosen for training gestures. Discrete gesture type allows VGB to train gestures using AdaBoost, which is a machine learning meta-algorithm to improve performance [10]. "Ignore Lower Body" was chosen to train all the start and end positions of the gestures, and lower body was considered for training "Standstill" position.

After creating a gesture using VGB, start and end positions of sign language gestures were tagged separately (see Figure 6). The blue frames in Figure 6 represent a positive training set of data, whereas, all other frames, which are untagged, are referred to as negative training data. These frames are weak classifiers for AdaBoost. For tagging data, VGB provides custom input parameters. The custom input parameters chosen for the start and end positions of gestures are shown in Figure 6. Building gestures in VGB result in .gbd files. These .gbd files are used in application to detect gestures.

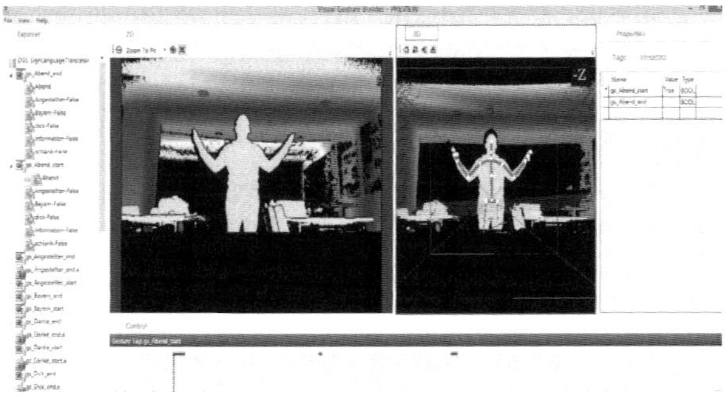

Figure 6. Clips tagged for "Abend_start" gesture

VGB view can be used to find out whether the start and end gestures of a sign language has been recognized correctly. It consists of all the gestures, which were tagged in VGB. When Microsoft Kinect SDK 2.0 captures the input, VGB view shows the confidence of gestures based on the input. A higher level of confidence shows more accuracy of the gestures performed by the user. Figure 7 is an example of a gesture performed using VGB view.

Project Settings

Name	Value	Type
Accuracy Level	0.95	FLOAT
Number Weak Classifiers at Runtime	1000	INT
Filter Results	True	BOOL
Auto Find Best Filtering Params	True	BOOL
Weight Of False Positives During Auto Find	0.5	FLOAT
Manual Filter Params: Num Frames To Filter	5	INT
Manual Filter Params: Threshold	0.001	FLOAT
Duplicate And Mirror Data During Training	False	BOOL
% CPU For Training	95	INT
Use Hands Data	False	BOOL
Ignore Left Arm	False	BOOL
Ignore Right Arm	False	BOOL
Ignore Lower Body	True	BOOL

Figure 7. Custom parameters for abend_start gesture

In Figure 8, the "dick" (in English: thick) gesture in DGS is performed. At first, a start position is detected followed by the end position. A spike shows the confidence of the start and end positions of the gesture.

Figure 8. An example of viewing .gbd file using VGB view

The VGB view allows developers to verify if the training is good enough to be used in an application. After the .gbd file was viewed using VGB view, it was added in our application to detect the start and end positions of gestures.

4.3 Normalization of coordinates

Microsoft Kinect for Windows v2 SDK 2.0 can track 25 body joints using its depth images. To determine the hand gesture motion, the following body joints in 2D – HandRight, HandLeft, ElbowRight, ElbowLeft, WristRight, WristLeft, ShoulderRight and ShoulderLeft were chosen as the joints of interest because they contribute to identifying hand gestures [2] in a sign language.

In this case, normalization is carried out by shifting the origin from the Kinect to the user body position. It is done to eliminate the variations in the joined coordinates due to the height of a person or his position in the camera's field of view [2]. The distance between joints "ShoulderLeft" and "ShoulderRight" are taken for the variations due to a person's size [2]. Thus, the joint "SpineShoulder" is selected as the origin of the user body position. Normalization is done by subtracting the shoulder elements from joints coordinates when a user is not in the center of depth image [2]. While normalizing, every frame is separated by the delimiter "@" and consists of twelve X and Y coordinates of joints of interest except "ShoulderRight" and "ShoulderLeft". While performing hand gestures, "SpineShoulder" is considered as origin, which is approximately the midpoint of "ShoulderRight" and "ShoulderLeft". These normalized coordinates are used as sequence X in sequence matching using DTW (see Sections 4.5 and 4.7).

4.4 Gesture Dataset

4.4.1 DTW Dataset

DTW dataset consists of .txt files, which are resulted from the Gesture Converter after Normalization of coordinates (see Section 4.3). The .txt files consist of X and Y coordinates of body joints for a gesture.

4.4.2 VGB Dataset

The VGB dataset consists of clips from Kinect Studio recordings where start position and end position of each sign language gesture were tagged separately and considered as separate postures. While creating a gesture project, start or end keyword was added as a suffix of the gesture. For example: "gs_Abend_start". The "Gesture Type" was chosen as Discrete (AdaBoostTrigger). It allows VGB to train gestures using AdaBoost machine learning technique. In Figure 5, "Angestellter-false" in "Abend_start" gesture consists of "Angestellter" gesture, which was tagged as a negative dataset. Unlike tagging start and end positions, negative tagging includes tagging of motion of a gesture. For every gesture, negative training of the gestures should be done to reduce false positives. Figure 5 shows tagging of

"Abend_start" gesture for training. Multiple portions of the same gesture are tagged to improve accuracy.

4.5 DTW-based Translator

The body joints provided by Kinect can be used for sequence matching using the Dynamic Time Warping (DTW) algorithm.

DTW is a technique to find an optimal alignment between two given sequences under certain restrictions [16]. A distance measurement between time series can be used to find similarity between them [22]. It is used to cope up with time deformation and different speeds of time-dependent data [16]. The time and space complexity of DTW is O(nm) [13], which means every point in a series compares every other point in a time series.

For a given two sequences $Q = (q_1, q_2, ..., q_i, ..., q_n)$ of length n and $C = (c_1, c_2, ..., c_j, ..., c_m)$ of length m, a cost matrix is constructed where the (i^{th}, j^{th}) element of the matrix contains the distance $d(q_i, c_j)$ between two points q_i and c_j, i.e., $d(q_i, c_j) = (q_i - c_j)^2$ [13].

Each matrix element (i, j) corresponds to alignment between the points q_i and c_j [13]. A warping path W is a set of matrix elements, which defines the mapping between Q and C [13]. The kth element of element W is defined as $w_k(i, j)$, where $W = (w_1, w_2, ..., w_k, ..., w_K)$ and where $max(m, n) \leq K < m+n-1$ [13]. K is the length of warp path [13][22]. The minimum distance of a warp path is called an optimal warp path [22]. Its distance can be calculated using [22]: if $w_k=(i, j)$, w_k+1 is equal (i', j'), where $i \leq i' \leq i+1$, and $j \leq j' \leq j+1$, then

$$\sum_{K=1}^{K} Dist(W) = Dist(w_{ki}, w_{kj}). \quad (1)$$

In (1) Dist(W) is the Euclidean distance of the warp path W and $Dist(w_{ki}, w_{kj})$ is the distance between two data points [22]. The value of a cell in a cost matrix is given by [22]:

$$D(i, j) = Dist(i, j) + min[D(i-1, j), D(i, j-1), D(i-1, j-1)] \quad (2)$$

The warp path to D(i, j) must pass through one of those three grid cells, and the least distance among the three neighboring cells are added to the Euclidean distance between the two points [22]. While filling the matrix, it is filled one column at a time from the bottom up, from left to right [22].

By using this approach, the cost matrix was plotted for two-time series. The normalized input from Kinect was captured in between standstill positions (sequence X in Figure 9) versus gesture from the DTW dataset (sequence Y) one at a time. The shortest distance (minimum cost) was calculated from the top row of the cost matrix. It was divided by the length of the gesture dataset sequence, with which it was compared against [4].

This resulted value was compared with a threshold value (t=2), which is defined manually. If the resulted value is less than or equal to t, the gesture is recognized.

4.6 Translation into Text

Since the gesture from Kinect (sequence X in Figure 9) is compared against multiple gestures in DTW dataset, only those gestures were chosen, which satisfies constraint (t less or equals to 2). DTW-based Translator returns a list of possible matches from the dataset for gesture input. Based upon the DTW principle, less cost results in more similarity in time series. Hence, the gesture, which has least cost was chosen to be a recognized gesture. After a gesture is recognized, the application gets the filename of the matched gesture, which is printed as the recognized gesture.

4.7 VGB with DTW-based Translator

DTW-based Translator utilizes high CPU and a significant amount of memory to compare the multiple gestures. Also, the application has to compute any gesture between standstill position even if they were not sign language gestures. The concept behind VGB with DTW approach is to avoid comparing every gesture in the DTW dataset for gesture recognition. It can be done by identifying the start position of the sign language gesture. If a start position is detected, it is highly probable that a user has signed a correct sign language gesture.

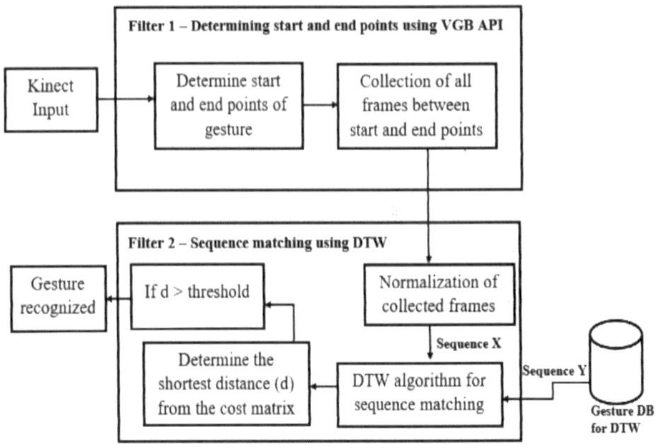

Figure 9. VGB-with-DTW-based Translator

In Figure 9, when the user body frame arrives as a Kinect input, each of these frames are processed by using the VGB API. It uses AdaBoost machine technique to recognize the start or end position of the sign language gestures. AdaBoost is a supervised machine learning algorithm [15], which generates a strong classifier out of the set of weak classifiers [10][12]. While training gesture datasets in VGB using AdaBoost, weak classifiers, i.e., angles using inferred joints, speed rejecting inferred joints, etc., are used to generate the strong classifier along with a confidence level. When a frame from Kinect is recognized as a gesture, VGB API returns the gesture name. When the start position of a gesture is detected, the application collects the body frames unless the end position of the same gesture is found. In the meantime, if it detects other gestures, the stored frames are cleared, and the collection of frames begins as soon as start position is detected again. After the frames are collected between start and end positions of the same gesture, they are normalized and passed for sequence matching using DTW. In this case, the application knows the gesture name and, by using this gesture name as a reference, it compares with only one gesture from DTW dataset, which matches the gesture. It was done to find if the motion of the sign language gestures were performed correctly. Using this technique, false positives, which were observed using the DTW-based Translator, can be significantly reduced.

V. RESULTS

The eleven gestures of DGS used in Germany: Abend, Angestellter, Bayern, Danke, Dick, Gebärdensprache, Information, München, Schlank, Un- möglich and Vater were used to compute the cost of computation and accuracy. These gestures, which were used as datasets for DTW and VGB were provided by an expert user. To compute the cost of computation and accuracy, "Abend"-gesture was chosen against the varying number of gestures in the dataset. For DTW–based Translator DTW threshold was chosen as 2, whereas for VGB-with-DTW based translator DTW threshold was chosen as 2.5.

In VGB-with-DTW based translator time taken to compute a single gesture in dataset includes the sum of time taken to compute start and end position of gesture from VGB along with time taken to compute the gesture in DTW dataset. Figure 10 shows time taken to compute the "Abend"-gesture using both approaches.

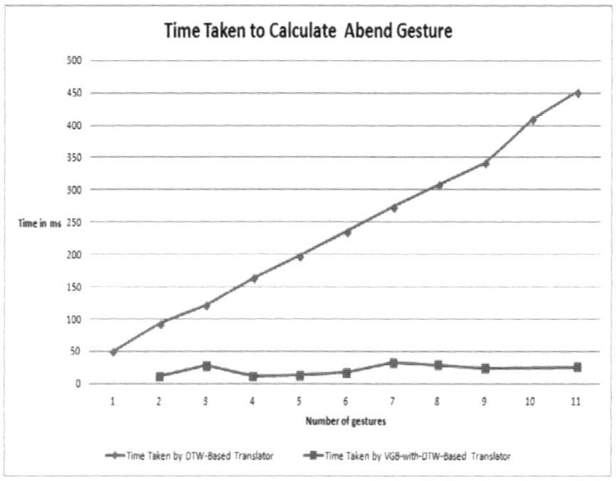

Figure 10. Time calculation for "Abend"-gesture using both approaches

5.1 Accuracy of DTW-based Translator

To compute the accuracy for DTW-based Translator, every gesture was performed 10 times by a novice user. Before performing the gestures, they were studied from the recordings of an expert user. Table 1 shows the number of detected, not detected, and false positives for the gestures using DTW-based Translator. The accuracy column shows accuracy in percentage for detected gestures. "Schlank" had 90% accuracy whereas "Unmöglich" had 40% accuracy.

TABLE I. ACCURACY OF DTW-BASED TRANSLATOR

Detected Gestures	No. of Obs.	Detected	Not Detected	False Positives	Accuracy(%)
Abend	10	6	3	1	60
Angesteller	10	7	3	0	70
Bayern	10	5	5	0	50
Danke	10	8	0	2	80
Dick	10	6	3	1	60
Gebärdensprache	10	5	5	0	50
Information	10	6	1	3	60
München	10	8	2	0	80
Schlank	10	9	1	0	90
Unmöglich	10	4	2	4	40
Vater	10	8	1	1	80
Total	110	72	26	12	
Overall Accuracy(%)		65.45	23.64	10.91	

Table 2 shows the gestures, which were recognized as false positives for DTW- based Translator.

TABLE II. GESTURES WITH FALSE-POSITIVE RECOGNITION

Detected Gesture	Recognized as
Abend	Gebärdensprache
Danke	Bayern
Dick	Unmöglich
Information	Dick
Unmöglich	Bayern, Danke
Vater	Bayern

Figure 11 is based on Table 1. For "Abend"-gesture, 6 gestures were detected, where one was false positive. The highest number of false positives were observed in "Unmöglich"-gesture, whereas the lowest number of false positives were observed in "Angesteller", "Bayern", "Gebärdensprache", "München" and "Schlank". The least detected gesture was "Unmöglich" whereas the most detected gesture was "Schlank".

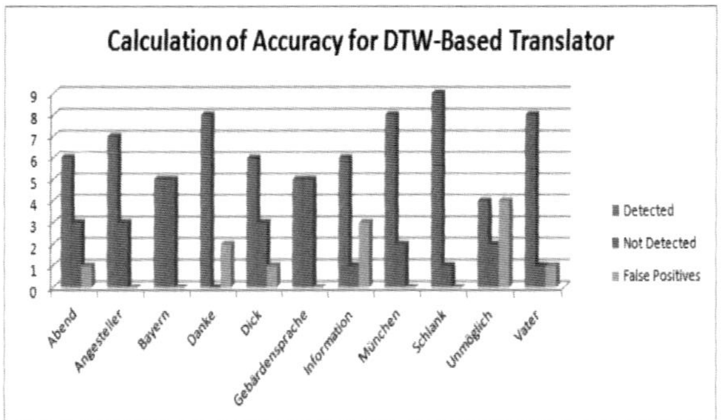

Figure 11. Calculation of Accuracy for DTW-based Translator

5.2 Accuracy of VGB-with-DTW-based Translator

Table 3 was calculated by performing a gesture several times by a novice user. "Abend" gesture was performed 15 times, but it was recognized only 4 times with no false positives. Some gestures like "Information" and "Vater" were not detected at all. The best-detected gesture was "Bayern", "Dick", and "München".

TABLE III. ACCURACY OF VGB-WITH-DTW-BASED TRANSLATOR

Detected gesture	No of obs.	Detected	Not detected	False Positives	Accuracy(%)
Abend	15	4	11	0	26.67
Angestellter	24	1	23	0	4.17
Bayern	15	7	8	0	46.67
Danke	14	4	10	0	28.57
Dick	14	6	8	0	42.86
Gebärdensprache	17	2	15	0	11.76
Information	23	0	20	3	0
München	12	5	7	0	41.67
Schlank	16	4	12	0	25
Unmöglich	23	6	17	0	26.09
Vater	18	0	18	0	0
Total	191	39	149	3	
Overall accuracy(%)		20.42	78.01	1.57	

Figure 12 shows the number of detected, not detected, and false positives for the gestures for VGB-with-DTW-based Translator recognized gesture.

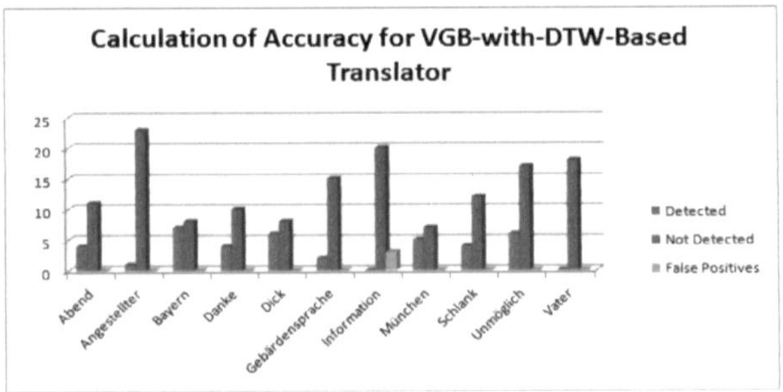

Figure 12. Calculation of accuracy for VGB-with-DTW-based Translator

5.3 Overall AccuraciesVGB with DTW-based Translator

DTW-based translator detected 65.45% of gestures with 10.91% false positives whereas VGB-with-DTW-based Translator detected 20.42% of gestures with 1.57% of false positives. More detections but also more false positives were observed in DTW-based Translator.

VI. DISCUSSION AND FUTURE WORK

In Figure 10, the time, which was taken to compute "Abend"-gesture using DTW–based translator, increased with increasing number of gestures in the dataset whereas VGB-with-DTW based translator almost remained same. This behavior was expected because DTW-based translator has to compare with more numbers of gestures on increasing the gestures in the dataset whereas VGB-with-DTW based translator has to compare with only one designated gesture. The constant outcome was expected for the VGB-with-DTW based translator, but some irregularities were observed in Figure 10. One of the possible reasons might be VGB not being able to detect the same frame as a start or end position of gestures in each observation. The accuracy of detected gestures of DTW–based Translator (see Table 1) was better than VGB-with-DTW based translator (see Table 3), although, some false positives were observed in DTW–based translator. From the false positive recognition (see Table 2) it can be inferred that:

- Usually, single-handed gestures have single-handed gestures as false positives. Similarly, two-handed gestures have two-handed gestures as false positives (Exception: "Dick").
- Most of the false positives were caused by "Bayern"-gesture. It was false positive for "Danke", "Unmöglich" and "Vater". If we observe the right-hand movement of "Bayern"-gesture, coordinates of right hand differ slightly because it is signed by forming small circles around the chest. The small variation in its coordinates might have resulted in false positive gesture for many cases.

From the accuracy of DTW-based Translator, it can be inferred that:

- Accuracy highly depended upon how user performed the gesture.
- Gestures involving long motions were difficult to recognize. For example, "Gebärdensprache", "Unmöglich".
- Short Gestures that included variation in coordinates were easier to recognize. For example: "Danke".
- However, lengthy gestures involving a greater variation of coordinates were difficult to recognize ("Abend", "Unmöglich").
- Long gestures affected Natural User Interaction of the user. It was observed that, while performing a long gesture like "Gebärdensprache", the gesture displayed in the application did not synchronize with the user body movement.
- When gestures were performed accurately, i.e., in accordance with the expert user, it was easier to recognize.
- The accuracy of VGB-with-DTW based translator was lower than DTW–based Translator. Some factors that may have affected its accuracy are:
- Detected gestures from VGB, i.e., start and end positions have very low confidence (<50%).
- The translator was not able to detect start and end points precisely. One reason might be due to a number of frames tagged in VGB. Several frames were considered for tagging standstill position, but only a small portion of frames was used for tagging start and end positions of gestures.
- "Angestellter_start" was not detected precisely, compared to "Angestellter_end". For example: the start position of "München", as well as the end position of "Unmöglich", were difficult to be detected. The reason might be that the start and end positions of a gesture closely resemble with other gestures.
- A single gesture "Bayern" was detected twice, because of multiple start and end points in the gesture. In such cases, the accuracy of this translator was even lower, because the partially completed gesture is not considered as a single gesture.

Nevertheless, this application is a proof of concept that VGB and DTW can be used for sign language recognition.

VII. CONCLUSION

In this paper, two different methods – DTW and VGB along with DTW were proposed to recognize dynamic sign language gestures.

To reduce complexity in application development, several constraints were taken into account, i.e., ignoring non-manual cues, the configuration of hands and considering only the signs that involve some motion. Using DTW–based translator-approach the input gesture was compared against all available gestures in dataset whereas in VGB–with–DTW–based translator, the concept of determining the start position and end position of a sign language were used to guess the correct gesture, which was then verified by DTW computation. The DTW-based translator had some false positive detections and the time computation increased with the increasing number of the gestures in the dataset. Usually, similar gestures were the false positives. Some latency was observed using this approach, but the accuracy was comparatively better than translator based on VGB–with–DTW–based translator. The key factor for the increase in accuracy was a small dataset, and the boundary condition (standstill) for the gestures were easily recognized. However, DTW–based translator is unrealistic for large numbers of the dataset. In VGB-with-DTW-based translator, false positive detections were significantly lower compared to that of DTW-based translator. But, the accuracy decreased significantly. The lower accuracy was mostly because of not being able to precisely detect start and end points of similar sign language gestures. This approach had less computation time because of less noise in the gesture. However, the accuracy also reduced significantly because of the low detection rate of start and end gestures.

From benchmarks of the translator applications, it can be concluded that the DTW-based Translator has higher accuracy (65.45%) than that of VGB-with-DTW-based Translator (20.42%). But, the VGB-with-DTW-based Translator performed better regarding CPU consumption than the DTW-based Translator.

References

[1] "Sign language". Available from http://wfdeaf.org/human-rights/crpd/sign-language; Last accessed 20.01.2018.

[2] S. Celebi, A. S. Aydin, T. T. Temiz, and T. Arici, "Gesture recognition using skeleton data with weighted dynamic time warping". In VISAPP (1), pp. 620-625, 2013.

[3] H. Cooper, E. J. Ong, N. Pugeault, and R. Bowden, "Sign language recognition using subunits". The Journal of Machine Learning Research 13, 1, pp. 2205-2231, 2012.

[4] "Dynamic time warping to recognize gestures". Available from https://social.msdn.microsoft.com/Forums/en-US/4a428391-82df-445a-a867-557f284bd4b1/dynamic-time-warping-to-recognize-gestures?forum=kinectsdk; Last accessed 20.01.2018.

[5] N. Gkigkelos and C. Goumopoulos, "Greek sign language vocabulary recognition using Kinect," presented at the Proceedings of the 21st Pan-Hellenic Conference on Informatics, Larissa, Greece, 2017.

[6] "Kinect tools and resources". Available from https://developer.microsoft.com/en-us/windows/kinect; Last accessed 20.01.2018.

[7] "Visual gesture builder: A data driven soultion to gesture detection". Available from https://onedrive.live.com/view.aspx?resid=1A0C78068E0550B5!77743&app=WordPdf; Last accessed 20.01.2018.

[8] K. Emmorey, "Language, cognition, and the brain: Insights from sign language research". Psychology Press, 2001.

[9] G. Fang, W. Gao, and D. Zhao, "Large-vocabulary continuous sign language recognition based on transition-movement models". In: IEEE Transactions on Systems, Man and Cybernetics, Part A: Systems and Humans, 37, 1, pp. 1-9, 2007.

[10] Y. Freund, and R. E. Schapire, "A decision-theoretic generalization of on-line learning and an application to boosting". In: Journal of computer and system sciences, 55, 1, pp. 119-139, 1997.

[11] P. A. Harling and A. D. N. Edwards, "Hand tension as a gesture segmentation cue". In: Proc. of Gesture Workshop on Progress in Gestural Interaction, pp. 75-88, 1996.

[12] T. Hastie, R. Tibshirani, and J. Friedman, "Boosting and Additive Trees". In: The Elements of Statistical Learning. Springer Series in Statistics. Springer, New York, NY, 2009.

[13] E. Keogh and C. A. Ratanamahatana, "Exact indexing of dynamic time warping". In: Journal of Knowledge and Information Systems, 7, 3, pp. 358-386, 2005.

[14] S. K . Liddell, "Grammar, gesture, and meaning in American Sign Language". Cambridge University Press, 2008.

[15] O. Mozos, C. Stachniss, and W. Burgard, "Supervised learning of places from range data using adaboost". In: Proc. of the IEEE International Conference on Robotics and Automation, pp. 1730-1735, 2005.

[16] M. Müller, "Dynamic time warping". Information retrieval for music and motion, Springer, 2007.

[17] S. Ong and S. Ranganath, "Automatic sign language analysis: a survey and the future beyond lexical meaning". In: IEEE Transactions on Pattern Analysis and Machine Intelligence, 27, 6, pp. 873-891, 2005.

[18] M. Oszust and M. Wysocki,. "Some approaches to recognition of sign language dynamic expressions with kinect". In Human-Computer Systems Interaction: Backgrounds and Applications 3. Springer, pp. 75-86, 2014.

[19] R. Pfau, M. Steinbach, and B. Woll, "Phonetics, phonology and prosody". In: Sign Language: An International Handbook, pp. 4-77, Walter de Gruyter, 2012.

[20] R. Pfau, M. Steinbach, and B. Woll, "Sign language: An international handbook". vol. 37, Walter de Gruyter, 2012.

[21] Quizlet LLC; Available from: http://quizlet.com/12296633/abc-1-asl-vocab-flash-cards; Last accessed 20.01.2018

[22] S. Salvador and P. Chan, "Toward accurate dynamic time warping in linear time and space". In: Journal of Intelligent Data Analysis, 11, 5, pp. 561-580, 2007.

[23] M. S. Santos, E. B. Pizzolato, S. Feuerstack, "A Real-Time System to Recognize Static Gestures of Brazilian Sign Language (Libras) alphabet using Kinect". In: IHC 2012 Proceedings, 2012.

[24] A. Sarkadi, "Vocabulary learning in dyslexia: the case of a hungarian learner". In: Language learners with special needs: An international perspective. Clevedon: Multilingual Matters 194, 2008.

[25] C. Sun, T. Zhang, C. Xu, „Latent support vector machine modeling for sign language recognition with Kinect." In: ACM Trans. Intell. Syst. Technol. 6, 2, pp. 1-20, 2015

[26] T. Starner and A. Pentland "Real-time american sign language recognition from video using hidden markov models". In: Proc. of the International Symposium on Computer-Vision, pp. 265-270, 1995.

[27] W. C. Stokoe, "Sign language structure: An outline of the visual communication systems of the american deaf". In: Journal of deaf studies and deaf education, 10, 1, pp. 3-37, 2005.

[28] W. C. Stokoe, D. C. Casterline and C. G. Croneberg, "Introduction to a dictionary of american sign language". In: Linguistics of American Sign Language, pp. 243-258, 2000.

[29] W. Vicars, "ASL University". Available from http://www.lifeprint.com; Last accessed 20.01.2018.

[30] J. Zhang, W. Zhou, and H. Li, "A Threshold-based HMM-DTW Approach for Continuous Sign Language Recognition". In Proc. of the International Conference on Internet Multimedia Computing and Service, pp. 237-240, 2014.

Basic Study for a New Analysis Method for Biological Signals to Evaluate in Human Walking

Tatsuo Hisaoka, Naoki Hashimoto, Yusuke Kobayashi, Masaya Hori
Tokyo Univ. of Science, Suwa
Engineering, management graduate course
Engineering, specialization in management
Chino-city, Japan
e-mail: {GH16608, GH16607, GH17608, GH17612}@ed.tus.ac.jp

Mayu Maeda, Hiroaki Inoue
Tokyo Univ. of Science, Suwa
Faculty of Engineering
Chino-city, Japan
e-mail: S314052@ed.tus.ac.jp
e-mail: hiroaki-inoue@rs.tus.ac.jp

Shunji Shimizu
Tokyo Univ. of Science, Suwa / Faculty of Engineering
Jichi Medical University / Psychiatric Course
Chino-city, Japan
e-mail: shun@rs.suwa.tus.ac.jp

Abstract—**Recently, in developed countries, especially in Japan, the population of elderly people has grown. The care load for elderly people has been steadily growing. Most important for such care is to provide support for elderly people in walking. There are many reports on analyses of Human Walking, but there are few commercially available products that are able to provide support for Human Walking. The utilization rate of such support is 8.7% in Japan. Therefore, it is bionic, and the development of expensive walk apparatus for such applications is necessary. The purpose of this study is to propose a new analysis method for biological signals to evaluate in human walking. Concretely, in this experiment, a new measurement system was developed for human walk movement analysis with an embedded system including a microcomputer chip and a motion tracking device. Using this measurement system, electrical muscular potential and the acceleration of toe or instep of foot. In our results, this measurement system was found to clearly discriminate the difference in walking movements when wearing a pair of sandal or not. We think that these data are useful to design guidelines for a new accessibility system for human walking.**

Keywords-Human walking; Surface myoelectric potential; Walk assisting apparatus; Analysis method; Biological signal.

I. INTRODUCTION

Recently, in developed countries, especially in Japan, the population of elderly people has grown. There is a high risk of falling among elderly people, with about a 28 to 35% chance of falls in those over 65 years old [1]. In severe cases, it may be a serious problem because their physical strength may be lowered due to bed rest and being bedridden may result. Especially preservation therapy is performed in 90% of such cases as a cure for degenerative joint disease and arthrogryposis. It is a serious problem in that chances of healing and recovery to a self-reliant life are less than 50% [2]. Methods for increasing functional base of support (FBOS), such as a cane for walk assistance and stabilization are effective for posture maintenance, but their rate of dissemination is poor [3]. As a result, rehabilitation stations are being expanded more frequently, and there seems to be a demand for lower limb orthotic conservative therapy. However, according to the research on age care payment costs, it was 8.7% in 2017 and, considering the present conditions of the diffusion rate of a walk aid being covered by nursing care insurance, cannot be said to be spreading [4]. Accordingly, our laboratory, aimed for the development of a walk aid which has a high bionic application level. In addition, we developed a new measurement system and, for walk movement analysis, introduced it and performed a surface electromyography (EMG) of the group of muscles being used in conjunction with the walk movement and simultaneous measurement of the acceleration of the foot part. Thus, the experiment extracts a quantitative index for the development of the walk aid and could in this way perform an analysis of the physical load and evaluation of the lower limb orthotic in a walking motion. Therefore, we tested footwear in which the load of the foot bottom was differentiated to be examined and reported [5].

The structure of this paper is Section 5. In Section 1, we describe the background, necessity and purpose of this research. In Section 2, we introduce a simple measurement system and experiment method. In Section 3, we explain using a figure how little foot subduction is taken. In Section 4, we will examine the results. Section 5 describes the usefulness of this experiment and future tasks.

II. Experimental Method

In this study, we tried to measure transformation of the arch of foot. The transformation of minute joint was ignored in the current measurement device such as force plate and the Three-dimensional motion capture system. Therefore, there are few examples that the transformation of the joints is considered in the development of welfare device. In order to measure the very small deviation of the foot during walking, we developed measuring system by using accelerometer and measured the walking movement.

1. Subjects

The subjects were five healthy men who had no history of orthopedic disease or neurological disease. Age, heights, weights, the average and standard deviation of age, height and weight was 23.8±0.9, 168.8±3.6cm, 66.5±9.9kg respectively.

2. Informed consent

We carried out this experiment with sufficient informed consent of the subjects after the approval of the Tokyo Univ. of Science, Suwa Ethical Review Board.

3. Measurement system

The use apparatus used Raspberry Pi 3 and MPU6050. The MPU6050 is a device that measures acceleration.
Specifications of the MPU-6050:

- Digital-output triple-axis accelerometer with a programmable full scale range of ±2g, ±4g, ±8g and ±16g (Table 1).
- The MPU-6050 then communicates with a system processor as a slave through an I2C serial interface.
- Chip built-in 16 bit AD converter, and 16 bits data output.
- A sampling rate that is programmable from 4 to 1,000Hz.
- Two I2C addresses.

The measurement system connected two MPU6050 to Raspberry Pi 3 and communicated using I2C. The program used python and executed things with Raspberry Pi 3. The range of measurement confirmed that ±16g was not necessary in a preliminary experiment. Therefore, the range of measurement was set to ±8g and had better precision. The sampling rate was measured at 1,000Hz. The data obtained from the sensor was corrected to the physical value by the following formula.

Acceleration = 16 bit value of sensor / LSB sensitivity [6].

The measurement data were saved to a PC through wireless communication of RaspberryPi3.

4. Method

A. Arrangement of accelerometer on the instep

Acceleration measurement of the instep was made by placing an accelerometer on the navicular bone to accord with Acceleration measurement of the arch. The x axis, the y axis and the z axis are of adduction direction, advancing direction, and the height direction to plus respectively.

B. Measurement of accelerometer on the instep

An accelerometer is put under the navicular bone to accord with the Acceleration measurement of the instep. The x axis, the y axis and the z axis are each of adduction direction, advancing direction, and the height direction to plus respectively.

C. Measurement by accelerometer on the instep

Acceleration at the time when hallux was stepping was measured. The accelerometer was adjusted to be placed

Table 1. The accelerometers sensitivity per LBS

Full Scale Range	LSB Sensitivity
±2g	16384 LSB/g
±4g	8192 LSB/g
±8g	4096 LSB/g
±16g	2048 LSB/g

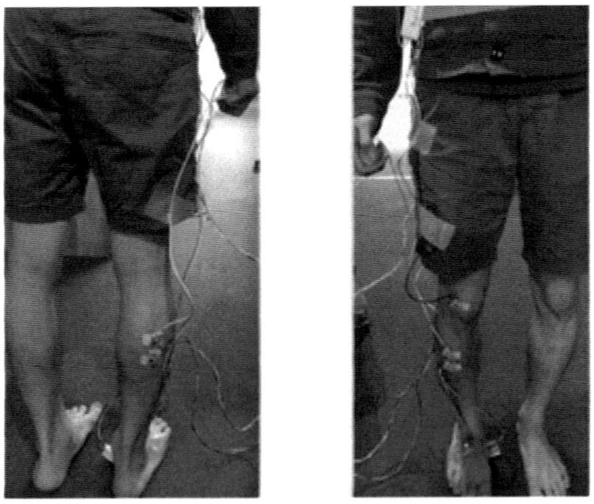

Figure 1. Surface EMG adhesion position

under the rough surface of the first metatarsal bone. The x axis, the y axis and the z axis are of adduction direction, advancing direction, the height direction to plus respectively.

D. Placement of surface electromyogram

The surface electromyogram (EMG) measured a muscular group (Tibialis anterior muscle, Gastrocnemius muscle) concerning the walk movement (Figure 1). In the experiment, a sufficient amount of fat and keratin was removed, and electrodes (Advance; LecTrode) were affixed.

E. The experiment method

The subjects attached two accelerometer and surface EMG meters to the lower limbs, and walked straight for approximately 10m indoors. During that time, we measured each eight times walking bare foot and wearing sandals.

A) The subject stands by in the standing position, starts measurement, and then starts to walk on the measurement person's signal.
B) The subject walks about 10 m.
C) The subject stops walking on the signal of the experimenter and waits in the standing position.
D) The subject keeps standing till there is a sign that the experiment has ended.

In addition, subjects were asked to press the switch at the time of heel contact and used as an indication of the start of the walk cycle. The accelerometer was connected with a microcomputer and saved acceleration data to the personal computer with a wireless connection.

EMG derived data with a multi telemeter (Nihon Kohden Tomioka Corp; Multi-telemeter), performed A / D conversion (ADinstrulmental; PowerLab), and saved EMG data to the personal computer (SONY; PCG-5M5N). The trigger input used an LED circuit of 5V output to synchronize with other data. While walking, the trigger was given to the examinee and was pressed when the toes left the ground and the heel made contact [7]. Furthermore, rectification, Root Mean Square analysis and examination was performed on the EMG data.

F. Analysis method

We thought of my legs as a simple model (Figure 2). From the motion picture at walking time, the angle from the center of gravity to the foot which was measured in advance from the front / side of the subject was mathematically examined. Compare the extension and deformation of the foot with the accelerometer and the extension / deformation at the resting standing position. Regarding the walking motion from terminal stance to loading, the position change due to acceleration was obtained by the following equation by integration. X is the variable distance, a is the acceleration obtained from the accelerometer, and g is the gravitational acceleration.

$$x = \sum_{i=0}^{t} \{\mathrm{T(i)} - \mathrm{T(i-1)}\}^2 \times a \times g \qquad (1)$$

III. EXPERIMETAL RESULTS

A. Measurment

As for experimental results, the acceleration of instep, arch and hallux was measured and a correspondence between the Tibialis anterior muscle and Gastrocnemius muscle could be confirmed.

Figure 3 shows the waveform of one subject accelerometer as a representative example. It represents one cycle from heel contact to heel contact. The vertical axis is the gravitational acceleration applied in each direction, the horizontal axis is time, x, y, z are the direction orthogonal to the traveling direction, the traveling direction and the height direction.

- Figure 3-a shows the results when placing acceleration on the instep and arch of the foot while walking with bare feet.
- Figure 3-b shows the results when placing acceleration on the instep and arch of the foot while walking with sandals.
- Figure 3-c shows the results when placing acceleration on the instep and the first toe while walking with bare feet.
- Figure 3-d shows the results when placing acceleration on the instep and the first toe while walking with sandals.

Figure 3 also shows the movement distance by one subject from the loading to the terminal stance as a representative example.

B. Analysis method

From the equation (1), we compare the changes in the long axis direction and the short axis direction of the foot with the micro displacement distance between the stationary state and the dynamic state. At that time, the area and norm were examined using the micro displacement distance.

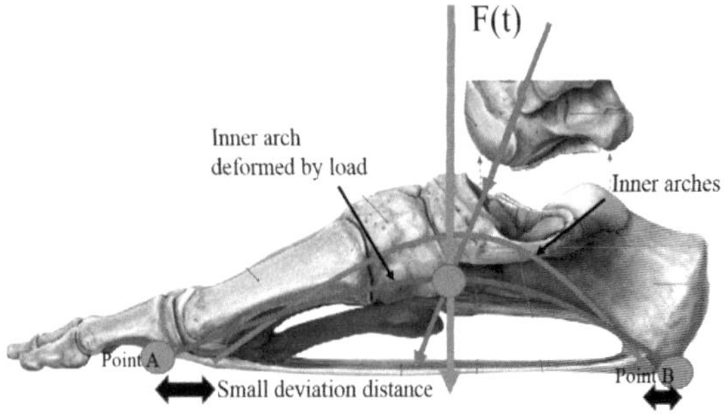

Figure 2. Simple skeleton model: Load response to feet as viewed from the side

This seems to be related to foot changes due to accelerometer load. In addition to not extending the elongation of the foot in one direction, it tends to elongate in the long axis direction due to individual differences and it tends to stretch in the minor axis direction, so compare the major axis direction, minor axis direction, area and norm.

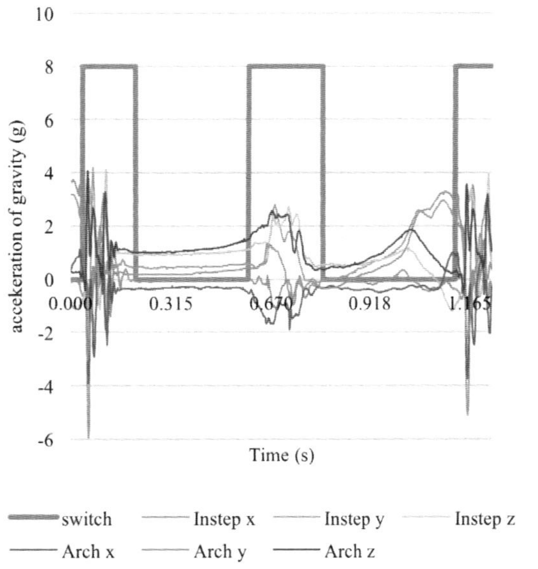

Figure 3-a. Walking with barefoot

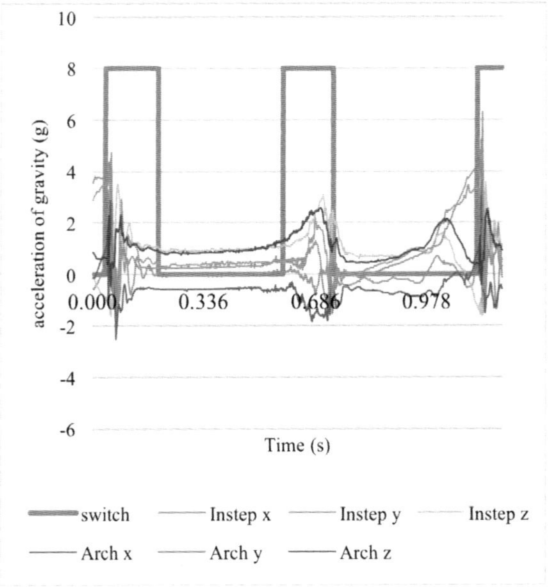

Figure 3-b. Walking with sandals

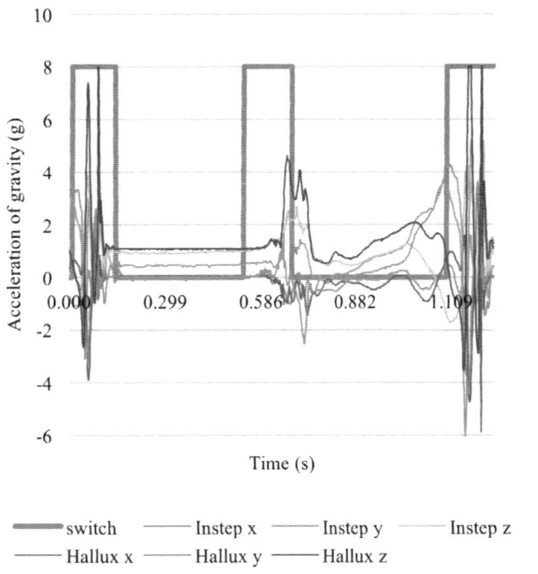

Figure 3-c. Walking with barefoot

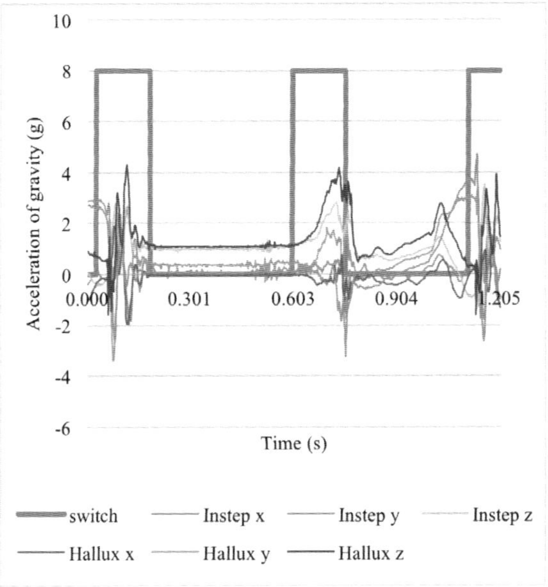

Figure 3-d. Walking with sandals

IV. Discussion

A. *Measurement*

In this research, we focused on the deformation of the arch during walking by using an accelerometer at walking in a force plate and a three - dimensional motion analyzer, and measured a minute displacement of the biological motion difficult to measure. We simulate a human body model that approximates a rigid body using a force plate and a three-dimensional motion analysis device used for the current gait analysis, and in many cases do not consider joints of the forefoot part. Therefore, at this time, there are no useful goods and welfare equipment. Thus, in order to measure minute displacement of walking feet, walking analysis was carried out using an accelerometer, and advanced bioengineering application was developed. We will explain experimental considerations on acceleration data, addition average, standard deviation, simple skeleton model, measurement deviation distance. Especially, consider area and norm. Regarding the arch change in the direction of travel and transverse direction by walking, norm and inner product value are obtained, and as a result of comparing the load change, the norm of the foot has a higher proportional relationship, the arch variable has the norm, I Found a possibility to be an indicator of the load evaluation on the foot.

This experiment yields the results that the hallux becomes the main axis from the moving distance of the instep, plantar arch, and hallux of the foot, and the possibility of center of gravity movement is considered.

According to Kanabe et al., "The hallux has supportive action at the position in front of the center of gravity". We think that the hallux also supports the center of gravity while walking. We consider that it is important not only to support the vertical direction but also to support the hallux, which is thought to have the support function of the center of gravity with respect to the horizontal force. The amount of change of

Table 2. Comparison with area

subjects	*Total load (mm^2)*	*Barefoot change due to acceleration (mm^2)*	*Acceleration of sandals and change during use (mm^2)*
A	32.0	1.85	1.23
B	130.0	$3.4*10^{-4}$	0.09
C	16.0	$1.8*10^{-4}$	0.04
D	20.0	0.81	0.17
E	18.0	0.13	1.38
F	18.0	18.44	1.16

Table 3. Comparison with norm

subjects	*Total load (mm)*	*Barefoot change due to acceleration (mm)*	*Acceleration of sandals and change during use (mm)*
A	90.0	2.77	7.25
B	25.0	0.43	0.73
C	17.0	0.03	0.16
D	19.0	1.93	0.93
E	18.0	0.76	2.72
F	13.0	3.69	2.63

the foot bottom is different from a bare foot in conjunction with having an insole or not.

In conclusion, this study proposed a new gait analysis method to measure microtremors of muscles and bones. In order to develop the insole which enables easy posture maintenance, we measured the parameters used as the index of the insole. The deformation of the arch that is difficult to measure with the method frequently used for biometric measurement was able to be grasped as the area and norm from the deviation distance. From this result, shock absorption of walking can be seen, and it is possible to quantitatively measure the change of the arch considering the bow of the foot which is greatly involved in the walking function. However, it is still inadequate to develop insole, which is the object of this research, and it is necessary to further improve the system, experiment and inspection, but it is necessary to further improve system, experiment and inspection by a simple and simple method suggesting the possibility.

V. Conclusion and Future work

In this experiment, the subduction of the foot during walking was measured using an accelerometer. I think that it is the first step of a system which can analyze walking anywhere, rather than using expensive equipment such as force plates or 3-dimensional motion analysis equipment. It can be used in limited space and is relatively inexpensive. Moreover, it is possible to observe the subduction of the foot and to estimate the subduction with the footwear. This study is relatively simple and can capture minute fluctuations of the foot. At the present stage, attention was focused on the vertical component at the time of grounding, aiming for new obstacles to the assistive devices by confirming minute fluctuations of the feet, but also comparing and examining the free legs and the horizontal component and further concrete Try to become an indicator. For that purpose, we will do further data analysis, discussion and proceed with development of sole for practical use.

References

[1] Orthopedics new patient investigation. Nonprofit foundation Japan orthopedics society 2012. [Online]. Available from: https://www.joa.or.jp/media/comment/pdf/investigation_2012 .pdf 2017.12.13

[2] M. Suzuki, "WHO Global Report on Falls Prevention in Older Age," Japan: QUALITY-CARE CO., Ltd. 2010.

[3] M. B. King, J. O. Judge, L. Wolfson, "Functional Base of Support Decreases With Age," Journal of Gerontoligy, vol. 49, pp. 258-263, 1. 11. 1994

[4] K. Kanabe, K. Kurosawa, Y. Nishida, Y. Nakata, et al, "The Study of Relationship between Toe and Dynamic Postural Control," Society of Physical Therapy Science (SPTS)., Vol.17, No. 3, pp. 199-204, 2002

[5] U. B Rao, B. Joseph," THE INFLUENCE OF FOOTWEAR ON THE PREVALENCE OF FLAT FOOT," Kasturba Medical College, Manipal: India, 1991

[6] InvenSense Inc, MPU-6000/MPU-6050 Register Map and Descriptions. [Online]. Available from: https://www.invensense.com/wp-content/uploads/2015/02/MPU-6000-Register-Map1.pdf. 2018.2.2.

[7] N, Yamazaki. ASHI NO JITEN. Asakura Publishing Co., Ltd. vol, 6. 2011

Fundamental Study for A Noise Reduction Method on Human Brain Activity Data of NIRS using AR Model

Toshiya Tsubota, Tomohiko Kuroiwa, Takuya Kiryu
Tokyo Univ. of Science, Suwa
Engineering, Management Graduate Course
Chino-city, Japan
e-mail: {GH16606, GH16604, GH17605}@ed.tus.ac.jp

Yu Kikuchi, Hiroaki Inoue
Tokyo Univ. of Science, Suwa
Faculty of Engineering
Chino-city, Japan
e-mail: S314015@ed.tus.ac.jp
e-mail: hiroaki-inoue@rs.tus.ac.jp

Fumikazu Miwakeichi
The Institute of Statistical Mathematics
Department of Statistical Modeling
Tachikawa-city, Japan
e-mail: miwake1@ism.ac.jp

Shunji Shimizu
Tokyo Univ. of Science, Suwa / Faculty of Engineering
Jichi Medical University / Psychiatric Course
Chino-city, Japan
e-mail: shun@rs.suwa.tus.ac.jp

***Abstract*—Currently, Near Infra-red Spectroscopy (NIRS) is used as a diagnostic aid for mental illness in hospitals [1]. In our previous study, we have already reported the relationship between human brain activity change and turning the corner while driving a car or carrying out human living motions, using NIRS [2][3]. In that research, it was very difficult to discriminate noise from measurement signals not only by using NIRS but also by using Magnetoencephalography (MEG), Electroencephalogram (EEG), and so on. In Particular, for a study to measure the brain activity related to tasks of memory or intention, the effects of the ratio of signal to noise are very important. Our experimental results show that our model removes the noise of the heartbeat and breathing motion from the brain activity data of NIRS.**

Keywords-Near Infra-Red Spectroscopy (NIRS); Auto Regressive (AR) model; signal to noise ratio.

I. INTRODUCTION

The study of brain science is being carried out on a global scale now. In the future, brain science research is expected to be applied to various fields, such as medical care and Brain-Machine Interface (BMI). Near Infra-red Spectroscopy (NIRS) is a device that can easily measure the limited functions of the brain. Currently, NIRS is used in hospitals as a diagnostic support device for depressive illness and epilepsy [1]. In general, psychiatric disorders are diagnosed by a doctor based on clinical symptoms and medical history. However, multiple cases have been reported in which it is extremely difficult for a doctor to make a diagnosis. NIRS is a device for measuring hemoglobin concentration contained in blood by using infra-red light. The areas in the cerebrum related to specific psychological phenomena and psychiatric disorders can be identified using a NIRS system based on the theory of brain function localization. We have been studying the quantitative evaluation method of brain activity using NIRS. We confirmed a statistically significant difference in specific areas of the brain related to movement. The following is an overview of our previous study.

1) Basic Study for New Assistive Technology Based on Brain Activity during Car Driving

In our previous study, we measured road sign recognition while driving and brain activities during left and right turns. In this experiment, we studied the cognitive mechanism of human spatial cognition and road signs. As a result, it was confirmed by statistical testing that brain activation signals were activated at different areas at the time of right turns and left turns [2].

2) Fundamental Study pn New Evaluation Method Based on Physical and Psychological Load in Care

In our previous study, "Standing-up movement" and "Sitting movement" which are essential for human life in rehabilitation and nursing care workplaces were performed multiple times, and changes in brain activity accompanying exercise were evaluated by statistical verification method. As a result, when the physical exercise load on the human body increased, a change in activity was confirmed at a specific brain area [3].

The above results are considered to have been experiments on sufficient ratio of signal to noise. NIRS is able to measure human brain activity under low physical restriction without being restricted by posture, vocalization, exercise, etc. NIRS has many advantages such as higher temporal resolution than functional Magnetic Resonance Imaging (fMRI). NIRS is suitable for the research on brain activities associated with mental tasks and behaviors. However, problems such as an accumulation of evidence and inadequate elucidation of mechanisms have been pointed out. In addition, NIRS includes heartbeat, breathing motion, and body movements as noise and is measured. This also applies to other brain activity measuring devices such as fMRI, MEG and, EEG. The problem influences studies measuring the brain activity related to the task of memory or intention.

In this study, the purpose of this paper, we attempt to reduce the artifacts generated by the heartbeat and breathing motion from the data of NIRS using the Auto Regressive (AR) model [4].

In Section I, the necessity of this paper is explained. In Section II, we report the method of this experiment and the calculation formula of the AR model used in this study. Section III reports the results obtained by applying the AR model to the NIRS data and ECG data obtained in this experiment. In Section IV, an FFT analysis was conducted to examine the validity of the results compared with the existing information. Section V summarizes the conclusion of this research and then summarizes future research subjects.

II. EXPERIMENTAL METHOD

In this study, we composed two experiments. In the first experiment, we measured the brain activity data and electrocardiogram (ECG) of the resting subjects using NIRS and Multi-Telemeter. These data included artefacts of heartbeat and breathing. In the second experiment, signal components for NIRS data were analyzed based on the ECG. Using the analysis results, we derived heartbeat artefact components from the NIRS data. Therefore, we could reduce the artefacts due to the heartbeats from NIRS data when we used a heartbeat artefact component. Finally, the breathing artefact components, presumed to be from the NIRS data, made a reduction in the number of artefacts caused the by breathing motion frequency.

1) *Near Infra-Red Spectroscopy (NIRS)*

NIRS is a device for measuring the density change of hemoglobin in cerebral neocortical blood flow at a depth of about 20 to 30 mm from the scalp using near infrared light. From the theory of localization of brain function, related brain areas are activated by human thought. At this time, the hemoglobin carries oxygen necessary for metabolism then, and the oxygen density throughout the bloodstream of the activated domain rises. The human body has characteristics that make it is easy for near infrared light to pass through, but the hemoglobin contained in the blood has the property of absorbing near infrared light. NIRS can estimate brain activity by measuring the difference between incident probe and detection probe [1].

2) *Auto Regressive (AR) model*

The AR model is a method to estimate future data from past data in time series data. To predict future data in the time series $\eta(t), t=1,\ldots,S$ it is necessary to construct a prediction model using information obtained from past data.

When only the most recent past data is used, we have:

$$\eta(t) = \alpha(1)\eta(t-1) + \varepsilon(t) \quad (1)$$

When using the past two data

$$\eta(t) = \alpha(2)\eta(t-1) + \alpha(1)\eta(t-2) + \varepsilon(t) \quad (2)$$

The above formula is quoted as an example. Generalizing this as a linear combination of past p-point data yields the following model

$$\eta(t) = \sum_{i=1}^{p} \alpha(i)\eta(t-i) + \varepsilon(t) \quad (3)$$

Here, $\varepsilon(t)$ is the prediction error (noise according to the normal distribution), p is the dimension of the model, and $\alpha(i)$ is the AR coefficient. The relationship between the AR coefficient, the frequency f of the stationary vibration and the sampling frequency Fs can be obtained by the following equation.

$$\alpha(1) = 2\gamma\cos\left(2\pi\frac{f}{Fs}\right), \alpha(2) = -\gamma^2 \quad (4)$$

Here, γ is a constant which corresponds to the attenuation factor. When using actual time series data, AR coefficients can be optimized by the least squares method or Yule-Walker method, and the dimension of the model can be determined by Akaike's information criterion [4] [5].

3) *Filtering using the AR model*

From (3), the AR model can be deformed as follows.

$$\varepsilon(t) = \eta(t) - \sum_{i=1}^{p} \alpha(i)\eta(t-i) \quad (5)$$

From (5) is a filter that inputs time series data and outputs prediction error. This prediction error is called innovation. When the frequency to be removed is predetermined, the AR coefficient is determined from (4) [4] [5]. The procedure for filtering using the AR model is shown below. Figure 1 shows the filtering method using the AR model.

1. Estimate the AR coefficient in the time series data of a certain section.
2. Estimate the AR model from the AR coefficient.
3. Calculate prediction error using the AR model.
4. Filter time series data using prediction error.
5. Measure unpredictable signal

A. Measurement of rest state by NIRS

In our previous study, we confirmed that NIRS data includes at least the effects of the heartbeat and breathing motion as noise [2] [3]. In this experiment, we measured brain activity and ECG of resting subjects with NIRS (Shimadzu Corporation FOIRE-3000) and Multi-Telemeter (NIHON KOHDEN CORPORATION WEB-5000). At this time, we assumed that the brain activity change of the subject was very small, and that NIRS data contained many artefacts due to heart rate and breathing exercise. At this time, we considered that the brain activity change of the subject was very small, and that NIRS data contained many artifacts due to heartbeat and breathing motion. The subjects were 10 adult men aged 22-24 years, sitting in a chair 60 cm away from the wall and gazing at the markers at eye height for 1 minute. At this time, the sampling frequency of NIRS was 20 Hz, and the sampling frequency of the ECG was 100 Hz. In addition, we did not give any special instructions to the subjects other than gaze the markers. Figure 2 shows the state of this experiment and NIRS.

B. Artefact reduction of NIRS data using the AR method

We filtered the measured NIRS data with the AR model [4]. At this time, the AR coefficient was obtained from NIRS data and ECG data. We analyzed the frequency of the ECG data and constructed a low pass filter. We reduced the frequency component of the heartbeat from NIRS data using a low pass filter. We extracted the artefact considered to be an influence on heartbeat from processed NIRS data using the AR model. We were later able to confirm the artefact occurred under the influence of respiratory movement. In order to remove this artefact, an AR model was created from the formula (4) using the frequency considered as respiratory motion from the FFT result of the NIRS data, and filtering was performed.

We carried out this experiment with sufficient informed consent of the subjects following the approval of the Tokyo Univ. of Science, Suwa Ethical Review Board.

III. EXPERIMETAL RESULTS

A. Measurement of rest state by NIRS

Heartbeat and breathing are deeply related to oxygen supply. In this experiment, we focused on the change of oxygenated hemoglobin in the NIRS data. Figure 3 and 4 show the NIRS data and ECG data of a subject. Figure 5 shows the FFT analysis results of the ECG data and NIRS data. In the ECG, a general waveform can be confirmed, and a waveform called an R wave when the ventricle contracts is recorded. From Figures 3 - 5, we confirmed the correspondence between the R wave and oxygen concentration change in NIRS data.

B. Artifact reduction of NIRS data using the AR method

For each data measured in Experiment A, the AR coefficient is calculated using the Yule-Walker method, and the data estimated from the AR model is compared with the measurement data. Figures 6 and 7 compare the AR model and measurement data for NIRS data and ECG data for 10 seconds to 20 seconds. Figures 8 and 9 show the prediction errors of the AR model and measurement data. Figure 10 shows the result of reducing the frequency component of the heartbeat from the NIRS data using the low-pass filter constructed from the result of the FFT analysis of experiment A. Figure 11 shows the result of extracting data considered as the influence of heartbeat from the NIRS data using the AR coefficient of the electrocardiogram data and the filtered NIRS data. We calculated AR coefficients from formula (4) using the frequency (0.2Hz) of the breathing motion of the average man. We estimated the AR model of respiratory motion using AR coefficient and filtered NIRS data. Figure 12 shows the AR model of breathing motion. In addition, Figure 13 shows the NIRS data from which the AR model of breathing motion and heart beat have been removed.

We were able to confirm the above results from the data of all subjects. Figures 15 to 25 show the results of other subjects.

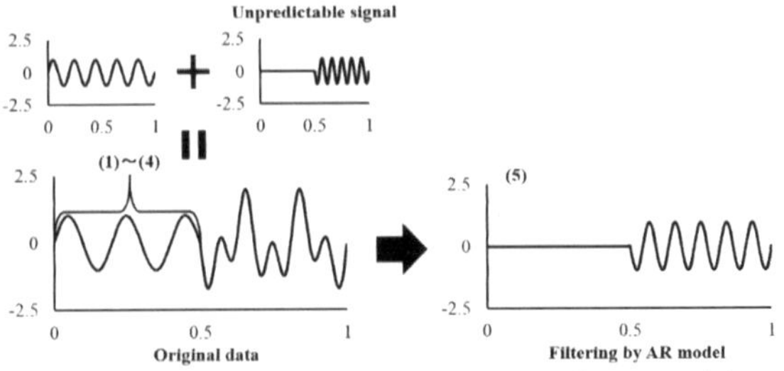

Figure 1. Conceptual diagram of noise removal by AR model

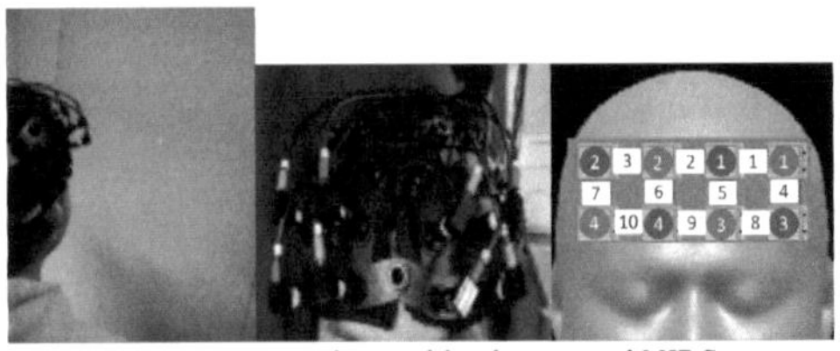
Figure 2. Experimental landscape and NIRS

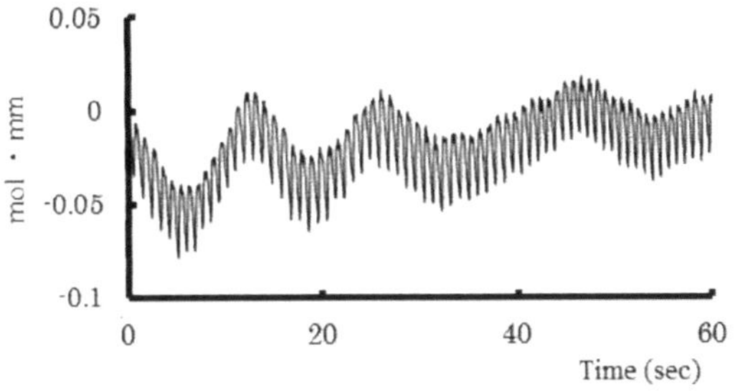

Figure 3. NIRS data measured by experiment

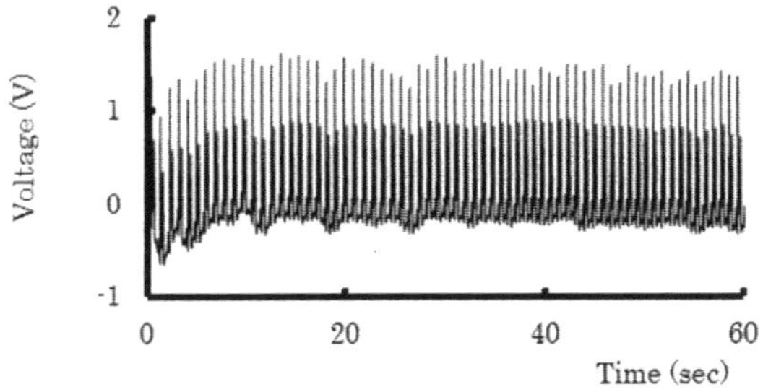

Figure 4. ECG data measured by experiment

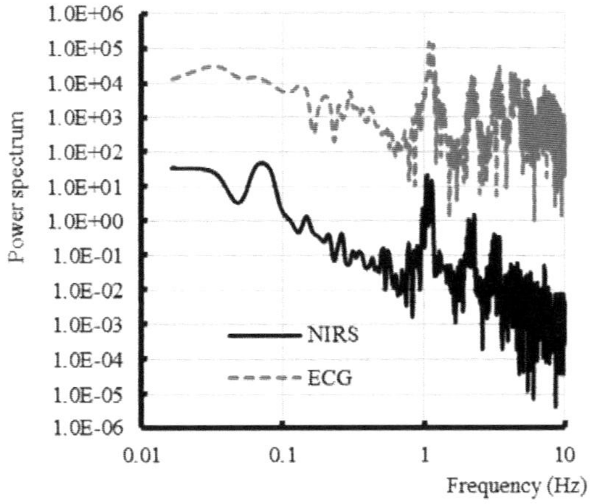

Figure 5. FFT analysis results of ECG data and NIRS data

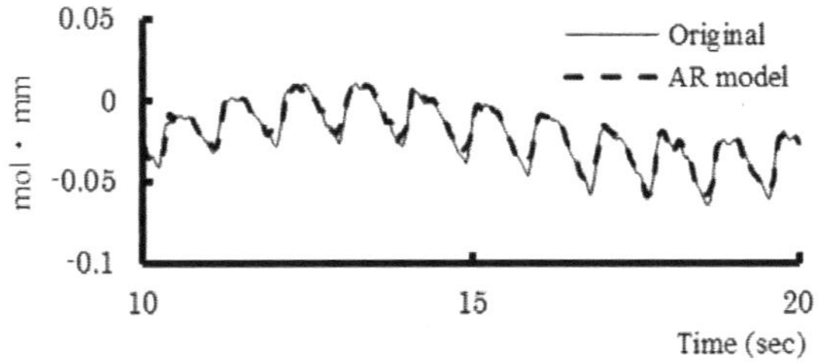

Figure 6. Comparison of NIRS data and AR model

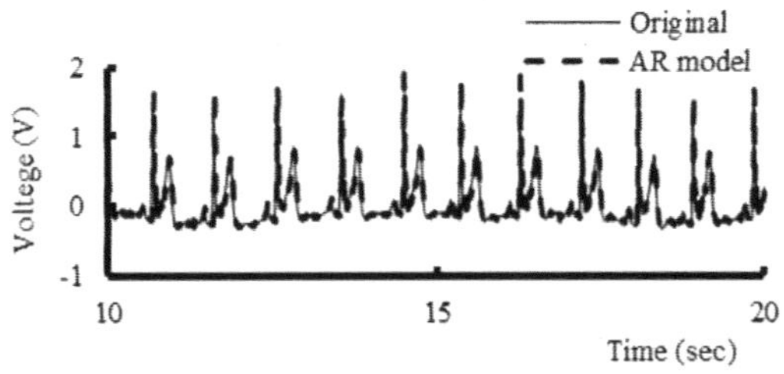

Figure 7. Comparison of ECG data and AR model

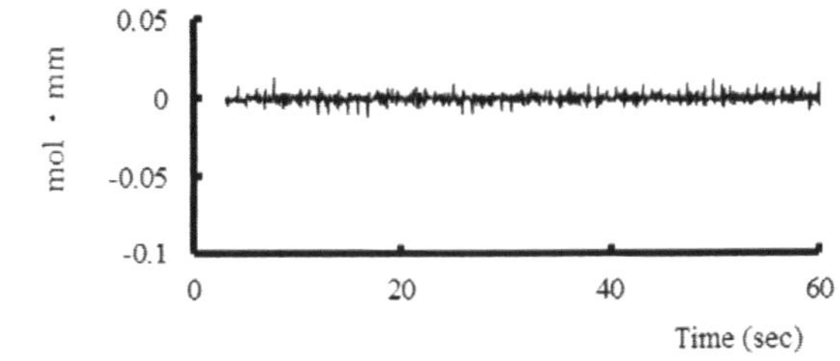

Figure 8. Prediction error of NIRS data and AR model

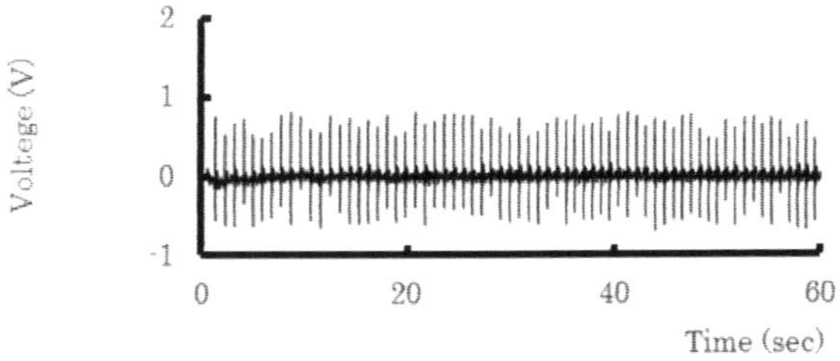

Figure 9. Prediction error of ECG data and AR model

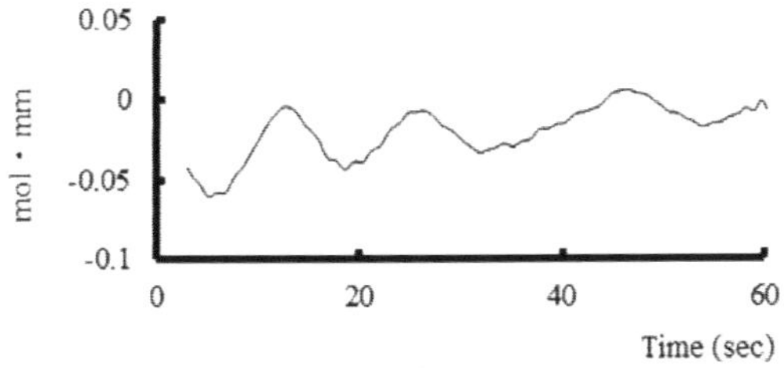

Figure 10. NIRS data calculated from the low pass filter

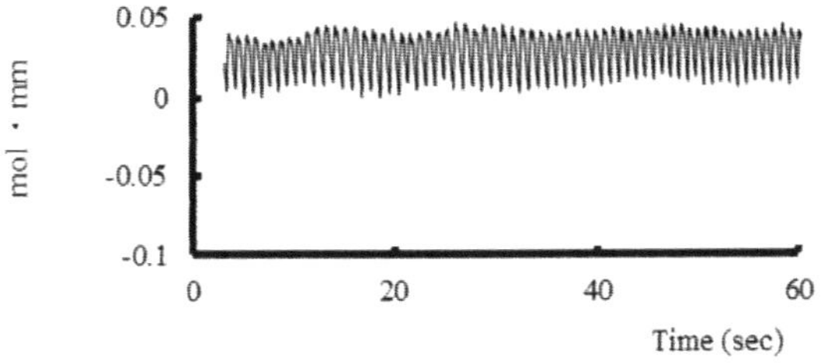

Figure 11. Data considered to be effects of heartbeat

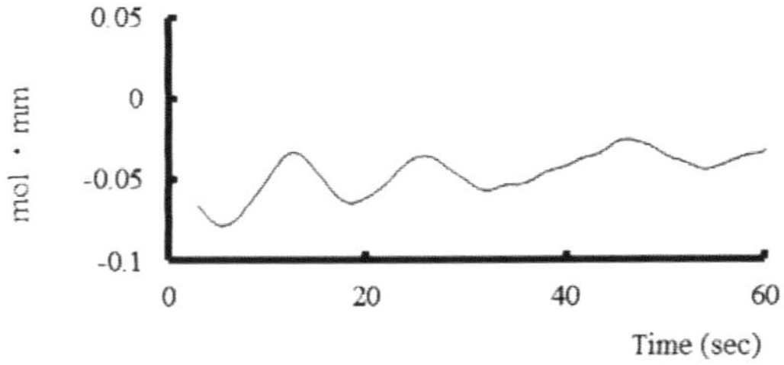

Figure 12. AR model by breathing motion

IV. Discussion

A. Measurement of rest state by NIRS

From the experimental results, we confirmed that the peaks of NIRS data and ECG data were nearly identical. In particular, we confirmed a characteristic peak near 1.1 Hz, which is considered as the period of the R wave in the ECG data. Furthermore, we confirmed that the amplitude component of the NIRS data is attenuated by the low pass filter produced based on 1.1 Hz. The above results were consistent with the frequency (0.85~1.5Hz [50~100 BPM]) of normal heartbeat of an average male in his twenties. However, the low-pass filter attenuated frequencies of 1.1 Hz or higher and had drawbacks such as not being able to remove breathing motion. Therefore, in Experiment B, filtering using the AR model was examined.

B. Artefact reduction of NIRS data using the AR method

Figure 14 shows the results of the FFT analysis of Figures 11 and 12. From Figure 14, the artefact due to breathing motion and the artefact due to a decrease in heartbeat from about 0.3 Hz as the difference in frequency components increases. We thought that the above results were related to the breathing frequency (0.2~0.3Hz [12~18BPM]) of adult males. As a result, Figure 12 has a very high possibility of being an artefact due to breathing motion. Also, Figures 5, 14 and 11 show a very high possibility of artefacts due to heartbeat. From the above results, Figure 13 considers that respiratory motion and heartbeat artefact could be removed from NIRS data. In this study, we succeeded in removing artifacts due to respiratory motion and heartbeat which could not be eliminated by a low pass filter using a method based on the AR model.

Figures 15 to 25 show the results of applying the AR method to NIRS data of other subjects. We confirmed the removal of the noise ingredient by a heartbeat and breathing motion from the NIRS data of all subjects. We measured brain activity of resting subjects. This study assumes that there is little change in brain activity. As a result, by removing the noise component from the NIRS data, the change of the NIRS signal was reduced.

V. Conclusion and Future Work

In this experiment, we measured the brain activity of the resting subjects. In other words, we supposed that a lot of noise ingredients were included in the NIRS data than a brain activity signal. We estimated the heartbeat artefacts and breathing motion artefacts included in noise using the AR model. We were able to estimate AR coefficients with high precision from ECG data. In addition, we were able to estimate the AR coefficient from the frequency that we set optionally. In this study, we succeeded in removing specific frequency components using the AR model estimated from AR coefficients. From these results, it is considered that high accuracy filter processing is possible using this study method. In the future, we will also consider ways to eliminate other noise factors (such as movement of the body). Moreover, by applying the proposed method to conventional studies, we aim to improve brain region identification and statistical accuracy which could not be clarified by conventional experimental methods.

References

[1] K. Kasai, M. Fukuda, N. Yahata, K. Morita, N.Fujii, "The future of real-world neuroscience: imaging techniques to assess active brains in social environments," Neurosci.Res., vol. 90, pp. 65-71, 2015.

[2] H. Inoue, F. Miwakeichi, S. Shimizu, N. Takahashi, Y. Yodhizawa, N. Hirai, "Basic Study for New Assistive Technology Based on Brain Activity during Car Driving," Article Published in International Journal of Advanced Computer Science and Applications(IJACSA)., Volume 5, Issue 11, 2014.

[3] H. Inoue, S. Shimizu, H. Ishihara, Y. Nakata, T. Tsuruga, F. Miwakeichi, "Fundamental Study to New Evaluation Method Based on Physical and Psychological Load in Care," International Journal of Advanced Computer Science and Applications (IJACSA)., Vol. 5, No. 11, 2014.

[4] F. Miwakeichi, "Extraction of Neural Activation from Biological Spatio-temporal Imaging Data using Autoregressive Model-based Filtering Technique," The Journal of Global Health., 00, 00, Nov, 2013.

[5] K. Akaike, S. Amari, G. Kitagawa, S. Kasima, H. Simodaira, "Akaikejyouhoukijyun AIC," Japan: Kyoritsu Shuppan Co., Ltd. 2007

[6] K. Sakatani, E. Okada, S. Hoshi,I Miyai, H. Watanabe, "NIRS -Fundamentals and Applications-," Japan: Shinkoh Igaku Shuppan Co., Ltd. 2012

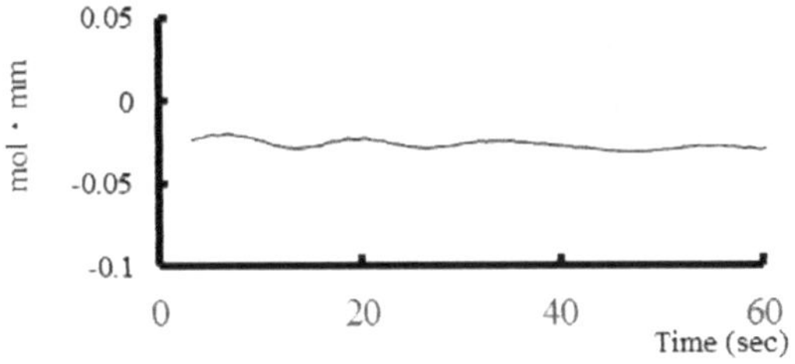

Figure 13. Filtered NIRS data

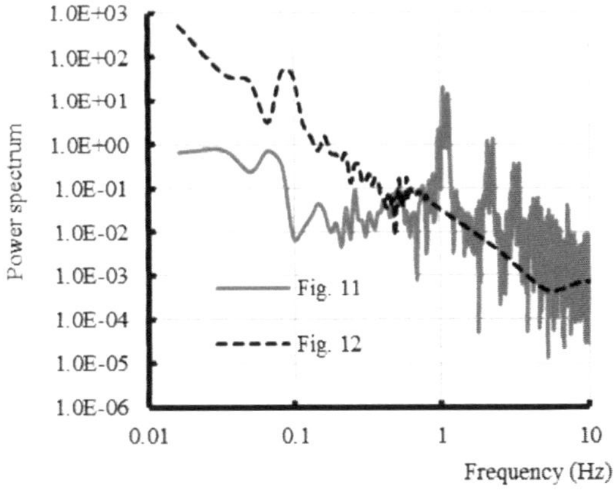

Figure 14. FFT analysis results of Fig. 11 and 12

- Subject B

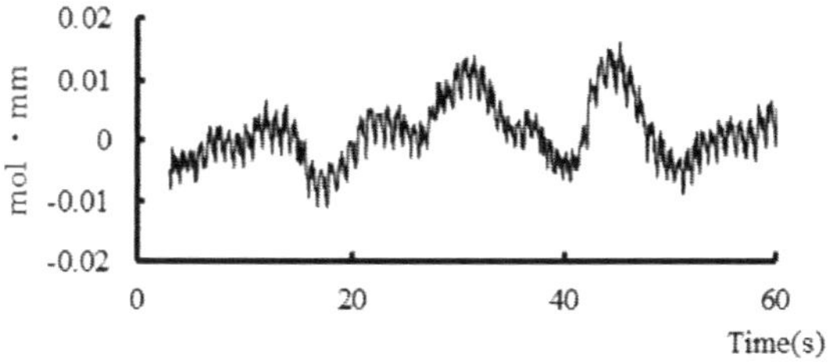

Figure 15. NIRS data of subject B

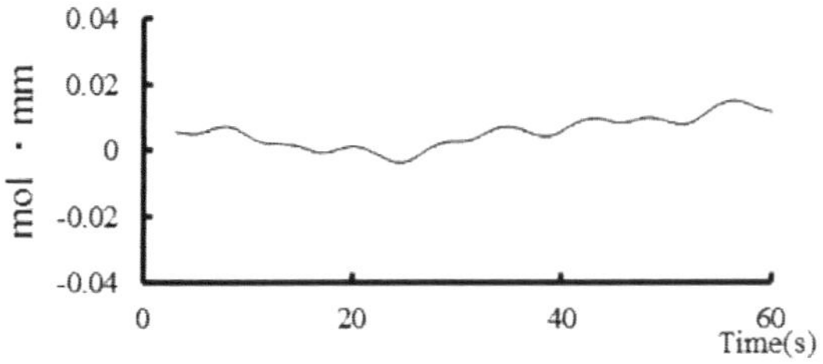

Figure 18. Filtered NIRS data of subject C

- Subject C

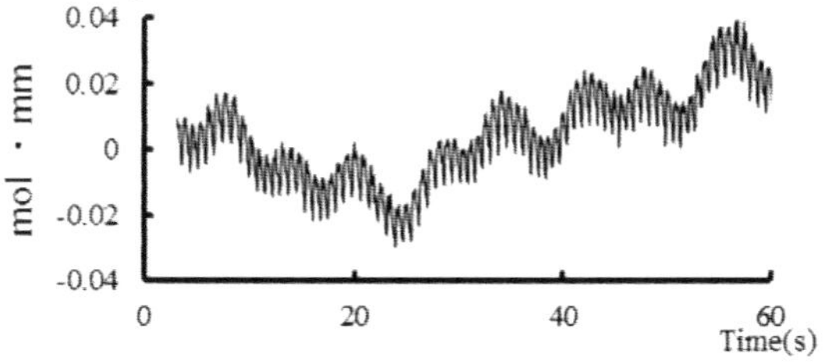

Figure 17. NIRS data of subject C

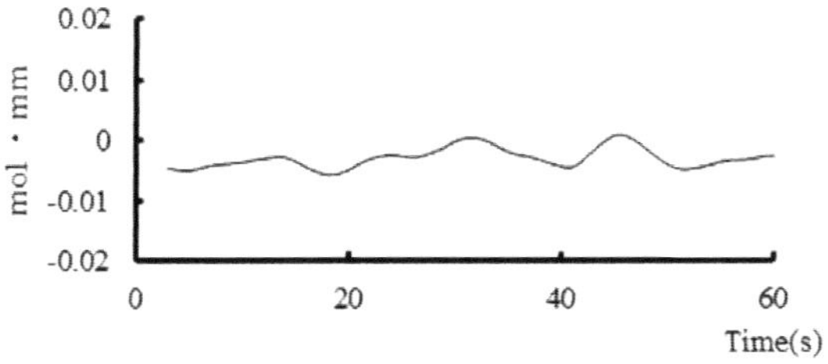

Figure 16. Filtered NIRS data of subject B

- Subject D

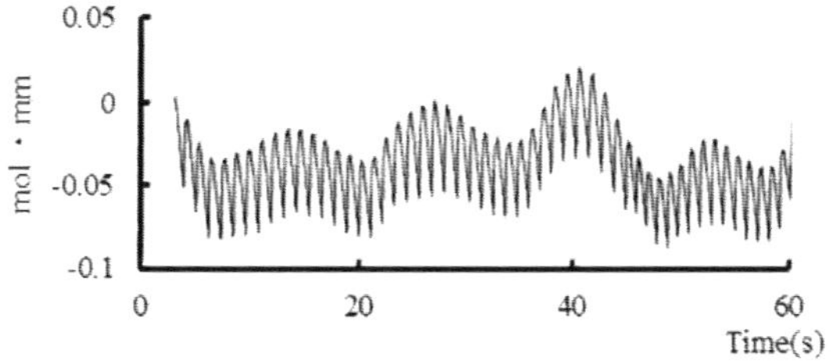

Figure 19. NIRS data of subject D

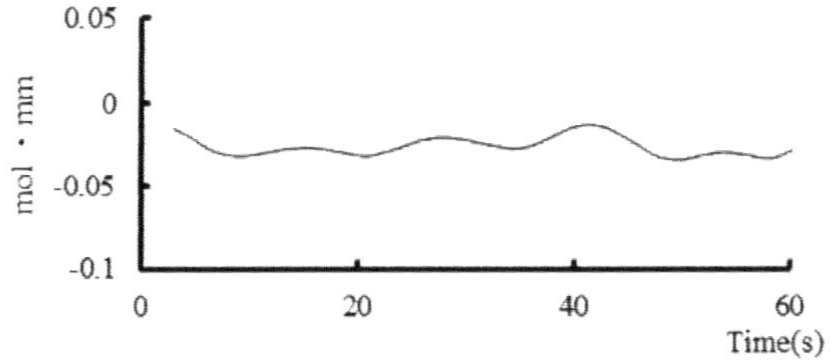

Figure 20. Filtered NIRS data of subject D

- Subject E

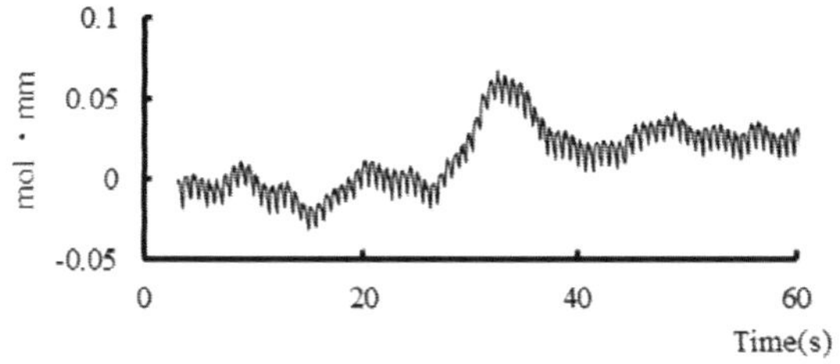

Figure 21. NIRS data of subject E

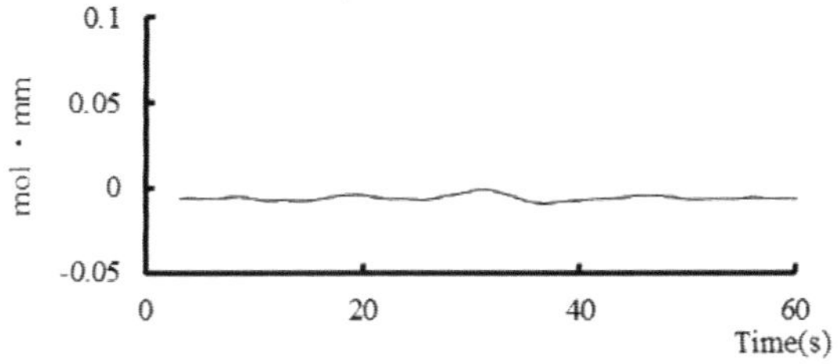

Figure 22. Filtered NIRS data of subject E

- Subject F

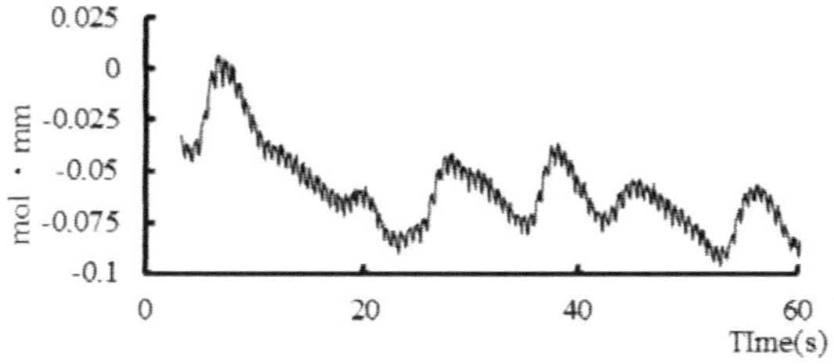

Figure 23. NIRS data of subject F

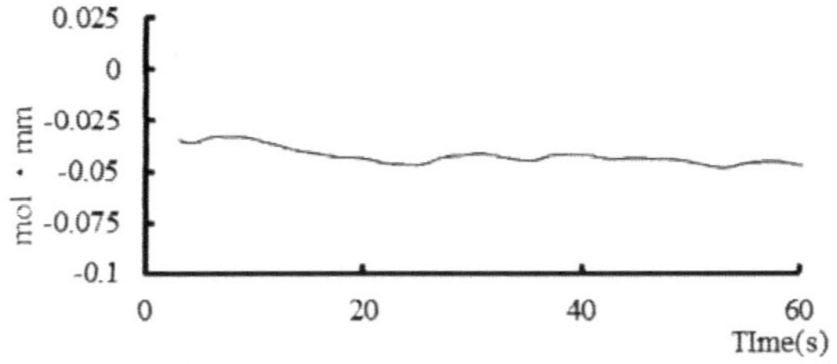

Figure 24. Filtered NIRS data of subject F

BrainSnake: Exploring Mode of Interaction in a Cooperative Multi-brain BCI Game Based on Alpha Activity

Marc van Almkerk*, Lena Brandl†, Rui Li‡, Pietro Romeo§ and Mannes Poel¶
Human Media Interaction
University of Twente, Enschede, The Netherlands
Email: m.vanalmkerk@student.utwente.nl*, l.brandl@student.utwente.nl†,
r.li-1@student.utwente.nl‡, p.romeo@student.utwente.nl§, m.poel@utwente.nl¶

Abstract—**This paper describes the design, development and evaluation of BrainSnake, a cooperative multi-brain closely-coupled brain-computer interface (BCI) game based on alpha activity. BrainSnake uses communication to address common shortcomings of BCI as an interaction modality. A within-subject study was performed to understand the value of communication in a BCI setting by putting players in both a "co-present" and "remote" condition. Results draw a complex picture of player experience but indicate that participants attributed more control over the snake character and less frustration to the co-present condition. Moreover, there was a preference for balancing communication and BCI input while playing the game. Recommendations for future design of cooperative multi-brain BCI games are derived.**

***Keywords*—brain computer interface; game design; multimodal interaction; user experience; communication.**

I. INTRODUCTION

In recent years, Brain-Computer Interfaces (BCIs) have been investigated as an input modality for user interfaces in recreational human-computer interaction (HCI), such as art [1] and games [2] [3]. At present, multi-brain BCI games enable multiple users to work towards the completion of cooperative or competitive tasks [4] [5]. However, BCI as an input modality still comes with a number of issues preventing it from becoming mainstream, such as delays in inputs, bad signal recognition, long training time, and cumbersome hardware [4]. Nevertheless, research on User Experience (UX) in games provides cumulative evidence that the use of (multi-brain) BCI as an interaction modality has considerable potential for the gaming community [3]–[6].

Research suggests that multi-player game setups may be preferred over single player mode with regard to fun and motivation [5]. However, to the best of our knowledge, no attention has been devoted to how people experience communication in multi-brain BCI games and how in-game communication should be implemented. This is due to the fact that Electroencephalography (EEG) recordings are easily disturbed by facial expressions, speech and bodily movements [4], limiting the scope of efficient modes of communication. This poses a challenge to BCI game designers.

We invite BCI researchers and game designers to view shortcomings of BCI in a new light. [6] makes a case for considering shortcomings of BCI in traditional BCI applications as in-game tasks and challenges from a game design point of view [6] [7]. One way to overcome these shortcomings is by using BCI as a complementary control modality. An example of such a BCI implementation is AlphaWoW, a variant of the popular videogame World of Warcraft, which calculates power in the alpha frequency (8-12 Hz) of the brain to control the shape-shifting ability of certain playable characters: when the user experiences stress, such as under in-game battle conditions, there is little alpha activity, and the character changes into a powerful bear form. Once the user starts to relax, alpha activity increases and the character reverts back to its natural elf shape [6]. However, such an implementation of a BCI is passive, i.e., the user is not directly controlling the game with brain activity. One of the easiest ways to control alpha activity is by closure of the eyes, however this introduces a counterintuitive control mechanism: alpha activity is increased when the subject closes their eyes, and by doing so, they give up visual feedback. Moreover, it takes a few seconds to induce higher alpha activity and for the system to detect it [4], preventing BCI players from playing fast-paced games.

Nonetheless, alpha activity is still worth exploring, since retrieving alpha band frequency is comparably uncomplicated without (extensive) training and it only requires a few electrodes for signal acquisition. Hence, inspired by Nijholt et al., we explore alternative ways of using BCI as a game input modality aimed at overcoming common shortcomings of alpha activity. For this, we propose "BrainSnake", a game with a novel design that uses both verbal player interaction and eye closure as main gameplay mechanics. Additionally, we investigate how the presence of direct communication, or the lack thereof, may affect playability and user experience of a multi-brain BCI game.

Section II of this article illustrates the design and implementation of BrainSnake and its novel interaction modality based on alpha activity. Section III describes the design and execution of a user study in which players evaluated BrainSnake under different inter-player communication conditions. Results of the user studies are reported and discussed in Section IV. Finally, in Section V, conclusions are drawn and recommendations for future designs of (alpha-based) BCI games are given.

II. GAME DESIGN

BrainSnake is based on the popular game "Snake", in which a snake character made up of dots has to collect pieces of

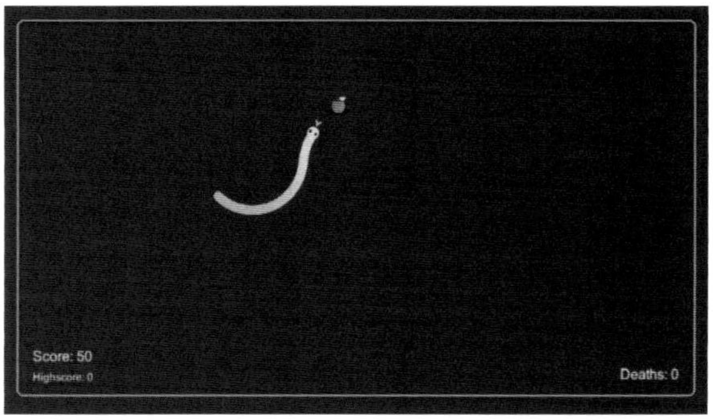

Figure 1. Screenshots from the final version of BrainSnake.

food on the screen whilst avoiding its own tail. The body of the snake grows by one dot for each piece of food collected, gradually increasing the difficulty of the game. Game over occurs when the snake eats its own tail (or hits one of the screen borders). BrainSnake adopts a similar gameplay in which two players have to collect apples by sharing control over the snake character. Both players control the snake avatar using their brain activities to turn either left or right. The complementarity-based control [8] was expected to elicit cooperative activities typical of closely-coupled games (e.g., "working out strategies together") which may be affected by the presence of communication (or lack thereof) [9]. Fig. 1 shows the graphical interface of the game, showing the snake avatar in yellow and collectable apples in red. Moreover, the current score, high score and the amount of deaths is visible in the bottom corners of the screen.

A. Gameplay and Interaction

The interaction of BrainSnake is designed to compensate three main limitations of alpha activity as an input modality. Firstly, alpha activity is most suitable for being used as a binary input despite being measured on a continuous scale, since it is difficult to regulate. Secondly, inducing and detecting alpha activity requires time, which results in a delay of a few seconds [4]. Thirdly, in order to induce alpha activity effectively, the subject has to close their eyes.

In the classic Snake game, the player has to choose, real-time, between "no action", "turn left" and "turn right" in order to direct the snake. This type of input combined with the delay in detecting alpha activity and lack of visual feedback over the game, would be likely to affect the playability of the game negatively and make players frustrated. To overcome this, BrainSnake featured a social component. Two players played the game together so that, whenever one player closed their eyes to induce alpha activity, the other player could act as the feedback provider communicating the state of the game to their partner. Game controls were designed such that, if there is no input from either player, the snake will move forward in its direction. One of the players can take 'control' over the snake by increasing their alpha activity. When this happens, the snake stops moving and goes into a "rotation mode". Depending on which player took control, the snake's head will rotate either left or right to a 90 degrees angle, as visualized in Fig. 2, in steps of 0.5 degrees per frame. When the controlling player opens their eyes - and reduces their alpha activity - the snake will be "released" and move forward again. When a player takes control over the snake, the alpha activity of the other player will be neglected and will have no influence on the gameplay. Additionally, the game uses audio assistance as another modality to indicate when the snake rotates, eats an apple, or when it dies. In contrast to the classic snake games, when the snake hits one of the borders of the screen, it bounces back instead of dying, reducing the overall difficulty of the game.

This interaction mechanism overcomes the earlier mentioned limitations of alpha-based BCI as (i) the binary (high or low) input is split over two players, (ii) the delay in response can be corrected by the other player (in the form of feedback) and (iii) there is an additional pair of eyes for the players to help them keep track of the state of the game. Additionally, this setup allowed to further stress the complementarity cooperative game pattern of BrainSnake: while it is possible to play the game without communication and rely on acoustic feedback only, even when the player's eyes are closed, talking to each other is expected to make the gaming experience more enjoyable [9].

B. Implementation

The implemented BCI system consisted of three subcomponents for EEG-data acquisition, data pre-processing and game visualization. For the data acquisition a BioSemi Active 2 [10] was used to buffer the raw EEG signals of 7 channels [C3, Cz, C4, P3, P4, O1 and O2] using a 7 to 12 Hz temporal filter to record the alpha waves. OpenVibe [11] was used to pre-process the data into a numeric representation of the alpha activity of the player. Lastly, the binary classification of the alpha activity (high or low) as well as the game visualization were done with the Unity game engine [12].

High or low alpha activity is detected by means of the incoming data-signal from OpenVibe. The signal was duplicated and filtered with an infinite impulse response filter to reduce

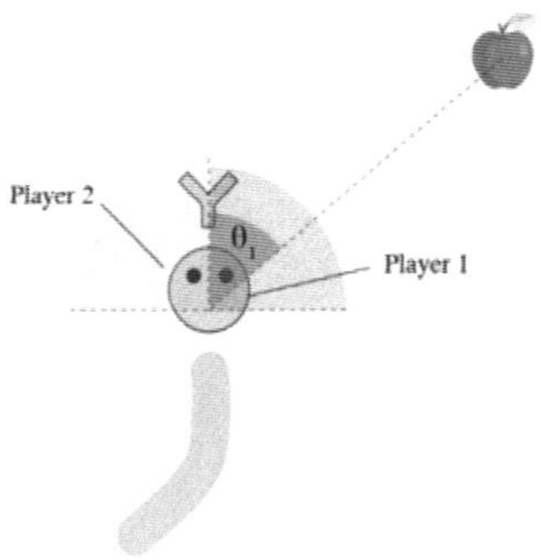

Figure 2. Players have joint control over the snake, one player rotates the snake's head left and the other player rotates it right. Rotation happens in steps over time (θ_1) till a 90 degree angle is reached, after which the snake will rotate back to its original position. Rotation continues till the player 'releases' the snake.

noise; it was then analysed alongside with the raw samples to determine high and low alpha activity according to a static, pre-determined threshold. When the filtered signal reached the threshold (for a certain amount of samples), the subject was classified as having high alpha activity, triggering the rotation mode in the game. By contrast, when the raw signals stayed below the threshold for a certain amount of time, the alpha activity was classified as low.

III. METHOD

A. Study Design

A within-subject experimental design was devised to investigate how players experienced different modes of communication in a BCI setup. This included two experimental conditions: (i) a "co-present setup", in which the two players were located next to each other, allowing them to communicate face-to-face while playing; and (ii) a "remote" set-up, in which the players were physically separated from each other by a wall and prohibited from communication. Fig. 3 illustrates the experimental setup of both conditions. Each participant experienced both conditions. The order of completion was counterbalanced. A within-subject design was chosen to allow participants to make well-informed comparisons between both modes of interaction. Player experience was assessed quantitatively using the Game Experience Questionnaire (GEQ) [13] once after each condition. Next to this, a semistructured interview was conducted at the end of the experiment to capture player experience qualitatively. Topics discussed in the interview included the seven core dimensions of the GEQ, user experiences regarding the different modes of interaction, difficulties encountered while playing BrainSnake, as well as user suggestions regarding improvements of inter-player communication.

B. Participants

A total of 12 participants (ten male, two female) aged 18 to 28 (M = 23.5, SD = 2.939) were recruited to take part in the experiment. Participants were all students from the University of Twente recruited through convenience sampling. Six pairs were formed with the intention of pairing up participants who did not know each other prior to the experiment. This was done to prevent relationship bonds from biasing the game experience of our participants.

C. Procedure

Prior to the experiment, participants were briefly introduced to their partner and asked to fill in a demographic questionnaire, including questions about their previous experience with games and BCIs. Moreover, participants were briefed on the experiment and instructed what was required from them in order to play the game. The participants were then equipped with a BioSemi cap and set up for a short individual training session. During training, the game is played in single-player with the snake only able to rotate in one direction. Once both participants reached enough confidence with the BCI, the multiplayer version of the game was introduced in one of the two experimental settings. In the remote condition, a partition wall was placed between the two players and earphones were used to ensure that no verbal communication would occur between the two players. Each game session lasted eight minutes and was followed by an administration of the GEQ. After both conditions were played, the BCI equipment was removed from each participant who was then asked to take part in an individual, audio recorded 20-minute interview aimed at further investigating dimensions from the GEQ as well as their personal experiences with the game in each condition.

D. Ethics

All participants were asked to sign an informed ethical consent form prior to the experiment. Participants were informed that they would be required to wear EEG equipment and that the data collected would be anonymised and only be used for research purposes. Moreover, participants were asked for consent to have their interview sessions audio recorded. This research was approved by the ethics committee of the University of Twente. No funding is received for this research.

E. Measurements

The GEQ consists of three modules: a core module which measures game experience on seven components calculated from 33 items: Immersion, Flow, Control, Positive and Negative Affect, Frustration, and Challenge. The remaining two modules, the social presence module (three components calculated from 17 items: Psychological Involvement - Empathy, Psychological Involvement - Negative Feelings, Behavioural Involvement) and the post-game module, assess psychological and behavioural involvement of the player with other social entities, and how players felt after they stopped playing, respectively. The post-game module was not included in this study because it is targeted at assessing naturalistic, rather than experimental gaming. All items of the GEQ are measured on a five-point Likert scale with answers ranging from 0 to 4. The GEQ was filled in by the participants after each condition. The interview schedule was partly inspired by the GEQ, covering six of the seven dimensions of the core module of the questionnaire. The dimension of Immersion was left out intentionally because immersiveness was not an aim of the developed game. Moreover, the interview schedule was targeted at exploring the communication between players and the suitability of either mode of communication for cooperative or competitive game settings.

IV. RESULTS & DISCUSSION

Internal consistency reliability was assessed for the relevant GEQ modules using Cronbach's alpha, the core module (co-present condition α = .807, remote condition α = .886) and the social presence module (co-present condition α = .856, remote condition α = .919). For the semi-structured interviews, a coding scheme was developed following a grounded theory approach to identify patterns, contrasts and similarities in participants' responses [14]. The coding scheme was informed by the measured constructs of the GEQ. Pattern-based inspection

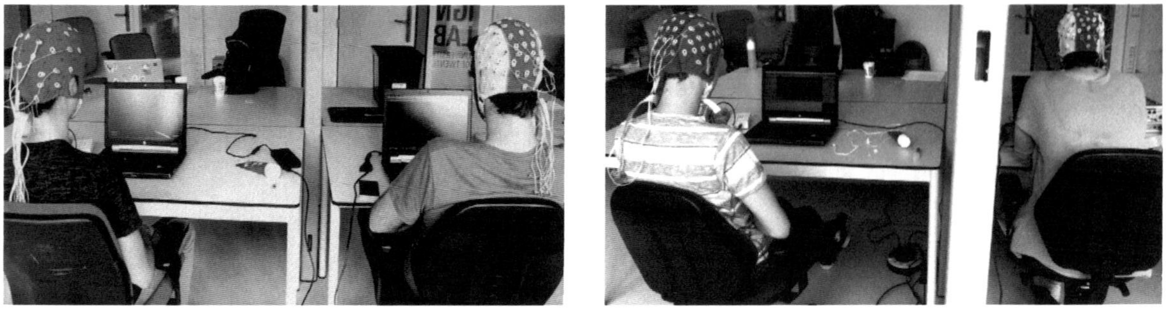

(a) (b)

Figure 3. Experimental setup for the co-present (a) and remote (b) condition.

was then performed based on the Cooperative Performance Metrics (CPMs) proposed by El-Nasr et al. [8]. As BrainSnake was designed following patterns typical of closely-coupled games [9], it was expected to raise a need for communication between the two players, reflected in CPMs such as "helping one another" and "working out strategies together" [8].

Results suggest that mode of communication did influence all the investigated aspects of player experience, although the obtained results draw a complex picture: player experience was affected, amongst other things, by individual differences and the level of harmony between players. This is also reflected in the high standard deviations of the GEQ core scores in Fig. 4. Similar results were obtained for the social presence module, as shown in Fig. 5. In the co-present condition, where direct verbal communication was allowed, participants tended to feel more psychologically and behaviourally involved with their partners. However, the obtained scores for the social presence components show great individual differences, whereas the results obtained from the semi-structured interviews give a more complete picture of how participants experienced playing BrainSnake and the interaction with their partners. In the remainder of this section, the results from the interviews are discussed.

A. Control

Eight participants explicitly indicated that they had a higher perceived control in the co-presence condition. Only one of the participants felt more in control in the remote condition, naming the lack of pressure from having to engage in communication with an unfamiliar person as a potential factor for this. P5-1: *"I was doing my thing, and let him do his thing, and it kinda worked better"*. It should also be noted that three of the participants felt that their partner was more in control of the character than they were, and that they were feeling overpowered by the other's level of control on the snake. P5-2: *"I felt that's because she kept turning, I could not turn... somehow, because she kept doing it, it was overpowering"*. This could be accounted as an instance of the *Got in each other's way* CPM [8] in which one player's actions slow down the other's.

B. Flow

Seven participants stated having experienced more flow in the co-present condition. Participants attributed the experience of flow to either i) the presence of their partner in the co-present condition, ii) being able to focus more on themselves and their actions in the remote condition, iii) the increasing skills level in the second game session (regardless of the experimental condition). The flow of one participant was actually compromised due to the increasing frustration throughout the course of the experiment. Despite the fact that the same written definition of flow was provided during each interview, the variety of responses suggests that each participant provided an answer according to their own mental model and personal concept of flow. As it turns out, the concept of flow is difficult to understand and might be more suitable for indirect assessment in subsequent research.

C. Frustration

Nine participants felt more frustrated in the remote condition. Two participants felt frustrated due to the absence of communication options in the remote condition. P5-2: *"I felt more frustrated because I couldn't verbally communicate with the other player"*. However, lack of control over the game character was named as the main source of frustration. P6-1: *"I felt like the system is just not picking up enough of what I want to do"*. This is in line with earlier research on user frustration due to malfunctioning control systems in HCI. For instance, Reuderink, Nijholt and Poel (2009) succeeded in inducing frustration in players of an adapted Pacman game by manipulating the user input and visual output of the game. Results obtained from the current study confirm the paramount importance of well-functioning game controls for minimising user frustration in HCI in general, and for BCI games in particular.

D. Challenge

A number of participants perceived both conditions as equally challenging, albeit for different reasons. Lack of communication in the remote condition added challenge for some, as one could not rely on their partner for the timing of the controls. P3-1: *"You can't work with each other, you can't*

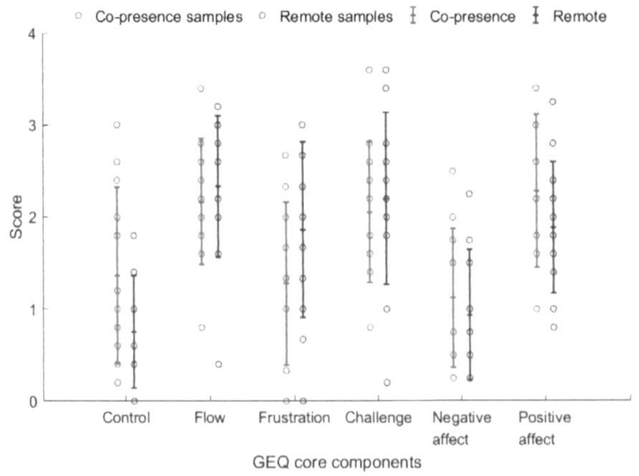

Figure 4. GEQ core component scores. High standard deviations are visible due to the individual game experiences of the participants.

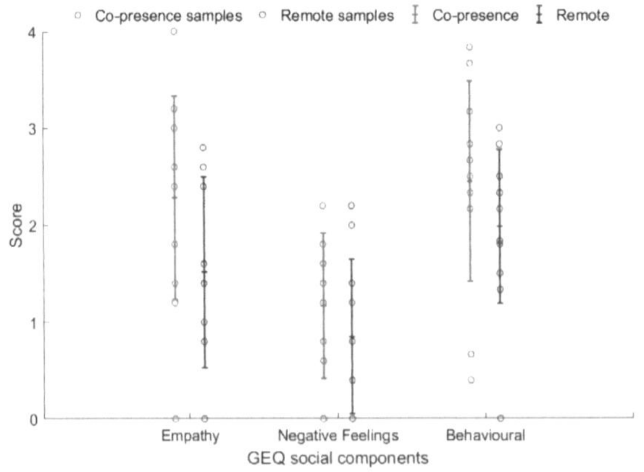

Figure 5. GEQ social component scores. Similar to the core components, high standard deviations are visible.

talk...". For others, managing communication while playing was regarded as more challenging since verbal communication distracted participants from entering a state of relaxation. P1-2: *"I felt more challenged in the first round because you had to communicate and actually motivate each other and talk to each other".* One of the participants mentioned that having to rely on communication added challenge because their partner was not "in sync" with them. P5-2: *"Because we had completely different ways of planning, then the communication made it really hard".* Others pointed out how not being able to communicate added the challenge of having to rely on intuition to anticipate the other player's moves. P1-1: *"The challenge was understanding the other player".*

E. Positive & Negative Affect

Overall, BrainSnake was well-received by the participants. Eight participants showed enthusiasm towards the BCI control mechanism, while four stated that they appreciated the cooperative nature of the game. P1-2: *"I liked the way you could play the game with another player. So you actually had to work together".* Two participants stated that they enjoyed the added challenge of having to rely on intuition to anticipate their partner's move in the remote condition. P3-2:*"I preferred the one where we were not allowed to talk to each other 'cause I think that's more challenging to get the feeling of what the other is doing".* When asked what they did not like about BrainSnake, five participants pointed out the earlier mentioned delay in detecting alpha activity and three participants indicated that they did not like having to close their eyes to perform a game action. P4-2: *"(...) that is not really what a player enjoys generally. You want to be able to track what you're controlling."*

F. Effect of communication on alpha based BCI

Ultimately, responses from around half of the participants suggest that there may have been a trade-off between communicating with a partner and being able to regulate levels of relaxation and focus in order to control the character. These participants stated that either communication made it harder for them to regulate their alpha activity, or that it would be preferable to keep communication to a minimum in order to keep one's mental state stable. P1-2: *"I was a bit more distracted in the first round, because you have to talk to each other and you can't only concentrate on what you're doing on the screen".* This could be accounted as another instance of the *Got in each other's way* CPM, although this could likely be influenced by individual differences. For instance, a few players seemed concerned about getting a high score and even the CPM of *worked out strategies* which involved keeping communication with their partner to a minimum. P6-1: *"We spoke about strategies, how to achieve the most points in the game. During the game, we tried to keep the communication to a minimum. I tried it, to not distract my partner when he had to go into relaxation".* Another participant, admittedly unfamiliar with gaming, only enjoyed playing BrainSnake in the co-present condition thanks to the communication component.

G. Limitations

One noteworthy limitation of the current study is the fact that participants were exposed to a cooperative game while being questioned about a hypothetical competitive game setting in the subsequent interview. Similarly, participants were offered only one form of communication during the game sessions, namely direct verbal communication, but subsequently they were asked about their preferences for hypothetical alternative forms of communication. Participants' statements regarding their preferences for either mode of communication for a competitive or cooperative game setting and their preferences for a specific form of communication have to be interpreted with caution. The inspection of CPMs was also performed based on user interviews rather than by analysing recorded gaming sessions, which made it difficult to identify metrics such as *laughter or excitement together* and *got in each others' way.* Future studies should consider investigating the effect of communication modalities on players' experience with novel BCI mechanisms in more detail, for instance by analysing recorded gaming sessions.

V. CONCLUSION

The current study exemplifies how game design allows users to play fast-paced BCI games using alpha activity, addressing common limitations associated with this input modality. Evaluation of the communication component of BrainSnake shows that most participants attributed more control over the snake character and less frustration to the co-present condition, albeit for different reasons. Moreover, most participants found playing in co-presence more enjoyable, while many felt that the lack of communication in remote added frustration and/or challenge to the game. Nonetheless, a few participants reported enjoying the extra challenge of not being able to communicate in the remote condition. Multiple participants suggested that there could be in fact a trade-off between direct communication and alpha based BCI, and players who self-reportedly worked well with each other worked out strategies which involved minimal use of communication in order to maintain focus. After having played BrainSnake, participants expressed their own ideas on alternative ways of communication (e.g., in-game visual and auditory cues) that could be implemented to enhance cooperation while compromising alpha activity as little as possible. Conceivably, the counterintuitive control mechanism of eye closure was received with mixed feelings: despite the fact that a few participants were intrigued by the interactive potential of this game mechanism, many regarded it as a main source of frustration.

Ultimately, BrainSnake was well-received and we suggest that novel gameplay mechanisms and dynamics departing from traditional gameplay should continue to draw genuine interest in the BCI game community. While individual and contextual differences in the way players experienced BrainSnake make drawing general conclusions difficult, the development of BrainSnake and insights from our participants' responses are of potential interest to those involved in the design and development of BCI games. In conclusion, the following recommendations are made:

- When using alpha waves or other BCI-paradigms as input modality for games, it is worth to think about creative compensations for its limitations as this can result in interesting new interaction modalities. For example, future work should look into assistive game mechanisms, such as one player having control over the movement of a character, while another player controls its speed or the direction of the camera [15]. This may potentially lead to improved game performance and enhanced immersion.
- Results indicate that closely-coupled cooperative BCI games based on alpha activity benefit from subtle, less intrusive ways of communication between players, while face-to-face verbal communication may disrupt one's levels of focus or relaxation causing players to get in each other's way more often. Future work should focus on extending this knowledge into other BCI-paradigms as well as exploring less intrusive ways of communication. For example, previous research shows that tactile feedback can be useful when the visual channel is highly loaded by a complex task [16] [17]. This may also benefit communication in BCI games.
- On the contrary, the use of direct verbal communication could be of potential interest for competitive BCI games based on alpha activity as, for example, verbal communication may allow for strategic manipulation of the opponent. Novel interaction modalities that allow to interfere with the opponent's ability to control the game are conceivable and worth investigating in the future.

REFERENCES

[1] B. Hamadicharef, M. Xu, and S. Aditya, "Brain-computer interface (bci) based musical composition," in *2010 International Conference on Cyberworlds*, Oct 2010, pp. 282–286.

[2] E. C. Lalor *et al.*, "Steady-State VEP-Based Brain-Computer Interface Control in an Immersive 3d Gaming Environment," *EURASIP Journal on Advances in Signal Processing*, vol. 2005, no. 19, pp. 706–906, Nov 2005.

[3] C. Mühl *et al.*, "Bacteria Hunt: Evaluating multi-paradigm BCI interaction," *Journal on Multimodal User Interfaces*, vol. 4, no. 1, pp. 11–25, Mar. 2010.

[4] D. P.-O. Bos *et al.*, "Brain-computer interfacing and games," in *Brain-Computer Interfaces*. Springer, 2010, pp. 149–178.

[5] L. Bonnet, F. Lotte, and A. Lécuyer, "Two brains, one game: Design and evaluation of a multiuser bci video game based on motor imagery," *IEEE Transactions on Computational Intelligence and AI in Games*, vol. 5, no. 2, pp. 185–198, June 2013.

[6] A. Nijholt, D. P.-O. Bos, and B. Reuderink, "Turning shortcomings into challenges: Brain–computer interfaces for games," *Entertainment Computing*, vol. 1, no. 2, pp. 85 – 94, 2009.

[7] A. Y. Kaplan, S. L. Shishkin, I. P. Ganin, I. A. Basyul, and A. Y. Zhigalov, "Adapting the p300-based brain-computer interface for gaming: A review," *IEEE Transactions on Computational Intelligence and AI in Games*, vol. 5, no. 2, pp. 141–149, June 2013.

[8] M. Seif El-Nasr *et al.*, "Understanding and evaluating cooperative games," in *Proceedings of the SIGCHI Conference on Human Factors in Computing Systems*, ser. CHI '10. New York, NY, USA: ACM, 2010, pp. 253–262. [Online]. Available: http://doi.acm.org/10.1145/1753326.1753363

[9] A. Beznosyk, P. Quax, K. Coninx, and W. Lamotte, "The influence of cooperative game design patterns for remote play on player experience," in *Proceedings of the 10th Asia Pacific Conference on Computer Human Interaction*, ser. APCHI '12. New York, NY, USA: ACM, 2012, pp. 11–20. [Online]. Available: http://doi.acm.org/10.1145/2350046.2350051

[10] BioSemi. (accessed on 22.05.2017) BioSemi. https://www.biosemi.com/ . [Online]. Available: https://www.biosemi.com/

[11] OpenVibe. (accessed on 22.05.2017) Software for Brain Computer Interfaces and Real Time Neurosciences. http://openvibe.inria.fr/. [Online]. Available: http://openvibe.inria.fr/

[12] Unity Technologies. (accessed on 22.05.2017) Unity. http://www.unity3d.com/. [Online]. Available: http://www.unity3d.com/

[13] W. IJsselsteijn, Y. de Kort, and K. Poels, "The game experience questionnaire," Eindhoven: Technische Universiteit Eindhoven, Jan. 2013.

[14] A. Strauss and J. Corbin, "Grounded theory methodology," *Handbook of qualitative research*, vol. 17, pp. 273–85, 1994.

[15] D. Coyle, J. Garcia, A. R. Satti, and T. M. McGinnity, "Eeg-based continuous control of a game using a 3 channel motor imagery bci: Bci game," in *2011 IEEE Symp. on Computational Intelligence, Cognitive Algorithms, Mind, and Brain (CCMB)*, April 2011, pp. 1–7.

[16] R. Leeb, K. Gwak, D. S. Kim, and J. d. R. Millán, "Freeing the visual channel by exploiting vibrotactile bci feedback," in *2013 35th Annual International Conference of the IEEE Engineering in Medicine and Biology Society (EMBC)*, July 2013, pp. 3093–3096.

[17] F. Cincotti *et al.*, "Preliminary experimentation on vibrotactile feedback in the context of mu-rhythm based bci," in *2007 29th Annual International Conference of the IEEE Engineering in Medicine and Biology Society (EMBC)*, Aug 2007, pp. 4739–4742.

Real-time Shape-based Sensory Substitution for Object Localization and Recognition

Hossein Pourghaemi, Torkan Gholamalizadeh, Ahmad Mhaish, Gökhan İnce and Damien Jade Duff
Faculty of Computer & Informatics Engineering
Istanbul Technical University, Turkey
Email: {anbardan16, torkan15, mhaish, gokhan.ince, djduff}@itu.edu.tr

Abstract—**In this paper, we present a new approach to real-time tracking and sonification of 3D object shapes and test the ability of blindfolded participants to learn to locate and recognize objects using our system in a controlled physical environment. In our sonification and sensory substitution system, a depth camera accesses the 3D structure of objects in the form of point clouds and objects are presented to users as spatial audio in real time. We introduce a novel object tracking scheme, which allows the system to be used in the wild, and a method for sonification of objects which encodes the internal 3D contour of objects. We compare the new sonfication method with our previous object-outline based approach. We use an ABA/BAB experimental protocol variant to test the effect of learning during training and testing and to control for order effects with a small group of participants. Results show that our system allows object recognition and localization with short learning time and similar performance between the two sonification methods.**

Keywords–sensory substitution; sensory augmentation; point clouds; depth camera; sonification; object tracking.

I. INTRODUCTION

Sensory substitution systems convert information from one sensory modality into another. They are potentially of great help for sense-impaired individuals, for example allowing individuals to locate and grasp objects [1], to navigate [2] or to appreciate visual patterns through sound [2][3]. They can also be used to answer questions about human perception [1].

We present a visual to auditory sensory substitution system, and we are concerned in particular with navigation, object recognition and object manipulation tasks. We would like users to be able to use the system to navigate with environmental awareness in unstructured environments, interpret novel objects from a distance, eat meals, and so forth.

The challenge in building such systems is in presenting sensory data to end users in a comfortable, learnable and understandable way. Until now, these systems have not reached a wide enough audience to supplant more basic but non-intrusive systems like the white cane or guide dog. We attempt to improve on these systems by using time-of-light and structured-light sensors which shortcut the problem of getting the depth of objects in a scene, and work by first extracting perceptual objects and spaces and then and generating meaningful sounds to allow their localization and recognition.

As a first step, we enabled users to localize single objects on a table top using simple spatial audio and tones to sonify direction and distance of objects [4]; next, we investigated different approaches to sonification of simulated 3D shapes [5]. An open research question is whether such sonification methods can be used in the real world; as such, in the current paper, instead of only sonifying simulated shapes, we test a new version of our system that enables localization and recognition of objects on the floor in an empty room. We allow

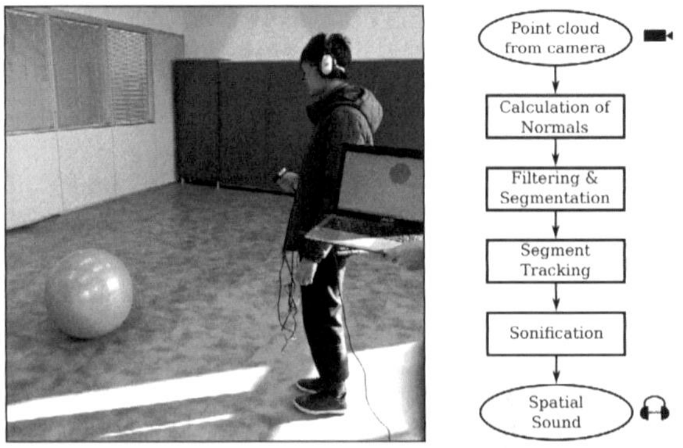

Figure 1. Left: Our system in use. Right: The data-flow pipeline of our sensory substitution system. Frames from the depth sensor are received at approximately $30Hz$ and are processed into sound.

users to move around freely and interact with objects actively using our system. The system in use during testing can be seen on the left of Figure 1.

In order to enable more sophisticated, longer lasting sounds to allow better discrimination of object parts, we build on previously developed object/part segmentation and background noise reduction techniques [4], implementing a scheme for consistently tracking object parts from frame to frame. We also realize a proto-object concept based on segmenting, tracking and sonifying multiple parts of objects separately so that users can understand the shape of objects as the assembly of their sonified parts. Finally, we improve the sonification approach to sonify not just the external contours (outlines) of objects, as previously done [5], but to completely sonify all internal contours of the object using a direct encoding of the full visible 3D shape of the object as sound waves. A summary of the flow of data for each frame in our real-time system can be seen on the right of Figure 1. We evaluated the performance of our system as it was being learnt and used, using a variant of an ABA/BAB test to capture the effect of learning, order effects, and to compare our different sonification approaches on a small sample of ten participants.

The rest of the paper is structured as follows. In Section II, we discuss related work. In Section III, we describe technical details, then experiments and results for localization and recognition problems in Sections IV and V, respectively. Finally, future work is discussed in Section VI.

II. RELATED WORK

A variety of sensory substitution systems exist, including tactile-tactile, visual-tactile and visual-auditory; our work is a *visual-auditory sensory substitution system*. As a system that can create non-speech sound from data, ours may also be considered a *sonification system*.

The most well-known visual-auditory sensory substitution/sonification system is the vOICe [1][3] system, which scans gray-scale image snapshots acquired from video left to right over time, mapping vertical location and intensity of pixels to frequency and amplitude of sound waves. It is possible to use this system to sonify depth images; in contrast, our system is built around the metric 3D structure of the scene as embodied in its point cloud, spatial audio, and the principle of real-time responsiveness. With respect to shape-focused systems, Yoshida et al. [6] sonify 2D shapes on a touch screen by allowing users to explore edges in the image with a finger, producing a sound using the same scheme as with the vOICe, but local to the finger. When the user loses the edges, cues help them find their way back. In See ColOr [2], a depth camera is used, and different instruments (like piano, flute, trumpet) with different properties and in different combination are used to represent different hues.

In the augmented reality work of Shelley et al. [7], users can touch simulated 3D objects and manipulate them with a visual-haptic interface with sound generated from the 3D contours of the object. The local curvature and cross-sections of objects are transmitted as frequency over a carrier wave that is either sinusoidal, a cello wavetable or modally synthesized, and with a haptic force feedback component.

Another close work in conception is the real-time navigation aid of Dunai et al. [8], which uses a stereo system to calculate depth images. After tracking and segmentation, objects with high importance like cars, humans, buildings, animals, and also free space 5 to 15 meters in range, are determined, and the closest object and free space are sonified with a synthetic instrument. Frequency, binaural cues and other sound properties represent distance, direction, and speed. The system is designed primarily as a salient hazard detector.

In our previous work [5], we presented two different approaches to 3D shape sonification: a method based on object recognition techniques commonly used in cognitive robotics applications that first recognizes an object and then chooses an instrument to sonify it accordingly, and a method in which sound waves are directly generated based on objects' outlines in an image - no attempt is made to account for the internal shape of objects. Moreover, that system was tested using artificially generated 3D objects on the problem of object recognition. In contrast, although using a simple sonification scheme, mapping object size or distance to frequency, the earlier incarnation of our system [4] was tested in real scenarios, on the problem of object localization. Conversely, the current paper proposes a scheme for sonifying the interior shape of an object, and compares it to the outline contour approach implemented previously [5]; moreover, here we also introduce new object tracking capabilities to adapt the approaches to real physical scenarios on both tasks - object localization and recognition.

III. TECHNICAL DETAILS

Figure 1 shows the full data-flow of our system, from acquisition of a point cloud from the depth sensor to its sonification, and reflects at a high level our software architecture.

Our system was conceived as an application of the sonification of shape in the context of sensory substitution, to make use of depth cameras like the Asus Xtion used in the current experiments, which can access the 3D structure of most indoor environments directly, in the form of depth images and point clouds. Indeed, advances in stereo vision, structure from motion, and depth from monocular cues are rapidly making the use of point clouds cheaper and more accessible.

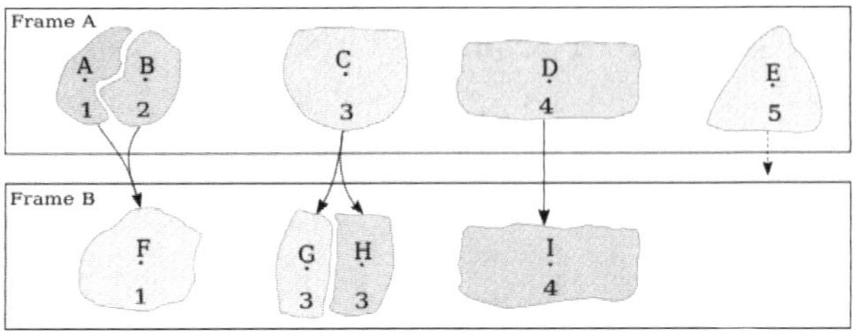

Figure 2. Example of the best association between segments in two consecutive frames (A and B). Letters show segment-ID, numbers show track-ID and black dots show the centroid of the segments. Each matched segment at frame t gets its track-ID number from its match at time $t-1$. If there is no match, it is given a new track-ID.

A. Filtering and Segmentation

Our original aim was to segment the point-cloud scene acquired by the camera into proto-objects based on structural edges between relatively smooth surface parts; these proto-objects we hereafter call segments. Segmenting objects in this way provides proto-objects that are relatively simple in terms of the local structure of their surface and as such suitable for later mapping on to sound primitives. As this is the first time this problem has been approached in the literature, in the first instance we adapted a common segmenting trick used in tabletop robotics [4] - removing the table from the scene and finding connected segments in the remaining point cloud.

In the current work, we return to the proto-object concept and segment and sonify multiple proto-objects in real-time based on sharp changes in the orientation of surfaces in an object, anticipating that their collective sound should help identify the object from which they are made. However, we do continue to filter out large planes, typically constituting walls and floor, to enable users to focus on object understanding.

B. Segment Tracking

In previous work [4], we were able to sonify an object by segmenting each new frame and playing a short sound interpolated from the previous sound. Since frames are received approximately every $\frac{1}{30}s$, and each frame is treated independently, we could only play sounds with a structure lasting $\frac{1}{30}s$. Moreover, because we sonified one segment/object at a time, we did not face problems with segments being confused with each other. However, in the present work we use improved kinds of sonification, in which sounds can last for several seconds, and we sonify multiple segments. We need to keep track of the identity of correct segments over multiple frames. Our approach is to keep the segmentation part of our pipeline but to associate segments over time using combinatorial optimization.

Figure 2 shows an ideal output of the tracker's data association. Due to noise, the sensitivity of camera to some materials, and the sensitivity of the segmenter to thresholds, objects might be segmented in different ways over time and the order in which segments are output from segmenter can change arbitrary from frame to frame. As can be seen in Figure 2 one segment (e.g., C) can split (into G and H) and two

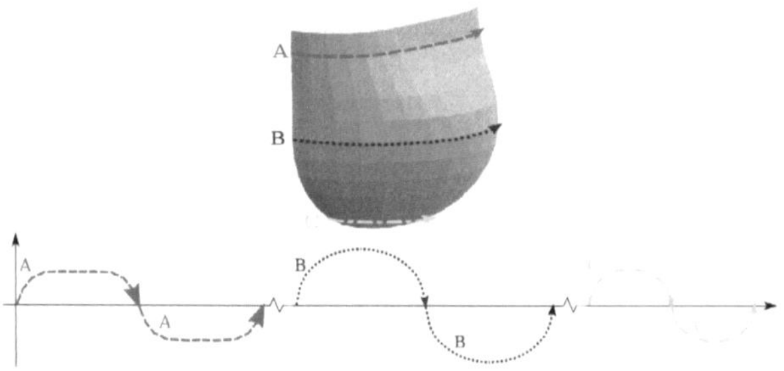

Figure 3. The proposed approach to shape sonification including internal contours. Top: The 3D object face, and selected superimposed internal contours from top to bottom (A,B,). Bottom: corresponding waveforms; combined, an entire waveform can be constructed.

segments (e.g., A and B), can merge (into F). Our tracker handles merging and splitting by amalgamating close segments if the amalgamated segment matches a previous segment well. This is essential because appearing and disappearing segments lead to ambiguous and confusing sound.

Our data association approach evaluates each set of associations based on a cost function, which takes into account the distance between centroids and the first moments of segments. These features are simple, fast to compute and sufficient for the task at hand. After generating possible associations and evaluating them, the association with best cost is selected, track-IDs are allocated and segments are sent to the sonification subsystem.

C. Sonification

The sonification subsystem takes as input the segments extracted by the segmentation and their IDs as applied by the tracking. It keeps track of which segments (IDs) are new, which have previously been seen, and which have disappeared. The cleanest sound was produced not by adjusting the sound over time but instead reproducing the sound associated with the segment as seen in the frame in which the sound started playing. Once a sound is finished playing, the segment can be sonified again. As long as an object is visible, the 3D location of the sound is updated according to the present centroid of the object and the initially calculated waveform is fed incrementally to the sound rendering subsystem in such a way as to minimize delay and artifacts, by tracking the expected frame-rate. If an object stops being visible its sound is faded out over the period of a frame (roughly $\frac{1}{30}s$).

We use two approaches to generating the waveforms used in the sonification: "external" and "internal" contour.

1) External Contour: This approach [5] works on the 2D organized point cloud extracted from each segment. This is essentially a calibrated depth image containing a channel for each of x, y and z coordinates. Point clouds remain organized in a 2D array even after segmentation and tracking in order to maintain our high frame-rate. The organized point cloud for each segment is a cropped window around the segment with a mask defining the segment shape.

The external contour approach works by tracing the outline (external contour) of the object in the organized point cloud to create a carrier wave which is subsequently frequency and amplitude modulated; the modulation is done by scanning the object top-to-bottom and using the width of the object at each vertical location to modulate the carrier [5].

2) Internal Contour: Gholamalizadeh et al. [5] discovered that the lack of interior shape information (inside the external contour) was one drawback of the direct sonification method compared to the indirect (recognition-based) method. We attempt to rectify that by extracting information about both external and interior contours of the segment/object to be sonified. The new method is visualized in Figure 3. The object is scanned top to bottom, and for each row of points (essentially a row of pixels), the object depth at each point becomes a sample in a waveform. Interpolation is done to increase and decrease the frequency/speed of the wave. Thus, the frequency of the sound will depend on the width of the object as it is scanned top-bottom and the exact shape of the waveform produced will depend on the horizontal cross-sectional shape of the object.

Important caveats are attached to the current instantiation of this approach. Firstly, it was planned that depths in the object be produced relative to the average depth of the object. However, for an object with no significant internal contours, such as a flat surface facing the camera, this produces no sound. We could normalize the amplitude of the wave but this then vastly amplifies noise. So instead of relative depth of each point, we use the depth from the camera center to the point. However, the depth to the camera greatly overwhelms any other value and produces essentially a square wave no matter the shape of the object. Thus, in order to transmit internal contours to the user, in addition to the above-described scheme, we average multiple rows of the object and use the resulting averaged 1D array to do amplitude modulation of the object while the relevant part of the object is being sonified. This results in a consciously discernible oscillation in the wave that serves to encode cross-sectional shape.

IV. Training and Experiments

We investigated the ability of users to localize and recognize objects in a restricted indoor physical scenario, comparing internal and external contour shape sonification approaches. For this purpose, we designed an experiment involving both localization and recognition tasks, where each of 10 participants (mean age 25, 9:1 male/female ratio) participated in either an ABA or BAB experiment. Due to the experimental nature of the prototype, we only worked with sighted individuals. 50% of participants had experience with a previous iteration of the system. Half of participants used the system with internal contour sonification (A), followed by the external contour sonification (B), and again the internal contour sonification (A). The other half of participants used the external (B) then internal (A) then external contour based sonification (B).

The main idea behind conducting ABA/BAB experiments is to investigate the order effect of conditions [9]. Since we have limited time with each participant as well as a limited number of participants, we wanted to evaluate both conditions with each participant - moreover, random-sample based experiments require an order of magnitude greater sample size compared to matched experiments. We also want to analyze the effect of experience with the system on performance. Before conducting each of the three tests in the ABA or BAB sequence, an independent training session was conducted. In each test, participants are asked to first localize a single object in their near environment and then recognize it.

For the localization task, blindfolded users were asked to localize an object placed in one of six possible locations by walking and pointing. A map of the environment and possible

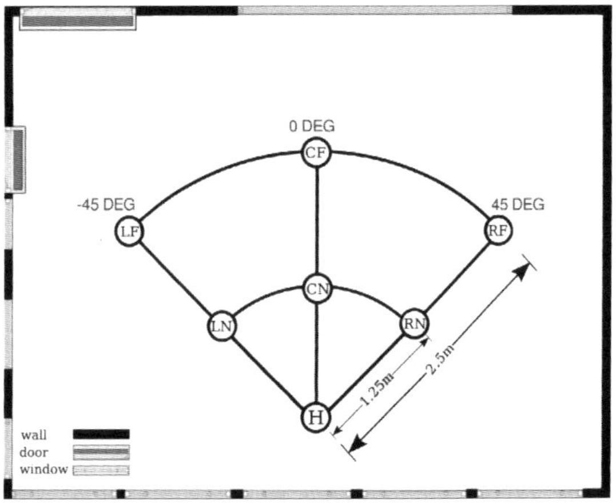

Figure 4. Map of the experiment room with six possible object positions. LN: left near, LF: left fat, CN: center near, CF: center far, RN: right near, RF: right far, H: Home location of the participant.

locations for objects is in Figure 4. After the localization task, users were asked to use the system to recognize the object.

Six arbitrary objects with disparate shape, size and complexity were chosen as an initial challenge to the capability of our sonification method. The objects and output of segmenter for each object are illustrated in Figures 5 and 6, respectively.

Next, training and test protocols are described.

A. *Training sessions*

The training protocol was exactly same for both encoding approaches (internal and external). First, a short verbal explanation of the system, encoding approaches, and the rules for experiments were given by the experimenter; this took five minutes. Then, three objects, namely box, drawer and bucket were placed in locations LF, CF and RF and participants were allowed to familiarize themselves with the system with open eyes, look at the objects from different view points, and listen to the sounds on the headphones; this took 12 minutes. Then, five minutes of training were allocated to learning about the localization task, where users were instructed to stay in the home location, scan the environment from left to right and down to up, walk towards objects and localize them. During all training sessions, users were allowed to move the camera freely with their hand, which was more comfortable for all users. They could see the output of the tracker on the computer display (as with Figure 6) and were suggested to also listen to the sound with closed eyes. After the first set of objects, a second set of objects - plant, stool and ball - were provided in locations LF, CF and RF, respectively. After learning with both sets of objects, users were allowed to interact freely with all objects placed at locations that they requested, for up to six minutes. As such, the maximum allowed training time for each test was $5 + 12 + 5 + 12 + 5 + 6 = 45$ minutes. These durations were selected considering the trade-off between our unpaid participants' time and the need to test our system with experienced users. The amount of time used to train with the system in these experiments is low compared to that which would be expected if the system were to be used day-to-day.

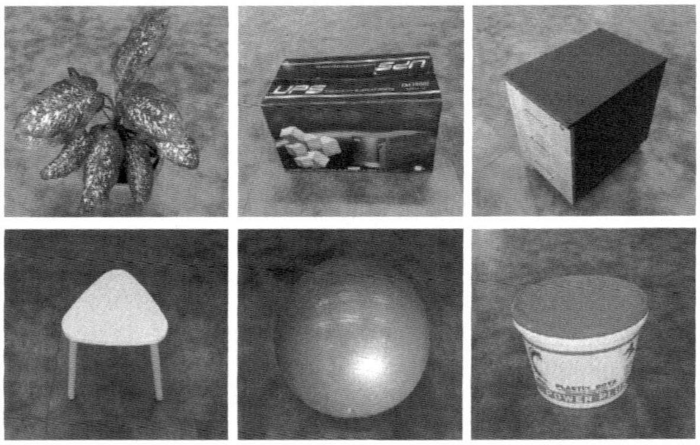

Figure 5. Set of objects used in experiments.

Figure 6. Segmented 3D images obtained from the objects in Figure 5. Top-left: plant, Top-middle: box, Top-right: drawer, Bottom-left: stool, Bottom-middle: ball, Bottom-right: bucket.

B. *Test sessions*

In test sessions, one randomly selected object was placed in a randomly selected location and blindfolded participants located at the home location were given three minutes to walk towards the object and localize it by pointing. Here, six trials with six different objects were conducted with each participant, plus an extra unrecorded trial with a random object, conducted to prevent the participant from guessing the object. Localization performance was evaluated as *precise*, *poor* or *failed* and participants were informed about the correctness of their answer. *Precise* localization meant the participant was able to point to the center of the object, *poor* localization meant the participant could point to the boundary of the object, and a *failed* localization meant the participant was unable to find the object. In the case of poor localization or failure, the experimenter helped the participant to precisely localize the object for the recognition phase of the test.

After localization of each object, participants were given two minutes to move the depth camera around the same object, listen to its sound and identify it. The experimenter then gave the correct answer, as participants were invariably curious considering their limited experience with the system during the training. The use of our ABA/BAB protocol controlled for the effect of experience during testing.

V. RESULTS

A. *Localization performance*

Figure 7 illustrates results of ABA and BAB experiments on the localization task for all participants. The internal approach with 73.3% precise localizations, 23.3% poor localizations and 3.3% failed localizations showed a similar performance to the external approach with 66.6% precise, 26.6% poor and 6.6% failed localizations (unpaired T-test, $N = 15$, $p = 0.31$). Localization performance for internal-external-internal and external-internal-external experiments increased by 22% and 30%, from the first to third test, respectively.

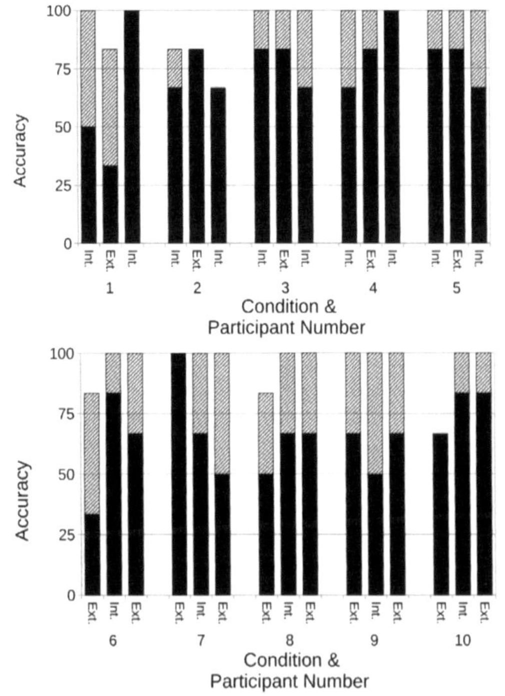

Figure 7. Results of ABA and BAB experiments for localization performance of all participants. Top: internal-external-internal order. Bottom: external-internal-external order. The black regions specify percentage of precise localizations and the shaded regions specify poor localizations.

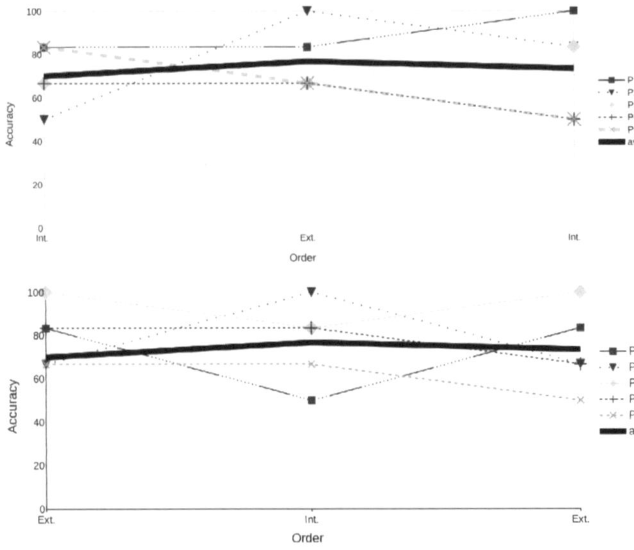

Figure 8. Results of ABA and BAB experiments for recognition performance of all participants (Pn: participant number n). Top: internal-external-internal order. Bottom: external-internal-external order.

For some objects, like plant, stool and bucket, the system had difficulty in detecting the objects when in distant locations like LF, CF or RF and when the user was at H. In these cases, participants tried to take a step forward and scan the environment again until they could find something. On the other hand, our system could detect the ball, drawer and box from the home position without a problem. For both approaches, participants reported that they had difficulty in localizing the drawer, because the large size of drawer created confusion. Therefore, the average localization time of drawer in both approaches was more than the average localization time for other objects. Moreover, among all experiments participants hit the object three times (1.6% of experiments); in two cases the object was the drawer and in one case bucket.

The system generated noisy sounds when the camera pointed at the walls and windows surrounding the test environment. In first training and then testing sessions, participants were confused when the system sonified segments related to part of the wall or window. Later, in the second and specially third tests, most participants showed that they can distinguish those noises, and they tried to change camera view to eliminate the noises and focus on the object.

B. Recognition performance

Results of ABA and BAB experiments for recognition performance of all participants can be seen in Figure 8. For the recognition task, results are independent of the order of conditions, with 4.7% improvement for internal-external-internal experiment and 8.3% deterioration for external-internal-external experiment, from the first to third test.

The internal contour approach, with an overall accuracy of 73%, did not show a significantly different performance from the external approach, with overall accuracy of 77% (unpaired T-test, $N = 15$, $p = 0.58$). Recognition accuracy showed individual differences. For example, one of the participants, who was a musician, obtained an accuracy of 100%, 83% and 100% on external, internal and external tests, respectively.

Participants, for both approaches, were encouraged to try to understand the logic of the encoding of object sounds. One of the strategies that participants were using for recognition was rotating the camera or going to other sides of the object to see it from different view points. These movements lead to different sounds for some objects due to the orientation-dependent top to bottom encoding in both approaches. It was observed that this cue helped users to distinguish between box and bucket in both approaches, and ball and stool in the external approach. Additionally, the other cue that was used heavily by users was the number of played sounds. By viewing some objects from different views, a different number of sounds could be heard. For example, by viewing a box from the front, just two sounds could be heard (one for the top segment and one for the side segment), whereas by viewing the same box from the side, three sounds could be heard (one for the top segment and two for side segments). On the other hand, for the ball and stool, just one sound could be heard. In the internal approach, some participants reported occasional interference of sounds of an object with multiple segments like box and bucket, making it hard for participants to distinguish number of segments. This led participants to confuse the stool with box and bucket. We attribute this effect to the square-wave nature of the internal contour encoding method we currently use.

For both approaches and for all objects, participants were able to successfully identify objects most of the time, as can be seen from the bold numbers in Table I. The two objects with the best recognition accuracy in both approaches were plant and ball, with 93% and 100% accuracy, respectively. The plant is distinctive because of a high number of segments

TABLE I. CONFUSION MATRICES FOR OBJECT RECOGNITION EXPERIMENTS. NUMBERS ARE PERCENTAGES ($N = 15$).

Internal approach		Response					
		plant	box	drawer	stool	ball	bucket
Actual	plant	**$93\frac{1}{3}$**					$6\frac{2}{3}$
	box		**60**	$6\frac{2}{3}$		$6\frac{2}{3}$	$26\frac{2}{3}$
	drawer		20	**$66\frac{2}{3}$**			$13\frac{1}{3}$
	stool		$33\frac{1}{3}$		**40**	$13\frac{1}{3}$	$13\frac{1}{3}$
	ball					**100**	
	bucket		$6\frac{2}{3}$	$6\frac{2}{3}$			**$86\frac{2}{3}$**

External approach		Response					
		plant	box	drawer	stool	ball	bucket
Actual	plant	**$93\frac{1}{3}$**		$6\frac{2}{3}$			
	box		**40**	$33\frac{1}{3}$	$6\frac{2}{3}$		20
	drawer		$6\frac{2}{3}$	**$86\frac{2}{3}$**		$6\frac{2}{3}$	
	stool				**$73\frac{1}{3}$**	$26\frac{2}{3}$	
	ball					**100**	
	bucket	$6\frac{2}{3}$	$6\frac{2}{3}$	$6\frac{2}{3}$	$6\frac{2}{3}$		**$73\frac{1}{3}$**

and the ball because of its size and recognizable contour. As expected, confusion is seen between objects similar in shape like box, drawer and bucket, the most confusions occurring between box and bucket, and also drawer and box in both approaches. Confusion between stool and ball also arises because of similarity of the contour of the two objects.

C. Learning and testing duration

Although we allocated a maximum of 45 minutes for training for each test, results shows that learning and using our system is possible in a shorter time. In both internal-external-internal and external-internal-external orders, the training time of participants decreased from the first test to the third test. In the internal-external-internal sequence ($N = 15$), the average training time for the first test was 23.5 minutes, which decreased by 47% for the third test; similarly, for the external-internal-external order ($N = 15$), time in the first test was 18.8 minutes, decreasing by 64% to the third test. Furthermore, the average time spent localizing and recognizing each object decreased from $181s$ by 22% and from $139s$ by 26%, from the first to third test. However, an unpaired T-test ($N = 15$, $p = 0.48$) verifies that there is no significant difference between internal and external contour in training and testing time.

D. Questionnaire

After the experiment, users were given a three-question questionnaire asking them to rate on a scale of one to five the quality of sound in each approach and the usability of our system. Most participants reported that they found the generated sound of the external contour approach (average score of 3.3 out of 5) more pleasant than the sound of the internal approach (average 2.6 from 5), most likely due to the fact that the internal approach always generated roughly a square wave (see the description of the method above), though participants acknowledged the suitability of the internal approach for sonifying the curvature of objects like a ball. With respect to usability, the average score was 3.2 out of 5, along with feedback that users considered that the system has usefulness in the current simplified scenario but cannot guess how it might be used with more objects and in more unstructured scenarios.

VI. CONCLUSION

This is the first time that sensory substitution from 3D shape has been attempted. An internal contour based encoding method for sonification of 3D objects was presented. This method is able to encode depth and curvature of objects, and is compared with our previous external contour based approach. A data-association based tracking system was introduced to enable the use of these sonifications in real interactive physical scenarios.

An ABA/BAB experiment was performed to evaluate the ability of blindfolded participants in localization and recognition of different objects, and to investigate order effects and the effect of experience. Results show similar performance of users in localization and recognition of objects in both approaches and quick mastery of the system. The internal approach was expected to show a better performance in recognition due to encoding more information but in its current iteration suffers from an inability to represent a variety of contours and produce harmonious sounds at the level of carrier wave.

The next steps in this work are developing the internal encoding to produce more pleasant and informative sound and exploring more approaches for dealing with background noises to make our system work in more general scenarios.

ACKNOWLEDGMENT

This work is supported by the Scientific and Technological Research Council of Turkey (TÜBITAK), Projects 114E443 and 116E167.

REFERENCES

[1] M. Auvray, S. Hanneton, and J. K. O'Regan, "Learning to perceive with a visuo-auditory substitution system: Localisation and object recognition with 'The vOICe'," Perception, vol. 36, no. 3, 2007, pp. 416 – 430, ISSN: 1468-4233.

[2] J. D. Gomez Valencia, "A computer-vision based sensory substitution device for the visually impaired (See ColOr)," Ph.D. dissertation, University of Geneva, 2014.

[3] P. Meijer, "An experimental system for auditory image representations," IEEE Transactions on Biomedical Engineering, vol. 39, no. 2, 1992, pp. 112–121, ISSN: 1558-2531.

[4] A. Mhaish, T. Gholamalizadeh, G. İnce, and D.J. Duff, "Assessment of a Visual-to-Spatial Audio Sensory Substitution System," in Proc. IEEE Conf. on Signal Processing and Communications Applications, 2016, pp. 245–248, ISBN: 978-1-5090-1679-2.

[5] T. Gholamalizadeh, H. Pourghaemi, A. Mhaish, G. İnce, and D. J. Duff, "Sonification of 3d Object Shape for Sensory Substitution: An Empirical Exploration," in ACHI 2017, The Tenth International Conference on Advances in Computer-Human Interactions, Mar. 2017, pp. 18–24, ISBN: 978-1-61208-538-8.

[6] T. Yoshida, K. M. Kitani, H. Koike, S. Belongie, and K. Schlei, "EdgeSonic: image feature sonification for the visually impaired," in Proceedings of the 2nd Augmented Human International Conference. ACM, 2011, p. 11, ISBN: 978-1-4503-0426-9.

[7] S. Shelley et al., "Interactive Sonification of Curve Shape and Curvature Data," in Haptic and Audio Interaction Design. Springer, Berlin, Heidelberg, Sep. 2009, pp. 51–60, ISBN: 978-3-642-04076-4.

[8] L. Dunai, G. Fajarnes, V. Praderas, B. Garcia, and I. Lengua, "Real-time assistance prototype - A new navigation aid for blind people," in IECON 2010 - 36th Annual Conference on IEEE Industrial Electronics Society, Glendale, Arizona, USA, Nov. 2010, pp. 1173–1178, ISBN: 978-1-4244-5225-5.

[9] C. Eilifsen and E. Arntzen, "Single-subject withdrawal designs in delayed matching-to-sample procedures," European Journal of Behavior Analysis, vol. 12, no. 1, 2011, pp. 157–172, ISSN: 1502-1149.

Programming in Natural Language: Building Algorithms from Human Descriptions

Alexander Wachtel, Felix Eurich, Walter F. Tichy

Karlsruhe Institute of Technology
Chair for Programming Systems Prof. Walter F. Tichy
Am Fasanengarten 5, 76131 Karlsruhe, Germany
Email: alexander.wachtel@kit.edu, felix.eurich@student.kit.edu, walter.tichy@kit.edu

***Abstract*—Our work is where the Software Engineering meets the Human Computer Interaction and the End User Programming to aim for a major breakthrough by making machines programmable in ordinary and unrestricted language. In this paper, we provide a solution on how new algorithms can be recognized and learned from human descriptions. Our focus is to improve the interaction between humans and machines and enable the end user to instruct programmable devices, without having to learn a programming language. In a test-driven development, we created a platform that allows users to manipulate spreadsheet data by using natural language. Therefore, the system (i) enables end users to give instructions step-by-step, to avoid the complexity in full descriptions and give directly feedback of success (ii) creates an abstract meta model for user input during the linguistic analysis and (iii) independently interprets the meta model to code sequences that contain loops, conditionals, and statements. The context then places the recognized program component in the history. In this way, an algorithm is generated in an interactive process. One of the result can be the code sequence for algorithm, like well-known selection sort. We present a series of ontology structures for matching instructions to declare variables, loop, make decisions, etc. Furthermore, our system asks clarification questions when the human user is ambiguous. During the evaluation, 11 undergraduate students were asked to solve tasks by using natural language, and describe algorithms in three classes of complexity. Overall, the system was able to transform 60% of the user statements into code. Far from perfect, this research might lead to fundamental changes in computer use. Rather than merely consuming software, end users of the ever-increasing variety of digital devices could develop their own programs, potentially leading to novel, highly personalized, and plentiful solutions.**

Keywords–Natural Language Processing; End User Programming; Natural Language Interfaces; Human Computer Interaction; Programming In Natural Language; Dialog Systems.

I. Introduction

Since their invention, digital computers have been programmed using specialized, artificial notations, called programming languages. Programming requires years of training. However, only a tiny fraction of human computer users can actually work with those notations. With natural language and end-user development methods, programming would become available to everyone and enable end-users to program their systems or extend them without any knowledge of programming languages. Programming languages assist with repetitive tasks that involve use of loops and conditionals. This is what is often challenging for users. Our vision should enable users to describe algorithms in their natural language and provides a valid output by the dialog system for a given description, e.g., selection sort of a set (See Algorithm 1). This vision forms the basis for our natural language user interface [1]. Already in 1987, Tichy discussed that Artificial Intelligence (AI) techniques are useful for software engineering, pointing out the potential of natural language processing [2] and natural-language help systems [3].

According to Liberman [4], the main question in the End User Development area of research is, how to allow non-programming users who have no access to source code, to program a computer system or extend the functionality of an existing system. In our prototype, we decided to address spreadsheets for several reasons:

- a lot of open data available, e.g. Eurostat [5] provides statistics for European Union that allow comparisons.
- well-known and well-distributed: Microsoft [6] announced the distribution of Office with 1.2 billion users worldwide. Furthermore, for humans the data in a table is easy to understand, complete and manipulate.

In general, spreadsheets have been used for at least 7000 years [7]. Myers [8] and Scaffidi [9] compared the number of end users and professional programmers in the United States. Nearly 90 million people use computers at work and 50 million of them use spreadsheets. In a self-assessment, 12 million considered themselves as programmers, but only 3 million people are professional programmers. The created spreadsheets are not only the traditional tabular representation of relational data that convey information space efficiently, but also allow a continuous revision and formula-based data manipulation. It is estimated that each year hundreds of millions of spreadsheets are created [10]. Our system consists of two main components: a user interface that gets natural language expressions from the user and a linguistic analysis framework. These components are explained below. This paper is structured as follows. Section II gives the overview of the current research and describes our goals. This is followed by the Section III, which presents the linguistic analysis that generates the meta model for given descriptions. In Section IV, the interpreter transforms the meta model to the control flows, conditional and loop statements. Section V evaluates the prototype and describes the setup and the results of a user study. Section VI presents related work in the research areas of programming in natural language, End User Programming and natural language dialog systems. Finally, Section VII presents a conclusion of our topic and future work.

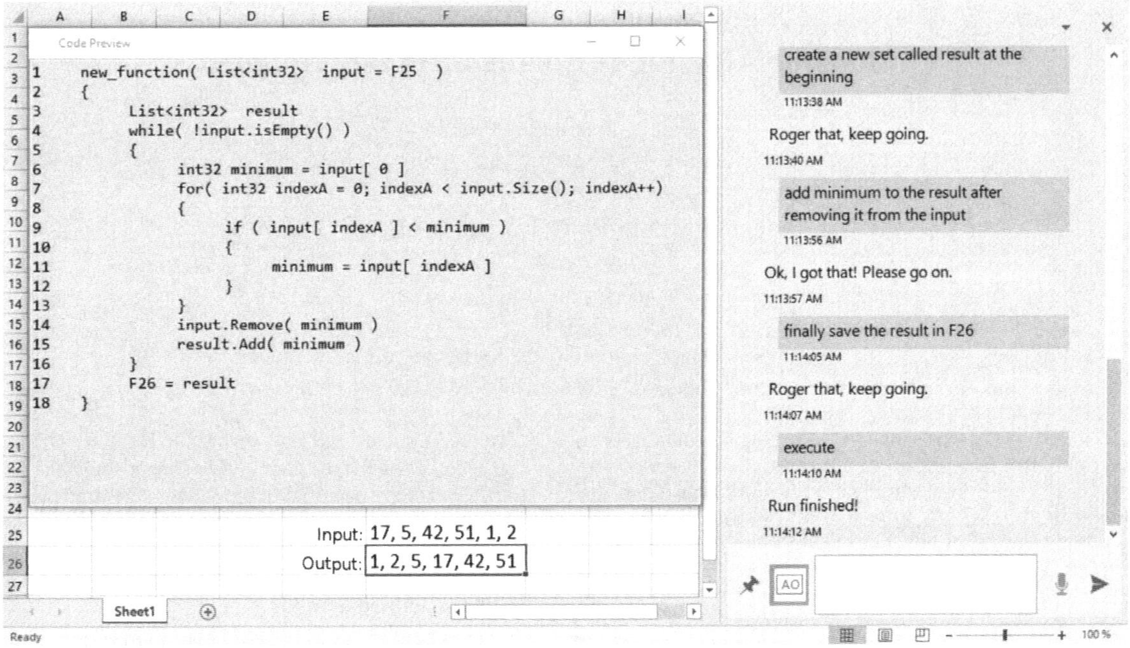

Figure 1. End user instructions of an algorithm are transformed to the code sequences and executed on a given set of numbers

II. CURRENT WORK AND RESEARCH GOALS

Our work is based on a dialog component implemented by [11] in 2015. It enables users to interact with our system and manipulate spreadsheet data via natural language. In early 2016, the system has been extended with an active ontology [1][12]. The idea of active ontology was first presented by Guzzoni [13]. In general, an ontology is a formal representation of knowledge. By adding a rule evaluation system, a fact store and sensor nodes to an ontology it becomes an execution environment rather than just a formal representation of knowledge. In late 2016, the natural language dialog system has been extended with a machine learning component, called Interactive Spreadsheet Processing Module (ISPM) [14]. It is an active dialog management system that uses machine learning techniques for context interpretation within spreadsheets and connects natural language to the data in the spreadsheets. First, the rows of a spreadsheet are divided into different classes and the table's schema is made searchable for the dialog system. In the case of a user input, it searches for headers, data values from the table and key phrases for operations. Implicit cell references like "people of age 18" are then resolved to explicit references using the schema. Using the ISPM, end users are able to search for values in the schema of the table and to address the data in spreadsheets implicitly, e.g., *What is the average age of people in group A?*. Furthermore, it enables them to select and sort the spreadsheet data by using natural language for end user software engineering, to overcome the present bottleneck of professional developers. In December 2017, we presented an overview about our current work in [15]. Therefore, we provided more details for the achieved design and implementation steps of our prototype.

In our current work, users describe algorithms (cf. [16]) in their natural language and get a valid output by the dialog system for a given description, e.g., selection sort of a set (See Figure 1). The functionality is aimed at users with no programming knowledge, as the system enables simple routines to be programmed without prior knowledge. This makes it easier for users to get started with programming. The system also illustrates the relationship between a natural statement and its code representation (See Figure 1), so it can also help to understand and learn a programming language.

$$Task : To\ sort\ a\ sequence\ of\ n\ numbers\ (a_1, ..., a_n)$$

$$\downarrow$$

User Input: the result is a vector. Initially it is empty. Find the minimal element of the set and append it to the vector. Remove the element form the set. Then, repeatedly find the minimum of the remaining elements and move them to the result in order, until there are no more elements in the set.

$$\downarrow$$

Algorithm 1 Pseudo code of selection sort.

```
procedure SELECTIONSORT( input as a set of numbers )
    result ← empty set
    while input IsNotEmpty do
        n ← length (input) - 1
        tmpMin ← 0
        for i ← 0 → n do
            if input[i] < input[tmpMin] then
                tmpMin ← i
        Add input[tmpMin] at the end of result.
        Remove element at index tmpMin from input.
```

$$\downarrow$$

$$Output : A\ permutation\ (b_1, b_2, ..., b_n)\ with\ b_1 \leq ... \leq b_n$$

III. Linguistic Analysis

In early 2017, we have done first steps on loops and conditionals [1]. In this work, we extend these active ontologies [1] that represent knowledge about the structure of natural language in the context of programming instructions and implementing a meta model layer, our system recognizes various programming concepts in user input and converts them into a meta language. The result of the analysis is a tree structure consisting of objects, whereby an object represents a recognized concept. These trees are built during the analysis from bottom up. The object structure contains three parts: whileIndicator, loopAction, and condition. The following sections describe the different steps on how our system creates shown WhileLoop object. Overall, it identifies the routines of the supported concepts, like statements, conditionals and loops, and provides functional overview of the linguistic analysis.

A. Reference Detection

The first step of the analysis is reference resolution. End users can provide the reference to variable as an individual pseudonym like the word "minimum" in *use 5 as minimum.* Furthermore, an implicit reference can be used such as *initialize it with 5* (See Figure 2). Dotted lines indicate sensor nodes which react if one of the attached word or word class [17] was detected in the input. A red mark around a node points to a key node which occurrence is essential for the parent node to trigger. The two inner node types: collect and select nodes, are marked with "C" and "S", respectively. The different types of nodes have different prerequisites for triggering. Leaf nodes unleash when a particular word is found in the input. Collecting nodes trigger when all required child nodes have been triggered and selection nodes trigger as soon as at least one child node triggers. When triggered, the recognized concept is passed on to the parent node as a new object [1].

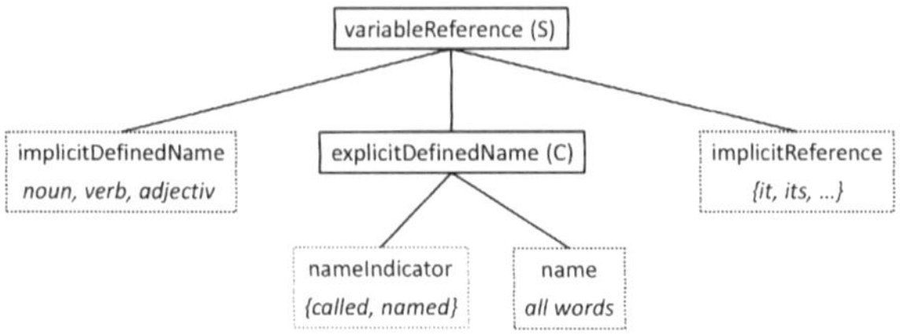

Figure 2. Ontology structure for variable references.

Detecting references to a quantity builds on the previous structure. Decisive for the recognition are descriptions of characteristics (`setIndicator`) which are linked to a variable reference. The simplest indicator is the occurrence of a size reference like the word *length*. In connection with a variable reference the presence of a reference to a quantity can be assumed. Another indicator is the detection of index referral. It's based on the identification of the explicit index as a constant number or reference (See Figure 3).

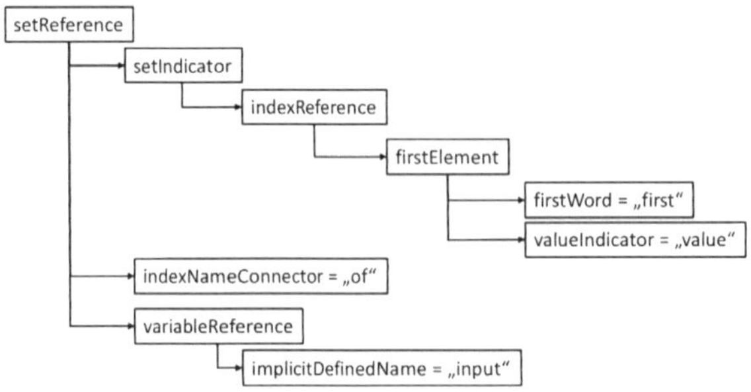

Figure 3. Result of "set the first element of the input to 0".

B. Statements

Built on the of reference recognition, declarations and actions are recognized by the linguistic analysis.

1) Declarations: In general, a new variable is defined explicitly by its name and a type. It is important to know that the type is not describing the data type, but the type of the variable, i.e., whether it's a simple variable or a set. In order to deal with formulations of the form "create a new set", the specification of a name is optional. If no name is found for the new variable, the system assigns one.

2) Actions: The current version of the system supports three types of actions, namely assignments, remove and add operations. All actions have the commonality that they have a direction. This is determined by the preposition and the verb used. On the basis of this information, the analysis can indicate which reference is the target and which is the parameter of the action. The set-up is the same for all actions and should be displayed on the basis of the assignment A possible entry for an assignment is the following "take the first value from the input as minimum". By the preposition "as" in combination with the verb "take" the analysis assumes that the target of the allocation is on the right side of the preposition. Therefore, the tree in Figure 4 is the output of the analysis. The other actions are also recognized according to this procedure.

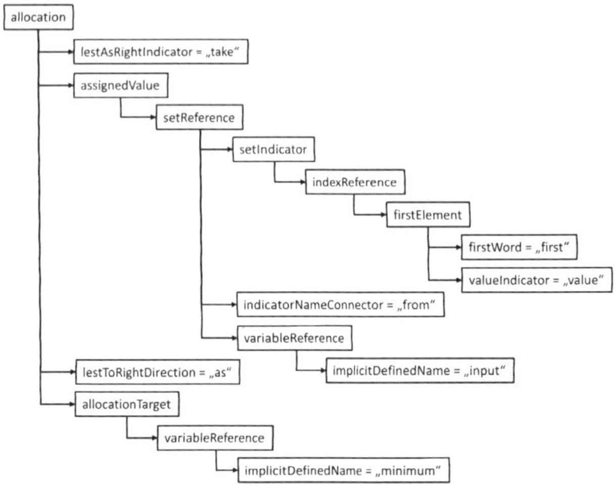

Figure 4. Result of the node `allocation` after the analysis of the entry "take the first value from the input as minimum".

C. Conditionals

Control structures such as looping and branching are essential elements of algorithms. By considering such concepts in the linguistic analysis, more complex algorithms like selection sort can be implemented with the system. As some control structures require the recognition of conditions, the logic used for this purpose should be briefly presented here. In general, a condition defies a property of a reference. Depending on the type of reference, different conditions can be set. In this work, a condition can be set for a simple value, a quantity of values and a quantity reference. Figure 5 shows the classification of the conditions. In a first subdivision, a distinction is made between conditions which relate to a single reference (`singleValueCondition`) and the composite condition (`multipleValueCondition`) which is the combination of several conditions by a conjunction such as "and" in "x is less than 3 and y is equal to 5". Furthermore, the individual conditions differentiate between statements that assign a condition to a value (`singleCondition`) and those with several premises for a value (`conditionChain`). The child nodes of `singleCondition` represent the three supported types of a condition. `limitedValueCondition` recognizes statements that compare two values. Conditions which relate to a quantity, e.g., "If the result is empty" are identified by `setConstrain`. `setCondition` recognizes the requirements of a property for certain elements of a set, such as "if all elements of the result are greater than 4".

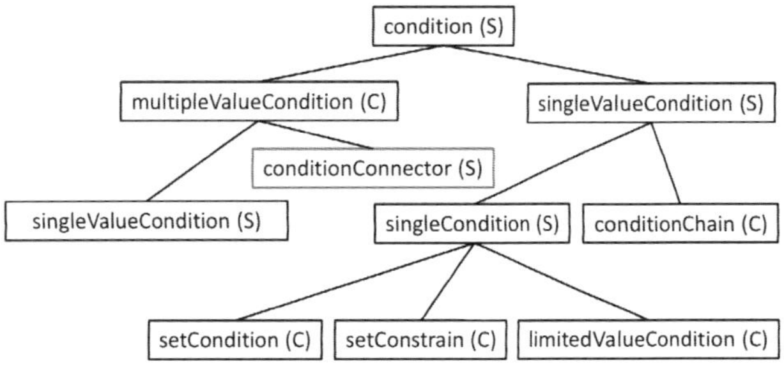

Figure 5. Ontology structure for the different conditions.

1) Single Value Condition: Assuming the input is "check if the result is less than 5". It is obvious that the user wants to check whether the value of the field "result" is less than the constant value 5. Analogously, it would also be conceivable to require equivalence or greater than 5. Of course, negated expressions such as "when the result at least 3 is not equal to minimum" must be recognized. For this purpose, a negative prefix, like "not", is searched for in the input. The `constantValueOrReference` node is represented a all previously discussed ways to reference a single value or a variable. Because of its identical structure, the `containRelation` is also part of this type of condition. The only difference is that a keyword such as "contain" is searched instead of the requested comparison operator.

2) Quantifier Condition: With these kind of conditions, formulations such as "check if all elements in the input are greater than 5" or "if any element of the input is smaller than 0" are correctly recognized Since the set reference to be checked is identified by the `setCondition` node, only the value has to be found in the subtree of `singleValueConditionWithoutLoop` instead of the value and the reference to be checked for the comparison. The already known structure of `possibleRelation` and `valueLimit` remains unchanged.

3) Constraint Condition: Entries such as "if the input contains any element" are handled by the `setConstrain` node. It is thus possible to check whether a quantity reference contains elements or not.

4) Condition Chain: The condition chain is a special compound condition, which requires several properties from a single reference. The decisive factor here is that only the first requirement has an explicit reference to the field to be examined. A possible input would be "if x is less than 5 or equal to 10". Instead of whole conditions, operators can also be linked. An example of this is the input "if x is smaller or equal to 4". In contrast to the linking of several conditions, only the last operator has an explicit reference to the limit.

D. Loops

In order to repeat an action, the user can link it to a condition or specify that it should be executed for each element of a set. Hence the analysis detects both `for` and `while` loops. The result of the ontology for a recognized `for` loop can be seen in Figure 6. Similarly, the result for the input "repeat all steps until the input is empty" will be computed.

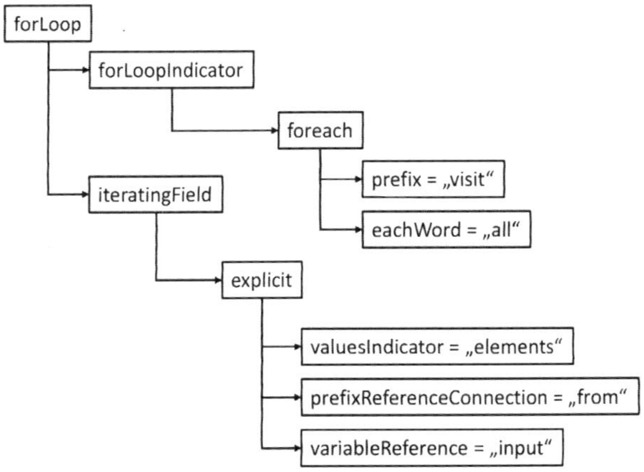

Figure 6. Result of the node `forLoop` after the analysis of the entry "visit all elements from the input".

E. Branches

Analogous to the branching in programming, the input is checked for conditional actions and possible alternatives. In fact, the system is able to trace and identify such user input like "if there is a value less than the minimum in the input use it as minimum".

F. Temporal Actions

Temporal actions are actions with an individual desired location. Both explicit position data and the definition of a temporal relationship to another action are taken into account during the analysis. As an explicit position, the start and end of the description is currently supported such as "at the beginning initialize the output with 0". The assignment of a temporal relationship requires, in addition to the action to be placed (`action`), the specification of a conjunction (after, while, before) and an anchor point (`anchor`). As an action or anchor point, the analysis allows both action descriptions, as well as concrete actions or references to earlier instructions. To identify the described component, the analysis looks for matching verbs and adds the corresponding section in the input as a description. It does not matter which action is already present in the program sequence and which is to be rearranged. This task is done by the interpreter. A possible entry for a temporal action would be "add minimum to the result after removing it from the input".

IV. Interpreter

In the following, the further processing of the object structure outputted by the ontology will be presented. The abstract process is shown in Figure 7. The successive processing steps are now to be considered in more detail.

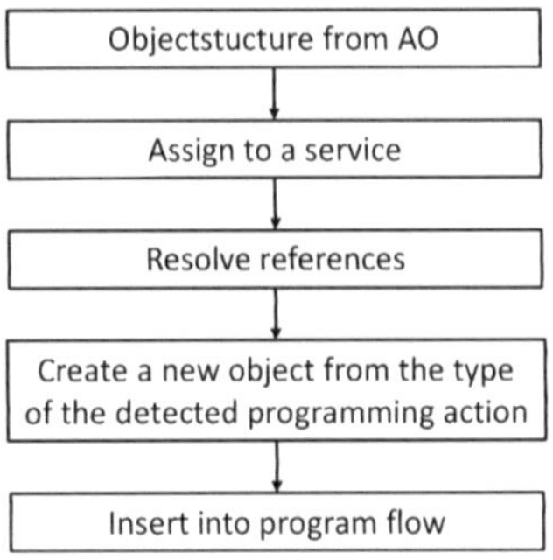

Figure 7. Abstract process in the Interpreter.

A. Interpreter Services

The transformation of the recognized concept was implemented with a micro service architecture. Every recognized programming concept has its own service, which knows what information is necessary for the transformation. In Figure 7, the result of the ontology is passed to the appropriate service on the basis of the detected action. The purpose of the services is to transform the existing information into an executable action. Regardless of the recognized statement, the main task is to resolve the specified references. After that they have to be linked to the action. For this purpose, a new object of the type of the action is generated and the resolved references are used (Section IV-D).

B. Reference Resolving

Similar to the organization of the detected actions, the references are also assigned to a service according to the recognized type. From the description of the linguistic analysis, three types are possible: constants, quantity references, and simple variable references. When searching for references, different information can be provided. Basically, the name of the reference or the indication that it is an implicit reference and the allowed field type must be given. Optionally, the required data type can be transferred. This is determined by the datatype of the first resolved reference. In the event of a directed action, this takes the assigned value. In addition to the data type, information can also be given as to whether the target is an action. All information is then processed by the context. This searches all currently available variables in the program code and returns the most likely reference. The distance to the current position in the code is taken into account as an additional quality criterion if the name is not explicitly mentioned. In these cases, if no existing reference can be assigned, it creates a new field with the data type of the assigned value. The procedure of resolving a target reference is shown in Figure 8.

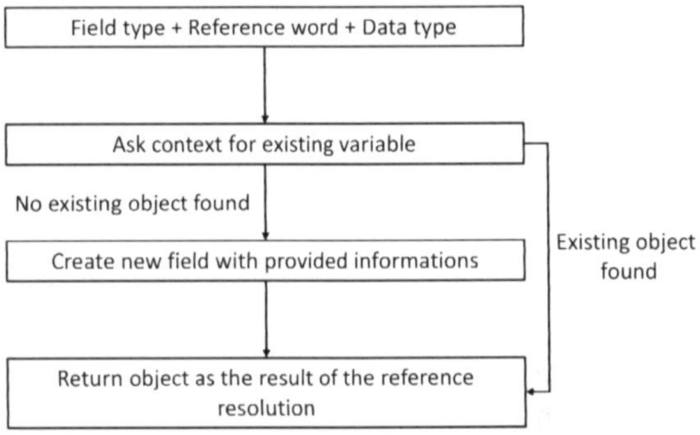

Figure 8. A reference resolution specified as the target of a directed action.

C. Context

The context module is the brain of the system and knows both the program sequence as well as the current position in it and offers functions to search for elements in it. Similar to [18], we solve an ordering problem that arises in natural-language programming. End users provide expressions involving "before", "after", "while", "at the end", and others. Our module represents the interface to the current excel document and thus allows the access to cells or area therein. It also knows the statement history and has a semantic understanding of the program code. This means that it knows at which position something was inserted last and what consequences this has on the accessible variables. Therefore, assigning an existing object in the program to a specified reference is an important task of the context. The procedure for resolving field references is shown in Figure 9. This function is called by the respective services as required.

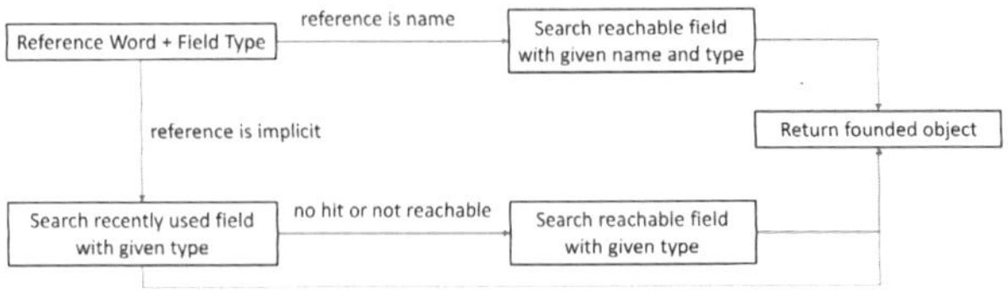

Figure 9. Sequence for resolving a reference in the context.

D. Data structure

The foundation on which both the context and the service structure work is a data structure which represents an object-oriented illustration of a programming language. Program sequences, actions, control structures and fields are implemented as classes. Functions are implemented as program sequences and contain references to the instructions placed in them. Analogous to this, control structures are constructed, which, depending on the type, additionally have a condition (`branches` or `while-loop`) or a reference to a quantity (`for-loop`). Actions define a processing rule and have appropriate references to fields that are necessary for execution. According to this concept, a program sequence can be represented as an object tree. The advantage of this implementation is the simple management and expansion of a resulting program sequence. Finally, in order to display the program code of the detected algorithm, each of the classes defines a method which dynamically generates the pseudo code of it. The execution is implemented in the same way. Each program component can be executed atomically. As a result of the structure as a tree, the entire program sequence can be drawn or executed by calling the respective method of the root object.

V. EVALUATION

In order to be able to make a statement about the quality of the system, the user study should be considered in addition to the unit tests carried out during the implementation.

A. Unit Tests

Due to the high complexity and complex dependencies, the active ontology was implemented with the process of test-driven development. The identification of individual concepts is ensured by a total of 132 defined entries. This results in a test coverage of 86%. The tests check whether the ontology delivers the expected output to an input. 57 test cases verify easy to recognize instructions, such as definitions, actions and unconditioned loops. 39 tests check the identification of various conditions. 36 defined inputs test the ontology for the detection of more complex instructions such as linking an action to a loop or condition.

In addition to the assurance of the functionality of individual concepts, complete algorithm descriptions are also tested by unit test. The following description of the switching sort algorithm shown in Algorithm 2 is tested.

Algorithm 2 Pseudo code of switching sort.

```
procedure SWITCHINGSORT(input)
    n ← length(input) − 1
    for i ← 0 → n do
        for j ← 0 → n do
            if input[j] > input[j+1] then
                tmp ← input[j]
                input[j] ← input[j + 1]
                input[j + 1] ← tmp
```

1. "check if any element of the input is higher than the next element"
2. "save it in an auxiliary variable"
3. "then the actual value should be set to the value of the next element"
4. "set the next element to the value of the auxiliary variable"
5. "do this for each element of the input"

In contrast to the above mentioned tests, the result of the ontology is not checked here, but the algorithm developed in the description has to sort a quantity of positive natural numbers. Thus, the function of the long-term memory and its interaction with ontology is ensured. In summary, the basic functionality is assured with the unit tests and at the same time it is shown that the system is able to process defined natural inputs correctly.

B. User Study

In order to gain an impression of the reliability of the system in relation to unknown and unrestricted formulations, a user study with a total of 11 participants was carried out. The participants were undergraduate computer science students and non-native English speakers. With six people, more than half of the participants described themselves as beginners in programming skills. Five participants described their skills at least as advanced. Seven of them have never used our system before. Four of the participants have already used previous version of our prototype in evaluations earlier. We were afraid that the prototype experts could sophisticate our evaluation results. At the end, they struggled the most during the evaluation trying to use our system in the old way, with old natural language structures.

1) Setup: The tasks of the study cover both the recognition of individual concepts as well as the processing of whole algorithm descriptions. In the first part the participants were asked to submit atomic descriptions of the supported programming elements. These includes definitions, assignments, conditions and loops. The second part again contained two tasks. In the first, the users should construct a process to find the largest element in a set of numbers and then write a step-by-step description of this on paper. The second task involved the pseudo code of a switching sort algorithm and claims the realization of this with the system. The reason for this subdivision is the insights that can be gained later. Interesting questionnaires are, for example, what influence the answer and the preview of the algorithm have on the course of the description and the achievement of the target.

2) Results: For a better overview of the results, the supported concepts were divided into three complexity classes. The tasks below are listed and assigned to the respective classes. Instructions describing a class three action are most difficult to detect.

1. Declarations, actions and for-loops:
   - Assigning a cell reference to a variable
   - Remove a value from a quantity
   - Save the value of a reference into a cell reference
   - Iterate over all elements of a quantity
2. Conditions and while-loops:
   - Check whether the value at a given position of a quantity is equal to 5
   - Check whether the value of a variable is already contained in a set
   - Do something until a given quantity is empty
   - Check if the value of a variable is less than three or greater or equal to five

3. Conditioned actions and conditioned loop action:
    - If the value of a variable is smaller than five write it to A3 otherwise store it into B3.
    - Remove all elements less than three from a quantity

Most of the tasks listed are code excerpts which have to be described. Figure 10 shows how reliable descriptions in the respective complexity classes have been correctly recognized. On average, the rate of detection of individual descriptions is 60%. It was noticeable in the analysis of the unrecognized inputs that many of the description could not be recognized due to the use of an unknown synonyms. For this reason, the descriptions were re-evaluated, this time replacing one word with a synonym. This time, a detection rate of 74% was achieved. A comparison of the individual classes is shown in Figure 10. The reason for the, in comparison to the other,

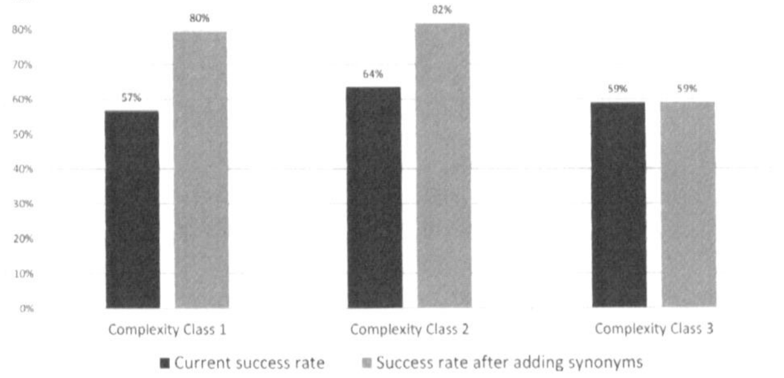

Figure 10. Result of the study for the individual complexity classes with and without synonyms

bad recognition rate in class three was that at the current time side additions are not considered. Therefore, no improvement could be achieved by taking synonyms into account. An input of complicity class three that could not be detected in the evaluation is "remove all elements from input which are smaller than 3". The condition is placed in a clause by using the phrase "which are". For the ontology, the distance between the referenced field name "input" and the condition is too large and therefore no relationship is detected. If the condition would be listed without a clause, as in "remove all elements from input smaller than 3", the input would have been correctly recognized.

In evaluating the results of a maximum-finding procedure given on paper, only two could be processed and executed correctly. Amazing after this modest success rate was that in implementing a switching sort algorithm with the system, seven out of eleven descriptions could be correctly processed and executed. From this contrast, the advantages of a dialog system and user feedback can be inferred. While this result demonstrate that our system is far from perfect it also shows that it is possible to correctly recognize programming instructions in natural language without restricting them beforehand. Knowing that nearly half of the unsolved tasks stemmed from unknown synonyms which are easy to fix the results we achieved are auspicious.

VI. Related Work

The idea of programming in natural language was first proposed by Sammet in 1966 [19], but enormous difficulties have resulted in disappointingly slow progress. One of the difficulties is that natural language programming requires a domain-aware counterpart that asks for clarification, thereby overcoming the chief disadvantages of natural language, namely ambiguity and imprecision. In recent years, significant advances in natural language techniques have been made, leading, for instance, to IBM's Watson [20] computer winning against the two Jeopardy! world champions, Apple's Siri routinely answering wide-ranging, spoken queries, and automated translation services such as Google's becoming usable [21][22]. In 1979, Ballard et al. [23][24][25] introduced their Natural Language Computer (NLC) that enables users to program simple arithmetic calculations using natural language. Although NLC resolves references as well, there is no dialog system. Metafor introduced by Liu et al. [26] has a different orientation. Based on user stories the system tries to derive program structures to support software design. A different approach regarding software design via natural language is taken by RECAA [27]. RECAA can automatically derive UML models from the text and also keep model and specification consistent through an automatic feedback component. A limited domain end-to-end programming is introduced by Le. SmartSynth [28] allows synthesizing smartphone automation scripts from natural language description. However, there is no dialog interaction besides the results output and error messages. One of the last research results have been presented by Wang [29]. They created a convenient natural language interface to perform user tasks. The system uses grammar rules that format natural language into a formal language. However, it is familiar with the pattern matching prototype that we have presented in late 2015 [11].

Paternò [30] introduces the motivations behind end user programming defined by Liberman [4] and discusses its basic concepts, and reviews the current state of art. Various approaches are discussed and classified in terms of their main features and the technologies and platforms for which they have been developed. In 2006, Myers [8] provides an overview of the research in the area of End-User Programming. As he summarized, many different systems for End User Development have already been realized [31][32][33]. However, there is no system such as our prototype that can be controlled with natural language. During a study in 2006, Ko [31] identifies six learning barriers in End User Programming: design, selection, coordination, use, understanding and information barriers. In 2008, Dorner [34] describes and classifies End User Development approaches taken from the literature, which are suitable approaches for different groups of end users. Implementing the right mixture of these approaches leads to embedded design environments, having a gentle slope of complexity. Such environments enable differently skilled end users to perform system adaptations on their own. Sestoft [35] increases expressiveness and emphasizing execution speed of the functions thus defined by supporting recursive and higher-order functions, and fast execution by a careful choice of data representation and compiler technology. Cunha [36] realizes techniques for model-driven spreadsheet engineering that employs bidirectional transformations to maintain spreadsheet models and synchronized instances. Begel [37] introduces voice recognition to the software development process. His approach uses program analysis to dictate code in natural language, thereby enabling the creation of a program editor that supports voice-based programming.

NLyze [38], an Add-In for Microsoft Excel that has been developed by Gulwani, Microsoft Research, at the same time as our system. It enables end users to manipulate spreadsheet data by using natural language. It uses a separate domain-specific language for logical interpretation of the user input. Instead of recognizing the tables automatically, it uses canonical tables which should be marked by the end user. Another Gulwani's tool QuickCode [39] deals with the production of the program code in spreadsheets through input-output examples provided by the end user [33]. It automates string processing in spreadsheets using input-output examples and splits the manipulations in spreadsheet by entering examples. The focus of his work is on the synthesizing of programs that consist of text operations. Furthermore, many dialog systems have already been developed. Commercially successful systems, such as Apple's Siri, actually based on active ontology [13], and Google's Voice Search [40][41] cover many domains. Reference resolution makes the systems act natural. However, there is no dialog interaction. The Mercury system [42] designed by the MIT research group is a telephone hotline for automated booking of airline tickets. Mercury guides the user through a mixed initiative dialog towards the selection of a suitable flight based on date, time and preferred airline. Furthermore, Allen [43] describes a system called PLOW developed at Stanford University. As a collaborative task agent PLOW can learn to perform certain tasks, such as extracting specific information from the internet, by demonstration, explanation, and dialog.

VII. Conclusion and Future Work

In this paper, we presented our work on a natural user interface which enables the end users to program in natural language. Based on active ontologies, programming concepts such as loops, conditionals and statements can be recognized in the analysis of the natural input. A meta model of the recognized concept, which contains relevant information, is then forwarded to the interpreter service provider. Here, the meta model is transformed into the target data structure with the help of a contextual knowledge. This corresponds to the object-oriented representation of a simple programming language. The context finally places the recognized program component in the history and informs the user of the detected action by updating the pseudo code. In this way, an algorithm is generated in an interactive process step for step, which can also be executed at the user's request.

In the evaluation of the prototype it was shown that the system is able to perform the required tasks. However, there is still a lot of work on our system needs to be done. The goal is the independent expansion of the language domain based on the basic vocabulary by means of a dialog system. In the following, such functions, algorithms, control structures and definitions to be recognized are summarized under description. The aim of this work is to ensure that system recognizes the synonyms entered by the user from a known description, learns it, assigns it to the known descriptions and saves it in a user-specific dictionary. This is intended as a local long-term memory for future input. Current work enables end users to describe algorithms and create code sequences as functions. Next step is to enable object-oriented programming [44]. Based on this, end users will also be able to interact with already existing objects, e.g., Excel tables, images, graphs, but also external connections, such as connecting to SQL tables. Such objects should be addressed directly and manipulated by natural-language input. In this case, our system analyzes big data and allows requests from different resources like tables, charts, and databases. End users could ask for information in their natural language that cannot be looked up in one step by the human.

Ordinary, natural language would enable almost anyone to program and would thus cause a fundamental shift in the way computers are used. Rather than being a mere consumer of programs written by others, each user could write his or her own programs [45]. However, programming in natural language remains an open challenge [22]. With natural language, programming would become available to everyone. We believe that it is a reasonable approach for end user software engineering and will therefore overcome the present bottleneck of IT proficients.

References

[1] A. Wachtel, J. Klamroth, and W. F. Tichy, "Natural language user interface for software engineering tasks," Tenth International Conference on Advances in Computer-Human Interactions, March 2017.

[2] W. F. Tichy, "What can software engineers learn from artificial intelligence," Computer;(United States), vol. 20, no. 11, 1987.

[3] ——, "NLH/E: A Natural Language Help System," the 11th International Conference on Software Engineering, 1989.

[4] H. Lieberman, F. Paternò, M. Klann, and V. Wulf, "End-user development: An emerging paradigm," in End user development. Springer, 2006, pp. 1–8.

[5] Eurostat, "European statistics database," last accessed March 17, 2018. [Online]. Available: http://ec.europa.eu/eurostat/data/database

[6] Microsoft, "By the numbers," last accessed March 17, 2018. [Online]. Available: https://news.microsoft.com/bythenumbers/planet-office

[7] M. F. Hurst, "The interpretation of tables in texts," 2000.

[8] B. A. Myers, A. J. Ko, and M. M. Burnett, "Invited research overview: end-user programming," in CHI'06 extended abstracts on Human factors in computing systems. ACM, 2006, pp. 75–80.

[9] B. M. Christopher Scaffidi, Mary Shaw, "Estimating the numbers of end users and end user programmers," in Proceedings of the 2005 IEEE Symposium on Visual Languages and Human-Centric Computing, ser. VLHCC '05. IEEE Computer Society, 2005.

[10] R. Abraham, "Header and Unit Inference for Spreadsheets Through Spatial Analyses," in IEEE Symposium on Visual Languages - Human Centric Computing, 2004.

[11] A. Wachtel, "Initial implementation of natural language turn-based dialog system," International Conference on Intelligent Human Computer Interaction (IHCI), December 2015.

[12] A. Wachtel, J. Klamroth, and W. F. Tichy, "A natural language dialog system based on active ontologies," in Proceedings of the Ninth International Conference on Advances in Computer-Human Interactions, 2016.

[13] D. Guzzoni, "Active: A unified platform for building intelligent web interaction assistants," in Web Intelligence and Intelligent Agent Technology Workshops, 2006. WI-IAT 2006 Workshops. 2006 IEEE/WIC/ACM International Conference on. IEEE, 2006, pp. 417–420.

[14] A. Wachtel, M. T. Franzen, and W. F., "Context Detection In Spreadsheets Based On Automatically Inferred Table Schema," ICHCI 2016: 18th International Conference on Human- Computer Interaction, World Academy of Science, Engineering and Technology, October 2016.

[15] A. Wachtel, "Programming Spreadsheets in Natural Language: Design of a Natural Language User Interface," Intl Journal on Advances in Software, Vol. 10, no. 3/4. Nice, France., December 2017.

[16] T. H. Cormen, Introduction to algorithms. MIT Press, 2009.

[17] K. Toutanova, D. Klein, C. D. Manning, and Y. Singer, "Feature-rich part-of-speech tagging with a cyclic dependency network," in Proceedings of the 2003 Conference of the North American Chapter of the Association for Computational Linguistics on Human Language Technology-Volume 1. Association for Computational Linguistics, 2003, pp. 173–180.

[18] T. Hey, "Deriving time lines from texts," in 3rd International Workshop on Realizing Artificial Intelligence Synergies in Software Engineering (RAISE'14), ser. ICSE. ACM New York, 2014.

[19] J. E. Sammet, "The use of english as a programming language," Communications of the ACM, vol. 9, no. 3, 1966, pp. 228–230.

[20] D. Ferrucci, E. Brown, J. Chu-Carroll, J. Fan, D. Gondek, A. A. Kalyanpur, A. Lally, J. W. Murdock, E. Nyberg, J. Prager et al., "Building watson: An overview of the deepqa project," AI magazine, vol. 31, no. 3, 2010, pp. 59–79.

[21] H. Liu and H. Lieberman, "Toward a programmatic semantics of natural language," in Visual Languages and Human Centric Computing, 2004 IEEE Symposium on. IEEE, 2004, pp. 281–282.

[22] C. L. Ortiz, "The road to natural conversational speech interfaces," IEEE Internet Computing, vol. 18, no. 2, 2014, pp. 74–78.

[23] B. W. Ballard and A. W. Biermann, "Programming in natural language:nlc as a prototype," in Proceedings of the 1979 annual conference. ACM, 1979, pp. 228–237.

[24] A. W. Biermann and B. W. Ballard, "Toward natural language computation," Computational Linguistics, vol. 6, no. 2, 1980, pp. 71–86.

[25] A. W. Biermann, B. W. Ballard, and A. H. Sigmon, "An experimental study of natural language programming," International journal of man-machine studies, vol. 18, no. 1, 1983, pp. 71–87.

[26] H. Liu and H. Lieberman, "Metafor: visualizing stories as code," in Proceedings of the 10th international conference on Intelligent user interfaces. ACM, 2005, pp. 305–307.

[27] S. J. Körner, M. Landhäußer, and W. F. Tichy, "Transferring research into the real world: How to improve re with ai in the automotive industry," in Artificial Intelligence for Requirements Engineering (AIRE), 2014 IEEE 1st International Workshop on. IEEE, 2014, pp. 13–18.

[28] V. Le, S. Gulwani, and Z. Su, "Smartsynth: Synthesizing smartphone automation scripts from natural language," in Proceeding of the 11th annual international conference on Mobile systems, applications, and services. ACM, 2013, pp. 193–206.

[29] S. I. Wang, S. Ginn, P. Liang, and C. D. Manning, "Naturalizing a programming language via interactive learning," arXiv preprint arXiv:1704.06956, 2017.

[30] F. Paternò, "End user development: Survey of an emerging field for empowering people," ISRN Software Engineering, vol. 2013, 2013.

[31] A. J. Ko and B. A. Myers, "Designing the whyline: a debugging interface for asking questions about program behavior," in Proceedings of the SIGCHI conference on Human factors in computing systems. ACM, 2004, pp. 151–158.

[32] S. Gulwani, W. R. Harris, and R. Singh, "Spreadsheet data manipulation using examples," Communications of the ACM, vol. 55, no. 8, 2012, pp. 97–105.

[33] A. Cypher and D. C. Halbert, Watch what I do: programming by demonstration. MIT press, 1993.

[34] M. Spahn, C. Dörner, and V. Wulf, "End user development: Approaches towards a flexible software design." in ECIS, 2008, pp. 303–314.

[35] P. Sestoft and J. Z. Sørensen, "Sheet-defined functions: implementation and initial evaluation," in International Symposium on End User Development. Springer, 2013, pp. 88–103.

[36] J. Cunha, J. P. Fernandes, J. Mendes, H. Pacheco, and J. Saraiva, "Bidirectional transformation of model-driven spreadsheets," in International Conference on Theory and Practice of Model Transformations. Springer, 2012, pp. 105–120.

[37] A. B. Begel, Spoken language support for software development. University of California, Berkeley, 2005.

[38] S. Gulwani and M. Marron, "Nlyze: Interactive programming by natural language for spreadsheet data analysis and manipulation," in Proceedings of the 2014 ACM SIGMOD international conference on Management of data. ACM, 2014, pp. 803–814.

[39] S. Gulwani, "Automating string processing in spreadsheets using input-output examples," in ACM SIGPLAN Notices, vol. 46, no. 1. ACM, 2011, pp. 317–330.

[40] J. R. Bellegarda, "Spoken language understanding for natural interaction: The siri experience," in Natural Interaction with Robots, Knowbots and Smartphones. Springer, 2014, pp. 3–14.

[41] J. D. Williams, "Spoken dialogue systems: Challenges, and opportunities for research." in ASRU, 2009, p. 25.

[42] S. Seneff, "Response planning and generation in the mercury flight reservation system," Computer Speech & Language, vol. 16, no. 3-4, 2002, pp. 283–312.

[43] J. Allen, N. Chambers, G. Ferguson, L. Galescu, H. Jung, M. Swift, and W. Taysom, "Plow: A collaborative task learning agent," in AAAI, vol. 7, 2007, pp. 1514–1519.

[44] N. Omar and N. A. Razik, "Determining the basic elements of object oriented programming using natural language processing," in Information Technology, 2008. ITSim 2008. International Symposium on, vol. 3. IEEE, 2008, pp. 1–6.

[45] W. F. Tichy, M. Landhäußer, and S. J. Körner, "Universal Programmability - How AI Can Help. Artificial Intelligence Synergies in Software Engineering," May 2013.

Usability Evaluation with Heuristics, Beyond Nielsen's List

Toni Granollers
Human-Computer Interaction and Data Integration Research Group (GRIHO)
Polytechnic Institute of Research and Innovation in Sustainability (INSPIRES)
University of Lleida
Lleida, Spain
email: antoni.granollers@udl.cat

***Abstract*— The work presented here is born of our extensive experience evaluating the usability of user interfaces and observing that some traditional methods need to be updated and improved. Here, we focus on the Heuristic Evaluation (HE) technique. It is one of the important topics in Human-Computer Interaction (HCI) when talking about usability evaluation. Different research works have been discussing the effectiveness of the current HE, but it is important to improve its effectiveness. A substantial improvement is presented, consisting of: (i) a new list of principles for evaluating any interface, (ii) a set of specific questions to be answered when analysing every principle, (iii) an easy rating scale for each question, and finally, (iv) a method to obtain a quantitative value, called the Usability Percentage. It gives a numeric idea about how usable the evaluated interface is. An experiment by a group of experts helped to validate the implications of the proposed solution.**

Keywords-usability; evaluation; heuristics; principles; user interface; human-computer interaction.

I. INTRODUCTION

Heuristic Evaluation (HE) is one of the most widely used methods for evaluating the usability of an interactive system. This technique became the most popular user-centred design approach in the 1990s but has become less prominent with the move away from desktop applications [3]. It is an effective method to assess User Interfaces (UI) by taking the recommendations based on User Centred Design (UCD) principles. These recommendations come in terms of design principles, heuristics, guidelines, best practices or user interface design patterns and standards [1] that are supposed to serve interface designers and evaluators.

Nevertheless, this technique has some aspects that, if improved, will increase its efficiency. For example, having to be concerned with the need for adapting the heuristic set to the specific features of each interactive system represents a drawback. Thus, evaluators must combine different recommendation sources to review the specific application domain. This involves either choosing Nielsen's list [10] (the most well-known and widely used), or a long reviewing process of guideline collections that inevitably causes conflicts between various resources [6]. In addition, each set uses different scoring systems to score the recommendations, so it is necessary to adjust it in the resulting set.

The process of combining different heuristic sets usually finishes up with an extensive list of duplicated recommendations, similar statements using different terms and potentially conflicting guidelines. A clean-up and selection process is then required to provide a reliable, consistent and easy to use heuristic set [1].

Furthermore, our experience reveals that, when someone uses Nielsen's list [10], it is often due to a lack of deep knowledge about it and, possibly, about the technique itself. This assertion is based on Nielsen's statement: "*these principles are broad rules of thumb and not specific usability guidelines*" [10], making the list itself impossible to be used to evaluate.

Another important aspect to be improved resides in the qualification method of the principles, providing very subjective and sometimes confusing final reports; HE combines the qualitative and quantitative results [12], but the qualitative results usually take on greater relevance. Attempts to improve quantitative outputs have been done in [1][2][9][14][20], among others. Other more ambitious works, such as work done by Masip et al. [6][7], offered a full framework that enables a semi-automatic process to provide the most adequate set of heuristics for each specific situation. It also classifies the heuristics (defining a User eXperience degree, UX-degree) in terms of different constraints and enables an automatic classification of the problems found (removing the post-evaluation meeting held by the evaluators) for a better, fuller process. Nevertheless, the rigorousness of this process makes it so complex that it is not widely used. Therefore, in this paper, we propose a substantial improvement in evaluating the usability of user interfaces, in the form of a new set of heuristics with a new evaluation method.

The article is organized as follows: Section 2 explains the sources of information consulted and the revision methodology. In Section 3, the new set of heuristics proposal is explained as well the new methodology for evaluating using it. Section 4 explains the experimentation carried out for validating the proposals. Section 5 presents our discussion and Section 6 concludes the article and provides future work plans.

II. COMBINING COMMON HEURISTIC SETS

A. Sources consulted

Since Schneiderman, in 1987, established his well-known *Eight Golden Rules of Interface Design* [18], and going via the no less well-known Nielsen's *Ten general principles for interaction design* [10] or Tognazzini's *First Principles of Interaction Design* [21], several authors have designed new sets (usually modifying Nielsen's list and/or adding new principles to evaluate specific aspects not covered) to help user interface designers and/or experts in their goal of enhancing usability. A complete review of several sets of usability heuristics created for specific domains by different authors can be found in [14] (specifically in the appendix A of this reference).

Nevertheless, the reality (mainly in private companies) is that when almost everybody refers to evaluate usability or UX with heuristics they refer to Nielsen's list.

In our case, after more than twenty years of experience involved in evaluation of interfaces, we decided to take Nielsen's and Tognazzini's lists to do this present work. We selected only these two because they are well-known references with unquestionable quality. So, there is no need to spend much time refining other sets or providing specific new ones. Moreover, as mentioned before (and confirmed by our own experience), Nielsen's list needed something more specific to be useful. Hence, we decided to complete it by combining both.

B. Methodology

Inspired by the recommendations found in Rusu et al.'s [14] and Quiñones's [13] works, the process followed for deciding our list of proposal principles was as follows:

1) **Revision** of the two chosen lists. The first step is to read carefully all the principles of Nielsen's and Tognazzini's lists. The revision has been done in terms of understanding the deep meaning of each principle.
2) **Compare** similarities. As the intention is to get a compact and complete solution for evaluating all kinds of user interfaces, we compared all the similarities in order to merge principles as much as possible.
3) **Integrate** these similarities. Previous comparison showed that some principles from both lists are identical while others are technically the same. The reader can identify these cases in marked cells (with the symbol "⇔") in the 2nd column in Table 1 TABLE I.
Also, in this step, we identified some cases from Tognazzini's list that can also be joined. The intention is not to question his proposal, only to have the shortest list possible without losing its efficiency. These cases are marked with the symbol "+" in the 4th column in Table 1; the following paragraphs explain the reasoning:

- "Use of Metaphors" and "Human Interface Objects" can be considered as a single principle because both have the objective of creating a mental connection between the user and an object. The user uses this object in his/her daily life that is associated with a functionality of the system.
- "Learnability" and "Anticipation". In Tognazzini's own words, anticipation tries to "bring to the user all the information and tools needed for each step of the process", a characteristic that is directly related with the learning curve, which defines learnability.

Additionally, both concepts can be understood with the capacity for minimizing the user's memory load by making objects, actions, and options visible. Hence, our decision of proposing the 5th principle "Recognition, rather than memory, learning and anticipation".

- Protecting the work and Saving the user's status can be grouped together as the purpose is for the user to continue working from where he was previously without losing his job. Regardless of whether there has been an unexpected failure of the system or the user who has closed the application. The main difference lies in how to prevent these errors, depending on whether an application is installed on the device or is consulted online. The 11th principle "Save the state and protect the work" serves to group these concepts together.
- Finally, Readability and Colour principles have been grouped together because both deal with design features to be easily seen and understood by every user. In fact, readability includes not only colour but fonts, typography or the text contrast with the background.

As a result, a final list with 15 general principles (or heuristics) resulting from mixing Nielsen's and Tognazzini's lists was created (see the far-right column of Table 1); this part is explained and expanded in [4].

TABLE I. RESULTING LIST OF PRINCIPLES. THE READER CAN OBSERVE THE CORRESPONDING PREDECESSORS.

Nielsen		Tognazzini			Resulting Principles
Visibility of system status	⇔	Visible Navigation	+	Discoverability	**1.- Visibility and system state**
Match between system and the real world	⇔	Human Interface Objects	+	Metaphors, Use of	**2.- Connection between the system and the real world, metaphor usage and human objects**
User control and freedom	⇔	Explorable Interfaces			**3.- User control and freedom**
Consistency and standards	⇔	Consistency			**4.- Consistency and standards**
Recognition rather than recall	⇔	Anticipation	+	Learnability	**5.- Recognition rather than memory, learning and anticipation**
Flexibility and efficiency of use	⇔	Efficiency of the User	+	Efficiency of the User	**6.- Flexibility and efficiency of use**
Help users recognize, diagnose, and recover from errors					**7.- Help users recognize, diagnose and recover from errors**
Error prevention					**8.- Preventing errors**
Aesthetic and minimalist design	⇔	Aesthetics	=	Simplicity	**9.- Aesthetic and minimalist design**
Help and documentation					**10.- Help and documentation**
		Protect Users' Work	+	State	**11.- Save the state and protect the work**
		Colour	+	Readability	**12.- Colour and readability**
		Autonomy			**13.- Autonomy**
		Defaults			**14.- Defaults**
		Latency Reduction			**15.- Latency reduction**

III. NEW SET AND EVALUATION PROPOSAL

A. Resulting set

As we have seen in the introductory section, to effectively use them for UI evaluations, we need "something more specific". This is also what every experienced usability/UX evaluator agrees upon. This "something more specific" are precise questions to be answered by the evaluators to assess every principle. Then, beyond the list of principles, a set of questions to evaluate every heuristic was created. In this case, 60 questions cover all the principles (Table 2 shows all the principles and their corresponding questions).

At this point, it is important to know two aspects: first, the list of questions arises directly from the analysis of our referents, mainly Tognazzini's, which is more expressive in this aspect, and second, the final list presented here is not the initial one. As it will be presented in Section IV, the experiment also served for testing the principles and their corresponding questions. The final list has the enhancements provided by the evaluator's feedback

TABLE II. HEURISTIC LIST PROPOSED WITH THEIR CORRESPONDING EVALUATION QUESTIONS

1.- Visibility and system state
- Does the application include a visible title page, section or site? - Does the user always know where it is located? - Does the user always know what the system or application is doing? - Are the links clearly defined? - Can all actions be visualized directly? (No other actions are required)
2.- Connection between the system and the real world, metaphor usage and human objects
- Does information appear in a logical order for the user? - Does the design of the icons correspond to everyday objects? - Does every icon do the action that you expect? - Does the system use phrases and concepts familiar to the user?
3.- User control and freedom
- Is there a link to come back to initial state or homepage? - Are the functions "undo" and "re-do" implemented? - Is it easy to come back to an earlier state of the application?
4.- Consistency and standards
- Do link labels have the same names as their destinations? - Do the same actions always have the same results? - Do the icons have the same meaning everywhere? - Is the information displayed consistently on every page? - Are the colours of the links standard? If not, are they suitable for its use? - Do navigation elements follow the standards? (Buttons, check box, ...)
5.- Recognition rather than memory, learning and anticipation
- Is it easy to use the system for the first time? - Is it easy to locate information that has already been searched for before? - Can you use the system at all times without remembering previous screens? - Is all content needed for navigation or task found in the "current screen"? - Is the information organized according to logic familiar to the end user?
6.- Flexibility and efficiency of use
- Are there keyboard shortcuts for common actions? - If there are, is it clear how to use them? - Is it possible to easily perform an action done earlier? - Does the design adapt to the changes of screen resolution? - Is the use of accelerators visible to the normal user? - Does it always keep the user busy? (without unnecessary delays)
7.- Help users recognize, diagnose and recover from errors
- Does it display a message before taking irreversible actions? - Are errors shown in real time? - Is the error message that appears easily interpretable? - Is some code also used to reference the error?
8.- Preventing errors
- Does a confirmation message appear before taking the action? - Is it clear what information needs to be entered in each box on a form? - Does the search engine tolerate typos and spelling errors?
9.- Aesthetic and minimalist design
- Is used a design without redundancy of information? - Is the information short, concise and accurate? - Is each item of information different from the rest and not confused? - Is the text well organized, with short sentences and quick to interpret?
10.- Help and documentation
- Is there the "help" option? - If so, is it visible and easy to access? - Is the help section aimed at solving problems? - Is there a section of frequently asked questions (FAQ)? - Is the help documentation clear, with examples?
11.- Save the state and protect the work
- Can users continue from a previous state (where they had previously been or from another device)? - Is "Autosave" implemented? - Does the system have a good response to external failures? (Power cut, internet not working, ...)
12.- Colour and readability
- Do the fonts have an adequate size? - Do the fonts use colours with sufficient contrast with the background? - Do background images or patterns allow the content to be read? - Does it consider people with reduced vision?
13.- Autonomy
- Does it keep the user informed of system status? - Moreover, is the system status visible and updated? - Can the user take their own decisions? (Personalization)
14.- Defaults
- Does the system or device give the option to return to factory settings? - If so, does it clearly indicate the consequences of the action? - Is the term "Default" used?
15.- Latency reduction
- Is the execution of heavy work transparent to the user? - While running heavy tasks, is remaining time or some animation shown?

B. Evaluation method

Formally, the HE method where evaluators rate every question to deliver a final report is considered. The intention is to combine the qualitative and quantitative findings, but usually the reports are mainly qualitative. So, some efforts have been made to improve the qualitative answer to the client.

For example, Nielsen [11] proposed a combination of three factors (frequency, impact and persistence) each of which must be rated on a scale of 5 values to assess the market impact of the problem according to its severity. Or, Rubin and Chisnell [10] whose problem severity's scale in a single parameter had 4 possible values (unusable, severe, moderate and irritant).

The previous examples, together with others that are not mentioned and our own experience, support the idea that existing quantitative proposals are not good enough. Nielsen himself declares that his proposal is a good measure but "*It is difficult to get good severity estimates from the evaluators during a heuristic evaluation session*" [11]. An idea also shared by UX professionals and researchers, such as Sauro [18], who argues that it is usually difficult to distinguish easily between too many rating levels.

In this research, we propose a simple but effective rating method. Our proposal has three main characteristics:

- A **4-option rating scale**: "Yes", "Neither", "No", and "Not applicable"

  Our experience demonstrates that evaluators find it exhausting when they must choose from a long list of values. This feature worsens as the evaluation time progresses, giving unreliable answers as the evaluators reach the last principles. We believe that by reducing the answers, as is proposed, this characteristic is minimized.

  Obviously, for each question, the evaluator can write as many qualitative comments as needed. They will reinforce the chosen selection and will provide hints to argue with other evaluators and for the programmers responsible to solve them.

- **Questions for the principles are interrogative questions written in a way that is favourable to usability**

  Literature and examples present design principles written in several forms: affirmative, negative, a mix of both or with and without question form, making (sometimes) confusion in the evaluator's work. A study presented by Masip et al. [7] revealed that evaluators prefer interrogative sentences because they are more intuitive, direct and easy for the evaluation job. Adopting this recommendation, all the principles in this proposal are written in question form.

  Moreover, all these questions are formulated in the way that when the answer is "Yes" it means that this feature represents good usability. Consequently, "No" represents the opposite, and "Neither" represents some value in between. The last possible answer, "Not applicable" is needed for those cases where this question has no meaning to the case.

  In fact, this is because we "*do not have to obsess too much over whether higher severity problems should have higher numbers or lower ones. It's the order that has meaning*" [18], what is really important is to find the mistakes.

- A final usability value, called "**Usability percentage**", UP.

  Apart from the qualitative insights, as we have seen in the introduction, some works [1][2][9][14][20] have been looking to complement them with a number to quantify how usable the evaluated interface is. This responds to one characteristic of human nature, always looking to quantify everything.

  In our case, it is important to know that there is no intention of giving a deterministic value with a hard meaning. Our aim is to give a kind of orientation about the level of usability of this interface.

  For this purpose, we will make use of the evaluators' answers to provide a final number. This is too simple, and we assign a numeric value to each possible answer. Thus, "Yes" is weighted with 1 point, "Neither" with 0.5 points and "No" with 0 points. "Not applicable" answers will not be taken into consideration, as if they do not exist.

TABLE III. 3 shows an example corresponding to the evaluation of the "Consistency and standards" principle. Here, one can observe how the values are taken in each case.

TABLE III. PUNCTUATION EXAMPLE WITH THE PRESENTED PROPOSAL.

4 - Consistency and standards		
Do link labels have the same names as their destinations?	Neither	0.5
Do the same actions always have the same results?	Yes	1
Do the icons have the same meaning everywhere?	Not applicable	-
Is the information displayed consistently on every page?	No	0
Are the colours of the links standard? If not, are they suitable for its use?	Yes	1
Do navigation elements follow the standards? (Buttons, check box, ..)	Yes	1

Finally, we add up all the values to obtain the final number.

With this, the maximum value is 60, corresponding with the case that all the questions have been answered with a "Yes". Nevertheless, as the "Not applicable" answer makes it impossible to know the maximum number for every evaluation, we translate this value to a percentage value, taking into consideration only the "Yes", "Neither" and "No" answers. It provides a number (a percentage) that enables the comparison among the assessments done by the other evaluators.

The value for the case of Table 3 is 3.5 that will be added to the final evaluation number. One should consider that, when translating to the percentage value, only 5 of the 6 questions will be taken into account (the 3rd answer is "Not applicable").

IV. EXPERIMENTATION

To validate our proposal, we designed an experiment that has a multipurpose goal. On the one hand, we want to obtain feedback from experienced evaluators to validate the heuristic list, the corresponding questions (see Table 1), the rating scale and the Usability Percentage (UP) final value. Secondly, we also wanted feedback about the questions to be answered by the evaluators when assessing every principle. And, finally, we wanted to have a real evaluation scenario that tests all the proposals. All together it should provide us with helpful comments and critiques.

For this, we planned a real evaluation. By that time, the faculty where we work had launched a completely redesigned website (http://www.eps.udl.cat) and the dean asked us about its usability. So, it was a perfect exercise to do. We could meet the request of our dean while being able to test the heuristic validation proposal.

We have recruited 7 evaluators, all them with valuable experience doing evaluations with heuristics: three with more than 10 years of experience, two with more than 5 years, one of whom developed her PhD completely in this specific field, and a PhD student that follows the previous one. The last student has less experienced, but is supervised by one of the seniors.

The evaluation process was very simple. Every evaluator received a spreadsheet file containing: a sheet for the project description and the evaluator data, 15 sheets (one for each principle) containing the principle and its questions, and a last sheet with the global calculation (blocked for the evaluator).

The questions on the principles sheets had to be answered with the score (one of the four available options) and with an additional cell for comments to describe the evaluator's feedback.

Table 4 shows the final scores of all the evaluators for every principle (this is what is shown in the last sheet). In this table, the important values are those along the bottom row, corresponding with the Usability Percentages.

Analysing these results, we can observe that, in general terms, the website evaluated has a good usability level. Figure 1 summarizes all the evaluations, the mean of all the evaluations is 77.5%, that means (or, could mean) a reasonably good usability level.

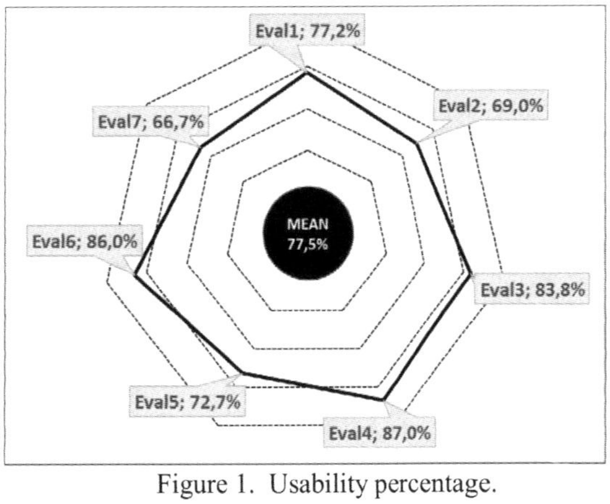

Figure 1. Usability percentage.

Moreover, if we want to be more precise, we can analyse the evaluation by each principle. Then, principles "*10 - Help and documentation*", "*11 - Save the state and protect the work*", "*14 – Defaults*" and "*15 - Latency reduction*" show the lowest; then, it is very easy to see what aspects are to be enhanced.

V. Discussion

Once this work was presented, the discussion was focused on what we learned from the experiment to validate the proposal presented here.

The first aspect to comment refers to the principles list. We are convinced that the new list is certainly an improvement on its predecessors. This position relies on (i) the basis of it is the result of shaking the most well-used list, Nielsen's, and another not so-well used, but more precise and complete list, Tognazzini's, and, (ii) on the comments provided by the evaluators who took part in the experiment. For example, the sentence "*this new list is a bit larger than Nielsen's, but it is much more complete*" had a unanimous consensus.

The second aspect is about the questions. Here, we must note that it is impossible to assess any single principle without the questions, hence their need. In our case, we delivered a list that also comes from the analysis of the two references used. We believe that these questions cover all the aspects to carry out a proper UI analysis. Certainly, they can be enhanced, but it is a reasoned and well-balanced list, with an appropriate number of questions for each principle.

The next characteristic refers to the rating method. Here, the first good decision was to write all the questions in question form and describe them with the same usability direction, the affirmative answer always representing good usability. This may seem unimportant, even trivial, but it is not usual to find it in the previous works. At the same time, it is a determinant for our score method. The second good decision was to simplify the rating scale. We know that larger scales allow evaluators to be more precise, but we also know that as the evaluation advances, the ratings for the last principles are less precise.

Both previous characteristics, i.e., the form of the questions and the rating method, enable us to quantify every evaluation done by the evaluators. It gives a global

TABLE IV. Results form all the evaluators

	Eval1	Eval2	Eval3	Eval4	Eval5	Eval6	Eval7
1- Visibility and system state	5	5	4	4.5	4	5	4
2 - Connection between the system and the real world, metaphor usage and human objects	3	2	4	4	3.5	4	2
3 - User control and freedom	3	2	3	2	2	1	1.5
4 - Consistency and standards	5	4	5	5.5	4	4	3.5
5 - Recognition rather than memory, learning and anticipation	5	4	4	5	5	5	4
6 - Flexibility and efficiency of use	5	3	3	6	3	5	3
7 - Help users recognize, diagnose and recover from errors	3	3	0	0	2	2	4
8 - Preventing errors	2	2	2	0	2	2	1
9 - Aesthetic and minimalist design	4	3	4	3	4	4	1
10 - Help and documentation	0	0	0	0	0.5	0	0
11 - Save the state and protect the work	2	0	0	1	1	0	0
12 - Colour and readability	4	3	2.5	4	4	2	2
13 - Autonomy	2	2.5	2	3	3	3	2
14 - Defaults	0	0	0	2	1	0	2
15 - Latency reduction	1	1	0	0	1	0	0
Usability Percentage (UP)	**77.2%**	**69.0%**	**83.8%**	**87.0%**	**72.7%**	**86.0%**	**66.7%**

evaluation point of view that we called the Usability Percentage (UP). This value must not be taken strictly as a full usability meaning, but as an orientation.

About this aspect, from the analysis of the experiment, beyond the result, we obtained the need to find the way to compare not only the UP, but the results of every single principle. Let us explain it: in Table 4, we see a lot of numbers that, at this moment, are slightly insignificant. These are the values obtained at every principle by every evaluator. They are used to calculate the UP, so are significant. But, we must find a way for comparing these values principle by principle. This will allow us to identify strengths and weaknesses and, then, to orientate the efforts for improving the usability of the interface. Certainly, this will be the next step to enhance our methodology.

VI. Conclusion and Future work

A new set of design principles has been presented with the intention to be used in Heuristic Evaluations. Additionally, a new methodology for evaluating completes the proposal, providing a quantitative rate named Usability percentage which complements the usual qualitative data provided by this type of evaluations. An experiment demonstrated how useful HE is and how easy it was to put our proposal into practise.

This is a work in progress in the sense that finding the specific strengths and weaknesses will make the system better and more useful. The proposed evaluation system is a potential candidate to replace existing methods. It is the simplification of the evaluation and the final value that make our system attractive.

References

[1] K. Baker, S. Greenberg, and C. Gutwin, "Empirical development of a heuristic evaluation methodology for shared workspace groupware". Proceedings of Conference on Computer Supported Cooperative Work, pp. 96–105, 2002.

[2] L. Bonastre and T. Granollers, "A Set Of Heuristics for User Experience Evaluation in E-commerce Websites". Proceedings of the Seventh International Conference on Advances in Computer-Human Interactions (ACHI 2014). ISBN: 978-1-61208-325-4, pp. 27-34, 2014.

[3] C. Cockton, "Usability Evaluation". The Encyclopedia of Human-Computer Interaction, 2nd Ed, Chapter 15. [Online]. Available from: www.interaction-design.org/literature/book/the-encyclopedia-of-human-computer-interaction-2nd-ed/usability-evaluation [retrieved: January, 2018].

[4] T. Granollers, "Usability evaluation with heuristics. New proposal from integrating two trusted sources". HCI International 2018. 20th International Conference on Human-Computer-Interaction.

[5] N. J. Lightner, "Evaluating e-commerce functionality with a focus on customer service".Communications of the ACM, 47 (1), pp. 88-92, 2004.

[6] L. Masip et al., "A design process for exhibition design choices and trade-offs in (potentially) conflicting user interface guidelines". Lecture Notes in Computer Science, vol. 7623, pp. 53-71. IFIP International Federation for Information Processing, 2012.

[7] L. Masip, M. Oliva, and T. Granollers, "OPEN-HEREDEUX: open heuristic resource for designing and evaluating user experience". Proceedings of the 13th IFIP TC 13 international conference on Human-computer interaction (INTERACT'11), P. Campos, N. Nunes, N. Graham, J. Jorge, and P. Palanque (Eds.), Part IV. Springer-Verlag, Berlin, Heidelberg, pp. 418-421, 2011.

[8] L. Masip, T. Granollers, and M. Oliva, "A Heuristic Evaluation Experiment To Validate The New Set Of Usability Heuristics". Proceedings of the 8th International Conference on Information Technology: New Generations, (Washington, DC, USA, 2011), IEEE Computer Society, pp. 429-434, 2011.

[9] A.B. Martínez, A. A. Juan, D. Álvarez, and M. C. Suárez, "WAB*: A quantitative metric based on WAB". Proceedings of the 9th International Conference on Web Engineering (ICWE 2009), LNCS Vol. 5648, pp. 485-488, Springer-Verlag Berlin Heidelberg. 2009.

[10] J. Nielsen, "10 Usability Heuristics for User Interface Design" [Online]. Available from: https://www.nngroup.com/articles/ten-usability-heuristics, 1995. [retrieved: January, 2018].

[11] J. Nielsen, "Severity Ratings for Usability Problems" [Online]. Available from: www.nngroup.com/articles/how-to-rate-the-severity-of-usability-problems, 1995. [retrieved: January, 2018].

[12] J. Nielsen, "Finding usability problems through heuristic evaluation". Proceedings of the SIGCHI conference on Human factors in computing systems (pp. 373-380). ACM, 1992.

[13] D. Quiñones, "A methodology to develop usability/user experience heuristics". Proceedings of the XVIII International Conference on Human Computer Interaction (Interacción '17). ACM, New York, NY, USA, Article 57, 2 pages. DOI: https://doi.org/10.1145/3123818.3133832, 2017.

[14] D. Quiñones and C. Rusu, "How to develop usability heuristics: A systematic literature review". Computer Standards & Interfaces, vol. 53, 2017, pp. 89-122, ISSN 0920-5489, https://doi.org/10.1016/j.csi.2017.03.009.

[15] P. C. Realpe, "Proceso de Diseño en Seguridad Usable y Autenticación mediante un enfoque Centrado en el Usuario". Doctoral Thesis, Universidad del Cauca (Colombia), 2017.

[16] J. Rubin and D. Chisnell, "Handbook of Usability Testing: How to Plan, Design, and Conduct Effective Tests". Ed. Wiley (2 edition), 2008. ISBN-13: 978-0470185483

[17] C. Rusu, S. Roncagliolo, V. Rusu, and C. A. Collazos, "A methodology to establish usability heuristics". Proceedings ACHI 2011: The Fourth International Conference on Advances in Computer-Human Interactions, pp. 59-62, 2011.

[18] J. Sauro, "Rating the Severity of Usability Problems" [Online]. Available from: https://measuringu.com/rating-severity, 2013. [retrieved: January, 2018].

[19] B. Shneiderman, "Designing the User Interface: Strategies for Effective Human-Computer Interaction". Addison-Wesley Publ. Co., Reading, MA, 1987.

[20] M. C. Suarez, "SIRIUS: Sistema de Evaluación de la Usabilidad Web Orientado al Usuario y basado en la Determinación de Tareas Críticas". Doctoral Thesis. Oviedo (Spain), 2011.

[21] B. Tognazzini, "First Principles, HCI Design, Human Computer Interaction (HCI), Principles of HCI Design, Usability Testing". [Online]. Available from: http://www.asktog.com/basics/firstPrinciples.html, 2014 [retrieved: January, 2018].

What's Hot in Interaction Design?

An International Survey of Practitioners' Views on Personas

Engie Bashir
Computer Engineering and Informatics
Middlesex University Dubai
Dubai, United Arab of Emirates
e-mail: e.bashir@mdx.ac.ae

Simon Attfield
Department of Computer Science
Middlesex University
London, United Kingdom
e-mail: s.attfield@mdx.ac.uk

Abstract— We report on findings from a 'state-of-practice' survey conducted with Interaction Design (IxD)/User Experience (UX) professionals called 'What's Hot in Interaction Design'. We focus on 20 items from the survey which elicited practitioners' usage of and attitudes towards personas. The survey items were derived from a review of academic and professional literature sources. The results show that practitioners think that personas have benefits, but come with associated resource demands and pitfalls, which we enumerate. We organize the results in terms of strength of opinion and discuss implications for methods, tools and curricula.

Keywords-personas; interaction design; persona usage; prioritising persona attitudes; theory and practice; tools and curricula.

I. INTRODUCTION

A persona is a user-model intended to support the design of a software product by anchoring design within a vision of intended users. Advocates argue that personas promote empathy and help focus design on the goals and characteristics of users. They are, however, not without detractors and although it has been 18 years since the publication of The Inmates are Running the Asylum [1], there has been little research to systematically elicit practitioners' attitudes about them.

In 1999, Cooper [1] introduced the idea of personas as a way of anchoring design within a vision of intended users. A persona is a kind of user-model—a *composite archetype* [2] drawn from behavioral data from users of an existing or intended digital product. A set of personas can be created where each represents a group of users with similar behaviors, attitudes, aptitudes, and needs. Methods for creating personas have been suggested by Cooper [2], Pruitt and Adlin [3], and Nielsen [4][5] with semi-automated methods also being proposed [6]–[8]. Personas have a role in the three phases of the User Centered Design (UCD): User Research & Requirements, Designing & Prototyping and Evaluation.

Despite the enthusiasm that some hold for personas, concerns have been raised about the resources required to create them [3][9]–[12] and their value to the design process [11]–[15]. A review of practitioners' attitudes towards personas via a selection of articles on professional websites revealed views ranging from strong advocacy to skepticism. To our knowledge, there has been little systematic research on attitudes towards personas held by the people who might use them—Interaction Design and User Experience professionals.

We conducted an online survey called 'What's Hot in Interaction Design' in order to elicit details of the current practices and attitudes of industry professionals. The survey spanned many topics of which personas was one. Our motivation was as a stimulus for considering new methods and tools, to inform university syllabus development, and simply to record current trends. The survey was in two parts: (1) an initial part about Interaction Design/User Experience practice in general ('main survey') which included 4 questions about personas, (2) an optional additional part ('persona survey') that had an additional 16 items (hereafter referred to 'A1' to 'A16' see TABLE I) which went into more detail about personas. Items were derived from a review of issues raised in the academic literature. The main survey was completed by 173 practitioners. 76 practitioners went on to complete the persona survey.

In this paper, we report results relating to persona use from both the main survey and the persona survey. We report an analysis of each item using significance testing and prioritize significant items using effect size (odds ratio) as a measure of relative strength of feeling.

In the next section (Section II), we review background literature which provided the basis for the persona survey items. In Section III, we discuss the survey and analysis method, and in Section IV we report the findings. In the final section, we summarize the results and discuss implications of our findings for interaction design practice.

II. LITERATURE REVIEW

A. *Overview on Personas*

Cooper introduced the idea of personas in 1999 [1]. Although a method for creating personas was not clearly articulated at that point, the idea attracted a good deal of attention. According to Cooper, personas offer a balance between formality and informality that carries more nuance than diagrammatic models through capturing users' goals, tasks, characteristics, and environments. The belief was that they could allow design teams from different disciplines and stakeholders to communicate about and empathize with the users and develop more focused designs. Methods for creating personas were subsequently offered that provided a structured approached to the development of personas. These included

Pruitt, Grudin and Adlins' 'role-based perspective' [3, 9]; Cooper, Reimann and Cronin's 'goal-directed perspective' [1]; and Nielsen's 'engaging perspective' [4]. Cooper, Reimann and Cronins' [1] method is a 7-step approach representing user-goals and including activities, attitudes, aptitudes, motivations, and skills towards a product. Pruitt, Grudin, and Adlin [3, 9] agreed on the benefits of personas suggested earlier, but propose personas as a complementary tool. Their method is a 5-step approach that looks into massive data and attempts to verify the quality and adequacy of persona representation. Nielsen [4][5], who observed variations in persona use, criticized some practitioners for failing to fully appreciate the potential of personas and for adopting marketing archetypes as personas. She offered the 'Engaging Persona' process, which is a 10-step approach aimed at establishing common ground on gathering data related to user needs, attitudes and aptitudes and includes details such as social background, psychological characteristics, and emotional relationship to invoke empathy and avoid stereotyping [16]. The method also included some steps that focus on how to make personas accepted and used by team members.

B. *Studies on Personas*

Some studies have explored experiences and outcomes of persona creation and use. Blomquist and Arvola [13], for example, observed a design team's first experience with personas. Methods for creating personas were relatively under-developed at that time and the authors found designers lacked confidence in using them for communication or design, concluding a need for expertise and integrating personas within existing knowledge and practice. Chang et al. [17] reported a small study with practitioners comparing attitudes of some who used personas and some of who didn't. The study found more positive attitudes towards personas from those who use personas who found it an essential tool for design. The study also found practitioners experimenting with new approaches. Later, Miaskiewicz and Kozar [18] elicited perceived benefits of personas from 19 experts (practitioners who created and used them) and derived a ranked list of 22 benefits, including: providing audience focus, helping to guide decisions, supporting collaboration, acting as a communication aid and guiding evaluation. Mathews et al. [15] reported a study of 14 practitioners and observed that those trained on Cooper's method tended to champion personas, whereas those trained in Engineering and Computer Science were 'moderate' persona users, and those trained in HCI and Design were pessimistic. The study also indicated benefits of personas in helping understand users' needs and context and establishing common ground.

A number of literature sources draw attention to the cost implications of personas creation. LeRouge [19] argued that despite their cost implications, when personas are successfully integrated into a design process by trained team members, the benefits outweigh the costs. Billestrup et al. [20] designed a questionnaire survey to investigate the knowledge and use of personas across 60 software development companies within a specific geographical region . The results revealed that more than half of the respondents had not heard of personas while the other respondents stated that personas were not well integrated into the development process. In addition, some problems related to time and budget constraints, limited knowledge with persona methods and inadequacy/ shallowness of persona descriptions were reported.

Based on an observational study of design team conversations, Friess [11] questioned the benefits of personas as a tool for communication. Fries' study showed that despite time and resources spent on developing and refining personas, they were only referred to briefly in designers' conversations. Fries, however, resists the conclusion that personas are not useful with the observation that members of the design team who created personas invoked them in conversations much more often than other team members and stakeholders. Tharon [12] commented on the result that, "Leaving the development of the personas to a select few on the team seems likely to ensure that those few are the only members of your team who will benefit from the time and money invested in the personas development."

C. *Personas and Empirical Methods of User Research*

It is agreed across the several methods of creating personas [2]–[4][6]–[8][10] that personas should be derived from user research. The approach suggested by Cooper [1][2] was solely qualitative, involving informal manual clustering of users (based on 'behavioral variables'). Such an approach has raised questions about possibilities of exploiting quantitative data [3][8]–[10], as well as issues of sample size [3][6][8]–[10][14], adequacy of personas in terms of validity and human bias[7][8][10][14], and time and budget implications [3][6][8]–[10][12][14][15][21]. In response to such issues, some have proposed the integration of quantitative research and/or automating clustering methods.

Pruitt, Adlin, and Grudin [3][9] were the first to combine quantitative and qualitative methods based on existing data about users. Their clustering method remained manual and was performed by experts in user research. They suggested validating personas through "sanity checks" and "foundation documents" to link them with the original gathered data. Later, Chapman's and Milham's [14] discussed the unexplored limitations of the former persona methods in terms of significance, accuracy, validity, human bias, and relation to the design of the product. The subsequent authors focused on bringing some automation to the process to increase objectivity, improve validity by increasing sample size, whilst also improving the efficiency of the method and making it less dependent on research expertise.

Mulder and Yaar [10] proposed a mixed method for web design personas starting with a quantitative analysis of large-scale market research and website log data and using semi-automated clustering techniques to create market segmentation/user profiles, followed by qualitative analysis such as interviews, field studies or usability tests. Following this, McGinn and Kotamraju [8] suggested designing a survey with agreed attributes to collect large-samples of customer data. *Factor Analysis* (FA) was used from the initial groupings, followed by interviews with selected users to reveal the goals and motivation and to validate group membership.

Maikenzie et al. [7] proposed *Latent Semantic Analysis* (LSA) for semi-automated clustering of qualitative interview transcripts data, proposing this method to be "more efficient, less subjective, and less reliant on specialized skills". Brikey, Walczak, and Burgess [6] reported a study that classified the methods of creating personas in terms of *manual qualitative techniques and semi-automated techniques (*LSA, FA, principal component analysis (PCA) and multivariate cluster analysis (CA)). The findings indicated that LSA semi-automated method, when compared to the manual qualitative method, is not affected by the quantity of data, requires less expertise in clustering, is faster and cheaper, and minimizes human bias. The study also showed that the three automated clustering techniques didn't agree with the cluster assignment done by experts.

In her 10-step approach, Nielsen [4] applies quantitative and qualitative research methods and considers manual clustering techniques (affinity diagrams and empathy maps) to be performed by qualified team members. These approaches each in its own capacity have exploited at least one of the following: sample size, adequacy of persona, time and budget; yet all of them need the expertise in quantitative/qualitative data analysis for clustering users.

D. Professional Literature

We also conducted a review of professional magazines and association websites for articles on personas. Here, mixed opinions can be found along with specific concerns which in many cases echo those expressed in the academic literature. For example, Sholmo G. [22][23], an interaction designer intern at Cooper design agency, remarks, "For every designer who uses personas, I have found even more who strongly oppose the technique." He reflects on his own conversion from negative attitude to positive once he started to develop and use personas "properly" in his work. He attempts to convince detractors to change their perceptions and promotes the use of personas for those who are unfamiliar with the process. Similarly Kellingley [24], another advocate for the development of personas, agreed with many of the criticisms under three headings: "Personas are time-consuming", "Personas are expensive", and "Personas need time to show ROI". However, he argues that more time and money would be spent on building and rebuilding products without considering user requirements and personas. Accordingly, the attempt to reduce cost and time by cutting back on user research and abandoning the use of personas does not hold. In the same way, Paul B. [25] discusses three reasons that lead some peers to adverse personas as design tools. First, the use of "Analytics", which he argues can reveal many insights about the design components based on users' interactions, overlooks how UX designers work and merely specifies user behaviors which is essential to the UX strategy. Second, A/B and multivariate testing assesses alternative designs in terms of quantitative results, but do not suggest how to reach the best design. Third, in an agile environment UX practitioners feel a burden when creating and designing personas because of time constraints, which again reveals that there is a need for better ways of fitting personas in the UX process.

III. Methods

A. Survey Design

The main survey contained 29 questions distributed across sections on: (1) demographics; (2) user research; (3) design and prototyping; (4) product development; and (5) evaluation. Section (1) contained questions asking the areas in which respondents had professional experience, the answers to which determined subsequent sections they were asked to complete. There were four questions about personas in the main survey across the remaining sections.

The persona survey contained 16 items. Each elicited agreement with a series of propositions on a five-point Likert scale. Each proposition represents a possible attitude towards personas. They were derived by collating reported findings and opinions (explicitly expressed or apparently assumed) appearing in a range of relevant academic sources (most appear in the literature review above) and a selection of industry blogs. The propositions are itemized in TABLE I. and each is mapped against its multiple sources.

Findings from previous studies were included because such studies were typically qualitative and/or longitudinal and based a small sample drawn from one specific contexts. In this sense, the survey can be seen as corroborating findings as well as opinions against a larger and more widely drawn sample. In some cases, sources contradicted each other. Here the survey can be seen as helping to resolve such conflicts. Thus, we believed we converged on a set of concerns that were relevant and might be profitably tested with reference to the experience of a larger sample of practitioners.

It is not uncommon for surveys to use both forward and reverse-keyed versions of items to control for possible acquiescence bias. However, Sonderen et al. [26] and Schriesheim & Hill [27] argue that there is little empirical evidence to support this recommendation and also demonstrate that it can increase respondent confusion and introduce difficulties in interpretation. In addition, including reverse-keyed items double the size of a survey which presumably can negatively affect completions and hence sample size. Hence, we opted for one item per proposition.

B. Participants and recruitment

The target population for the survey was UX/IxD practitioners. Respondents were recruited by non-probabilistic convenience sampling via invitations to online interest groups, and by snowball sampling via the researchers' professional networks. The requirement of working as a UX/IxD practitioner was included in invitations. Respondents were asked to give job titles as part of the survey and these were subsequently reviewed for relevance prior to analysis.

C. Data Analysis

Responses to each Likert item were coded on a scale of 1 to 5 where 1 = *strongly disagree*, 2 = *disagree*, 3 = *neutral*, 4 = *agree*, 5 = *strongly agree*. For each item, a lower bound one-sample, one-tailed sign test was performed to assess agreement according to the following hypotheses:

H0: The population median response is equal to or less than neutral ($\eta<=3$) (i.e., non-agreement)

H1: The population median response is greater than neutral ($\eta> 3$) (i.e., agreement)

Given the multiple tests, Benjamini and Hochberg [28] method was used to control for inflated type I error rate ($\alpha_{adjusted}$ =.040625). The odds ratio (OR) -an unstandardized effect size statistic- was also computed for each item and to ultimately organize the responses in terms of strength of expressed opinion.

TABLE I. THE 16 STATEMENTS USED AS ATTITUDINAL MEASURES TOWARDS PERSONAS

A1: Personas are time consuming to create/use. **Agree:** [3][8]–[10][12][19][20].**Disagree:** [6][7]
A2: Personas are expensive to create/use. **Agree:** [3][8]–[10][19][20]**Disagree:** [6][7]
A3: Representative personas require a lot of data. **Agree:** [3][8]–[10][19].**Disagree:**[17][29]
A4: Personas require expertise in qualitative research to create. **Agree:** [2][3][9][10][13][17][19]. **Disagree:** [6][7]
A5: Personas require training in persona methods. **Agree:** [2]–[4][8]–[10][15][19]
A6: Collaborating around personas is difficult. **Agree:** [3][9][13]. **Disagree:** [13]
A7: Personas are often not properly used by teams. **Agree:** [11][12]. **Disagree:** [3][7][13]
A8: Personas often represent extreme archetypes **Agree:** [2][10][21]
A9: Personas often lack important information related to goals, needs, behaviors, and attitudes. **Agree:** [20]. **Disagree:**[1]–[5][9][10]
A10: Persona sets often incorporate redundancy (multiple personas referring to the same characteristics).**Agree:** [2][3]
A11: Personas are helpful for understanding users' needs and context. **Agree:** [1]–[6][9][10][19][21]. **Disagree:** [13]
A12: Personas are helpful for making design decisions. **Agree:** [2][3][5][7][9][10][21]. **Disagree:** [13]–[15]
A13: Personas are helpful for implementing and building **Agree:**[2][3][5][9][10][19][21]
A14: Personas are helpful for evaluation. **Agree:** [10][18][19][21].**Disagree:**[20]
A15: Personas are helpful for communicating with stakeholders and team members. **Agree:** [1]–[5][7][9][10][19][21].**Disagree:** [11]–[13]
A16: The personas I use are usually well formed and adequate. **Disagree:** [20]

IV. RESULTS

A. Demographics

The main survey and the persona survey were completed by 173 and 76 practitioners, respectively, with the following self-reported demographics (number in main survey/number in persona survey):

- Job Titles: UX Designers (52/21), UX Researchers (27/13), Senior User Experience Designers (23/13), User Interface Designer / Information Architect (7/2), and others (64/27);
- Years of experience: > 5 yrs (79/36), 3 -5 yrs(45/17), 1 -2 yrs (26/11), < 1 year (23/12);
- Countries: UK (56/30), USA (35/13), Sweden (12/7), India (11/2), Norway (8/3), UAE (8/3) and 43/18 others;
- Organization size: 20-99 employees (34/14), 1000-4999 employees (31/13), 10000+ employees (24/13), 100-499 employees (24/6), 5000-9999 employees (20/8), 1-4 employees (12/3), 10-19 employees (9/5), 500-999 employees (8/8), 5-9 employees (6/6).

Respondents worked with digital products in the areas: websites (134/63), mobile solutions /applications (121/52), consumer technology (73/35), enterprise solutions (67/33), accessibility (62/24), visualization of big data (44/25), smart objects/devices (IOT)(31/10) and, tabletops/multi-touch surfaces (24/8), wearable technology (19/5), Robotics & AI (16/4), A/R (14/3), VR (11/2), others (35/14)

B. Persona Use

Of the 173 practitioners who completed the main survey 111(64%) reported using personas in some capacity. Of 105 respondents involved in user research, 78 (74%) reported using personas to represent/communicate user needs based on research studies. Of 109 respondents involved in design and prototyping, 69 (63%) reported using personas for motivating design ideas/decisions and 44 (40%) reported using persona-based inspection for creating/refining the concepts of design. Of 113 respondents involved in evaluation, 34 (30%) reported using persona-based inspection methods.

C. Results from the Personas Survey

We report responses to the items in the persona survey, including results of a one-sample sign test used to assess agreement with each proposition. In each of the bar charts (Fig. 1—16), the left end of the red arrow indicates the lower bound of the 95% confidence interval and the dot indicates the estimated population median. Note that in a number of cases these values are the same.

A1: Personas are time-consuming to create/use

Fig. 1 shows that the attitudes to this item were mostly positive with median and mode of 4. 62% responded on the 'agree' side of neutral (4 or 5) and 25% responded on the 'disagree' side of neutral (1 or 2). A one-tailed sign test was **highly significant** (p=.0004 and p-adjusted=0.03125) supporting H1 (agreement). The odds ratio was 2.5.

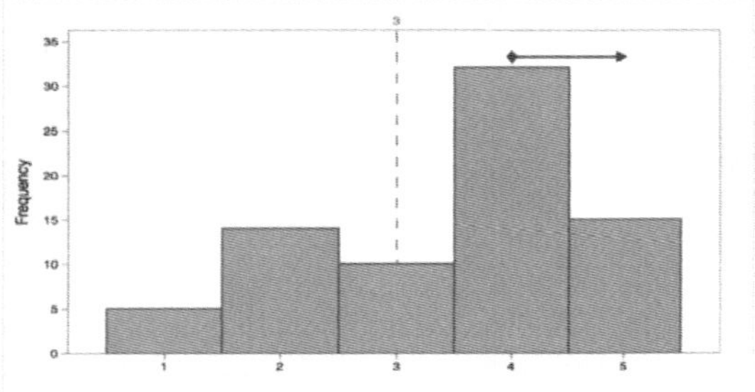

Figure 1. Personas are time-consuming to create/use

Conclusion: Practitioners tend to agree that personas are time-consuming to create/use.

<u>A2: Personas are expensive to create/use</u>

Fig. 2 shows that the attitudes to this item were fairly even around neutral with a median of 3 and mode of 4. 34% responded on the 'agree' side of neutral (4 or 5) and 25% responded on the 'disagree' side of neutral (1 or 2). A one-tailed sign test was **non-significant** (1-tailed *p*=.7052 and *p-adjusted*=0.046875) supporting H0 (non-agreement). The odds ratio was 0.9.

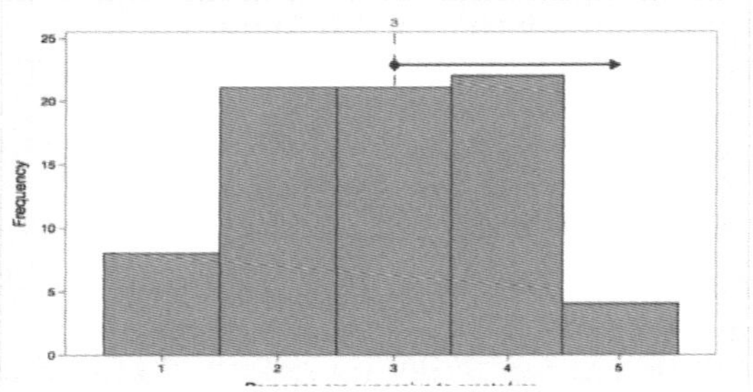

Figure 2. Personas are expensive to create/use

Conclusion: Practitioners tend **not to** agree that personas are expensive to create/use.

<u>A3: Representative personas require a lot of data</u>

Fig. 3 shows that the attitudes to this item had a median and mode of 4. 54% responded on the 'agree' side of neutral (4 or 5) and 16% responded on the 'disagree' side (1 or 2). A one-tailed sign test was highly significant (1-tailed *p* <.0001 and *p-adjusted*=.003125) supporting H1 (agreement). The odds ratio was 3.4.

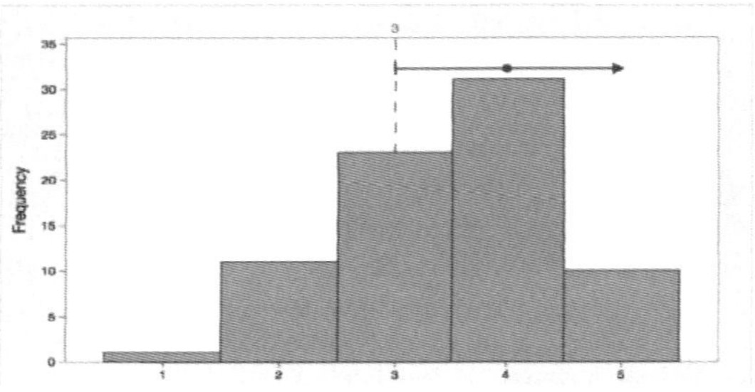

Figure 3. Representative personas require a lot of data

Conclusion: Practitioners tend to agree that representative personas require a lot of data.

<u>A4: Personas require expertise in qualitative research to create.</u>

Fig. 4 shows that the attitudes to this item had a median and mode of 4. 72% responded on the 'agree' side of neutral (4 or 5) and 14% responded on the 'disagree' side (1 or 2). A one-tailed sign test was highly significant (1-tailed *p* <.0001 and *p-adjusted*=.00625) supporting H1 (agreement). The odds ratio was 5.

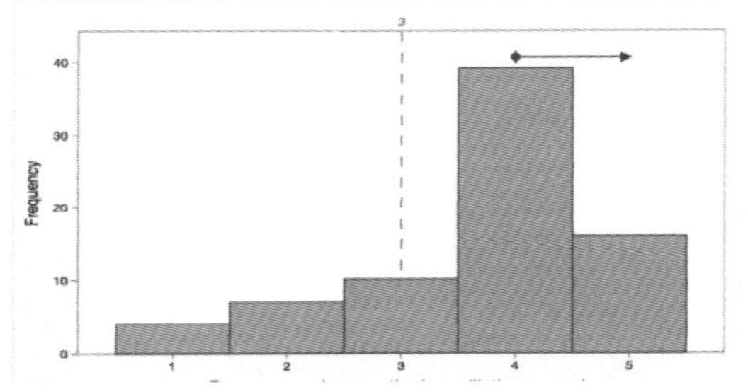

Figure 4. Personas require expertise in qualitative research to create

Conclusion: Practitioners tend to agree that personas require expertise in qualitative research to create.

<u>A5: Personas require training in personas methods</u>

Fig. 5 shows that the attitudes to this item had a median and mode of 4. 66% responded on the 'agree' side of neutral (4 or 5) and 13% responded on the 'disagree' side (1 or 2). A one-tailed sign test was highly significant (Z = 3.846, 1-tailed *p*<.0001 and *p-adjusted* =.00937) supporting H1 (agreement). The odds ratio was 5.

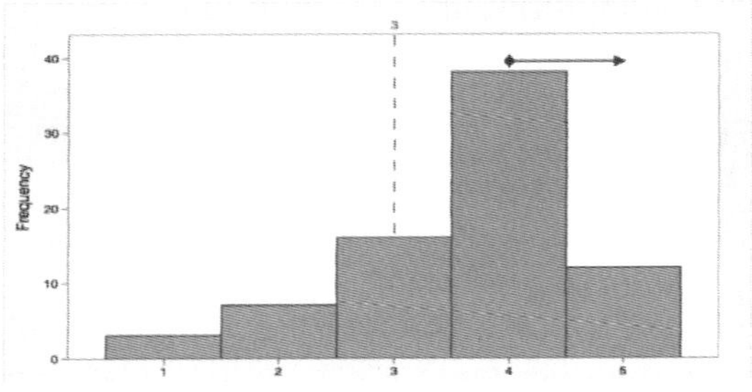

Figure 5. Personas require training in personas methods

Conclusion: Practitioners tend to agree that personas require training in personas methods.

<u>A6: Collaborating around personas is difficult</u>

Fig. 6 shows that the attitudes to this item had a median of 3 and mode of 2. 34% responded on the 'agree' side of neutral (i.e., 4 or 5) and 39% responded on the 'disagree' side (1 or 2). A one-tailed sign test was non-significant (1-tailed *p*=.748 and *p-adjusted*=.05) supporting H0 (neutral or disagree) with an odds ratio (OR≈0.9).

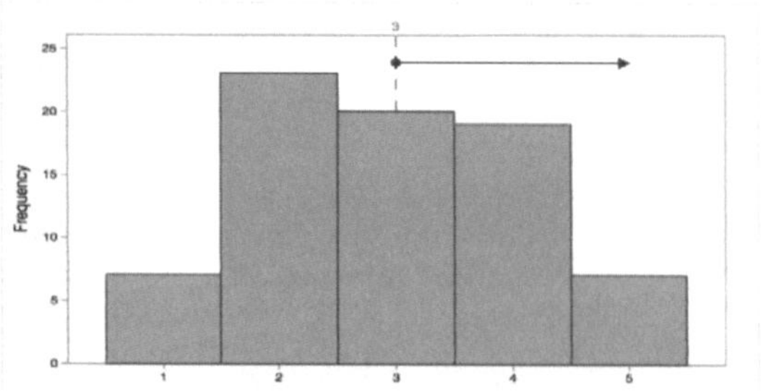

Figure 6. Collaborating around personas is difficult

Conclusion: Practitioners tend **not to** agree that collaborating around personas is difficult.

A7: Personas are often not properly used by teams

Fig. 7 shows that the attitudes to this item had a median of 4 and mode of 5. 78% responded on the 'agree' side of neutral (i.e., 4 or 5) and 4% responded on the 'disagree' side (1 or 2). A one-tailed sign test was highly significant (1- tailed $p<.0001$ and *p-adjusted*=.00125) supporting H1 (agreement). The odds ratio was 19.7.

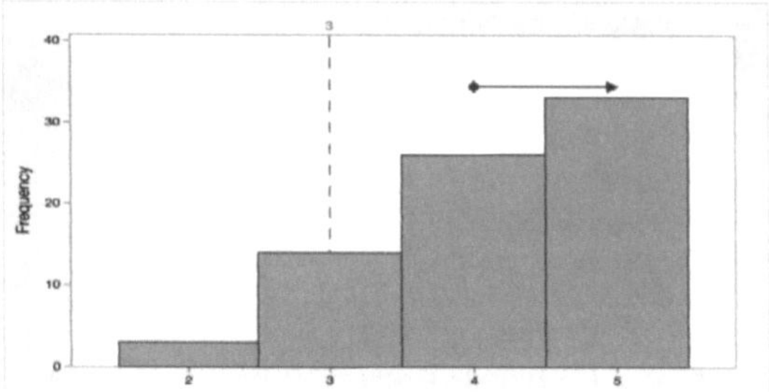

Figure 7. Personas are often not properly used by teams

Conclusion: Practitioners tend to agree that personas are often not properly used by teams.

A8: Personas often represent extreme archetypes

Fig. 8 shows that the attitudes to this item had a median and mode of 3. 43% responded on the 'agree' side of neutral (4 or 5) and 22% responded on the 'disagree' side (1 or 2). A one-tailed sign test was found to be significant (1-tailed p=.025 and *p-adjusted*=.0344) supporting H1 (agreement) with an odds ratio of 1.9.

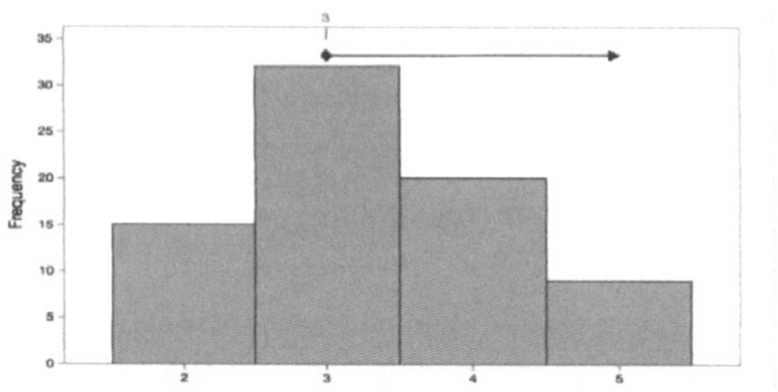

Figure 8. Personas often represent extreme archetypes

Conclusion: Practitioners tend to agree that personas often represent extreme archetypes.

A9: Personas often lack important information related to goals, needs, behaviors, and attitudes.

Fig. 9 shows that the attitudes to item had a median and mode of 3. 42% responded on the 'agree' side of neutral (4 or 5) and 26% responded on the 'disagree' side (1 or 2). A one-tailed sign test was found to be non-significant (1-tailed p=.064 and *p-adjusted*=.0438) supporting H0 (neutral or disagree) with an odds ratio of 1.6.

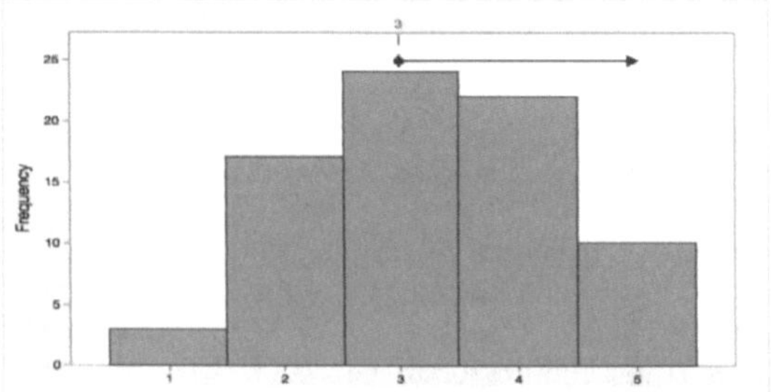

Figure 9. Personas often lack important information related to goals, needs, behaviors, and attitudes.

Conclusion: Practitioners tend **not to** agree that personas often lack important information related to goals, needs, behaviors, attitudes.

A10: Persona sets often incorporate redundancy

Fig. 10 shows that the attitudes to this item had a median and mode of 3. 42% responded on the 'agree' side of neutral (4 or 5) and 26% responded on the 'disagree' side (1 or 2). A one-tailed sign test was found to be significant (1-tailed p=.064 and *p-adjusted*=.0438) supporting H1 (agreement). The odds ratio was 1.8.

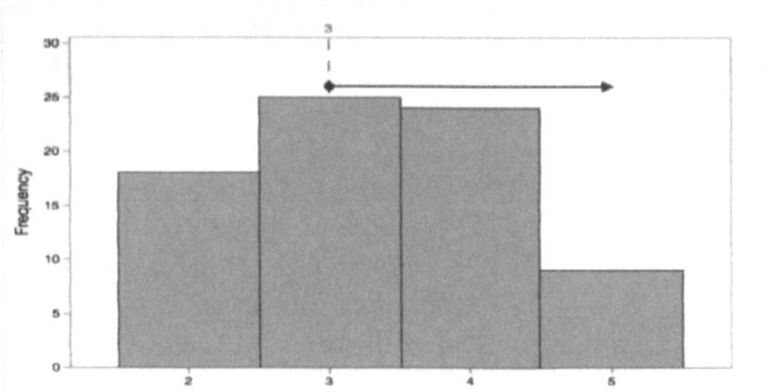

Figure 10. Persona sets often incorporate redundancy

Conclusion: Practitioners tend to agree that personas often incorporate redundancy.

A11: Personas are helpful for understanding users' needs and context

Fig. 11 shows that the attitudes to this item had a median and mode of 4. 83% responded on the 'agree' side of neutral (i.e., 4 or 5) and 8% responded on the 'disagree' side. A one-tailed sign test was highly significant (1- tailed $p<.0001$ and *p-adjusted*=.015625) supporting H1 (agreement). The odds ratio was 10.5.

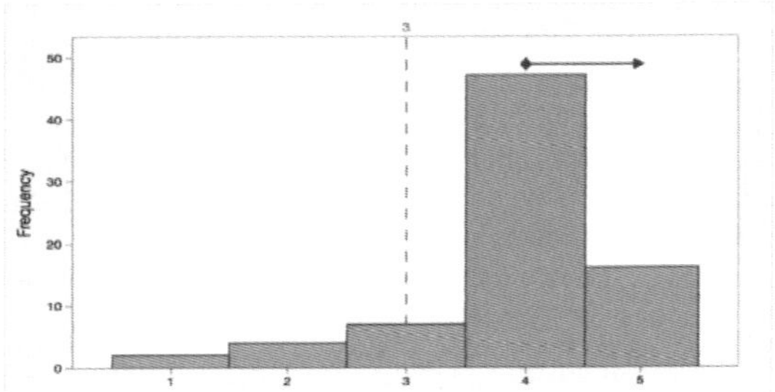

Figure 11. Personas are helpful for understanding users' needs and context

Conclusion: Practitioners tend to agree that personas are helpful for understanding users' needs and context.

A12: Personas are helpful for making design decisions

Fig. 12 shows that the attitudes to this item had a median and mode of 4. 72% responded on the 'agree' side of neutral (i.e., 4 or 5) and 11% responded on the 'disagree' side (1 or 2). A one-tailed sign test was highly significant (1-tailed $p<.0001$ and *p-adjusted*=.01875) supporting H1 (agreement). The odds ratio was 6.9.

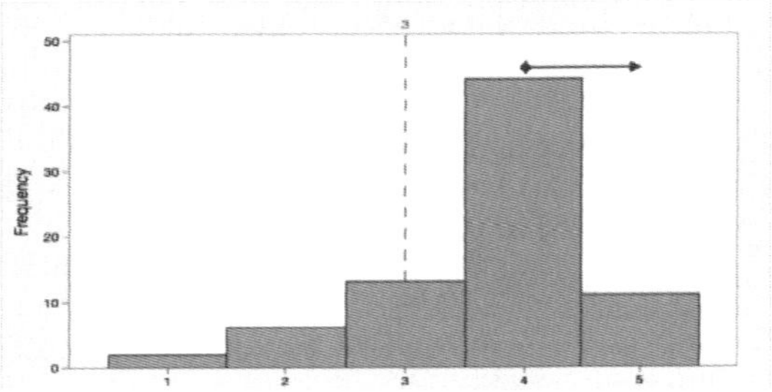

Figure 12. Personas are helpful for making design decisions

Conclusion: Practitioners tend to agree that personas are helpful for making design decisions.

A13: Personas are helpful for implementing and building

Fig. 13 shows that the attitudes to this item had a median of 3 and mode of 4. 47% responded on the 'agree' side of neutral (4 or 5) and 28% responded on the 'disagree' side (1 or 2). A one-tailed sign test was highly significant (1-tailed $p=$ .0318 and *p-adjusted*= .040625) supporting H1 (agreement). The odds ratio was 1.7.

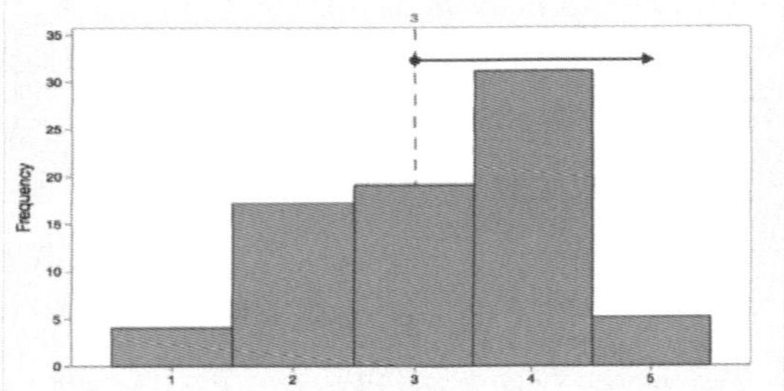

Figure 13. Personas are helpful for implementing and building

Conclusion: Practitioners tend to agree that personas are helpful for implementing and building.

A14: Personas are helpful for evaluation

Fig. 14 shows that the attitudes to this item had a median and mode of 4. 68% responded on the 'agree' side of neutral (i.e., 4 or 5) and 12% responded on the 'disagree' side (1 or 2). A one-tailed sign test was highly significant (1-tailed $p=.0318$ and *p-adjusted*= .021875) supporting H1 (agreement). The odds ratio was 5.8.

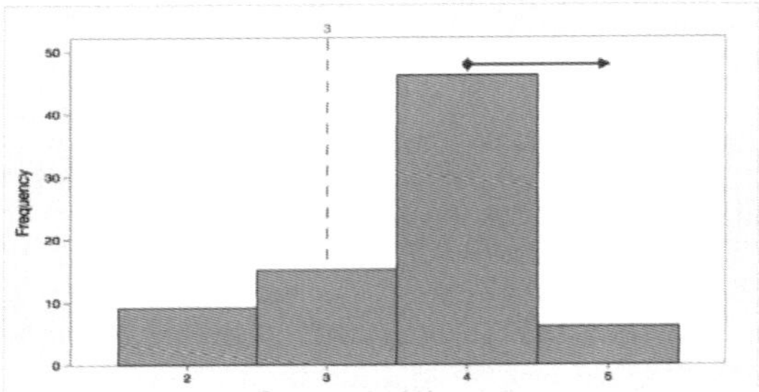

Figure 14. Personas are helpful for evaluation

Conclusion: Practitioners tend to agree that personas are helpful for evaluation.

A15: Personas are helpful for communicating with stakeholders and team members

Fig. 15 shows that the attitudes to this item had a median and mode of 4. 75% responded on the 'agree' side of neutral (4 or 5) whilst 11% responded on the 'disagree' side (1 or 2). A one-tailed sign test was highly significant (1- tailed $p<0.001$ and *p-adjusted*= .025) supporting H1 (agreement). The odds ratio was 7.1.

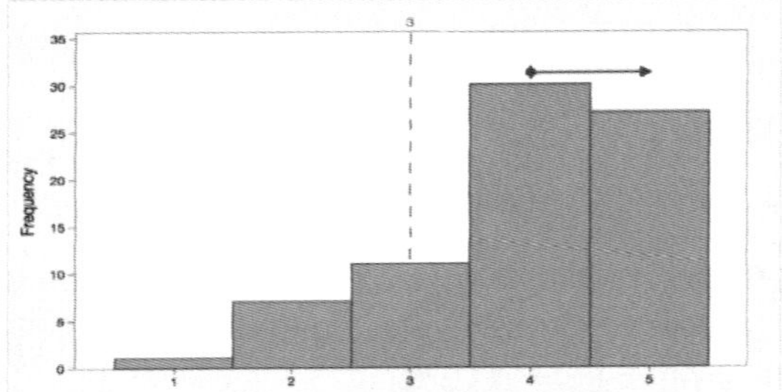

Figure 15. Personas are helpful for communicating with stakeholders and team members

Conclusion: Practitioners tend to agree that personas are helpful for communicating with stakeholders and team members.

A16: Personas I use are usually well formed and adequate

Fig. 16 shows that the attitudes to this item had a median of 3 and mode of 4. 49% responded on the 'agree' side of neutral (4 or 5) and 16% responded on the 'disagree' side (1 or

2). A one-tailed sign test was highly significant (1-tailed $p=0.003$ and $p\text{-}adjusted= .028125$) supporting H1 (agreement). The odds ratio was 3.

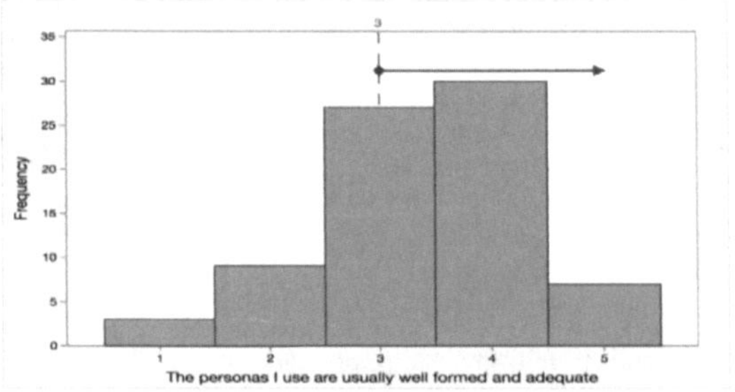

Figure 16. Personas I use are usually well formed and adequate.

Conclusion: Practitioners tend to agree that the personas they use are usually well formed and adequate.

We use the odds ratio to judge relative strength of opinion. TABLE II shows the items ordered by odds ratio. We use descending order (most strongly held view at the top). The 13 significant items are displayed first followed by the 3 non-significant items (A9, A2, A6).

V. CONCLUSION

Existing persona studies are typically qualitative/ethnographic or case studies. They tend to involve small samples of practitioners with findings developed inductively. These studies are valuable for raising issues, but any generalization is problematic. Also, the claims in the literature are also diffused, uncorroborated and cannot be prioritized.

The 'What's Hot in Interaction Design' survey, with the additional persona survey component, represents one of the largest studies of personas that we know of to-date. It allows a quantitative analysis of the views of a large number of practitioners in relation to issues previously raised in the literature and which in many cases were a source of disagreement. It does this in a way that allows generalization and comparison between issues (i.e., prioritization). The results show that persona use is quite prevalent amongst IxD/UX practitioners, particularly to capture the results of user research but also to support design activities and to some extent, to support evaluation.

Practitioners revealed strong opinions relating to challenges that are faced with personas such as the need for expertise in persona methods and expertise in qualitative research, as well as questions of user sample size and the amount of data required to create personas. However, the main challenge (high OR) turns out to be that, in the practitioners' views, personas are not properly used by teams.

Although previous research (TABLE I) included an agreement about financial costs (A2) and collaboration effort (A6), our findings show that practitioners had an overall neutral opinion towards them. The former might be explained by the fact that practitioners are more affected by time implications than they are by implications for budgets. The latter might be explained, not by a lack of collaboration difficulties, but by a lack of collaboration. On the other hand, our findings and literature tend to disagree on the question of personas lacking important information related to goals, needs, behaviors, and attitudes.

TABLE II. PRIORITY OF ATTITUDES TOWARDS PERSONAS BASED ON THE DESCENDING ORDER OF OR RATIOS.

Priority	Attitude	OR
1	A7: Personas are often not properly used by teams.	19.6
2	A11: Personas are helpful for understanding users' needs and context	10.5
3	A15: Personas are helpful for communicating with stakeholders and team members	7.1
4	A12: Personas are helpful for making design decisions	6.9
5	A14: Personas are helpful for evaluation	5.8
6	A5: Personas require training in persona methods.	5
7	A4: Personas require expertise in qualitative research to create.	5
8	A3: Representative personas require a lot of data.	3.4
9	A16: The personas I use are usually well formed and adequate.	3.1
10	A1: Personas are time consuming to create/use.	2.5
11	A8: Personas often represent extreme archetypes	1.9
12	A10: Persona sets often incorporate redundancy (multiple personas referring to the same characteristics)	1.8
13	A13: Personas are helpful for implementing and building	1.7
14	A9: Personas often lack important information related to goals, needs, behaviors, and attitudes	1.6
15	A2: Personas are expensive to create/use.	0.9
16	A6: Collaborating around personas is difficult.	0.9

Our overall findings also provide an indication for the need for persona methods and tools that address the problem of using personas by teams and other challenges whilst maintaining personas benefits. It elicits the requirements for a personas tool that can support practitioners in their work and target the reported practitioners' issues.

In future work, we plan to follow up on the findings reported here by exploring them more deeply in an interview study with IxD/UX practitioners and which will be helping further in the design/development of a persona tool. And as educators, given that personas are usually perceived as beneficial in the UCD, we would do well to include personas in our university syllabi but to find approaches that overcome or at least educate students about the challenges of resources and common pitfalls.

REFERENCES

[1] A. Cooper, *The inmates are running the asylum*. Sams, 1999.

[2] A. Cooper, R. Reimann, D. Cronin, and A. Cooper, *About face 3 : the essentials of interaction design*. Wiley Pub, 2007.

[3] J. Pruitt and T. Adlin, *The persona lifecycle : keeping people in mind throughout product design*. Elsevier, 2006.

[4] L. Nielsen, "Personas," in *The Encyclopedia of Human-Computer Interaction*, 2nd ed., Aarhus: The Interaction Design Foundation, 2014.

[5] L. Nielsen, K. S. Nielsen, J. Stage, and J. Billestrup, "Going Global with Personas," 2013, pp. 350–357.

[6] J. Brickey, S. Walczak, and T. Burgess, "Comparing Semi-Automated Clustering Methods for Persona Development," *IEEE Trans. Softw. Eng.*, vol. 38, no. 3, pp. 537–546, May 2012, doi: 10.1109/TSE.2011.60.

[7] T. Miaskiewicz, T. Sumner, and K. A. Kozar, "A latent semantic analysis methodology for the identification and creation of personas," in *Proceedings of the 26th SIGCHI Conference on Human Factors in Computing Systems*, 2008, pp. 1501–1510.

[8] J. McGinn and N. Kotamraju, "Data-Driven Persona Development," in *SIGCHI Conference on Human Factors in Computing Systems*, 2008, pp. 1521–1524.

[9] J. Pruitt and J. Grudin, "Personas: practice and theory," in *Proceedings of the 2003 conference on Designing for user experiences - DUX '03*, 2003, p. 1.

[10] S. Mulder and Z. Yaar, *The user is always right : a practical guide to creating and using personas for the Web*. New Riders, 2007.

[11] E. Friess, "Personas and Decision Making in the Design Process: An Ethnographic Case Study," in *CHI*, 2012.

[12] T. W. Howard, "Are personas really usable?," *Commun. Des. Q. Rev.*, vol. 3, no. 2, pp. 20–26, Mar. 2015, doi: 10.1145/2752853.2752856.

[13] Å. Blomquist and M. Arvola, "Personas in Action: Ethnography in an Interaction Design Team," 2002.

[14] C. N. Chapman and R. P. Milham, "The Personas' New Clothes: Methodological and Practical Arguments against a Popular Method," *Proc. Hum. Factors Ergon. Soc. Annu. Meet.*, vol. 50, no. 5, pp. 634–636, Oct. 2006, doi: 10.1177/154193120605000503.

[15] T. Matthews, T. Judge, and S. Whittaker, "How do designers and user experience professionals actually perceive and use personas?," in *Proceedings of the 2012 ACM annual conference on Human Factors in Computing Systems - CHI '12*, 2012, p. 1219.

[16] P. Turner and S. Turner, "Is stereotyping inevitable when designing with personas?," *Des. Stud.*, vol. 32, no. 1, pp. 30–44, 2011, doi: 10.1016/j.destud.2010.06.002.

[17] Y. Chang, Y. Lim, and E. Stolterman, "Personas: From Theory to Practices," in *Proceedings of the 5th Nordic conference on Human-computer interaction building bridges - NordiCHI '08*, 2008, p. 439.

[18] T. Miaskiewicz and K. A. Kozar, "Personas and user-centered design: How can personas benefit product design processes?," *Des. Stud.*, vol. 32, no. 5, pp. 417–430, 2011, doi: 10.1016/j.destud.2011.03.003.

[19] C. LeRouge, J. Ma, S. Sneha, and K. Tolle, "User profiles and personas in the design and development of consumer health technologies," *Int. J. Med. Inform.*, vol. 82, no. 11, pp. e251–e268, 2013, doi: 10.1016/j.ijmedinf.2011.03.006.

[20] J. Billestrup, J. Stage, L. Nielsen, and K. S. Hansen, "Persona Usage in Software Development: Advantages and Obstacles," in *The Seventh International Conference on Advances in Computer-Human Interactions Persona*, 2014.

[21] F. Long, "Real or Imaginary: The effectiveness of using personas in product design | Frontend," in *Proceedings of the IES Conference*, 2009.

[22] G. Sholmo, "A Closer Look At Personas: A Guide To Developing The Right Ones (Part 2) — Smashing Magazine," *smashingmagazine*, 2014. [Online]. Available: https://www.smashingmagazine.com/2014/08/a-closer-look-at-personas-part-2/. [Accessed: 02-Feb-2018].

[23] G. Sholmo, "A Closer Look At Personas: What They Are And How They Work | 1 — Smashing Magazine," *smashingmagazine*, 2014. [Online]. Available: https://www.smashingmagazine.com/2014/08/a-closer-look-at-personas-part-1/. [Accessed: 02-Feb-2018].

[24] N. Kellingley, "Common Problems with User Personas | Interaction Design Foundation," 2015. [Online]. Available: https://www.interaction-design.org/literature/article/common-problems-with-user-personas. [Accessed: 02-Feb-2018].

[25] P. Bryan, "Are Personas Still Relevant to UX Strategy? :: UXmatters," *UXmatters*, 2013. [Online]. Available: https://www.uxmatters.com/mt/archives/2013/01/are-personas-still-relevant-to-ux-strategy.php. [Accessed: 01-Feb-2018].

[26] E. Sonderen, R. Sanderman, and J. C. Coyne, "Ineffectiveness of Reverse Wording of Questionnaire Items: Let's Learn from Cows in the Rain," *PLoS One*, vol. 8, no. 7, p. e68967, Jul. 2013, doi: 10.1371/journal.pone.0068967.

[27] C. A. Schriesheim and K. D. Hill, "Educational and Psychological Measurement Controlling Acquiescence Response Bias by Item Reversals: the Effect on Questionnaire Validity," *Sociol. Methods Res.*, vol. 21, no. 1, pp. 52–88.

[28] J. A. Ferreira, J. A. Ferreira, and A. H. Zwinderman, "On the Benjamini-Hochberg method," *ANN. Stat.*, pp. 1827--1849, 2006.

[29] D. Norman, "Ad-Hoc Personas & Empathetic Focus - jnd.org," *jnd.org*, 2004. [Online]. Available: http://jnd.org/dn.mss/ad-hoc_personas_empathetic_focus.html. [Accessed: 01-Feb-2018].

Exploring the User Security Experience of Mobile Payment in China

Jiaxin Zhang and Yan Luximon*
School of Design
The Hong Kong Polytechnic University
Hung Hom, Hong Kong
e-mails: jx.zhang@connect.polyu.hk, *yan.luximon@polyu.edu.hk

Abstract— **Mobile payment services are in widespread use in China, but with them come growing concerns about security. Although the security of mobile payment has been demonstrated, a sample of user experience derived from real world data must be collected to understand the complex use context. This study aims to contribute to the current research by providing qualitative data through in-depth semi-structured interviews. The research explores the user security experience in a variety of use contexts by investigating mobile payment services in a mature market. The findings showed that users view their security experience as composed both financial and privacy aspects. The key user experience for mobile payment security was divided into five components: online mobile transaction, in-store payment, peer-to-peer payment, payment interaction in the physical world, and the network environment. Useful elements were also identified for enhancing security experience for mobile payment. Investigating security experience and user needs when designing mobile payment systems in context will provide a more holistic picture of the security needs surrounding mobile payment.**

Keywords-mobile payment; security; user experience; use context.

I. INTRODUCTION

Advances in mobile technology have led to the increased popularity of mobile services in recent years. Mobile payment is vital to the development of mobile services, allowing for numerous diverse electronic transactions, such as online and offline purchasing, payment of bills and peer-to-peer transfer [1][2]. As China is one of the largest mobile payment markets in the world, it has drawn a great deal of attention from both practitioners and researchers [3]. According to the 40th China Statistical Report on Internet Development [4], there are 502 million mobile payment users in China. 90% of users (463 million) use mobile payment in offline situations, resulting in a variety of use contexts; these include payments made at physical stores, large retailers, vending machines, restaurants, hotels and public transportation. Mobile payment platforms, such as Alipay and WeChat Pay [5] have not only reduced the use of cash, but have also provided other supporting functions, including account and money management, location information and financial services, which enhance user experience while using mobile payment [2]. It is not surprising that mobile payment has become a part of everyday life in China. However, this widespread adoption has created multiple transaction scenes, leading to increasing security concerns in both the financial and privacy aspects [6][7].

This paper focuses on the security experience of mobile payment in a well-developed mobile services market, where various mobile payment scenarios can be identified and discussed. The purpose of this study is to investigate the specific user experiences of mobile payment to explore the associated factors and use contexts related to specific security experience. The study also tried to determine the user perspective of mobile payment security. The findings of this research could provide a comprehensive understanding of users' security needs in different mobile payment scenarios and past experiences of the users in a mature market of mobile payment. The following sections of this article are organized as follows: Section II introduces the state of the art in mobile payment and security research. Section III describes the method applied for the study. Section IV outlines the participants' demographic information and results of the interview. Section V compares the current results with previous research outcomes. Section VI presents the conclusion of the main findings and indicates the possible fields for future research.

II. STATE OF THE ART

Previous studies have found a strong relationship between perceived security of electronic commerce and user attitudes toward its adoption [7]-[9]. Research studies have reported that security risks have been an important factor influencing customer's willingness in using mobile payment in China [10]. Although this consumer "adoption" study has demonstrated the importance of mobile payment security, simply using "adoption" research to investigate the impact of mobile payment security might not be effective enough for evaluating the overall situation and gaining broader insights about this area [11].

With the increasing adoption of mobile services, researchers have emphasized on the importance of studying the relationship between use context and security of mobile payment. For instance, Figge [12] is concerned about information confidentiality regarding the context computation. Since consumer information is sent out for improving mobile services in different use contexts, service providers could access to a lot of personal information. Dahlberg et al. [11] have mentioned the research value of understanding use context and security in mobile payment, and suggested the need to map the use context of mobile payment with security methods, which can be regarded as a promising research area.

Today, the use context of mobile payment in China is more and more complex, as the platforms such as Alipay and WeChat Pay have created a mobile lifestyle rather than simply providing a service. This calls for studies to understand of security experience of mobile payment usage in a particular situation. As compared to provious empirical studies, interviews can help in collecting data regarding user attitude and experience regarding the daily use of mobile payment services in use contexts. This contributes to an overall understanding of the formation of security experience depending on the scenarios and provides insights for enhancing mobile payment interaction.

III. METHOD

Semi-structured in-depth interviews were adopted for this research to investigate the user security experience of mobile payment in order to form a holistic understanding of the phenomenon.

A. Participants

In order to identify the most cases across various payment scenarios, we conducted the research in a mature market to collect as much user experience as possible. We recruited 10 participants (5 male and 5 female users) in Guangdong province in China, where mobile payment services are widely used.

B. Interview Design

A semi-structured in-depth interview was conducted for each participant individually. Each interview ranged from 25 to 45 minutes, depending on the participant's experience in the topic. The interview was conducted either in person or by phone. Before the interview, each participant completed a questionnaire on their demographic information as well as their experience with using mobile payment, including the platforms they had used, the frequency and duration of use and the transaction amount per month. At the beginning of the interview, all participants were asked if they believe mobile payment is secure. Next, we asked participants about their security concerns when using mobile payment. The purpose of these two questions was to determine what users want to protect most when using mobile payment, thus allowing us to identify user concerns regarding mobile payment security more accurately. Participants were then required to think about previous secure or insecure experiences in different use contexts of mobile payment. Finally, the interviewer asked participants what factors they believed to influence their perception of security in mobile payment, and to identify their reasons. All interviews were recorded for data analysis.

C. Data Analysis

The coding method applied in this study is that of Strauss, which requires grounding to the data [13]. First, the voice data were transcribed to text. We examined the data, made notes and coded according to three themes: security concerns in mobile payment, security experience and use context and other elements related security experience. Labels and themes were developed based on each topic to create categories and generate theory.

IV. RESULTS

The findings that emerged from the interview are as shown. The results section presents a detailed explanation of how user security experience is formed, as well as the important elements that influence it.

A. General Information

The average age for participants is 25.6 years (SD=2.12; age range: 21-29). All participants had experience using mobile payment, such as WeChat Pay, Alipay, UnionPay Online, Apple Pay, Baidu Wallet, JD Pay, Tenpay, 99 Bill or Mobile Banking. 70% are customers with more than 3 years' experience using mobile payment; 20% are users with 1-3 years' experience; and 10% have less than 1 year of experience. The percentage of monthly expenditure through mobile payment ranges from 7.5% to 100% of their monthly income.

B. Security Concerns in Mobile Payment

All participants were asked at the beginning "*Do you think it is secure to adopt mobile payment service and what are your security concerns with it?*" 5 participants (50%) responded that they believe it is secure, while 4 participants (40%) believe it is insecure. 1 participant (10%) stated that it depends on the reputation of the service provider. 8 participants (80%) said that they considered both financial and privacy aspects; of these, 3 participants concluded that financial security was more important, 2 participants stated that information security was more essential, and 3 participants thought that financial and information security are equally important. 2 participants considered only one or the other of financial or information security. Surprisingly, 2 participants (20%) stated that they had few worries regarding potential financial loss, due to the small amounts of their transactions and high popularity of the mobile payment platform.

TABLE I. PRIVACY INFORMATION CONCERNS

Privacy Information concerns	
Privacy information	***Frequency***
Phone number	7
ID number	5
Consumption record	3
Address	2
Cookies	2
Account	1
Job information	1
Name	1
Financial information	1

According to the above responses, most participants emphasized the importance of their privacy. We explored the reasons for this with further questions, and 3 participants said it was because relationships can be traced through information. For example, they believe that a person's mobile payment account could reflect a behavior pattern, or a dishonest browsing history might have a negative influence on their personal credit. Participants also mentioned the specific privacy information they would be reluctant to disclose, as shown in Table I.

C. *Security experience and use context*

This section describes the security experience mentioned by participants in the interview process in order to present a comprehensive picture of security in daily life. We explored the security experience of our participants mainly by asking "*In what situation do you use mobile payment service*" and requiring them to "*describe secure and insecure use contexts of mobile payment usage according to your own experience*". In the case of mobile payment platforms, such as WeChat Pay and Alipay, participants in our study indicated a variety of user experiences that structured their perception of the security of these systems. Based on our analysis, user experience can be divided into five payment situations: online mobile transaction, in-store payment, peer-to-peer payment, payment interaction in the physical world and network environment. Online transaction focuses on payment scenarios made entirely on a mobile device. In-store payment involves a face-to-face transaction between merchants and consumers, while peer-to-peer payment describes a transfer made between parties with relatively strong ties. Payment interaction in the physical world involves payment between users and machines in the public space, and the final category refers to users' selection of network environment for mobile payment.

1) Online mobile transaction: The major experiences with online mobile transaction are associated with online shopping. In this situation, participants responded with two security considerations. The first relates to payment system usability. A system that runs smoothly and can provide efficient feedback during a transaction is necessary to ensure a positive user security experience. The second user security experience derives from the reputation of the merchant or payment service developer. In the case of developer reputation (with 70% of participants' concern), participants mainly worried about the security of their information. In terms of merchant reputation (with 50% of participants' concern), most of participants worried about the quality of goods bought online. Of note, 2 participants stated that insurance for account security was provided by certain platforms, such as WeChat Pay, Alipay and JD Pay, which enhanced their perception of the security of the system.

We also asked our participants to compare the platforms they have used in order to further understand the relationship between user experience and reputation. Alipay and WeChat Pay are the most popular mobile payment platforms in China. 5 respondents (50%) stated their belief that both of them are secure, while 5 respondents (50%) perceived that their security levels are different. 3 respondents indicated that frequency of use of a platform influenced their perception of security, which could lead to their belief that either Alipay or WeChat Pay is securer. Another factor is the different brand images of Alipay and WeChat Pay. U2 participant explained, "*Alipay looks like a large platform with various kinds of merchants in it. I am afraid that my privacy will be stolen and my money is insecure... Compared with Alipay, WeChat Pay is a platform for transferring between friends...Also, I usually use WeChat to keep in touch with my friends. I prefer to use WeChat Pay in my daily life since it is convenient and secure.*"

2) In-store payment: In the context of the physical store, mobile payment systems enable consumers to pay by scanning a merchant's QR code or by having their account's QR code scanned by a merchant. In the first case, users scan a QR code provided by the merchant, then input the charge as well as a password to settle the payment (Figure 1). In the second case, merchants input the amount of money first, while the consumer provides their account's QR code for the merchants to scan (Figure 2). This second transaction can be settled without the user inputting a password. The security experience is formed through the interaction between merchant and customer, as well as the physical environment. 2 participants (20%) said they felt insecure when paying by having their QR code scanned by merchants. They worried that merchants would charge them an amount of money higher than the actual price; in addition, this method of payment does not require their password to pay. These factors decrease their perception of security.

In addition, 2 participants (20%) felt the physical environment could be a risk for mobile payment users. Since surveillance cameras are installed in public places, users cannot avoid being recorded every time they input their password. U9 gave a detailed description of the situation: "*There are surveillance cameras in supermarkets or banks. When I use mobile payment to pay in these places, I input my passwords in a hurry sometimes. The charging process needs to be quick, so I am not able to use my hand to cover it, or my phone screen is too large to cover. My password would be easy to record.*"

Figure 1. User scanning merchant's QR code for payment

Figure 2. Merchant scanning customer's QR code for payment

3) Peer-to-peer payment: One particular advantage of mobile payment is that it supports peer-to-peer transfer, leading to the convenience of transaction between individuals. Peer-to-peer payment can occur between strangers, such as buying food at a kiosk or paying a taxi bill, or between friends, such as sharing a dining fee or sending "gift money" [14]. Specifically, 1 participant (10%) mentioned their belief that the method of transferring money within a chat group is secure, where sender and recipient already know each other. This method allows immediate feedback, as well. U2 added that transactions among friends provide a much more secure experience in terms of mobile payment. For this reason, the participant prefers to use WeChat Pay rather than Alipay for peer-to-peer payment, as WeChat is also a chat application. In the case of payment between strangers, the participant stated that it is better to pay using paper money than to use mobile payment at a kiosk, because this might avoid the privacy being stolen.

4) Payment interaction in the physical world: The adoption of mobile payment has encouraged the development of self-service equipment, such as ticket machines, vending machines and bike sharing. This allows transactions not only from person to person, but also between man and machine. In this study, however, we found particular concerns when participants interacted with these machines in the physical world, as the transaction context has become more complex.

This consideration is not only restricted to the user interface, but also applies to the physical environment. Mobile payment for bike sharing was mentioned by several participants. Currently, users can pay to share bikes in the city by scanning a QR code using a mobile payment system. Unlike the QR code scanning that happens between users in person, self-service payment in public places may pose more risks. One concern is about the legitimacy of QR codes (Figure 3). When a QR code is used for payment in a public place, it is possible for users to become involved in fraudulent activities. For example, 2 participants stated they cannot tell whether a QR code is the original or one pasted on by criminals in order to steal the users' money.

Figure 3. Scanning a bike-sharing QR code in a public place

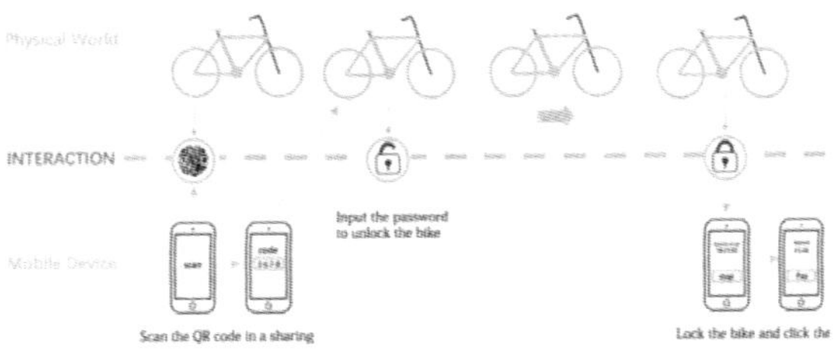

Figure 4. Payment settled in Mobike system

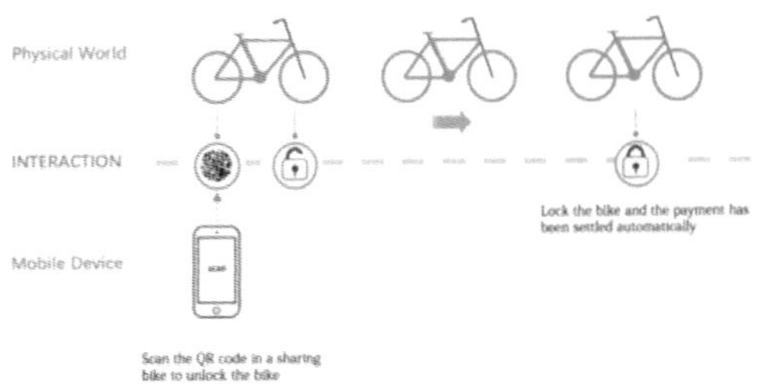

Figure 5. Payment settled in OfO system

Another concern is usability. Users have less experience when adopting a mobile payment system in a new context. The various payment processes across different services can cause an insecure experience. For example, in the bike-sharing system OfO, users must manually stop the charges after they return a bike, while Mobike (another bike-sharing system) stops charging the user automatically after returning a bike (Figure 4 and Figure 5). One participant worried that the manual system (OfO) might overcharge them if they forget to stop the charges after returning a bike. However, another participant thought the automatic system (Mobike) might secretly charge more than it should, as the system does not allow users to confirm the amount before payment is settled. This inconsistent process is likely to create an insecure experience, as users need more time to adapt to various payment processes despite the similar use context.

5) Network environment: Our research showed that participants are also concerned about the network environment when using mobile payment. 70% of participants emphasized that they would not use mobile payment on public Wi-Fi networks to avoid risk, while 5 participants (50%) said they would not connect to public Wi-Fi at all. It is clear that the mobile wireless network is a necessary trusted context for mobile transactions.

D. *Other elements that relate to the security experience*

In addition to user security experience, participants also mentioned other possible elements that influence the perceived security of mobile payment. 5 participants (50%) expressed the need for the customization of mobile payment platforms in order to improve their security experience. Different use contexts should be tailored to the particular user in terms of authentication methods for mobile payment. For instance, users require more complicate authentication methods (multi-factor authentication) to protect the payment of large transaction amount, while they want simpler methods to facilitate the payment of a small transaction amount. Participants also revealed that they are not being told what personal information is being disclosed by mobile payment platforms, but that they need to be made aware so that they can make choices that avoid disclosures of privacy. Another consideration is that designers need to think about users' capability of customizing the user interface. One participant said, *"If there are too many user settings, it will be a mess. I would be afraid that the device cannot run smoothly. Also, I will forget my settings."*

What is interesting to note is that participants developed certain self-directed approaches to help themselves "feel more secure" when using mobile payment, such as hiding unfamiliar functions in the platform, regularly deleting records of mobile payment usage on their device, linking a credit card to their mobile payment user account or using two-step authentication on two different devices.

V. DISCUSSION

A. Security concerns

We investigated user concerns about security in mobile payment in both the financial and privacy aspect. As users connect with various kinds of services, including food take-out or delivery services, DiDi taxi, online and offline purchasing and social media, personal data is collected by mobile payment platforms to understand the particular user's behavior pattern and provide a more efficient service. A previous study revealed that social network services can expose user behavior patterns, known as privacy disclosure patterns [15]; our research found that users believe mobile payment platforms pose a similar risk to user privacy [16]. Based on the responses of our participants, a focus on intent to disclose private information through mobile payment, rather than concerns about financial losses, might have a more effective impact on user security experience. While some participants discussed the personal information they provided on mobile payment platforms, future research could investigate the importance of different types of personal data accessed by mobile payment systems and the possible consequence of privacy disclosure in mobile payment.

B. Weakening or strengthening user security experience

In examining the use context of mobile payment, we identified experiences that could strengthen or weaken perceived user security in particular situations. According to our participants' responses as well as the previous research [17], reputation is an important factor in the adoption of mobile commerce, especially in online shopping. A good reputation guarantees the security of possession and privacy. A readily available payment record will enhance the user's security experience, while delayed feedback or lack of information will weaken it. Regarding the payment process, participants added that when they pay without a password or have their codes scanned by a merchant to pay, they felt insecure. This is because they cannot confirm the transaction amount before the payment settled. These scenarios indicate that users expect to have better control over managing their accounts or the transaction process in order to enhance their security experience when using mobile payment. Unlike actual control, which refers to the capability of changing a situation, perceived control emphasizes the user's feeling of their ability to maintain a coming event [18]. Previous studies have demonstrated the importance of perceived control on security problems in other contexts [18][19]. The results presented in this study lead us to recommend more studies to investigate the influence of perceived control in mobile payment.

In addition, users felt more secure when money was transferred to their friends, rather than to strangers or merchants. Similar to the findings of a previous study [20], participants perceived the social relations in WeChat to be based on real life, while the social relations in Alipay are mostly based on virtual situations. The strong ties built in a user's actual life develop a sense of trustworthiness in mobile payment. According to previous studies [21], social influence can not only affect the user's intention of adopting mobile payment by enhancing its perceived usefulness, but also reducing user's perceived risk of mobile payment. The responses in this study reveal a relationship between social influence and perceived security in mobile payment.

C. The need for customization in the security experience

The interviews revealed the need for customization to enhance the security experience of mobile payment. Based on our results, setting authentication methods according to the use context holds the greatest attraction for participants. Authentication methods are a vital issue when it comes to the tradeoff between convenience and security in technology usage [22]. While customization of authentication methods is crucial for a positive security experience, use context is an important element. In this case, tailoring would occur according to "location, time or resources" [23]. The complex nature of mobile payment usage means designers must consider the extent to which users be given permission to customize the platform, in terms of the user's cognitive capabilities and the limitations of the mobile device. The creation of self-directed approaches in order to feel secure as reported by participants in the interviews may present possible solutions to this problem. Under this approach, a method of participatory design could be created to study the details for customization. Designers could learn from users' experience and knowledge, formed within the use context, in order to develop a comprehensive understanding of the users' needs [24].

VI. CONCLUSION AND FUTURE WORK

Although mobile payment has been adopted across many aspects of life in China, users have security concerns in different use contexts. In this study, we explored users' perspectives of mobile payment security in various use contexts, and discussed factors that could enhance user security experience. Through the interview process, we identified five use contexts for mobile payment to present a more holistic picture of mobile payment in China The study finding also recognized the need of design customization for improving the security. The result of this research could provide a reference to enhance security experience design according to users' needs and different use contexts in mature markets of mobile payment, while its effectiveness in developing markets of mobile payment will still require to be verified.

Future research on the user security experience of mobile payment can be focusing on determining what can be user security concerns in various payment scenarios and categorizing their security experience for better experience design.

ACKNOWLEDGMENT

The authors would like to thank the support of the UGC Funding Scheme from the Hong Kong Polytechnic University.

REFERENCES

[1] L. Goeke and K. Pousttchi, "A scenario-based analysis of mobile payment acceptance," Mobile Business and 2010 Ninth Global Mobility Roundtable (ICMB-GMR), 2010 Ninth International Conference on, IEEE Press, Jun. 2010, pp. 371-378, doi: 10.1109/ICMB-GMR.2010.81

[2] T. Oliveira, M. Thomas, G. Baptista, and F. Campos, "Mobile payment: Understanding the determinants of customer adoption and intention to recommend the technology," Computers in Human Behavior, vol. 61, pp. 404-414, Mar. 2016, doi: doi.org/10.1016/j.chb.2016.03.030

[3] A. Y. L. Chong, "Understanding mobile commerce continuance intentions: an empirical analysis of Chinese consumers," Journal of Computer Information Systems, vol.53(4), pp. 22-30, Dec. 2015, doi: dx.doi.org/10.1080/08874417.2013.11645647

[4] CNNIC, the 40th China Statistical Report on Internet Development, 2017, http://www.cnnic.net.cn/hlwfzyj/hlwxzbg/hlwtjbg/201708/P0 20170807351923262153.pdf [retrieved: Feburary, 2018]

[5] iiMedia Research, The report for mobile payment market research of the first half year of 2017, retrieved from: http://www.iimedia.cn/53957.html [retrieved: Feburary, 2018]

[6] G. de Kerviler, N. T. M. Demoulin, and P. Zidda, "Adoption of in-store mobile payment: Are perceived risk and convenience the only drivers?" Journal of Retailing and Consumer Services, vol. 31, pp.334-344, May 2016, doi: doi.org/10.1016/j.jretconser.2016.04.011

[7] P. G. Schierz, O. Schilke, and B. W. Wirtz, "Understanding consumer acceptance of mobile payment services: An empirical analysis," Electronic commerce research and applications, vol. 9(3), Aug. 2009, pp. 209-216, doi: doi.org/10.1016/j.elerap.2009.07.005

[8] M. H. Shah, H. R. Peikari, and N. M. Yasin, "The determinants of individuals' perceived e-security: Evidence from Malaysia," International Journal of Information Management, vol. 34(1), Nov. 2013, pp. 48-57, doi: dx.doi.org/10.1016/j.ijinformgt.2013.10.001.

[9] C. Kim, W. Tao, N. Shin, and K. S. Kim, "An empirical study of customers' perceptions of security and trust in e-payment systems," Electronic commerce research and applications, vol. 9(1), Jun. 2009, pp. 84-95.

[10] W. Xu, "The Study of WeChat Payment Users Willingness Factor," Journal of Service Science and Management, vol. 10(3), Jun. 2017, pp. 251-259, doi: 10.4236/jssm.2017.103021

[11] T. Dahlberg, J. Guo, and J. Ondrus, "A critical review of mobile payment research," Electronic Commerce Research and Applications, vol. 14(5), Jul. 2015, pp. 265-284, doi: doi.org/10.1016/j.elerap.2015.07.006

[12] S. Figge "Situation-dependent services —a challenge for mobile network operators," Journal of Business Research, vol.57(12), Dec 2004, pp. 1416-1422, doi: doi.org/10.1016/S0148-2963(02)00431-9

[13] A. L. Strauss, Qualitative analysis for social scientists. Cambridge, UK: Cambridge University Press, 1987

[14] Y. M. Kow, X. Gui, and W. Cheng, "Special Digital Monies: The Design of Alipay and WeChat Wallet for Mobile Payment Practices in China," IFIP Conference on Human-Computer Interaction, Springer Press, Sep. 2017, pp. 136-155, doi: 10.1007/978-3-319-68059-0_9

[15] K. Li, Z. Lin, and X. Wang, "An empirical analysis of users' privacy disclosure behaviors on social network sites," Information & management, vol. 52(7), Jul. 2015, pp. 882-891, doi: dx.doi.org/10.1016/j.im.2015.07.006

[16] Y. Zhuang, A. C. M. Leung, and J. Hughes, "Matching in Proximity Authentication and Mobile Payment EcoSystem: What Are We Missing?" International Workshop on Radio Frequency Identification: Security and Privacy Issues, Springer Press, Jul. 2017, pp. 163-172, doi: 10.1007/978-3-319-62024-4_12

[17] K. Siau and Z. Shen, "Building customer trust in mobile commerce," Communications of the ACM, vol. 46, Apr. 2003, pp. 91-94, doi: 10.1145/641205.641211

[18] N. Hajli and X. Lin, "Exploring the security of information sharing on social networking sites: The role of perceived control of information," Journal of Business Ethics, vol. 133(1), Sep. 2014, pp. 111-123, doi: 10.1007/s10551-014-2346-x

[19] D. L. Huang, P. L. P. Rau, and G. Salvendy, "Perception of information security," Behaviour & Information Technology, vol. 29(3), Nov. 2008, pp. 221-232, doi: dx.doi.org/10.1080/01449290701679361

[20] Y. Qu, W. Rong, Y. Ouyang, H. Chen, and Z. Xiong, "Social Aware Mobile Payment Service Popularity Analysis: The Case of WeChat Payment in China," Asia-Pacific Services Computing Conference, Springer Press, Dec. 2015,pp. 289-299, doi: https://doi.org/10.1007/978-3-319-26979-5_22

[21] S. Yang, Y. Lu, S. Gupta, Y. Cao, and R. Zhang, "Mobile payment services adoption across time: An empirical study of the effects of behavioral beliefs, social influences, and personal traits," Computers in Human Behavior, vol. 28(1), Sep. 2011, pp.129-142, doi: 10.1016/j.chb.2011.08.019

[22] N. Gunson, D. Marshall, H. Morton, and M. Jack, "User perceptions of security and usability of single-factor and two-factor authentication in automated telephone banking," Computers & Security, vol. 30(4), Dec. 2010, pp. 208-220, doi: 10.1016/j.cose.2010.12.001

[23] Y. E. Lee and I. Benbasat, "Interface design for mobile commerce," Communications of the ACM, vol. 46(12), Dec. 2003, pp. 48-52, doi: 10.1145/953460.953487

[24] M. J. Muller, "Participatory design: the third space in HCI," in Human-Computer Interaction: Development Process, A. Sears and J. A. Jacko, Eds. Boca Raton: CRC Press, pp. 165-180, 2007.

Cybersecurity Awareness Training provided by the Competence Developing Game GHOST

Johannes A. König, Martin R. Wolf
Lab for IT Organization and Management
Aachen University of Applied Sciences
Aachen, Germany
email: koenig@fh-aachen.de, m.wolf@fh-aachen.de

Abstract—**This paper introduces a Competence Developing Game (CDG) for the purpose of a cybersecurity awareness training for businesses. The target audience will be discussed in detail to understand their requirements. It will be explained why and how a mix of business simulation and serious game meets these stakeholder requirements. It will be shown that a tablet and touchscreen based approach is the most suitable solution. In addition, an empirical study will be briefly presented. The study was carried out to examine how an interaction system for a 3D-tablet based CDG has to be designed, to be manageable for non-game experienced employees. Furthermore, it will be explained which serious content is necessary for a Cybersecurity awareness training CDG and how this content is wrapped in the game.**

Keywords-Cybersecurity; Awareness; CDG; Serious Game; tablet game; business simulation.

I. INTRODUCTION

The use of digital systems is crucial in modern companies and one effort of digitization is to use these digital systems more efficiently. Through these efforts, more and more analog processes are no longer available. By that, nowadays almost all relevant records are stored in databases or on cloud based file servers. Accordingly, the analog data management will be reduced to minimum, if that has not already happened.

Of course, a well functioning digital working environment is required to ensure that the data are always available. If data are accessible everywhere and always for employees, then assailants are able to use these infrastructure, too. This issue is getting worse because nowadays, in modern digitalized systems, employees are owners of the keys necessary for data access. Consequently, it is no longer necessary for an assailant to attack the IT-infrastructure (IT = Information technology) or the IT-department. He can focus his attack directly on the data-using persons, e.g., with fishing-mails, social attacks, manipulated flash drives, etc. Despite this issue, this kind of always available data management is indispensable for modern companies.

As a result, it is essential to train non-IT personnel how to avoid cybersecurity risks arising within their daily digitalized work [1]. Already today, employees are often the biggest threat in the cybersecurity chain [2]. To offer an effective cybersecurity awareness training, it is important to establish a continuous training cycle to establish a long term behavior change (req. 7 (see Section II)). It should be noted that too many topics in too short time increase the risk to overwhelm the exercisers which is also a reason for a long training cycle. Basically, a successful cybersecurity awareness training has to solve two tasks. On one hand, it has to attract the attention of the participants for a defined time period. On the other hand it has to convey the training content as efficiently as possible. Unfortunately, most of today's trainings solutions show weaknesses in dealing with both aspects. A very suitable solutions to address both aspects is the use of interactive computer based training methods (req. 6 (see Section II)) [1]. The use of gaming concepts in serious situations provides the possibility to transfer the motivation of a gaming situation into a serious learning context. In addition, games provide an environment which allows to choose risky or intentional wrong strategies just to figure out what will happen. Generally, there are three major kinds of games with a serious approach: Serious Games, Business Simulation/Games and the approach of Gamification. Further, there are different gradations of, e.g., serious games, which are not consistently defined [3].

However, instead of questioning 'What defines a particular game kind?' König and Wolf suggest to focus on the question 'What characteristics of which game kind are well suited for a specific application' [4]. For this, they provide the umbrella term Competence Developing Game that encompasses all 'serious' game types (digital and analog): 'A Competence Developing Game (CDG) is a game that has the primary purpose to teach knowledge, skills and personal, social and/or methodological abilities, in work or study situations and in professional and personal development of the game player, by retaining the motivation of a gaming situation' [3].

Accordingly, this paper examines what features a digital CDG must have in order to enable a cybersecurity awareness training for (German) business users. Further, it shows how a specific CDG, in which these features have been realized, looks like. The game is called GHOST: Gamified Hacking Offence Simulation-based Training (see [18]).

In Section II, the target audience will be determined in more detail, to understand their preferences and requirements. Section III addresses these requirements to determine a suitable CDG game kind. In Section IV, it will be explained how a game interaction interface design for a huge audience group like, 'business users', could look like. In addition, in Section V, a study that examines game interaction systems will be briefly presented. Section VI describes the CDG GHOST which results from all previous considerations. Section VII offers a conclusion and an overview about future work and use.

II. FINDING REQUIREMENTS BY UNDERSTANDING THE AUDIENCE

A study in German enterprises determined that the three most common reasons for employee related trainings are: the development of employee skills, increasing employee motivation and job satisfaction, and strengthening the employee-company relation (req. 1). The study also determined the obstacles that inhibit employee trainings. The identified top-two reasons not to train although there is a need are: no time available to dispense employees (43,8%) and missing internal capacity to organize a training (42,6%) [5]. A second study in German companies identified training costs and also the time issue as main reasons not to train employees. The three most common training methods are learning at the place of work (46%), external courses (28%) and in-house courses (<28%) [6].

In the case of learning at the place of work, the time an employee needs to be dispensed is limited to the actual duration of the training, because there is no traveling time (obstacle: no dispense time available) (req. 2.a.). The absence of traveling time is linked to the absence of traveling costs (obstacle: training costs) (req. 2.c.). By that, the organizational complexity of the training is also reduced, as employees must be covered shorter, and they are more easily accessible in crisis situations, etc. (obstacle: organizational capacity) (req. 2.b.). Accordingly in the case of a continuous training cycle, as needed for a cybersecurity awareness training and therefore for GHOST, learning at the place of work seems particularly advantageous. These considerations clarify why learning at the place of work is the most popular training method and therefore it should be the method of choice for GHOST (req. 2).

In addition to these employer-focused considerations, the CDG GHOST is after all played by employees. As explained in Section I, more or less every employee who uses digital systems for work reasons should participate in a cybersecurity awareness training. By that, the target audience is broad (req. 3). Since the GHOST-Research-Project is granted by a German ministry (Federal Ministry of Education and Research), the German employee sector was considered in first place. According to a report by the Federal Institute for Vocational Education and Training, the average German trainee is 19.7 years old. The report shows the first grouping called "16-year-olds and younger". The average age of all employees was 43 years in 2016, with a relatively balanced distribution between women (~ 47%) and men (~ 53%) [7]. In summary, it can be stated that the vast majority of the target group is> = 16 years and <67 years old, the average age is 43, and women and men are similarly distributed.

As already mentioned, the use of a CDG as a training instrument has the advantage that the motivation of a game situation can be transferred in a serious context. In order to use this advantage a CDG must entertain players in a fun way while keeping the serious content in focus. This aspect requires a CDG that matches the tastes and abilities of the target audience. But because of the diversified target group, it is nearly impossible to construct a CDG that fulfills the individual game taste of each subject. On the other hand, the development of many games that meet the individual taste of each player would be expensive and it would stand in opposite to the obstacle: 'costs'. Following these remarks, a CDG that addresses a broad audience always represents a compromise in game design.

To find the major common denominator of each CDG-Player the 'Pyramid Assessment Framework for 'Competence Developing Games'' ('PACDG-Framework') was studied with this objective. The PACDG-Framework represents a tool that delivers the capability to analyze different game kinds in a standardized way. To do so, the framework covers, among other things, the entire player perspective of a CDG [4], as it was proposed (also) in the well-known MDA-framework for conventional entertainment games [8]. However, the PACDG-Framework covers the CDG-Player perspective in the three steps: "Experience", "Aftereffect" and "Impact". The last two steps refer to the same idea: A CDG should lead to competence acquisition, where the competences should help to solve at least one real life problem (req. 4). The step "Experience" is all about the player's claim to participate in an emphatic and positive gaming experience. In order to meet this claim, a high, entertainment game equivalent, quality must be delivered (req. 5).

Therefore, a CDG-based training that is accessible for all employees who use digital systems for work reasons should…:

- Req. 1. …develop skills, increasing motivation / satisfaction, strengthening the job relation.
- Req. 2. …take place at the place of work to reduce
  - a. time expense and release time,
  - b. organizational overhead and by that
  - c. costs.
- Req. 3. …be accessible for every target group member.
- Req. 4. …help to solve a real life problem.
- Req. 5. …be similar in quality to an entertainment game.

Additionally a CDG for a cybersecurity awareness training should…: (see Section I)

- Req. 6. …use interactive computer based training methods.
- Req. 7. …occur in a continuous training cycle.

III. GAME TYPE SELECTION

As discussed in Section I and II, the use of interactive computer based training methods is suitable for a cybersecurity awareness training. By that, a serious game, a business simulation (supported by a computer based simulation model) or a gamified work environment could be used (fulfill req. 6). Furthermore it is of course possible to develop a CDG in one of the named kinds with an entertainment game comparable quality (fulfill req. 5).

However, every well designed cybersecurity awareness training will match the requirements 1 and 4 too. It is because the main CDG purpose would be to lead to competence acquisition, where these competence acquisition refers to the ability to perceive possible IT-Security threats (fulfill req. 1). As IT-Security issues are a real life problem, of course, such competences would support to solve a real life problem (fulfill req. 4). Therefore it can be assumed, that a capable development team has the ability to develop a CDG from one of the named game kinds that has the potential to fulfill the requirements 1, 4, 5 and 6.

So to choose the most suitable CDG game kind it is necessary to determine whether the requirements 2, 3 and 7 can be fulfilled.

„'Gamification' is the use of game design elements in non-game contexts“[9]. As a result, for the gamification solution a deeply integration of game elements into the computer environment of the employees would be necessary. Based on such integration, e.g., correct behavior such as scanning a flash drive or locking the screen during a longer period of inactivity could be rewarded with points (fulfill req. 2a-b). This solution would enable a permanent and time neutral training without the need of learning to handle the training instrument (fulfill req. 3 and 7). However, the necessary development effort would be high (game element integration in every used program and operating system) and the privacy protection question would need clarification (not fulfill req. 2c). In addition, the extensive system intervention could have unforeseeable consequences on the IT security of the manipulated operating systems and programs. For these reasons a gamification solutions does not seem suitable for a cybersecurity awareness training.

A closed 'Business Simulation' is characterized by the participants being placed into a well-defined and prepared action situation. A model calculation (the simulation) assesses the decision effects on the game environment. Further the model communicates the success of each action to the players [10]. Since a business simulation is similar to a board game the majority of the employees should not have any problem to handle the game (fulfill req. 3). In addition, many simulation games are turn-based anyway and thus predestined for a long continuous game cycle (fulfill req. 7). The problem here is that even if it is possible to organize multiple business game session at the work (fulfill req. 2a), fixed dates have to be coordinated between different employees plus the necessary setup and dismantling of the business game have to be organized in time (not fulfill req. 2b-c). That means, a business simulation can also not fulfill all requirements.

The third alternative are 'Serious Games'. Serious Games are video games where the primary purpose is not entertainment, enjoyment or fun, which does not mean that Serious Games are not entertaining. They just have another primary purpose, in kind of an ulterior motive [11]. A video game has the advantage of being fully flexible in terms of time. Further no coordination is required between employees nor an organization of the game setup and it can also take place at work (fulfill req. 2a-c) However, it is difficult to realize a continuous training cycle without a turn-based design and such a design is not intended for Serious Games (not fulfill req. 7). But indeed it is the only approach that has the potential to fulfill requirement 2.

At this point, a CDG reveals its strength. The solution is to mix up the game kinds. Serious Games are the only game type that fulfills the requirements 2a-c, but the turn-based design of business simulations supports a continuous game cycle. Accordingly the solution is to develop a Serious Game with Business Simulation (turn-based) game mechanics (see Section VI). Therefore, only the mix out of a Serious Game and a Business Simulation has the potential to fulfill requirements 1 to 7.

Due to this design choice, the biggest problem with meeting the requirements will be requirement 3 in which a CDG is demanded that is playable for every target group member. In requirement 5, the demand for a quality which is similar to an entertainment game is formulated. It needs to be kept in mind that not all members of the target group have experience with video games. It must therefore be ensured that requirement 3 can be met without losing number 5. Therefore, it is necessary to find an interaction-interface for a high quality video game that does not require any video game experience. Section V will introduce a case study that was performed to evaluate how a game interface has to be designed to meet requirement 3 even when the game uses a 3D-Environment to fulfill requirement 5. Section IV explains the game interface development and the case study design.

IV. DEALING WITH THE GAME INTERACTION ISSUE

Germany is the largest video game market in Europe with sales of 2.8 billion euros in 2015. Overall, the video game players are distributed as follows: PC / laptop 18.4 million players, smartphone 17.2 million players, console 15.6 million players, tablet 11.5 million players, handheld 8.3 million players. It should be noted that smartphones and tablets both use gaming apps, which means gaming apps with 23 million players in total have the largest player community [12]. Accordingly to that information even in the aimed target group the amount of people who have experience with gaming apps should be higher than with other video game mediums.

In addition, it can be stated that touchscreens as used in smartphones and tablets have significantly changed the world of games in a short period of time. Modern touchscreen devices show a very intuitive interaction design that allows even children to use such a device successfully.

To explain why touchscreen devices are intuitive to such strong extend, a look at the three-layered brain model is helpful. To use a tool (in a computer context a tool means a device like a keyboard, a mouse, a game controller, etc.) humans have to make use of their neocortex. The cerebrum represents the highest layer in the brain model. In contrast, for 'touches', as needed during the use of a touchscreen device, humans only need to use the reptilian brain, which is represented in the lowest layer in the three-layered brain model [13]. Both aspects, (a) the widely use of gaming apps and (b) the intuitive aspect of modern touchscreen devices lead to the conclusion that a gaming app based CDG is the right choice for GHOST. Considering the broad target audience it is further reasonable to use a tablet based gaming app because of the larger screen size compared to a smartphone.

According to the last Section, a CDG should be similar in quality to an entertainment game (req. 5). Modern gaming apps with the scope to be played over a longer period of time (as it is planned in GHOST) implement a three-dimensional, high quality looking game environment regardless of the genre (see e.g. Lara Croft Go, Lego Star Wars, Jam League, Modern Combat, Asphalt, Bothers: a tale of two sons, etc.). By that, GHOST has to be a three-dimensional tablet based CDG. On the other hand, GHOST has to be accessible for every target group member (req. 3). Thus, an appropriate game interaction system has to be found, that allows three-dimensional tablet based playing even for people who have never played a video game in their live. However, there are well established interaction systems for videogames that are also adapted for touchscreen devices.

The three most common used are 1st-Person, 3rd-Person and God view. The idea behind the 1st-Person perspective is that the player sees through the eyes of his player-character (PC) [14]. In conventional video games, the player controls the PC with mouse and keyboard [15]. Touchscreen based 1st-Person games are usually implemented in landscape mode. To control the PC the left and right thumb are used. The left thumb is used in the lower left area of the screen to control the movement of the PC. The right thumb is used in the lower right area of the screen to control the viewing direction [16].

In games that implement a 3rd-person perspective, a camera is used, which is aligned to the top of the PC to show him completely. Sometimes 3rd-person is implemented with „Trailing" option, then the camera is anchored at head height behind the PC. In classic video games, the control is similar to 1st-person games [15] the same applies to the touch screen control.

A God View perspective, also referred to by the terms 'overhead', 'top down' and 'God Eye', provides a perspective in which the game map is shown from above. Usually the control is realized with the mouse [14]. Touchscreen-based God View games are often implemented by touching directly on the device. In such case the 'touch' on the device is equivalent to a mouse click. Additionally manipulations of the camera perspective are done by the usual multi-touch gestures (e.g., two-finger zoom). Consequently, any 3D gaming interaction system known from the Computer/Laptop can be adapted for touch screen based games.

It has to be noted, that the 1st-person and 3rd-person solution only replace mouse and keyboard through two equivalent virtual generated tools. By that, according to Schell [13], neocortex participation is still needed and whereby the advantage of a touchscreen solution is not exploited. Only the 'God View' interaction systems provide a solution that's natively transforms touch into interaction. As a result, this kind of game interaction should be manageable for inexperienced players and therefore is the right solutions for a touchscreen based CDG and GHOST.

However, this question cannot be clarified for the intended target audience based on the state of scientific research. There is a lack of empirical research that investigates the suitability of existing touch screen-based control and camera tracking paradigms for 3D serious games. However, since a well-functioning interaction system is elemental for the CDG success, a corresponding study has been carried out that will be briefly discussed in the next Section.

V. INTERACTION SYSTEM FOR A TOUCHSCREEN BASED CDG

A. Discussion of possible interaction systems

The main objective of the study is to investigate wheatear it is possible to find an interaction-interface for a high quality tablet based video games that does not require any video game experience. Such an interaction-interface would connect requirements 3 and 5 that seem as if they exclude each other. The presence of such an interface would open the possibility to develop a cybersecurity awareness training that fulfills all seven requirements in the first place.

From a theoretical point of view, a game that responds as intuitive as possible on touch screen input should be advantageous for the players. As shown in the last Section even the 'God View' interaction system relies on not intuitive multi-touch gestures for camera control. For that reason, a new interaction system for the GHOST prototype was designed.

These 'optimized' called interaction system provides the PC control via finger touch. The PC automatically moves to the location of the map where the map was touched. Even the interaction with game objects or non-player characters (NPC) works this way. If a player, e.g., touches a game object his PC will automatically move to the point next to the object. After arriving at this point an interaction dialog opens automatically. To remove the maybe not intuitive camera control the whole game map is divided in different camera zones (partly multiple zones in one room). Each zone provides its own static camera perspective. If the player controls his avatar from one camera zone to another, the camera angle changes automatically. The player is not aware of where the zone boundaries are, the camera angle change just happens. To help the CDG-Player's orientation, there is also a second 'optimized+' called interaction system where the camera change from one position to the next one appears in a smooth move.

Additionally to the three mentioned interactions systems (1st-Person, 3rd-Person, God View) both versions were examined in a blind study. For this purpose, a small game was designed where the participant had to find six game objects or NPCs to interact with. At the beginning of the test a participant is set in a game environment (a space ship) with six rooms and two corridors. The participant does not get any map because the study also refers to the orientation ability. Finally the time needed to complete the interaction tasks was measured.

A total of five mini games, called 'demo versions', because they based on the GHOST source code, were developed:

- Demo1: 1st-Person
- Demo2: 3rd-Person
- Demo3: God View
- Demo4: optimized+
- Demo5: optimized

Deviating from the previous explanation of 3rd-Person interaction-systems the 3rd-Person PC control was changed. Usually the PC is controlled with the left and right thumb as in a 1st-Person tablet game.

Indeed, the interaction system in Demo2 uses a touch based PC movement control as in the 'optimized' demo versions. In addition, camera rotation was enabled by integrating a two-finger-rotate gesture for camera rotation. The classic two thumb control is still used in Demo1. Figures 1 to 4 are screenshots made of each demo version, respectively.

Figure 1. 1st-Person interaction system with dynamic appearing 'activate'-button for object interaction (Demo1).

Figure 2. 3rd-Person interaction system before and after two-finger-rotate (Demo2).

Figure 3. Good-View before and after gesture based camera rotation (Demo3).

Figure 4. Adjacent camera zones in the optimized (+) interaction system (Demo4&5).

B. *Summary of Study Results*

TABLE I. SUBJECT DISTRIBUTION

	subject distribution				
	Demo1	*Demo2*	*Demo3*	*Demo4*	*Demo5*
age<=37	7	7	7	7	6
age>37	6	6	6	6	6
$\bar{x}$ age	39	38	40	41	41
SD age	17	16	16	15	15
n woman	6	6	6	6	6
n men	7	7	7	7	6
n	13	13	13	13	12

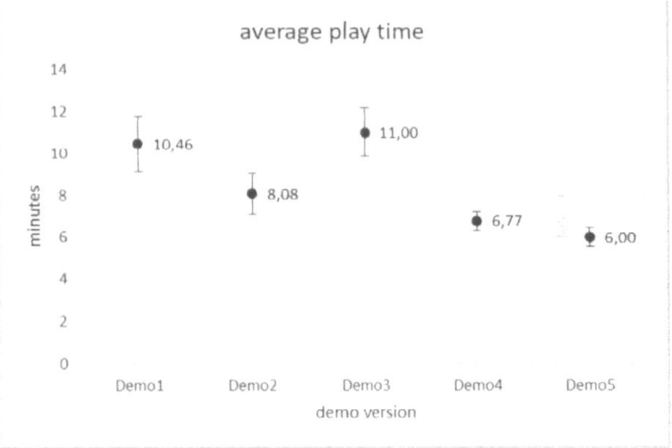

Figure 5. Average play time and 95% confidence interval.

In total 64 participants participated in the study. Table I provides information about the exact distribution of the test subjects to the individual demo versions.

An ANOVA was calculated and, by that, proved that the playtime differences are statistically significant ($\alpha = .05$; $F_{(4,59)} = 4{,}26$; $p < 0{,}0011$) . Figure 5 shows the average playtime for each demo version. It can be seen, that the playing time of the demo version 4 and 5 are the shortest ones. As a result, the assumption that an intuitive interaction system simplifies the access to the game can be confirmed. By that, the 'optimized' or 'optimized+' interaction systems are the most suitable solutions for the GHOST-Prototype. Moreover the results show that there are performance differences between the groups <=37 and >37 and that demo version 4 and 5 minimize these differences.

VI. GHOST: A CDG BASED CYBERSECURITY AWARENESS TRAINING

Following the remarks of this paper, GHOST is a turn-based, tablet-based, serious game like, Competence Developing Game, which provides a cybersecurity awareness training for end users in companies. Furthermore, in GHOST a new intuitive interaction systems was implemented. By that, it has the potential to fulfill the seven requirements which were derived in chapter two.

Whether GHOST meets these requirements depends on the game design. First of all the game design tracks two aspects. It creates the space to experience which personal actions are positive respectively negative for the cybersecurity. Second, it demonstrates which and why IT-department activities are necessary and meaningful. By that, it allows the end user to notice missing activities in his/her company and in addition it will increase the employee's acceptance for such activities.

In case of a cybersecurity training too many topics in a short time period increase the risk to overwhelm the exercisers [1]. Therefore in the beginning each game round (playtime 30 to 60 min) treats only one serious topic. The IT risks are hidden between other tasks and rarely occur, as in reality. In order to evaluate which serious content should find its way into the GHOST CDG, Annex 'A' of ISO 27001 was analyzed (ISO/IEC 27001: Information technology – Security techniques – Information security management systems – requirements, see [17]). In Table II, the serious topic of each game round is presented.

The idea behind GHOST's game design is to minimize the organizational effort. By a trick, GHOST still provides player the illusion of playing together. Every GHOST training is designed for 8 players in two groups at the same time. The training consists of 16 units (game rounds) in total. However, each round gets a specific time period in which the round is active and ready for play. In this period each player can choose the moment to play the round individually. At the end of the time period the GHOST-System calculates, based on each individual result in a group, a common group result which is the starting point for the next round. If, e.g., a player misses to participate in one round the whole group result will be weakened. This kind of game design uses the business simulation advantages like group motivation and the enforcing of a specific continuous training cycle without the disadvantages of complicated appointment organization. Nevertheless GHOST allows even real multiplayer experience. The Round 7&8 as 15&16 require all 8 players to participate the training at the same time. Each group has to be in one physical room, the merging of the groups takes place via internet. These real multiplayer rounds serve as highlights of the complete training cycle. However, since two multiplayer rounds are played at one appointment, accordingly only two appointments must be arranged. As a result GHOST provides 16 play rounds and only requires the coordination of two appointments, which results in a huge reduction of the organizational effort compared to business simulations. Table II shows the assignment between serious content and game rounds.

As already mentioned, the serious content in GHOST is hidden between other tasks. To assure a simple knowledge transfer between the game environment and the real world it seems to be obvious to build an office environment inside the game. Accordingly, the player would solve everyday work tasks inside the game world to come across serious content from time to time. This would result in a game that simulates an office for a game player whose position is currently an office, means playing-office in the office.

TABLE II. GAME ROUNDS

Round	*Serious topic*
1	Screen lock
2	Handling of foreign flash drives
3	Phishing-Mails
4	Backups
5	Mobile Devices (especially Smartphones)
6	Websites, software installation, own IT infrastructure
7&8 (MP)	Passwords, Information encoding, Emergency response, Environmental Security, Backups
9	Access rights
10	Environmental Security, safe workplace
11	Virus prevention, Keylogger, Work delegation
12	Network Devices, Audits,
13	Log files, Access Right Management
14	Quiz Round
15&16 (MP)	Flash drive, Information encoding, Phishing-Mails, Malware, Passwords, Emergency response

MP = Multiplayer

This would most likely ruin the fun aspect of the game, what would gamble away the main advantage of a CDG, the transfer of the motivation of a game situation to a serious context. For this reason, the game was moved 50 years into the future. The players find themselves in a science fiction scenario on a space ship named GHOST. They experience a journey of sixteen laps (one lap one round) and figure out quickly that someone tries to sabotage the mission by infiltrating the ship's computer systems.

As a crew member each player has to handle a lot of day-to-day tasks, which are intentionally similar to 2017 tasks in a normal office. Nevertheless, a player has to be constantly on guard while interacting with the computer systems or other aspects in his environment. The assailant could start the next cyber-attack in any moment, with any strategy.

VII. CONCLUSION

GHOST is a novel approach to perform a cybersecurity awareness training for end users in companies. As shown in Section II such a training should fulfill at least seven requirements to match employer and employee expectations. However, this paper shows that the exploitation of the CDG concept provides the necessary resources to develop a suitable game design. It turns out, however, that the game control, due to the large target group, requires a closer examination. Therefore a study was carried out that solving this issue (evaluate req. 3). How the serious game content was systematically developed out of the well-known ISO 27001 is also explained.

Summarized a GHOST training can take place at the place of work to reduce the time expense. Since an extensive preparation is not needed the organizational overhead is reduced. Both aspects also reduce the training costs (req. 2a-c). Because of its sophisticated empirical evaluated (see Section V) interaction systems even employees without any game experience can participate the training (req. 3). In addition, this interaction system helps GHOST to have an entertainment game look and feel (req. 5). The turn-based, business game inspired, game design allows further a continuous training cycle, that is made possible with a computer-based training (req. 6 and 7). Moreover, the social significance of - and the increased attacks on- IT systems leave no doubt on the real life relevance of the underlying problem (req. 4).

In this discussion, only requirement 1 was left unmentioned. Requirement 1 demands a CDG to help an employee to develop skills, to increase his motivation and satisfaction and to strength the job relation. As already shown requirement 1 aspects have been taken into account throughout the GHOST development. Nevertheless requirement 1 can only be substantiated by field studies. However, the GHOST prototype will be ready for use in short future. Accordingly, for the experimental verification of the GHOST aftereffect a field study is already planned and will be performed in April 2018. The study will provide the possibility to validate the GHOST aftereffect and, by that, to prove the fulfillment of requirement 1 that is not addressed in this paper. After the evaluation of the GHOST aftereffect GHOST will be used for cybersecurity awareness trainings in real life.

REFERENCES

[1] A. Nagarajan, J. M. Allbeck, A. Sood and T. L. Janssen, "Exploring game design for cybersecurity training", Cyber Technology in Automation, Control, and Intelligent Systems (CYBER), IEEE International Conference, pp. 256-262, 2012.

[2] S. Culp, "Cyber Risk: People Are Often The Weakest Link In The Security Chain", Forbes, [Online]. Available: https://www.forbes.com/sites/steveculp/2016/05/10/cyber-risk-people-are-often-the-weakest-link-in-the-security-chain, Last access: 27.10.2017, 2016.

[3] J. A. König and M. R. Wolf, "A New Definition of Competence Developing Games," ACHI 2016, pp. 95-97, 2016.

[4] J. A. König and M. R. Wolf, "The Pyramid Assessment Framework for 'Competence Developing Games'", HCI International, pp. 232-237, 2016.

[5] S. Seyda and Werner, „IW Continuous Vocational Training Survey 2014 - Companies Show In-creased Committed and Invest more in Enhancing their Employees' Skills", Cologne Institute for Economic Research, 2014.

[6] Gesellschaft für Innovationsforschung und Beratung mbH., „Empirical monitoring to the qualification situation in the German economy" (original foreign title:„Empiriegestütztes Monitoring zur Qualifizierungssituation in der deutschen Wirtschaft"), Berlin: Federal Ministry for Economics Affairs and Energy, 2014.

[7] BIBB, "Data Expose to the Vocational Training Report 2017 – Information and analysis in on the development of vocational training" (original foreign title: „Datenreport zum Berufsbildungsbericht 2017 - Informationen und Analysen zur Entwicklung der beruflichen Bildung"), Federal Institute for Vocational Education and Training, 2017.

[8] R. Hunicke, M. Leblanc and R. Zubek, "MDA: a formal approach to game design and game research" In: Proceedings of the Challenges in Games AI Workshop, Nineteenth National Conference of Artificial Intelligence, 2004.

[9] S. Deterding, D. Dixon, R. Khaled and L. Nacke, "From game design elements to gamefulness: defining "gamification"", Proceedings of the 15th International Academic MindTrek Conference: Envisioning Future Media Environments. Finland: ACM, pp. 9-15, 2011.

[10] U. Blötz, "Business Games and Serious Games in Vocational Training" (original foreign title: „Planspiele und Serious Games in der beruflichen Bildung"), Bertelsmann, 2015.

[11] D. Michael and S. Chen, "Serious Games: Games That Educate, Train, and Inform," Thomson Course Technology PTR, 2005.

[12] GTAI, "The Gaming Industry in Germany", Berlin: Germany Trade and Invest, supported by Federal Ministery for Economics Affairs and Energy, 2016.

[13] J. Schell, "The Art of Game Design – A Book of Lenses", 2. Edition, mitp, 2016.

[14] L. N. Taylor, "Video games: perspective, point-of-view, and immersion", Master Thesis - University of Florida, 2002.

[15] D. A. Bowman, E. Kruijff, J. J. LaViola Jr. and I. Poupyrev, "3D User interfaces: Theory and Practise", Addison Wesley, USA, 2005.

[16] T. Hynninen, "First-Person Shooter Controls on Touchscreen Devices: a Heuristic Evaluation of Three Games on the iPod Touch", Master Thesis - University of Tampere, department of Computer Sciences, 2012.

[17] ISO/IEC 27001:2013 - Annex A, information technology - Security techniques - Information security management systems – Requirements, 2013.

[18] Lab for IT-Organization and Management, "Gamified Hacking Offence Simulation-based Training", [Online]. Available: http://itom.fh-aachen.de/index.php/forschung/ghost, Last access: 10.03.2018, 2018.

Proposal and Evaluation of Kinect-based Physical Training System for Special Needs Education

Hiroki Matsuda, Hidemi Yamachi, Fumihiro Kumeno
Department of Computer and Information Technology
Nippon Institute of Technology
Japan, Miyashiro
email: zuimu1010@gmail.com, yamachi@nit.ac.jp, kumeno@nit.ac.jp

Kotomi Shiota
Organization for University Research Initiatives
Waseda Universityline
Japan, Totsukamachi
email: shiota@aoni.waseda.jp

***Abstract*- Microsoft Kinect is a motion sensing device for video games with potential applications in rehabilitation or physical training systems. Many studies have shown the effectiveness of Kinect-based physical training systems, particularly for promoting concentration and movement in special needs education. However, the availability of such systems in the special needs education field in Japan is currently very limited. We developed a Kinect-based physical training system for special needs education and provided it to schools for evaluation. To clearly estimate the system efficacy, we developed a motion analyzer utilizing the open-source software OpenPose. Using the motion analyzer, we were able to evaluate the system's efficacy. In this paper, we report an overview of the system and the results of the evaluation.**

Keywords-motion sensor; Kinect; physical training system; special needs education; OpenPose.

I. INTRODUCTION

Recently, several motion sensor device types have been developed for use in video game systems, such as the Nintendo Wii Fit, Microsoft Kinect, and Leap Motion. These devices are also useful for rehabilitation or physical training assistance systems, and many research reports have been published on the efficacy of such motion sensor devices.

Lange et al. reported that Kinect's high accuracy of tracking and feedback on performance was important in games developed as rehabilitation tools for adults with neurological injuries [1]. Kayama et al. focused on decreasing elderly adults' dual-task ability as a risk factor for falls [2]. They developed a game based on tai chi exercises using Kinect to improve dual-task ability and evaluated the game over a 12-week period in 41 elderly individuals. They reported that the exercise was effective in improving cognitive functions. Chang et al. reported that the Kinect-based rehabilitation system significantly improved motivation for physical training and exercise performance among young adults with motor disabilities [3]. Bartoli et al. adapted an on-the-market, motion-based touchless game for use with Kinect to assist the education of five children with autism and confirmed the efficacy of this teaching tool using standardized therapeutic tests [4]. Fu et al. evaluated the efficacy of a Kinect-based game system for the rehabilitation of 112 children with mental disorders. They compared the children's' pediatric evaluation of disability inventory scores before and after training [5] and found significantly improved results.

Few studies have specifically studied the use of such tools in the special needs education fields. Chang et al. compared the effectiveness of the Kinect system and the high fidelity OptiTrack optical system [6] and showed that Kinect was effective enough as a rehabilitation tool for use in both clinical and home environments. Altanis et al. also found that a Kinect learning game was effective for children with gross motor skill problems and motor impairments [7]. Boutiska et al. successfully used a game called "Kinect Adventures" as an auxiliary learning tool for teaching "Mnemonic Techniques" in children with autism [8]. Freitas et al. developed a Kinect-based motor rehabilitation game to analyze the evaluation feedback from users to repeatedly inform appropriate upgrades [9].

Kinect is most often used as a motion sensor device in such studies because of its low cost and usage possibility without extra attachment devices or markers. However, developing effective Kinect-based rehabilitation systems is not easy. This has led some researchers to use on-the-market games that might discourage continued use by individuals with special needs. Greef et al. discussed the efficacy of Kinect-based games as rehabilitation tools for children with motor skill problems [10], emphasizing that on-the-market games usually revolve around competitions based on mastery skills. Hence, on-the-market games for children with special needs may result in feelings of exclusion. To provide interesting games for such individuals, they recommend developing Kinect games designed according to user requirements. Contrarily, a commercial suite of Kinect-based educational games known as Kinems [11] already exists. These games are targeted at not only typically-developing children, but also at children with learning disabilities. Some researchers have already investigated the efficacy of these games. Kosmas et al. provided empirical evidence that Kinems games enhance motor performance in children with learning disabilities and motor impairments [12]. Kourakli et al. conducted analyses in inclusive classrooms at two primary schools with 20 children having special educational needs. They concluded that these games have a positive impact on children's academic performances and improve their cognitive, motor, and academic skills [13]. Tsiakalou et al. also showed that Kinems games can improve academic performance, motor skills, and executive functions like short-term memory, problem solving, concentration, and attention in children with special needs [14]. Some Kinems games have an embedded monitoring and reporting system that provides teachers the ability to enrich the quantity and quality of information about the children's specific needs. Retalis et al. used Kinems in a study involving children with ADHD learning disabilities [15] and found a statistically significant pre- to post game improvement in their nonverbal intelligence scores. Additionally, an in-depth examination of learning and kinetics showed an improvement in the children's executive functions and cognitive skills.

The Japanese Ministry of Education (MEXT) actively promotes the use of Information and Communication Technology (ICT) devices as educational tools [16]. Several studies related to special needs education have reported an excessive use of notebook and tablet PCs for communication training or rehabilitation; however, there is a limited mention of motion sensor devices such as Kinect. On the National Institute of Special Needs Education website [17], the discussion about ICT devices and their applications in special needs education does not include any information on motion sensors [11]. In 2013, Microsoft Japan and Tokyo University's Research Center of Advanced Science and Technology collaboratively developed the observation and access with Kinect (OAK) [12], a software that aims at supporting children with severe disabilities by identifying their tiniest movements and utilizing those as switches for electronic devices or communication needs. Although OAK can also be used for rehabilitation, it does not provide it's software development kit; therefore, it is impossible to adapt its function to other applications.

We developed a Kinect-based physical training system and provided it to special needs education teachers in seven classrooms of three schools for evaluation. Comments were gathered from the teachers and users, and the system was accordingly revised. Most comments were highly positive, and many teachers reported that the system promoted unusual physical movements that had not been previously seen among the children.

Besides such positive evaluations, numerical data is still required for evaluating the objective of the system. Numerical data was obtained by comparing the player's skeleton positions and the angles formed by connecting skeletons of two video images presented with or without the system. For this analysis, we developed a motion analyzer utilizing OpenPose [18], an open-source software that provides human skeleton position data from video images. We applied the system to a child with motor skill problems and evaluated the data obtained from the system.

Our design goals of this system is as follows.

For trainees (children with disabilities):

1. Inducing a trainee's motivation to move their body as much as they can.
2. Making the training with the system enjoyable for trainees.
3. Developing a trainee's potential ability of their physical body motormovements.

Figure 1. Application outlook

For trainers (special needs education teachers):

1. Easy to use - no need for training before use the system.
2. Easy to customize the system for each trainee condition.
3. Easy to recognize the effect of the training.

Based on these goals, we evaluate our system and specify the effectiveness and problems to be solved of the system.

The structure of this paper is as follows. In Section 2, we provide an overview of the physical training system. In Section 3, evaluations and suggestions from several teachers who have used the system are presented. In Section 4, we describe an outline of the motion analyzer and the results applied to a child with motor skill problems. Finally, we provide concluding remarks and suggestions for future prospects in Section 5.

II. SYSTEM SPECIFICATIONS

The Kinect-based system was developed to motivate movement in children with autism and mental disorders who are able to independently move around. The system displays a video image of the player captured by the Kinect camera with randomly allocated graphical targets, such as balls, other shapes or animals, superimposed on the screen. When the player touches a target, it disappears with a sound and a point is awarded. The game lasts until all the targets have been eliminated (Figure 1). To clearly identify the relationship between the touching motion and target elimination, the target changes its shape before disappearing. When Kinect recognizes the player, red circles appear on the players hands. The game can also be used without a finish point. For example, by selecting the target-manipulate mode, players can hit targets with a rock-shaped hand, break them with scissors, and catch them with paper. In this mode, recognizable pictures, instead of red circles, are displayed on the player's hand (Figure 2(g)).

The game can be customized according to the training purpose or the child's needs. The customizable parameters are listed below:

- Number of targets (Figure 2(a))
- Finish point
- Target size (Figure 2(b))
- Touch-area size (Figure 2(c))
- Type of targets (Figure 2(d))
- Size and position of target area (Figure2(e))
- Body parts used for touching (head, right or left hand, and right or left foot; Figure 2(f))

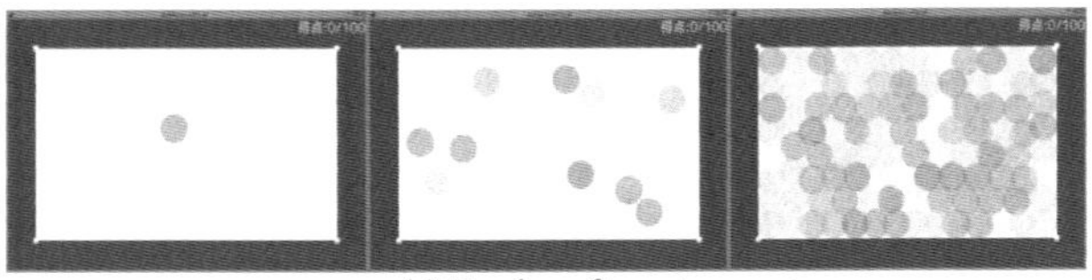

(a) Number of targets

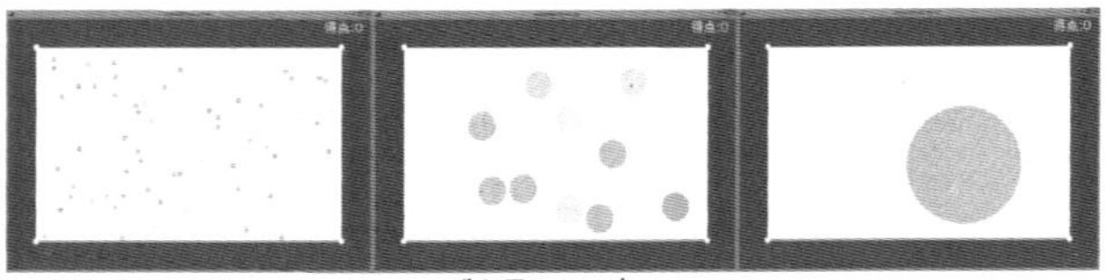

(b) Target size

(d) Touch-area size

(e) Types of targets

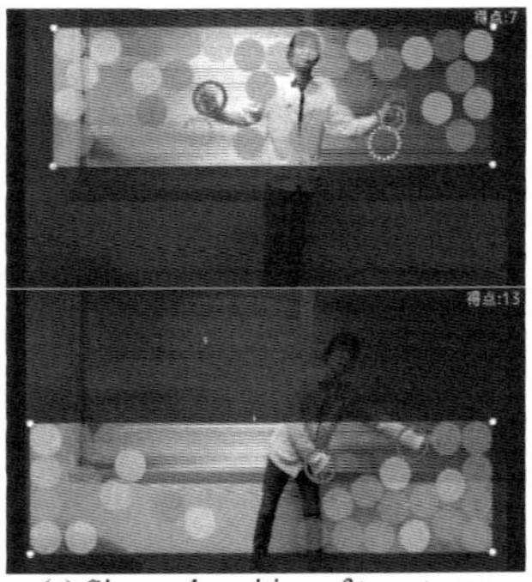

(e) Size and position of target area

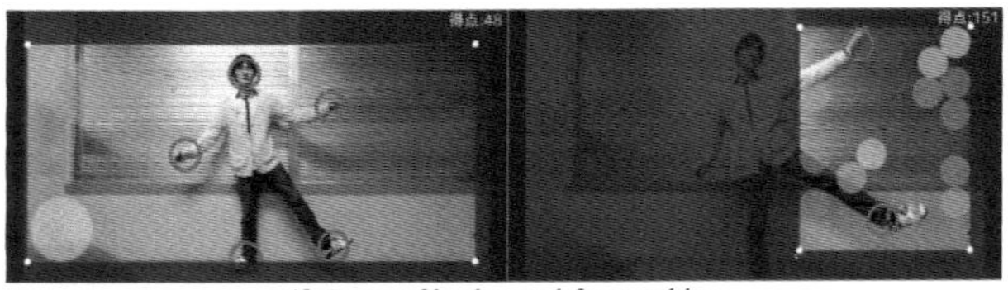

(f) Parts of body used for touching

(g)Target manipulation modes
Rock: catch, Scissors: break, Paper: hit

Figure 2. System specifications

As shown in Figure 2(e), the user can change the size and position of the area where the targets will appear. This function allows the player to concentrate on a specific area and move toward the area. The last parameter (Figure 2(f)) allows the player to use only the left or right hand or all body parts to touch the targets. These settings are saved as a text file for each player and are retained for the next time they play.

III. TEACHERS' EVALUATION AND SUGGESTIONS

The Kinect-based physical training system was provided to seven classes in three Japanese special education schools and reports were gathered on its usefulness and popularity. There were no questionnaires used because the evaluation criteria were expected to be different depending on the disability situation of each child, the aim of the session, and the education method of each teacher. The collected comments are given in the Appendix.

The teachers used large monitors, 50 inches or more, and each practice was 10 to 15 minutes depending on children's situation. The disability situations of the children of these classes were as follows.

- Case 1 contained two children: Child A, aged 10 years, with autism spectrum disorders and mild intellectual disability; Child B with cerebral palsy.
- Case 2 contained five children aged 15 years, four with developmental disability and one with autism
- Case 3 included five classes.
  Class (1) contained .three children aged 15 years, with intellectual and physical disability.
  Class (2) contained three 3 children aged 3with cerebral palsy.
  Class (3) contained three 3 children aged 7 years with severe multiple disabilities.
  Class (4) contained one child aged 8 years with cerebral palsy.
  Class (5) contained one child aged 14years with muscular dystrophy.

Here, we describe the teachers' comments.

According to the comments in the cases 1, 2 and (1), (2), (4), (5) of Case 3, children, who could move around by themselves and recognize that the targets disappeared when they touched them enjoyed the game intensely by extending their arms, lifting them over their heads, or jumping. All teachers commented that the children seldom used those movements. In class 3 (2), there was one child who was so energetic that he became exhausted. These comments show that the game system successfully induced children's motivation to move their body and most of them seemed to enjoy the training.

However, the comment of Case 3 (4) (see Appendix) identifies the difficulty of recognition of the target for a child with milder disability. In Case 2 and Case 3 (3), there was also recognition difficulty for children with severe disabilities. This explains the suggestion of making the targets static and showing them one at a time.

The first suggestion of Case 2 arises from the issue of Kinect sensor. The first version of Kinect recognized two people and the second version recognized six. But neither could distinguish each person. In order to distinguish each person frame by frame, we need to use markers of some kind.

The second suggestion of Case 2 pointed out that for hand shapes to be recognized by Kinect, it is necessary to have the hands face toward Kinect. This movement was one of the difficulties faced by most of the children. Even if they can fold their wrists, intellectual disability makes it hard to understand the function of Kinect. Some children were unable to make the scissor shape.

IV. RESULTS ANALYSIS

It is challenging to compare motions made with or without the system for evaluating the system performance. Although Kinect can easily recognize the position of human skeleton data, most special needs education schools and classes are not in a situation to use Kinect anytime they want. Thus, in some cases, we must use a video footage of the children's motion for comparison of motions made with and without the system. To help evaluate the system, we developed a motion analyzer that can compare differences in motion between two videos. The motion analyzer uses OpenPose, an open-source software that recognizes human poses and reports skeleton position data. OpenPose obtains position data from the base of the neck and both sides of the hips in each video, and superimposes the points by zooming from one to the other. Through this process, OpenPose can calculate the motion angles of the shoulders, elbows, or other joints and compare the difference in angles between the two videos (Figure 3).

We used motion videos of a child with limb and trunk dysfunction caused by cerebral palsy and hydrocephaly. He also suffered from paralysis on the right half of his body. The

Step 1: Original videos — Step 2: OpenPose Output — Step 3: Motion Analyzer

Figure 3. Analysis process

TABLE 1. ANGLES OF SHOULDERS AND ELBOWS DURING EACH MOTION

Joint	Pattern	Before	After	Standard
Right shoulder	A	120.3(67%)	167.4(93%)	180.0
	B	47.0(35%)	102.1(76%)	135.0
	C	37.9(28%)	120.8(89%)	135.0
	D	117.8(65%)	132.8(74%)	180.0
Right elbow	A	72.8(60%)	13.1(93%)	0.0
	B	5.0(97%)	5.4(97%)	0.0
	C	14.3(92%)	10.0(94%)	0.0
	D	56.1(69%)	24.4(86%)	0.0
Left shoulder	A	139.5(77%)	178.3(99%)	180.0
	B	21.3(16%)	119.9(89%)	135.0
	C	22.9(17%)	114.3(85%)	135.0
	D	141.1(78%)	150.8(84%)	180.0
Left elbow	A	58.7(67%)	2.8(98%)	0.0
	B	49.4(73%)	23.5(87%)	0.0
	C	6.6(96%)	15.2(92%)	0.0
	D	16.2(91%)	26.5(85%)	0.0

child underwent a calisthenics training with a teacher for a year. This calisthenics training is very popular in Japanese compulsory education and it includes whole body basic

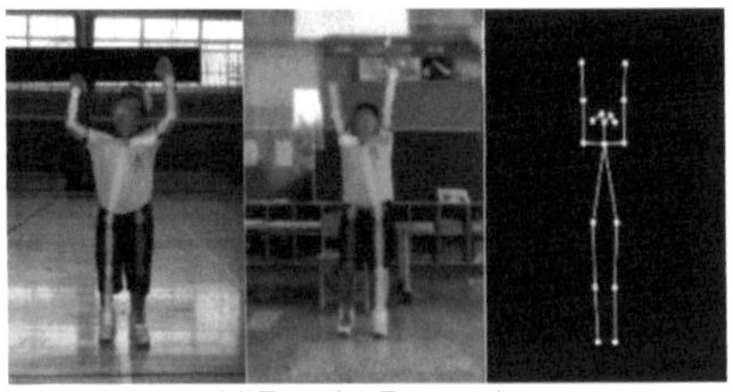

(a) Exercise Pattern A: Raise arms next to the ears

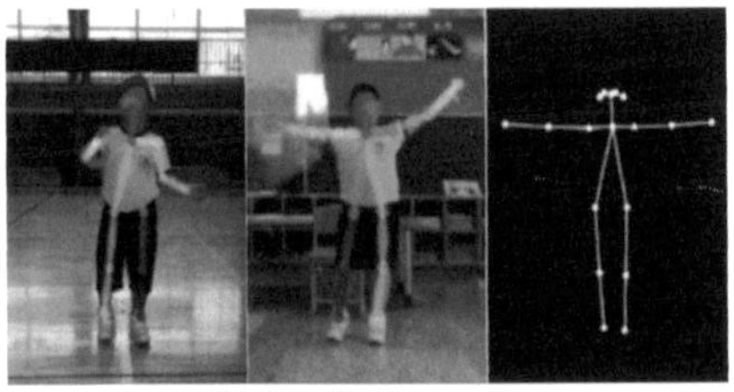

(b) Exercise Pattern B: Arms at shoulder level

(c) Exercise Pattern C: Arms swinging above the shoulders

(d) Exercises Pattern D: Raising arms and standing on toes

Left: before, Center: after, Right: standard

Figure 4. Motions with and without the system

motions with familiar rhythm and the words. At the beginning of the training, he could not move his body to the rhythm. After training, he was able to move to the rhythm; however, his ability to move his muscles showed no improvement, according to the teacher. The teacher used the Kinect system with the child for 15 minutes per week from April to July 2017. The two videos, with and without the system, were recorded in July 2017. Based on the rhythm of the calisthenics training, we fit the same timing of both video scenes. The motions with and without the system that were compared are listed in Figure 4 (a)–(d), and the angles of the shoulders and elbows for each motion are shown in TABLE 1. The "Standard" in TABLE 1 indicates the ideal angle for each motion and each percentage indicates the standard angle.

Figure 4 (a) depicts that the child showed great improvement in extending his arms upward. As observed in

Figure 4 (b), his motion also considerably improved, except for his left elbow. However, as observed in Figure 4 (c) and (d), better results were obtained with the system.

The results support that the system induced the child's active movements and performance. The teacher informed that the child had never shown such extending actions before. In this study, we focused only on the upper half of the child's body. In future studies, it will be necessary to expand the analysis to whole body motion and to observe more number of children. We also need to revise the system to record the motion video and data directly.

V. CONCLUSION AND FUTURE WORK

We developed a Kinect-based rehabilitation system for special -needs education and provided it to schools for evaluation. In order to clearly estimate the system efficacy, we also developed a motion analyzer utilizing the open-source software, OpenPose. We then evaluated the effectiveness of the system efficacy using this motion analyzer.

The Kinect-based physical training system was provided to seven classes in three Japanese special education schools and reports were gathered on its usefulness and popularity. Many teachers rated the system as highly valuable for children with disabilities. The feedback and suggestions offered by the teachers provided insights into ways the system could be made more effective and more popular.

We also developed a motion analyzer using the open-source software OpenPose, which recognizes human poses and reports their skeleton position data. Using the analyzer, we analyzed videos of motions performed by a child with limb and trunk dysfunction, with and without the rehabilitation system. In most cases, the child's motions improved upon Kinect-based system usage. The child's teacher reported never having seen him make such movements before. It is clear that the system induced these active movements in the child.

In this research, we only analyzed the upper part of the body. In the future, we will need to analyze whole body motion. Additionally, we applied and analyzed the system to data for only one child. However, we have provided several schools with the Kinect systems as we mentioned in Section 3. We are going to request the teachers for gathering motion datas and share the analysis results for improving the system better and developing the best way of utilizing it.

REFERENCES

[1] B. Lange et al., "Development and Evaluation of Low Cost Game-Based Balance Rehabilitation Tool Using the Microsoft Kinect Sensor," Engineering in Medicine and Biology Society, EMBC, Annual International Conference of the IEEE, pp.1831-1834, 2011.

[2] H. Kayama et al., "Effect of a Kinect-based Exercise Game on Improving Executive Cognitive Performance in Community-Dwelling Elderly: Case Control Study," 7th International Conference on Pervasive Computing Technologies for Healthcare and Workshops. IEEE, pp. 362-365, 2013.

[3] Y. J. Chang, S. F. Chen, and J. D. Huang, "A Kinect-based system for physical rehabilitation: A pilot study for young adults with motor disabilities," Research in developmental disabilities, pp. 2566-2570, 2011.

[4] L. Bartoli, C. Corradi, G. Garzotto, and M. Valoriani, "Exploring motion-based touchless games for autistic children's learning," IDC '13, Proceedings of the12th International Conference on Interaction Design and Children, pp. 102-111, 2013.

[5] Y. Fu, J. Wu, S. Wu, H. Chai, and Y. Xu, "Game System for Rehabilitation Based on Kinect is Effective for Mental Retardation," In:MATEC Web of Conferences 22, 01036, 2015.

[6] C. Y. Chang et al., "Towards pervasive physical rehabilitation using Microsoft Kinect," 6th International Conference on Pervasive Computing Technologies for Healthcare (Pervasive Health) and Workshops, pp. 159-162, 2012.

[7] G. Altanis, M. Boloudakis, S. Retalis, and N. Nikou, "Children with Motor Impairments Play a Kinect Learning Game: First Findings from a Pilot Case in an Authentic Classroom Environment," Interaction Design and Architecture(s) Journal - IxD&A, N.19, pp. 91-104, 2013.

[8] E. Boutsika, "Kinect in Education: A Proposal for Children with Autism," Procedua Computer Science 27, pp.123-129, 2014.

[9] D. Q. Freitas et al., "Development and Evaluation of a Kinect Based Motor Rehabilitation Game," Proceedings of SBGames, 2012, pp. 114-153, 2012.

[10] K. J. F. Greef, E. D. Spek, and M. M. Bekker, "Designing Kinect games to train motor skills for mixed ability players," Games for Health: proceedings of the 3rd european conference on gaming and playful interaction in health care, pp. 197-205, 2013.

[11] Kinems Learning Games, http://www.kinems.com/ [retrieved: January, 2018]

[12] P. Kosmas, A. Ioannou, and S.Retalis, "Using Embodied Learning Technology to Advance Motor Performance of Children with Special Educational Needs and Motor Impairments," European Conference on Technology Enhanced Learning, EC-TEL: Data Driven Approaches in Digital Education pp.111-124, 2017

[13] M. Kourakli et al., "Towards the improvement of the cognitive, motoric and academic skills of students with special educational needs using Kinect learning games," International Journal of Child-Computer Interaction, Vol. 11, pp. 28-39, 2017

[14] F. G. Tsiakalou, "Teachers exploring the potential of Kinems movement-based learning gaming platform in 2 SEN schools in UK," Presented at the 11th Autism-Europe International Congress, organised by The National Autistic Society in Edunburgh UK, pp.16-18, 2016.

[15] S. Retalis et al., "Empowering Children With ADHD Learning Disabilities With The Kinems Kinect Learning Games," European Conference on Games Based Learning; Reading Vol. 2, pp.469-477, 2014.

[16] http://kyozai.nise.go.jp/ (in Japanese) [retrived: January, 2018]

[17] http://doit-japan.org/doat/oak/ (in Japanese) [retrived: January, 2018]

[18] https://github.com/CMU-Perceptual-Computing-Lab/openpose [retrived: January, 2018]

APPENDIX

- Case 1:

Child A: Aged 10 years; with autism spectrum disorders and mild intellectual disability.

Child B: Aged 10 years; with cerebral palsy.

Teacher's evaluation: Child A actively moved his body. While aiming at targets, he checked his body position and tried to touch them by his extending arms or jumping. Because child B had palsy affecting his left arm, which he usually does not use, his movement for touching was limited. He enjoyed the game a lot.

Suggestions: To reduce clumsy body motion because of disability, the children need synergetic motion trainings for their hands and legs, for example, by letting them touch static targets in turn.

- Case 2:

Five children, four with developmental disability and one with autism

Teacher's evaluation:

- It was clear that the child had visual field constrictions, which was evident from his movement during the game.
- By projecting the large screen (120 inches), children were well motivated.
- Trying to touch targets made children careful about their body positions.
- Using animal picture targets drew more attention.
- Children showed unusual motions like crouching down or taking long strides toward left and right.
- They played with more intention and for longer than other activities.
- Many children can play at the same time.
- Suggestions:
- When Kinect does not recognize a child, he is confused.
- For some children, making a rock, scissor or paper hand is difficult, particularly the scissor hand.
- Too many targets make it difficult for children to concentrate on a specific one.
- It would be useful to designate the positions and the turns of the targets as they appear.
- System preparation takes lot of time.

- Case 3: Comments were obtained from 5 classes.

(1) Three children aged 15 years, with intellectual and physical disability

Teacher's evaluation:

- Usually they tend to be inactive, but the game induced them to move independently, extending their arms or crouching down.
- One child could not understand the causal relationship between touching and disappearing targets; however, when the animal picture targets were shown, he understood the relation.

Suggestions:

- By fully showing targets on the screen, we may be able to find the child's gazing point and their visibility range.

(2) Three children aged 3with cerebral palsy

Teacher's evaluation:

- They very eagerly played the game and one child got exhausted.
- The game was used once a week for 5 weeks. Children became more active than before.

Suggestions:

- No suggestions.

(3) Three children aged 7 years with severe multiple disabilities

Teacher's evaluation:

- They could not recognize the targets and just slightly moved their hands.
- It was difficult for them to notice whether they touched the target or not.

Suggestions:

- In order to make the targets easier to recognize, make the targets blink or develop other strategies.
- It is difficult for the children to concentrate on the game if there are many things on the backdrop.
- Making the targets appear one by one would help children recognize each target.

(4) One child aged 8 years with cerebral palsy

Teacher's evaluation:

- The child actively played at first, but lost interest later.
- Recognizing the target did not seem easy for her.

Suggestions:

- Many such games should be developed.

(5) One child aged 14years with muscular dystrophy

Teacher's evaluation:

- He usually does not lift his arm above his shoulder, but here, he lifted his arm over his head.
- Changing the target site helps train children to move their arms in various directions.

Suggestions:

- No suggestions.

Fiction Design of a 3D Tutor for and with School Children

Monica Landoni
Faculty of Informatics,
Università della Svizzera italiana, USI
Lugano, Switzerland
e-mail: monica.landoni@usi.ch

Fabrizio Gramuglio
FOREVER Identity
New York, USA
e-mail: fabrizio.gramuglio@gmail.com

Emiliana Murgia
ICS Antonio Stoppani
Milano, Italy
e-mail: emilianamurgia@gmail.com

Giorgio Manfredi
FOREVER Identity
New York, USA
e-mail: giorgio.manfredi@rumbletumbleweed.com

Abstract—**In this paper, we describe the fiction design approach we are using in collaboration with school children and teachers in order to produce a 3D Tutor. We introduce the actors and procedure we are following with particular emphasis on the activities devised to engage children in the various stages of design and produce the necessary output for each of the facets of the 3D Tutor. Our assumption is that making learning more fun will increase the overall level of children's engagement and their motivation towards it. Thus, we describe how children are helping us to design a 3D Tutor able to cater for individual learning styles as well as being fun to work with. Finally, we discuss how this ongoing experience with collaborative fiction design is providing us with directions towards the first prototype of our 3D Tutor.**

Keyword-E-learning Interaction; 3D Tutor; Collaborative Design; User Requirements; Fiction Design.

I. INTRODUCTION

Technology is used to support teaching and learning in many ways. Here, we are exploring the design of a 3D Tutor to act as a teachable agent to engage primary school children. Teachable agents are defined by Biswas et al. [1] as a "...computer agents that students teach, and in the process, learn themselves". Children asked to teach them are forced to structure their knowledge, take responsibility for its delivery and reflect upon it. All essential steps in the learning process. Both the social and emotional dimensions of teachable tutors are still under study, and our work contributes to this research by exploring the impact of one of its possible manifestations, that in the shape of 3D holographic tutor.

Our assumption is that, by involving children in the definition of the look and feel of their teaching tutor-agent, they could help us design one that better satisfies their needs. Besides, given that our tutor will learn from children, we would start our exploration by revisiting the list of qualities proposed by Buskin et al. [2] and focusing on few of the most highly ranked in that study. Thus, we wanted to find out whether for our pupils, as for the older students in that study, it is important that their 3D Tutor *should be enthusiastic about learning, promotes crucial thinking, approachable, respectful, creative, has realistic expectations*. By engaging children and teachers as co-designers, we came up with the first set of user requirements for a prototype of a 3D Tutor together with a list of desirable qualities for making it an ideal teaching agent. We start by providing a very brief account of previous works on co-design with children and explorations of the social and emotional dimensions of teachable agents. We then provide a description of our study, and finally draw some initial conclusions based on the evidence gathered.

II. RELATED WORK

In the literature describing how co-design can help the design of effective digital tutors for children, we found inspiration from the work by Herberg et al. [3] involving children in the identification of qualities for an ideal robot tutor. Among the many approaches to collaborative design, particularly suitable for young children is fiction design, where "something that creates a story world... has something being prototyped within that story world, ... does so in order to create a discursive space." [4].

Moving on to consider research on the design of teachable tutors [1], Ogan et al. [5] go on to explore the social dimension of teachable agents and report on how having a friendly, equal approach, where the tutor and the child align themselves to be peers, together with being able to use informal interactions, including mutual teasing, is conducive to successful learning experiences. On the contrary, keeping a formal distance has a negative effect on the overall experience. While most of the available literature reports on pro and cons of having robots to play the role of the tutor, we set out to explore an alternative, that of a 3D holographic entity.

The 3D Tutor is a 3D character animated in real-time, able to interact through different senses (touch, voice, vision) and to convey dialog, emotions and lessons. It is responsive and adaptive: it can diagnose end users' conditions (e.g., he/she may be tired), preferences, needs and peculiarities/ environment conditions (e.g., preferred language, currently available bandwidth, etc.) in real time. In this way, we separate the content of the lesson to be taught (Knowledge) from the means used to convey this content (Teaching methodology) and interact with students. Using Artificial Intelligence, the 3D Tutor can choose the right question/topic;

using Artificial Empathy, the 3D Tutor has the ability to recognise users' emotional state and engagement to react in the proper way. Thus, the content is adapted to both the conditions of the student and the particular device used (mobile device, web, classroom). With the 3D Tutors, teachers can explore new ways to present subjects to students, as well as encourage students to find the learning style that suits them including the adoption of the teaching agent paradigm. The concept of a 3D Tutor is based on that of Human-like Interaction (HLI) [3]. HLI implies the use of all dimensions of human language, not only written or verbal communication but also gestures, postures and expressions. Starting from the concept that transmitted messages between humans contain both an informative (rational) value and an emotional value, the human form is the best way to synthesize them.

III. OUR STUDY

Here, we describe our experience in involving children in the design of a 3D Tutor to assist them in their learning as teaching agent. We included in our study 154 children in primary 2, aged 7 to 8, from two schools, one in Italy and one in the Italian speaking part of Switzerland, and 9 teachers. One of them, playing the role of digital creative, worked very closely with the researchers when proposing procedures and protocols for engaging the children. We applied a make-believe approach, where we created a fictional world supported by narrative and acting. This helped to generate intrinsic motivation in pupils to take part in the various activities necessary to inform our design process, and provide us with the necessary insights to define the look and feel of our 3D Tutor. While the design process is still ongoing, by having completed the first two phases: the *meeting the Alien* and the *Looking and Feeling like a Human Being,* both described below, we have gathered a wealth of data and experience to share with our community.

The use of an alien in anthropomorphic form has made it easier to encode a series of messages that, otherwise would have been very complex to transmit to our co-designers. For example, the message of non-aggression was conveyed to the children in an intuitive way by having the alien assume the posture of a timid person: it often looked down at its feet, rocking slightly on its heels.

IV. FICTION DESIGN WITH CHILDREN

Our design scenario includes an unusually large number of children, more than 150. Teachers behaved as co-designers and proposed, adapted and conducted the various design related activities. Researchers acted as facilitators and made sure teachers had all the technological support for the make-believe approach. Head-teachers and parents in both schools were informed and asked to keep up with the fictional setting, without revealing what was really happening. Our main assumption was that children as young as 7 to 8 had the necessary flexibility towards reality, yet still had the ability to embrace mystery and magic.

V. MEETING THE ALIEN

The first meeting was staged in a theatre (Fig. 1) and resulted in a memorable event for children, as reflected in the quality and quantity of their comments. Children had received an email via their school head-teacher, wherein a group of scientists was asking for their help to make sense of a mysterious message from space. On reading it, children immediately accepted to take part in the adventure. They had also been invited by their teachers to prepare questions beforehand to ask the alien, in the assumption the children could understand the answers. This was the beginning of the make-believe narrative adopted in the study.

Figure 1. Meeting the Alien

The second step was the encounter with Olo-Disk, as the name of the alien was finally revealed ("discolo" is an Italian old fashioned term for naughty child).

The event was carefully staged, with a couple of researchers playing the role of lab scientists, wearing white coats in a dark room. Finally, in a surreal silence, Olo-Disk appeared, remote, and different but intentionally never dangerous, (see Fig. 2). Looking often down to his/her feet, with a subdued attitude and using a never heard concoction of Italian, Finnish and Cantonese with a prevalence of "ɑ:" sounds, s/he had clearly a non-threatening appearance.

Figure 2. Our friendly Alien

S/he started to explain that, while travelling in space s/he was attracted by a blue planet (Earth), but s/he was aware that his/her physical features were not adequate to come and visit it. That was why s/he was trying to communicate with scientists: s/he needed their help to know how to transform her/himself to be like humans. Immediately after the meeting, children were asked to engage with some simple exercises, individually and in groups, in order to explore how they felt and reflect on their experience. They were invited to select one single word that, summarised the experience of meeting Olo-Disk and then, as group, to put forward some more words linked with the event. These were then copied on a poster size paper, to be shared with others.

Pupils were asked to make a drawing, to represent the most important element of the day (Fig. 3). The purpose of these exercises was to make children reflect and fix their memories of the day.

Their artifacts were then analysed by teachers and researchers, looking for signs of engagement and participation. We searched for expressions of surprise, curiosity, fear and excitement, between those used in the two word based exercises.

Figure 3: The experience in one drawing – English for "In un disegno"

For drawings as in Fig. 3 we adopted and adapted a coding scheme from Xu at al [2], see Table 1.

TABLE 1: CODING SCHEME FOR DRAWINGS

Element	Evidence	Score
Participation	Children, self portraits	Score: Absent (0) or Present (1)
Visual Magic	Portrait of the Alien: size, color, appearance, lights	Not evident (0), Possibly Evident (1) Evident (2) Highly Evident (3)
Interactive Magic	Questions and answers, communication, sound, gestures	Not Evident (0) Possibly Evident (1) Evident(2) Highly Evident (3)

VI. ACTIVITIES

It is worth noticing how all activities were designed to be in line with existing curriculum. Even if the stimulus was coming from a request issued by Olo-Disk, it was up to the teachers to interpret it and guide the children in a process of problematisation of the request to result in a stronger form of engagement with the new learning activity. After the first meeting, a new message came directly to the children. Olo-Disk needed their help to look and behave like a human being.

A. *Looking and Feeling like a Human Being*

In order to answer this new request, a series of activities were elaborated by the different teachers and proposed to the children.

The teachers and children from the Italian Swiss school devised a variety of multidisciplinary exercises. As there was only one class engaged in the process, all children were involved in all activities that spanned across disciplines. Children worked on emotions and prepared drawings portraying those they felt stronger, as in Fig. 4 ("I am Leone, and I am happy"; "I am Valeria and I am happy" is written in Italian in the picture). These drawings were analysed in terms of dominant emotions, and assisted in the definition of the look and feel of the interface for our 3D Tutor. During their art class, they also prepared outfits for Olo-Disk to look like a human being, different ones in case Olo-Disk were a female or a male being. These artifacts contributed to define the appearance of our 3D Tutor.

Figure 4: Emotions

The English teachers wanted to contribute to the project, by discussing with children what kind of information would be useful to Olo-Disk. They decided to share with Olo-Disk their knowledge of the solar system in English, given that they had to use the universal translator to communicate anyway. In order to make it more fun and engaging for Olo-Disk, children and teachers decided to organize a play where each pair of pupils would act as one planet and describe it to Olo-Disk, by using a mixture of words and gestures. Teachers reported on how committed children were, as they felt this task would help Olo-Disk in his/her quest. In particular, knowing that their play was being recorded and sent to Olo-Disk, made them learn their lines faster and each put as much effort as possible in order to share their newly acquired knowledge with their friend.

In Italy, the six classes were teamed in pairs. In order to answer the main question, about what makes us human, each pair fully explored one of the three facets of our 3D Tutor: *corpus* (physical facet), *indoles* (emotional facet) and *societas* (social facet). Children in every class worked first in small groups, each focusing on a specific sub-facet. All contributions were then combined. To give Olo-Disk enough information for becoming similar to a human being. The indoles team worked to sort out which emotions Olo-Disk had to learn, detailing in which conditions they are generated. Finally, the classes who worked on societas, identified conventional relationships and related behaviours among people.

During the activities, the teachers let children free and encouraged them to consider every possible solution. Thus, few members of the "corpus" team- wrote an email to Olo-Disk asking if he/she really wanted agree to transform him/herself, explaining that they didn't mind if he/she was so peculiar, adding also that they were available to help her/him to travel the world without transforming him/herself.

All the 154 children, across the two schools, were invited to work using the same tools: drawings, content tables and text, to organize and summarize in writing the conclusions reached and their achievements for each activity. Desktop computers and interactive whiteboard where part of the resources available to them, when helping their friend Olo-Disk.

VII. NEXT STEPS

In the immediate future, we will complete the analyses of all data gathered and use that output to inform the production of the first prototype of our 3D Tutor. This will be presented to the children by the end of the current school year, 2017-2018, when they will meet Olo-Disk with his/her new look and behavior. Children will also be sent a message from the scientists, thanking them for all the work done and showing them how, this was used to help Olo-disk to answer his/her quest on how to become human. In the new autumn semester, 2018-2019, we will then involve the same children as assessors in its evaluation and proceed toward the production of incremental prototypes. These will expand the 3D Tutor in three directions:

- by providing an authoring tool for teachers and children to add educational material;
- by expanding on the sensorial experience with Olo-disk, acquiring the ability to see and touch.
- by enhancing Olo-disk's ability to master the use of language and rhetoric.

VIII. CONCLUSIONS

The introduction of artificial tutors in education is still under debate and presents many open issues. We believe that by following an appropriate design approach, we can deliver a 3D Tutor to enhance the learning experience, starting from primary school. We tested our hypothesis by involving seven classes of primary school 2nd grade children and their teachers across two countries, in a collaborative fiction driven design process. Even if the process is still ongoing, its outlook is encouraging. Usually, the introduction of new technology in educational activities brings high levels of engagement. Thus, it was not a surprise that children reacted with vibrant enthusiasm from the very beginning of the project. Guided by an effective make-believe narrative, the children immediately adopted the tutor as one of them. By analyzing the discourse in class and interviewing the teachers, it was clear that Olo-Disk was never perceived as a "teacher" but a companion or a friend, a truly *approachable* teachable agent. One of the teachers commented on the fact that Olo-Disk had become such an important member of the class, so much so that children were asking her to find more time during the day for activities linked to him/her, as these stimulated their *creativity*. Children felt Olo-Disk was *enthusiastic about learning* as s/he valued and *respected* them. They never felt under pressure for his/her requests, as these responded to *realistic expectations,* while at the same time, *promoted crucial thinking*, as when children pondered whether the transformation was really necessary.

Besides, the combination of the HLI approach with fiction design, in a collaborative setting involving children, has proved successful in keeping a high level of motivation and producing a large number of artifacts. These will serve as input for the user requirement phase of our project. The analysis and interpretation of all the heterogeneous data gathered from drawings to acting, from word chains to discussions in focus groups and teachers' interviews is proving to be a stimulating activity too. Our 2nd grade children have fully engaged with all the proposed activities and we are looking forward to them moving on to next step, and acting as evaluators for our project.

ACKNOWLEDGEMENTS

We thank the schools, teachers, parents and above all the children who brought enthusiasm and magic to the study.

REFERENCES

[1] G. Biswas, K. Leelawong, D. Schwartz, N. Vye and The Teachable Agents Group at Vanderbilt, "Learning by Teaching a New Agent Paradigm for Educational Software", Applied Artificial Intelligence, vol. 9, issue 3-4, pp. 363-392, 2005.

[2] W. Buskist, J. Sikorski, T. Buckley and B. K. Saville, "Elements of masterteaching" in The Teaching of Psychology: Essays in Honor of Wilbert J. McKeachie and Charles L. Brewer. , S. F. Davis and W. Buskist, eds. Mahwah New Jersey: Erlbaum, pp. 27-39, 2002.

[3] J. S. Herberg, D. C. Behera, and M. Saerbeck, "Eliciting ideal tutor trait perception in robots: pinpointing effective robot design space elements for smooth tutor interactions", HRI '13: Proc. of the 8th ACM/IEEE international conference on Human-robot interaction, IEEE Press, Piscataway, NJ, USA, pp. 137-138. 2013.

[4] J. Lindley, "Researching Design Fiction With Design Fiction", C&C '15: Proc. of the ACM SIGCHI Conference on Creativity and Cognition, pp. 325-326, 2015.

[5] A. Ogan, S. Finkelstein, E. Mayfield, C. D'Adamo, N. Matsuda, and J. Cassell, ""Oh dear Stacy!": social interaction, elaboration, and learning with teachable agents", CHI 2012: Proc. of the SIGCHI Conference on Human Factors in Computing Systems, ACM, New York, NY, USA, pp. 39-48, 2012.

[6] D. Xu, J. C. Read, G. Sim and B. McManus, "Experience it, draw it, rate it: capture children's experiences with their drawings", IDC '09: Proc. of the 8th International Conference on Interaction Design and Children, pp. 266-270, 2009.

[7] J. van Oijen and F. Dignum, "Agent communication for believable human-like interactions between virtual characters", Proc. of the 11th International Conference on Autonomous Agents and Multi-agent System, vol. 3, pp. 1181-1182 , 2012.

The User-Focused Storybuilding Framework for Competence Developing Games

A Design-Framework considering the basics of an educational game's story

Johannes A. König, Veronika Völker, Martin R. Wolf
Lab for IT Organization and Management
Aachen University of Applied Sciences
Aachen, Germany
email: koenig@fh-aachen.de, veronika.voelker@alumni.fh-aachen.de, m.wolf@fh-aachen.de

Abstract—**During the development of a Competence Developing Game's (CDG) story it is indispensable to understand the target audience. Thereby, CDGs stories represent more than just the plot. The Story is about the Setting, the Characters and the Plot. As a toolkit to support the development of such a story, this paper introduces the User-Focused Storybuilding (short UFoS) Framework for CDGs. The Framework and its utilization will be explained, followed by a description of its development and derivation, including an empirical study. In addition, to simplify the Framework use regarding the CDG's target audience, a new concept of Nine Psychographic Player Types will be explained. This concept of Player Types provides an approach to handle the differences in between players during the UFoS Framework use. Thereby, this article presents a unique approach to the development of target group-differentiated CDGs stories.**

Keywords-CDG; Competence Developing Game; Serious Game; Video Game; Story; Narrative; Player Types; Player-Types; User-Focused Storybuilding Framework; UFoS.

I. INTRODUCTION

Recently, games have become more and more important for serious education in private or business situations. Entertaining gaming situations are inherently motivating and, as such, could be utilized to deliver a specific message to their audience in an entertaining way [1]. For this purpose, not only business simulations (often board game based) are in use, also video game based solutions (e.g., serious games) are common. Every game with a serious intention, regardless if it is a video game or a board game, can be described as a Competence Developing Game (CDG). In detail, a CDG is characterized by the endeavor to teach its players a competence and utilize the motivational and entertaining nature of games to do so [2].

Zyda [3] refers to "Bing Gordon, chief creative officer of video and computer games developer Electronic Arts [...] [who] defines video games as 'story, art, and software'" [3]. The first aspect 'story' distinguishes between a board game or a business simulation compared to a video game based CDG. Here, a video game tells a complex continuous and sometimes changing story presented by technology. Meanwhile, a board game or a business simulation presents an often minimalistic story using printed game material or a facilitator. Nevertheless, Ritterfeld explains that the quality of a game with a serious intention has to be similar to an entertainment game to be successful [4]. The other two aspects 'art' and 'software' are comparable in their roots. Art, for instance, includes the visuals of a game. Software may pertain to executable files, but for board games it can be understood as resource to create the cards, board, etc. Art and software need to be implemented by a development team. To do so, the team needs tools. In the case of video games, the team uses programming languages to produce a new piece of executable software. Board game developers use physical materials to create a touchable and playable game. Consequently, only the game's story differentiates deeply between analog and digital games. By that, story is one of three main game components and the only component that differs greatly between the game types under the CDG umbrella term. Because of that, an explicit CDG story Framework is useful. There are different approaches for story development (see e.g.: [8][14][16][18]), but there is no approach that was developed specifically for CDG story design so far.

Story, in fact, is one of the key components of video games [3]. It creates background information and context for many of the actions taken within a game. It can also serve as a motivator and a means of maintaining interest in the game and understanding of the sequence of events occurring within it. Therefore, story should be crafted to compliment the rest of the game. Also, in CDGs, it supports and underlines the serious intention and connects with the audience. To support a CDG's developer to design a story in a standardized way, this paper presents the User-Focused Storybuilding (short UFoS) Framework for CDGs.

The Framework thus supports the development of the game story on paper. By that, the UFoS Framework has to be applied before using game engines like Unity [23], Unreal [24] or their board game equivalents. The result of this application can even support to decide whether a video game based CDG, a board game based CDG or a mix up will be the best choice.

The structure of this paper will be as follows: In Section II of this paper, the Framework itself with all its components will be explained, elaborating its content and visual representation. Section III will provide an overview and explanation of the Nine Psychographic Player Types, placing a focus on the psychographical attributes of a Player. Section IV explains how to apply the Framework as a development tool for the basic elements of a story. In Section V, the derivation of the Framework will be discussed, examining how its components were chosen and designed and why those particular components belong to the Framework.

Section VI seeks to explain the origin of the Player Types, including the taxonomies used to craft the different categories and the process of developing them. Section VII concludes the paper by examining the need for further research and the possibilities and advantages of the UFoS Framework.

II. The UFoS Framework

The UFoS Framework serves as a guideline to create the basics of a CDG's story that can motivate players. It entails six components (Serious Content, Plot, Characters, Setting, Presentation, and Player), which are examined individually in the process of story creation. Therefore, these six components cover all aspects of a video game-based CDG's story. In the following paragraphs the components are briefly described (for the Framework derivation see Section V).

The first story component is the **'Serious Content'**, based on the word 'Serious' in the 'Serious Game' term. This aspect deals with the intention behind the game. It is usually one of the first elements to be described in the process of developing a CDG [5]. The Serious Content describes the real life problem that the game is attempting to solve. The competence the game is aiming to teach is derived from this. The Serious Content is the game's purpose and its primary focus and, as such, other components of a CDG have the objective of underlining it. The next story component is the **'Player'**. This component covers the audience of the game. It is different from the other components, as it is the only element that the designer cannot create but merely describe. The Players exist independently from the game, whereas every other element does not. The Player is defined by two different parts: *'Demographics'* and *'Psychographics'*. Demographics describe external attributes, such as age and gender [6]. Psychographics describe inner attributes, such as preferences or life styles [6].

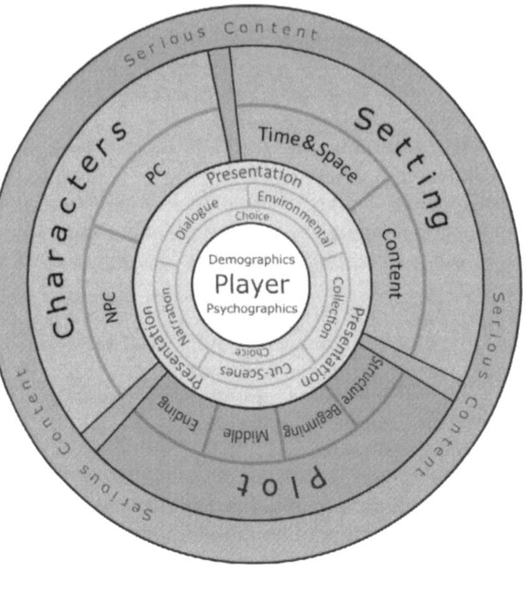

Figure 1. The UFoS – Framework for CDGs

Both parts need to be considered when describing the Player as both influence how a game story is designed. Additionally, understanding and describing the Player will enable the developer to craft a powerful gaming experience for their specific target audience. The whole story of a digital CDG serves as a bridge between the components 'Serious Content' and 'Player'.

The three components in between are the Plot, the Characters and the Setting. These components are the heart of every digital CDG's story. The amount of influence they have on the whole story varies depending on the nature of the components 'Player' and 'Serious Content', as will be discussed later (see Section IV).

The **'Plot'** describes the sequence of events happening in the game. It starts with the beginning of the game and ends with its conclusion. As seen in [7] and [8], the Plot has an overall *'Structure'*, as well as three parts: The *'Beginning'*, the *'Middle'* and the *'End'* [7][8].

The **'Characters'** are the entities living within the game. These are separated into the *'Player Character'* (PC), an entity controlled by the player to navigate through the game; and the *'Non-Player Characters'* (NPCs), entities controlled by an Artificial Intelligence [7][9]

The **'Setting'** describes the *'Time & Space'* of the game. This can be very realistic or very unrealistic and entail other elements, such as the laws it follows [10]. Time and Space are only the frame conditions of the Setting. Everything else, like its laws or specific areas, are its *'Content'*, which is influenced and defined by those two initial parameters [6].

As already mentioned, the level of influence of the three components depends on the Serious Content and the Player and is individually crafted for each game. This is the case because detailing all elements in the same amount could potentially overwhelm players, especially those who are not willing to invest time and energy into a game story [7]. Therefore, the developer needs to select a focus, which is in line with the determined intention of the game (Serious Content) and, if possible, caters to its target audience (Player). So, the level of detail required for each component varies from CDG to CDG. Therefore, components of a lower priority should also be considered later during a game story development process.

The final component of a story is its **'Presentation'**, also called 'Discourse'. A story's presentation refers to the question of how something is shown within the game [11]. It describes the way how the five previously established components are explained and presented to the Player. The literature describes different possibilities to present a CDG to its players. The decision of the right style of presentation for a specific CDG, again, depends on the intention of the game, as well as the preferences of the target audience.

Presentation is divided into the areas 'Plot' and 'Choice'. Video games provide the player varying amounts of choices; some of them influence the events and some of them do not [6]. Choices can be presented in different ways, ranging from on-screen options to subtle decisions. Different degrees of subtlety can cause different effects, as more obvious choices can be utilized to demonstrate cause and effect and less visible ones can be exhibit how easy it is to make wrong decisions or miss certain things in some scenarios.

However, keeping the serious mission of every CDG in mind, the different options the player can take have to be considered carefully, because the decision made by a player in the game's world may support building competences the player is able to use in the real world. By that, 'Choices' support achieving the serious mission of a CDG in a very direct manner. Additionally, there a several ways to present the Plot.

A common way of a plot's presentation is *'Narration'*. It is about telling a story via text and speech [12]. Another plot presentation opportunity is *'Dialogue'* [13], a method of conveying information via the interactions between two or more characters in the game, shown with either text, sound or both. An overarching category of presentation deals with visual storytelling. This term describes methods in which, rather than explaining story with words, the audience witnesses the events directly by observing the characters, or is provided with images or other visual cues that deliver context and clue them into the happenings of the story [14]. For this kind of visual storytelling there two more possibilities: *'Cut-Scenes'* (not interactive sequence, breaking up the gameplay) [15] and *'Environmental Storytelling'*. The latter describes a technique which uses certain environmental features to tell a story. For instance, puddles in the street as a signal for rain having fallen [16]. The last plot presentation method is called *'Collection'*. Collection takes place when the pick up or the interaction with a game object triggers a narrative sequence [17], and several of these interactions and triggers exist, or are required to understand the narrative.

The six components are arranged in a circle as their order depends on the CDG's purpose and players and therefore, from a generic view, there is no hierarchy between them. However, the components of the Setting, the Characters, the Plot and the Presentation separate the Serious Content on the outside from the Player on the inside. This is because the Serious Content serves as a frame for the other components, not only determining several of their attributes, but also providing possibilities and limitations to them. The Player, on the inside of the Framework, is the target of the Serious Content, so the components should be designed to allow the Serious Content on the outside to have the optimal way to the Player, on the inside. Figure 1 shows the visual representation of the Framework. The derivation of the Framework will be explained in Section V.

III. The Nine Psychographic Player Types

As will be shown in Section IV, there are phases and steps, which support the use of the six Framework components. The Player and their preferences have to be considered. This means that a developer has to make choices that match the likes and dislikes of different Psychographic Player Types.

The Nine Psychographic Player Types are a method of grouping Players of a game by psychographic attributes (for their derivation, see Section VI). They were jointly developed with the Framework and are essential for the application of the Framework as shown in Section IV. The Player Types are:

1. The **Narrator**. This category defines people with a strong interest in observing dramatic sequences of events. They take pleasure in strong narratives and well-written plotlines.
2. The **Challenger**. Challengers primarily play video games for their problem-solving qualities. They enjoy difficulty and examining a problem or puzzle from multiple angles before solving it.
3. The **Socialite**. Socialites enjoy the social aspects of games, such as playing with friends or interacting with realistic Non-Player Characters.
4. The **Explorer**. This group represents people who enjoy discovering things. They thrive on a sense of wonder and act in pursuit of it, exploring and uncovering. This exploration is not limited to areas but extends to the discovery of new methods or abilities.
5. The **Expressionist**. These players play for the chance to express themselves within the game. They wish to have control over what happens and generally influence the game.
6. The **Dreamer**. The Dreamer plays to escape everyday life temporarily. They wish to fully immerse themselves in the game world and become part of it for a while, taking in the various sensations offered by it.
7. The **Daredevil**. These players, like Challengers, enjoy difficult games. However, their motivation to play them is not the careful consideration of problems, but instead the thrill and suspense provided by certain obstacles. They also enjoy Horror games as these are suspenseful and thrilling by nature.
8. The **Winner**. This category describes players who deem winning to be one of their primary goals or their only goal. They also enjoy difficulty in games, as it makes the experience of winning more rewarding. There is less merit in winning something easy than winning something difficult.
9. The **Collector**. Collectors like collecting and completing. This does not only refer to quests or objects in games, but also describes the act of finding or doing everything a game has to offer.

Of course, no person can be described as only one Player Type. Humans' desires and their psychology are far too complex to be labeled accurately with nine terms. Instead of assigning one description to each person, this approach attempts to describe possible motivations while considering that each player falls into different categories to different degrees [6]. For instance, one person may enjoy a strong narrative (Narrator), while also playing the game to escape everyday life (Dreamer) and following the drive to collect everything in the game (Collector). But they despise puzzles (Challenger) and thrills (Daredevil). Each player has an individual profile of Player Types, with some of them being stronger motivators and influencers of behavior than others. A group of people can be defined by their common predominant Player Types. One person can fall into many categories this way, each of them defined by one of the Player Types that influences them the most. This approach at classifying them acknowledges the multitude of possible motivators and influencers, while also maintaining the ease of identifying people with labels.

It is important to understand which Player Types are predominant in the audience. Due to their different motives, natures and drives, people categorized as different Player Types have different priorities and preferences regarding several elements of a game's design; this includes the story [6], as will be discussed later.

IV. HOW TO USE THE FRAMEWORK

A. *General description*

In Section III all components of a game story and their positions within the UFoS Framework were explained. In addition, the Nine Psychographic Player Types were introduced, which simplify the Framework application. Now, it is important to understand how the UFoS Framework could be used during the story design of a CDG.

There are different phases in the process of the story development. They all correspond with one or more of the components described in the previous Section. Each phase contains several steps to be followed to create the basis of a CDG story.

The first phase exists to establish the Serious Content which, as previously mentioned, must be determined first to design every other element to underline and support it.

The second phase deals with determining the Player, the audience of the game. It requires a definition of their demographic traits, as well as their psychographic profile, which can include up to nine different psychographic player types (see Section III). This phase has to take place after the definition of the Serious Content, because the teaching goal implies a specific target audience. Sometimes, when a CDG is developed, several of the traits of the Players are already pre-determined (e.g., if the intention is to play the game with employees of a company, they have to be at least 18 years old). It has to, however, occur before developing several of the other components, as the definition of the Player will influence design choices that affect them.

The third phase is used to determine the priorities of the Setting, the Plot and the Characters. As previously mentioned, a developer should prioritize one of the three components over the other two, to focus on that one in more detail. So, the developer should establish a priority list, which includes the components Setting, Plot and Characters. This third phase requires the developer to not only prioritize one component, but to furthermore determine which of the other two is the second and which is the least important, creating a hierarchy. This list is utilized to make design choices and determine the level of detail each component gains in the design process. Since the priorities determine some of the design choices of the other aspects, phase three needs to occur at this time. However, since setting the priorities largely depends on the Serious Content and the preferences of the Player, it cannot take place sooner.

The fourth phase is the largest one. It is about designing the now prioritized components Setting, Plot and Characters. This phase is repeated multiple times. Due to the varying order of the elements, some of the steps may require information from steps or elements that have not yet been developed. In such instances, the developer will have to make a note and move on with the following steps and return to the missing or incomplete ones during the next iteration, to complete them with the information gained and developed within their successor steps. As mentioned, not only their order is determined by the assessment of the priorities, but their level of detail, as well. That does not necessarily mean that the development team cannot give each element a lot of details. It merely indicates how much detail should be actively presented to the Player in the game and how much detail should be relevant and a part of the overall product (this relationship is explained in the second Section of this Section with an example).

The fifth and final phase deals with presentation. Once all other elements have been determined, the developer has enough knowledge to understand in what capacity which things have to be presented to the Player throughout the CDG interface.

Table I shows that each of these phases contains steps describing the precise actions the developer must take. These steps include a brief descriptive title.

Furthermore, there are three pieces of information that are not included in Table I because of spatial limitations: Required internal information, Required external information and the Instruction. The first two columns describe which information is needed to perform the instructions. This additional content can be found in [22].

It should be noted, that the information provided in this paper is not adequate to use the story Framework. If the Framework is to be used, it is absolutely necessary to download the pdf file from [22] and follow its instructions step by step.

As can be seen in the linked pdf document, the actions that have to be taken in each step depend on the Psychographic Player Type the game wants to serve. Therefore, during the use of the Framework (carry out the Framework step by step) it will be necessary to understand the preferences of the CDG's players. This knowledge is required for many steps and displayed in the Framework in the 'required internal information' area. To provide a handle for the different player characteristics, Nine Psychographic Player Types where defined through conceptual and empirical research (see Sections III or V). These Player Types refer not only to digital CDGs, but also to entertainment video games.

TABLE I. THE PHASES AND STEPS OF THE UFOS FRAMEWORK

Phases	UFoS Steps for CDGs
Phase 1: Defining the Serious Content	Serious Content – Step 1: Determine the intention
	Serious Content – Step 2: Define the Serious Content
Phase 2: Defining the Player	Player – Step 1: Demographic Factors
	Player – Step 2: Define the Psychographic Player Type
Phase 3: Determining Priorities	Priorities – Step 1: Set the Priorities
Phase 4: Performing Setting, Characters and Plot	Setting – Step 1: Requirements
	Setting – Step 2: Realism
	Setting – Step 3: Accessibility
	Setting – Step 4: Debriefing
	Setting – Step 5: Simplicity
	Setting – Step 6: Size
	Setting – Step 7: Laws
	Setting – Step 8: Player Influence
	Characters – Step 1: Existence of NPCs
	Characters – Step 2: Character Focus
	Characters – Step 3: NPC roles
	Characters – Step 4: NPC character Profiles
	Characters – Step 5: NPC backstory
	Characters – Step 6: NPC memories
	Characters – Step 7: NPC affective State and Actions
	Characters – Step 8: NPC relationships
	Characters – Step 9: PC observer
	Characters – Step 10: PC grade of Personality
	Characters – Step 11: PC customization
	Characters – Step 12: PC motivations
	Characters – Step 13: PC player Character Personality
	Characters – Step 14: Relationships
	Plot – Step 1: Linearity
	Plot – Step 2: Outline
	Plot – Step 3: Time Constraints
	Plot – Step 4: Serious and Non-Serious Content
	Plot – Step 5: Exposition
	Plot – Step 6: Tutorial
	Plot – Step 7: Hook
	Plot – Step 8: Obstacles
	Plot – Step 9: Plot Points
	Plot – Step 10: Choice
	Plot – Step 11: Impact of Choice
	Plot – Step 12: Illusion of Freedom
	Plot – Step 13: Climax
	Plot – Step 14: Resolution and endings
Phase 5: Defining Presentation	Presentation – Step 1: Plot
	Presentation – Step 2: Choice

B. *Exemplary use*

To illustrate this process, one can examine a fictional example. This will create a better understanding of the Framework use and underline the connections between different parts of the process. The preferences of the Player Types that will be mentioned here are shown in the UFoS Framework document [22].

The fictional example in this case is a CDG that seeks to teach the employees of various companies IT-Security. The game writer, tasked with developing the story, utilizes UFoS.

In Phase 1, they must describe the Serious Content. The description of the project already does this loosely. The Serious Content is IT-Security. However, the game writer needs to define what parts of IT-security the game will entail and which it will exclude. They examine some standards and risks described by the ISO/IEC 27001 and formulate scenarios that will be depicted by the game. Then they continue with Phase 2.

Phase 2 requires them to define the Player. The Serious Content determines some of the demographic traits. Since its IT-Security in companies, the Players have a broad age range from 18 to around 65, are of all genders, and can be at various stages of life. To establish the Player Types within the audience, the game writer conducts a survey questioning the employees of multiple companies. The results e.g., show that the primary Player Types in the target audience are Narrators, Explorers, Dreamers and Winners.

In Phase 3 the game writer has to establish the priorities between the three large components Setting, Characters and Plot. They decide that the most important component to depict IT-Security is Plot, as this entails showing behavior and consequences. In IT-Security this means showing what type of behavior can lead to security breaches. The preferences of the Narrators, Explorers, Dreamers and Winners underline this decision. The game writer is unsure which to set as second most important component. The Setting can provide themes of environmental security whereas Characters allow dealing with social engineering. Because Explorers prefer Characters over Setting and the other Player Types are indifferent, the writer selects Characters.

Phase 4 deals with the three large components. First, the game writer writes the Plot, as this is the component they prioritized. They write a basic outline for the Plot in which a group of people has to master IT-Security to overcome some large obstacle. They realize that they need to establish the Setting to get into more detail. They match the Plot to the time constraints, decide on a pattern to include Serious Content and write everything, keeping IT-Security and the preferences of the Player Types in mind. Next is the design of the Characters. The game writer decides to include NPCs, as Characters is of the second highest priority and IT-Security can benefit from it. Additionally, all of the found Player Types enjoy them. For social engineering, a part of IT-Security, the game writer places the focus on the NPCs. They then write characters that match the requirements posed by the Serious Content, the Player Types, and the Plot. The Plot, for example, demands that certain people exist to carry out certain actions, which are roles that the game writer has to consider.

Once the Characters are developed, the game writer deals with the Setting. They decide to set the story in a spaceship in the future as this is a topic all people of the target audience understand. Also, it can portray all needed elements of IT-Security (e.g., technology, etc.). After the Setting is developed, they go back and fill in more details in the Plot, such as describing which NPC is used in which situation and what elements of the Setting are employed in which way. Once all Steps are finished, Phase 4 is concluded.

In Phase 5 the game writer decides to present the Plot via Cut-Scenes and Dialogue, as these methods cater to all Player Types in the audience.

The game writer documents all their decisions in one comprehensive document, creating the basic story of their CDG.

V. Derivation of the Framework

The Framework is based on the previously explained components of story. These were derived by examining a list of elements of story and modifying it to be simpler and to meet the requirements of an interactive medium. The initial list of elements consisted of 11 elements found and arranged by Miller, director of the World Storytelling Institute [18]:

1. "Characters (decisions and follow-through)
2. Place
3. Time (continues, or jumps, flashbacks?)
4. Storyline (also known as, plot).
5. Sensory Elements: Smells, Flavours, Colours, Textures, etc.
6. Objects. Such as: Clothing. A costume. A piece of fabric.
7. Characters' physical gestures, and attitudes.
8. Emotions in the story (for the characters, the teller, and the listeners).
9. Narrator's Point of View. (Who is telling the story? [...])
10. Narrator's Tone of Voice, Attitude, Style (casual, formal, other?).
11. Theme (Meaning, moral, message, idea)." [18]

This list was selected as a starting point, as Miller is a very credible source. Additionally, his list entails several steps that were only partially covered in other lists and sources. This list is altered in the following paragraphs, as it only matches stories in general not stories in CDGs, specifically.

Several of these elements can be combined into one, more broadly defined element. The first element, Characters and the seventh element Character's physical gestures, and attitudes, can be merged into one bigger element of Characters with all their traits and behavior. The elements place and time can be combined in one element Setting. This also seems to be important, since the state of a place can only be described under the consideration of time.

Miller understands the Storyline as a sequence of events, that occur within the story [18]. To reduce misunderstanding between storyline and story, the term Plot will be used instead.

Sensory Elements are stimuli which affect the audience [18]. But usually, the development of these kind of elements is task of other departments than the story department [7]. For that reason, they do not occur in the actual story developing process, so that they are omitted for simplifying reasons.

Objects are things that appear in the Plot or the story [18]. They do not add enough to the whole story construct to process them separately.

The following two elements: Narrator's Point of View and Narrator's Tone of Voice et al. will also be summarized under the element Characters. This is because a distinction between two types of Characters can be made: The PC, an entity controlled by the Player, and the NPCs, characters who are controlled by Artificial Intelligence. The elements pertaining to the Narrator are included in the definition of the PC, as their perspective determines the audience's point of view, and their comments, attitude etc. (see [9]) reflect a narrator's tone of voice.

The eleventh and final element is Theme. Theme is described as a combination of the preceding ten, it is the driving force behind the game [18]. In a CDG this driving force has to be the Serious Content of the game and as that it will be maintained.

By shortening the list in that way, it will be easier for the developer to work with and understand the elements. The resulting list looks as follows:

1. Characters
   a. Non-Player Characters
   b. Player Characters
2. The Setting
3. The Plot
4. Serious Content

As shown, these elements cover a whole CDG story. By that, they shape the base of the UFoS Framework as shown in the Sections II and III and represent four of the six Framework components. Beyond these elements, the center of the UFoS Framework consists additionally of the components Player and Presentation. The following Section explains the derivation of this both components.

Miller wrote about Story and Storytelling in general. In addition to his definition, some elements that are not part of traditional storytelling must be considered when dealing with CDGs or video games in general. While each story requires a form of presentation, games are one of the only mediums with as many different possibilities of presenting story as they have.

One of the missing components is the Presentation of a digital game story. There are several ways to do so, the possibilities are hardly limited. This fact is e.g., shown in the 'Preverbal phenomenon'. This phenomenon is based on the consideration that a narrative can be understood without the use of language [11]. By that, every element inside a CDG can contribute to the whole game story construct, but it does not necessarily have to. Of course, it is not possible to cover a huge amount of story presentation methods, but to assist a story developer at work the UFoS Frameworks deals with five common plot presentation methods: Narration [12], Dialogue [13], Cut-Scenes [14], Environmental Storytelling [15] and Collection [16], which were already explained in Section II.

Another aspect of a game story presentation is that game stories are not static. In interactive media, as opposed to books or movies, the audience has the possibility to influence the course of events happening in the game.

To provide interactive content to the player, games offer 'Choices' e.g., in form of several textual options on screen or by putting the player in an open world, allowing them to do whatever they want [6]. Of course, this kind of freedom has to be considered during the story development. A game designer has to be sure that the story is presented in the right sequence and that every path of the game leads to a consistent story. In a dynamic game environment these conditions result in very high requirements on the story presentation. Choices have to be considered during the whole game development to perform well during the story presentation. For the above reasons, as part of Presentation, Choices have been included in the Framework, to ensure the timely integration into the story development process.

The other missing component is the Player. While every medium has an audience, interactive media needs to consider it more strongly as the player has to play to drive the story forward and has to be invested in the gameplay. Because the story aspects of gameplay are presented through the Setting, the Characters and the Plot, the Player should be considered while developing these components. Therefore, these three elements are the most vital as they make up the true content of the story. The Player, represented by the Psychographic Player Types, was integrated into the Framework, too. The derivation of the types is explained in the next Section.

1. Serious Content
2. The Player
3. The Setting
4. Characters
    a. Non-Player Characters
    b. Player Characters
5. The Plot
    a. Choices
6. Presentation

VI. DERIVATION OF THE PSYCHOGRAPHIC PLAYER TYPES

In this Section, it will be explained how the different Psychographic Player Types were created and what taxonomies were examined in order to do so. Understanding what the Player Types are and how their traits were defined aids in understanding Players and their desires as such, since the derivation provides insights into several attempts at categorizing and defining human desires and preferences. Considering the expertise and observations of different people provides a more objectively true and thorough insight into the minds of the audience.

The Player Types were derived from preexisting taxonomies and attempts to group the motivations and desires relating to games. The selected taxonomies are some of the few grouping players by psychographic attributes and all examine this theme from slightly different angles (Types, Pleasures, Motives), without repeating their point of view. 21 categories with their origins in three different taxonomies were examined. Their traits and attributes were analyzed to determine similarities and differences. They were then grouped by those traits to create new, sometimes more broadly defined, Player Types. The comparison of the different categories and resulting Psychographic Player Types can be seen in Table II.

Here, the different taxonomies are depicted in columns. Each cell contains one or more of their categories. The rows show which categories share similarities and were therefore combined, with the resulting Player Type of each comparison being presented in the right-most column.

TABLE II. PLAYER TYPES DERIVATION

Bartle's Taxonomy of Player Types [20]	**LeBlanc's Taxonomy of Game Pleasures [21]**	**The Aesthetic Motives of Play [19]**	**The Psychographic Player Types** (result)
	Narrative	Narrative	**The Narrator**
Achiever, Killer	Challenge	Problem-Solving	**The Challenger**
Socializer	Fellowship	Social	**The Socialite**
Explorer	Discovery	Curiosity	**The Explorer**
	Expression	Agency	**The Expressionist**
	Submission, Fantasy, Sensation		**The Dreamer**
		Thrill-Seeking, Horror	**The Daredevil**
Achiever		Victory	**The Winner**
Achiever, Explorer		Acquisition	**The Collector**

While sometimes different categories from different taxonomies were combined to create a Player Type, occasionally some categories of one taxonomy were fused into one Player Type with a broader definition.

The only category that is absent is the "Luck Motive" of the "Aesthetic Motives of Play" [19]. This is because, on one hand, that motive is describes as a desire for fairness and equal opportunities, which every person has to a degree. On the other hand, Players of a CDG should not rely on luck to achieve victory, as this does not underline the learning and improvement of a skill or competence.

From these Player Types, as well as the Framework components, a need for empirical research arises to ensure that these conceptually derived elements indeed exist as assumed through the literature examination. However, because the player preferences are crucial during the use of the UFoS Framework (represented through Player Types), a study has been designed to link Player Types to Player preferences.

This study was created in form of an online survey. First, the participants were asked to select up to two motivations factors to play video games from a list of nine motivations, corresponding to the Nine Psychographic Player Types. This information was utilized to group the participants into the Player Types. They were then asked several questions related to each Framework component, asking for preferences, likes and dislikes regarding video game stories.

Overall, the study includes 37 questions. The first 8 questions refer to demographic characteristics, like age and gender, but also to general video game subjects as the main reasons to play (Player Type) or whether the participant has ever played to learn. The following 5 questions relate to the Setting, followed by 9 questions about Characters, 8 about the Plot, 4 about Choices plus 2 about Presentation. Finally, there was one question referring to the desired balance between Characters, Plot and Setting.

118 people participated in the survey. Among them, all the Player Types were represented as seen in Figure 2. Each subject was assigned to up to two Player Types.

To validate the preferences and differences in preferences between each Player Type, the data records were grouped by Player Types. These grouped records were used to analyze for each question whether the average-answer of a certain Player Type is 'within the average' of all answers, 'above the average', 'below the average', 'strongly above the average' or 'strongly below the average' of all answers. By that, it was possible to determine whether the Player Types deviate greatly from another or whether they are very similar.

The analysis of the congruence in answers between Player Types determines that the highest congruence in answers in between two different Player Types is at 53.73%. The Player Types in question are the Narrator and the Dreamers. This means that for 53.73% of all answers, these two Player Types answered very similarly. In other words, if a game developer creates a game story to cater to Narrators, he would also be catering to Dreamers about 53.73% of the time. This means that about half of the time the Dreamers would not be as satisfied with the design choices as they could be. This, in return, means that no two Player Types are similar enough to combine them into one. It can be interpreted as a confirmation that considering several types is meaningful.

To ensure that the differences in the Player Types are statistically significant, the answers to every item grouped by the Player Types were replaced by numbers from 1 (strongly below the average) to 5 (strongly above the average). This creates a scale from 1 to 5 for every answer, representing how much each Player Type agrees with the average answer. An ANOVA calculated with these data shows with $\alpha = .05$ a p-value $< .0002$ with $F_{(8;252)} = 3.963$ and a critical F-Value = 1.975. By that the H_0 hypotheses "there are no differences in between the Player Types" with a level of significance of $\alpha = .05$ is to be rejected. Table III shows in how many cases the questions between two Player Types are "very similar" and, by that, in reverse the differences between the Player Types.

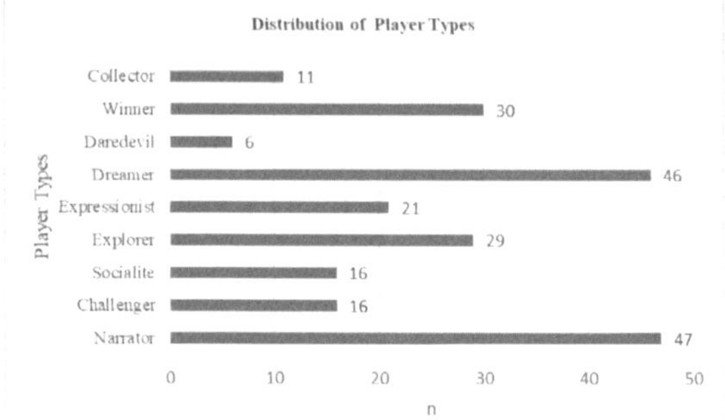

Figure 2. Player Type distribution

TABLE III. NUMBER OF 'VERY SIMILAR' ANSWERS IN BETWEEN PLAYER TYPES

	Na	Ch	So	E	Ex	Dr	Da	Wi	Co
Na									
Ch	**43%**								
So	31%	40%							
E	**53%**	40%	35%						
Ex	**43%**	**44%**	40%	**43%**					
Dr	**54%**	**50%**	**43%**	**52%**	**45%**				
Da	37%	30%	25%	32%	37%	29%			
Wi	40%	**44%**	34%	**43%**	38%	**45%**	28%		
Co	28%	26%	28%	32%	32%	32%	29%	33%	

Values >40% are bold printed

Therefore, many of the steps shown in Table I contain a note explaining what to do when dealing with which Player Type, allowing for the designer to optimize the story for the Player Types they uncovered in their audience. These notes are accessible as 'instructions' in [22]. These instructions are developed from the literature and only integrated into the Framework, if they were validated by the study. Therefore, the integrated concept between the UFoS Framework and the Psychographic Player Types provides a designer with the possibility to develop an audience optimized and entertaining CDG-Story. The entire concept has to be carried out iteratively. This ensures that the player preferences characterized by the Player Types are incorporated into all areas of the story and are noticed in all story developing phases. In this way (as shown in Section IV) the components Characters, Setting and Plot are influencing each other depending on the targeted Player Type.

However, a detailed review of the 37 questions, grouped according to the Player Types, in this paper is not meaningful in terms of the scope of this publication. It is planned to publish a detailed review in another publication with a different focus.

VII. CONCLUSION

A Framework that has the power to create an entire motivating CDG's story is explained in this paper. The Framework supports CDG story designers to ask themselves the necessary questions in the right moment and to take solidly based decisions in the right order. During that process, game story designers are encouraged to define their target audience. Therefore, due to the use of the UFoS Framework, it can be ensured that a story was created in which everything is included, and the right priorities were set. By that, the possibility to use CDGs for research topics is enhanced because the influence of the CDG's story on the research will be decreased.

The paper illustrated the Framework dependencies by utilizing a fictional example, establishing that it's possible to use the Framework in the field and underlining the connections in between the components. In addition to providing a simple use of the Framework, Nine Psychographic Player Types were described. Furthermore, it was explained how to use the Framework and where to get additional information and detailed procedures to do so.

Subsequently, the derivation of the UFoS Framework and the Nine Psychographic Player Types was described. For that reason, an empirical study was presented that validates the existence of the Player Types and the different characteristics. A story designer has to integrate these characteristics, depending on the Player Types and the current Framework phase or step.

However, it is required to further test and specify the Player Types and the UFoS Framework.

Currently, it is only statistically significantly proven that there are at least the nine identified Player Types; it could be possible that there are more yet unknown. Because the current nine Types were discovered during a literature analysis, an explorative empirical study will be useful to identify more types, if there are any. In addition, possible connections between the Player Types and demographic traits should be sought to more easily group a potential audience into the Player Types. Yet, the only method is close observation of the audience and asking them to evaluate their own motivations to play as has been done in the survey.

Although the Framework was carefully derived from the literature, it is only proven by concept, excluded from the step-instructions. Therefore, the next step will be a use of the Framework during a CDG development process to prove the concept as whole in a real development situation.

Furthermore, the UFoS Framework has been developed to get used by game story designers. So far it is not possible for laymen to develop a CDG story with the Framework. Enabling this could be the focus of future developments. It would require a deep understanding of every detail and aspect of a CDG story, but it would allow many scientists to perform CDG-based experiments even in small or low budget research groups.

In summary, the User-Focused Storybuilding Framework for Competence Developing Games provides a powerful tool to develop CDG stories.

REFERENCES

[1] D. Michael and S. Chen, "Serious Games That Educate, Train, and Inform," Thomson Course Technology PTR, 2006.

[2] J. A. König and M. R. Wolf, "A New Definition of Competence Developing Games," ACHI 2016, pp. 95-97, 2016.

[3] M. Zyda, "From visual simulation to virtual reality to games," IEEE Computer Society (Computer), Volume:38, Issue: 9, 2005, P. 25-32.

[4] U. Ritterfeld, *Serious Games: Only Quality is Fun* (Original foreign title: *Serious Games: Nur Qualität macht Spaß),* [Online]. Available at: http://www.checkpoint-elearning.de/article/5425.html [retrieved: January, 2018]

[5] J. A. König and M. R. Wolf, "The Pyramid Assessment Framework for 'Competence Developing Games'," HCI International, pp. 232-237, 2016.

[6] J. Schell, "The Art of Game Design: a Book of Lenses," Burlington: Morgan Kaufmann, 2008.

[7] S. Rogers, "Level up the Guide to great Video Game Design," Chichester: John Wiley & Sons, 2010.

[8] S. Field, "Screenplay: The Foundations of Screenwriting," Delta, Revised ed., 2005.

[9] A. M. Freed, *Alexander Free.* [Online]. Available from: http://www.alexanderfreed.com/2014/01/13/craft-sessions-character-viewpoint-and-audience-sympathy/ [retrieved: January, 2018]

[10] Anon, *Dictionary,* [Online]. Available from: http://www.dictionary.com/browse/setting [retrieved: January, 2018]

[11] R. Nakatsu, M. Rauterberg, and P. Ciancarini, "Handbook of digital Games and Entertainment Technologies," Signapore: SpringerReference, 2017.

[12] P. Hühn and R. Sommer, *The living handbook of narratology.* [Online]. http://www.lhn.uni-hamburg.de/article/narration-poetry-and-drama/ [retrieved: January, 2018]

[13] S. King, "On Writing," Charles Scriber's Sons, 2000.

[14] T. C. Caputo, "Visual Storytelling: The Art and Technique," Watson-Guptill Publications, 2003.

[15] M. Aaron, "Design, User Experience, and Usability. User Experience Design for diverse Interaction Platforms and Environments," Springer, 2014.

[16] A. Pitzer, *Harvey Smith on environmental Storytelling and embedding Narrative.* [Online] Available from: http://niemanstoryboard.org/stories/harvey-smith-onenvironmental-storytelling-and-embedding-narrative/ [retrieved: January, 2018]

[17] J. Wöbbeking, *4Players.* [Online] Available from: http://www.4players.de/4players.php/dispbericht/Allgemein/Test/30907/816 87/0/Gone_Home.html [retrieved: January, 2018]

[18] E. Miller, *Theories of Story and Storytelling.* [Online]. Available from: http://www.storytellingandvideoconferencing.com/ [retrieved: January, 2018]

[19] K. Karpouzis and G. N. Yannakakis, "Emotion in Games," Switzerland: Springer, 2016.

[20] R. A. Bartle, *MUD.* [Online]. Available from: http://mud.co.uk/richard/hcds.htm#1 [retrieved: January, 2018]

[21] R. Hunicke, M. LeBlanc, and R. Zubeck, "MDA: A Formal Approach to Game Design and Game Research," Workshop on Challenges in Game AI, AAAI, 2004, pp.1-4 doi: http://dx.doi.ord/10.1.1.79.4561.

[22] Lab for IT-Organization and Management, "Gamified Hacking Offence Simulation-based Training", [Online]. Available from: http://www.itom.fh-aachen.de/pdf/UFoS-Framework.pdf Last access: 12.03.2018, 2018.

[23] Unity Technologies, "Unity", [Online]. Available from: https://unity3d.com/ Last access: 12.03.2018, 2018.

[24] Epic Games, Inc. "Make Something Unreal", [Online] Available from: https://www.unrealengine.com/en-US/what-is-unreal-engine-4 Last access: 12.03.2018, 2018.

TeamAR – Generic Interface for Cooperation Using Augmented Reality

Dawid Pacholczyk
Department of Software Engineering
Polish-Japanese Academy of IT
Warsaw, Poland
dpacholczyk@pjwstk.edu.pl

Mariusz Trzaska
Department of Software Engineering
Polish-Japanese Academy of IT
Warsaw, Poland
mtrzaska@pjatk.edu.pl

Abstract—**Thanks to technology, the world is getting smaller and smaller every day. We are moving towards the model in which we do not have to be in the same place where our employer is located. Remote, scattered teams are something that we encounter every day. In our research, we explore methods and strategies that will allow to increase the efficiency of teamwork using augmented reality. We are looking for a way to bring a low-cost software platform that will allow to create augmented reality sessions and bring 3D objects into the world of each person. These objects should be shared but should also be independent on some level for every participant. Such platform can help with the problem of availability of augmented reality for a wider audience. This paper provides an overview of research done in this field and our thoughts related to the topic and description of a working prototype.**

Keywords-Augmented reality; Collaborative augmented reality; Cooperation.

I. INTRODUCTION

Augmented Reality (AR) allows users to see the real world together with some generated, virtual objects. Using this technology, we are capable to present not only simple 2D overlays, but also complex 3D structures and animations. There is an old saying: "A picture is worth a thousand words". If we can present complex structures and animation as a part of our world, why not use them to improve our communication and teamwork?

In our research, we are looking for ways to improve remote cooperation and resolve the problem of low availability of AR. Our goal is to create a generic platform that will allow to start a quick AR session without any programming or need for special equipment. This project is intended for companies, their teams and average users.

In our opinion, it is much easier to just present a complex object and experience it through some interactions rather than trying to explain it. For each participant, we want to provide their own perspective in addition to the shared state of the scene. During the presentation, each person can reach his/her own goal without disturbing the rest of the team. We want to maximize the efficiency of the team and minimize the technology adoption cost.

Such platform can have a positive influence on elements such as: lowering the cost of creating complex mockups, or new kind of low cost user experience tests. In the design sector, it helps with easier presentation as well as keeping low costs. Positive influences of the platform are also envisioned for the education and entertainment sectors.

The rest of the paper is structured as follows. Section 2 covers the background. We describe how ideas related with cooperation using AR evolved in time. In Section 3, we describe the concept that stands behind *TeamAR*, what are the goals that we want to achieve. Section 4 describes the implementation details and architecture that was developed for *TeamAR* prototype. As this is the first prototype of our platform, in Section 5 we describe the future work that stands in front of us. Section 6 is the conclusion, the summary of what we already achieved and what possibilities are created thanks to our system.

II. BACKGROUND

Augmented reality is a very broad field for research. Over the past few years, several studies explored the usage of augmented reality in our everyday actions, starting from simple usage like games [16][17], entertainment [8], productivity [29][30], through more complex tasks like data visualization [33], repairing [31] to logistic support [32].

Our system was inspired by several previous research projects in augmented reality and possibilities to use them for collaboration and teamwork.

Shared space [1] presented how AR can become a powerful tool in face-to-face meetings. It was one of the first significant steps in this field. Shared space allows a group of people to work in one room on common 3D objects. Users must be equipped with a HMD (Head Mounted Display). The workflow, and objects attached to a 2D marker are predefined. Each user sees the same object as every other in the room, they can share, and move the markers in the same way as they would do with normal elements of the environment. Shared space showed how much AR can help us to enrich our communication, and methods of work.

Our project took the lead in finding the solution for removing one of the biggest obstacles, which is lack of flexibility, and strong need of highly qualified staff. We also want to provide a possibility to work remotely if needed.

Project *Studierstube* [14] increased mobility of the AR systems. Authors built a mobile workstation, combined with optical see-through HMD. Thanks to that, multiple users can cooperate with each other, working on the same 3D objects with shared state. Each user has its own version of the object, set in an individual coordinate system. Thanks to that, one user will not affect the visible state of the second user.

Although this project was built using a laptop, modern mobile hardware is powerful enough to reduce the weight and size of AR devices. From this work, we can specify five key advantages, and elements that need to be met in similar platforms. Those elements are: virtuality, augmentation, cooperation, independence, and individuality.

Cooperative AR is not only helping in communication itself, it can be much more than that. For example, *Transvision* [12] is focused on supporting designing tasks. It is based on computer generated images displayed on palmtop (video see-through strategy). The augmentation helps designers as it combines two important elements: the possibility of an easy and cheap design change and physical contact between participants.

Similar task was taken by the team of the *ARVita* [13] project. It shows how AR can help engineers in their everyday work, by adding new powerful tools which they can use. Our work methods evolved from simple notes, and plans, through photos, up to 3D/4D Computer Aided Design (CAD) models. *ARVita* is trying to go one step further, namely, it adds a 3D animation to the physical world to give us a better perspective on the work that needs to be done. This idea allows to prepare complicated simulations and to watch them in full 3D from different perspectives.

Many researchers are aware of the benefits, and possibilities which AR can deliver in terms of cooperation whether face to face or remote. Augmented reality can even improve our chances to save lives in the face of crisis. In [3], there is an example how AR can be used to coordinate work of different organizations, and how it can help to make the best decision based on very dynamic circumstances. Despite the fact that the described scenario is not very flexible, and it is hard to reproduce in a short period of time, the results of this research are very promising. It is worth noting that such a system can be enriched with remote collaboration. We believe that decreasing the access time to specialists can help people particularly in crisis situations. Unfortunately, this solution is faces similar problems to those previously mentioned: lack of flexibility, time consuming tasks needed for preparation of the scenario, complicated hardware. In our project we are trying to remove those complications.

The natural path of the evolution of collaboration using AR is to allow a remote user to access the same state of the object. We can see such first attempts in [2], where the authors implement a simple Tetris game that allows more than one user. This research makes us aware how hard it is to achieve such goal. It reveals key problems such as sharing the object state, anchoring it in a fixed place, and performing some interaction. Those tasks, as a single case are quite easy to resolve, the true challenge is to combine everything into one platform. Similar to other research, this one uses markers for setting objects in the scene and uses the same technique to support the interaction.

MARS [11] presents a path which shows how we can work in teams on separate tasks to achieve a common goal. This project allows to send extra information from people in the office (indoor) to a person in the field (outdoor). Everything is displayed on HMD (see-through). Such a concept provides multiple possibilities from engineer support during assembly tasks, providing help for the soldiers on the battlefield. Similar approach, but from a different perspective, was presented in the project called *God-like interaction* [27]. It also focused on putting users in two groups:

- Indoor users that have access to a tabletop projector display system,
- Outdoor users with Tinmith mobile augmented reality system [28].

In the case of these studies, it is interesting that we can put different real objects in the perspective of the outdoor user, by capturing them in a series of photos focused on the table surface. Those objects are sent to the outdoor user and reconstructed on his/her display. Such an approach allows us to put virtual signposts, alerts, extra information, etc. We can also inform about important places to visit or areas that should be avoided.

Both *MARS* and God-like interaction draw attention to the fact that such systems have enormous potential to help during different crisis situations. We can treat indoor users as crisis staff (see also [3]), and the outdoor users as the rescue brigade. Thanks to augmented reality we are able to send to the people in the field much more information than only voice messages. We can mark where they should go, where they can find something important, etc.

All presented research projects have one thing in common, namely interaction. Regardless of what kind of project we are building, what hardware we will use, we always need a way to interact with objects that augment our reality. This is the very basic concept of AR. Nowadays, we have access to multiple tools which allow us to work in teams irrespective of location (Google Docs [22], Office 365 [23], etc.). We need to remember that working on different computers, even in the same place and on simple tasks, can create problems. Lack of the same perspective, and a common view, limits ways of our communication, e.g., we have no option for using simple gestures or pointing at objects.

Another thing common to the presented projects, is a method of setting virtual elements in the real world. To make AR as much natural as possible, we need to achieve full transparency. Objects should behave in a predictable way, with a fixed position "glued" to the part of the scene. In many of presented papers, simple 2D markers were used to handle this as a well-known strategy. One of the disadvantages of this pairing the marker with an object preparing it, before we can start the work. In [15], we can see an attempt to do it in a more generic way. A shared vision system is a platform that allows to use dynamic markers made from the first frame from camera view and track it to display a 3D model on it. The whole thing is shared between thanks to a database in the cloud.

We cannot forget about the latest products of Apple, and Google: ARKit [36], and ARCore [37]. Using standard smartphones, we are able to prepare a simple map of planes in our environment, remember it, and place objects on them. Augmentation is very natural, and the results give a new hope in terms of popularization of AR. This solution provides the full virtualization of our perspective, virtual objects are placed on a virtual plane, we can interact with them physically.

Last but not least, let us remember that one of the best reference is how the market accepts a technology. It is hard to push such a complicated technology to people that are not related to science or any research. That is why a simple mobile game is the best scenario. Online, multiplayer game is a fantastic example of a remote collaboration between users in different locations. For example, Ingress [16], or Pokemon GO [17]. Both games are based on a simple concept, but putting them all together in a single application, available for over 2 billion devices [18], give us easy to use augmented reality solution for everyone. Both games convert the real world into a playground for every player. Their foundation is a collaboration between multiple users in the real time. They interact with each other physically, and they can interact with the same virtual objects on map. Massive popularity of those games shows how big impact augmented reality can have on our lives. Those simple games are a small proof of the fact that people can and want to collaborate using new technologies, and that using proper approach to the scenario can give a fantastic result.

III. TEAMAR - CONCEPT

In this section, we will describe concept of our system *TeamAR*. We will describe the ideas, goals, and things that we want to achieve regardless to the current state.

A. Concept

In this section we will describe concept of our system *TAR* (Team Augmented Reality). We will describe the ideas, goals, and things that we want to achieve regardless to the current state.

Our project is focused on achieving the following goals:

- First, and most important. *TeamAR* is a project that must be usable in real life scenarios. We are focused on preparing usable prototype that can be easily implemented in every company, and different environments, that can get value from it. Every decision made must be compatible with this requirement.
- The system must be easy to use, and flexible. It must allow multiple users to work on a shared task.
- No extra programming needed. User only configures a session with selected markers, and objects. All participants join the defined session using its identifier. The whole process is supported by our platform.
- No extra hardware, except a smartphone, is needed. Using a head-mounted display (HMD) or special sticks with marker for manipulating is unnatural, and may cause problems with configuration, or may act as a deterrent for new users. We also want to avoid additional devices, because currently available ones are expensive, uncomfortable, and hard to get. That is why our goal was to create a platform that will use smartphones nly.
- Ready "on-fly". *TeamAR* must be easy to use and easy to manage. That means that application must be able to learn new patterns and objects during the runtime. No recompilation and even no restart of application should be necessary.
- The whole system must be mobile. We do not want the user to be limited to just one place and surrounded by cables.

B. Platform

TeamAR is based on the SaaS model. We built a web application for managing session and user synchronization. We used a standard smartphone with Android OS for working with the sessions (augmentation). Thanks to that, we could solve four major problems:

1) User perspective

- **Access to hardware** – nowadays, almost everybody has a smartphone. We want to make our project as flexible, and easy to access, as possible.
- **Interaction layer** – as we showed in the previous parts, there is no common, easy for user, and a hardware-free way to interact with the generated objects. Thanks to a screen of a smartphone, we get such a layer without any extra devices. Besides that, this platform is already well-known to users, so there are hardly any barriers to entry.
- **Progress** – software (Android), and hardware (smartphone) platforms will evolve in a natural way. Thanks to that we will obtain new capabilities without cost increases.

2) Software perspective

Easy management – thanks to choosing a SaaS platform, we have a platform that allows to create and edit sessions, as well manage them. The platform is scalable, accessible, efficient, and reliable

C. Augmentation

TeamAR uses smartphones, built-in cameras, and sensors. The output is seen on the screen (video see-through strategy) after augmentation with virtual objects. To pin an object in space we use 2D markers. When the user looks at the card with a pattern, computer vision recognizes it, links with the 3D object from the session, and displays it on the card. The details of the current state of the implementation are described further in the paper along with more technical details of future development. We selected the 2D markers approach, because they are easy to use. They can be sent as a link, and displayed on the screen, or just printed. Every team can have their own set of markers, and just connect them with different objects in a new session or even update the reference in the current session.

D. Collaboration

TeamAR will allow user to refer to every physical element that he/she would normally use in a normal face-to-face meeting, like personal notes. Thanks to AR, he/she will also be able to refer to objects that normally would be impossible to use. This project will combine most important elements from the two worlds: virtual, and physical.

Furthermore, our project will allow teams to work remotely or stationary in the same room. No extra configuration will be needed. Thanks to the same objects base, and state sharing, they will see the same things independently from the location of each user.

E. Interaction

As we already mentioned, we decided to use a popular software, and hardware platform. It provides a well know, widely used interaction layer: the screen. The combination of mobility, good user experience, and an easy to use device provides a flexible tool to work with. The application will allow interaction with all virtual objects. This information can be synchronized between all participants of the session. As you can see the interaction is very similar to pointing at an element during a normal face to face meeting. This approach makes possible to avoid dedicated programming for every scenario.

IV. Implementation

In this section we want to describe our current state of the development.

As mentioned in the previous part of this paper, *TeamAR* is based on two main parts:

- Web application - responsible for creating/updating the session, sharing, and synchronizing the state of each object.
- Mobile application - marker recognition, displaying objects, and interaction. Speaking briefly, it is used for augmentation.

We prepared a tool (web application) that allows to create a session (Figure 1). Even a user without any technical skills can prepare a configuration of the meeting that will use AR technology. Users can upload a set of 3D objects and connect each of them with a specific 2D marker. Such configuration will be propagated to every user in the session.

Every person who possesses the identifier of the session can connect from the level of a mobile application and participate in the meetings. Thanks to our approach it is not important if that person is in the same room or in the other parts of the world. Everything he/she needs is a stable internet connection (mobile connection is enough) and 2D markers related with the session printed or displayed on a screen. Application learns new patterns during the runtime and displays the 3D objects on proper markers basing on the configuration that it received.

We decided to use 2D markers over the current solutions like ARKit [36] or ARCore [37], due to the fact that it is more natural. Secondly, ARKit and ARCore are available on a small number of costly smartphones, and, as we want to create as available as possible platform, it is very a important factor that we had to take into account. Both mentioned solutions are very interesting and have big potential, but they create more virtual environment. Virtual objects are mapped and placed on virtual planes. These methods limit ways of interaction between participants of meetings, and even between specific persons, and virtual objects, for example a person cannot lift the marker as he would lift a physical object to have a better look at it.

We used *Firebase Cloud Messaging* as part of our infrastructure for easy and real-time synchronization of actions performed on the objects. If the host changes color of the selected object, or if he/she marks an object it will be instantly synchronized to all devices that are currently in the session. Each participant will see the action in the same way as he/she would see when someone points at a physical object in the room.

A. Communication

We use a cloud service to implement fast, real-time, and reliable communication layer between the web application, and the mobile device. As a cloud service, we selected *Firebase Cloud Messaging (FCM)* [34]. The main reason for this selection is that, we plan to support other mobile platforms, and FCM is a cross-platform solution. The whole architecture and communication pattern is visualized on Fig. 2.

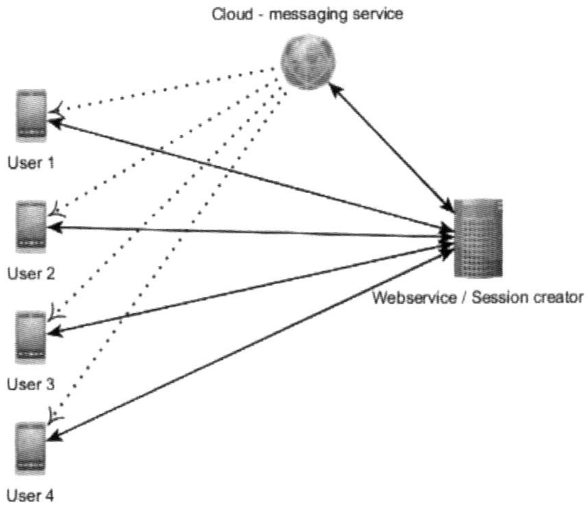

Figure 1. Presentation of infrastructure scheme

The web application is divided into two parts. The first one, contains a user interface. It is used to manage the sessions. It will be deployed, and available for users as service.

The second one is a REST API used for communication between mobile application and the database, and/or cloud. Thanks to the modular architecture, our system is easy to maintain, develop, and upgrade in the future. We also achieved a situation in which we are not tied up to a specific technology. As we have mentioned before, we are working on creating a proper concept of team collaboration with the use of augmented reality, not on specific technology. With better tools, better technology, we can replace single modules of our system, keeping all functionalities intact. We believe that minimizing dependency on current solutions, and technological trends is the key to our goal.

B. Data exchange

One of the most important decisions that we had to make, was selecting proper types of data used by the system for session configuration, both for the marker, and the 3D object. Selected type for each of these elements had to meet the specific requirement: a popular format already available on the market. To make the whole platform easy to implement in a company/team, we need to avoid situations when the selected data format is not known or hard to process; easy to use by a common user. Integrating users with the session should be as easy as possible to lower the entry barrier.

Because of the above requirements, we have focused on types that can be transformed and saved as a text file.

For the 3D object format, we selected Wavefront .obj file [35]. It is easy to use, easily accessible, it allows to create simple objects without any experience on the user side. Wavefront file is a text file that can be uploaded to our application and stored in the database. Reading this format is fast, and Android platform delivers native tools to work with it.

Another important fact is that such 3D models can be uploaded to software like Unity3D and used in different types of application. This corresponds perfectly with our main assumption about using *TeamAR* in a real-life scenario. Such objects can be prototyped, shared, and discussed before performing other time-consuming actions.

Furthermore, this format is very universal and easy to send. All this combined creates a perfect selection for our platform. As it is text data we can in easily update mobile application with the information about new objects. The format is light, therefor we do not need a high-quality internet connection, all calculations are performed on the device locally basing on the provided data. Wavefront format is universal, so when we will migrate out application to other operating systems, we will already have proper tools.

C. Augmentation

Our augmentation is based on video-see through HMD concept. In this case we deliberately ignored the HMD for the reasons mentioned earlier in the text. The application generates 3D objects based on the definition of the model received from the API. Actions performed on each object are shared, every change to the object is synchronized between users in session but the perspective is individual. Each user can independently observe the object without making any impact on the perspective of any other user.

Each object is located only on one 2D marker. The marker can be printed and put on the table or displayed on the screen (Figure 2). This ensures flexibility. Beside that a new object can be connected to the same marker and overwrite previous settings. Thanks to that, there is no need to prepare a big number of markers, users can easily update current state of the session and work comfortably having just a few or even one marker.

D. Interaction

In the early stage of the project we decided to implement a simplified model of interaction based on a toolbox. Thanks to that, during our tests new users had quick overview of actions that can be performed. This also made the whole interface very natural. There is a possibility that this will be a standard form of interaction for *TeamAR*. The decision will be based on collected feedback.

Currently, our toolbox allows to perform simple actions: highlighting selected objects. It is especially important when the host wants to focus the audience`s attention on a specific object in the session with many different structures. The user can also perform color changing action, which allows to make a fast grouping of objects basing on a selected color. The user is able to change the color of each object that is available in the session. This feature was implemented to simplify discussion about multiple structures.

Of course, the state of all objects can be reset to the default one using the reset action.

The whole "action framework" is easy to extend and we will experiment with more types of actions which will increase capabilities of *TAR*.

V. FUTURE WORK

Our future work will be focused on extending the functionalities of the prototype and delivering it to users.

We plan to create interaction based on touching particular fragments of the object and confront it with the current solution. Although we do not limit ourselves only to one technology, as we are working more on the concept, and the philosophy of making Augmented Reality more accessible rather than on specific software type.

In the current version, the interaction is limited to basic operation like highlighting and changing the color of a specific object. Of course, the whole solution works "out of the box". No extra programming from the user is needed.

We will use the history of performed actions to allow disconnected, and/or new users to start the session with the same state of the object as each of the users.

After that we plan to perform some usability tests comparing the performance of standard cooperation versus AR collaboration.

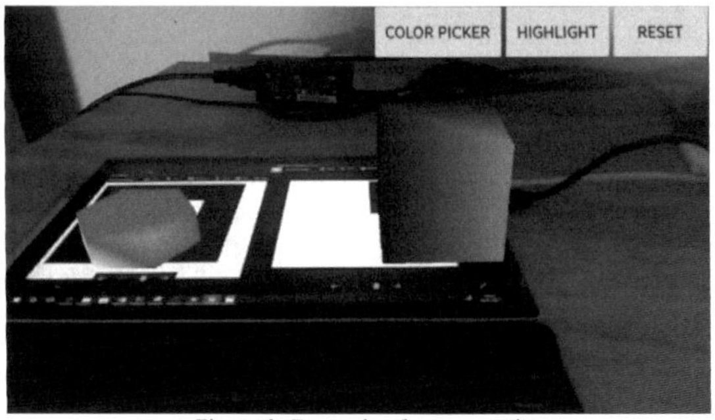

Figure 2. Example of augmentation

VI. CONCLUSION

Collaboration with the use of augmented reality is a very important area of technology. In our opinion, this is the direction that should be chosen to improve of remote work/teams in many professions. Various scenarios force different approaches, but our goal is to create a platform which will give the most possibilities.

It is obvious that hardware will change in time, also the approach may be a bit different because of the evolution of the technology, but the concept in most cases will remain unchanged. Similar situation can be observed in many researches quoted in this paper. Even some of our solutions were inspired by research made almost 20 years ago. Of course, nowadays they can be greatly enhanced with modern technologies and more powerful hardware.

This paper has two main contributions. The first one is to present the current state of the AR solutions for teams. We try to identify weaknesses and strengths.

The second one is related with the following question: why should anybody want to build such a system? We believe that our prototype answers that question. Most of the systems that we have presented in the *Background* section is complicated, hardware dependent, connected with preprogramming concrete scenario of usage, created only for a specific purpose. We fully understand that *TeamAR* will not cover every possible scenario, but it hopefully provides a set of general purpose tools. It can help popularize augmented reality thanks to lowering the entry threshold.

We hope that vision of such interesting and fascinating area of research like collaboration in AR, will encourage other teams and researchers to search new fantastic ways of interaction between people. We are sure that such systems will shape our future.

REFERENCES

[1] M. Billinghurst, I. Poupyrev, H. Kato, and R. May, "Mixing realities in Shared Space: an augmented reality interface for collaborative computing," 2000, vol. 3, pp. 1641–1644.

[2] R. Wichert, "Collaborative Gaming in a Mobile Augmented Reality Environment." ResearchGate. Accessed May 12, 2017.

[3] S. Nilsson, B. J. E. Johansson, and A. Jönsson, "A Co-Located Collaborative Augmented Reality Application," In Proceedings of the 8th International Conference on Virtual Reality Continuum and Its Applications in Industry. New York, NY, USA: ACM, pp. 179-184, 2009.

[4] "Proceedings of the IASTED International Conference, Computer Graphics and Imaging", IASTED/ACTA Press, pp. 249-252, 1998

[5] H. Regenbrecht *et al.*, "Using Augmented Virtuality for Remote Collaboration," *Presence: Teleoperators and Virtual Environments*, vol. 13, no. 3, pp. 338–354, Jun. 2004.

[6] D. Schmalstieg and G. Hesina, "Distributed Applications for Collaborative Augmented Reality," IEEE Comput. Soc, pp. 59–66, 2002.

[7] W. Matcha and D. R. A. Rambli, "Exploratory Study on Collaborative Interaction through the Use of Augmented Reality in Science Learning," *Procedia Computer Science*, vol. 25, pp. 144–153, 2013.

[8] J. Gimeno, R. Olanda, B. Martinez, and F. M. Sanchez, "Multiuser Augmented Reality System for Indoor Exhibitions," in *Human-Computer Interaction – INTERACT 2011*, vol. 6949, P. Campos, N. Graham, J. Jorge, N. Nunes, P. Palanque, and M. Winckler, Eds. Berlin, Heidelberg: Springer Berlin Heidelberg, pp. 576–579, 2011.

[9] M. Diaz, M. Alencastre-Miranda, L. Munoz-Gomez, and I. Rudomin, "Multi-User Networked Interactive Augmented Reality Card Game," IEEE, pp. 177–82, 2006.

[10] S. Kasahara, V. Heun, A. S. Lee, and H. Ishii. "Second Surface: Multi-User Spatial Collaboration System Based on Augmented Reality," ACM Press, pp. 1–4, 2012.

[11] T. Höllerer, S. Feiner, T. Terauchi, G. Rashid, and D. Hallaway, "Exploring MARS: Developing Indoor and Outdoor User Interfaces to a Mobile Augmented Reality System," Computers & Graphics 23, no. 6, pp. 779–785, December 1999.

[12] J. Rekimoto, "Transvision: A hand-held augmented reality system for collaborative design," Jan-1996. [Online]. Available: https://www.researchgate.net/publication/228929153_Transvision_A_hand-held_augmented_reality_system_for_collaborative_design. [Accessed: 23-May-2017].

[13] S. Dong and V. R. Kamat, "Collaborative Visualization of Simulated Processes Using Tabletop Fiducial Augmented Reality," IEEE, pp. 828–37, 2011.

[14] G. Reitmayr and D. Schmalstieg, "Mobile Collaborative Augmented Reality," IEEE Comput. Soc, pp. 114–23, 2001.

[15] S. Khana, Z. Rehman, F. Virani, and M. Vadnagarwala, "Shared Vision System." Procedia Computer Science 79, pp. 525–532, 2016.

[16] https://www.ingress.com/ [retrieved: 11, 2017]

[17] http://www.pokemongo.com/en-us/ [retrieved: 10, 2017]

[18] http://www.androidcentral.com/there-are-over-2-billion-active-android-devices-today [retrieved: 11, 2017]

[19] Proceedings of the First International Symposium on Mixed Reality (ISMR '99). Mixed Reality – Merging Real and Virtual Worlds, pp. 261-284. Berlin: Springer Verlag.

[20] L. Alem and Jane Li, "A Study of Gestures in a Video-Mediated Collaborative Assembly Task," Advances in Human-Computer Interaction, pp. 1–7. 2011.

[21] https://www.microsoft.com/en-us/hololens [retrieved: 11, 2017]

[22] https://en.wikipedia.org/wiki/Google_Docs,_Sheets_and_Slides. [retrieved: 9, 2017]

[23] https://products.office.com/en-US/what-is-office-365 [retrieved: 9, 2017]

[24] Fussell, R. Susan, L. D. Setlock, E. M. Parker, and J. Yang, "Assessing the Value of a Cursor Pointing Device for Remote Collaboration on Physical Task," ACM Press, 2003.

[25] W. Piekarski and B. H. Thomas, "An object-oriented software architecture for 3D mixed reality applications," pp. 247–256, 2003.

[26] D. Kirk and D. S. Fraser, "Comparing Remote Gesture Technologies for Supporting Collaborative Physical Tasks," ACM Press, 2006.

[27] D. Kirk and D. Stanton Fraser, "Comparing remote gesture technologies for supporting collaborative physical tasks," p. 1191, 2006.

[28] D. Kirk and D. S. Fraser, "The Effects of Remote Gesturing on Distance Instruction," 301–10. Association for Computational Linguistics, 2005.

[29] A. Stafford, W. Piekarski, and B. Thomas, "Implementation of god-like interaction techniques for supporting collaboration

between outdoor AR and indoor tabletop users," pp. 165–172, 2006.
[30] W. Piekarski and B.H. Thomas, „An Object-Oriented Software Architecture for 3D Mixed Reality Applications," IEEE Comput. Soc., pp. 247-256, 2003.
[31] http://www.gereports.com/game-augmented-reality-helping-factory-workers-become-productive/
[32] https://www.youtube.com/watch?v=4ue4Gw1A67c [retrieved: 11, 2017]
[33] http://www.dailymail.co.uk/sciencetech/article-2543395/The-end-mechanic-Smart-glasses-make-possible-fix-car-engine-just-looking-it.html [retrieved: 11, 2017]
[34] A. Cirulis and E. Ginters, "Augmented Reality in Logistics," Procedia Computer Science 26, pp. 14–20, 2013.
[35] C. Parker and M. Tomitsch, "Data Visualisation Trends in Mobile Augmented Reality Applications," ACM Press, pp. 228–31, 2014.
[36] https://firebase.google.com/docs/cloud-messaging/ [retrieved: 8, 2017]
[37] https://en.wikipedia.org/wiki/Wavefront_.obj_file [retrieved: 8, 2017]
[38] https://developer.apple.com/arkit/ [retrieved: 11, 2017]
[39] https://developers.google.com/ar/ [retrieved: 11, 2017]

Real-Time Recognition of Human Postures for Human-Robot Interaction

Zuhair Zafar, Rahul Venugopal*, Karsten Berns

Robotics Research Lab
Department of Computer Science
Technical University of Kaiserslautern
Kaiserslautern, Germany
Email: {zafar,berns}@cs.uni-kl.de, venugo@rhrk.uni-kl.de*

***Abstract*—To function in a complex and unpredictable physical and social environment, robots have to apply their intellectual resources to understand the scene in an efficient and intelligent way, similar to humans. Especially when interacting with humans, this cognitive task becomes more challenging. The work in this paper is focused on recognizing human actions and postures during daily life routines in real-time to understand human motives and emotions during a dialogue scenario. Using depth data, a real-time approach has been proposed that uses human skeleton joint angles to recognize 19 different human postures (standing and sitting). Feature vectors are constructed after pre-processing of joint angles. A supervised learning mechanism has been used to train the classifier using Support Vector Machine. Approximately 30000 training samples have been created for training purpose. The system recognizes all the postures accurately provided the skeleton tracker is working precisely when tested on the database. During live testing, the system reports 98.2% recognition rate, proving the potential of the proposed approach.**

Keywords–Human-robot interaction; skeleton data; human posture recognition; feature vector; classification.

I. Introduction

Human posture recognition is an active research topic in the field of human-robot interaction. In addition to being used in the context of humanoid robotics, recognition of human postures has many applications in human assistive systems and in the automobile industry. The basic objective is to enable humanoid robots to work side by side with humans during daily life. In order to realize this goal, robotic systems must have the capability to differentiate human(s) from the cluttered environments. In addition to detecting humans, these systems should also analyze their posture, actions, emotions, motives and overall behavior. This, in turn, helps the robots to be more intelligent and resourceful when interacting with humans. Human behavior can be analyzed using human's nonverbal communication. According to [1], two thirds of our communication consists of non-verbal communication and only one third of our communication consists of verbal content. Nonverbal communication consists of facial expressions and bodily cues. Human posture represents an important part of the nonverbal communication.

Human posture and body movement play significant role in the perception of interaction partner. Humans use different hand gestures and body postures to express their internal emotional state in different situations. In humans, postures provide significant information through nonverbal cues. Psychological studies have also demonstrated the effects of body posture on emotions. This research can be traced back to Charles Darwin's studies of emotion and movement in humans and animals [2]. A massive study and research has been conducted in 1970s on the significance of body language in which the main area of focus was leg-crossing, defensive posture and arm-crossing, suggesting that these nonverbal behaviors depict feelings and attitude. Posture can also rely on the situation, i.e., people change their postures depending on the situation. Currently, many studies have shown that certain patterns of body movements are indicative of specific emotions [3][4]. Researchers have studied sign language and found that even non-sign language users can determine emotions from only hand and body movements [5]. For example, anger is characterized by forward body movement [6].

Posture recognition plays an important role in expressing human emotions. Many scientists believe that all the variations of postures are due to the change in emotions and play significant role in human evolution. Human emotions are always difficult to understand and there are many factors that influence human emotions. The art of recognizing human emotions had gained its importance long back and is, currently, studied actively [7]. Some behavioral cues can be easily recognized from postures. For example, a person scratching his head during interaction shows thinking behavior. Similarly, crossed arms posture shows that the interlocutor is reserved and is trying to block himself from opening to other person.

However, the challenge is to recognize complex human postures in cluttered environment in real-time, especially, those set of postures which are used in daily life in human-human interaction scenarios. For example, crossed arm, pointing with left or right arm, casual or attentive standing posture, relaxing posture, thinking or shrug posture, etc. On the contrary, every region or culture has its own different postures which, sometimes, are totally opposite in meaning in some another culture. One of the major challenges in recognizing human postures is diversity in people performing postures. People from different culture are expressing the same posture in different ways as compared to others. In addition, postures are also dependent on the height and human physique variations which make them more challenging to recognize. Moreover, sitting postures appear different from standing postures and need separate classifier for the posture recognition task.

Numerous ways have been reported in the literature to recognize human postures. Some of these methods use wearable sensors to extract the psychological parameters like electroencephalography (EEG) data, skin temperature, accelerometer readings, etc. However, these methods require special sensors to wear all the time and sometimes require training how to use them. In contrast, approaches using visual information from the visual sensors are more natural means of recognition of human posture. However, this work explores recognition of human postures using RGB and depth (RGB-D) sensor. This work uses ASUS Xtion [8], installed on a humanoid robot, ROBIN [9] to extract distance data. With the help of OpenNI and NiTE library, the system is able to extract human skeleton joints. These joints are then pre-processed and converted into angles to make the system invariable to human height or physique. Feature vectors are generated using angle information between each joint and classified using Support Vector Machines (SVM). The major contribution of the paper is the accurate and automatic recognition of human postures in real-time using kinect-like sensor. Our approach reports close to 100% results when the human skeleton is tracked accurately in real-time in cluttered environment. Moreover, the system is also capable of distinguishing between standing and sitting human postures using human height analysis. In the following sections, we describe the overall approach and experimental results in detail.

The rest of the paper is organized as follows: related work is discussed in Section 2, Section 3 discusses human posture recognition approach and classification in detail. Experimental results and performance evaluation are discussed in Section 4. We conclude the paper in Section 5.

II. Related Work

Research on posture recognition using skeleton data began in the 1990s and is still being carried on. Generally, posture recognition approaches can be separated in two broad categories: (a) wearable sensors based posture recognition and (b) posture recognition using vision based sensors. Wearable sensors include gloves and other commercially available products that are used to extract different statistical and geometrical information of the limbs or body when worn. Few of these devices namely Sensewear, ActiGraph and ActivPal have been used by Wang et al. [10]. They address challenges like data imbalancement, instant recognition and sensor deployment in order to achieve an overall accuracy of 91% for sitting, standing and walking postures. Similar approaches using wearable sensors have been reported with higher accuracy. However, these require sensors to be worn. Latter approaches use vision sensors for the recognition of human postures. The advantage of this approach is twofold: first, these approaches are noninvasive; and secondly, they are also cost-efficient. Humans can perform their gestures and postures in front of a camera sensor without any other device attached to their bodies for posture recognition tasks.

Posture recognition via vision sensors can be further divided into two categories namely camera based posture recognition and RGB-D sensor based posture recognition. Numerous works have been reported in the literature that use monocular camera to estimate human pose and human action. The most general approach is to extract features from images based on the structure of the human body, e.g., skin color or face position [11]. However, this approach impose restrictions on features such as clothes and orientation. There are other methods to extract silhouettes and edges as features from the image [12][13]. However, they rely on the stable extraction of the silhouettes and edges. Moreover, they perform poorly in self-occlusion.

In order to address these shortcomings, researchers use depth sensors to extract human joint positions. S. Nirjon et al. [14] describe a system, called Kintense, which is real-time system with a high accuracy to detect human aggressive actions, e.g., hitting and pushing that are relevant for games. The system has been trained using supervised and unsupervised machine learning techniques. The sensors calculate distance between body and the cameras, skeleton joints and speed at which an action is performed. Deep learning and neural networks are used to eliminate false positives and to identify actions that are not labeled. Real-time testing has been performed by deploying the system in more than one multiple-person household which illustrates the sensitivity of the system towards unknown and unseen actions. The real-time system proves that the accuracy of the system is more than 90% [14].

Using RGB-D sensor, Zhang et al. [15] extract joint positions of a human with the help of Microsoft Kinect. In order to make it independent of human size, each joint position is normalized using its neighboring joint to make a feature. This feature vector which consists of all normalized joints is then classified using SVM. A total of 22 postures are recognized with 3 different classifiers. The drawback of this approach lies in normalization of joint positions. Although authors claim that the system is invariant to human size, it would not be invariant to human height or size of the limbs completely as normalization only adjusts joint values with its neighboring joint.

Another similar work has been conducted by Ivan Lilloa et al. [16] to recognize human activities using body poses estimated from RGB-D data. The system modules are classified into three different levels which include geometry and motion descriptors at the lowest level, sparse compositions of these body movement at the intermediate level, spatial and time stamped compositions used to represent human actions involving multiple activities at the highest level. The work is related to dictionary learning method and their framework focuses on vector quantization using k-means to cluster low-level key point descriptors for dictionary learning [17]. The model developed uses an alternative quantization methods, discriminative dictionaries, or different pooling schemes [18]. Sparse coding methods have also been used for alternative quantization methods. These methods have mostly focused on non-hierarchical cases where mid-level dictionaries and top-level classifiers are trained independently [17]. Niebles et al. [18] extend this model to the case of action recognition. In contrast to former approach, the model is limited to binary classification problems and reports good accuracy only in a constraint scenario.

In previous related work, the required data is captured either from images or videos and the processing is done to create the feature vector. Feature vector represents the data in a form such that the system can be trained. Many classification techniques have been used in classification of the training dataset, such as SVM, neural networks and deep learning techniques. After the classification, the system can be tested offline using existing database or online testing in real-time scenario. Most of these approaches are used only to recognize standing postures or actions. Additionally, these approaches are not robust to real-time recognition of human postures with

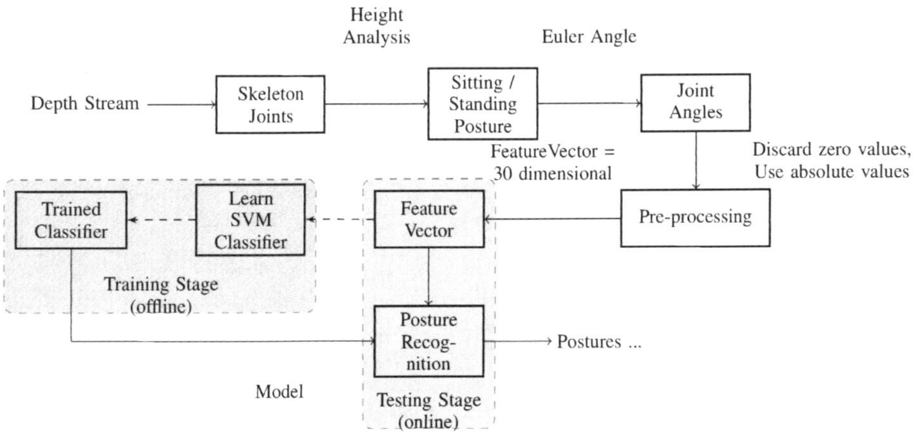

Figure 1. Working schematics of the approach. Using depth stream and NiTE Library, skeleton joints are detected. Based on the height, system classifies the subject either standing or sitting, after which joint angles are computed from joint positions to construct a 30 dimensional feature vector for classification.

more than 10 classes. In this paper, we have proposed an approach that is robust to real-time recognition of postures and can differentiate between standing and sitting postures. Moreover, it can recognize 19 postures used in daily life routine. The detailed analysis of the proposed approach is discussed in following sections.

III. Human Posture Recognition

Visual perception in complex and dynamical scenes with cluttered background is a challenging task which humans can solve remarkably well. However, it performs poorly in this kind of challenging scenarios for a robot perception system. One of the reasons of this large difference in performance is the use of context or contextual information by humans. Furthermore, robot has to perform its computations as fast as possible due to the notion of real-time. As a result, most of the time robot perception system is hampered with low resolution images. There is a need to develop such perception system which can cater complex environments and work efficiently.

This paper presents an approach that uses depth data along with NiTE library to detect human joint positions and then convert them into meaningful angles for feature vector generation task. The resultant feature vector is quite unique for each posture and is invariant to height, body shape, illumination, proximity and appearance of human. The working schematics of the proposed approach is presented in Figure 1. Our proposed approach reports high accuracy for both sitting and standing postures. The system is able to recognize overall 19 gestures real-time when classified by using multi-class SVM. Each module of the approach is described in the following sub-sections.

A. Depth Image

Instead of using monocular camera, ASUS Xtion is employed in order to utilize depth data. The advantage of using such devices with depth sensor lies in the segmentation of human skeleton using OpenNI and NiTE Library. Segmenting humans on the basis of silhouette and edges might work in a constraint scenario but it behaves poorly when applied in dynamic environment. In contrast, human can be detected and tracked efficiently using depth sensor in constantly changing scenario with a lot of different daily life objects involved. This sensor can work efficiently in the range of 0.5 to 3.5 meter.

B. Skeleton Data and Joint Positions

Fifteen different skeletal joint positions of human can be extracted in real-time using OpenNI and NiTE libraries. These joint positions are quite accurate and tracked over time. Furthermore, NiTE middle ware library allows multiple human tracking and joint positions extraction in real-time. In order to extract joint positions reliably, the whole human body should be clearly visible to RGB-D sensor with no complete occlusions of body parts. The disadvantage in using joint positions is the dependence on correct detection of human skeleton. Due to partial occlusions of limbs, the module can report ambiguous skeletal information which effects the joint position values. Figure 2 shows tracked humans with their respective skeletal joints.

Figure 2. Multiple tracked humans and their skeletal joints. (Image used from www.openni.ru/files/nite/index.html)

C. Sitting or Standing Postures

Before recognizing postures, the important step is to detect whether human is standing or sitting. The simplest way is to analyze the height of human with respect to its z distance from the sensor. Empirical studies have shown that the relation between these two entities is linear. For example, if human is near to the sensor, he/she appears taller and similarly, if human is away from the sensor, he/she appears short. To make it height and scale invariant, the system uses the depth data (z distance) to normalize the height of the person. If the human head joint has the value more than the set threshold value, system would classify it as standing posture. If he/she has the head joint position value less than the set threshold, the system would classify it as sitting.

D. Joint Angles

The major disadvantage in using joint positions for feature extraction task is that they are variant to positions, height and limbs variations. This type of features might report better results when the position and height of the human would be fixed. However, these features behave poorly when dealing with varied height or dynamic humans. In order to solve this problem, researchers have proposed an approach that calculates distance of each joint from torso to make a feature vector. Although this type of feature extraction reports better results, it is still dependent on the height of the person.

In order to address this shortcoming, this paper proposed a unique method to extract features. Instead of using joint position for feature extraction task, these joints positions are converted into angles between each two joints. The benefit of using angles is that they are not dependent on the position or height or human physique, instead they compute directions between each joint. The direction between each joint would be similar for a short person and a tall person if they are expressing the same posture. Euler angles are used to convert the joint positions to angles. Following (1) - (3) are used to compute angle between joint a and b.

$$angle_x = \tan^{-1}\frac{(a_y - b_y)}{(a_x - b_x)} \tag{1}$$

$$angle_y = \tan^{-1}\frac{(a_z - b_z)}{(a_y - b_y)} \tag{2}$$

$$angle_z = \tan^{-1}\frac{(a_x - b_x)}{(a_z - b_z)} \tag{3}$$

The angles are then converted from Radian to degrees using (4).

$$angle_x^{\circ} = angle_x * 180/\pi \tag{4}$$

E. Pre-processing and Feature Extraction

In total, 15 joint angles can be calculated for each posture. However, it has been observed that certain joints do not contribute in deciding the posture. Joint angles between knee and foot, or hip and knee do not add useful information for posture recognition task. The reason lies in the postures, recognized in this work, are not effected by joint angles of lower body. During this pre-processing stage, the number of angles recorded are reduced to 10.

On the other hand, NiTE library can detect and track human but it is not able to distinguish whether human is facing towards the camera or his/her back facing the camera. This makes the direction of angles totally opposite. In order to make the system invariant to human facing direction, we take the absolute value of all the joints, thus making the features more consistent for the same class. Joint angles with values $0°$, $90°$, $180°$ or $270°$ in 10 consecutive frames are also discarded. After empirical studies, it has been found out that when part of the limb or body is occluded, skeleton tracker reports $(0, 0, 0)$ joint position. This leads to false recognition, therefore, the instances are discarded. 10 joint angles are then used to construct a feature vector. Since every joint angle has x, y, z values, the feature vector for a single depth observation becomes 30 dimensional.

F. Classification

Classification is an important step in any recognition task. The major task of classification stage is to differentiate each class or category accurately based on the knowledge gained during the training stage. Numerous classification algorithms have been presented in machine learning, e.g., neural networks, decision trees, random forests, convolution neural network, etc. This work uses SVM, a supervised learning algorithm, for the classification task. An SVM model is a representation of the examples as points in space, mapped so that the examples of the separate categories are divided by a clear gap. New examples are then mapped into that same space and predicted to belong to a category based on which side of the gap they fall [19]. The benefit of SVM lies in the regularization parameter which if set accurately, avoids over-fitting. Moreover, it uses the kernel trick, i.e., it can build an expert knowledge about the problem by engineering the kernel. SVM generalizes on high dimensional feature set quite well given that the database is also huge.

This paper uses multi-class SVM classification. More than 2100 instances are used during training stage for each posture and 40000 instances for the whole training data are used for 19 classes. 10 different subjects, from different ethnicity (Indian, Pakistani, German, Italian and Turkish), featured in the training dataset. Linear kernel with regularization parameter $C = 0.4586$ is used during SVM training. Figure 3 shows 3D graphical plots of joint angles between *right_shoulder-right_elbow* and *right_elbow-right_hand*. It can be seen that the classes are easily distinguishable based on the angle between two joints. With the contribution of other joints angles between joints, the problem is easily classified by SVM linear kernel.

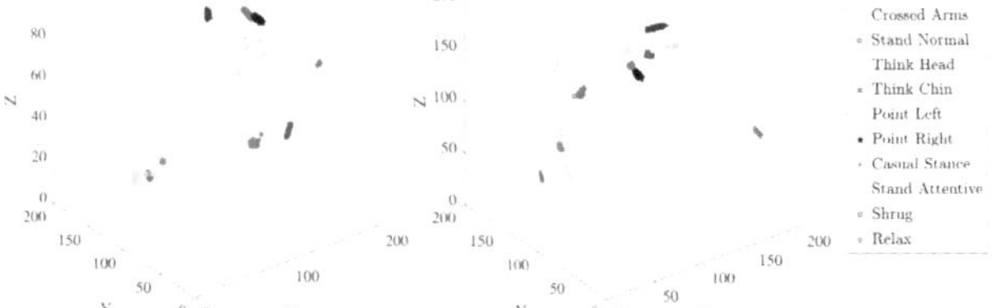

Figure 3. Samples from training data in 3D plane for each class marked with different color. (a) Angle values between right shoulder and right elbow (b) Angle values between right elbow and right hand.

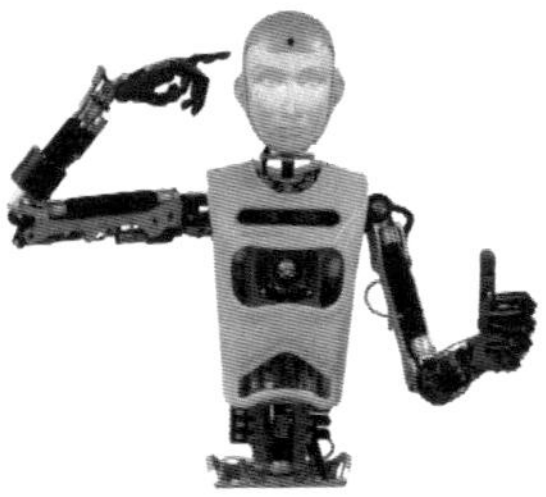

Figure 4. ROBIN - Humanoid robot of TU Kaiserslautern

TABLE I. STANDING POSTURES AND THEIR RECOGNITION RATES

	Postures	Recog. Rate (%)
1	Crossed Arms	100
2	Open Arms	100
3	Standing Normal	97.33
4	Think (Hand on the Head)	98.67
5	Think (Hand on the Chin)	95.1
6	Point with Left Hand	100
7	Point with Right Hand	100
8	Casual Stance	100
9	Standing Attentive	90.27
10	Shrug	100
11	Relax (Hands behind the neck)	100
	Average	**98.3**

IV. EXPERIMENTATION AND EVALUATION

The goal of the system is to recognize human postures in real-time robustly in order to realize human-robot interaction. The humanoid robot, named ROBot-human-INteraction (ROBIN), is used in order to evaluate the posture recognition system. ROBIN has been developed by Technical University of Kaiserslautern [9] as shown in Figure 4. It consists of intelligent hands that can express almost any gesture. Single whole arm has 14 degrees of freedom that uses compressed air to perform any action. Head and torso of ROBIN also have 3 degrees of freedom. The backlit projected face is able to express different expressions and emotions. Additionally, ROBIN can speak in English and German using text-to-speech software. ASUS Xtion is installed on the chest of ROBIN, which is used for all the perception tasks, e.g., posture recognition, gestures recognition, etc. ROBIN has its own processor that can handle all the movements of joints. In the following subsection, a detail analysis of postures and experimentation are discussed.

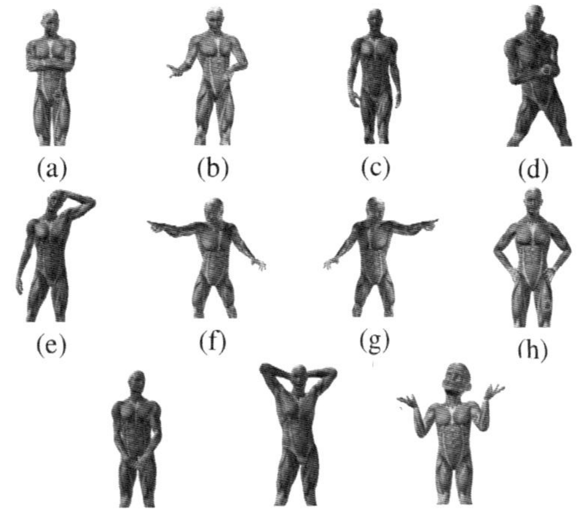

Figure 5. Standing postures (a) Crossed Arms (b) Open Arms (c) Stand Normal (d) Think (Hand on chin) (e) Think (Hand on Head) (f) Point Right (g) Point Left (h) Casual Stance (i) Attentive (j) Relax (k) Shrug. Pictures are used from *www.posemaniacs.com*

A. Recognized Human Postures

Postures are categorized mainly as sitting and standing. Overall 11 postures are recognized for standing and 8 postures have been recognized for sitting. Different postures recognized are crossed arms, open arms, think (hand on the head), think (hand on chin), pointing (with left hand), pointing (with right hand), standing/sitting normal, shrug, relax, casual posture and attentive posture. Figure 5 shows different postures for standing that are recognized by the system. Similar postures for sitting are also recognized by the system. Total of 10 subjects featured in the training stage. For each class and each subject, at least 300 instances are collected with a little bit of movement and varied styles.

B. Experimentation

There are generally two ways to conduct experiments. Experimentation or testing of the system can either be done on the testing dataset or testing can be done real-time directly on the ROBIN. We have conducted both these experiments in this work to evaluate the system. 25% of the dataset have been separated from the training data before training. This dataset serves as test dataset to evaluate the system. Since the recorded dataset has no false skeleton tracking, the system reports 99.4% recognition rate. This shows the potential of the approach when the provided dataset is accurate.

For the second experiment, ROBIN is used to recognize postures in real-time. Once ROBIN recognizes the posture, it indicates by saying the name of the posture. In order to avoid any bias, new subjects have been used to express postures in front of ROBIN. Subjects have been instructed in the start about the postures which ROBIN can recognize. However, the knowledge about performing each posture has not been shared with them in order to evaluate the system potential to generalize varied postures. Every subject performs each posture at least 30 times. Table I and Table II show the recognition rates of standing and sitting postures respectively.

TABLE II. SITTING POSTURES AND THEIR RECOGNITION RATE

	Sitting Postures	Recog. Rate (%)
12	Sitting Normal	98.33
13	Crossed Arms	95.28
14	Think (Hand on the Head)	96
15	Think (Hand on the Chin)	94.5
16	Point with Left Hand	100
17	Point with Right Hand	100
18	Shrug	100
19	Relax (Hands behind the neck)	100
	Average	**98.01**

Figure 6. Subject is interacting with ROBIN using Postures.

C. Performance Evaluation

As shown in Table I and Table II, ROBIN is able to recognize human postures with an average accuracy of 98%. For standing postures, the recognition rate for each class is above 90%. Attentive posture reports low accuracy as compared to others because of the fact that the hands are too close to the body and therefore, the algorithm considers hands as part of the body for skeletal joints detection. Thinking postures are sometimes confused between each other and show recognition rates above 95%.

For sitting postures, it has been found out that when the person is sitting, the skeleton of whole body is not visible. In order to address this issue, ROBIN uses torso pitch angle to tilt its body in the front. In this way, the whole skeleton of human is visible. Due to sitting posture, sometimes human skeleton tracker does not work accurately to localize limbs and positions. Therefore, some of the postures show relatively less recognition rate than standing postures. Nevertheless, ROBIN is able to recognize human postures accurately in real-time with an accuracy of more than 98%. Since the system uses only depth data, issues regarding lighting condition, image resolution, texture variations are avoided. This enhances the accuracy considerably as compared to approaches using color image to recognize human postures. Figure 6 shows experimental environment where subject is interacting with ROBIN using postures.

V. Conclusion and Future Work

Identification of human postures is a complicated task based on the situation and interacting environment. Recognition of human postures has many applications in modern human-robot interaction developments. This can be applied for the purposes, e.g., natural interaction, gaming, developing assisted systems, surveillance systems, entertainment purposes and educational purposes. This paper presents an approach which uses RGB-D sensor for posture recognition. Depth information is used to extract joint positions. These joint positions are then converted into joint angles in order to make the system invariant to height, scale, position or physique of the person. Feature vectors are generated based on refined joint angles. SVM is used for classification of 19 different sitting and standing postures. System reports 100% recognition rate on a dataset with no false skeleton tracking and 98% when tested real-time in a cluttered and dynamic environment.

For future work, this approach can easily be extended for recognition of more postures. Additionally, using color image along with the depth can provide texture information, which can be utilized when the skeleton tracker does not work accurately.

References

[1] P. Noller, Nonverbal Communication in Close Relationships, 0th ed. SAGE Publications, Inc., 2006, pp. 403–421.

[2] B. D. Bruyn, "Review: The history of psychology: Fundamental questions," Perception, vol. 32, no. 11, 2003, pp. 1409–1410.

[3] N. Dael, M. Mortillaro, and K. Scherer, "Emotion expression in body action and posture," vol. 12, 11 2011, pp. 1085–101.

[4] J. Montepare, E. Koff, D. Zaitchik, and M. Albert, "The use of body movements and gestures as cues to emotions in younger and older adults," Journal of Nonverbal Behavior, vol. 23, no. 2, Jun 1999, pp. 133–152.

[5] I. Rossberg-Gempton and G. D. Poole, "The effect of open and closed postures on pleasant and unpleasant emotions," The Arts in Psychotherapy, vol. 20, no. 1, 1993, pp. 75 – 82, special Issue Research in the Creative Arts Therapies.

[6] S. Oosterwijk, M. Rotteveel, A. Fischer, and U. Hess, "Embodied emotion concepts: How generating words about pride and disappointment influences posture," vol. 39, 04 2009, pp. 457 – 466.

[7] L. Al-Shawaf, D. Conroy-Beam, K. Asao, and D. M. Buss, "Human emotions: An evolutionary psychological perspective," Emotion Review, vol. 8, no. 2, 2016, pp. 173–186.

[8] A. Xtion, "Xtion pro live — 3d sensor — asus global," 2018, online; accessed 2018-03-12. [Online]. Available: https://www.asus.com/3D-Sensor/Xtion_PRO_LIVE/

[9] R. R. Lab, "Robin: Robot-human interaction," 2018, online; accessed 2018-01-31. [Online]. Available: https://agrosy.informatik.uni-kl.de/robots/robin00/?L=1

[10] J. Wang et al., "Wearable sensor based human posture recognition," in 2016 IEEE International Conference on Big Data (Big Data), Dec 2016, pp. 3432–3438.

[11] M. W. Lee and I. Cohen, "A model-based approach for estimating human 3d poses in static images," IEEE Transactions on Pattern Analysis and Machine Intelligence, vol. 28, no. 6, June 2006, pp. 905–916.

[12] A. Agarwal and B. Triggs, "3d human pose from silhouettes by relevance vector regression," in Proceedings of the 2004 IEEE Computer Society Conference on Computer Vision and Pattern Recognition, 2004. CVPR 2004., vol. 2, June 2004, pp. 882–888 Vol.2.

[13] J. Malik and G. Mori, "Estimating human body configurations using shape context matching," in Proceedings of the 7th European Conference on Computer Vision-Part III, ser. ECCV '02. Springer-Verlag, 2002, pp. 666–680.

[14] S. Nirjon et al., "Kintense: A robust, accurate, real-time and evolving system for detecting aggressive actions from streaming 3d skeleton data," in 2014 IEEE International Conference on Pervasive Computing and Communications (PerCom), March 2014, pp. 2–10.

[15] Z. Zhang et al., "A novel method for user-defined human posture recognition using kinect," in 2014 7th International Congress on Image and Signal Processing, Oct 2014, pp. 736–740.

[16] I. Lillo, J. C. Niebles, and A. Soto, "Sparse composition of body poses and atomic actions for human activity recognition in rgb-d videos," Image and Vision Computing, vol. 59, 2017, pp. 63 – 75.

[17] Y. L. Boureau, F. Bach, Y. LeCun, and J. Ponce, "Learning mid-level features for recognition," in 2010 IEEE Computer Society Conference on Computer Vision and Pattern Recognition, June 2010, pp. 2559–2566.

[18] J. C. Niebles, C.-W. Chen, and L. Fei-Fei, Modeling Temporal Structure of Decomposable Motion Segments for Activity Classification. Berlin, Heidelberg: Springer Berlin Heidelberg, 2010, pp. 392–405.

[19] S. Tong and E. Chang, "Support vector machine active learning for image retrieval," in Proceedings of the Ninth ACM International Conference on Multimedia, ser. MULTIMEDIA '01. New York, NY, USA: ACM, 2001, pp. 107–118.

Smart Home Resource Management based on Multi-Agent System Modeling Combined with SVM Machine Learning for Prediction and Decision-Making

Kalthoum Zaouali
National School of Engineering of Tunis-ENIT
University Tunis El Manar
Tunis, Tunisia
e-mail: zaoualikalthoum@gmail.com

Mohamed Lassaad Ammari
Department of Electrical and Computer Engineering
Laval University
Quebec, Canada
e-mail: mlammari@gel.ulaval.ca

Mhamed Tabka, Amine Choueib
Chifco Company
Tunis, Tunisia
e-mail: mhamed.tabka@chifco.com, amine.chouaieb@chifco.com

Ridha Bouallegue
Sup'Com, Innov'Com Laboratory
Carthage University
Tunis, Tunisia
e-mail: ridha.bouallegue@supcom.rnu.tn

***Abstract*—The challenges of the Internet of Things (IoT) in a Smart Home are the monitoring of energy consumption and the automation of the household appliances connected to the Wireless Sensor Networks (WSN). The Smart Home monitoring technology has recently received great attention in the areas of IoT, home automation and WSN monitoring. Many companies seek to address a wide range of important issues including data mining and analysis, energy saving, comfort and security. The Smart Home application is inherently dynamic in the sense that it forms time-series data with real-time changing behavior. We seek to extract and analyze this incoming data to provide and predict useful features for the decision-making system in a Smart Home. This paper describes a new methodology of Smart Home data mining analysis based on Support Vector Machine (SVM) learning for a proposed Multi-Agent System (MAS). The key ideas are to represent the WSN behavior exchange by the modeled MAS, then to predict and classify features using the SVM regression model. Based on the cross-validation performed on the training data-set, the SVM model parameters are optimized for each combination of features. We demonstrate the validity of our methodology in the scenarios of emerging data recognition using a real "Smart Life" database.**

Keywords–Smart Home; distributed control; home automation; multi-agent systems; machine learning; support vector machine; time-series prediction.

I. INTRODUCTION

Nowadays, human beings always seek refuge, relaxation, security and prosperity at home, hence influencing the quality of life. The development of integrated electronic features to reduce costs has opened new perspectives of automation controls and monitoring of habitat that appears to be a task of great social importance. In the recent years, computer technology has been applied to the creation of Smart Homes in order to improve the lives of people at home. A Smart Home is an entity integrated with diversified automation, communication, and control service functions that collaborate in a convenient manner via intelligent tasks to provide many services, such as energy management, comfort, security and monitoring. The field of Smart Home is multidisciplinary with variations in architectures, dissimilar devices and systems, and diverse application and features [1]. In a Smart Home environment, the inter-operation unpredictability is one of the fundamental reasons behind uncertainty in the interoperability among these systems having diverse requirements, information exchanges and federated routine.

Home automation solutions range from overviewing information about energy consumption, presence and weather data in illustrative forms, automating and monitoring appliances either locally or remotely. Traditional strategies of building control are no longer efficient and smart to ensure the dynamic pricing of electricity and the demand response application for residential customers. To overcome this fundamental limitation and to solve such complex and dynamic decision processes, a Multi-Agent System (MAS) is required to provide intelligent energy management and home automation.

The MAS is a distributed artificial intelligence system that allows the intercommunication and the interaction between intelligent agents. The interactions of these entities of agent technology are made by the perception of the environment and by executing actions according to their decisions in order to conduct them and to study their varied situations. The agents must cooperate to achieve the overall goals as they have only a partial representation of their environment. The reactivity and pro-activity actions of the MAS are depicted by sensing and interpreting the changes in the environment in real-time [2].

Home automation can be addressed through the prediction and analysis of appliances' data, offering support for more advanced applications, such as activity recognition. The automatic human activity recognition requires new context-aware domestic smart services, such as controlling voice in Smart Home. Chahuara et al. [3] investigated an on-line activities of daily living recognition device from non-visual, audio and home automation sensors. The performances of this smart service were determined by comparing several learning models, such as hidden Markov model, the conditional random fields, the sequential Markov logic network, the Support Vector Machine (SVM), the random forest and the non-sequential Markov logic network.

Predicted time-series data can be investigated for energy consumption data mining, home automation and also home-owner activity and behavior forecasting. Data history clusters are utilized by machine learning, which take into account the effects of the previous device states. Therefore, we propose a MAS using the SVM approach to predict and classify features. Currently, Smart Home owners have trouble to daily control and manage the various heterogeneous smart sensors and devices. One of the greatest challenges in the current Smart Home field is to deal with the collaborative control problem of these heterogeneous smart devices using a home automation platform.

Our contribution is to propose a universal Smart Home automation platform architecture based on a multi-agent system and predictive software for decision making. The proposed system provides heterogeneous devices' connectivity, collaborative agents' communication, human-devices' interaction and appliances' auto-control to improve the Smart Home automation system. In this paper, we represent the ability to predict the behavior of Smart Home owners by monitoring the daily appliances' usages. Indeed, we develop a robust, flexible and intelligent platform integrating temporal contextual information based on the incoming sensor data. The developed prototype is used to forecast daily power consumption and to estimate human actions in a Smart Home. We test the performance of our system using statistical metrics, and the experimental results are encouraging. The model features are updated based on the time series analysis.

The MASs consist of an intelligent distributed artificial system integrating Internet of Things (IoT) aspects and human cognition for Smart Home automation. The proposed architecture is based on a virtual multi-agent platform incorporating services to provide Wireless Sensor Networks (WSN) interconnectivity. This design makes it possible for Smart Homes to include organizational aspects of human activities, improving the auto-control and auto-programming of appliances. The autonomous agents fixed in devices consume and provide different services to offer more distributed and complex functionalities and capabilities.

The proposed MAS should guarantee the platform scalability, and flexibility and efficient and intelligent communication with the ability to add new functionalities for the layer of user applications. The main functions are the fusion of incoming information from heterogeneous sources. The suggested system must be able to monitor automatically the Smart Home and to predict the household energy consumption through a predictive model with input variables regarding the weather and space information, appliances' state, power consumption and the time. The WSNs are used to analyze the command of electrical appliances and the interactions between different sensors in order to automatically make decisions on a daily basis.

The rest of the sections of this paper are structured as follows. Section II describes the system architecture overview of the proposed system modeling for home automation. Section III defines the predicting incoming time-sequence data models. We explain the experiments and results by considering the proposed method in Section IV. Section V presents the conclusion and some future work.

II. Related Work

A Smart Home should meet the requirements of homeowners, including security, weather information, consumption measurements and remote control of different categories of smart products. According to the rapid anticipation for the Smart Home, several commercial intelligent IoT solutions are involved for home automation using smart sensors as a universal remote-control software-defined Smart Home appliance that can be handled safely by homeowners [4].

Smart Home applications are generally based on the IoT and cognitive dynamic systems. Feng et al. [5] investigated a cognitive interactive people-centric IoT in the Smart Home to improve human life quality with intelligent control of its setting by considering perception actions that would contribute to the interactive IoT ecosystem.

Viswanath et al. [6] proposed the design of an IoT system for real-time residential smart grid applications focused on a large number of home devices communicating through a universal IoT home gateway, a cloud back-end server, and user interfaces offering services as well as energy management, demand response management, dynamic pricing, energy monitoring, home automation and home security.

The MASs are a preferred approach addressing complex systems that rely on classical artificial intelligence extended to a distributed computing environment and the sharing of tasks, resources and knowledge. Their totally decentralized nature makes them particularly suitable for this type of systems. The MASs allow working on the overall operation of a system by focusing on the component entities and their interactions. However, MASs are applied increasingly in various fields of real life due to the technological revolution and the intensive use of Internet services by large companies. Several constraints are questioned because of this application domain diversity. Among these constraints we can cite the difficulty of specifying and systematically modeling applications, the problems related to the concepts of resource allocations and the complexity of negotiation and inter-cooperation between agents.

Several researches identify information security requirements that impact critical societal services ranging over transport, home automation, energy management, industrial control, and health services and their perceptions and attitudes on the IoT security [7]. The fields of telecommunications and information may also be based on MASs for network management, remote management of Smart Home and information knowledge. In industry, the MASs are operated in production automation processes, smart cards and cooperative robots. Manufacturers often try to achieve the effective resolution of issues targeted as the complexity of real-mode systems. These issues provide an intellectual challenge to researchers who seek to maintain soft constraint systems using agents. Thus, realizing the integration of control, maintenance and technical management of automation system based on MASs can lead to the resolution of the various industrial problems. Recently, the MASs are utilized for crop irrigation monitoring allowing farmers to rationalize the amount of resources that optimize crop needs. The system offeres an economical solution combining intelligence and context-awareness by merging heterogeneous data from the WSNs [8]. Tele-medicine also applies MASs in the supervision and assistance of the elderly sick. They are obviously used in the field of logistics and information on trips [9].

Smart grid architectures consist of many autonomous systems with partial knowledge that have to cooperate and communicate in order to solve complex problems. The MAS is a mature and efficient mechanism that provides many features imperatively required for smart grid applications to solve their distributed nature problems. However, it is still difficult to provide a generic perspective on smart grid architectures. Dynamical MASs have been used for the systematic modeling of the cyber and electrical grids to provide flexibility. Other solutions for smart grid architectures have been explored using a MAS to develop a decision-making support for distributed power generation [10] and for managing electric vehicles' charging stations [11]. Sun et al. [12] proposed a multi-agent system framework for home automation, based on belief, desire and intention model for an agent individual behavior design, a regulation policy-based multi-agent collaboration behavior design and a Petri-net method for system analysis and evaluation.

As dynamic contributors to smart grids, Smart Home systems have ensured interactive communication that affects the electricity demand, generation, and bills, leading to a reduction in the total demand curve. Smart Grid modeling is based on a multi-agent system that designs each Smart Home as an autonomous agent making rational decisions for power generation, storage, and trading features founded on the expected utilities they offer. The individual decisions of these home agents significantly reduce electricity costs, which encourages conventional homes to purchase their own local generation-storage systems and to benefit from the different operational conditions.

Integrating the IoT with Cloud computing and Web services, Javed et al. [13] investigated model-based wireless sensor nodes for Smart Home monitoring and HVAC using machine learning like the artificial neural network to estimate setpoints for controlling the heating, ventilation, and cooling of the Smart Home while reducing human intervention.

The energy consumption cost reduction requires a dynamic demand response and distributed energy resource management. Therefore, home automation trends towards IoT and ambient intelligence technologies for device self-control. Ruta, et al. [14] put forward a distributed multi-agent framework for home and building automation and energy management, based on a semantic improvement of domotic standards using the discovery and orchestration of formal annotation-based resources to support the semantic characterization of user profiles and device functionalities. In [15], the authors suggested an adapting automation architecture for activity recognition in Smart Home based on semi-supervised learning algorithms and Markov models combining the data observations and the feedback of users decisions. Jose et al. [16] studied the various security issues and verification approaches to improve Smart Home security. They proposed a device fingerprinting algorithm that considered the device's geographical location, username and password of utilizers as well as the device used to access the home.

III. MULTI-AGENTS SYSTEM MODELING FOR HOME AUTOMATION

Using an agent language like Java Agent Development (JADE) framework, the MASs are able to share information, to exchange messages and to solve complex problems. The JADE is a software framework fully implemented in Java language to simplify the development of the MAS using graphical tools for debugging and deployment according to the Foundation for Intelligent Physical Agents (FIPA) standard and the Agent Communication Language (FIPA-ACL) specifications [17]. The FIPA interaction protocols between agents are being developed to define a standard communication structure ensuring the conduct of conversations between these agents. These protocols use a manager agent to offer the performance of a task in terms of appropriate resources and expertise by selecting the best proposal returned and then begins the necessary exchanges with the elected official. An agent asks another agent to perform an action and inform the initiator about the structure in which agents exist and operate [18].

A. *Agents Functionalities*

In the MAS-based Smart Home setting, we use four containers where each container is a room of the house embedded in a main container (Smart Home container) as shown in Figure 1. These containers interact to estimate the presence of owners and their provided activity in each Smart Home room. Every container consists of a set of agents instances' that represent the equipment or environment variables (temperature, humidity, etc.) responsible for learning the habits, equipment states, environmental conditions and situations of the home owners in order to supervise, control and take appropriate actions. Each agent has a specific role. The proposed MAS

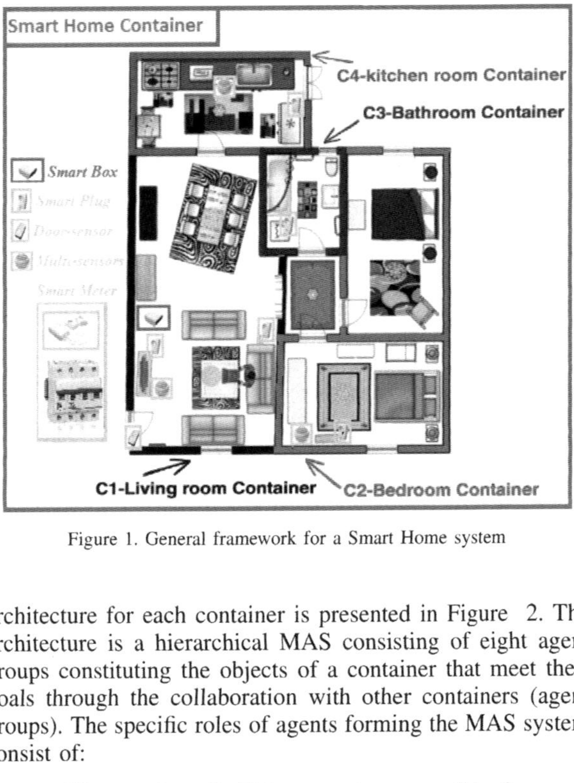

Figure 1. General framework for a Smart Home system

architecture for each container is presented in Figure 2. The architecture is a hierarchical MAS consisting of eight agent groups constituting the objects of a container that meet their goals through the collaboration with other containers (agent groups). The specific roles of agents forming the MAS system consist of:

- "Sensor Agent": This agent is responsible for monitoring and controlling environment sensors by receiving messages from the same container agents and saving them in the database. These messages can be transmitted to the "Electrical Outlet Agent", the "Air Conditioner Agent" and the "Lamp Agent" in order to predict the user actions.
- "Electrical Outlet Agent": This agent receives the data sent by the "Sensor Agent" and uses it as an input of

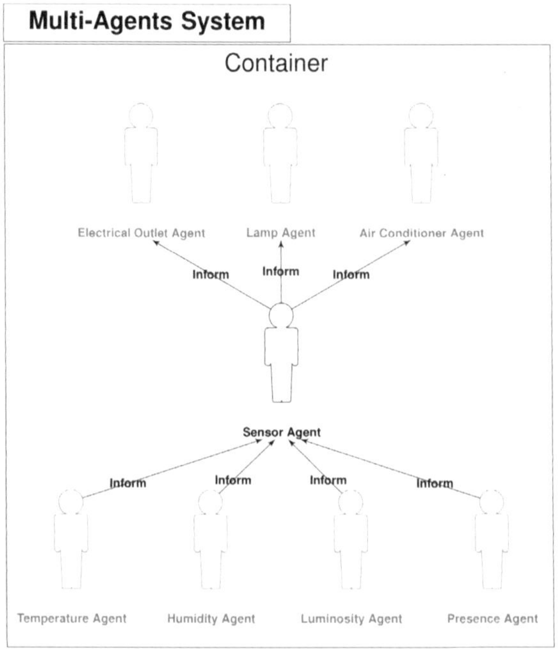

Figure 2. Proposed MAS-based architecture for Smart Home automation

the SVM classifier to predict the decision states of the electrical outlet.

- "Air Conditioner Agent": The following agent receives the data sent by the "Sensor Agent" and uses it as an input of the SVM classifier to predict the states of the air conditioner.
- "Lamp Agent": The required data to predict the states of the lamp are sent by the "Sensor Agent". The "Lamp Agent" uses this information as an input of the SVM classifier.
- "Temperature Agent": It treats the prediction of the temperature variable for a defined period using the SVM machine learning. Then, the results are sent to the "Sensor Agent" embedded in the same container.
- "Humidity Agent": It predicts the humidity variable for a defined period using the SVM machine learning. The results are sent to the "Sensor Agent" embedded in the same container.
- "Luminosity Agent": It predicts the luminosity variable for a defined period using the SVM machine learning. The results are sent to the "Sensor Agent" embedded in the same container.
- "Presence Agent": It predicts the presence state for a defined period using the SVM machine learning. The results are sent to the "Sensor Agent" embedded in the same container.

IV. Predicting Incoming Time-sequence Data Model

A. SVM model for prediction and making-decision

In order to predict and classify the measured results, numerous methods are applied. The SVM method seems to be better suited to this problem saw his ability to handle a small amount of data. The SVM models have been widely used to solve classification and regression problems.

1) Classification function: The SVM separates the different classes of data, by a hyperplane corresponding to the following decision function:

$$f(\mathbf{x}) = sign(\langle \mathbf{w}, \phi(\mathbf{x})\rangle + b) \tag{1}$$

where $\mathbf{x}$ is a set of observations, $\mathbf{w}$ is the vector of coefficients and b is a noise constant.

This supervised machine learning seeks to deduce the function $\Phi : \mathbf{x} \subset \Re^d \rightarrow \{-1; 1\}$ from a set of observations that will correctly classify a maximum number of vectors $\mathbf{x}_i$ by describing the optimal hyper-plane between the two classes: Considering two classes of points, scored -1 and 1, we have a set of N vectors $\mathbf{x}_i \in \mathbf{X} \subset \Re^d, i \in [1, N]$ (d is the input space dimension) with their associated class $y_i \in \{-1; 1\}$.

The constrained quadratic optimization problem can be solved by $\mathbf{w} = \sum_i \alpha_i \Phi(\mathbf{x}_i)$ in terms of a subset of training patterns N. The classifier capacity results in the assignment of a new unknown point in the right class.

The classification function is given by the minimum of the following function:

$$f < \mathbf{w}, \xi >= \min \frac{1}{2} \|\mathbf{w}\|^2 + C \sum_i (\xi_i) \tag{2}$$

subject to:

$$y_i(\langle \mathbf{w}, \Phi(\mathbf{x}_i) + b) \geq 1 - \xi_i\rangle$$

$$\xi_i \geq 0$$

where C is a pre-specified value, and ξ_i are the class variables. Due to the rich theoretical bases and the possibility of transferring the problem to a large space of features, the SVM can provide a good generalization performance. The sensors send pairs of values and activities forming the training set.

This nonlinear binary classification problem requires a maximum optimization model based on the Lagrange multipliers technique and the Kernel function. The SVM classifier manages its nonlinear nature by replacing each scalar product of the weight of activities in a dual form with the Kernel function. The SVM solution $\mathbf{w}$ can be shown using the kernel method as follows:

$$\mathbf{w} = \sum_i y_i \alpha_i \Phi(\mathbf{x}_i)$$

The support vectors' coefficients occur when a point $(\mathbf{x}_i, y_i)$ meets the constraint found by minimizing the following equation:

$$\mathbf{W}(\alpha) = \sum \sum_{j=1} \alpha_i - \frac{1}{2} \sum_{i=1} \sum_{j=1} (\alpha_i \alpha_j y_i y_j K(\mathbf{x}_i, \mathbf{x}_j)) \tag{3}$$

subject to:

$$0 \leq \alpha_i \leq C$$

$$\sum_i y_i \alpha_i = 0$$

2) Regression function: When the SVM are used in regression problems to predict real values, we will talk about the "Support Vector Regression" (SVR) technique. Let consider all of training points $(\mathbf{x}_1, y_1)...(\mathbf{x}_N, y_N)$ where $\mathbf{x}_i \in \mathbf{X} \subset \Re^d, i \in [1, N]$ and the output target $y_i \in \mathbf{Y} \subset \Re^1, i \in [1, N]$, with the condition $C \succ 0$ and $\epsilon \succ 0$. The SVR can also perform regression and estimate the accuracy by computing the scale parameter $\mathbf{y} = f(\mathbf{x})$, where f(**x**) is the estimated decision function. This function ignores errors that are smaller than a certain threshold $\epsilon \succ 0$, thus creating a tube around the true output. The optimal regression function of the two subjects

$$\langle \mathbf{w}, \Phi(\mathbf{x}_i) \rangle + b - y_i \leq \epsilon - \xi^-$$
$$y_i - \langle w, \Phi(x_i) \rangle + b \leq \epsilon - \xi^+$$

is given by:

$$f < W, \xi >= \min \frac{1}{2} \|w\|^2 + C \sum_i (\xi_i^-) + C \sum_i (\xi_i^+) \quad (4)$$

where C is a pre-specified value, and ξ_i^-, ξ_i^+ are gap variables representing upper and lower constraints on system outputs. The dual form of SVR using the Kernel function is:

$$\max_{\alpha,\alpha^*} W(\alpha, \alpha^*) = \max_{\alpha,\alpha^*} \sum_{i=1} \alpha_i^*(y_i - \epsilon) - \alpha_i(y_i + \epsilon)$$
$$- \frac{1}{2} \sum_{i=1} \sum_{j=1}^{l} (\alpha_i^* - \alpha_i)(\alpha_j^* - \alpha_j) K(x_i, x_j) \quad (5)$$

with $\sum_{i=1} (\alpha_i^* - \alpha_i) = 0$ et $0 \leq \alpha_i, \alpha_i^* \leq C$.
The result regression function of the resolution of the above equation by determining the Lagrange multipliers α_i, α_i^* is given by:

$$f(x) = \sum_{SVs} (\bar{\alpha_i} - \bar{\alpha_i^*}) K(x_i, x_j + \bar{b}) \quad (6)$$

with:

$$\bar{b} = -\frac{1}{2} \sum_{i=1}^{l} (\alpha_i - \alpha_i^*)(K(x_i, x_r) + K(x_i, x_s)) \quad (7)$$

$$< \bar{w}, x >= \sum_{i=1}^{l} (\alpha_i - \alpha_i^*) K(x_i, x_j) \quad (8)$$

Our research provides the opportunity to learn the behavior of a resident of a Smart Home from all detected usual tasks. The appropriate equipment, according to the "Electrical Outlet Agent", the "Air Conditioner Agent" and the "Lamp Agent", request the "Sensor Agent" to look for specific data to select the equipment criteria grouped by the "Temperature Agent", the "Humidity Agent", the "Luminosity Agent" and the "Presence Agent". The "Sensor Agent" returns the requested list which will be processed by the equipment agents. Finally, the results that meet the needs of the resident return to the "Sensor Agent". The interactions between agents performing the learning algorithm are illustrated by sequence diagrams shown in Figures 3 and 4.

After making its predictions, the MAS sends notifications

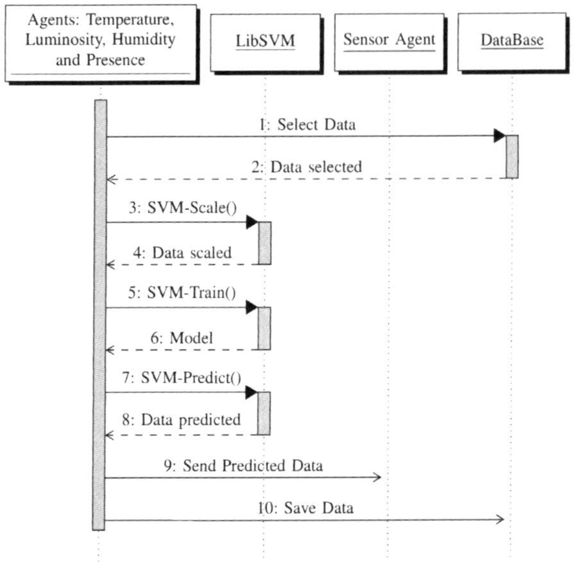

Figure 3. Interaction sequence diagram for temperature, luminosity, humidity and presence agents

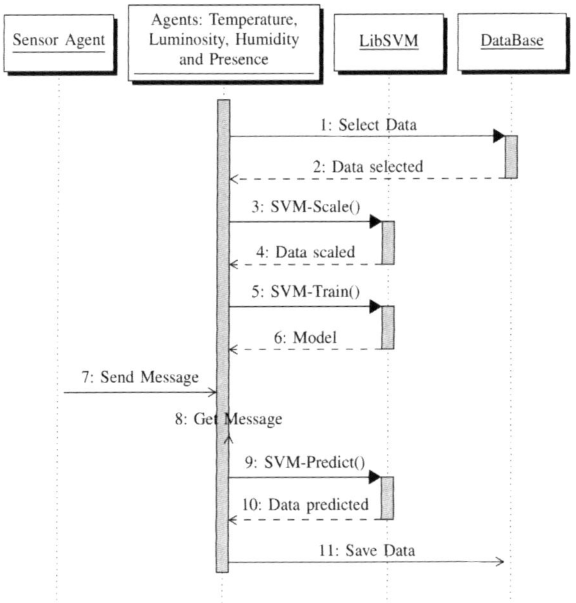

Figure 4. Interaction sequence diagram for Sensor Agent

to the user who can consult the list of predicted tasks. Following its consulted results, the user can react by canceling, confirming or changing the date and the system will finally save these changes.

B. Quality and precision criteria

To assess the quality of our models, we will mainly look at their respective predictive performances measured by the Mean Squared Error (MSE). As a matter of fact, we are working with hourly-normalized data and we will model each hour independently from one another, which is a common choice given the type of data, hence leading to a model of 24 separate daily hours. Indexing the respective MSE criteria of these models by the instant $i = 0, ..., 23,$ to which they are associated, and given their respective observations $y_1, i, ..., y_N$,i, these models return 24 t-day-ahead predictions, defined as the expectations of the predictive distributions, i.e., for $i = 0, .., 23$:

$$\mathbf{x} = \frac{1}{N} \sum_{i=1}^{N} (\hat{y}_i y_i)^2 \tag{9}$$

In our case study, we managed to set up a training set of three months in 2015 so as to predict the values of the different variables for June 2016.

V. Experiments and Results

The features are obtained from the WSN installed in the Smart Home. These features are classified using the SVM machine learning. The development of the classifier takes place using the LIBSVM library of the framework JADE. The LIBSVM toolbox generates a structure containing the type of the SVM, the kernel type, the number of support vectors, the number of classes, the class labels and the offset. It is employed both in the training and testing phases. Several SVM structures are trained on all the possible combinations of signals. A prediction can be obtained with a combination of previously predicted signals.

In our case study, the SVM machine learning is made in four steps (LIBSVM functions):

1) "SVM-Scale" function for data normalization.
2) "SVM-Train" function for training data to obtain a prediction model.
3) "SVM-Predict" function using the model to make predictions about the classes or the values in the case of regression.
4) "SVM-Test" function to calculate the model performance. In this step, we select the data whose class or values are known (for regression) and we use the model to predict their class and value, and in the end, we compare the two real and predicted classes (or the real and predicted values). To assess the quality of the predictions obtained in the "SVM-Test", the MSE is used as a measure of a prediction error.

We choose to use as "Input-Attributes" the time and the date and as "Input-Labels" the class or the regression values for the prediction of power consumption, presence, open/close and environment variables (temperature, humidity and luminosity). The SVM model parameters are specified in Table I. We construct an SVM learning scheme to predict the environment variables and power consumption in a Smart Home. We use the "Smart Life" datasets for validating the performance of our proposed architectures. The "Smart Life" datasets consists of independent datasets collected from a couple of apartments for a year using different sensors. The sensors are installed in everyday objects, such as refrigerator, and light switches, etc. We thoroughly analyze a full year historical data and utilize them to configure a large number of input and output datasets for the SVM learning. The proposed SVM-based prediction model can simultaneously predict the future amount of time-series data. Throughout the experiments, the proposed SVM-based prediction model shows the highest prediction accuracy, compared to other prediction models, such as the conventional time-series and the artificial neural network models. As a result, these prediction data can be effectively utilized for behavior recognition and energy management systems in Smart Home.

Using the MSE function to calculate the performance of the SVM predictor, we show in Figure 5 and Figure 6 that the prediction for the time series with low intensity of harmonic variations, as the temperature variable ($MSE = 8.57$), is more performant than the high intensity of harmonic variations, like the humidity variable ($MSE = 18.6948$). The Performance of the SVM model for the air conditioners' operating status regression is perfect with an $MSEvalue = 0.57$, describing the conformity of the predicted equipment state values to the real ones. These simulations confirm the performance of the SVM predictor, compared with the real values, as shown in Figure 7.

We propose the SVM machine learning to automate the

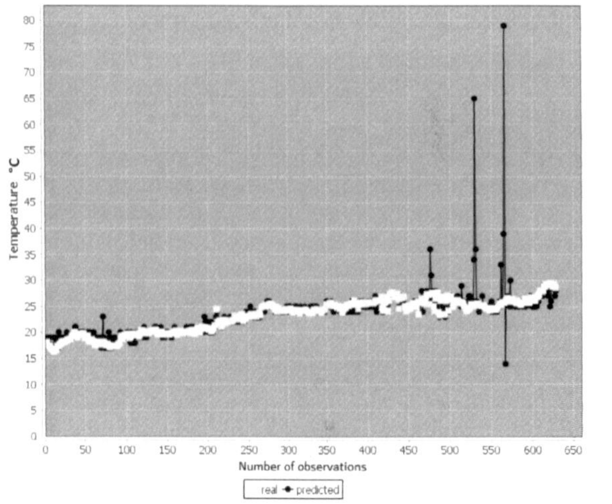

Figure 5. Performance of SVM model for temperature prediction (MSE= 8.57)

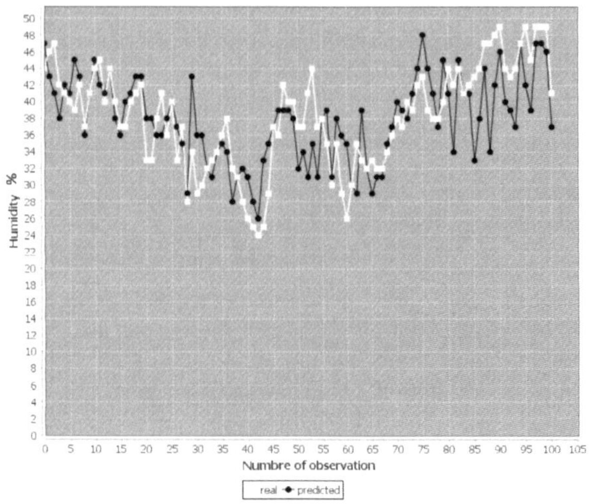

Figure 6. Performance of SVM model for humidity prediction (MSE= 18.6948)

TABLE I. SVM MODEL PARAMETERS FOR EACH VARIABLE

			State	Presence	Door-sensor	Temperature	Humidity	Luminosity	Power
SVM-Train	Inputs	*Attributes*	Hour	Hour	Hour	Hour	Hour	Hour	Hour
			Minute	Minute	Minute	Minute	Minute	Minute	Minute
			Day of the month	Day of the month	Day of the month	Day of the month	Day of the month	Day of the month	Day of the month
			Day of the week	Day of the week	Day of the week	Day of the week	Day of the week	Day of the week	Day of the week
			Week of the month	Week of the month	Week of the month	Week of the month	Week of the month	Week of the month	Week of the month
			Month	Month	Month	Month	Month	Month	Month
			Year	Year	Year	Year	Year	Year	Year
		Labels	Class '0' : OFF Class '1' : ON	Class '0' : Absence Class '1' : Presence	Class '0' : Close Class '1' : Open	Real values	Real values	Real values	Real Values
	Outputs	*Model*	Regression Model	Regression	Regression	Classification	Classification	Classification	Classification
SVM-Predict	Inputs	*Attributes*	Hour	Hour	Hour	Hour	Hour	Hour	Hour
			Minute	Minute	Minute	Minute	Minute	Minute	Minute
			Day of the month	Day of the month	Day of the month	Day of the month	Day of the month	Day of the month	Day of the month
			Day of the week	Day of the week	Day of the week	Day of the week	Day of the week	Day of the week	Day of the week
			Week of the month	Week of the month	Week of the month	Week of the month	Week of the month	Week of the month	Week of the month
			Month	Month	Month	Month	Month	Month	Month
			Year	Year	Year	Year	Year	Year	Year
	Outputs	*Labels*	Class '0' : OFF Class '1' : ON	Class '0' : Absence Class '1' : Presence	Class '0' : Close Class '1' : Open	Real values	Real values	Real values	Real Values
SVM-Test	Inputs	Attributes	Hour	Hour	Hour	Hour	Hour	Hour	Hour
			Minute	Minute	Minute	Minute	Minute	Minute	Minute
			Day of the month	Day of the month	Day of the month	Day of the month	Day of the month	Day of the month	Day of the month
			Day of the week	Day of the week	Day of the week	Day of the week	Day of the week	Day of the week	Day of the week
			Week of the month	Week of the month	Week of the month	Week of the month	Week of the month	Week of the month	Week of the month
			Month	Month	Month	Month	Month	Month	Month
			Year	Year	Year	Year	Year	Year	Year
		Labels	Class '0' : OFF Class '1' : ON	Class '0' : Absence Class '1' : Presence	Class '0' : Close Class '1' : Open	Real values	Real values	Real values	Real Values
	Outputs	*Performance*	MSE	MSE	MSE	MSE	MSE	MSE	MSE

process of air conditioning in a home as a case study. We use the SVM machine learning to predict the ambient temperature and the condition and value of the power of the air conditioner at a specific date-time. These recorded features will be useful for the decision-making and automatic control of the air conditioner. The SVM classifier determines the temperature set point belonging to a predefined regression class. The experimental results on the real world application "Smart Life" demonstrate the effectiveness of our approach in case of linear classification and regression. The SVM model has a remarkable learning ability in a distributed intelligence system.

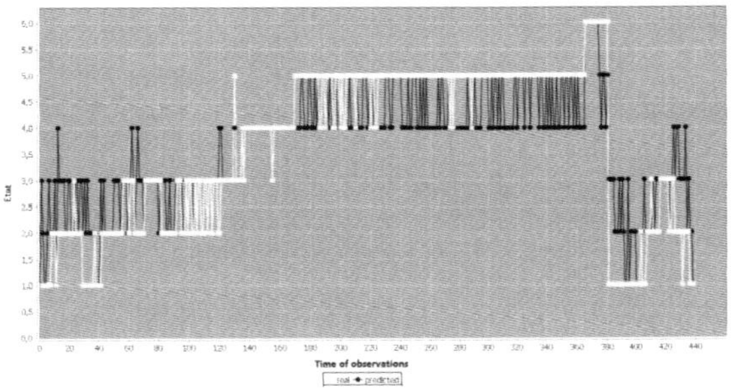

Figure 7. Performance of SVM model for air conditioner operating state regression (MSE= 0.57)

VI. Conclusion and Future Work

In this paper, we have started by introducing the IoT and the MASs and their applications to design our MAS architecture for Smart Home automation. Indeed, we have proposed a new active learning algorithm based on the SVM approach adopted to solve the problem of prediction and multi-class classification of WSN devices installed in a Smart Home. The technical experience requires to manipulate the proposed Smart Home scenario with the machine learning algorithm, the MAS system and the Android mobile system. Our solution must be well integrated into the professional company IoT application. For future work, we will use a hybrid algorithm combining the hiden Markov model and the SVM model for features' prediction and the decision tree model for making decision to remotely control intelligent households via an Android application. Nevertheless, we can extend the realization of this project by enriching the use of more accurate intelligent sensors. In addition, we can optimize our solution using a consistent big-data learning base for real-time prediction of sequential data.

Acknowledgment

This work is part of a PhD thesis supported by "PASRI-MOBIDOC" Project financed by the EU, "Chifco" company, "Innov'COM" laboratory, and National School of Engineering of Tunis-ENIT.

References

[1] M. A. C. Lozada and F. D. la Rosa R., "Simulation platform for domotic systems," in Proc. IEEE Colombian Conf. Communications and Computing (COLCOM), Jun. 2014, pp. 1–6.

[2] Y. Zhang, Q. Wu, X. Tang, Q. Wu, and Z. Ma, "Progresses for multi-agents system models," in Proc. 2nd Int Computer and Automation Engineering (ICCAE) Conf, vol. 3, Feb. 2010, pp. 44–48.

[3] P. Chahuara, A. Fleury, F. Portet, and M. Vacher, "On-line human activity recognition from audio and home automation sensors: Comparison of sequential and non-sequential models in realistic smart homes1," Journal of Ambient Intelligence and Smart Environments, vol. 8, no. 4, 2016, pp. 399–422.

[4] Y.-W. Lin, Y.-B. Lin, C.-Y. Hsiao, and Y.-Y. Wang, "Iottalk-rc: Sensors as universal remote control for aftermarket home appliances," IEEE Internet of Things Journal, vol. 4, no. 4, 2017, pp. 1104–1112.

[5] S. Feng, P. Setoodeh, and S. Haykin, "Smart home: Cognitive interactive people-centric internet of things," IEEE Communications Magazine, vol. 55, no. 2, 2017, pp. 34–39.

[6] S. K. Viswanath and et al., "System design of the internet of things for residential smart grid," IEEE Wireless Communications, vol. 23, no. 5, 2016, pp. 90–98.

[7] M. Asplund and S. Nadjm-Tehrani, "Attitudes and perceptions of iot security in critical societal services," IEEE Access, vol. 4, 2016, pp. 2130–2138.

[8] G. Villarrubia, J. F. D. Paz, D. H. Iglesia, and J. Bajo, "Combining multi-agent systems and wireless sensor networks for monitoring crop irrigation," Sensors, vol. 17, no. 8, 2017, p. 1775.

[9] R. M. Saleem, A. Muhammad, and A. M. Martinez-Enriquez, "Remote patient monitoring and healthcare management using multi-agent based architecture," in Proc. Ninth Mexican Int Artificial Intelligence (MICAI) Conf, Nov. 2010, pp. 118–123.

[10] M. H. Cintuglu and O. A. Mohammed, "Simulation of digitalized power system using pmu and intelligent control," in Proc. IEEE Industry Applications Society Annual Meeting, Oct. 2013, pp. 1–8.

[11] C. Yilmaz, S. Albayrak, and M. Ltzenberger, "Smart grid architectures and the multi-agent system paradigm," ENERGY, 2014, pp. 90–95.

[12] Q. Sun, W. Yu, N. Kochurov, Q. Hao, and F. Hu, "A multi-agent-based intelligent sensor and actuator network design for smart house and home automation," Journal of Sensor and Actuator Networks, vol. 2, no. 3, 2013, pp. 557–588.

[13] A. Javed, H. Larijani, A. Ahmadinia, and D. Gibson, "Smart random neural network controller for hvac using cloud computing technology," IEEE Transactions on Industrial Informatics, vol. 13, no. 1, 2017, pp. 351–360.

[14] M. Ruta, F. Scioscia, G. Loseto, and E. Di Sciascio, "Semantic-based resource discovery and orchestration in home and building automation: A multi-agent approach," IEEE Transactions on Industrial Informatics, vol. 10, no. 1, 2014, pp. 730–741.

[15] A. B. Karami, A. Fleury, J. Boonaert, and S. Lecoeuche, "User in the loop: Adaptive smart homes exploiting user feedbackstate of the art and future directions," Information, vol. 7, no. 2, 2016, p. 35.

[16] A. C. Jose, R. Malekian, and N. Ye, "Improving home automation security; integrating device fingerprinting into smart home," IEEE Access, vol. 4, 2016, pp. 5776–5787.

[17] U. Siddiqui and et al., "Elastic jade: Dynamically scalable multi agents using cloud resources," in Proc. Second Int Cloud and Green Computing (CGC) Conf, Nov. 2012, pp. 167–172.

[18] J. Britz, J. Frey, and J. Alexandersson, "Bridging the gap between smart home and agents," in Proc. Int Intelligent Environments (IE) Conf, Jun. 2014, pp. 31–38.

Numerical Approach to Simulation of Nanoprinting Processes

Tatiana Kudryashova[1], Viktoriia Podryga[1,2], and Sergey Polyakov[1,3]
[1] Keldysh Institute of Applied Mathematics RAS, Moscow, Russia
[2] Moscow Automobile and Road Construction State Technical University, Moscow, Russia
[3] National Research Nuclear University MEPhI, Moscow, Russia
e-mail: kudryashova@imamod.ru, pvictoria@list.ru, polyakov@imamod.ru

Abstract **– This work-in-progress paper proposes a new numerical approach for the simulation of technological process of obtaining surfaces with given properties. This problem is relevant for many industrial applications. In medicine, nanotechnology enables us to create plasters, to implement bioprinting or to construct microsensors that will be used to detect cancer cells in the body. The paper describes a numerical method that helps to analyze different possibilities of producing functional surfaces coated with noble metal nanoparticles. Such surfaces may have many uses. Firstly, it is known that silver, aurum and other noble metals have a strong antibacterial effect. Secondly, the electrical conductivity of a noble metal is greater in comparison with the other metals. A set of numerical experiments have been done and their results are reported in this work.**

Keywords – multiscale mathematical models; numerical methods; nanotechnology problems; noble metal nanoparticles; nanoprinting in medical applications.

I. INTRODUCTION

In the late 2000s and early 2010s, in most developed countries, the potential for further growth of productivity in the world economic and technological sectors was limited [1]. Recovery of high rates of productivity in the economy and its profit can not be achieved only through macroeconomic measures. At present, the answer to the challenge of preserving competitiveness and achieving high rates of productivity should be given by the scientific, technological and innovation policies pursued by industrialized countries. The purpose of these policies is to stimulate development and implementation of advanced technologies, whose performance significantly exceeds the characteristics of traditional technologies.

The traditional and new mathematics, mathematical methods, numerical methods based on multiscale models, differential equations and classical physics underlie the development of the novel technologies.

Nowadays, clearly identified directions that can be considered technologically mainstream include: information technology, biotechnology, nanotechnology, ecological technology, and cognitive technology. They represent a new technological interface between humans and their environment [2]. The progress of these directions defines technological development and its rate corresponding to the modern world challenges.

Nanotechnology plays an important role in industrial and natural processes in a variety of fields including engineering, production of consumer goods, public health and biology. The creation of micro- or nanostructures on the substrate surface not only changes its topography, but can substantially modify the properties of the substance. By creating structures similar to natural objects, we can control their properties without changing their chemical nature.

Multicolored butterfly wings are painted in all colors of the rainbow without any paints, geckos know how to run on steep walls without using glue, the leaves of some plants can purify themselves and repel droplets of water without chemical treatment. All this is possible thanks to the hierarchically structured topography of biological objects and can be reproduced with the help of nanotechnology [3]-[7].

The typical size of noble metal particles is equal to 5-50 nm. These nanoparticles are the strongest biocidal agents and are used in biosensors and numerous assays. Nanostructure materials with noble metal nanoparticles can be used as biological markers for quantitative detection. For example, silver nanoparticles are incorporated in apparel, footwear, paints, wound dressings, appliances, cosmetics, and plastics for their antibacterial properties [8]. The unique properties of silver nanoparticles make them attractive for numerous areas.

It is known that materials can be modified with noble metal nanoparticles, using plasma treatment or cold gas spraying. In contrast to other technologies, this enables the creation of materials with different bactericidal properties and also high hydrophilicity/hydrophobicity. For example, the ability to absorb body moisture is an important hygienic indicator.

In this paper, we study the nanoprinting processes at low and room temperatures (100-350 K). Cold rarefied gas accelerated to supersonic speed is used for transportation of noble metal nanoparticles to a hot substrate.

In our previous works, we analyzed jet flows, streams in microchannels and other gas dynamic problems using a new multiscale approach [9]-[12]. This approach combines the traditional hydrodynamic models (we use quasigasdynamic equations [13],[14]) with Newton's dynamics equations for individual particles. In this paper, we use direct molecular dynamic simulation [15]-[18].

This paper is organized as follows: Section II states the current problem and gives some literature references to preview works. In Section III, we describe what methods are used in the research, and we consider the main macroparameters of the system. Section IV presents the preliminary results of the current research. Section V presents conclusions that can be drawn from the testing results and addresses future work as well. The future study will exceed the scope of this research. Also, the next steps and future plans of this study are described in this section.

In the paper an approach for the cold gas spraying process of the nanoparticles on substrate is discussed.

II. STATEMENT OF THE PROBLEM

In the present work, the process of acceleration of a metallic nanocluster by a supersonic gas flow is considered. The purpose of this particular procedure is to allow the metal clusters to reach a predetermined constant velocity, which will allow these clusters to adhere to a hot substrate in case of contact with it. The procedure is illustrated in Figure 1, which shows a fragment of the spraying system.

To describe the acceleration of the nanocluster, we used the equations of two-component molecular dynamics [18]:

$$m_l \frac{d\mathbf{v}_{l,i}}{dt} = \mathbf{F}_{l,i}, \quad \frac{d\mathbf{r}_{l,i}}{dt} = \mathbf{v}_{l,i}, \quad i = 1,\dots,N_l, \quad l = a,b, \quad (1)$$

where i is the particle number, l is the particle type (a – molecules of gas, b – atoms of metal in the nanocluster), N_l is the total number of particles of type l, m_l is the mass of particle of type l, $\mathbf{r}_{l,i} = (r_{x,l,i}, r_{y,l,i}, r_{z,l,i})$ and $\mathbf{v}_{l,i} = (v_{x,l,i}, v_{y,l,i}, v_{z,l,i})$ are the position vector and the velocity vector of the i -th particle of type l, $\mathbf{F}_{l,i} = (F_{x,l,i}, F_{y,l,i}, F_{z,l,i})$ is the resultant force acting on this particle.

The forces include the component of i -th particle interaction with the surrounding particles and the component responsible for external action:

$$\mathbf{F}_{l,i} = -\nabla_{\mathbf{r}_{l,i}} U + \mathbf{F}^{ext}_{l,i}, \quad i = 1,\dots,N_l, \quad l = a,b. \quad (2)$$

Here, $\mathbf{F}^{ext}_{l,i}$ is the force of interaction with the environment, U is the total potential energy and it depends on choosing the interaction potential of molecules. The potential energy of the system is represented as a function that depends on the coordinates of considered particles and describes the interaction between the particles of the system. Selecting a specific type of interaction potential is based on a comparison of the mechanical properties of the computer model of potential and real material. To solve equations (1) and (2), it is necessary to consider all options of interaction l with l' for $l = a,b$ and $l' = a,b$. As an example, the potential functions for modeling the interactions between the gas molecules and the metal atoms of the nanocluster can be considered, which were used in [19].

For closure of (1) and (2), the periodic boundary conditions were used.

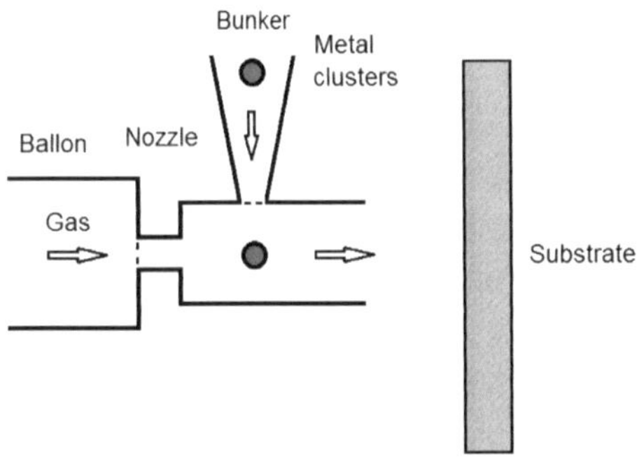

Figure 1. Fragment of spraying microsystem.

An initial state of the gas and the metal systems corresponded to the condition of thermodynamic equilibrium at a predetermined temperature and pressure.

III. METHOD OF STUDY

A numerical algorithm for integration of equations (1) and (2) is based on well known Verlet's scheme [20]:

$$\begin{cases} \mathbf{v}^{n+1/2}_{l,i} = \mathbf{v}^{n}_{l,i} + \dfrac{\mathbf{F}^{n}_{l,i}}{2m_{l,i}}\Delta t, \quad \mathbf{r}^{n+1}_{l,i} = \mathbf{r}^{n}_{l,i} + \mathbf{v}^{n+1/2}_{l,i}\Delta t, \\ \mathbf{v}^{n+1}_{l,i} = \mathbf{v}^{n+1/2}_{l,i} + \dfrac{\mathbf{F}^{n+1}_{l,i}}{2m_{l,i}}\Delta t, \quad i = 1,\dots,N_l, \quad l = a,b. \end{cases} \quad (3)$$

Here, Δt is the integration step (in time), n is the step number, $\mathbf{F}^{n+1}$ is the value of the force at this step.

At the initial time, the coordinates and velocities of all particles are set. Further, at each time step, the equations of motion are solved; new values of the force vectors, new coordinates and velocities are computed. Calculations are carried out taking into account the boundary conditions and the external impact on the system in areas where this impact is present.

Kinetic energy of thermal motion E_T, kinetic energy E_K and total energy E of the system are calculated separately for particles of each type $l = a,b$ as follows:

$$\begin{gathered} E_K = \sum_i E_{K,l,i}, \quad E_T = \sum_i E_{T,l,i}, \quad E = E_K + U, \\ E_{K,l,i} = m_{l,i}\left|\mathbf{v}_{l,i}\right|^2/2, \quad E_{T,l,i} = m_{l,i}\left|\mathbf{v}_{l,i} - \mathbf{v}_l\right|^2/2, \quad (4) \\ \mathbf{v}_l = \frac{1}{N_l}\sum_i \mathbf{v}_{l,i}, \quad i = 1,\dots,N_l, \quad l = a,b. \end{gathered}$$

Here, $E_{K,l,i}$ is the kinetic energy of the particle with number i, $E_{T,l,i}$ is the thermal kinetic energy of the particle with number i, $\left|\mathbf{v}_{l,i}\right|$ is the velocity vector length of i -th particle of l type, $\mathbf{v}_l = \left(v_{x,l}, v_{y,l}, v_{z,l}\right)$ is the center-of-momentum frame velocity for particles of type $l = a,b$.

Gas or metal particle system temperature T and pressure p are defined as follows:

$$T = \frac{2}{d}\frac{\langle E_T \rangle}{N k_b}, \quad p = \frac{1}{3}\left(p_{xx} + p_{yy} + p_{zz}\right),$$
$$p_{\alpha\alpha} = \frac{1}{V}\sum_i m_i \left(v_{i,\alpha} - v_\alpha\right)^2 + \frac{1}{V}\sum_i \sum_{j>i} r_{ij,\alpha} \cdot F_{ij,\alpha}. \quad (5)$$

Here, d is the number of particle freedom degrees, k_b is the Boltzmann constant (further unless otherwise is stated $d = 3$), V is the volume of the system, $\mathbf{r}_{ij} = \mathbf{r}_i - \mathbf{r}_j$, $\mathbf{F}_{ij}$ is the force of interaction between i-th and j-th particles, α is coordinate x, y or z accordingly. The particle type index has been removed from the formula for clarity of expression.

The initial state of the gas and metal microsystem was realized by thermostating.

IV. RESULTS AND DISSCUSSION

As a model problem, the problem of acceleration of a nickel cluster by nitrogen molecules was considered. The dimensions of the cubic-shaped cluster were 24^3 crystals or 8.475^3 nm^3, and the number of atoms was 55296 (see Figure 2). The initial position of the cluster center was at the point $(266.97, 34.14, 34.14)$; sizes were measured in nanometers. The acceleration was carried out by injecting a small portion of gas into the system. In this case, a gas microsystem containing 82904 molecules was used. The microsystem was under normal conditions ($T = 273.15K$, $p = 101325Pa$). Approximately a half of these molecules were pre-accelerated to speeds of 14 Mach (see Figure 3).

The performed calculation was related to the analysis of the evolution of a shock wave and its interaction with the nanocluster and resting gas molecules. Figure 3 shows the longitudinal velocity distributions of the gas near the region occupied by the nanoclusters; values are averaged over the coordinate y. They illustrate some details of the acceleration process. At the beginning of this process, the front of the shock wave is scattered near the cluster. But the cluster itself does not move much. Then, it begins to accelerate slowly and evenly up to a certain limiting speed (see Figures 4 and 5). The magnitude of this velocity is related to the amount of gas incident on the cluster and its total momentum. If the value of the total momentum of the gas is small, it will take a very long time to accelerate the system to a certain average speed. From the law of conservation of momentum, we can estimate the value of the total average velocity:

$$\mathbf{v}^{(\infty)} = \frac{m_a N_a^*}{\left(m_a N_a + m_b N_b\right)} \mathbf{v}^{(0)}, \quad (6)$$

where $\mathbf{v}^{(0)}$ is the average initial velocity of accelerated nitrogen molecules, N_a^* is the number of such molecules.

The numerical algorithm was implemented as a parallel program using the MPI [21] and OpenMP [22] standards. Model calculations were performed on K60 cluster with processors Intel Xeon E5-2690 v4 @ 2.60GHz and a total performance of 60 TFlops.

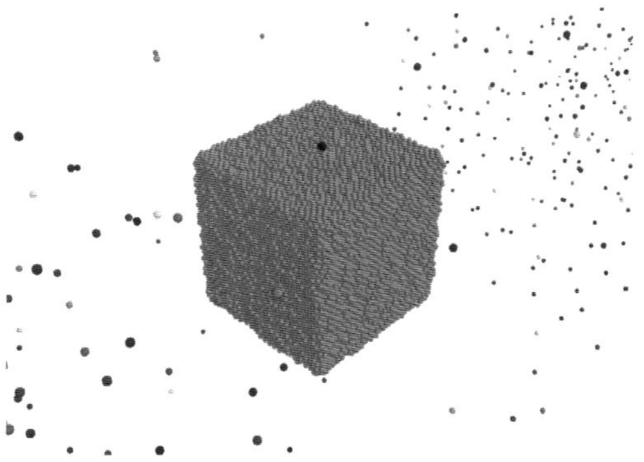

Figure 2. 3D image of the nanocluster and gas molecules at the beginning of the acceleration process.

(a)
(b)
(c)

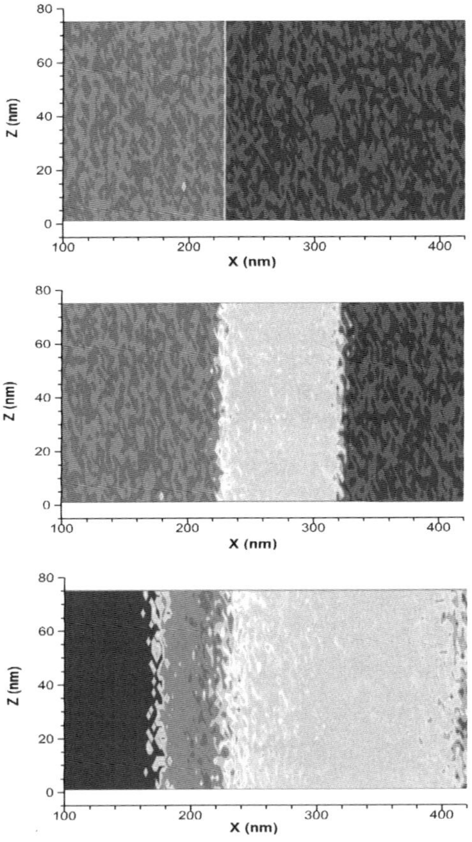

Figure 3. Distributions of the longitudinal velocity of the gas averaged over the coordinate y at time points 0, 18, 38 ps (a, b, c).

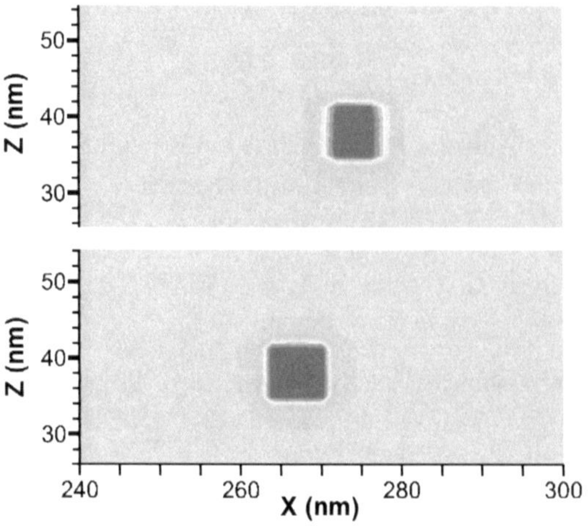

Figure 4. Position of the nanocluster at initial time (from below) and at time point 350 ps (from above). Coordinates are measured in nanometers.

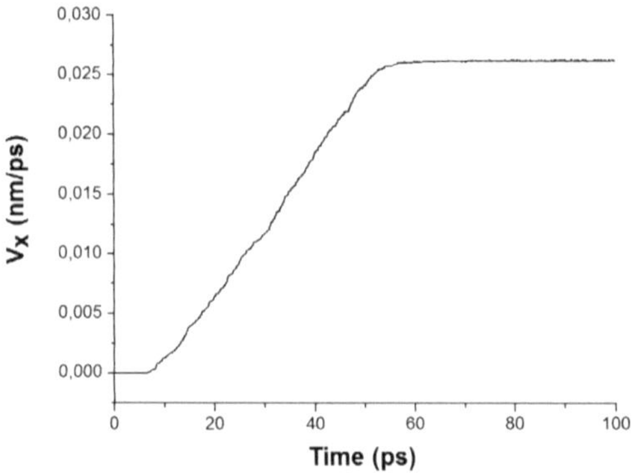

Figure 5. Evolution of the longitudinal velocity of the cluster.

V. CONCLUSION AND FUTURE WORK

In this paper, we considered only the first stage of the process of spraying and deposition of nanoparticles on a substrate associated with the acceleration of a single nanocluster. The numerical approach based on the direct molecular modelling was used for this purpose. The continuation of this work will be connected both with the interaction of the cluster accelerated to a certain velocity with the substrate, and the general spraying processes, in which a lot of clusters participate. In the future, we will consider the nanoparticles of other metals. In this general problem, it is proposed to use the multiscale technology developed in previous works of the authors.

ACKNOWLEDGMENT

This work was partially supported by Russian Foundation for Basic Research (grants No. 16-07-00206-a, 17-01-00973-a).

REFERENCES

[1] V. Knyaginin, The New Technological Revolution. URL: https://csr.ru/wp-content/uploads/2017/10/novaya-tehnologicheskaya-revolutsiya-2017-10-13.pdf

[2] https://www.techopedia.com/definition/29894/nanotechnology-biotechnology-information-technology-cognitive-science-nbic

[3] M. V. Kiryuhin, B. M. Sergeev, A. N. Prusov, and V. G. Sergeev, "Photochemical reduction of silver cations in a polyelectrolyte matrix," High-molecular compounds. Series B, vol. 42, no 6, pp. 1069–1073, 2000.

[4] B. Nolting, "Biophysical nanotechnology," in Methods in Modern Biophysics. Berlin, Heidelberg: Springer, pp. 147–163, 2004.

[5] E. Gazit, Plenty of Room for Biology at the Bottom: An Introduction to Bionanotechnology. London: Imperial College Press, 2007.

[6] L. Mädler and S. K. Friedlander, "Transport of nanoparticles in gases: overview and recent advances," Aerosol and Air Quality Research, vol. 7, no. 3, pp. 304–342, 2007.

[7] R. M. Zadegan and M. L. Norton, "Structural DNA nanotechnology: from design to applications," Int. J. Mol. Sci., vol. 13, no. 6, pp. 7149–7162, 2012.

[8] S. J. Oldenburg, Silver Nanoparticles: Properties and Applications. URL: https://www.sigmaaldrich.com/technical-documents/articles/materials-science/nanomaterials/silver-nanoparticles.html

[9] Yu. Karamzin, T. Kudryashova, V. Podryga, and S. Polyakov, "Numerical Simulation of the Gas Mixture Flows Using Hybrid Computer Systems," Proc. of the Ninth International Conference on Engineering Computational Technology (ECT 2014), Stirlingshire, UK: Civil-Comp Press, Sept. 2014, paper 28, pp. 1–14. doi:10.4203/ccp.105.28.

[10] T. Kudryashova, Yu. Karamzin, V. Podryga, and S. Polyakov, "Two-scale computation of N2-H2 jet flow based on QGD and MMD on heterogeneous multi-core hardware," Advances in Engineering Software, ELSEVIER, in press, online 31 March 2016. doi:10.1016/j.advengsoft.2016.02.005.

[11] V. O. Podryga, Yu. N. Karamzin, T. A. Kudryashova, and S. V. Polyakov, "Multiscale Simulation of Three-Dimensional Unsteady Gas Flows in Microchannels of Technical Systems," Proc. of the Seventh European Congress on Computational Methods in Applied Sciences and Engineering (ECCOMAS 2016), June 2016, vol. 2, pp. 2331-2345.

[12] T. Kudryashova, V. Podryga, and S. Polyakov, "HPC-simulation of gasdynamic flows on macroscopic and molecular levels," in Nonlinearity. Problems, Solutions and Applications, vol. I, chap. 26, L. A. Uvarova, A. B. Nadykto, and A. V. Latyshev, Eds. New York: Nova Science Publishers, pp. 543–556, 2017.

[13] B. N. Chetverushkin, Kinetic Schemes and Quasi-Gasdynamic System of Equations. Barcelona: CIMNE, 2008.

[14] T. G. Elizarova, Quasi-Gas Dynamic Equations. Berlin, Heidelberg, New York: Springer-Verlag, 2009.

[15] M. P. Allen and D. J. Tildesley, Computer Simulation of Liquids. London: U.K.: Oxford Univ. Press, 1989.

[16] D. C. Rapaport, The Art of Molecular Dynamics Simulation. Cambridge: Cambridge University Press, 2004.

[17] J. M. Haile, Molecular Dynamics Simulation: Elementary Methods. New York: Wiley, 1992.

[18] D. Frenkel and B. Smit, Understanding Molecular Simulation: from Algorithms to Applications. San Diego: Academic Press, 2002.

[19] J. E. Lennard-Jones, "Cohesion," Proc. Phys. Soc., vol. 43, no. 5, pp. 461–482, 1931.

[20] L. Verlet, "Computer "experiments" on classical fluids. I. Thermodynamical properties of Lennard-Jones molecules," Physical Review, vol. 159, no. 1, pp. 98–103, 1967.

[21] Official documentation and manuals on MPI. URL: http://www.mcs.anl.gov/ research/projects/mpi/

[22] Official documentation and manuals on OpenMP. URL: http://www.openmp.org/resources/openmp-books

Workflow Representations for Human and Artificial Agent Collaborations

Georg Weichhart
Flexible Production Systems, PROFACTOR GmbH
Cognitive Robotics and Shop Floors, Pro2Future GmbH
Steyr, Austria
email: georg.weichhart@Pro2Future.at

Andreas Pichler, Christian Wögerer
Robotic and Assistive Systems
PROFACTOR GmbH
Steyr, Austria
email: Givenname.Surname@PROFACTOR.at

Abstract— **In this initial research, we are taking a look at process representation and process modelling approaches for collaborative robotics. We take a system-of-systems view and apply work stemming from business process management, workflow systems to enable interoperable workflows. Initial requirements and research needs are identified for planning, executing interoperable process models, which are representing tasks shared among multiple human and artificial systems.**

Keywords- Collaborative Robotics; Enterprise Interoperability; Process Modelling; Business Process Management.

I. INTRODUCTION

In the past, production companies have been focusing on optimizing with the goal to increase efficiency and effectiveness. Modern paradigms like the S^3 (Sensing, Smart, Sustainable) Enterprise [1] envision a networked, flexible production system capable of quick adaptation to evolving situations and changing customer demands. This paradigm is suitable for increasing production in Europe, due to the need for late customization of products while still having limited transport times.

The sensing part of the S^3 Enterprise paradigm implies the capability of hardware devices, machines to transmit information about themselves and the surrounding they are aware of. This is needed to be able to react to changes. The smart part implies that intelligent algorithms are in place across the enterprise, being able to either make information available to decision makers, or make decisions on their own rule set. Flexibility often comes at the cost of complexity. Still, decision are to be taken fast. The sustainability part implies evolution and the need of continuous adaptation to heterogeneous factors. Where one important factor here is the customer demand.

Collaborative robotics is one technical approach that conceptually fits into the S^3 Enterprise worldview. Such production systems are highly adaptive, equipped with a number of sensors, and are driven by highly intelligent algorithms. From an interoperability point of view, a unifying model is needed that allows both systems (worker agent, robotic agent) to map their own (mental) models to the unifying one. The unifying level is needed, due to the (obvious) different requirements of the systems, which inhibit integrated approaches. Research in interoperability is concerned with the infrastructure needed that allows lose coupled systems. Here, the systems are the humans and the robots. Both remain independent but need a common understanding.

The remaining parts of this paper are structured as follows. In Section 2, we make research questions explicit. Two exemplary existing business process modelling and execution languages are used to exemplify the modelling of complex human robot interactions. These are presented in Section 3. We conclude this work in Section 4.

II. MODELS OF COLLABORATIVE PROCESSES

A unifying model supports loose coupling of independent systems. This increases flexibility as systems might change without influencing others. A unifying level has to provide all features that are needed for the systems' interactions.

To be able to connect independent systems through a unifying level, it must be possible to translate or map system internal models to the common one. The complexity of the overall system increases, and more effort is needed to reach interoperability than to reach integration through a single model.

To understand the requirements for interoperable process models we want to answer the following two questions. What is the overall goal for the model? What are scenarios / functions that need to be covered to reach that goal?

A. *Goals of Process Models for Human Robot Collaboration*

As the two considered systems (humans, robots) are active, these are referred to as *agents* in the following [2]. The term *agent* signifies that the systems have some sort of intelligence allowing the agents to act autonomous. Agents have control over their actions, allowing the execution of tasks concurrently.

A unifying model has to be useable for the execution phase and for the planning phase of process. It must support interaction and synchronization of human and artificial agents during planning, execution of the common process.

- *Execution Phase*: The execution of process steps may be implemented by humans, or artificial agents, or both. This affects the readability, understandability and usability of the model. Execution of process steps needs to be synchronized across concurrently acting actors.

- *Planning Phase*: Manual design of process segments as well as automated (re-)planning needs to be possible to support changes and adaptation.

In situations requiring ad hoc adaptation, the phases might be dynamically switched. This implies that re-planning has to respect partially executed plans. At any time the unifying character, allowing the systems to interact, needs to be intact. Workers for example, need to understand the workflow executed by the robot.

B. *Degree of Collaboration*

To understand detailed requirements for situations where systems interact, we analyze human robot interaction with respect to the synchronization of work between human and artificial agents [3]:

- *Binary interaction (Start / Stop)*: Simple interaction (like pressing start / stop) of the worker with the robot. The activities of both agents are synchronized through a simple task where the worker uses control buttons. The robot is passive in the sense of obeying the command without further interaction.
- *Coexistence interaction*: This is a situation, where both agents operate next to each other but have no shared tasks or pieces of work. Hardly any synchronization is required. Both agents must make sure to not interfere with the other agent's work. Some sort of collision detection and avoidance is required.
- *Assistance interaction*: Robot is assisting the human. The robot serves without following individual goals, obeying commands of the user. Synchronization between the two agents takes place through the transmission of commands from the human to the robot, with limited feedback by the robot.
- *Cooperation interaction*: This describes a situation where human and robotic agents, share a work-piece. The synchronization of both agents takes place through the location of the work. Both agents need to be aware where and when the respective other agent works on a part of the work piece. The agents must not perform any steps that interfere with the other's work. This requires some understanding about the other agent's currently executed and immediate next tasks.
- *Collaborative interaction*: Here, human and robotic agents share a task. The synchronization of both agents is not limited to a work-piece, but activities are synchronized. Timing and location, where the tasks are executed, are of importance. Also, the upcoming activities of the collaborator. Both (the human and the robot) need a detailed understanding of the activities including their timing.

III. PROCESS DESIGN APPROACHES

In the following, we take a look at different approaches which fall into two categories. Task centric approaches considered are for example Business Process Management Notation (BPMN), and ARIS [4], communication oriented approaches are for example Subject-oriented Business Process Management (S-BPM) [5], and Agent-oriented Business Process Management (ABPM) [6].

A. *S-BPM*

S-BPM (Subject-oriented Business Process Management) is a process approach, used for manual design of processes, which are executed by humans. Recently extensions have been researched to mix human and artificial agents [7,8].

S-BPM allows to model two aspects, the subject-interaction, and the subject behavior. Subject Interaction Diagrams (SID) show the message flows between subjects. Subject Behavior Diagrams (SBD) show the individual control flow of a single subject. These two diagrams are on two different levels of abstraction. Subjects may be interpreted as roles of agents that prescribe the behavior of that role in a wider process context.

Figure 1 shows a S-BPM process. On top, a subject interaction diagram is presented. The grey boxes are "Collaborator" represent subjects. A subject is similar to a role in a process. It shows the interface where information objects are exchanged, between the subjects. The second part of Figure 1. shows two subjects next to each other, and their internal behavior. Three types of activities are possible: (1) Act (yellow; marked with F), (2) Receive Business Object (green; marked with R), (3) Send Business Object (red; marked with S). One start activity is marked with a "play" triangle; multiple stop activities marked with square.

A formal implementation of S-BPM exists [4, 9] based on Abstract State Machines [10]. Part of that formalization is given in listing 1 below.

Listing 1.: ASM Implementation for verification & automated execution [9]

BEHAVIOR (*subj* , *state*) =
  if SID_*state*(*subj*) = *state* **then**
    if *Completed*(*subj* , *service*(*state*), *state*) **then**
      let edge = $\text{select}_{\text{Edge}}$ ({*e* ∈ *OutEdge*(*state*) | *ExitCond*(*e*)(*subj* , *state*)}) in
        PROCEED (*subj* , *service*(*target*(*edge*)), *target*(*edge*))
    else PERFORM (*subj* , *service*(*state*), *state*)
  where
    PROCEED (*subj* , *X* , *node*) =
      SID_*state*(*subj*) := *node*
      START (*subj* , *X* , *node*)

The ASM-based Listing 1 is interpreted as follows: Every subject is in a particular state (SID_State). A transition from one state to the next happens when the execution of a service is finished. Service here includes the three activities (send, receive, act). The rule PERFORM is executed until the predicate *Completed* confirms the service has been completed. The next edge to be followed for the next state, is selected by the $select_{Edge}$ function.

To conclude, S-BPM has both, a human read-able representation, and a formal representation.

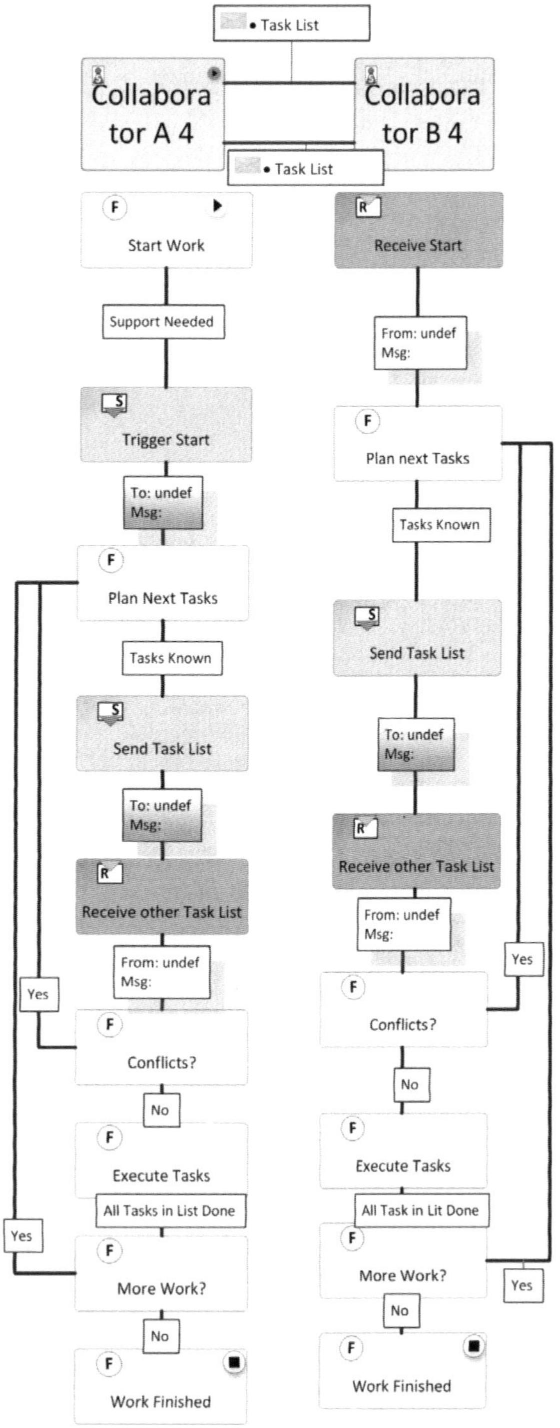

Figure 1. Example of a process model for human robot collaboration [11].

B. BPMN

The Business Process Management Notation (BPMN) is the de-facto standard for representation of processes in the business world [12]. Version 2.0 has been accepted as ISO standard. BPMN 2.0 includes support execution of BPMN process models, and a serialization standard has been added [13]. Some execution engines support the simulation of processes.

Agents' roles may be modelled as pools, and lanes within a pool (see Figure 2). Message flows are used to synchronize tasks in different lanes. This allows the implicit definition and usage of message exchange protocols as standard interfaces between certain "roles". In contrast to S-BPM, this is not explicit in a separate model.

Swimlanes are used to separate different entities working on a process. The yellow diamonds indicate "or" gateways; Green round symbols are start events, where for the robot this is a message based event. Messages sent around are modelled explicitly on the same level. Red circles are stop events.

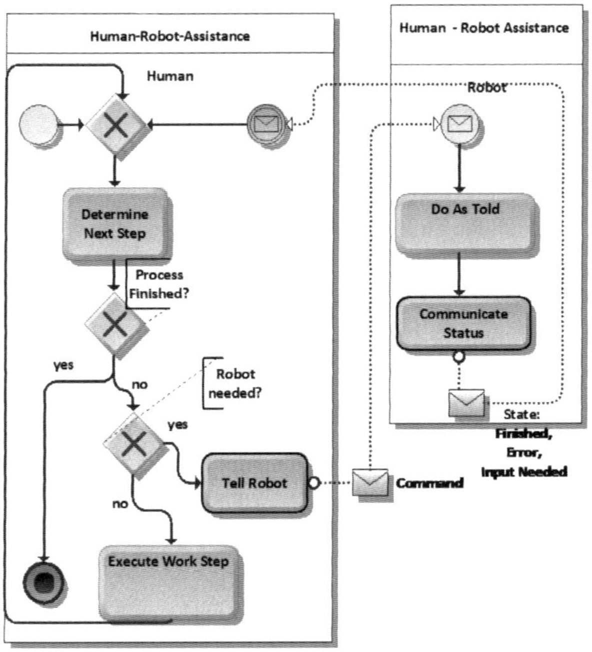

Figure 2. Example of a process model for human robot assistance.

However, BPMN is a large, and feature-rich modeling language. Unfortunately, this feature richness provides problems in practical environments. Most users do not know the exact definition, and usage of all concepts, model constructs [12]. All existing *execution* engines execute only a limited set of concepts. The automated translation from a modelled process to an executable one is at least cumbersome, and dependent on the actual used engine [13].

These problems partially stem from a missing formal semantics, and a missing formal execution environment [14].

For BPMN, we may conclude that while it is well known standard, it is only of limited suitability for communicating the processes to robots. However, an execution environment might take a subset of the BPMN standard, and use that subset to communicate to humans, and robots. Yet, no prior work exists helping in selecting required modelling constructs.

IV. CONCLUSIONS

Given the increase of flexibility required for getting production back to Europe, the number of work environments with human robot collaboration is expected to rise.

Current research focuses on the interaction part of robots with humans in linear, simple processes. However, in the near future, the complexity of processes is expected to rise. This implies the need for communication of these processes to the humans as well as to the robots.

In this initial work, we have analyzed two approaches to business process modelling and execution. For each, we have provided a brief description with respect to its suitability to communicate a complex process to both, the human and the robot.

We will continue this research in the near future, in order to understand the contributions of process models in flexible and interoperable production environments.

ACKNOWLEDGMENT

The research, described in this paper, has been partially funded by the European Union and the state of Upper Austria within the strategic economic and research program “Innovative Upper Austria 2020” and the projects "Smart Factory Lab" and "DigiManu".

REFERENCES

[1] G. Weichhart, A. Molina, D. Chen, L. Whitman, & F. Vernadat, “Challenges and Current Developments for Sensing”, Smart and Sustainable Enterprise Systems Computers in Industry, vol. 79, pp. 34-46, 2016.

[2] G. Weichhart, W. Guédria, and Y. Naudet, "Supporting Interoperability in Complex Adaptive Enterprise Systems: A Domain Specific Language Approach," Data and Knowledge Engineering, vol. 105, pp. 90-106, 2016.

[3] A. Pichler, S. C. Akkaladevi, M. Ikeda, M. Hofmann, M. Plasch, C. Wögerer, and G. Fritz, “Towards shared autonomy for robotic tasks in Manufacturing”, Procedia Manufacturing, vol. 11, pp. 72-82, 2017.

[4] IDS Scheer AG, „Handbuch zur ARIS-Methode“, Saarbrücken, 2000.

[5] A. Fleischmann, W. Schmidt, C. Stary, S. Obermeier, and E. Börger, “Subject-Oriented Business Process Management”, Springer, 2012.

[6] A. Fleischmann, U. Kannengiesser, W. Schmidt and C. Stary, “Subject-Oriented Modeling and Execution of Multi-Agent Business Processes”, Intelligent Agent Technology, The 2013 IEEE/WIC/ACM International Conference on, 2013.

[7] M. Neubauer, and C. Stary, (Eds.) “S-BPM in the Production Industry” Springer International Publishing, 2017

[8] M. Neubauer, F. Krenn, D. Majoe, and C. Stary, “Subject-orientation as design language for integration across organisational control layers”, International Journal of Production Research, vol. 55, pp. 3644-3656, 2017

[9] H. Lerchner, and C. Stary, “An Open S-BPM Runtime Environment based on Abstract State Machines”, in IEEE 16th Conference on Business Informatics, pp. 54-61, 2014

[10] E. Börger and R. Stärk, “Abstract State Machine - A Method for High Level System Design and Analysis”, Springer Verlag Berlin Heidelberg, 2003.

[11] G. Weichhart, “Representing Processes of Human Robot Collaboration”, S-BPM-ONE Workshop Proceedings, CEUR Workshop Proceedings, 2018 (to appear).

[12] M. Chinosi, and A. Trombetta, “BPMN: An introduction to the standard”, Computer Standards & Interfaces, vol. 34, pp. 124 – 134, 2012.

[13] M. Geiger, S. Harrer, J. Lenhard, and G. Wirtz, “BPMN 2.0: The state of support and implementation”, Future Generation Computer Systems, vol. 80, pp. 250 – 262, 2018.

[14] P. Wohed, W. M. van der Aalst, M. Dumas, A. H. ter Hofstede, and N. Russell, “On the Suitability of BPMN for Business Process Modelling”. Proceedings 4th International Conference on Business Process Management, Springer, vol. 4102, pp. 161-176, 2006.

MMAssist_II- A Lighthouse Project for Industrial Assistance

Assistance in Production in the Context of Human – Machine Cooperation

Christian Wögerer
Matthias Plasch
PROFACTOR GmbH
4407 Steyr, Austria
email: christian.woegerer@profactor.at
email: Matthias.plasch@profactor.at

Manfred Tscheligi
Sebastian Egger-Lampl
AIT Austrian Institute of Technology GmbH
Center for Technology Experience, 1220 Vienna, Austria
email: manfred.tscheligi@ait.ac.at
email: sebastian.egger-lampl@ait.ac.at

Abstract—**In this paper, we present MMAssist_II, a national Austrian flagship project for research, development and establishment of assistance systems, which could be used as a tool box for different applications. Besides a fundamental understanding of demands for such assistance units also a demonstration in industrial near production settings including an extensive evaluation is part of the project. Therefore, a mighty consortium of 9 scientific partners and 16 industrial partners join the consortium.**

Keywords - industrial assistance; collaborative robotics; reusable assistance systems.

I. INTRODUCTION

Initial situation: Austrian production companies manufacture goods of high quality and have a staff of well-trained employees. However, companies currently face technological and societal challenges to which they have to react to in order to continually provide competitive goods on an international level. These challenges include the demand of customers for individualized products, which leads to smaller lot sizes and faster production cycles. At the same time, production machines are more and more connected and equipped with sensors. This leads to an increased information density and more complexity for the workers, which induces a higher workload and stress. Furthermore, Austria is experiencing a demographic change. As Austrian citizens get older, they stay longer in employment. All of these trends, as well as the goal to keep up the high quality of produced goods, lead to an increased need of optimized assistance for the worker in the factory.

In Section II, this paper is presenting the general aspects of the project flowed by Section III describing the technical concept of MMAssist_II. In Section IV, the available basic technologies are presented. The paper ends with Section V were we present the first results after 6 months project duration.

II. THE PROJECT MMASSIST_II

A. General project description

The lighthouse project MMAssist_II [1] will form a national research network with an international scientific board in order to find recognition and acceptance within the Austrian economy.

Goals and innovation: The goal of the project partners in **MMAssist_II** is to research and implement modular, reusable assistance systems for employees in production companies. Therefore, the project partners will work on the exemplary uses cases *Maintenance and Service*, *Arming of Machines and Simultaneous Handling of Multiple Machines*, and *Assembly* to analyze the technical and socio-economic requirements for assistance systems in these areas. Based on a strongly context-oriented requirements analysis, the partners will implement so-called "Assistance Units", which are modular components for assistance systems. Assistance Units are defined in a way that they can be applied to different application contexts. The partners will implement a software framework to enable a dynamic configuration and interaction of Assistance Units, thus forming an assistance system for a given application. To configure an Assistance Unit, different input and output modalities, as well as modules for context generation are needed, which will also be developed in the project. In order to measure and evaluate the efficiency and feasibility of the project's approach, the partners will implement lab-based prototypes of defined Assistance Units and evaluate them in real production environments.

Expected results: The project partners expect to gain a profound empirical and socio-technical understanding of the demands and requirements for assistance systems in the production context. These systems will consist of reusable, scientifically grounded Assistance Units that are thoroughly evaluated. The implemented assistance systems will be evaluated, by workers of production companies, in real production environments. This will lead to findings about the acceptance and user experience of workers who use assistance systems and a measurable reduced workload of the workers.

B. Key facts

MMAssit_II was launched in May 2017 and will run until April 2020. The project involves 25 different partners from research and industry, which are key players for research and manufacturing in Austria [2]. The partners expertise covers the whole manufacturing value chain from basic research to industrial manufacturing of high tech products and services. This consortium was set up to have all necessary competences without any overlap in research, and besides technical capacities there is also social-economic knowledge available. The industrial partners cover a wide range of different technical branches and provide real use cases to demonstrate the results in a production near environment. Key facts are shown in Figure 1.

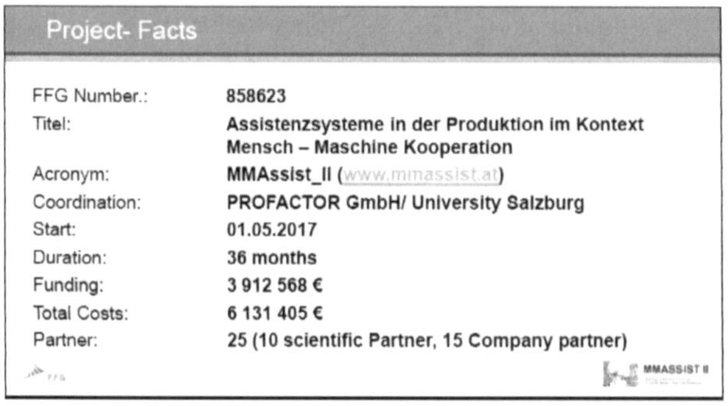

Figure 1. Key facts of the MMAssist_II project

C. *Objectives*

The goal of the project partners in MMAssist_II is to explore assistance systems for employees in production environments and to develop these systems. This is necessary to overcome future technical and socio-technical challenges for production, by setting new paradigms of industrial assistance. Figure 2 shows challenges for future.

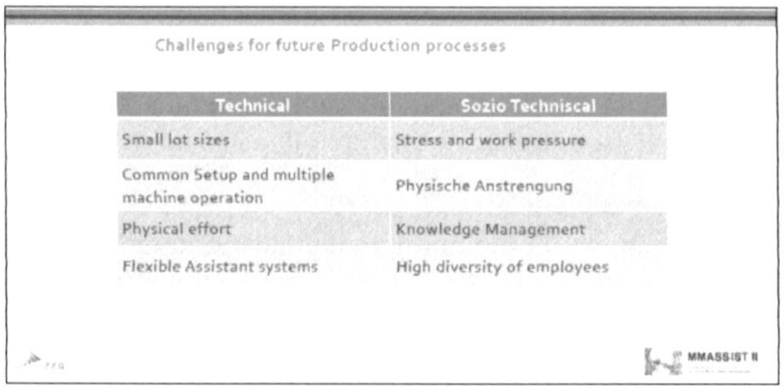

Figure 2. Challenges for Future production processes

These assistance systems should be tailored to the needs of employees for their special context. It is also the goal of the project partners, to develop more than only specialized solutions and assistance systems. Moreover, the assistance systems being developed are relevant for Austrian production companies in general. Therefore, the project partners have defined the following objectives.

OBJECTIVE 1: Exploration of modular, reusable assistance systems. The project partners will develop assistance systems that can be used not only for the specific individual cases, but are applicable in different contexts and for different applications. The purpose is to establish a general approach for implementing assistance systems for employees in manufacturing companies. This system should be open and able to motivate other companies to include there products and developments into the system later on.

OBJECTIVE 2: Context oriented detection of assistance needs. Methods are developed, to enable the identification of the assistance needs of people in the vicinity of the machines from machine point of view. The purpose is to explore intelligent assistance systems, which offer targeted assistance only if it is needed. An important point is the acceptance by the workers and therefore a neutralized information exchange has to be implemented.

OBJECTIVE 3: Improve the work and assistance experience. As a major goal, the project partners will implement assistance systems that increase positive factors of work and assistance experience while they are used, and reduce negative factors. Thus, it will be achieved that the systems are accepted by users and contribute to an improvement of their daily work.

OBJECTIVE 4: Applicability in real production environments. The project partner aims to use the implemented assistance systems application at the industrial partner's production facilities and to evaluate in terms of productivity, acceptance through the staff and ergonomics. This evaluation should prove that the assistance systems are also usable in real production environments and beyond the project. For this reason leading companies are included into the project development from the beginning to secure a real industrial relevance and industrial standards of the developed assistance systems.

III. PROJECT CONCEPT

The goal of MMAssist_II is to fundamentally research and characterize assistance in a production context. Based on this, optimized assistance systems for future working places focused on the human worker („Human-Centered Workplace") will be developed, implemented and evaluated in an industrial environment. Basis for the implementation are so called „Assistance Units" – which are modular components for assistance systems. Assistance Units are defined in a way that they can be applied to different application contexts. The partners will implement a software framework to enable a dynamic configuration and interaction of Assistance Units, thus forming an assistance system for a given application.

A. *Motivation*

The central motivation shown in Figure 3 is the development of Assistance Units (Unit 1...n) based on available and adapted basic technologies (for example mixed reality methods, Visualization of complex data, object recognition, scene interpretation and others). These Assistance units are implemented in a software framework and the best fitting Assistance Units for an application are composed to an assistance system that is tailored for the given production context. The Assistance Units and the assistance systems are implemented, tested and evaluated in different Use Cases, first in the labs of the partners and then in "semi" real production environment. Also some tests in real environment are planned.

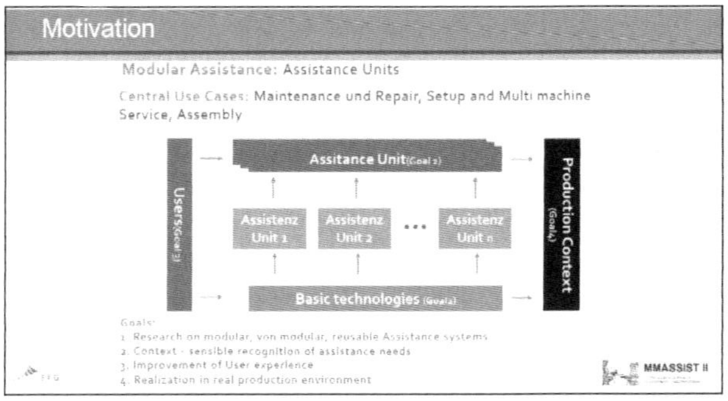

Figure 3. MMAsist_II Motivation

B. Assistance Units

A generalized description of an **Assistance Unit** is shown in Figure 4 considering the example of an Assistance Unit for assembly. Any assistance has, in addition to a clear title and a short description of the unit, primarily a definition which knowledge source is needed by the Assistance Unit to work correctly. These sources of knowledge can be for example information about the condition of the employee that is available on the machine, or process data, such as installation instructions. Among the needed data also the information, when the Assistance Unit must be activated, based on the context information of the employee and the process, is required. A second central element of an Assistance Unit is a description of "how and by which equipment" the employee can make submissions to the Assistance Unit, and also the output form, in which way the information of the machine is given to employees. So, the main components of an Assistance Unit are name, Assistance/Assistant task (Type), Knowledge source, Input form, Input device, Output form and Output device.

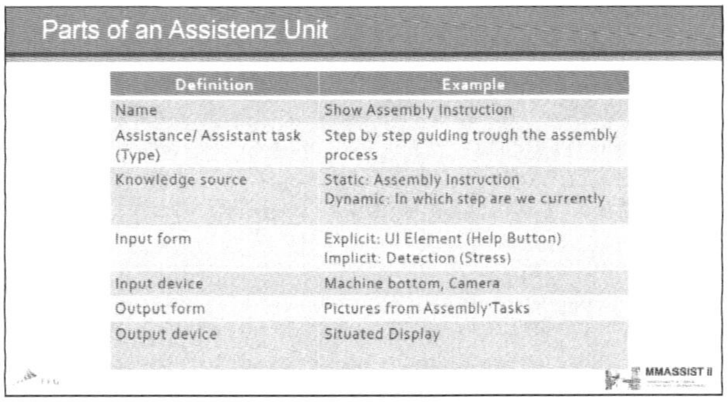

Definition	Example
Name	Show Assembly Instruction
Assistance/ Assistant task (Type)	Step by step guiding trough the assembly process
Knowledge source	Static: Assembly Instruction Dynamic: In which step are we currently
Input form	Explicit: UI Element (Help Button) Implicit: Detection (Stress)
Input device	Machine bottom, Camera
Output form	Pictures from Assembly Tasks
Output device	Situated Display

Figure 4. Assitance Unit description

C. Workpackage structure

The work package structure for MMAssist_II in context with the aim of the project is shown in Figure 5. 10 different Work packages including the project management and leaded by experienced project managers are the key for a successful project implementation. Workpackages are on different TRLs (Technology readiness level) and are well connected to each other. The detailed structure of the Workpackages is shown in Figure 5.

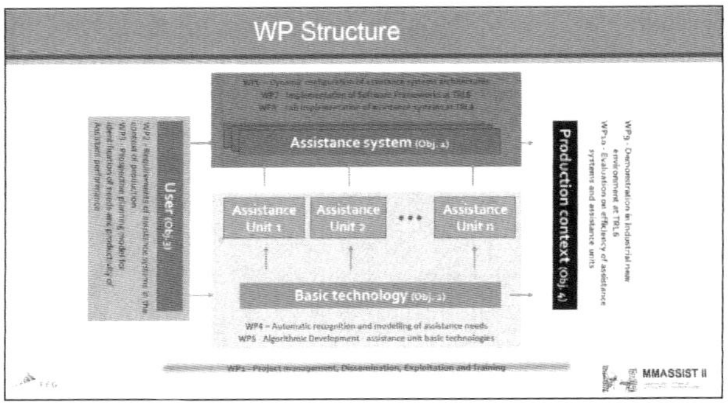

Figure 5. Work package structure

WP (Workpackage) 1 summarizes the tasks of the project related to the management of the project and the dissemination of project results. AP2 parses the requests of Assistance Units and assistance systems in the context of production from the point of view of the users and from a technical perspective. A planning model for the identification of assistance needs will be developed in WP3. Moreover, a model for structured preparation of work content and an employee model will be designed. Based on the theoretical results of WP2 and WP3, Assistance Units are explored in WP4. With these units assistance can be detected automatically. WP5 develops basic algorithms for Assistance Units. In WP6, partners develop approaches for the dynamic configuration of Assistant Units for specified use cases. A software framework is developed to implement the dynamically configured assistance systems in AP7. This framework is basis for WP8, in which assistance is prototypically implemented in laboratory environments. The assistance systems in real environment are implemented in WP9 at the facilities of the industry partners. Finally, the implemented assistance systems are evaluated in WP10.

D. System architecture

Core unit of the technical system architecture shown in Figure 6 are the single "Assistance Units" which are integrated to an overall assistance system via the Software Framework. The assistance system has interfaces to sensors that allow, together with a direct user input, a context recognition for the identification of assistance needs. Derived cognitive or physical assistance is provided via the respective Assistance Units. The overall system also has interfaces to external legacy systems (especially ERP & MES), which can retrieve, for example, job information and machine structural analysis.

Task management module manages the orders that can be adopted or entered directly via the administration interface from external systems, and informs the users about a specific job and corresponding support performance. The user management module enables central management of user master data and roles of all Assistance Units and interacts with a skill database that stores relevant skills of employees for the respective tasks. In the asset database, resources or appropriate references are stored, which can be consumed by the assistance units. The content management system has the purpose to take care of digital resources that need to be imported in an appropriate form, edited, saved, updated, illustrated and re-exported.

A knowledge data base provides process knowledge from and also knowledge about the relevance and quality of certain assets. Here, employees can assess for a specific resource, which was offered by the assistance system in one specific step, how helpful it was, or correct a proposed sequence by the system.

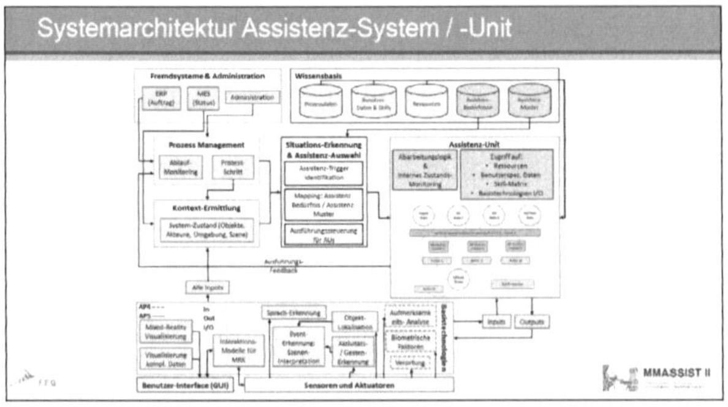

Figure 6. System architecture

IV. BASIC TECHNOLOGIES

In the MMAssist_II project, 9 scientific partners from Austria provide different basic technologies shown in Figure 7 for various Assistance Units. Either these technologies are ready for implementation or they were developed ready for use. The most challenging problem is the interfaces between this basic technologies and the software framework. Main basic technologies are:

Object recognition, Event recognition and scene Interpretation by Technical University Vienna [3]: A system to generate hypotheses on the current state and events happening in Human Robot Collaborative scenarios (HRC) is being developed. The software modules will be based on existing approaches and software libraries for object modelling and object pose recognition, concepts to describe events in HRC scenes, and fusion of data streams including action recognition, robot states and object recognition.

Mixed Reality methods by Evolaris [4]: Focus of this work is to develop methods to augment visual information using Head Mounted Displays (HMDs) and modes for the user to interaction with the HMD (data input). A major challenge is given through the requirement of selecting appropriate information given the current context and individual needs of the user.

Visualization of complex data by Fraunhofer Austria [5]: The main focus is developing approaches to enable real-time visualization of large amount of data, e.g., complex CAD models, on thin clients (data glasses). Moreover, a model-based tracking approach based on CAD data is developed, to facilitate position-stable augmentation of data in industrial environments.

Interaction for robot-based Assembly processes by PROFACTOR [6]: Within this technology package, concepts to enable intuitive interaction in HRC scenarios will be developed. Major challenges include the implementation of flexible models to enable fast adaptation of process knowledge and adaptation of the human-robot interaction (user specific needs), avoiding explicit programming.

Acoustic Interaction by Joanneum research [7]: The main goal is to develop speech-interfaces to enable intuitive interaction with assistance systems in an industrial setting. In order to maximize user friendliness, the interfaces are not restricted to a collection of commands and can cope with different dialects and languages. Acoustic feedback is used to inform the user about the states of the assistance system.

Iterative Interaction Design by AIT [8] and PLUS [9]: The goal is to implement a Research through Design (RtD) based process, where prototypes for current and present interaction models/modes are developed by potential end-users. This generated, valuable feedback serves as input to an iterative development process for assistance system interaction design.

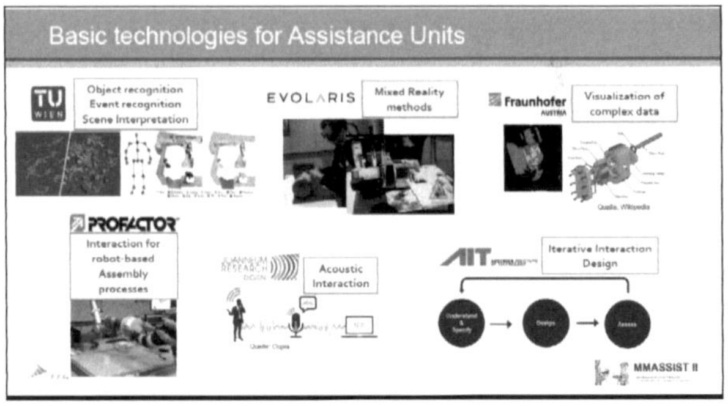

Figure 7. Basic technologies avialable for MMAssist_II Assitance Units

V. FIRST RESULTS

As the project has started in May 2017, the work performed in the first 6 months was focused on requirements and finding a set of basic technologies as described in chapter IV. Also a more detailed definition of the use cases and the Assistance Units, which will be implemented, was done. This led to 3 different Use Cases with 7 Assistance Units in total.

- **Service and maintenance (Use CASE 1)**
  - Notification of maintenance protocols (Assistance Unit 1)
  - Communication with Experts (Assistance Unit 2)
- **Setup and multi machine service (Use CASE 2)**
  - Guiding through setup process (Assistance Unit 3)
  - Multi machine service (Assistance Unit 4)
- **Assembly (Use CASE 3)**
  - Notification of Assembly instructions (Assistance Unit 5)
  - Part delivery (Assistance Unit 6)
  - Assembly instructions review (Assistance Unit 7)

A requirement Analyses based on the needs of Users of the assistance systems in the context of production was done. The goal was to capture the requirements from a technical and a socio- economic view. First steps were done so far:

- Determine the requirements for assistance units: data collection is almost completed; current data will be analyzed and interpreted.
- Conceptual design and modeling of Assistance Units to the subsequent implementation: an adequate conceptual base model for the taxonomy of Assistance Units and situation patterns was identified and is now further developed for the project problems.
- Investigation of job satisfaction and acceptance by the use of Assistance Units: an existing framework for the project was adapted. A data collection tool to raise job satisfaction was developed.
- Analysis of relevant safety and security factors within the use of Assistant Units: Data collection was carried out and a knowledge base was developed.

VI. CONCLUSION

The main expected results is a software framework which connects all main basic technologies to Assistance units which could be used to create a Use Case sensitive Assistance system adapted to the needs of the workers. This is an open system which could be enlarged by contributing (and other interested) companies.

The main challenge is to find a software solution and architecture which is able to handle the interface problematic between the single sub systems.

Besides first promising results, it is a challenge to manage a research project with 24 partners and to find a common solution for a lot of different companies.

ACKNOWLEDGMENT

This work has been supported by the Austrian Research Promotion Agency [10] in the program "Production of the Future" funded project MMAssist II (FFG No.: 858623) and the Austrian Ministry for Transport, Innovation and Technology (bmvit) [11].

REFERENCES

[1] MMAssist_II: Avialable online at www.mmassist.at [accessed March 2018]

[2] MMAssist_II partners: Avialable on http://www.mmassist.at/partner/wissenschaftliche-partner/ and http://www.mmassist.at/partner/unternehmenspartner/ [accessed March 2018]

[3] Technical University Vienna: https://www.acin.tuwien.ac.at/en/ [accessed Februar 2018]

[4] Evolaris: https://www.evolaris.net/en/ [accessed March 2018]

[5] Fraunhofer Austria: https://www.fraunhofer.at/en.html [accessed January 2018]

[6] PROFACTOR GmbH: https://www.profactor.at/en/ [accessed March 2018]

[7] Joanneum Research: https://www.joanneum.at/en/ [accessed March 2018]

[8] AIT: https://www.ait.ac.at/en/about-the-ait/center/center-for-technology-experience/ [accessed March 2018]

[9] PLUS: https://www.uni-salzburg.at/index.php?id=38601&L=1 [accessed February 2018]

[10] FFG – Avialable online at https://www.ffg.at/ [accessed March 2018]

[11] BMVIT- Avialable online at www.bmvit.gv.at/en/index.html [accessed December 2017]

Approaches to a Practical Implementation of Industry 4.0

Ahmed Elkaseer
Institute for Automation and Applied Informatics
Karlsruhe Institute of Technology, Karlsruhe, Germany
Faculty of Engineering, Port Said University, Egypt
e-mail: ahmed.elkaseer@kit.edu

Hazem Ali
Intel Germany GmbH
Nürnberg, Germany
e-mail: Hazemx.ali@intel.com

Mahmoud Salama
Department of Computer and Systems Engineering,
Faculty of Engineering, Ain Shams University, Cairo, Egypt
e-mail: g16091591@eng.asu.edu.eg

Steffen Scholz
Institute for Automation and Applied Informatics
Karlsruhe Institute of Technology, Karlsruhe, Germany
e-mail: steffen.scholz@kit.edu

Abstract—**The arrival of Industry 4.0 has popularised the concept of smart interactions between humans and the physical world that could realise the synergistic integration of intelligent manufacturing assets. However, a systematic and cogent approach to the practical and profitable application of Industry 4.0 is still missing. This paper presents practical approaches to the application of Industry 4.0 to manufacture with the aim of strengthening its competitiveness and meeting the growing serious challenges that threaten its profitability and survival. Precision Additive Metal Manufacturing is utilised in this study for demonstration purposes. A conceptual framework combined with two practical modules available in the market, a "native-design" and "Plug and Play", is proposed. These approaches offer flexible prototypes with sequential procedures that ultimately would allow for easy employment of Industry 4.0, and will help remove technical barriers to the development of manufacturing industry in the domain of Industry 4.0.**

Keywords-Industry 4.0; IoT; Cloud-based big data analytics; CPS; precision additive metal manufacturing

I. Introduction

Although European industrial sectors continue to receive significant investment, unfortunately, the generated profit does not follow the same positive trend, which negatively influences their growth. Figure 1 illustrates the relative proportions of world global manufacturing outputs for gross domestic products (GDP) between 2003 and 2011 [1]. It is clearly seen that while the share of global manufacturing output for USA and European manufacturing communities have lessened consistently, the Chinese share has had a strong upward trend.

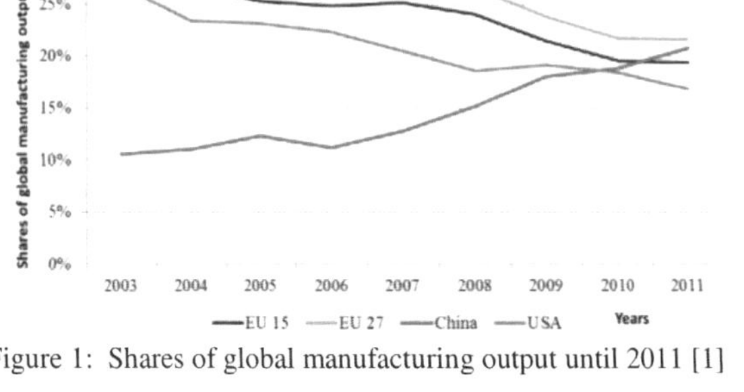

Figure 1: Shares of global manufacturing output until 2011 [1]

This observation certainly reflects the fierce competition between the well-established manufacturing communities in USA and Europe, and the new superpower player, China, who can offer highly competitive industrial products of good quality at low cost, due to lower expenses (both labour and operating costs) [2]. This has driven some European manufacturers to invest outside Europe in other growing economies. This objectively works against the advancement of European industry and poses serious threats to European economies. In view of this situation, the transition to the fourth industrial generation "Industry 4.0" has become indispensable as a robust solution for the survival of European industry [3]. In particular, the existing capabilities of conventional manufacturing technologies are no longer adequate to face the current industrial challenges. This has motivated manufacturers and researchers to develop different approaches to implement Industry 4.0 for a range of industrial applications, which would ultimately strengthen the competitiveness of the European economy [4].

Literally, the term "Industry 4.0" stands for smart manufacturing, involving Data Acquisition, Cyber-Physical Systems (CPSs), Internet of Things (IoT), Cloud/Edge Computing, Big Data Analytics (BDA), and Enterprise Resource Planning (ERP) [3]-[5].

Since information is the key factor in implementing Industry 4.0, data acquisition techniques play an important role in any proposed approach [5]. Different convenient algorithms have been utilised for sensing, acquiring, and processing of signals. However, CPSs are central in Industry 4.0, to monitor and control physical processes. The industry basically builds a seamless link between the mechanical and digital systems combined with a data exchange system onto the CPS [6]. The digital system can be designed based on convenient hybrid approaches using hardware components such as embedded systems and computers with integrated software solutions.

In Industry 4.0, communication technology is empowered by the IoT, which enables system components, processed products and people to concurrently exchange information [7][8]. This technology allows for acquiring massive data, where its analysis can be performed via cloud computing and BDA. This facilitates modelling, simulation, and virtualisation of the manufacturing process [7]. However, cloud computing and BDA are also used to feed the

Manufacturing Execution Systems (MES), in order to monitor the work in progress and enables the simultaneous connection of partners, suppliers, customers and other stakeholders [9][10].

Some of these components have already been utilised on an industrial scale. However, the synergistic integration of the aforementioned fragments is the most challenging issue that still needs addressing, and could eventually offer a smart solution to manufacturing problems [10]. A capable and insightful approach on how to apply Industry 4.0, practically and profitably, is still not available. The aim of this paper is to provide a generic practical model on how to implement Industry 4.0. Therefore, metal additive manufacturing, as a good example of the digital manufacturing method, is utilised in this study to improve obtainable precision and accuracy of the manufacturing processes. This research was inspired by project Precision Additive Metal Manufacturing (PAM²).

The following sections of this paper are organised as follows. First, some of the expected benefits and challenges that are associated with the implementation of Industry 4.0 are discussed. After that, a theoretical Industry 4.0 model followed by two practical approaches are detailed. Finally, conclusions are drawn and future perspectives presented.

II. INDUSTRY 4.0: BENEFITS AND CHALLENGES

The 4th industrial revolution, currently in-progress, has been promoted by the advent of recent advanced information- and communication-driven technologies, aiming at realising the potential of cross-linking intelligent manufacturing operations with automated near real time data acquisition and simulation technologies, see Figure 2. This offers the possibility of instantaneous identification of physical problems with the almost concurrent production of necessary corrective actions which are expected to optimise the performance of the entire manufacturing system [11][12]. The expected outcomes of the implementation of Industry 4.0 in manufacturing processes and the challenges associated with this implementation are presented in the following sub-sections.

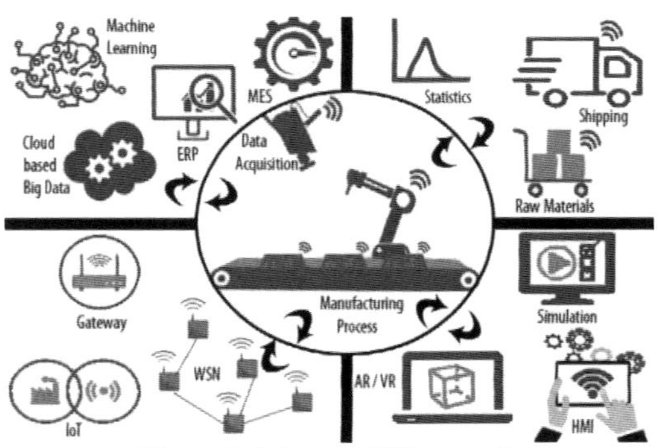

Figure 2: Industry 4.0 Framework

A. Benefits

The added value to the manufacturing processes can be seen in the following four phases.

1. Virtual design and pre-manufacturing validation

For additive manufacturing technology, Industry 4.0 offers an upgraded version of the design tool, which especially integrates virtual reality (VR) and augmented reality (AR) into the design environment. In particular, computer-aided design (CAD) will be able to interface with VR and AR to present in virtual form the physical product, and thus enable assessment of the design prior to actual manufacturing [13].

2. Corrective actions of manufacturing process

Any fabrication process depends on a controller to secure a stable response under different process conditions. Industry 4.0 presents smart pilot actions based on the CPS and cloud computing. In particular, CPS works to transfer physical parameters (thermal, power, and geometry) to the cloud to be processed, where optimal control decisions will be sent back to the physical system. If the information indicates an issue such as too high power consumption, then the system has to take an appropriate action.

3. Self-decision and big data analytics

Smart decision making is an advantage of Industry 4.0. The ultimate goal of deploying widespread sensors is to achieve smart decision making through comprehensive data collection. The realisation of smart decision making requires real time information sharing and collaboration. Big data and its analytics play an important role in smart decision making tasks, including data-driven modelling, data-enabled predictive maintenance, ERP and marketing.

B. Challenges

Although applying Industry 4.0 will generate new opportunities and provide enormous benefits, it will not be a bed of roses. There are some challenges that need addressing prior to swinging into action.

Industrial challenges generally can be understood to act as a barrier to the advancement of manufacturing technology and the challenges generally increase in complexity over time. On the other hand, to move forward, industrial capability has to grow beyond existing levels, and this is what Industry 4.0 is intended to help accomplish.

The following areas are examples of potential challenges to realising Industry 4.0:

1. Ensure integrity

Integration compatibility is one of the main issues to be considered when applying Industry 4.0. As previously stated, Industry 4.0 has different elements, which need to be suitably integrated to attain the best possible performance of the developed system. In particular, it is a communication challenge to tune the sub-systems' components (nodes) to work in synchronised time domains based on the desired priorities.

2. Ensure security

Since massive data sets with important and confidential information will be exchanged, strenuous effort must be taken to ensure secure data processing among and between Industry 4.0 systems; Data Acquisition, CPSs systems, IoT, Cloud computing, BDA, and ERP. The encryption used must resist cipher analysis (attack), which poses formidable challenges on the level of security and data protection.

3. Power consumption

Reducing power consumption is of significant importance to stakeholders, and is considered one of the major priority parameters in a good design. Generating an optimal design to reduce power consumption without affecting the work performance is still a major design issue.

C. Industry 4.0: Human-Machinery Interaction

The industry 4.0 will introduce entirely different ways of smart interaction between human and the physical world. Especially, Industry 4.0 provides a user-friendly interface for humans to remotely interact with machines. Advancement of Industry 4.0 allows users to have remote interaction with manufacturing processes, and to enhance the manufacturing parameters using this interface. HMI will be developed for mobile, web, and other techniques [6]. Based on the developed techniques on HMI, the HMI will dramatically change the way people work together and also the interaction among industrial partners. Thus, attention should be paid to the working environment to persuade people to accept the new procedures and changes. The results of using HMI is playing an important role in using the productivity and manufacturing process optimisation such as enhancing of monitoring, reporting, quality control, and other manufacturing process.

Human machine interaction in industry can also take place on-site. On site interface/control can be implemented via local area network (LAN). Both aforementioned interactions, remote and on site interfaces, could be realised via contact and non-contact methods. Examples of Contact HMI are Graphical User Interface (GUI), Menu Driven Interface, Command Line Interface (CLI) and Touch Sensitive Interface. However, Hand Gesture Recognition and Voice Driven Interface (Voice recognition) are methods of non-contact HMI, as shown in Fig. 3. To utilise one or more of the formerly mentioned techniques, an algorithm has to be designed that consideres constraints related to machine, operation, work-piece and safety environment.

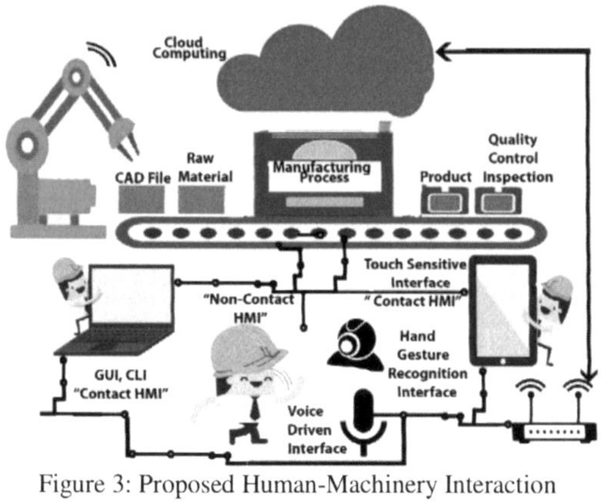

Figure 3: Proposed Human-Machinery Interaction

III. THEORETICAL APPROACH

German chancellor Angela Merkel in a visit to the Siemens "smart" factory in February 2015, defined Industry 4.0 as "the fusion of the online world and the world of industrial production" [12]. Technically, Industry 4.0 can be simply defined as the digitising of the manufacturing processes combined with real time data acquisition to server computing, cloud and/or edge, where the acquired data is processed and analysed to simulate the real world [5][6].

One of the main objectives of developing manufacturing solutions based on Industry 4.0 concepts is to monitor industrial processes in order to optimise them.

Virtual simulation can be conducted based on real time data acquisition to enable monitoring of the real state of the manufacturing process. This real time monitoring helps to reduce the time taken for maintenance, with the added possibility of almost instantaneously taking necessary corrective measures, by either human to machine, or learned algorithms to the machine, as shown in Figure 4.

Figure 4 illustrates proposed approaches to implementing Industry 4.0 in additive manufacturing processes. The approach starts with the Data Acquisition module, where an invasive or non-invasive sensor takes a measure of the relevant industrial parameter to be then digitised. Data Acquisition is the process of sensing, sampling, acquiring and measuring an electrical or other physical signal representing the real world and converting it into numeric values so that it can be analysed using statistical techniques.

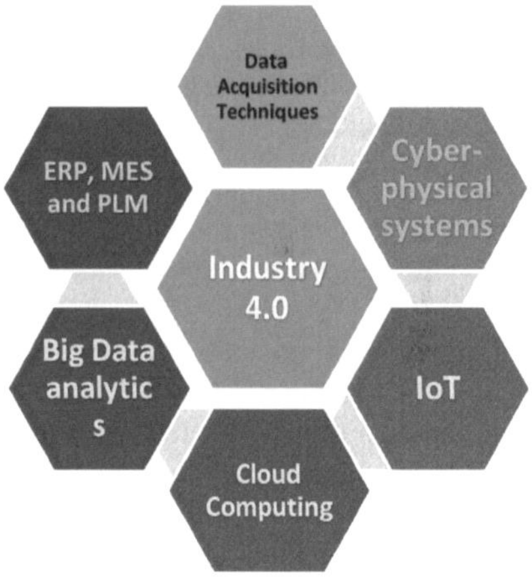

Figure 4: Industry 4.0: theoretical approach

The data acquisition is considered as the input of the CPS which processes information received and analyses it to perform the digitalised manufacturing process as a real-time simulation. This simulation is the core of the monitoring process using the CPS approach.

IoT plays an important role on the approach, as shown in Figure 4. The IoT technology helps the nodes (products, machines parts, controllers, users, and manufacture districts) to exchange the information in a way that increases the efficiency of the manufacturing process. The collected information helps human/machine learning algorithms to solve serious decision/estimation problems. The proposed study interlinks with the IoT based on a cipher algorithm sufficiently robust to protect against security threats. Also, the proposed IoT platform and software algorithms are designed for low power consumption.

Edge computing "refers to the enabling technologies allowing computational processing to be performed at the edge of the network, on downstream data on behalf of cloud services and upstream data on behalf of IoT services" [15]. Based on the above definition, edge computing can be described as a computing technique for processing acquired data from machines (IoT devices) and generating a pre-analysis/ simulation at the edge of the network (on site) before sending it to the cloud computing to avoid latency problems, while cloud computing consumes time but gives stable and independent analysis and simulations. In the proposed Cyber-Physical world, edge/cloud computing will play a significant role in managing the IoT data received for processing and to feed the simulation process.

Machine Learning is a computational algorithm based on statistics and mathematical optimisation that allows for prediction, classification, recognition or decision-making [16]. Decision making using clustering of data is important in modern industrial applications. Besides, pattern recognition for validation and verification of the processing conditions (raw materials, product status during the industrial process) has received great attention by manufacturers. However, so-called deep learning such as Convolution Neural Networks (CNN) has been implemented recently in order to recognise images/frames during the industrial process [17]. Herein, machine/deep learning will be utilised to analyse the collected data and identify the proper actions to be taken for the ERP based on the predicted and estimated needs of the manufacturing scenario. The simulation process will be used to optimise the manufacturing processes by getting fully remote monitoring/interfacing of, e.g., laser direct metal deposition (LMD) or other additive processes by detecting possible defects and enhancing product quality.

IV. Practical Approach

A. *Native design approach*

The proposed design of the Industry 4.0 has been developed based on the theoretical criteria presented in the previous section. In this approach, humans can interact with multiple nodes (data acquisition, industry 4 sub-systems, products, and raw materials). These nodes can exchange data between themselves through a communication physical layer based on LoRa technology [18]. Also, each node can send or receive the data to/from a LoRa gateway wirelessly and the data can be stored on the cloud for analysis. There will be communication between user and cloud data via a Long-Term Evolution (LTE) gateway. Also, there can be communication between a human and the LTE gateway through, for example, a mobile phone. The proposed overall processes are as a shown in Figure 5.

In this design, the proposed data acquisition technique and CPS are used for extracting relevant features of the product during its fabrication by additive manufacturing. The process will be simulated based on the output of the data acquisition which, here, is a non-invasive data acquisition technique. The algorithms are based on computer vision, where the camera works to capture frames of the results of the additive manufacturing during production, and processes them into information form. This information will, for example, contain the physical geometrical shape, temperatures and colours during the process [6].

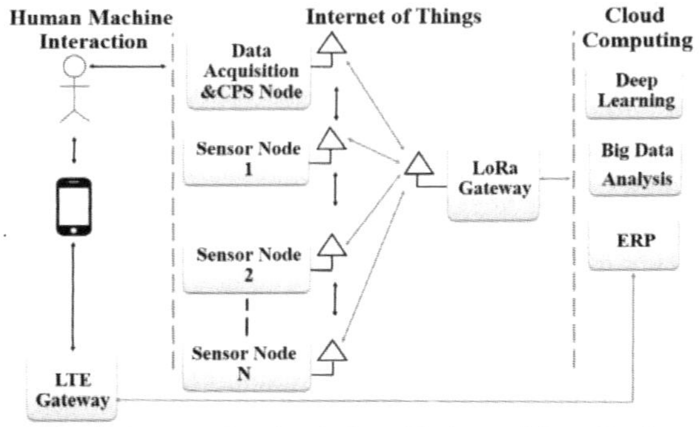

Figure 5: Proposed native design of Industry 4.0 application

The proposed sensing elements for the above approach are 2D/3D cameras, and a thermal camera. The data acquisition algorithms will work on embedded applications in visual computing. A Jetson TX1 Developer Kit enables embedded vision systems based on a GPU NVidia core structure, as shown in Figure 6. The benefits of the proposed design based on the Jetson TX1 are the low power consumption based on the Linux low power management solution of a NVidia GPU [19]. Also, it's supported to interact with the camera module interface, as shown in Figure 6. The processing speed of the GPU NVidia is significantly higher than other models, which is crucial for investigating the process properly [20]. The device comes with a large assortment of porting interfaces, to interact with other peripherals, as shown in Figure 6. The proposed design of the CPS/inspection will be interfacing between 2D/3D cameras and thermal camera with the Jetson for extracting the relevant feature within the production process. LoRa is the proposed hardware for the communication physical layer for IoT nodes. The wireless sensor network (WSN) structure is illustrated in Figure 5.

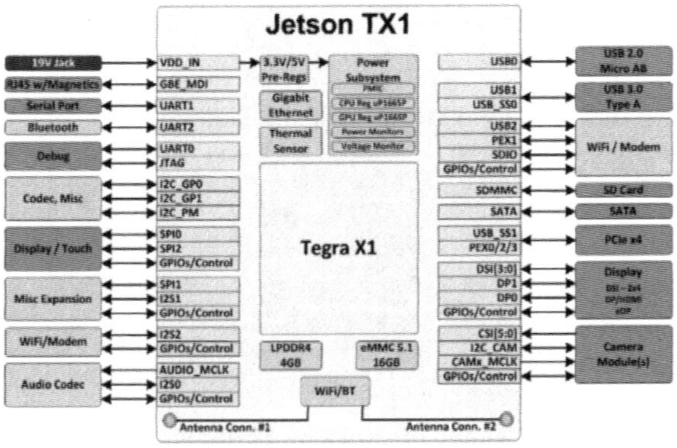

Figure 6: Block diagram of Jetson TX1 with its interfaces [13]

The proposed software will extract features of the image/frame (of the additive manufacturing product) based on a convenient image processing algorithm. Furthermore, the feature will be compared with the feature as stored in the CAD file and an inspection result generated for quality control. The software will be supported with a wide range of libraries such as Computer vision, Deep learning and Linux platforms, based on the Jetson SDK [20].

Thus, the manufacturing process and products' states information will be extracted using computer vision system then it will be presented in form of Virtual Reality (simulation) approach. All these developments will be performed based on the Jetson kit.

The working scenario will be as follows:

1. CAD file received (Client Request).
2. Software sends the CAD file to a machine.
3. Product is being built by AM based on CPS and Inspection system;
   3.1 Captures frames for the process and acquires the manufacturing data such as (temperature, physical and so on).
   3.2 Compares the processing part with the design.
   3.3 Simulates the process based on acquired data.
   3.4 Interacts with LoRa gateway to upload simulation to the cloud and feedback will be sent to the manufacturing system.
4. Data will be analysed on the Cloud then sent as reports to quality control inspection.
5. Cloud can query any data from the nodes such as (conditions of the machine, maintenance issue, etc.)
6. Deep learning works to estimate the maintenance issues and the capacity of production at certain time and quality inspection for raw martials and product.

B. Plug and Play approach

This model is built according to the Reference Architectural Model of Industry 4.0 (RAMI 4.0), see Figure 7. RAMI 4.0 describes the hierarchical levels of a manufacturing system networked via the Internet, the lifecycle of systems and products, and the IT structure of the Industry 4.0 components. The hierarchical levels are almost the same as the layers of the pyramid of automation.

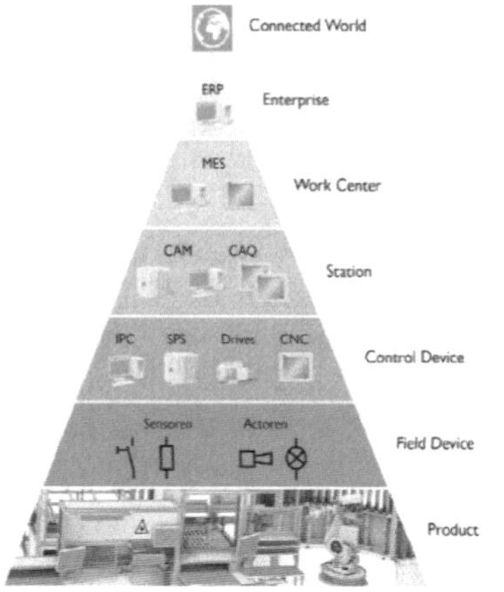

Figure 7: Industry 4.0 productive process pyramid

There is a wide range of commercial brands available in the industrial market that can be utilised to implement an Industry 4.0 approach; these include Siemens, Allen Bradley, Mitsubishi, Omron, Schneider, GE Fanuc, Beckhoff, Moeller, Hitachi, ABB, Phoenix, and Bosch- Rexroth. However, it would be very difficult to construct a generic model for each brand. In this implementation, specific brands are proposed because of their compatibility, availability and market share. In particular, Siemens and Beckhoff, as the big brand names, have been chosen in building our approach to Industry 4.0.

1- The proposed model starts by linking the physical world with the virtual world, the so-called CPS, to monitor the manufacturing processes, and the collected information will be processed using big data analytics. To achieve this step, two hardware solutions are proposed:

A. Siemens SIMATIC IOT2000 which can facilitate data processing/exchange between the manufacturing system and cloud-based data.

B. Beckhoff EK9160 IoT Bus Coupler offers a plug and play module that can simply transmit all control data to all common cloud systems, in a timely and cost effective manner. This allows I/O data to be parameterised via an easy-to-configure website on the device, for sending to a cloud server.

2- For Additive manufacturing, it is recommended to add motion and axis control option for the 3D printer. To achieve this step, two hardware solutions are proposed:

A. Siemens SIMOTION, which provides high-end motion control system, features optimal performance for all machine concepts as well as maximum modularity.

B. Beckhoff CX2040 motion control system will give high-performance and can be used for interpolating 3-D path movements.

3- To perform an integration between the manufacturing data of the physical systems and ERP;

A. The MindSphere Siemens Cloud is a cloud-based IoT operating system that will connect products, machines and systems to interface with the ERP system and will perform any required exchange of data between automated components. The system uses the SAP S/4HANA open cloud platform enabling users to operate, extend and develop the applications in the cloud.

B. The Beckhoff EK9160 coupler will support most of the main cloud systems; Amazon Web Services (AWS), Microsoft Azure and SAP HANA. It will also support the private cloud systems included in many company networks.

4- To enable Physical systems to interact with the real world, particularly to allow for real time simulation and visualisation of the manufacturing process:

A. Siemens provides software, entitled; "SEMATIC inside TIA portal" supports real time visualisation and simulation for manufacturing processes. In addition, NX software offers real time visualisation and sophisticated depiction which is a valuable asset for the product development process.

B. Beckhoff TwinCAT3 supports real time visualisations of the manufacturing process for HMI and Web processing. It allows for analysis, visualisation, diagnosis and recording of variables both external and internal.

5- Finally, CPSs need to increase their experience of utilising machine learning and data mining algorithms.

A. MindSphere Siemens Cloud offers its MindConnect Library on edge devices; providing secure advanced analytics in close proximity to the equipment. MindConnect is suitable for use with descriptive, prescriptive, diagnostic and predictive analytics. Cloud connectivity can be enhanced by combining MindConnect with edge applications in integrated software/hardware environments.

B. Beckhoff TwinCAT Analytics, is able to store process data for each cycle synchronously, this can be invaluable for easy and informative analyses of the processes involved. The software can be expanded with C/C++ and MATLAB for enhancing the analytics application via Mathworks toolboxes for machine learning and optimisation.

Figure 8 summarises the proposed approaches to the practical implementation of Industry 4.0.

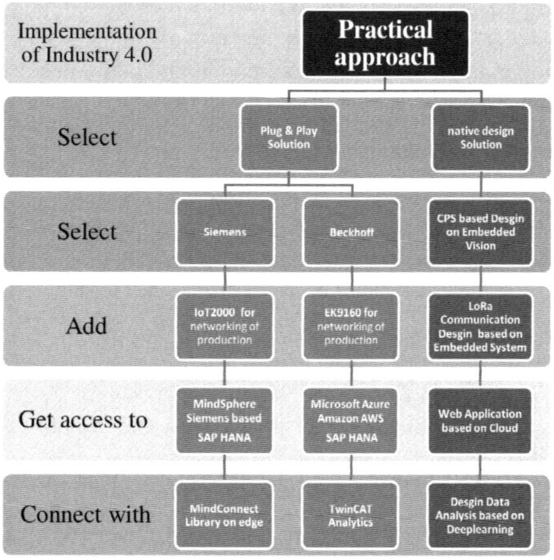

Figure 8: Native approach vs. Plug and Play approach

V. CONCLUSIONS

This paper has presented practical approaches to implant Industry 4.0 in the additive manufacturing process to increase the flexibility, competitiveness and profitability of the manufacturing systems. However, it is also proposing new ways of human machinery interaction. Next step comprises an implementation of M2M communication for Additive manufacturing. Moreover, RFID will be utilised to manage an interaction between machine and product/raw material.

ACKNOWLEDGMENT

The authors would like to thank the European Commission for funding the PAM² project under H2020-MSCA-ITN-2016 Program, Grant Agreement No 721383.

REFERENCES

[1] European Commission, Competitiveness report 2013: no growth and jobs without industry, MEMO/13/815. http://europa.eu/rapid/press-release_MEMO-13-815_en.htm

[2] G. Erber, "German-Chinese Economic Relation: Opportunities and Risks," DIW Economic Bulletin, 2012 2(3), pp. 27-31

[3] A. Dujin, C. Geissler, D. Horstkotter, "Industry 4.0: the new industrial revolution, How Europe will succeed", Roland Berger Startegy Consultants, 2014

[4] A. Gilchrist, "Industry 4.0: The Industrial Internet of Things", Apress, 2016, ISBN 9781484220474.

[5] R. Zhong, X. Xu, E. Klotz, et al "Intelligent Manufacturing in the Context of Industry 4.0: A Review" , Engineering, 2017, ,3, pp. 616-630

[6] P Zheng, H. Wang, Z. Sang, et al, "Smart manufacturing systems for Industry 4.0: Conceptual framework, scenarios, and future perspectives", Front. Mech. Eng., 2018, pp. 1–14

[7] P. Verma, R. Verma, A. Prakash, et al., "Machine-to-Machine (M2M) Communications:A Survey", Journal of Network and Computer Applications, 2016, 55, pp. 83–105

[8] J. Lin, W. Yu, N. Zhang, et al, "A Survey on Internet of Things: Architecture, Enabling Technologies, Security and Privacy, and Applications", IEEE Internet of Things Journal, 2017, 4(5), pp. 1125-1142

[9] J. Lee and H. Kao, "Service innovation and smart analytics for Industry 4.0 and big data environment", Procedia CIRP, 2014, 16, pp. 3-8

[10] B. Denkena and T. Morke, "Cyber-Physical and Gentelligent Systems in Manufacturing and Life Cycle: Genetics and Intelligence – Keys to Industry 4.0.", 2017, ISBN 9780128126004.

[11] J. Hull, "The Second Industrial Revolution: The History of a Concept", Storia Della Storiografia, 1999, 36, pp. 81–90

[12] D. Klitou, J. Conrads, M. Rasmussen et al "Digital Transformation Monitor Germany: Industrie 4.0" European Commission, European Union, January 2017

[13] D. Imkamp, J. Berthold, M. Heizmann, et al., "Challenges and trends in manufacturing measurement technology – the "Industrie 4.0" concept", Journal of Sensors and Sensor Syatems, 2016, 5, pp. 325–335

[14] R. Babiceanu and R. Seker "Big Data and virtualization for manufacturing cyber-physical systems: A survey of the current status and future outlook", Computer in industry, 2016, 81, pp. 128-137

[15] W. Shi, J. Cao, Q. Zhang, et al., "Edge Computing: Vision and Challenges" , IEEE Internet of Things Journal, 2016, 3(5), pp. 637-646

[16] S. Arthur, "Some Studies in Machine Learning Using the Game of Checkers", IBM Journal of Research and Development, 1959, 3, pp. 211-229

[17] A. Karpathy, G. Toderici, S. Shetty, et al., "Large-scale Video Classification with Convolutional Neural Networks", CVPR, 2014, pp. 1725-1732

[18] M. Rizzi, P. Ferrari, E. Sisinni, et al , "Using LoRa for industrial wireless networks", IEEE (WFCS), 2017, pp. 1-4

[19] A. Das, M. Walker, A. Hansson et al, "Hardware Software Interaction for Run-time Power Optimization: A Case Study of Embedded Linux on Multicore Smartphones" IEEE, ACM (ISLPED), 2015, pp. 165-170

[20] NVIDIA® Jetson™ TX1 Supercomputer-on-Module Drives Next Wave of Autonomous Machines "https://devblogs.nvidia.com/nvidia-jetson-tx1-supercomputer-on-module-drives-next-wave-of-autonomous-machine

How Can a User-Centered Design Bring Innovation in a Business Intelligence Platform?

Elodie Rival
Bertin IT-AMI Software, Centre Recherche et Développement, France
e-mail: elodie.rival@orange.fr

Céline Mateev, Nicolas Maranzana
Arts et Métiers ParisTech, LCPI
France
e-mail: celine.mateev@ensam.eu
e-mail: nicolas.maranzana@ensam.eu

Abstract—**We live in a world of data, in a constant flow of information. In business intelligence, data support a key role in decision-making and innovation. Digital tools are used to help business intelligence experts in research of insight. However, these tools are often difficult to use for a novice and are not fully adapted to every activity field. In this study, we propose to apply a user-centered design method for business intelligence tool redesign. We have integrated the user as a co-designer from the ideation phase to the evaluation of the solution. We present here the developed method and the mobilized tools necessary to generate a novel, efficient and generic interface for business intelligence experts.**

Keywords-user-centered design; data visualization; design method; evaluation method.

I. INTRODUCTION

With the Big Data advent, we are confronted with a huge production of digital information. Big Data is defined as: "*a new generation of technologies and architectures, designed to economically extract value from very large volumes of a wide variety of data, by enabling the high velocity capture, discovery, and/or analysis*" [1]. Therefore, it can be approached in a technical way, for instance, with algorithms, but it can also be addressed towards the end users, their operations and their needs. This represents the end-user approach that will be favored here, through the user-centered design process. End users are strategic or marketing stakeholders of companies from different fields (such as aeronautics, pharmaceuticals, transport, etc.,) but they are driven by a common aim: collecting as much data as possible on their markets to adapt their strategy and decision-making. For example, they want to visualize key information during a meeting and show them to their boss in a quick and efficient manner. We performed an intervention based on principles of user-centered design [2] and using its relevant tools and resources.

The context of the study was an intervention within a software edition company. Collaborators were using a business intelligence platform including complex functionalities from meta-analysis to news reading. This software was composed of several functionalities to share, organize, analyze, collect and search information. However, this version was restrictive, not intuitive and therefore not fully satisfying for the business intelligence expert. In this context, the company was looking for developing a new software to improve multidimensional data manipulation. We identified the following multidimensional data concerns:

- The origin of the information: type of media, of network, etc.
- The characteristics of the information: date, transmitter, linked concepts, etc.

In this study, we aimed at developing a new tool to support the daily work of the business intelligence expert and improve the decision-making by allowing an intuitive browsing within a complex network of data. To reach our goal, we used the user-centered design method.

The rest of the paper is structured as follows. In Section 2, we present a state of the art to define business intelligence and to specify the human needs and habits in this domain. We also identify the cognitive principles involved in visualization and data processing to improve those activities in an appropriate manner. Then, in Section 3, we define our method of intervention. Finally, in Sections 4 and 5, we perform a study to build a relevant solution for the end-user and to evaluate and to readjust it quickly.

II. STATE OF THE ART

A state of the art will first allow us to define the terms of business intelligence and data visualization. In the second step, we will present the research question discussed in this paper.

A. Business intelligence

Business intelligence is defined as a "*process implementing, recurring and methodical devices to collect, process and disseminate information to its operation. It is a systematic activity, equated to an active environmental monitoring*" [3]. Gathering competitive or strategic information for a company is a major challenge that provide added value, and sustains the growth of the company [4]. To this end, several software solutions: Digimind, AMI Enterprise Intelligence (Figure 1), Synthesio, etc. have been developed, offering advanced setting and information analysis of one or more topics of interest. The information is valuable for decision makers and must give insights quickly to push for action and to optimize decision-making. We extracted from the literature a first taxonomy of tasks governing information analysis. It consists of the following categories [5]: Observation, Navigation, Manipulation and Comparison to which we added one more: Restitution. We translated functionally these categories into the tasks performed by the user during the analysis [6]: Give an overview, Filter, Zoom, Details on demand, Associate, Provide a historical, Extract. After collecting a dataset, the user will first implement visual exploration strategies [7] and by then get new knowledge from the data by completing specific tasks. The decomposition of these strategies gave us a first insight of users' needs to analyze data and to proceed to decision-making.

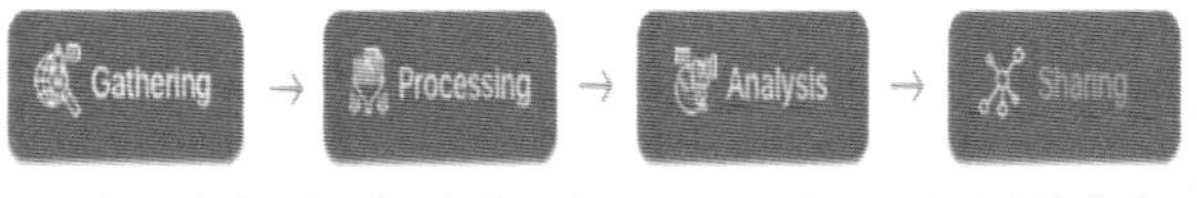

Figure 1. Business Intelligence AMI EI Software process

B. Business intelligence and Data visualization

This project is at the crossroads of two subjects: Business Intelligence and Data visualization. We are already familiar with some theories about visualization and architecture information of a Human Computer Interaction (HCI), for instance with the Gestalt Theory [8], whose basic premise is: *"in front of the complexity of our environment, the brain will try to get in shape, to give a meaningful structure to what it perceives to simplify and organize"*. Therefore, it was important to ensure excellent presentation and organization of information, and to introduce visual variables in user interface design regarding the user perspective [9]. The laws proposed in Gestalt Theory guide designers to arrange information in a relevant way. In addition, the system acts as a guide for the user by intuitive interaction, involving for instance icons and labels, mostly known as "Affordance" [10]. The functions of icons and labels must be clearly represented and quickly understandable. For instance, we can switch a cursor's representation to indicate the possibility of "grabbing" an object and moving it to another. Affordance is highly attractive from the perspective of data visualization as it facilitates decision-making and thus improves usability and usefulness of the system.

To provide functional implementations based on user as a human, we investigated cognitive sciences in detail. We focused on the user's needs to interact with a dataset and to provide better performance. The Active Reading consists in transforming the "reader" into an "actor" [11]. This is possible by offering a degree of freedom in document manipulation thanks to specific enrichment such as graphic signs and text annotations. The user can actively read and produce a modified or "enhanced" version of the source document. Thus, during a second reading, important information will be easier to find and draw more attention. The main constraint of this process remains the homogenization of these signs between different operators, particularly for the purpose of sharing information. Indeed, it is important that all operators share a common understanding of the codes used. The notion of Active Reading is strongly linked to the concept of ownership defined as "*the progressive internalization of technical and cognitive skills at work, in individuals or groups who handle daily technology* "[12]. Consequently, the daily use of technology allows suitable changes by creating new uses. This concept must bring designers to think about their project in a prospective way such as we have done here. Interestingly, it is common to say "I see" when we realized something instead of "I understand" since vision is the first sense we used, that provide us valuable knowledge on how information is assimilated [13]. Graphical characteristics (orientation, color, texture and movement) are seen without effort. For this reason, it is a source of information that promotes efficiency and should not be ignored. There are many forms of presentations to be considered, particularly movement that can be used such as a dynamic information. We chose vision as a central element of our project so we will be sensitive to those pieces of information during all our intervention.

C. Research question

The state of the art has allowed us to promote the importance of visualization and perception in the context of business intelligence and manipulation of a large and heterogeneous amount data. As part of this work, the research question focuses on how to effectively adapt a user-centered design method to design and evaluate a business intelligence platform?

III. METHOD

To define our intervention methodology, we used the User-Centered Design (UCD) [14] [15], which is frequently used in the field of ergonomics [3] [16] [24]. The project was divided into four main stages, regarding the UCD method: 1- specify the context of use, 2- specify requirements, 3- create design solutions, 4- evaluate design.

For each step of the method, we mobilized tools that allowed us to (1) introduce the users at the beginning of the design process and (2) produce intermediate solutions on an iterative and incremental way in order to permit their evaluation by the users. The users were first introduced in the design process as informant. Then, they became the most important stakeholder during the design of solution and its validation. These two phases were built on an iterative manner. The user contribution was progressive and participated to the success and strength of our intervention (Figure 2).

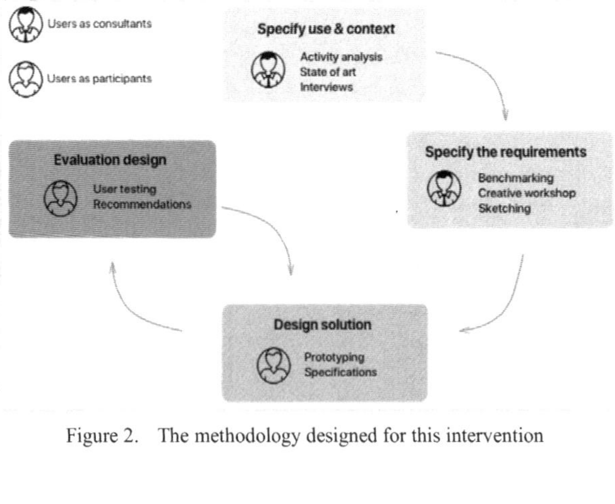

Figure 2. The methodology designed for this intervention

We opted for a method close to the MVP (Most Viable Product). This method consists of proposing a simple version of a product with basic features and allowing it to evolve using user's feedbacks. It is an agile design approach, which, if it remains close and keeps listening to users, provides very convincing results [23].

After the presentation of the general approach we will present in details the steps that bring us to the development of the final solution.

IV. EXPERIMENTATION

To reach a pertinent solution for the interface users, we first worked with them on the usage context.

A. Phases 1 and 2: Specify the context of use and the requirements

In this step of the design process, we drew from the literature all relevant information to specify better users' needs, such as the vision process, the active reading process [11], the preference for dynamic information, etc. We also gathered complementary and specific information during users' interviews, about their preferences on the composition of the modules, the importance of the analysis page, the difficulties to use some features such as key concepts, etc. Then, we realized a benchmark to determine the add value that we can propose on this market.

Creativity workshops were integrated in our intervention. We settled up a brainstorming with 4 developers, 3 managers and 3 designers with the following lead question: "How to improve the manipulation and the interaction with Big Data?"

We focused on the two working axis that emerged from this work: elements about the representation of information and elements about the interface interaction. Recommendations were associated to these two axis and are presented in the table below:

TABLE I. 2 AXIS RECOMMENDATIONS

	Recommendations
Interface interactions	- Save, export and share data - Drag / drop of a value from a chart to another, allowing zooming to obtain more details - Ability to lock the widget filters to keep a scope unchanged, as a context of the analyze - Comments on data
Representing information	- Multiplicity of graphics - Filter display - Widget layout

For the interface redesign, we focused on the analysis mode because it represents the most difficult part for the users but also because it covers the highest number of interaction elements and information representation. Indeed, interviews with users allowed us to identify difficulties linked to the analysis mode as it is not interactive and it does not allow the reading of several graphics at the same time to compare and study the interaction between several criteria (Figure 3).

During the analysis configuration, the expert has to use 3 tab pages to set up one analysis (Figure 4). Once again, the presence of these 3 tab pages prevents the expert to have a synthetic and global vision of the elements of the analysis. Moreover, the language used is not adapted to random users but only to experts.

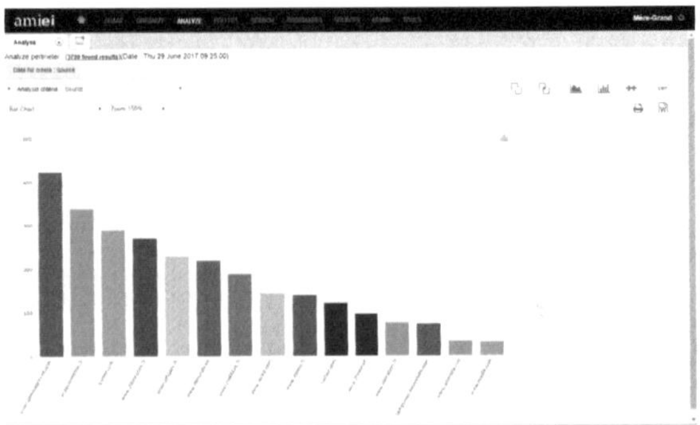

Figure 3. Screenshot of the current page of Analysis

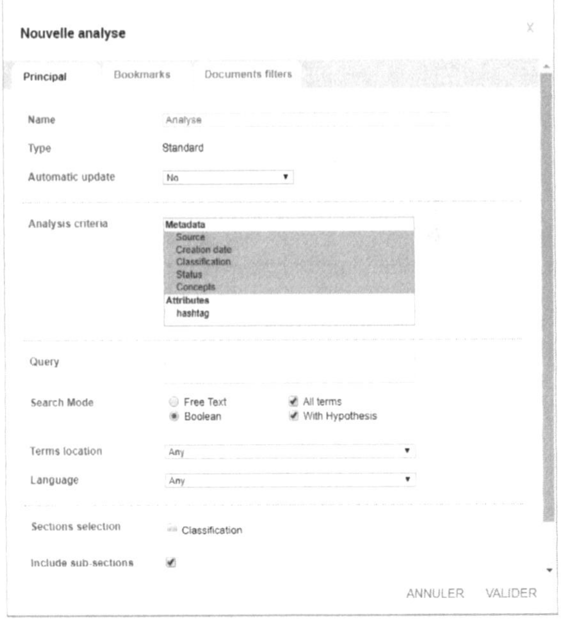

Figure 4. Screenshot of the setting of Analysis

A work of synthesis brought us to the first functional prototype that combine insight from the literature and users' interviews [17][18]. To start the experimentation, we developed an interactive prototype with a dedicated software: Axure, and implemented our solution on the Analyze module of AMI EI software.

B. Phases 3 and 4: Create and evaluate design solution

During all prototyping, we confronted the solution to our research findings to readjust the conception. The first version was composed of functionalities such as save, export, share, filter, widgets addition and also new interaction such as drag and drop. Although we made an important research on users' needs, we also included the specificity of AMI EI to accomplish the business goal. The evaluation phase started with a presentation of the prototype to expert clients to gather feedbacks and advices about the functional architecture. We decided to include "Recommended analysis", working such as an analysis template, to reach user of different expertise level. We also included a rapid and simple way to access to the filters of the analyze (Figure 5).

For the evaluation, we made two different tests with different users: expert evaluation and end users testing.

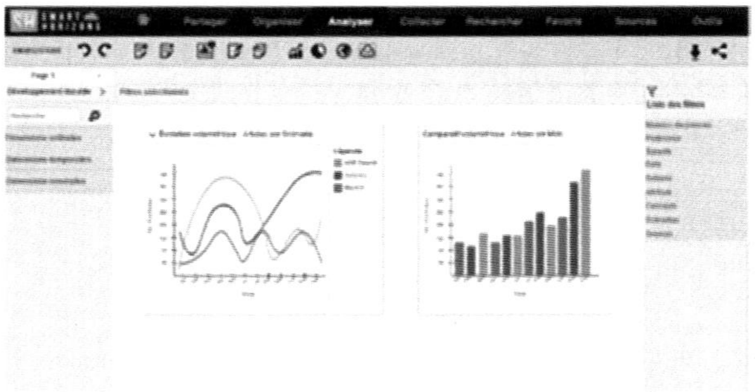

Figure 5. Screenshot of recommended Analysis page

1) Experts evaluation

The evaluation was realized in two steps: a demonstration of the prototype and a test scenario. First, we performed a demonstration of the prototype to five AMI expert customers. During the recorded interview, the experts guided us to a more fluent architecture. For instance, instead of dissociating the family of criteria with their children, the experts proposed a simpler way to present criteria all together. They particularly enjoyed multiples widgets on a same page, the use of a shortcut to add widgets and the direct manipulation offered by the drag and drop interaction. They also raised the importance of text document's consultation during analyze. Following this, we conducted iterations and established a test scenario composed of tasks such as starting an analysis, adding criteria to it, filter with these criteria, dragging and dropping a value from a widget to another. We engaged a second expert's review and received positive feedbacks and validated the overall behavior with a second phase of iteration before user testing. Each iteration phase took about a week.

2) End users testing

Prior to the user testing, a protocol was written and included:

- The objective of the test: improve the navigation and manipulation of a large dataset
- The scope: the analyze module
- The context: 1h of testing by ConfCall with recording
- Several scenarii, based on the information analysis tasks: starting an analysis, adding criteria to it, filter with these criteria, dragging and dropping a value from a widget to another.
- Material and human resources: AMI EI customers
- Final questionnaire

The testing sessions began with a presentation of the scope project and the objective. Then, the participants could performed the scenario of tasks. In line with the low number of users of the current Analysis module, we could only meet five testers. However, their profiles were varied by their level of expertise and by their work field (Aviation, Defense and Security, Automobile, University Research). Moreover, according to Nielsen, 80% of usability problems can be observed with a panel of five users [19].

3) Results

Two tasks, adding a widget and locking a graphic, required a demonstration to three out of five testers before the functionality can be well understood. However, all features were considered useful and relevant. The more popular ones were: plurality of widgets on a same a page, preprogrammed analysis models, drag / drop, sharing, annotation and export tools. All users also highlighted a better usability compared to the current model and suggested some improvements to pass the next step with a even more intuitive interface. At the end of each task, we asked them whether the interface met their needs in day-to-day job and all participants answered positively. Finally, they had to evaluate the global interaction on a scale of 10 (10 meaning the highest score for the best interaction). These feedbacks and score were formalized through the final questionnaire (Table II).

TABLE II. SYNTHESIS OF FINAL QUESTIONNAIRES

	CURRENT Analyze Module	TESTED Analyze module
Evaluation	4.6/10	7/10
Strengths	Advanced settings Capacity to provide the source statistics, subjects, etc.	Clear language Solves the main defect of the current module, the visual creation is more natural and accessible
Weaknesses	Difficulties to use some features such as key concepts	Filtering a graph from another one is not intuitive but training helps

A third phase of iteration was performed taking into accounts the result of user testing. The page was redesigned to increase relevance and customization possibilities (Figure 6).

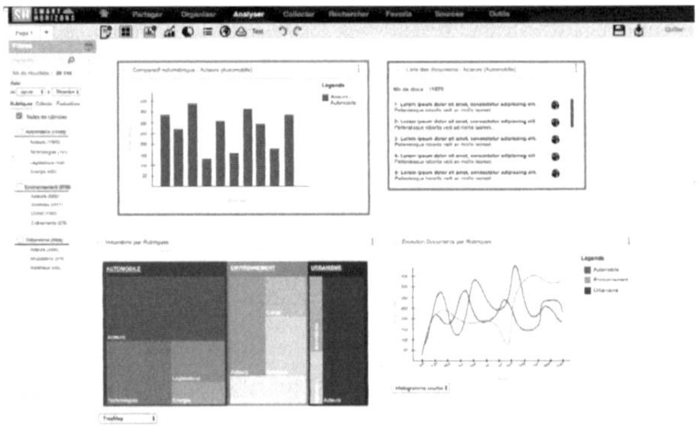

Figure 6. Screenshot of optimized Analysis page after final questionnaires

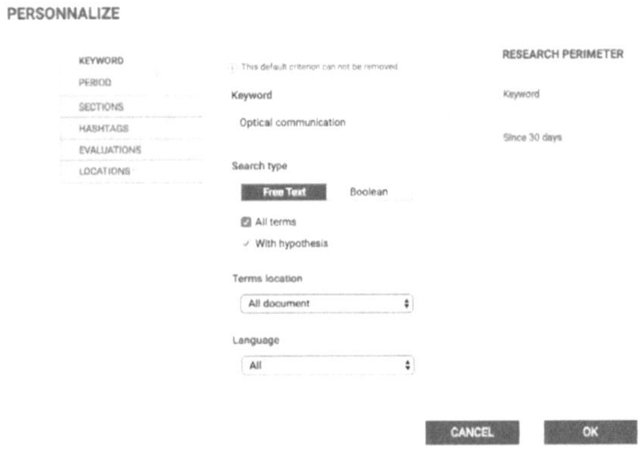

Figure 7. Screenshot "Personalized my research perimeter"

The different areas of improvement were specified in a document restoring observations during user testing and their recommendations and requests. This document was accompanied by own specifications for the development of the solution. Using "checklists", we described each feature and each section of the interface [20][21]. We collected rich feedback from users and the overall behavior can be validated and new iterations implemented. The solution continued to evolve until the presentation to the development team. We interviewed five more users, experts in Business Intelligence analysis, and developed solids use cases helpful to determine *"who (actor) does what (interaction) with the system, for what purpose (goal), without dealing with system internals"* [22].

The stakeholders decided to integrate this module in the new platform of consultation developed by AMI Software. Therefore, with an input of his choice, the user can visualize the following information:

- its change over time in the collection of data
- the set of documents associated to it within all the documents collected
- the set of the most relevant concepts lies to it

In addition, with all evolutions of the solution (after a fourth phase of iterations) the user can:

- Add a widget: the navigation bar was transformed into a floating button that follows the user throughout his scrolling on the page without being too visually ubiquitous.
- Analysis criteria are gathering on "Perimeter of research" and personalized according to users' needs. The selection is quite free and sub-criteria of a family can be chosen. The content is more distinguishable too (Figure 7). The comparison with the figure 4 and the settings of the actual analysis show clearly the progress made on an individual widget filters is also available and manageable for customizable views.

We decided to include "Share" and "Save" on a second phase of development. Preprogrammed models will also be included later, as we want to build them with the help of the daily use and a better knowledge on this need.

We defined an included analysis interface in an existing product and offered a simple interface with innovative interaction and meaningful representation. This design allows users (and even those who are far to be experts on Business Intelligence) to manipulate information to prepare a reunion with an important client or to make advanced market analysis and to spot a trend.

V. CONCLUSION AND FUTURE WORK

The "user-centered" approach established in this project gave an effective response to the problem "How to effectively adapt a user-centered design method to design and evaluate a business intelligence platform?"

The combination of a scientific and technological research, multidisciplinary team and an iterative process leads to a prototype that respects the model of ergonomic Graphical User Interface:

- meets ergonomic criteria (usability),
- innovates in line with needs and goals of end users (relevance and usefulness),
- Supports technical constraints of IT developers.

Our project is also influenced by contributions of data visualization and manipulation fields. The motion was introduced as a vehicle for information first, but also as a facilitator for handling this information (drag/drop). The crucial aspect of information architecture was enhanced by providing smooth navigation with clear design. This categorization allows the user to adapt quickly to the interface and to identify interactions. Through an analysis of the professional activity of end users, we have implemented innovative features and provided a relevant and intuitive solution.

Ongoing features on the prototype assert the stakeholders' satisfaction toward UX Designer's work. Those features included more Social Media Analysis, which is increasingly used in market analysis. Based on the work of Wu, Rosen & Schaefer [24], it will be interesting to determine how to detect communities or influencers in such networks. Indeed, it is important to involve all resources necessary to make the product evolve. During the presentation to the development teams, it will be crucial to make sense and to attach a clear goal in each feature [25].

REFERENCES

[1] J. Akoka, I. Comyn-Wattiau and N. Laoufi, *Research on Big Data – A systematic mapping study*, Computer Standards & Interfaces, vol. 54, part 2, pp. 105-115, 2017.

[2] L. L. Constantine, L. A. Lockwood, *Software for use: a practical guide to the models and methods of usage-centered design. Pearson Education,* 1999.

[3] G. Cliquet, *Method of innovation in the era of web 2.0* (phD thesis, Arts et Métiers ParisTech), 2010. Available from: https://pastel.archives-ouvertes.fr/pastel-00542938

[4] P. Alpar, T. H. Engler and M. Schulz, "Influence of social software features on the reuse of Business Intelligence reports" in Information Processing & Management, 51(3), pp. 235-251, 2015.

[5] C. Daassi, , L. Nigay and M. C. Fauvet, "Visualization process of temporal data" in *International Conference on Database and Expert Systems Applications*, Springer Berlin/Heidelberg, pp. 914-924, 2004.

[6] B. Shneiderman, "The eyes have it: A task by data type taxonomy for information visualizations" in *Visual Languages*, Proceedings IEEE Symposium on. IEEE, 1996.

[7] D. Keim, G. Andrienko, J.-D. Fekete, C. Görg, J. Kohlhammer and G. Melançon, *Visual analytics: Definition, process, and challenges,* Springer Berlin/Heidelberg, 2008.

[8] G. Humphrey, "The Psychology of the Gestalt" in *Journal of Educational Psychology*, 15(7), 1924.

[9] J. Silvennoinen, "Towards Essential Visual Variables" in *User Interface Design. 7th International Conference on Advances in Computer-Human Interactions,* Barcelona. pp. 229 - 234, 2014.

[10] E.J. Gibson, *The concept of affordances in development: The renascence of functionalism,* 1982.

[11] M.J. Adler and C. Van Doren, *How to read a book,* Ed. Simon and Schuster, 1976.

[12] M. Certeau (De), *The invention of everyday life*, Paris: UGE (réédition 1990), 1980.

[13] C. Ware, *Information visualization: perception for design,* Ed. Elsevier, 2012.

[14] ISO 9241-210: 2010. Ergonomics of human system interaction-Part 210: Human-centred design for interactive systems

[15] J.J. Garrett, *The elements of User experience – User-centered design for the Web*, New Riders, 2002.

[16] C. Abras, D. Maloney-Krichmar and J. Preece, "User-centered design" in *Bainbridge, W. Encyclopedia of Human-Computer Interaction, Thousand Oaks: Sage Publications,* 37(4), pp. 445-456, 2004.

[17] K. T. Ulrich and, S. D. Eppinger, *Product design and development.* Boston, MA: McGraw-Hill/Irwin, 2004.

[18] L. S. Jensen, A. G. Özkil and N. H. Mortensen, "Prototypes in Engineering Design: Definitions and strategies" in *DS 84: Proceedings of the 14th International Design Conference (Design'16), Cavtat, Croatia,* 2016.

[19] J. Nielsen, "Usability inspection methods" in *Conference companion on Human factors in computing systems (CHI'96)*, ACM, 1994.

[20] G. Pahl, W. Beitz, J.Feldhusen, and K. H. Grote, Engineering Design, *A Systematic Approach*, Ken Wallace and Lucienne Blessing translators and editors, 2006.

[21] S. Pugh, *Total design: integrated methods for successful product engineering*, Wokingham: Addison-Wesley, 1991.

[22] R. Malan and D. Bredemeyer, *Functional requirements and use cases,* Bredemeyer Consulting, 2001.

[23] L. Schwartz, , A. Vagner, S. Kubicki, and T. Altenburger, "Feedback on the definition and design of innovative mobile services" in *Proceedings of the 13th International Conference on Human Computer Interaction with Mobile Devices and Services (MobileHCI'11), ACM*, 2011.

[24] D. Wu, D. Schaefer and D. W. Rosen, "Cloud-based design and manufacturing systems: a social network analysis" in *International Conference on Engineering Design (ICED'13). Seoul, Korea, 2013.*

[25] I. Michailidou, C. Von Saucken and U. Lindemann, "Extending the product specification with emotional aspects: introducing user experience stories" in *International Conference on Engineering Design (ICED'13). Seoul, Korea,* 2013.

How Do User Experience Experts Organize Their Knowledge of User Experience Criteria?

Josefina Isabel Gil Urrutia[1,2,*]
Eric Brangier[1]
[1]Psychologie Ergonomique et Sociale de l'Expérience Utilisateurs (PErSEUs)
Université de Lorraine – UFR SHS
Metz, France
email: josefina.gil_urrutia@allianz.fr (*)
email: eric.brangier@univ-lorraine.fr

Laurent Cessat[2]
[2]Direction des Développements et de la Maintenance, Département Digital & Mobile
Allianz France Solutions & Services
Paris La Défense, France
email: laurent.cessat_2@allianz.fr

Abstract— **This paper presents a study where 17 User Experience professionals assessed and categorized a set of User Experience/Human-Computer Interaction criteria. We examined how they organize their cognitions around a suggested set of 58 criteria based on 7 significant theoretical dimensions: accessibility, usability/practicality, emotions & motivation, persuasion, cultural factors, management of the experience and socio-organizational factors. We aimed to determine whether the experts' cognitions would mirror these same theoretical considerations and, if so, to what extent. For this purpose, we analysed their classifications of the criteria during an open card-sorting task, limited to 7 groups. Results show a repartition of the criteria among the following standardized categories: (1) Utility & Usability; (2) Marketing Strategy; (3) Hedonism; (4) Organizational factors; (5) Emotional & Cognitive Stimulation; (6) Control & Personalization; and (7) System characteristics. We found that the groups created by the participants were conceptually rather similar throughout their categorizations and that they were rather close to the founding theoretical dimensions we had originally considered. Implications for our theoretical model's architecture are discussed.**

Keywords-user experience; holistic criteria-based approach; card-sort; dimensions; multidimensional model.

I. Introduction

Throughout history, ever-changing consumer requirements, economic models and technology have had a determining role on the evolution of the field of Human-Computer Interaction (HCI)/User Experience (UX). This has resulted in different issues being addressed at given times, as well as in different recommendations being made. Consequently, we are currently confronted with an overflow of frameworks, approaches, concepts, recommendations -so called criteria- which results in an ever increasing complexity of our practice [17].

It is with this in mind that we have taken upon ourselves to propose a holistic criteria-based approach in the field of HCI/UX to aid in the process of designing and/or evaluating user interfaces/products/services and that would encompass all aspects relevant for its truly holistic comprehension and conceptualization [6].

However, we must now reflect upon a possible organization of the myriad of relevant principles. To do this, we opted to examine how UX professionals organize their cognitions regarding a proposed range of criteria.

Considering UX as a multi-dimensional system, and based on the definition of UX suggested by [17], we opted for a selection of criteria based on 7 dimensions that we consider paramount in UX. These dimensions cover different aspects of HCI, ranging from sensory-motor factors, to cultural aspects, as well as cognitive, emotional and persuasive elements, among others. Each dimension is represented by a subset of criteria: 5 are based on pre-existing sets of guidelines; the remaining 2, we created based on the literature. These are:

- Accessibility: Web Content Accessibility Guidelines [15];
- Usability: Bastien & Scapin ergonomic criteria [1];
- Emotions and Motivation: de Vicente & Pain emotions & motivation detection model traits and states [2];
- Persuasion: Nemery & Brangier persuasion criteria [9];
- Culture: Schwartz basic human values [14];
- Management of the experience: created based on the literature [7], [10]-[13];
- And socio-organizational factors: also based on the available literature [4], [5].

Given the substantial number of criteria (58; detailed presentation in [6]), along with their inherent redundancies and interdependencies [6], [17]-[18], it seems difficult to mentally organize them in a coherent and relevant manner. Therefore, in order to determine a viable architecture for our suggested model, it is necessary to study how UX experts would mentally represent and organize said lot of criteria.

How do UX experts organize their knowledge of UX criteria? Two research questions were addressed here:

- On one hand: whether or not UX experts - who regularly use these criteria - all have the same mental organization of the set.
- On the other hand: whether their cognitive organizations of the criteria are in line with that provided by the authors of the different theoretical criteria grids. Or, on the contrary, whether the organization of the criteria depends on other factors that need to be elucidated and interpreted.

This study aimed to determine how UX experts would envision, apprehend and structure the proposed set of UX criteria through a card-sort exercise: would the card sort reveal categories stable enough throughout the experts? Would the general classification of criteria produced by experts overlap itself or correspond with the original theoretical guidelines proposed by their original authors? and if so, to what extent?

This paper therefore focuses on an experiment -which was part of a broader research project- where UX experts had to classify 58 recognized criteria in strictly 7 groups. Section 2 presents the methodology used. Thereupon, the results will be summarized (in section 3) followed by their discussion (in section 4) and we will conclude with our future work in Section 5.

II. METHOD

A. Participants

17 HCI/UX Design experts (6 women, 11 men; mean age 44 (standard deviation (SD)=8.6)) took part in this experiment. Among them, 11 are specialized in Ergonomics/Cognitive Psychology, 4 in Computer Science and the remaining 2 in Communications and Media. Participants were required to have at least 10 years of experience in the field of HCI/UX in order to be eligible for this study (mean ($\bar{x}$)=17.53; SD=6.05). 11 of them are academics, 4 are consultants and 2 are both. 10 have a PhD, and 7 have a Master's degree. The experts received a small compensation for their participation.

B. Material

This study used the same deck of 58 cards described in [6], each containing the name and definition of a criterion from the set. A pen and extra plain 5x5cm cards were always at the participants' disposal in case they wished to create (a) new card(s). Also, plain white 5x20cm index cards were made available to create the category name tags.

The researcher who conducted the experiment used a camera and a recorder to document the data.

C. Procedure

Sessions were un-moderated and carried out individually. No duration limit was imposed; they lasted 10 to 20 minutes.

Participants were presented with the card-deck. They were asked to do an open card-sort in strictly 7 groups (which corresponds to the number of theoretical sets of guidelines considered). They were asked to name the categories they had created and to explain the logic on which they had based their sortings. These debriefings were recorded and later transcribed for reference during the analysis and interpretation of the data.

Participants were allowed to exclude the criteria they considered irrelevant and/or to create (a) new card(s) indicating a name and definition when considered necessary.

III. RESULTS

Following [3], we analysed each participant's classification to create standardized categories that would sum up the range of classifications done by the experts. Furthermore, [3] automatically generated the items by standardized categories matrix.

Also, with an adapted version of [8], we generated the global distance matrix. Using R-3.3.2 [16], we carried out a Hierarchical Cluster Analysis (HCA) with Ward's clustering method and a Multi-Dimensional Scaling (MDS) based on Kruskal's non-metric MDS.

A. Standardized Categories for the Criterion Distribution

Table 1 recaps the 18 pertinent standardized categories we created for the analysis of the different participants' categorizations (plus the "Excluded/Irrelevant" category).

TABLE I. STANDARDIZED CATEGORIES CREATED FOR THE ANALYSIS (GENERATED USING [3])

Standardized Categories	Sorters who used this	Total cards in this category	Unique cards	Agree -ment
Utility, task-system suitability, achieving the goal, efficacy	5	30	21	0.29
Usability/Pragmatismer gonomic criteria, efficiency	12	163	37	0.37
Utility & Usability / Efficacy & Efficiency	2	43	26	0.83
Hedonism, Pleasure, Emotions	14	138	41	0.24
Adaptability of the system	9	90	42	0.24
Organizational Factors	9	63	20	0.35
Socio-organizational factors	2	12	9	0.67
Persuasion, Incitement, Pervasive design	11	71	28	0.23
Marketing Strategy/ Customer Relationship Management	13	88	21	0.32
User Effort	1	6	6	1.00
Personalization/ Customization	4	23	15	0.38
Mastering/Control over the system	3	20	19	0.35
Security/Reliability-User's Protection	8	53	26	0.25
User onboarding	4	43	28	0.38
Emotional & Cognitive Stimulation for self-development	7	48	24	0.29
Social, moral and/or cultural factors	5	21	12	0.35
Technical aspects/ Robustness	3	16	14	0.38
Others/Unknown	6	28	23	0.20
Excluded/Irrelevant	6	15	14	0.18

The agreement values found are rather low ($\bar{x}$=0.38; SD=0.22). However, the occurrence of the standardized categories is quite high ($\bar{x}$=6.59; max=14) By instance, as much as 14 participants created a category conceptually-linked to "Hedonism, Pleasure, Emotions". So, though it remains questionable as to which criteria belong to which category, the fundamental categories underlying the organization seem to be of general-understanding among the participants.

B. Hierarchical categorization of the 58 criteria

Next, we performed a HCA on the overall distance matrix. By reading of the items by standardized categories matrix, we were able to interpret the resulting dendrogram, in order to identify and label the clusters of criteria found (Fig. 1).

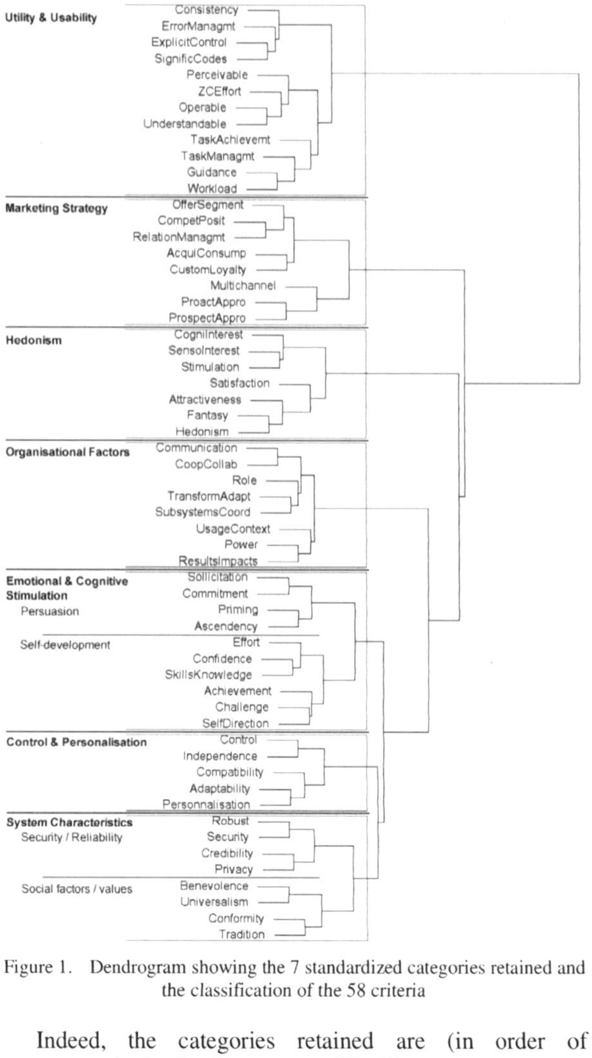

Figure 1. Dendrogram showing the 7 standardized categories retained and the classification of the 58 criteria

Indeed, the categories retained are (in order of appearance in the dendrogram; see Fig. 1):

1. Utility (task-system suitability, achieving the goal, efficacy) & Usability/Pragmatism (ergonomic criteria, efficiency) containing the items: Perceivable, Operable and Understandable from [15], Consistency, Error Management, Explicit Control, Significance of Codes, Guidance and Workload from [1], Zero Customer Effort from the management of the experience dimension, as well as Task Achievement and Task Management from the socio-organizational dimension;
2. Marketing Strategy/Customer Relationship Management encompassing 8 of the 9 elements created for the management of the experience dimension, namely: Offer Segmentation, Competitive Positioning, Relationship Management, Acquisition-Consumption, Customer Loyalty and Recommendation, Multichannel/Omni-channel, Proactive Approach and Prospective Approach;
3. Hedonism, Pleasure, Emotions comprising the criteria: Cognitive Interest, Sensory Interest, Satisfaction and Fantasy from [2], Stimulation and Hedonism from [14], and Attractiveness from [9];
4. Organisational Factors: including 7 of the 10 elements created for the socio-organisational dimension (Communication, Cooperation/Collaboration, Role, Transformation-Adaptation, Sub-systems coordination, Context of use, Results & Impacts) and Power, from [14];
5. Emotional & Cognitive Stimulation for self-development: structured around two subgroups - one containing elements in relation to "persuasion, incitement, pervasive design" (Solicitation, Commitment, Priming and Ascendency, all from [9]), and the other to "self-development" (Effort, Confidence, Challenge from [2], Skills & Knowledge from the socio-organisational dimension, as well as Achievement and Self-direction from [14]);
6. Control & Personalization, a combination of two subgroups: "personalization/customization" and "mastering/control over the system" linked to user's need and desire for self-expression and self-direction. The former is composed of the elements Control and Independence both from [2]; the latter is composed of Compatibility and Adaptability from [1] and Personalisation from [9]. These criteria were often linked to notions of Utility and/or Usability and of "Adaptability of the System";
7. And, lastly, what we chose to name "System's characteristics" based on the analysis of the debriefings, a category including the subgroups "Security/Reliability-User's Protection" (Robust from [15], Security from [14], as well as Credibility and Privacy from [9]), and "Social Factors/Values" of the system (Benevolence, Universalism, Conformity and Tradition, all taken from [14]).

These results are very similar -as to the groupings and the naming of the groups- to those from our previous paper [6] where the participants were asked to do an open-card sort without a limited number categories. The results showed an average repartition in 7.71 groups (SD=1.65; min=5; max=11) and the categories retained were: 1) Utility & Usability; 2) Hedonism, Pleasure, Emotions; 3) Persuasion, Incitement, Pervasive design; 4) Emotional & Cognitive

Stimulation for self-development; 5) Marketing strategy/Customer Relationship Management; 6) Security/Reliability-User's protection; 7) Organizational factors; and 8) Social, moral and/or cultural factors.

However, regardless of the similarity, three main findings are worth mentioning.

Firstly, this exercise yielded differences in the granularity of the classification: depending on whether the participant had previously done more or less than 7 groups, they would often either divide one (or more) in two, or, assemble two (or more). For example, this was the case for participants who had previously created a group for "Efficacy", another one for "Efficiency", and who assembled the two in order to create one named "Usability/Utility/Ergonomic Criteria" (or vice-versa). Likewise, the same phenomenon happened with the categories "Organizational factors" and "Social factors" – though only 2 participants assembled them together and thus this does not reflect in the categories retained. Moreover, however seldom, certain participants would pick-and-choose certain criteria in order to *extract* an entirely new category (e.g., "Marketing Strategy", by participant n°13).

Furthermore, compared to the groupings found in [6], only 3 *migrators* were found; while the rest remained pretty much the same ("migrators" being items that moved from one category to another):

- Compatibility (ergonomic criterion; [1]) moved from "Utility & Usability" to the group "Control & Personalization";
- Achievement (cultural criterion; [14]) moved from "Social factors" to the "Self-development" subgroup in the category "Emotional & Cognitive Stimulation for self-development";
- And, to a certain point, Self-Direction (cultural criterion; [14]) that moved from the subgroup "mastering/control over the system" to the "self-development" subgroup – which are subgroups of the "Emotional & Cognitive Stimulation for self-development" category.

This indicates a permeability/porosity of the frontiers and evidences certain variability in the interpretation of the criteria –like further discussed below.

Lastly, these results highlight the variability in the interpretation of the criteria and of the card-groupings, with regard to the criteria's attributes and their category affiliations. For example, the group of criteria labelled "Social Factors/Values" previously (in [6]) interpreted as characteristics of the user or of the context of use, is interpreted here as characteristics of/expected from the system (e.g., "a benevolent system", "a traditional system").

C. Categories' Relationships and Proximity

The dendrogram (Fig. 1) revealed a close link between the categories (7) "System characteristics" and (6) "Control & Personalization" which in turn revealed a link to the category (5) "Emotional & Cognitive Stimulation for self-development". The following group to link to the dendrogram is the (4) "Organizational Factors", next, the (3) "Hedonism, Pleasure, Emotions", then, the (2) "Marketing Strategy/Customer Relationship Management", and lastly, the (1) "Utility (task-system suitability, achieving the goal, efficacy) & Usability/Pragmatism (ergonomic criteria, efficiency)".

This structure might be due to stronger cohesiveness values within the last 4 categories listed above. This is especially true for the category "Utility & Usability" given the importance of its perceived distance (graphically represented in the tree diagram).

D. Spatial Representation and Structure

The MDS required a three-factor analysis in order to obtain significant enough results (stress=17.06%). The spatial representation drawn from this analysis is presented in a two-dimensional plot in Figure 2.

The spatial representation and repartition of the criteria throughout the MDS showed a structural resemblance to that of our previous study [6]. Indeed, the results here allude to the same ternary structure with the three outermost groups (Utility & Usability, Organisational factors, Hedonism, Pleasure and Emotions; representing the functional, experiential and contextual pillars of UX) merging towards elements of technological persuasion and user stimulation.

Additionally, by graphical reading, the same two possible factors justifying the structure stand out:

- Along the x-axis, a first one seeming to correspond to the nature of the experience, ranging from the functional experience to the experiential experience;
- The other one along the y-axis seeming to be the level the criterion intervenes on: the user, the system or the context of use.

Further analyses are required to verify this and to identify the third factor.

However, three new findings stick out. First, the system is more visibly represented via the category "System characteristics" that occupies a significant area between the Organizational factors and the Utility & Usability categories. Second, the category "Control & Personalization" seems to bridge "Utility & Usability" and "System characteristics" as well as the former and "Emotional & Cognitive Stimulation for self-development". Lastly, in the same manner, the group "Marketing Strategy" seems to link the elements pertaining to organizational factors and social factors/values of the system to the remaining elements, serving as a sort of intermediary between the two.

E. Additional Elements of Analysis

Six participants excluded 13 unique cards from their sortings. Only the criterion "Challenge" was excluded by two participants – which has a negligible impact as to its perceived relevancy for our model.

No one suggested adding any new criteria.

IV. Discussion

This paper presents a study where UX professionals assessed and categorized a suggested set of UX/HCI criteria in order to elucidate whether the basis for their categorizations would overlap with the original theoretical dimensions considered, if so, to what extent, or whether it would be based on other factors that would need to be revealed.

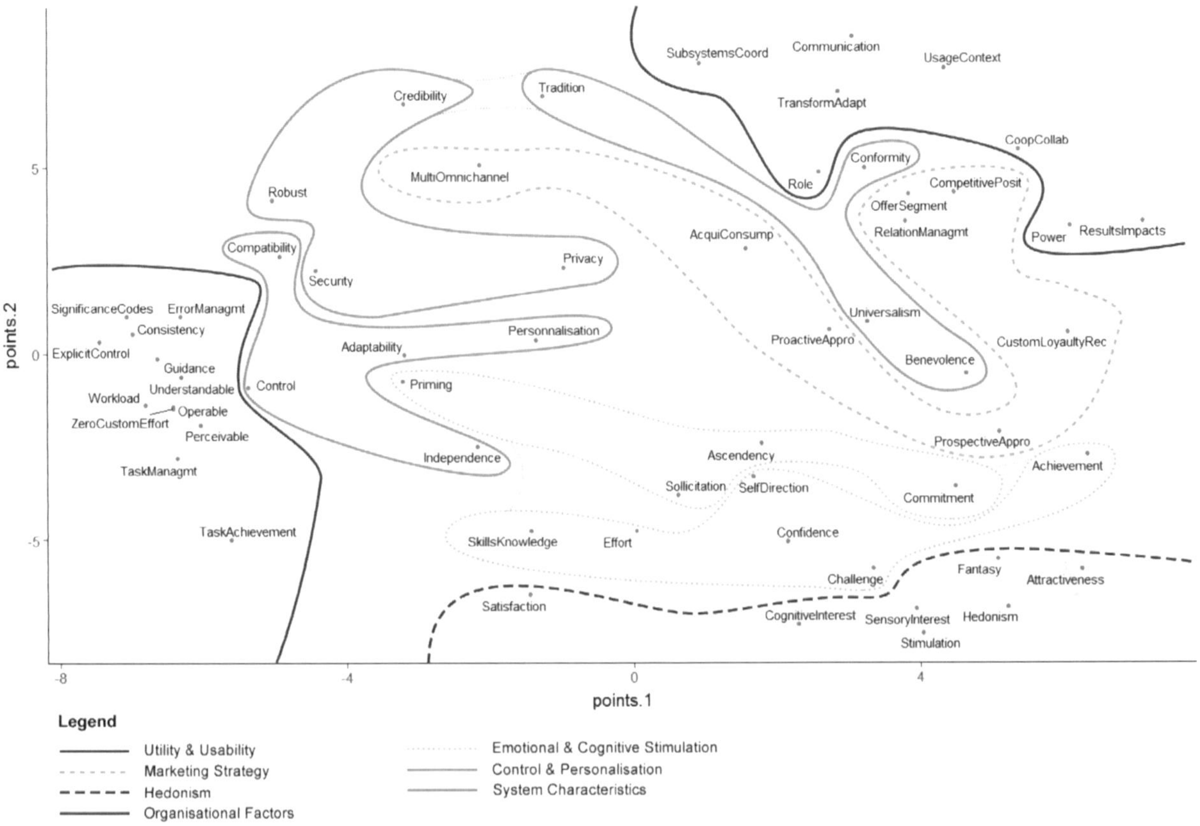

Figure 2. Multi-Dimensional Scaling plot using 3 factors (stress=17.06%) showing the overall categorization among 7 standardized categories.

Four/Five of the seven categories retained from the analysis indicate a relative correspondence to the initial theoretical dimensions. Besides from the categories "Utility & Usability", "Marketing strategy/Customer Relationship Management" and "Organizational factors" being evidently analogous to the usability, management of the experience and socio-organizational factors dimensions, one/two more categories deserve further attention. Indeed, the categories "Hedonism, Pleasure, Emotions" and "Emotional & Cognitive Stimulation for self-development" are also related to our emotions & motivation dimension – even though a distinction was clearly made by the participants, who opted to make two separate categories. Similarly, the subgroup "persuasion, incitement, pervasive design", contained within the "Emotional & Cognitive Stimulation for self-development" (though it was a category in and of itself in [6]) is in line with yet another one of our theoretical UX dimensions (Persuasion). Thus, despite the rather low agreement values, and though not entirely in line with the 7 dimensions considered, the participants' resulting mean categorization is fundamentally quite close to our theoretical considerations.

Moreover, this study shed light as to differences in the granularity of the classifications. This shows that various possible levels of categorization of the criteria can be made which raises questions as to what the optimal architecture for a holistic criteria-based model of UX would look like; between a high/macro-level or a low/micro-level (more detail-oriented) approach.

Results also revealed the porosity/permeability of the frontiers between the categories as well as a considerable variability as to the interpretation of the criteria and of the groupings. Indeed, certain criteria were attributed varying characteristics and, depending on this, were allocated to varying categories – evidencing a criterion's multiple possible impacts on UX as well as the systemic nature of UX. Other than the three *migrators* identified and described above, this was particularly the case for Schwartz's cultural values [14]. Undeniably, these elements were subject to the most varying interpretations possible; participants describing/manipulating them as social/cultural factors, as system characteristics expected by the user, as factors of motivation, etc.

The spatial representation reinforced the idea of a ternary structure built around the three basis of the experience (functional, experiential and contextual elements) merging towards technological persuasion and user stimulation. But this time the system is more markedly represented and, as supported by the proximity among the categories in the tree diagram, it is closely linked to elements of user control & personalization which in turn are strongly linked to emotional & cognitive stimulation for self-development.

Lastly, we found that three factors underlie the participants' cognitive organizations reflected through this sorting exercise; one being the nature of the experience, one seeming to be the level the criterion intervenes on; the last one remains to be clarified.

V. Conclusion and Future Work

Generally speaking, human-machine interactions have been studied within the framework of research related to software ergonomics, which aims at adapting the software to the user as it deals with information. In other words, the goal is to adapt the computer's behaviour, i.e., its external manifestations, to the user's cognitive functioning seeking to offer the most efficient, pleasant, satisfactory and least restrictive assistance possible. By extension, software ergonomics also needs to produce knowledge about how users work, interact and think. This knowledge includes many criteria that we seek to better understand and organize in a relevant manner in order to propose a structured model.

When HCI experts are asked to categorize these criteria, it appears that:

- The criteria grids are mentally reassembled in a way that certain criteria are stable and invariant of their category, while others are not, so they *migrate* towards other categories;
- The criteria most stable and consistent with their category are those related to usability;
- The criteria are subject to varying interpretations and they might be attributed different characteristics leading to categorization differences;
- The standardized categories created and retained during the analysis of the data, are conceptually similar to a certain point to the initial theoretical considerations we chose for the suggestion of the 58 criteria;
- The two main factors justifying the categorization and its resulting spatial representation seem to be the nature of the experience (functional vs. experiential), and the level of impact of the criterion (user, system, context of use).

While research on UX factors and criteria is continuing, we think this research is necessary to summarize perception of UX criteria as assessed by UX experts.

Currently, two studies are underway in which we are evaluating the applicability of our holistic criteria-based approach, in both HCI design and evaluation practices. Our next task will be to define a generic toolkit to organize the criteria so that they can be used in interface design and evaluation.

Acknowledgment

We thank Hervé Mémain and Yadira Colin for their valuable contributions to this paper.

References

[1] J. M. C. Bastien and D. L. Scapin, "Ergonomic criteria for the evaluation of human-computer interfaces". (Technical report N° 156). Rocquencourt, France: INRIA Rocquencourt, 1993.

[2] A. de Vicente and H. Pain, "Informing the Detection of the Students' Motivational State: an Empirical Study," Proceedings of the Sixth International Conference on Intelligent Tutoring Systems, 2002.

[3] D. Maurer. *Card Sort Analysis Spreadsheet Template*. [Online] [retrieved: November, 2016] Available from: http://rosenfeldmedia.com/books/card-sorting/

[4] K. Eason, "Sociotechnical systems theory in the 21st Century: another half-filled glass," Sense in Social Science: A collection of essays in honour of Dr. Lisl Klein, Broughton, United Kingdom, pp. 123-134, 2008.

[5] R. Eskl, A. Sole, and Presses universitaires de France, "Automation strategies, work organisation and social relantionships in large companies in the tertiary sector". Réseaux, 4(18), pp. 7-18, 1986.

[6] J. I. Gil Urrutia, E. Brangier, and L. Cessat, "Is a holistic criteria-based approach possible in user experience?: Study of the classification of 58 criteria linked to UX," In: A. Marcus, W. Wang (Eds.): DUXU 2017, Part I, LNCS, vol. 10288, pp. 395-409, 2017, Springer Verlag DOI: 10.1007/978-3-319-58634-2_29

[7] P. Klaus, B. Edvardsson, and S. Maklan, "Developing a typology of customer experience management practice–from preservers to vanguards," In 12th International Research Conference in Service Management, La Londe les Maures, France, 2012.

[8] M. Rice. *Co-occurrence Matrix*. [Online] [retrieved: November, 2016] Available from: http://www.informoire.com/taxonomy/co-occurrence-matrix-announcement/ and from http://www.informoire.com/co-occurrence-matrix/

[9] A. Nemery and E. Brangier, "Set of Guidelines for Persuasive Interfaces: Organization and Validation of the Criteria," Journal of Usability Studies, Vol. 9, Issue 3, pp. 105-128, 2014.

[10] P. Neveu and V. Alasluquetas, "White paper: Approaches, Routes and Customer experiences : 10 best practices of companies inspired by their customers," Ginger & Different Factory [Online] [retrieved: June, 2016] Available from: http://docplayer.fr/13137085-Demarches-parcours-et-experience-clients.html

[11] A. Palmer, "Customer experience management: a critical review of an emerging idea," Journal of Services marketing, 24(3), 196–208, 2010.

[12] B. J. Pine and J. H. Gilmore, "Welcome to the experience economy," Harvard business review, 76, 97–105, 1998.

[13] M. Schofield, "Applying the Kano Model to Improve UX," Computers In Libraries, 36(8), 28, 2016.

[14] S. H. Schwartz, "Basic human values : Theory, measurement, and applications," Revue française de sociologie, 47(4), 929-968, 2006.

[15] World Wide Web Consortium Recommentation 11 December 2008. *Web Content Accessibility Guidelines (WCAG) 2.0.*. [Online] [retrieved: June, 2016] Available from: http://www.w3.org/TR/2008/REC-WCAG20-20081211/ Latest version available at http://www.w3.org/TR/WCAG20/

[16] R Core Team, "R: a Language and Environment for Statistical Computing", R Foundation for Statistical Computing, Vienna, Austria, 2016, Available from: https://www.R-project.org/

[17] E. Brangier, M. Desmarais, A. Nemery, and S. Prom Tep, "Evolution of the heuristic inspection: towards an integration of accessibility, usability, emotion and persuasion?," Journal d'Interaction Personne-Système, 4(1), pp. 69-84, 2015.

[18] J. I. Gil Urrutia, E. Brangier, V. Senderowicz and L. Cessat, "Beyond "Usability and User Experience", Towards an Integrative Heuristic Inspection: From Accessibility to Persuasiveness in the UX Evaluation," In: T. Ahram, C. Falcão C. (Eds.) Advances in Usability and User Experience. AHFE 2017. Advances in Intelligent Systems and Computing, vol 607. Springer, Cham

The Impact of Visual Aesthetic Quality on User Engagement during Gameplay

Uttam Kokil
Kennesaw State University
Marietta Campus, GA 30060. U.S.A
E-mail: ukokil@kennesaw.edu

Abstract—**The aim of this study was to examine player behavior in two different levels of visual aesthetic quality of a tablet game user interface. First, the tablet game was created by applying user centered design principles, such as prototyping and usability testing in an iterative manner. The game was then modified into two different visual aesthetic conditions – monochromatic (low quality) and in full color (high quality) to serve as response stimuli. The first objective examined the effect of visual aesthetic quality on user engagement using the user engagement scale (UES). The four components of user engagement are *reward, aesthetics, focused attention*, and perceived *usability*. It was observed that three of the user engagement components, *reward, aesthetics* and *usability* significantly predicted *perceived high visual aesthetic quality* interface. In addition, three user engagement components, reward, aesthetics and focused attention, supported *perceived visual aesthetic quality* for the low-quality interface. This result was further substantiated by investigating the effect of perceived usability in the same experimental condition using the *AttrakDiff* questionnaire. The main finding of this study reveals that high visual aesthetic quality user interfaces are perceived to be usable whereas low visual aesthetic interfaces are not. There was also a significant difference in the level of *overall user engagement* between the two game interfaces, as participants found the high visual aesthetic quality to be more engaging.**

Keywords-tablet gaming; user experience; user interface design; user engagement; perceived usability; visual aesthetics.

I. INTRODUCTION

The ubiquitous property of tablet gaming has contributed to a wider demographic of users [1] [2]. Clearly the rate of tablet adoption is due to an innovation that has been perceived to have a greater relative advantage by the end-users, as per the Diffusion of Innovations Theory [3]. Digital games arise from a wide spectrum of genres, classifications, and categories; technology acts as a catalyst for the changing medium of game interaction, from consoles to touch screen devices. In fact, traditional keyboard and console-based games are dramatically shifting to the more affordable touch-screen games for tablets and mobile devices [4]. The advent of touchscreen computing has revolutionized the field of Human Computer Interaction (HCI) as it has become part of our everyday life and experience [5]. The mobile platform has tremendous scope for developing newer types of games, targeted to a broader demographic of users [1]. Designing digital games for a broader audience is complex in the sense that all users have their own preference and motive in terms of game genres, such as action, adventure, or serious games. There is unanimous acceptance among researchers and practitioners in the HCI field that applications must be designed with the inclusion of non-task-related concepts [6], which Mahlke [7] positions as non-instrumental quality and other researchers describe as hedonic components [8]–[11]. Instrumental quality is also referred to as the pragmatic aspect of product quality which incorporates functionality, usability, practicality, and utility; non-instrumental quality on the other hand encompasses visual aesthetics, and hedonic qualities such as pleasure, enjoyment, and fun. Therefore, it becomes pertinent to design "engaging experiences" in products, to captivate and enrich user experience (UX) by adding playful and fun features in games [12]. A method to engage end-users is to create user-centric applications based on user needs and satisfaction.

HCI practitioners have linked UX to components beyond instrumental quality to include hedonic, visual aesthetics, affective, emotions, and "experiential" technology-interaction [13]–[15]. The roles of instrumental and non-instrumental qualities in products have been closely studied over and again by several scholars [7] [16]–[18]. There has been no consensus on the relationship between usability and visual aesthetics in the domain of product design, or interactive design. Some researchers have lengthily discussed the concept of what is "*beautiful is usable,*" signifying that a "beautiful" object influences usability [19], while other scholars have shown that there is no relationship between usability and visual aesthetics [20] or the factors are independent from each other [7]. User engagement is part of a positive UX [21]. Carr [22] explains that game players are able to make choices and important decisions during gameplay by virtue of the visceral characteristics of visual elements. This implies that users make judgment based on both cognitive and emotional capabilities [23], induced by visual elements [24]. It becomes essential to examine user perceptions and behavior during gameplay interaction. This will provide a deeper insight why users are attracted and engaged to play games [7]. The main objective of this study is to examine the effect of visual aesthetic quality on four components of user engagement [25] in tablet game interfaces. According to extant literature, no distinction has been made concerning the level of visual aesthetics in products that have an impact on usability. The second objective attempts to bridge the knowledge gap by providing insights to identify the level of visual aesthetics in user interfaces that influence usability. Section II provides an overview of the literature review. Section III justifies the methods, including data gathering procedure. Section IV elucidates the analysis and results portion. Section V concludes the paper.

II. Literature Review

It has been argued that the components associated with usability, such as effectiveness, efficiency and satisfaction alone cannot be a sole predictor of UX. The inclusion and assessment of hedonic and experiential attributes concerning human technology interaction such as pleasure, fun, enjoyment, and engagement are necessary to close the loop [26]. A game interface connects a player's experience to the gaming system; hence it becomes imperative to understand user engagement, UX, and emotional outcome, along with the characteristics of the tablet user interface. It is clear that mobile devices have a set of new features (touch screen, camera, GPS, etc.) over game consoles that offers different mode of interactions. According to Cyr et al. [27, pp. 951], aesthetics has demonstrated to have a "positive effect on user perception on mobile system's ease of use, usefulness and enjoyment." However, the impact of the degree of visual aesthetic quality (low or high) on perceived usability is not clear.

O'Brien and Toms [25] conducted a study in the e-commerce domain to explore the hedonic and utilitarian motivation with regards to user engagement in the online shopping domain. The hedonic and utilitarian motivation and engagement include both functional and pleasurable aspects of UX and the hedonic qualities of product attributes, such as entertainment and utilitarian concepts including efficiency, cost, and functional attributes influence user engagement. Consequently, several studies have been conducted to assess user engagement in the domains of video games [28], online news [29] [30], and web searching [31]. UX examines the quality of information interactions from users' perspective [21]. User engagement forms part of UX, as the positive side of user interaction is accentuated, whereby technology can entice and motivate the user towards product use [32]. User Engagement is defined as a user-product relationship encompassing an emotional, cognitive and behavioral bond that prevails over time [6]. User Engagement encompasses the initial reaction of users towards technology [33] as well as the continuous use and re-engagement with the information system over time [34] [35]. Engagement is determined by factors like visual aesthetics, system usability, user involvement and evaluation of the experience [34]. It was recommended that the term "engagement" should replace "satisfaction" as the latter does not signify the experience a user is drawn into a user interface [36]. User attitude towards the system is part of engagement and focused on the thoughts of individual users [37], "feelings" [38], "their degree of activity" [37], and "during system use [39]". O'Brien and Toms [40] devised the UES scale to measure user engagement by assessing user perspective of *perceived usability, aesthetics, novelty, felt Involvement, endurability*, and *focused attention*. In this study, it was recommended to combine *novelty, felt involvement and endurability* into one factor called *reward,* because they all formed part of the hedonic aspects. By contrast, perceived usability, aesthetics and focused attention emerged to be typically different from each other in the UES scale study. Wiebe et al. [28] recommended to use fewer constructs in the UES scale. Hence, the UES scale was reduced to four factors: *perceived usability, aesthetics, focused attention and reward* [29].

A description of the user engagement scale components is provided as follows. Researchers have associated, *endurability* to an experience in which users will remember the most gratifying moments during an activity, and will most likely repeat those activities again [41]. It is also associated to user loyalty. *Novelty* covers a new idea or concept pertaining to game narrative or storytelling, or a creative method for a player to interact with the game user interface, which may give rise to elements of surprise or excitement during gameplay. It arouses a user sense of curiosity [42]. *Felt involvement* is described as a fun experience which sustains user interest in an interactive environment which may arise from an emotional connection between the interface and the user [28]. *Focused attention* is defined as a high-level concentration and absorption of one's mental state into an activity, which resonates with the flow theory, whereby the notion of time is lost when a user is fully immersed into the activity at hand [26]. Aesthetics appeals to the senses. Engholm [43] defines aesthetics as the "sensuous qualities, the emotions, moods, and experiences" that occur while interacting with a product. Visual aesthetics refers to the appearance the user interface, depicted as the top-most visible surface layer of the UX model [44]. Perceived usability is defined as the ease of use, the practical side of a product use, with goals such as efficiency, effectiveness, and user satisfaction in specific contextual use (ISO 9241-11).

III. Methodology

The objectives of this study were: (i) to examine the relationship between visual aesthetic quality and perceived game usability (ii) to examine the impact of visual aesthetic quality on game engagement. A convenience sample frame of fifty-six participants were recruited for the first objective on a university campus in the US. Thirty-five participants took part in the second objective. The within-subject tests minimized error variance individual differences between treatments. Participants were randomly assigned to each treatment to create equivalent conditions and to control extraneous variables across conditions. Participants selected for this study were between 18–35 years old. Perceived game usability data were collected using the dimensions related to pragmatic quality (PQ) of the *AttrakDiff* instrument. The dimensions related to visual aesthetics quality (AT) of the *AttrakDiff* instrument were used to gather data related to the perceptions of visual aesthetics [25]. PQ is comprised of seven bi-polar items, and is related to the perceived usability assessing ease of use. Similarly, AT consists of 7 bi-polar items, aimed to measure the perceived visual aesthetics of the game user interfaces. The procedure involved a within-subjects test whereby the same participant interacted with both game versions. Each participant was randomly assigned to play either the low or high visual aesthetic game version in order to ensure high internal validity; according to *Law of Probability*, this ensures that two equivalent groups are created [27]. A high visual aesthetic quality of an iOS adventure game was primarily created; the same interface was modified into a low-quality visual aesthetic condition by violating the Principles of Design, such as rendering low-bits graphics and reducing the contrast between foreground elements and the background. Each game session lasted for 10 minutes. At the end of each game session, participants were instructed to complete the 7-items of the PQ and the 7-items of the VA section of the *AttrakDiff* instrument, and the 31-items of the *User Engagement Scale (UES)* questionnaire. The original UES is a self-report instrument which consists of the following constructs: *usability, aesthetics, focused attention, novelty, endurability, felt involvement* to capture user engagement. In this study, data from the three constructs *novelty, endurability* and *felt involvement* were combined as a single construct called *reward.*

IV. RESULTS AND ANALYSIS

The first objective of this study was to examine if a variation of the visual aesthetic quality (low or high) a game user interface influences perceived game usability. The *perception of usability* data was first inspected for normality of distribution and verified for ANOVA assumptions. The boxplots did not reveal any extreme outliers or skewness. The bell-shaped curve, though slightly skewed to the right, confirmed that the data were normally distributed. During the preliminary analysis, it was noted that the variability of the *perceived usability* for the high-quality visual aesthetic quality was higher than the low visual aesthetic quality version. The perceived usability result was reported using *AttrakDiff-(PQ)* while the perceived visual aesthetic quality result was reported using *AttrakDiff-(AT) (Hassenzahl, 2003).*

It was important to verify if the ***perceived visual aesthetic quality*** of the two game conditions were different. The result demonstrated that the *perception of visual aesthetic quality* was statistically significant, $F(1,51)=76.997$, $p<0.05$, n=52. The null hypothesis is rejected, inferring that there is a significant difference of perceived visual aesthetics between the quality for the two game user interfaces. The descriptive statistics reveal that the high visual aesthetic quality interface had a mean value of 4.89 whereas the low visual aesthetic quality was rated at 3.91; the boxplot shows that high visual aesthetic quality interface had a higher variability, slightly skewed to the right. The partial eta-squared, $n_p^2 = 0.602$, and according to Cohen's [45] guidelines, is considered a large effect. It is deduced that 60.2% of the variance in the dependent variable, perception of visual aesthetics, is accounted by the independent variable, visual aesthetic quality.

A one-way repeated measures ANOVA was conducted to compare the mean values of **perceived game usability** in the two levels of user interfaces, low and high visual aesthetic quality. IBM SPSS result for the PQ dependent variable shows $F(1, 55)=0.196$, $p=0.660$, n=56. For the low visual aesthetic interface, the mean value of the *perceived game usability* was rated at ($\mu=4.84$, SD 0.74) whereas for the high visual aesthetic interface, the mean value for the *perceived usability* was ($\mu=4.88$, SD 0.79). Given that *p*-value>0.05, this implies that the perception of usability of both conditions of the game interfaces was not statistically significant, as both the low and high visual aesthetic quality were deemed to be equally usable. It was deduced that there was no effect-size, as per Cohen's guidelines [45], given that partial eta-squared, $n_p^2 = 0.004$, which indicates that the independent variables, low and high visual aesthetic qualities, did not influence the dependent variable, perceived usability.

Pearson Regression Analyses were conducted to have a deeper understanding of the relationship between (i) the independent variable – *perceived high visual aesthetic quality* of game interface, and the dependent variable - *perceived game usability* (ii) the independent variable – *perceived low visual aesthetic quality* of game interface, and the dependent variable, *perceived game usability.*

The relationship between ***perceived game usability***, as measured by *AttrakDiff-(PQ)*, and ***perceived high visual game aesthetics***, as measured by *AttrakDiff-(AT)*, was investigated using Pearson product-moment correlation coefficient. Preliminary analyses were performed to ensure no violation of the assumptions of normality, linearity and homoscedasticity occurred. There was a weak, significant positive correlation between the two variables, $r=0.298$, n=55, $p=0.035$. The high visual aesthetic quality significantly supports perceived usability, as $p<0.05$. Given the value of $R^2=0.089$, 8.9% of the variation in the response variable could be explained by the high visual aesthetic game version. It is reasonable to deduce that high visual game aesthetic quality has an effect on perceived game usability.

In addition, the relationship between ***perceived game usability***, as measured by *AttrakDiff-(PQ)*, and ***perceived low visual game aesthetics***, as measured by *AttrakDiff-(AT)*, was investigated using the Pearson product-moment correlation coefficient. There was a weak, positive correlation between the independent variable, *perceived low visual aesthetic quality*, and the response variable, *perceived usability*, $r=0.193$, n=49, $p>0.05$ 9 ($p=0.185$). Low visual game aesthetics did not significantly support the predicted perceived game usability. Given the value of $R^2=0.037$, it is deduced that 3.7% of the variation in the response variable was accounted for by the independent variable. Therefore, it may not reasonable to rely on this equation to predict perceived game usability using the low aesthetic quality version of the game user interface. It is deduced that low visual game aesthetic quality does not have an influence on perceived game usability.

The **second objective** was to evaluate the impact of visual aesthetic quality on user engagement in the same experimental setting. A repeated one-way ANOVA data analysis of the UES questionnaire revealed that there was a statistically significant difference of user engagement level between the two game versions, F(1,34)=18.05, p<0.05, multivariate partial-eta squared 0.348. Following the commonly used guidelines proposed by Cohen [45, pp.284–7], (0.01=small, .06=moderate, 0.14=large effect), this result suggests a very large effect size. This result comprises all the four components of the UES instrument. Users were more engaged in the high visual aesthetic version of the game user interface, which scored a mean value of μ=2.92 (SD 0.49) as compared to μ=2.67 (SD 0.45) for the low visual aesthetic version.

TABLE I. DESCRIPTIVE STATISTICS UES COMPONENTS

UES Dimension	Mean		Significant value 0.05	F-statistics
	Low Visual Aesthetics	*High Visual Aesthetics*		
Overall UES	μ=2.67 (SD 0.45)	μ=2.92 (SD 0.49)	*p*<0.05	F (1,34) =18.05
Reward	μ=2.99 (SD 0.69)	μ=3.24 (SD 0.75)	*p*=0.003	F (1,34) = 10.09
Focused Attention	μ=2.39 (SD 0.91)	μ=2.45 (SD 0.92)	*p*=0.467	F (1,34) = 0.540
Aesthetics	μ=2.77 (SD 0.53)	μ=3.78 (SD 0.40)	*p*<0.05	F (1,34) = 53.78
Usability	μ=3.53 (SD 0.52)	μ=3.65 (SD 0.49)	*p*=0.111	F (1,34) = 2.68

Four individual dimensions of UES were individually compared as shown in Table I. All the user-engagement constructs (*reward, focused attention, aesthetics, usability*) were rated higher for the high-quality visual aesthetic game user interface version, implying that participants were more engaged in that version. Participants found a significant difference between the low and the high visual interface in the case of *aesthetics* and *reward*, *p*<0.05. There was no significant difference in the case of perceived *usability* and *focused attention* between the two game conditions.

In order to examine if the components of user engagement were influenced by each condition of visual aesthetic quality of game user interfaces, a multiple regression analysis was conducted to predict the continuous dependent variable, *perceived visual aesthetic quality,* based on the following four multiple independent variables: *reward, focused attention, aesthetics, and usability*

In the case of the **high visual aesthetic quality**, there was linearity as assessed by partial regression plots and a plot of *studentized* residuals against the predicted values. There was independence of residuals, as assessed by a Durbin-Watson statistic of 2.455. Homoscedasticity was present, as assessed by visual inspection of a plot of *studentized* residuals versus unstandardized predicted values. No evidence of multicollinearity was found, as assessed by tolerance values greater than 0.1; the Collinearity Tolerance ranges from 0.325 to 0.681. The assumption of normality was met as assessed by the Q-Q plot. As shown in Table II, three components of user engagement, namely *reward (p=0.001), aesthetics (p<0.005)* and *usability (p=0.008),* (except *focused attention, p=0.096*) significantly predicted *perceived high visual aesthetic quality* of the game user interface, $F(4, 34)= 7.739$, $p<0.005$. R^2 for the overall model was 50.8% with an adjusted R^2 of 44.2%, a large effect size according to Cohen (1988).

TABLE II. PEARSON CORRELATIONS COEFFICIENTS BETWEEN HIGH VISUAL AESTHETIC QUALITY INTERFACE (HQ) AND UES COMPONENTS

	Perceived Visual Aesthetics (HQ)	Aesthetics	Focused Attention	Usability
Aesthetics	0.671**			
Focused Attention	0.226	0.374*		
Usability	0.401*	0.378*	-0.018	
Reward	0.525**	0.590**	0.691**	0.377*

** *p*<0.005; * *p*<0.05

TABLE III. PEARSON CORRELATIONS COEFFICIENTS BETWEEN LOW VISUAL AESTHETIC QUALITY INTERFACE (LQ) AND UES COMPONENTS

	Perceived Visual Aesthetics (LQ)	Aesthetics	Focused Attention	Usability
Aesthetics	0.404*			
Focused Attention	0.440**	0.548**		
Usability	0.222	0.079	0.123	
Reward	0.631**	0.535**	0.606**	0.463**

** *p*<0.005; * *p*<0.05

In the case of the **low visual aesthetic quality**, there was linearity as assessed by partial regression plots and a plot of *studentized* residuals against the predicted values. There was independence of residuals, as assessed by a Durbin-Watson statistic of 1.916. Homoscedasticity was present, as assessed by visual inspection of a plot of *studentized* residuals versus unstandardized predicted values. No evidence of multicollinearity was found, as assessed by tolerance values greater than 0.1. This implies that there was no evidence that two or more independent variables were correlated to each other, as the Collinearity Tolerance ranges from 0.424 to 0.726. The assumption of normality was met as assessed by the Q-Q plot. As shown in Table III, three components of user engagement, namely *reward* ($p<0.005$), *aesthetics* ($p=0.008$) and *focused attention* ($p=0.04$), (except *usability*, $p>0.05$) significantly predicted *perceived low visual aesthetic quality* of the game user interface, $F(4, 34)= 5.214$, $p=0.003$. R^2 for the overall model was 41.0% with an adjusted R^2 of 33.1%, a medium effect size according to Cohen (1988).

V. CONCLUSION

The above results add an important contribution to the field of HCI. High visual aesthetic quality of game interfaces has an impact on perceived usability, whereas interfaces with low visual aesthetic quality are not perceived to be usable. The results from Table 1 show that visual aesthetic quality had an impact on the *overall user-engagement* which was significantly different in each condition. The high visual quality game interface was more appealing as the colorful and crisp graphics sustained users' interests; the look and feel of the game elements were perceived to be more user usable. Emotional visceral responses, which emanate from our subconscious minds, are elicited by virtue of the game aesthetic quality. Colors, attractiveness and layout are essential design aesthetic elements that can immerse a player during mobile gameplay [46]. The level of overall user-engagement was greater in the high visual aesthetic quality.

Moreover, two components namely *reward* and *aesthetics* were perceived to be significantly different, as part of the engagement level in the two experimental conditions. This implies that a high visual aesthetic game user interface influences users' perception of *endurability*, *novelty* and *felt involvement,* holistically referred as *reward*, signifying that there were aspects of the high visual aesthetic interface that were self-motivating, gratifying, exciting, fun and surprising. This kind of engagement level prompted the users to play the game again in order to derive those unique experiences.

By contrast, the mean value of the two other components of user-engagement, *focused attention* and *perceived usability,* were not significantly different, and were perceived to be equivalent in either game interface. This leads to the conclusion that there are other factors besides visual aesthetics such as game mechanics and game narrative in tablet games that might have influenced *focused-attention* and *perceived usability*.

A limitation of the current study is that it may not be generalizable to other game types due to the relative small sample size. Further research is required to examine how game characteristics and components such as game mechanics and narrative may affect *focused attention* and *usability* in game interfaces. For future work, a larger sample size should be considered, including random selection of participants to increase externa validity of the experiment. This study can also be repeated with different cultural and/or demographic populations. This current study builds upon a previous work in progress research study that was presented at ACHI 2016.

REFERENCES

[1] C. Feijoo, J. Gomez-Barroso and S. Ramos, "An analysis of mobile gaming development: The role of the software platforms," *ICIN*, 11–14 Oct 2010, pp. 1-7.

[2] M. Ziefle, "Information presentation in small screen devices: The trade-off between visual density and menu foresight," *Applied Ergonomics*, vol. 41, no. 6, pp. 719-730.

[3] E. M. Rogers, "'Diffusion of innovations,", 5th ed., Free Press trade paperback ed., 2003.

[4] M. Oshita and H. Ishikawa, "Gamepad vs. touchscreen: A comparison of action selection interfaces in computer games," Proceedings of WASA, Workshop at SIGGRAPH Asia 2012, pp. 27-31.

[5] T. Schiphorst, "soft(n): Toward a somaesthetics of touch," *In ACM CHI EA '09 Extended Abstracts on human factors in computing systems*, Boston, MA, USA, April 04–09, 2009, pp. 2427-2438.

[6] S. Attfield, G. Kazai, M. Lalmas, and B. Piwowarski, "Towards a science of user engagement," In *ACM WSDM'11, Workshop on User Modelling for Web Applications*, Hong Kong, China. February 9–12, 2011, pp. (n.d).

[7] S. Mahlke, "*User Experience of Interaction with Technical Systems*," Ph.D. dissertation, The Technische Universität, Berlin, Germany, 2008.

[8] M. Hassenzahl, "The Effect of Perceived Hedonic Quality on Product Appealingness," *International Journal of Human-Computer Interaction*, vol. 13, no. 4, 2001, pp. 481-499.

[9] M. Hassenzahl, "The Interplay of Beauty, Goodness, and Usability in Interactive Products," *Human-Computer Interaction*, vol. 19, no. 4, 2004, pp. 319-349.

[10] P. van Schaik and J. Ling, "Modelling user experience with web sites: Usability, hedonic value, beauty and goodness," *Interacting with Computers*, vol. 20, no. 3, 2008, pp. 419-432.

[11] M. Hassenzahl and A. Monk, "The Inference of Perceived Usability From Beauty," *Human-Computer Interaction*, vol. 25, no. 3, 2010, pp. 235-260.

[12] K. Overbeeke, T. Djajadiningrat, C. Hummels, S. Wensveen and J. Frens, "Lets make things engaging," in *Funology: from Usability to Enjoyment*, Blythe, M.A., Overbeeke, K., Monk, A.F., Wright, P.C, (Eds.) Kluwer Academic, Dordrecht, 2005, pp. 7–17.

[13] J. Forlizzi and S. Ford, "The building blocks of experience: An Early Framework for Interaction Designers," *Proceedings of the 3rd conference on designing interactive systems: Processes, Practices, Methods, and Techniques, AC, New York, NY. USA,* 2000, pp. 419-423.

[14] M. Hassenzahl and N. Tractinsky, "User experience - a research agenda," *Behaviour and Information Technology*, vol. 25, no. 2, 2006, pp. 91-97.

[15] P. Desmet and P. Hekkert, "Framework of product experience," *International journal of design,* vol. 1, no. 1, pp. 57-66, 2007.

[16] A. Sonderegger and J. Sauer, "The influence of design aesthetics in usability testing: Effects on user performance and perceived usability," *Applied Ergonomics*, vol. 41, no. 3, pp. 403-410, 2010.

[17] J. Silvennoinen, M. Vogel, and S. Kujala, "Experiencing visual usability and aesthetics in two mobile application contexts," *Journal of Usability Studies, 10, (1),* pp.46-62, 2014.

[18] M. Hassenzahl, "The thing and I: understanding the relationship between user and product," In *Funology: from usability to enjoyment,* M. Blythe, C. Overbeeke, A. F. Monk, and P. C. Wright (Eds.) Dordrecht: Kluwer Academic Publishers, 2003, pp. 31–42.

[19] T. Lavie and N. Tractinsky, "Assessing dimensions of perceived visual aesthetics of web sites," *International Journal of Human - Computer Studies*, vol. 60, no. 3, pp. 269-298, 2004.

[20] M. Hassenzahl and A. Monk, "The Inference of Perceived Usability from Beauty," *The Human Computer Interaction,* vol. 25, no. 3, pp. 235–260, 2010.

[21] H. O'Brien and E. Toms, "Examining the generalizability of the User Engagement Scale (UES) in exploratory search,"*Information Processing and Management,* vol. 49, no. 5, pp. 1092-1107, 2012.

[22] B. Carr, "Applying cultural and critical theory to video game aesthetics," *Southern Mass Communication Journal*, vol. 27, no. 3, pp. 1–25, 2012.

[23] D. Norman, D, Emotional Design: *Why we love (or hate) everyday things.* New York: Basic Books, 2004.

[24] E. Amit, S. Gottlieb, and J. D. Greene, "Visual versus Verbal Thinking and Dual-Process Moral Cognition, " in *Dual-Process Theories of the Social Mind*, Chapter 23, J.W. Sherman, B. Gawronski, and Y. Trope, Eds. New York: Guilford Press, 2014, pp. 340-354.

[25] H. O'Brien and E. Toms, "The development and evaluation of a survey to measure user engagement", *J. Am. Soc. Inf. Sci.*, vol. 61, no. 1, pp. 50-69, 2010.

[26] E. Yom-Tov, M. Lalmas and H. O'Brien, *Synthesis Lectures on Information Concepts, Retrieval, and Services.* San Rafael, CA: Morgan and Claypool Publishers, 2014.

[27] D. Cyr, M. Head and H. Larios, "Colour appeal in website design within and across cultures: A multi-method evaluation," *International Journal of Human Computer Studies*, vol. 68, no. 1, pp. 1-21, 2010.

[28] E.N. Wiebe, A. Lamb, M. Hardy and D. Sharek, "Measuring engagement in video game-based environments: Investigation of the User Engagement Scale," *Computers in Human Behavior*, vol. 32, Mar, pp. 123-132, 2014.

[29] H. O'Brien and P. Cairns, "An empirical evaluation of the User Engagement Scale (UES) in online news environments," *Information Processing and Management*, vol. 51, no. 4, Jul, pp. 413-427, 2015.

[30] H. L. O'Brien and M. Lebow, "Mixed-methods approach to measuring user experience in online news interactions," *Journal of the American Society for Information Science and Technology*, vol. 64, no. 8, Aug, pp. 1543-1556, 2013.

[31] H. L. O'Brien and E.G. Toms, "Examining the generalizability of the User Engagement Scale (UES) in exploratory search," *Information Processing and Management*, vol. 49, no. 5, Sep 1, pp. 1092-1107, 2013.

[32] J. Webster and H. Ho, "Audience engagement in multimedia presentations," *ACM SIGMIS Database: the DATABASE for Advances in Information Systems*, vol. 28, no. 2, Apr 1, pp. 63-77.

[33] A. Sutcliffe, "Designing for User Engagement: Aesthetic and Attractive User Interfaces," *Synthesis Lectures on Human-Centered Informatics*, vol. 2, no. 1, Jan, pp. 1-55, 2009.

[34] H. L. O'Brien and E.G. Toms, "What is user engagement? A conceptual framework for defining user engagement with technology," *Journal of the American Society for Information Science and Technology*, vol. 59, no. 6, Apr, pp. 938-955, 2008.

[35] R. D. Jacques, "The nature of engagement and its role in hypermedia evaluation and design," Doctoral Thesis. South Bank University, London, 1996.

[36] W. Quesenbery, "Dimensions of Usability: Defining the Conversation, Driving the Process," *Proceedings of the UPA 2003 Conference*, Scottsdale, AZ, June 23-27, 2003

[37] B. Laurel, *Computers as Theatre.* Reading, MA, USA: Addison-Wesley, 1993.

[38] R. Jacques, J. Preece and T. Carey, "Engagement as a Design Concept for Multimedia," *Canadian Journal of Learning and Technology / La revue canadienne de l'apprentissage et de la technologie*, vol. 24, no. 1, Jan 15, pp. 49, 1995.

[39] A. Norman and S.W. Draper, *User Centered System Design*, Hillsdale, NJ: Lawrence Erlbaum, 1986.

[40] H. L. O'Brien and E.G. Toms, "The development and evaluation of a survey to measure user engagement," *Journal of the American Society for Information Science and Technology*, vol. 61, no. 1, Jan, pp. 50-69, 2010.

[41] J. C. Read, S. J. MacFarlane, and C. Casey, "Endurability, engagement and expectations: Measuring children's fun," *Interaction design and children*, vol. 2, pp. 1-23, 2002.

[42] H. L. O'Brien, E.G. Toms, E. K. Kelloway and E. Kelley, *Developing and evaluating a reliable measure of user engagement, Proceedings of the American Society for Information Science and Technology*, Columbus, OH, USA, vol. 45, no. 1, 2008, pp. 1-10.

[43] I. Engholm, "Digital style history: the development of graphic design on the Internet," *Digital Creativity*, vol. 13, no. 4, pp. 193-211, 2002.

[44] J. J. Garrett, *The elements of user experience*, 2nd ed., Berkeley, CA: New Riders, 2011.

[45] J. Cohen, *Statistical Power Analysis for the Behavioral Sciences*, 2nd ed., New Jersey: Erlbaum: Hillsdale, 1988.

[46] J. Merikivi, V. Tuunainen, and D. Nguyen, "What makes continued mobile gaming enjoyable?" *Computers in Human Behavior*, vol. 68, pp. 411–421, 2017.

Time Before Negative Emotions Occur While Waiting for a Reply in Text Messaging with Read Receipt Functionality

Shogo Kato
School of Arts and Sciences
Tokyo Woman's Christian University
Tokyo, Japan
e-mail: shogo@lab.twcu.ac.jp

Yasuyuki Ozawa
Faculty of Education
Meisei University
Tokyo, Japan
e-mail: ozawa.yasuyuki@gmail.com

Yuuki Kato
Faculty of Arts and Sciences
Sagami Women's University
Kanagawa, Japan
e-mail: y-katou@star.sagami-wu.ac.jp

Abstract—**In text messaging via smartphone, many users feel pressure to rapidly exchange messages. This study investigates reply speeds in smartphone messaging, focusing on messaging with read receipt functionality. This function allows the sender to see when a recipient has read a sent message. Using a questionnaire completed by 213 female college students in Japan, we investigate the time before negative emotions are felt while waiting for a reply. Results showed negative emotions arise in significantly less time when waiting for a reply to a read message than an unread one.**

Keywords—reply speed; read receipt function; emotion; text messaging.

I. INTRODUCTION

People looking at their phones while walking are now a common sight on the street and in train stations [1]. Although they do so for a variety of reasons, it seems that many are texting while walking in order to quickly reply to received messages [2]. In text messaging with mobile phones and smartphones, many users feel pressure to rapidly reply [3]. However, there are few studies examining response speed in text-based communication. To clarify demands for rapid responses in text messaging, this study investigates reply speeds in messaging via smartphones and assesses the time before negative emotions arise while waiting for a reply.

In text-based communication such as conventional email, there is no interaction while a message sender waits for a reply. However, messaging apps such as Facebook Messenger and LINE have read receipt functions, which notify senders when recipients have read a sent message, allowing senders to know that recipients have read the message before any reply arrives [4]. In such exchanges, many senders are concerned not only about the time spent waiting for a reply, but also about the time until the read receipt appears [4]. For example, the sender may suspect that the recipient is ignoring the message if the read receipt is not displayed after an extended time ("ignored unread"), or if no reply is received long after the read receipt has been displayed ("ignored read"). Conversely, recipients may worry about being misunderstood for leaving messages in an "ignored unread" state when they cannot read messages immediately, or in an "ignored read" state when unable to immediately reply to read messages. We hypothesize that read receipt functions are strongly associated with interaction speed. Therefore, this study focuses on relations between this display function (which does not exist in conventional mobile phone messaging or email) and requirements for response speed.

The study used a questionnaire survey to investigate the time before negative emotions occur while waiting for a reply in text messaging on smartphones. This covered messaging with read receipt functionality, such as Facebook Messenger and LINE, and wait times were categorized as *read* status or *unread* status. The questionnaire focused on four representative negative emotions often mentioned in interpersonal communication research: sadness, anxiety, anger, and guilt. We recognized that a variety of additional factors are likely involved, such as message content and context, but as it is difficult to conduct a survey that covers all possible factors, we focused on two kinds of message recipients: friendships [5] and family relationships [6].

The rest of the paper is structured as follows. In Section 2, we present method of this study. In Section 3, we present results of this study. Finally, we conclude in Section 4.

II. METHOD

Survey participants were 213 Japanese female students (mean age = 18.67; SD = 0.94; age range, 18–22 years) at universities in the Tokyo area. The participants in this survey were limited to young women, because young women are more inclined to maintain human relationships through text messaging, and prefer and use messaging more than do men (e.g., [7]). All participants possessed their own smartphone and regularly used text messaging applications with read receipt functionality. Participation in this survey was voluntary. This survey was conducted in July of 2017. Participants were asked to answer a paper-based questionnaire.

The questionnaire asked "At noon, you send a text message to two recipients (*family and relatives* and *friends*), from whom you expect a response. Once sent, the message is immediately displayed as read. While waiting for a response, how long will it take for each of the four negative emotions to arise in you? How long would it take for each of the four negative emotions to arise if the message remained unread?" Each questionnaire item was answered using ten times of day: 1 = Until 13:00, 2 = Until 15:00, 3 = Until 17:00, 4 =

Until 19:00, 5 = Until 21:00, 6 = Until 23:00, 7 = Until 01:00, 8 = Until the next morning, 9 = Until noon the next day, 10 = Later than noon the next day. Each of the four negative emotions and each of the two recipient types were measured. Because answers are provided on an ordinal scale, the resulting data are subject to nonparametric analyses.

III. RESULTS

To compare time before each emotion occurs while waiting for a reply from recipients in *read* and *unread* statuses, we conducted the Wilcoxon signed-rank test using time-zone option responses for each of the two recipients and for each of the four negative emotions. Results indicated significant differences between *read* and *unread* status for each recipient and for each negative emotion. Table 1 shows the times before each of the four emotions occur while waiting for a reply from each of two recipients in *read* and *unread* status. We regarded the period from option 1 to 7 as "the same day as the message was sent" by considering option 7 (until 01:00) to mean the same thing as "by bedtime." The main results were the following three points: 1) For both recipient types, negative emotions arise in significantly less time when waiting for a reply to a *read* status message than one with an *unread* status. (Though only a marginal difference in occurrence of guilt when waiting for a reply from *family and relatives*). 2) When messages are in *read* status, anxiety occurs when no reply arrives from *family and relatives* on the same day. 3) When a message is in *unread* status, anxiety occurs when no reply arrives from *family and relatives* on the same day.

To find differences between sadness, anxiety, anger, and guilt with respect to the time before these four negative emotions occur while waiting for a reply from each of the recipients in each of the statuses, we conducted multiple comparisons among these emotions for each condition of the two recipients × the two statuses. The main results were the following four points: 1) Anxiety arises in significantly less time than does sadness ($p < 0.001$), anger ($p < 0.001$), or guilt ($p < 0.001$) when waiting for a reply from *family and relatives* for both *read* and *unread* statuses. 2) Anger arises in significantly less time than does guilt ($p < 0.001$) when waiting for a reply from only *family and relatives* for both *read* and *unread* status. 3) There is no significant difference between sadness and anger in the time before these emotions occur while waiting for a reply from only *family and relatives* for both *read* and *unread* statuses. 4) There is no significant difference between anxiety and sadness in the time before these two emotions occur while waiting for a reply from only *friends* for *read* status.

IV. CONCLUSION

The study clarified that sadness, anxiety, anger, and guilt arise in significantly less time when waiting for a reply to a read status than an unread status from all recipients. That is, senders experience negative emotions when they do not receive replies from recipients who were able to read the sender's message. Among the four emotions, anxiety and sadness tend to occur early, while anger and guilt tend to take longer. We observed that when waiting for a reply from family and relatives, anxiety occurred in a shorter time in both read and unread status. Relationships with family are more intimate than friends, so senders may be more prone to worry about accidents or illness when messages remain unread for a long period, resulting in faster experience of anxiety. There is also likely a strong emotional dependence of young people on their families. Late replies may therefore more easily lead to anger and subsequently to anxiety. We also found that when waiting for a reply from friends, sadness occurred more quickly in the read status. While family relationships are strong, friendships may be relatively fragile [8], and the ending or erosion of such relationships results in sadness. Senders may interpret a lack of reply as indication of a decline in recipients' interest in them, resulting in a faster experience of sadness.

In future work we will gather scenes in which users intentionally manipulate reply speeds and analyze them in detail. In addition, this study solely surveyed young Japanese women. To generalize the results obtained in this study, we should examine the influence of differences in gender, culture, and generation.

ACKNOWLEDGMENT

This work was supported by JSPS KAKENHI Grant Numbers 15K01089, 15K01095.

REFERENCES

[1] E. M. Lamberg and L. M. Muratori, "Cell phones change the way we walk," Gait & Posture, vol. 35, no. 4, pp. 688-690, 2012, doi:10.1016/j.gaitpost.2011.12.005.

[2] D. C. Schwebel, L. A. McClure, and B. E. Porter, "Experiential exposure to texting and walking in virtual reality: A randomized trial to reduce distracted pedestrian behavior," Accident Analysis & Prevention, vol. 102, pp. 116 -122, 2017, doi:10.1016/j.aap.2017.02.026.

[3] Y. Kato and S. Kato, "Reply speed to mobile text messages among Japanese college students: When a quick reply is preferred and a late reply is acceptable," Computers in Human Behavior, vol. 44, pp. 209-219, 2015, doi:10.1016/j.chb. 2014.11.047.

[4] Y. Kato, "Ignoring read and unread text messages: Basic survey on the LINE messaging application's read receipt function," Journal of Information and Media Studies, vol. 2, pp. 17-32, 2016 (in Japanese with English abstract).

[5] J. A. Hall and N. K. Baym, "Calling and texting (too much): Mobile maintenance expectations, (over) dependence, entrapment, and friendship satisfaction," New Media & Society, vol. 14, no. 2, pp. 316-331, 2012, doi:10.1177/ 1461444811415047.

[6] A. Lepp, J. Li, and J. E. Barkley, "College students' cell phone use and attachment to parents and peers," Computers in Human Behavior, vol. 64, pp. 401-408, 2016, doi:10.1016/ j.chb.2016.07.021.

[7] A. M. Kimbrough, R. E. Guadagno, N. L. Muscanell, and J. Dill, "Gender differences in mediated communication: Women connect more than do men," Computers in Human Behavior, vol. 29, no. 3, pp. 896-900, 2013, doi:10.1016/j.chb.2012.12.005.

[8] B. Jin, "Hurtful texting in friendships: Satisfaction buffers the distancing effects of intention," Communication Research Reports, vol. 30, no. 2, pp. 148-156, 2013, doi:10.1080/ 08824096.2012.763026.

TABLE I. TIMES BEFORE EACH OF THE FOUR EMOTIONS OCCURS WHILE WAITING FOR A REPLY IN READ AND UNREAD STATUSES.

Recipient Type	Status	Sadness			Anxiety			Anger			Guilt		
		Median (IQR)	z	p	Median (IQR)	z	p	Median (IQR)	z	p	Median (IQR)	z	p
Family and Relatives	Read	10 (4.5 – 10)	-4.73	<0.001	6 (3 – 10)	-3.02	<0.01	10 (5 – 10)	-4.13	<0.001	10 (9 – 10)	-1.88	<0.10
	Unread	10 (6 – 10)			7 (4 – 10)			10 (7 – 10)			10 (9 – 10)		
Friends	Read	9 (4 – 10)	-6.27	<0.001	8 (4 – 10)	-5.41	<0.001	10 (6 – 10)	-4.75	<0.001	10 (7 – 10)	-3.08	<0.01
	Unread	10 (7 – 10)			9 (6 – 10)			10 (9 – 10)			10 (8 – 10)		

Note. IQR = interquartile range; z = z-value of Wilcoxon signed-rank test; p = significance probability of Wilcoxon signed-rank test.

Perceived Usefulness of Features of Stickers in Text Messaging:

Effects of Gender and Text-Messaging Dependency

Yuuki Kato
Faculty of Arts and Sciences
Sagami Women's University
Kanagawa, Japan
e-mail: y-katou@star.sagami-wu.ac.jp

Shogo Kato
School of Arts and Sciences
Tokyo Woman's Christian University
Tokyo, Japan
e-mail: shogo@lab.twcu.ac.jp

Yasuyuki Ozawa
Faculty of Education
Meisei University
Tokyo, Japan
e-mail: ozawa.yasuyuki@gmail.com

Abstract—**In text-based communication via social media, users can communicate using not only emoticons and emoji, but now also a third type of graphical symbol called "stickers." This study focused on role of stickers in communication. A questionnaire was developed, which asked subjects to individually rate the usefulness of 25 features of stickers on a Likert-like scale. Using this questionnaire, a survey targeting 211 Japanese college students was conducted. Data obtained from the questionnaire were compared by gender and degree of text-messaging dependency for each question item. Results indicated significant effects of dependency and gender.**

Keywords—sticker; emoticon; perceived usefulness; text-messaging dependency; gender differences; text messaging.

I. INTRODUCTION

In recent years, a new type of graphical symbol called a "sticker" has appeared in social-media-based text messaging applications [1]. This study focuses on the role of this new type of graphical symbol. Stickers play a role in transmitting emotions, similar to emoticons and emoji, but they also serve other functions [2]. Research comparing the features of emoticons, emoji, and stickers found that whereas emotional transmission is the main role of emoticons and emoji, stickers can also change the flow of communication and serve as an alternative to text messages [3]. This previous research [3] generated a detailed list of sticker features by administering a survey to hundreds of Japanese young adults who own smartphones and routinely use LINE messenger. Participants were asked to provide free-text descriptions of the usefulness of stickers. To examine the role of stickers in greater detail, a questionnaire was administered that contained questions related to each of these features.

Previous research has examined gender differences with respect to emoticon use [4]. For example, various researchers have suggested that women use more emoticons in computer-mediated communication. Conversely, another study showed that, compared with women, men use more emoticons in blog posts [5]. Results related to gender differences in emoticon use are thus mixed [6]. A previous study examined the usefulness of emoticons, emoji, and stickers, and showed gender differences in usefulness ratings of these three symbol types [3]. The authors suggested that ratings were influenced by text-messaging dependency [7] in addition to gender. Namely, since symbols serve various roles, multifaceted effects of gender and dependency may appear within each role. This study separately examines these effects for each feature of stickers.

We prepared a questionnaire asking subjects to rate the multiple features of stickers on a Likert-like scale based on that employed in the previous study [3]. Using this questionnaire, we surveyed 211 Japanese college students. Data obtained from this questionnaire were compared by gender and degree of text-messaging dependency for each question item corresponding to each feature.

II. METHODS

Survey participants were 211 Japanese students (110 women, 101 men; mean age = 19.09; SD = 2.34) at universities in the Tokyo area. All participants possessed their own smartphone and regularly used messaging applications capable of exchanging stickers, such as LINE.

We constructed questionnaire items based on previously identified sticker features [3]. This was done by consensus of the authors. This resulted in a 25-item questionnaire that asked participants to rate each sticker's usefulness feature

TABLE I. TWENTY-FIVE-ITEM QUESTIONNAIRE ON STICKERS

- Using stickers makes it easy to convey emotions.
- Stickers make it easy to interpret emotions.
- Using stickers can convey facial expressions.
- Stickers show the facial expression of the sender.
- Stickers can express messages that cannot be expressed in words.
- Stickers can express subtle nuances.
- It is possible to see the intent of the message just by looking at the sticker.
- Stickers are cute.
- The variety of stickers is abundant.
- Using stickers can end a prolonged exchange.
- Stickers accentuate textual exchange.
- It is possible to express user preferences with stickers.
- Using stickers makes interactions cheerier.
- A text message is already included in the stickers (so inputting characters is unnecessary).
- Using stickers makes interactions fun.
- Using stickers facilitates interaction.
- Using stickers can change the topic.
- Introducing newly found stickers is fun.
- Sending stickers is a catalyst for interaction.
- Sending stickers can buy time to prepare text messages.
- Using stickers speeds up interaction.
- The stickers themselves become the conversation topic.
- Stickers are playful.
- Stickers can entertain recipients.
- Lighthearted communication is possible using only stickers.

using a 7-point Likert-like scale from 1 (*not useful at all*) to 7 (*very useful*). These items are listed in Table 1.

We measured messaging dependency using an abbreviated 15-item version of the Text-Message Dependency Scale [7] modified by the authors. This scale comprises emotional reaction, perception of excessive use, and relationship maintenance subscales. Each subscale involves five questions scored on a 5-point Likert-like scale from 1 (*strongly disagree*) to 5 (*strongly agree*).

III. Results

To investigate the influence of gender and degree of text-messaging dependency on each usefulness rating, we assigned gender (male or female) and dependency group (high or low) as between-subjects factors. We then performed a two-way analysis of variance for each item. Results indicated a significant main effect of gender for only the following items: "Using stickers makes it easy to convey emotions," ($F(1, 207) = 5.49$, $p < 0.05$, $\eta_p^2 = 0.03$); "Stickers are cute," ($F(1, 207) = 10.97$, $p < 0.001$, $\eta_p^2 = 0.05$); "Using stickers can end a prolonged exchange," ($F(1, 205) = 4.25$, $p < 0.05$, $\eta_p^2 = 0.02$); and "A text message is already included in the stickers," ($F(1, 206) = 14.05$, $p < 0.001$, $\eta_p^2 = 0.06$). Each of these significant differences indicate that women appreciate these features more than men do.

A significant main effect of dependency group was only seen for the following items: "Stickers can express messages that cannot be expressed by letters," ($F(1, 204) = 5.63$, $p < 0.05$, $\eta_p^2 = 0.03$); "The variety of stickers is abundant," ($F(1, 206) = 7.10$, $p < 0.01$, $\eta_p^2 = 0.03$); "Using stickers makes interactions cheerier," ($F(1, 205) = 4.05$, $p < 0.05$, $\eta_p^2 = 0.02$); "Sending stickers is a catalyst for interaction," ($F(1, 207) = 6.97$, $p < 0.01$, $\eta_p^2 = 0.03$); "The stickers themselves become the topic," ($F(1, 207) = 7.53$, $p < 0.01$, $\eta_p^2 = 0.04$); and "Lighthearted communication is possible using only stickers," ($F(1, 206) = 6.79$, $p < 0.01$, $\eta_p^2 = 0.03$). Each of these significant differences indicates that the high-dependency group appreciated these features more than the low-dependency group did. In addition, a significant main effect of the dependency group was seen in "Using stickers can convey facial expressions," ($F(1, 207) = 6.17$, $p < 0.05$, $\eta_p^2 = 0.03$). However, this significant main effect is qualified by the significant interaction of gender × dependency group, $F(1, 207) = 4.15$, $p < 0.05$, $\eta_p^2 = 0.02$. To rate this feature, we performed a simple main effect test using Bonferroni's adjustment to investigate differences among the dependency groups for each gender. The results suggested that the high-dependency group rated this feature as more useful than did the low-dependency group among men ($p < 0.01$), but there was no significant difference among women.

Only the following items were significant in the gender × dependency group interaction: $F(1, 207) = 4.22$, $p < 0.05$, $\eta_p^2 = 0.02$ in "Stickers can express subtle nuances"; and $F(1, 205) = 8.28$, $p < 0.01$, $\eta_p^2 = 0.04$ in "Using stickers facilitates interaction." We performed simple main effect tests using Bonferroni's adjustment to investigate differences among the dependency groups in each gender. The results showed that men in the high-dependency group rated these features as more useful than did those in the low-dependency group ("Stickers can express subtle nuances," $p < 0.05$, "Using stickers relieves interaction," $p < 0.01$), but there were no significant differences among women.

IV. Discussion

Regarding ratings of sticker roles, we found that some ratings are influenced by gender and some by degree of dependency. Further, there are both overlapping and unique parts within the scope of these influences.

Some features in which gender differences were found are functions common to both conventional emoticons and emoji. Many previous studies have found that women have higher affinity for emoticons and emoji than do men, while other research has shown no gender difference, or even opposing findings [6]. This study, which focused on stickers, may explain the mixed results related to emoticons and emoji. Gender differences were seen in the ratings of some sticker roles that are common with emoticons and emoji, but there were also effects of text-messaging dependency.

Roles related to the overall impact on interaction, such as "Sending stickers is a catalyst for interaction," and "The stickers themselves become the conversation topic" appear to be roles unique to stickers [2][3]. There was no gender difference for these roles. The Text-Message Dependency Scale [7] measures how people perceive their usage of text messages along with their attitudes toward compulsive text-messaging in the context of interpersonal relationships. In particular, high-dependency groups tend to fear disruption of relationships in the absence of text messages [7]. Therefore, the high-dependency groups may be more careful in maintaining interactions via text messaging, and use stickers to accomplish this.

Acknowledgment

This work was supported by JSPS KAKENHI Grant Numbers 15K01089, 15K01095.

References

[1] A. M. F. Yousef and G. Rößling, "How to design good educational blogs in LMS?," CSEDU 2013 - The Sixth International Conference on Computer Supported Education, pp. 70-75, 2013.

[2] S. S. Wang, "More than words? The effect of Line character sticker use on intimacy in the mobile communication environment," Social Science Computer Review, vol. 34, pp. 456-478, 2016, doi:org/10.1177/0894439315590209.

[3] S. Kato, Y. Ozawa, and Y. Kato, "Comparison of perceived usefulness of emoticons, emoji, and stickers in text messaging via smartphone," Proceedings of the International Symposium on Teaching, Education, and Learning ISTEL-Winter 2018, pp. 16-21, 2018, ISSN: 2409-1855

[4] T. Luor, H. P. Lu, L. L. Wu, and Y. H. Tao, "The effect of emoticon in simplex and complex task-oriented commu nication: An empirical study of Instant Messaging," Com puters in Human Behavior, vol. 26, no. 5, pp. 889-895, 2010, doi:10. 1016/j.chb.2010.02.003.

[5] D. F. Witmer and S. L. Katzman, "On-line smilies: Does gender make a difference in the use of graphic accents?," Journal of Computer-Mediated Communication, vol. 2, no. 4, 1997, doi/10.1111/j.1083-6101.1997.tb00192.x/full.

[6] D. Derks, A. H. Fischer, and A. E. Bos, "The role of emoticon in computer-mediated communication: A review," Computers in Human Behavior, vol. 24, pp. 766-785, 2008, doi:10.1016/j.chb.2007.04.004.

[7] T. Igarashi, T. Motoyoshi, J. Takai, and T. Yoshida, "No mobile, no life: Self-perception and text-message dependency among Japanese high school students," Computers in Human Behavior, vol. 24, pp. 2311-2324, 2008, doi:10.1016/j.chb.2007.12.001.

Fear, Feedback, Familiarity… How are These Connected?

– Can *familiarity* as a design concept applied to *digital feedback* reduce *fear*?

Diana Saplacan, Jo Herstad
Department of Informatics
University of Oslo, UiO,
Oslo, Norway
email: {diana.saplacan, jo.herstad}@ifi.uio.no

Abstract—**This paper is a reflective paper discussing *fear*, and the emotions associated with it, felt by the elderly while using modern technologies. The pattern of *fear* emerged from our initial research activities. The preliminary results presented here are part of the pre-study phase within the Multimodal Elderly Care Systems (MECS) project, which focuses on the design of a safety alarm robot for the elderly. Here, we explored various design issues that elderly encounter in their daily interaction with various modern technologies. One of the explored issues is *digital feedback*, the subject of this paper. The aim of our exploration was to look at what potential design implications that digital feedback may have on the elderly's interactions with these technologies, such as triggering the feeling of *fear* when using them, and what we could learn from those when designing a robot safety alarm. Finally, we propose *familiarity* as a central design concept for designing feedback.**

Keywords-fear; digital feedback; elderly; modern technologies; familiarity.

I. Introduction

In this paper, we chose to address the feeling of *fear*, and the emotions associated with it, felt by the elderly while using modern technologies, such as smartphones and computers. More specifically, we chose to use here the term *fear* as an umbrella term for derivatives emotions, such as *angst, anxiety, concern, doubt, dread, unease, uneasiness, worry, aversion, fright, phobia, presentiment* [1]. We exemplify this through situations experienced by them, in their daily lives' interactions with these modern technologies. Specifically, we focus on situations where the users do not understand how to perceive the digital feedback received. This may hinder them to understand correctly these technologies, as well as discouraging them to use those. We discuss situations where the feedback provided is *improper*, and where *there is not provided any feedback at all*, e.g., *lack of feedback*.

The preliminary results presented here are part of the pre-study phase within the Multimodal Elderly Care Systems (MECS) project, which focuses on the design of a safety alarm robot for the elderly. We explored elderly's interaction with various modern technologies in their daily lives, such as smartphones and computers. The aim of our exploration is twofold. On one hand, we look at what potential design implications that *digital feedback* may have on the elderly's interactions with these technologies, such as triggering the emotion of *fear*. We do this by bringing empirical evidence from our fieldwork. And, on the other hand, we look at what we could learn from those when designing a safety alarm robot. There, we propose *familiarity* as a central design concept when designing digital feedback.

But why should one focus on the phenomena of *feedback*? Introducing modern technologies in the homes of the elderly, such as robots, requires close scrutiny of the design of current technologies used by them. Understanding what issues the elderly experience in their daily lives with these technologies will help us to develop our understanding prior to designing new ones, such as a safety alarm robot. Further, various societal challenges, such as the aging of the workforce, as shown by [2][3], invoke consequences within the healthcare field. As for Norway, by 2050, there will be an increase of 21% in the elderly population [4]. Furthermore, the active working force will not be able to tackle the healthcare needs imposed by this increase (ibid p. 20), and yet among the action plans taken at the European Union's level, regarding this societal challenge, is the digitalization of health through the use of Information Communication Technologies (ICT's), so-called eHealth [5]. Moreover, several studies address directly or indirectly the issue of the *digital divide* between users with ICT literacy and those with reduced ICT literacy. Elderly are often included in the group of users with reduced ICT literacy as shown in [6]–[9]. Yet, all of the above yield at how important it is to rethink how we design new modern technologies, including digital *feedback*, for the elderly as the target users.

The rest of this paper is organized as follows. Section II describes briefly the case. Section III introduced the central concepts used in this paper, *feedback, fear,* and *familiarity*, by looking at what others have done. Section IV provides a description of the methodology used. Section V presents *preliminary results* from the MECS project, whereas Section VI discusses those, and proposes familiarity as an essential design concept to be considered when designing digital feedback for modern technologies. Finally, Section VII presents the conclusion, a summary of the paper and future work.

II. Case Description

Multimodal Elderly Care Systems project [10] focuses on exploring ways of developing in-motion digital technologies, such as a safety-alarm robot, for the independently living elderly (≥65 years). Among our project collaborators is Kampen Omsorg Pluss [11], an organization providing accommodation facilities for the independent living elderly. It has 91 apartments, where the residents can rent them on their own, or together with their partner. The building also has a reception, where the staff is available 24/7, in case of emergencies, or otherwise they arrange the social, cultural and another type of events for them. In addition, the facilities have a library, a restaurant publicly open, a gym, and an open area where usually the residents would have coffee every evening at 5 PM, presentations, and performances. As a part of our MECS pre-study, we have conducted three group interviews (n=3), and several individual interviews (n=6, only three included in this work, out of which 1 is a pilot-interview). These research activities are related to the use of modern technology. We present some partial results in this paper.

III. Related Work

In this section, we present three central concepts used in this paper: *digital feedback, fear,* as a feeling triggered by the use of modern technology, and *familiarity,* proposed as a possible design concept solution in preventing fear of new digital technologies.

A. On Digital Feedback

The term *feedback* was initially used within control theory and cybernetics [12] and was described as "the circularity of action" between "the parts of a dynamic system" (p. 53). Later, the same term was used within learning theory, as a form of improving the learning of the students, or the teaching quality. In this case, the feedback could refer to a *dialogical* one, between humans, or between humans but mediated by systems (e.g., learning platforms), or between humans and systems, as in human-computer interaction (HCI) (e.g., getting direct feedback from the systems). [13] showed five clusters of characteristics of feedback from learning theories, such as descriptive, task-related characteristics, time-related, affective and emotional, as well as characteristics related to its effects on learners (p. 5). Here, we are interested in the affective and emotional characteristics. Further, according to [14] in [15], within the HCI field, "feedback refers to a system's response to users' action". Users are here also the learners of the system they interact with. [16] showed that feedback is important when errors should be minimized (p. 688-689). Within *affective computing*, defined as "computing that relates to, arises from, or influences emotions" [17, p. 1], feedback is represented as *bio-* or *multimodal feedback*. Bio-feedback is related to the improvement process, over time, of health and performance [18], where one gets information (e.g., *feedback)* on this process. Multimodal feedback refers to the representation of feedback through visuals, audio, haptic, or video forms etc., and it is often discussed in relation to design for vulnerable groups [19]–[21]. This type of feedback is often discussed as a part of affective computing. Sometimes, feedback *becomes affective* by *design* through its multimodality, whereas in other cases it *becomes affective as a result of how the user experiences it*. In this paper, we look at how *visual feedback* becomes *affective feedback*, when the users, here the elderly, do not understand it. As an effect of the visual feedback received in their interaction with the modern technology, they start having *feelings* of *fear* when using it. The term is used here as an umbrella term for the feelings associated with it. In the next subsection, we explain it further.

B. On Fear

Within the field of Human-Computer Interaction (HCI), one of the areas dealing with the notion of *fear* is affective computing. [17] classified *fear* as one of the basic emotions (p. 540, fig. 3), among the eight: *joy, acceptance, surprise, sadness, disgust, anger, anticipation,* and *fear*. Etymologically, *fear* can be "the emotion of pain or uneasiness caused by the sense of impending danger, or by the prospect of some possible evil." [22]. Among its synonyms are angst, anxiety, concern, doubt, dread, unease, uneasiness, worry, aversion, fright, phobia, presentiment [1].

Multiple studies on learning show that individuals, being young or old, *fear* to deal with modern technologies. This occurs either due to their lack of motivation or interest, a high threshold between the knowledge possessed and the challenge at hand, or due to the health condition of the individuals. In [23] it was identified that *obstacles* in the learning process affect their interest in learning. Here, if the individuals' motivation is sufficiently strong, they will eventually learn the technologies, whereas if it is lacking, there is a lower chance for learning to deal with those. [24] shows that emotional factors affect elderly's technology acceptance in their homes, and a technology shall fulfill their "functional, *emotional*, and social needs" (p. 711, emphasis added). [25] emphasizes the importance of *motivation*, that will determine the elderly people use modern technology, such as smartphones, computers, or robots. To this, the author adds: the importance of the elderly's health condition, in terms of *mood and depression; self-efficacy and coping* when dealing with different situations, i.e., the elderly shall *feel* they have a locus of control over their environment (here the digital environment); and the importance of *wellbeing and happiness (positive computing),* a subfield of *affective computing,* which deals with "the design and development of technology to support psychological wellbeing and human potential." [26, p. 2]. However, in this study, we do not deal with modeling of *fear* as explained in other psychological or medical studies [27], [28], neither with specific ranges of it as in [29]. Can then digital *feedback* motivate or demotivate the elderly to use the modern technologies? We describe, in the next subsection, familiarity, a concept that we propose as central when designing for the elderly users.

C. On familiarity

Familiarity is often described as "a state" that feels "friendly or intimate, a friendly interaction; close friendship, intimacy" [22]. The concept is borrowed by several researchers from Heidegger's *Being and Time* [30, p. 405] (354), which describes it as "[knowing] its way about" (p. 405 (354)). [31] argues that *familiarity* consists of "dispositions to respond to situations in appropriate ways" (p. 117). Later, [32] has used this concept to explain that *familiarity* with technology "has been found to be something important – if not crucial – in the general relationship that people have with it and their attitudes towards it". Now, this becomes even more essential for the elderly's relationship with technology, as they might not have had the same opportunities of experiencing it during their "development years" (p. 464). The study presented by [16] was conducted with 50 people with different backgrounds and showed that "familiarity is the key" when learning to deal with digital technologies, being "a form of understanding", of "getting involved" with the technology, without requiring an extra effort when "doing things" (p. 468-469). Similarly, [33] have used this concept in their study of older adults learning to use computers. The authors' advise that one should aim for "human-centered design" (compare to *"user-centered-"* and *"technology-centered design"*), where the design of technologies shall "aim to build on the prior skills, self-perceptions and aspirations of older people as competent individuals" (p. 29). In the same way, [34] describes *familiarity* as the "engagement, understanding, and an intimate or close relationship between the [humans] and the technology" (p. 89). Here, the authors propose implicitly to look at *positive computing* as *salutogenesis,* as a way of focusing on the factors that contribute to well-being and health, rather than "treating" or "fixing" a disability, incapability or weakness (p. 91).

IV. METHODOLOGY

According to [35], interpretive research is afforded through "language, consciousness and shared meanings" (p. 2). Boland (1985) in (ibid) says that "the philosophical base of interpretive research is hermeneutics and phenomenology". Further, we follow one of Ricoeur's thesis [36], that hermeneutics builds upon phenomenology (p. 85). We interpret the textual data that using a hermeneutical approach. We explain the data gathering- and data analysis *methods* as it follows.

A. Data gathering

During our pre-study phase, we were particularly interested in the participant's own understanding of the concept of robots, and other modern technologies such as smartphones and tablets, as well as their experiences with those. We have conducted multiple research activities, gathering data through various research methods, including three semi-structured group interviews, a pilot semi-structured interview, and individual semi-structured interviews. The details are shown in Table I below.

TABLE 1. OVERVIEW PARTICIPANTS

Research activity	Number of participants	Gender distribution
3 group interviews	15	8 females, 7 males
Pilot interview	1	Female
Individual interviews	2	Female
Total	18	

The participants are elderly (≥65 years), part of the MECS project, recruited through MECS' partner organization. Some of the participants participated in multiple research activities, whereas some did not. The participants have different backgrounds and present different levels of interest in modern technologies. No family members were interviewed.

The interviews covered multiple types of modern technologies. The same interview guide was used for the first and second group interview. A pilot interview guide was then developed, and together with the initial group interview guide, served later as a base for the third group interview. These were later used as a base for the individual interviews.

Complementary to these, we have attended informal meetings with the elderly at the Kampen Omsorg Pluss' facilities, and other relevant presentations, in order to familiarize ourselves with the environment and the residents, e.g., the elderly. However, for this contribution, we do not cover all the themes and pattern found in our material. We focused instead on the pattern explored in this paper, *digital feedback* and *fear*.

B. Ethics

This study is part of the MECS-project. MECS is complying with the ethical guidelines from the Norwegian Center for Research Data (reference number: 50689). The participants were recruited through MECS's partner organization. They were given information about the study, prior the study started, through a formal presentation. Prior starting the research activities, the information was given again, and the participants chose to participate on a voluntary basis after reading the informed consent. They were informed that they can withdraw at any time, without any consequences for them. The data is stored on TSD (Services for Sensitive Data) at University of Oslo, Norway.

C. *Data analysis*

Our data analysis can be structured into two types: (1) through the researchers' positionality, and (2) through a thorough analysis following several stages of filtering. Both are described below.

(1) Positionality of the researchers and data analysis.

The researchers are considered here non-detached from the data gathered during the research activities, such that their positionality influence at some degree the results [37]. For instance, there were considered here researchers' *first impressions* on the data gathered on how elderly understand *robots* and their experiences with various technologies. These types of *first impressions* would result in post research activity notes that were immediate to the field activity. [38] calls this method *headnotes* as [39], which, according to the author, describe "experiences, impressions, encounters, and evaluations that are continuously present in [the] memory" (p. 32). In the same way, in MECS, the researchers would either discuss the perceived outcomes of the activity, immediate to it or write down those in the form of reflections. These would be later used in (2).

(2) The second type of analysis is a thorough one, that follows several stages.

According to [40], "analysis is less a matter of something emerging from the data, of simply finding what is there; it is more fundamental a process of creating what is there by constantly thinking about the import of previously recorded events and meanings" (p. 168). In this way, the process of analysis started already while being in the field, as a form of doing *some* preliminary work [37, p. 134], as described in *(1)*. This has been followed by a multiple stage analysis process, where the data went through some analytical filters. We illustrate the process of data analysis as a three-tier process, as shown in Figure 1.

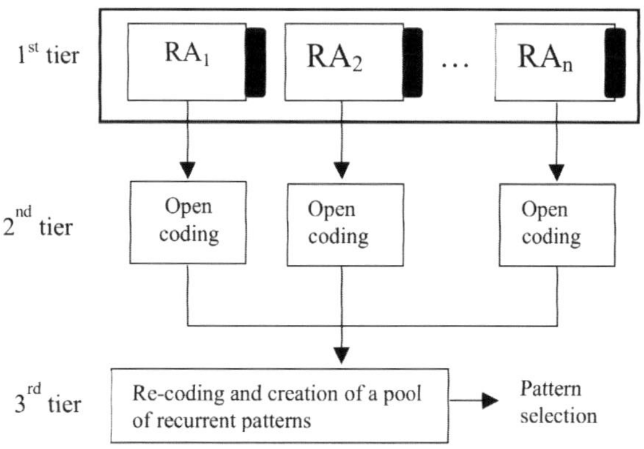

Figure 1. Data Analysis Process

The first tier embeds the research activities (annotated as RA): group interviews, pilot-interview, and individual interviews. The filled-in rounded squares, at the end of each RA, represent the *headnotes,* or preliminary-work did right after each activity in the form of discussions and reflections, as explained in (1). The second-tier is described as *open-coding*. Here, the *raw data* became textual data, in the form of transcribed interviews, notes, or interview summaries. Several of the researchers involved in MECS project has analyzed hermeneutically the data, on their own, and created codes through *open coding,* by reading the material "line-by-line to identify and formulate all ideas, themes, or issues they suggest, no matter how varied and disparate" [40, p. 143]. This resulted in a variety of scattered *patterns*, on one hand, due to our variation in research activities, and on the other hand, due to researchers' own research interests that had some influence on the research activities and their outcome. For instance, the researchers analyzed the data on their own, and thereafter share the analysis both through documents and orally, during a formal analysis meeting. However, this is valid for the first two group interviews, whereas the rest were analyzed independently by the main author of this paper. Noticing that *feedback* and *fear* were present patterns in the data, but also due to own interest, the main author of this paper chose to go through the data again, but also to analyze further the next research activities. Some of the researchers were either not part of the next research activities, or other research areas to focus on, therefore we cannot claim an inter-rater reliability of the study. However, following [38], validity, in this case, is not of "a particular concern", as the study focuses on gathering user-requirements for the safety-alarm robot. Therefore, one would need first to get insights into the participants' understanding of modern technologies before creating the safety alarm robot (ibid, p. 212). In addition, some relations were developed between the RA, in an iterative way, based on the findings from previous activities. This is not shown in Figure 1, but a concrete such example is the understanding of *what a robot is.* The elderly understood the concept of a robot, either as something they have seen on TV's, such as a humanoid robot, or semi-autonomous vacuum cleaners and lawnmower – this is what a *robot* is for them. For limiting our scope, we do not cover these relations here, although we are aware of those. In the third tier of the analysis process, the main author of this paper went again through the whole research material collected, for partially merging the data collected in order to get a holistic view of it, and partially, with the purpose of a second filtering and re-coding. In the end, based on the recurrent pattern available, *fear* has been selected to be discussed in this paper. In Figure 2, we show the details of each of the tiers.

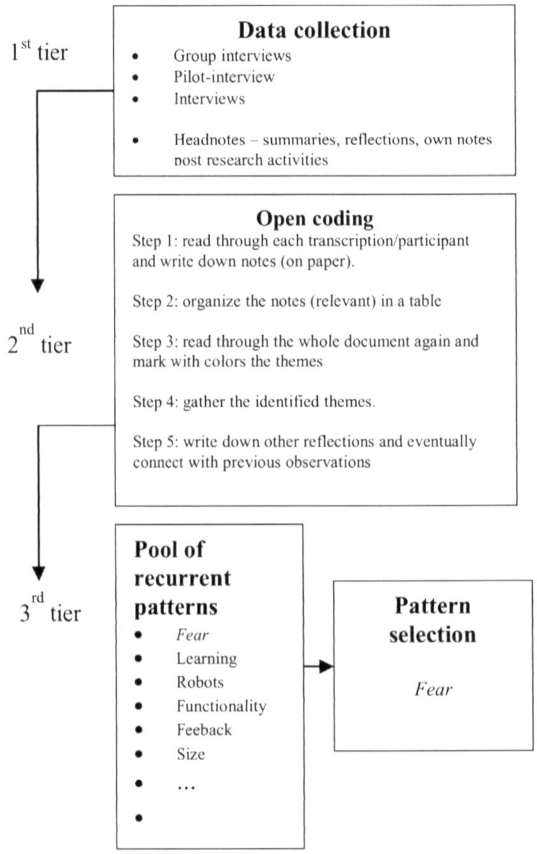

Figure 2. Data Analysis Process – Detailed View

V. Preliminary Results of Feedback and Fear

We illustrate in the next paragraphs two types of situations from our research: technology providing improper feedback where the user (here the elderly) does not know how to proceed, and the technology not providing any feedback at all, e.g., lack of feedback. We showcase each of these through real-life situations experienced by the elderly in their daily interaction with modern technologies, i.e., *stories from the elderly*.

A. *Situation 1: Providing improper feedback*

"*SMS shows full. Do I need to buy a new phone?*" - One of the participants tells about her experience with the mobile phone and the feedback of SMS - full blinking icon. She would tell that she is not able to store any new photos received from her children or grandchildren. The participant feared that she had to buy a new phone and losing the photos because of the feedback is shown by the phone. Regarding the design issue here, we can look at how the elderly may perceive the digital feedback gotten from the technology.

"*I couldn't start it—but it was so much more.. among others, the screen.. disappeared and so..*" - Another participant explains her experience with a semi-autonomous vacuum cleaner which can be controlled by an app. During a power outage, the app controlling the domestic robot stopped working. The participant got a message that the app "*cannot connect to the cloud services*".

"*Where is the 'No' option when updating software?*" - Another situation described by one of the participants is related to the feedback received when a software shall be updated. The participant explained that she is tired of getting constant updates, and points out that an *exit* option does not exist. She would get either the option '*Now*' or '*Later'*, but not a '*No'* option. She contacted the company providing the operating system via a *handwritten* letter and asked about this option. To her surprise, got called up by the customer service, and got offered help on *how to deal with the two options available, 'Now'* and *'Later'*, but the company had no regard in planning to introduce a *No-option*. The participant explained that she knew how to deal with the updates, but what she wanted was that the feedback should embed a '*No'*-option alternative. Regarding this design issue, this has to do with the continuous update of software and the point of view of the elderly on these "*never-ending*" updates. This example illustrates a situation where feedback messages do not provide enough options.

"*It was just standing still there. Or when I pressed on it there it says something about cloud-service. It didn't do anything, but I thought you will come tomorrow*" - Another participant explains a situation with controlling a semi-autonomous vacuum cleaner through an app, which did not provide sufficient feedback. Using the wording "*cloud-services*" can confuse a user not-knowing what it means. The user, in this case, relied on the researchers help to come along the next days.

B. *Situation 2: The software does not provide any feedback at all, e.g., lack of feedback*

"*You were terribly afraid of doing something wrong*" - In one of our interviews sessions, one participant describes that when she learns using new technologies, she is so afraid of *doing something wrong*. A concrete example is that the technology, being it smartphone or tablet, does not provide any feedback on how to "*get back to basics*": "*so you were very afraid that .. I did not feel I could come back to the base. But I was afraid to do something wrong.*"

By this, the participant means that the applications are built in such a way, that one is expected to have that intuitive knowledge, but for new learners, it can be difficult to understand how to navigate within an app, and one can easily "get stuck". She explained about her experience when using a streaming TV-channel app and its search function: "*I think now I will do this... Huuuu (exhales heavy) and I do not get it.. and there are many of you who have explained to me. (laughs) But it goes so fast!*".

"I have an example absolutely horrible. I had to print something on 3 pages.. and the printer goes fine.. and it prints and it prints and it prints. I cannot afford it. In the end, I had a lot of printed files.." - Another participant explains an experience with a printing machine, where no feedback was provided at all. She had to call an organization that provides IT services for the elderly users, in order to be able to stop the machine. Another participant agreeing on the story, says: "*It can get so difficult when one does not understand [what's happening].*"

VI. DISCUSSION: FEEDBACK AND FAMILIARITY

In this section, we unpack the pattern of *fear* emerged from our data, based on its derivatives, e.g., associated emotions. The pattern is unpacked with regard to *digital feedback*, and how it is experienced by the elderly. We assigned this based on our phenomenological interpretation and understanding of what has been communicated. This is strictly our phenomenological interpretation, and we are aware that other interpretations are possible. But first, we typecast the situations described to the corresponding derivative of the emotion of fear, as shown in Table II.

TABLE II TYPECAST SITUATIONS – AND FEAR

Situation	**Typecast**	**The emotion of fear and its derivatives**
Situation 1	Not providing proper feedback	Concern (here for buying a new phone), doubt (from getting a black screen), unease, uneasiness and presentiment when the technology *provides improper feedback*
Situation 2	Not providing any feedback at all	Angst, anxiety, concern unease, uneasiness, fright, phobia, worry – when there is *lack of feedback*

We can observe from concrete situations presented in the previous section and typecast in Table 1 above how feedback, from digital technologies, being it improper, or lacking completely, may generate at some degree the emotion of *fear*, or feelings associated with it. This is due to either not knowing what happened, or how to proceed further.

[42, p. 75] propose *familiarity* as a design aspect in order to enhance the usability of the digital technology, pointing out that "usability alone does not guarantee that the technology will be used (Hirsch, Forlizzi et. al 2000)" (p. 86). Even in our study, the aspect of usability was indicated, but *feeling unsafe* (aka feeling *fear*) is still an indicator of using or not the technology. For instance, one of the participants points out on his concrete experiences with new digital technologies: "*As soon as I feel unsafe regarding the technology, I put it aside."*'; "*First, I do not need it to.. go [meaning learning it] in deep.. and secondly, I am afraid... I feel unsafe, yes..*"

Hence, here we could identify two aspects: on one hand the aspect of familiarity through the feeling of safety, and *functionality,* the value provided by the technology in itself.

But concrete experiences have to be complemented by the allocation of the 'appropriate resources' if one should follow the zone of proximal development (ZPD) theory on learning [43]. What if the only 'appropriate resources' might be the technology in itself, or as [31, p. 431] puts it: "~The medium is the message."? Specifically, in our case, digital *feedback* can be considered as a *carrier* of design concepts, such as *familiarity*. As we show in our findings, feedback might be either *improper or lacking completely*. This also implies that the elderly's concrete experiences with technologies are not supported through design. But how can familiarity be applied to in practice to digital feedback? We discuss further both situations described in *Section VI Preliminary Results.*

A. Familiarity with a design concept for situation 1) – providing improper feedback

First, a solution for providing proper feedback is, for instance, through clear messages, avoiding the use of single modalities of feedback representations, such as the blinking icon for showing the status of *full messages.* Although, there are situations when this type of feedback is supported by a text informing the user about "full messages", it does not guide the user on how to proceed further. One solution is to decrease the gap, e.g., the zone of proximal development, between what the user knows, and what has to be achieved, i.e., deleting messages, by providing *proper feedback.* Specifically, we mean by *proper* feedback, *descriptive* and *relevant feedback:* this can simply be done through a text that points out how to proceed further, as for instance: "*SMS full. You need to delete some of your SMS before you can receive new ones.*"; or by including more step-by-step guidelines: "*SMS full. You can solve this by 1. Go to your SMS messages. 2. Click long on one of the SMS from the list. 3. Mark the checkbox of those SMS you wish to delete. 4. Select delete.*" In this way, we decrease the gap between what is not familiar to the user, and what it is.

Second, one can provide proper feedback, by avoiding the use of technical terminologies, such as "*it cannot connect to the cloud-services*". Many of the elderly do not know what a "cloud-service" is. Using such technical terminology discourages them from using the technology. Instead, one could build upon the concept of *familiarity,* starting from the assumption that one does not know what the "*cloud service*" is. This can be done either through simple visualization or animations or through further explanations in plain English. Second, this type of feedback can be supported by additional alternatives, showing step-by-step how one could connect to the service: "*Have you checked out your internet connection – is your router turned on? Go to..",* without assuming that the users know how to get around, giving them step-by-step feedback on how to proceed further.

Third, in the case of not providing enough alternatives example, one can provide proper feedback through giving more explanations on *why* one has to proceed in a certain way, e.g., such as updating the software when the *"No"*-option is not available. Another way of doing it is through actually making these updates invisible to the user. In that case, the interaction should be robust enough, so the user does not end up in not getting any feedback at all, as described in Situation 2), which is also discussed next.

B. *Familiarity with a design concept for situation 2)- not providing feedback at all, e.g., lack of feedback*

One can provide proper feedback before the breakdown situation, when the user gets stuck, by indicating the user where it is, or by preventing such a situation and offering feedback in time. This can be done by building upon the *familiarity* of the user – what does the user might not know, and how can the design prevent breakdown situations? This way of enhancing the user experience in its interaction with modern technologies is sometimes referred as *feed-forward* [40][41]. This approach relates to *showing the way forward* on how the user shall proceed, prior an event occurred as an effect of the user's interaction with the modern technology. In the next paragraphs, we provide a few examples.

First, a solution example is used for instance in Android Operating Systems, when it is required in a text field, an input from the user. Some designs allow so-called *hints*, which are non-editable texts that are shown in the background of a text field, indicating the user what to enter in the respective field. This way of providing feedback to the user counteracts eventual *deviations* in the user's interaction with the technology, prior to the interaction occurring.

Second, another example is shown by autofill functions, for instance, in a web-browser, where the text fields are filled in with information, based on historical data – name, email addresses, home address, zip code, phone number etc. that have been used as input on that respective computer.

Third, a similar example is also the auto-complete input function, that learns based on the user's past inputs.

The second and third examples of built-in feedback are examples, on *supporting* the user interaction with the technology, *on the go*. As the technology learns more about *its* user, it can also give *appropriate* feedback for that specific user. Appropriate feedback is based in this case on elements that are already *familiar* to the user.

These type of approaches are also often discussed in literature of universal design, as *simple and intuitive use,* and as *perceptible information* (see principles 3 and 4 in [46]–[48]).

C. *Some final reflections and wrap-up*

One study, [49] shows that feedback increases performance encourages reflection "by increasing knowledge and awareness of behaviors and their impact", and has motivational consequences (p. 63). In this way, feedback, not only encourages what [50] calls 'reflection on action' on "evaluating [own] past behavior", but also 'reflection-in-action', "the analysis of behavior as it occurs" [49]. One should take into account feedback's properties such as: the technology, the content, timing, modality, duration, frequency, presentation, user experience [49], as well as spatiality between the user and the technology in itself, which is important when interacting with robots, as reported by [15]. Could then it be so that if the technology embeds a better design of feedback (compare to *improper,* or *lacking completely* as shown in this study), would eventually contribute to the learning experience of the user (e.g. elderly)? We argue that if users such as elderly would be provided with *enough* and *proper* feedback, with respect to the properties enumerated earlier, the zone of proximal development will provide the user with sufficient resources for the learner, in such way that the learner will feel *safer* to use the technology. In its turn, this will contribute to the familiarity of the user with the technology, reducing the threshold between the user's prior knowledge and the challenge at hand.

VII. CONCLUSION AN D FUTURE WORK

In this paper, we have presented: what affective implications the design of digital feedback in modern technologies may have on the elderly users while they use those, such as triggering the emotion of *fear*; and proposed familiarity as a central design concept to be considered when designing for the elderly users. We started the paper by introducing the reader to three central concepts: *digital feedback, fear* and the emotions associated with it, and *familiarity.* Digital feedback is presented here as visual feedback received by the elderly in their interaction with the modern technologies. We argued that *feedback* can be affective *by its design*, through multimodality, or *become affective* as a result of how it is experienced by the users, here the elderly. We exemplified this through the use of the umbrella term for *fear* and the feelings associated with it, e.g., derivatives, such as *angst, anxiety, concern, doubt, dread, unease, uneasiness, worry, aversion, fright, phobia, presentiment* [1]. After presenting our methodology, as an interpretative phenomenological one, the methods used and our analysis, we showcased this through empirical data. Thereafter, we discussed theoretically *familiarity* as a design concept that should be considered when designing *feedback* in modern technologies. We argue that having *familiarity* in mind when designing new technologies, can bridge the gap between the elderly's zone of proximal development and the challenge at hand while learning new technologies. Yet, specifically, we encourage to consider feedback as the *carrier* of the *familiarity* design concept, which would support the elderly's learning process of interacting with new modern technologies. However, we do not address here the issue of cognitive impairments, or representations of visual feedback through other visual ways (e.g. animations). We propose this be further investigated through concepts such as *universal design*. Specifically, we intend to explore this further through focusing on the principle five of universal design, namely *tolerance for error,* and build further upon it. Based on our theoretical findings, we hope, in the future, to contribute to the design of modern technologies that will encompass the patterns explored here. Based on our reported work so far in the MECS project, we plan to build further upon *familiarity* design concept while designing the safety alarm robot for the elderly. More concrete, in a second phase of the project, we introduced semi-autonomous vacuum cleaners robots in the home of the elderly, in order to learn more about their daily interaction with a robot. The partial results presented here, as well as the second phase of the project, are part of the MECS project phase where we get insights on the elderly's understanding of robots and welfare technologies, as well as of the gathering requirements phase. We plan to continue our work in this sense, in order to get a deeper understanding of the pattern explored here.

ACKNOWLEDGMENT

This work was part of the MECS project funded by the Norwegian Research Council IKTPluss Program (Grant agreement no: 247697). We would like to thank our project funders, partners, especially to Kampen Omsorg Pluss, the project manager, Jim Tørresen, colleagues (Trenton Schulz and Rebekka Soma, as well as to the Robotics and Intelligent Systems Group at UiO), and to students involved in this project (Magnus Søyland, Vegard Dønnem Søyseth).

REFERENCES

[1] Dictionary.com, "Thesaurus.com | Meanings, and Definitions of Words at Thesaurus.com," *Thesaurus.com*, 2016. [Online]. Available: http://www.thesaurus.com/, http://www.thesaurus.com/. [Retrieved: November 2017].

[2] Eurostat, "Population structure and aging - Statistics Explained," *Population structure and aging*, 20-Jul-2017. [Online]. Available: http://ec.europa.eu/eurostat/statistics-explained/index.php/Population_structure_and_ageing. [Retrieved: November 2017].

[3] SSB, "Next million reached set to be the fastest," *ssb.no*, 2017. [Online]. Available: http://www.ssb.no/en/befolkning/statistikker/folkfram/aar/2016-06-21. [Retrieved: November 2017].

[4] J. Ramm, "Health and care. Use of services among the elderly," *ssb.no*, 2013. [Online]. Available: http://www.ssb.no/en/helse/artikler-og-publikasjoner/eldres-bruk-av-helse-og-omsorgstjenester. [Retrieved: January 2018].

[5] European Commision, "eHealth Action Plan 2012-2020: Innovative healthcare for the 21st century," *Digital Single Market*, 07-Dec-2012. [Online]. Available: https://ec.europa.eu/digital-single-market/en/news/ehealth-action-plan-2012-2020-innovative-healthcare-21st-century. [Retrieved: January, 2018].

[6] J. A. Delello and R. R. McWhorter, "Reducing the Digital Divide: Connecting Older Adults to iPad Technology," *J. Appl. Gerontol.*, vol. 36, no. 1, pp. 3–28, Jan. 2017.

[7] Y.-H. Wu, S. Damnée, H. Kerhervé, C. Ware, and A.-S. Rigaud, "Bridging the digital divide in older adults: a study from an initiative to inform older adults about new technologies," *Clin. Interv. Aging*, vol. 10, pp. 193–201, Jan. 2015.

[8] T. Halbach and T. Schulz, "MobileSage - A Prototype Based Case Study for Delivering Context-Aware, Personalized, On-Demand Help Content," presented at the CENTRIC 2013, The Sixth International Conference on Advances in Human-oriented and Personalized Mechanisms, Technologies, and Services, 2014, vol. International Journal on Advances in Intelligent Systems, 7, nos. 1–2, pp. 267–278.

[9] M. Anerson and A. Perrin, "1. Technology use among seniors," *Pew Research Center: Internet, Science & Tech*, [Online]: http://www.pewinternet.org/2017/05/17/technology-use-among-seniors/, [Retrieved: January 2018].

[10] "MECS," *Multimodal Elderly Care Systems (MECS), About the project*, 17-Oct-2016. [Online]. Available: http://www.mn.uio.no/ifi/english/research/groups/robin/research-projects/mecs/. [Retrieved: January 2018].

[11] KO+, "Kampen Omsorg+ - KirkensBymisjon," 2017. [Online]. Available: http://www.bymisjon.no/Virksomheter/Kampen-omsorg/. [Accessed: 24-Mar-2017].

[12] W. R. Ashby, *An Introduction to Cybernetics*. London, U.K.: Chapman & Hall LTD, 1957.

[13] M. Thurlings, M. Vermeulen, T. Bastiaens, and S. Stijnen, "Understanding feedback: A learning theory perspective," *Educ. Res. Rev.*, vol. 9, no. Supplement C, pp. 1–15, Jun. 2013.

[14] B. Shneiderman, *Designing the User Interface: Strategies for Effective Human-computer Interaction*. Boston, MA, USA: Addison-Wesley Longman Publishing Co., Inc., 1986.

[15] D. Saplacan and J. Herstad, "A Quadratic Anthropocentric Perspective on Feedback - Using Proxemics as a Framework," in Lynn Hall; Tom Flint; Suzy O'Hara & Phil Turner (ed.), *Proceedings of the 31st International BCS Human Computer Interaction Conference (HCI 2017)*. British Computer Society (BCS). 1. Sunderland, U.K., 03-Jul-2017.

[16] C. Lewis and D. A. Norman, "Human-computer Interaction," R. M. Baecker, J. Grudin, W. A. S. Buxton, and S. Greenberg, Eds. San Francisco, CA, USA: Morgan Kaufmann Publishers Inc., 1995, pp. 686–697.

[17] R. W. Picard, "Affective Computing in M.I.T Media Laboratory Perceptual Computing Section Technical Report," MIT Media Laboratory, Perceptual Computing, Cambridge, MA 02139, Technical Report 321, 1995.

[18] L. Chittaro and R. Sioni, "Affective computing vs. affective placebo: Study of a biofeedback-controlled game for relaxation training," *Int. J. Hum.-Comput. Stud.*, vol. 72, no. 8–9, pp. 663–673, Aug. 2014.

[19] Akshita, H. Alagarai Sampath, B. Indurkhya, E. Lee, and Y. Bae, "Towards Multimodal Affective Feedback: Interaction Between Visual and Haptic Modalities," in *Proceedings of the 33rd Annual ACM Conference on Human Factors in*

Computing Systems, New York, NY, USA, 2015, pp. 2043–2052.

[20] M. Kächele *et al.*, "On Annotation and Evaluation of Multimodal Corpora in Affective Human-Computer Interaction," in *Multimodal Analyses enabling Artificial Agents in Human-Machine Interaction*, 2014, pp. 35–44.

[21] M. Schels, M. Kächele, M. Glodek, D. Hrabal, S. Walter, and F. Schwenker, "Using unlabeled data to improve classification of emotional states in human-computer interaction," *J. Multimodal User Interfaces*, vol. 8, no. 1, pp. 5–16, Mar. 2014.

[22] OED, "fear, n.1," *Oxford English Dictionary Online*. Oxford University Press, [Retrieved: January 2018]

[23] G. Boulton-Lewis, "Education and Learning for the Elderly: Why, How, What," *Educational Gerontology*. pp. 228–231, 2010.

[24] M. Díaz, J. Saez-Pons, M. Heerink, and C. Angulo, "Emotional factors in robot-based assistive services for elderly at home," in *2013 IEEE RO-MAN*, 2013, pp. 711–716.

[25] J. Gallego-Perez, M. Lohse, and V. Evers, "Robots to motivate elderly people: Present and future challenges," in *2013 IEEE RO-MAN*, 2013, pp. 685–690.

[26] R. A. Calvo and D. Peters, *Positive Computing: Technology for Well-Being and Human Potential*. The MIT Press, 2014.

[27] J. Lethem, P. D. Slade, J. D. G. Troup, and G. Bentley, "Outline of a fear-avoidance model of exaggerated pain perception—I," *Behav. Res. Ther.*, vol. 21, no. 4, pp. 401–408, Jan. 1983.

[28] J. J. L. M. Boselie and J. W. S. Vlaeyen, "Broadening the fear-avoidance model of chronic pain?," *Scand. J. Pain*, vol. 17, pp. 176–177, Oct. 2017.

[29] P. J. Lang and L. M. McTeague, "The anxiety disorder spectrum," *Anxiety Stress Coping*, vol. 22, no. 1, pp. 5–25, Jan. 2009.

[30] M. Heidegger, *Being and time*. Oxford, U.K.: Blackwell Publishers Ltd, 1967.

[31] H. Dreyfus, *Being-in-the-world: A Commentary on Heidegger's Being and Time, Division I*. Massachusetts Institute of Technology, 1991.

[32] G. Van de Walle, P. Turner, and E. Davenport, "A study of familiarity," in *Human-Computer Interaction-INTERACT*, 2003, vol. 3, pp. 463–70.

[33] P. Turner and G. van de Walle, "Familiarity as a basis for universal design," *Gerontechnology*, vol. 5, no. 3, pp. 150–159, Jan. 2006.

[34] J. Herstad and H. Holone, "Making Sense of Co-creative Tangibles Through the Concept of Familiarity," in *Proceedings of the 7th Nordic Conference on Human-Computer Interaction: Making Sense Through Design*, New York, NY, USA, 2012, pp. 89–98.

[35] M. Myers D., "Qualitative Research in Information Systems," *MISQ Discovery*, 1997.

[36] P. Ricoeur, "Phenomenology and Hermeneutics," *Noûs*, vol. 9, no. 1, pp. 85–102, 1975.

[37] M. Crang and I. Cook, *Doing Ethnographies*. SAGE Publications, Inc., 2007.

[38] G. Verne, "'The winners are those who have used the old paper form'. On citizens and automated public services," University of Oslo, Oslo, Norway, 2015.

[39] S. Ottenberg, "Thirty Years of Fieldnotes: Changing Relationships to the text," in *The Making of Anthropology, R. Sanjek*, Cornell University Press, 1990, pp. 139–160.

[40] R. M. Emerson, R. I. Fretz, and L. L. Shaw, "Processing Fieldnotes: Coding and Memoing (Chapter 6)," in *Writing Ethnographic Fieldnotes*, Chicago, and London: University of Chicago Press, 1995, pp. 142–168.

[41] J. Lazar, J. H. Feng, and H. Hochheiser, *Research Methods In Human-Computer Interaction*. West Sussex, United Kingdom: Jon Wiley & Sons Ltd, 2010.

[42] S. G. Joshi and H. Bråthen, "Supporting new interactions with past experiences anchored in materials," *IADIS International Journal on Computer Science and Information Systems*, vol. 2, 11 vols. pp. 74–89, 2016.

[43] B. Nardi and J. Harris, "Strangers and Friends: Collaborative Play in World of Warcraft," in *Proceedings of the 2006 20th Anniversary Conference on Computer Supported Cooperative Work*, New York, NY, USA, 2006, pp. 149–158.

[44] G. Freitag, M. Tränkner, and M. Wacker, "Enhanced Feed-forward for a User Aware Multi-touch Device," in *Proceedings of the 7th Nordic Conference on Human-Computer Interaction: Making Sense Through Design*, New York, NY, USA, 2012, pp. 578–586.

[45] M. B. Alonso, J. Stienstra, and R. Dijkstra, "Brush and Learn: Transforming Tooth Brushing Behavior Through Interactive Materiality, a Design Exploration," in *Proceedings of the 8th International Conference on Tangible, Embedded and Embodied Interaction*, New York, NY, USA, 2013, pp. 113–120.

[46] Centre for Excellence in Universal Design, "The 7 Principles | Centre for Excellence in Universal Design," 2014. [Online]. Available: http://universaldesign.ie/What-is-Universal-Design/The-7-Principles/.[Retrieved: January, 2018].

[47] North Carolina State University, "Guidelines for Use of the Principles of Universal Design." NCSU, revised 2002-1999.

[48] "Web Content Accessibility Guidelines (WCAG) 2.0." [Online]. Available: https://www.w3.org/TR/WCAG20/. [Retrieved: January, 2018].

[49] S. Hermsen, J. Frost, R. J. Renes, and P. Kerkhof, "Using feedback through digital technology to disrupt and change habitual behavior: A critical review of current literature," *Comput. Hum. Behav.*, vol. 57, pp. 61–74, Apr. 2016.

[50] D. A. Schön, *The reflective practitioner: how professionals think in action*. New York: Basic Books, 1983.

A Study on Visualization of User Reviews

Eric Yang
Department of Digital Media Design
National Yunlin University of Science and Technology
Yunlin, Taiwan
E-mail: yangyueric@icloud.com

***Abstract*—User reviews is a research method with increasing application in the application ('app') industry in recent years because it allows development teams to better understand users' needs and ideas through user review analysis. However, deciding how to interpret the massive daily incoming user review data and how to sort them into useful information is a challenge that development teams must address. This study combined the architecture of an app with the excellent information communication capability of information visualisation and compiled a priority list of version releases based on function areas mentioned in user reviews, allowing development teams to create strategies for updates and emergency resolution, as well as designing apps to meet users' expectations, and to therefore achieve better user experience. Subsequent to a heuristic evaluation, the three most important suggestions were made: 1. Improve the enrichment of the visualisation chart; 2. Increase follow-up evaluation; and 3. Understand the reasons and context that lead users to like apps. Experts that participated in the evaluation believed that the visualisation chart generated in this study allows developers to better understand users' real needs, to be able to focus on the more serious issues related to system structure, and assign them with higher priority for repair such that product evaluation will be enhanced resulting in more download volume and profits. The experts also believed that if visualisation charts can be enhanced with more flexibility and user reviews will be followed up with ongoing evaluation, the approach suggested in the present study will surely prove to be very useful in the app market application.**

Keywords-user review analysis; structured system; information visualization; negative feedback.

I. INTRODUCTION

As the mobile app market continues gaining momentum, more developers are now paying attention to user reviews. Consumers usually consult others for opinions to better understand their products or services of interest and to support their purchase decisions [17]. To allow consumers the opportunity to preview an app before downloading it, the user reviews and Feedback section is located on the app product download page in each app store download platform to provide reference to consumers before downloading. The section also serves as a channel for developers to make corrections to the app based on the user feedback and to meet the needs of consumers in the market.

Vu et al. [15] pointed out that conducting manual analyses of user reviews is a huge challenge because for a popular app, there are as many as thousands or tens of thousands of reviews daily, and therefore, it would be very time-consuming to read through all the reviews. In addition, user reviews are generally messy due to misspelling, the use of acronyms, abbreviations, emojis, and others. C. Iacob et al. [8] also agreed that users often use unconventional expressions when writing reviews, which can be very brief and unstructured and do not usually follow syntax and punctuation rules. This implies that merely relying on computer programming to sort out and analyse user reviews is not feasible. Rather, a certain level of artificial judgment is needed in the preliminary sorting of messy raw reviews before further computer processing should be performed to ensure the accuracy of the results that are generated. Thus, the question of how to filter out invalid reviews to pinpoint authentic errors for correction and set the stage for generating accurate results in subsequent computer processing is an issue that development teams must address.

[7], [9] argued that product characteristics or product functions identified in user reviews are conducive to manufacturers in making adjustments to respective characteristics or functions. In [11], semantics used in user reviews were analysed for classification based on directional product characteristics in reviews. Subsequent evaluation was then conducted to sort out the good reviews from the bad based on product characteristics. The respective experimental results showed that this methodology is effective to developers, as keywords extracted from product characteristics help developers quickly locate problem areas and understand the situation. Linking user reviews with the system functionality and characteristics of an app will certainly help developers expedite the sorting of messy user reviews to a certain extent, resulting in the ability to make up for negative user reviews.

In addition, [10] revealed that among the review ratings that included the keyword 'shortcoming' in the feedback, the percentages of ratings from 5-star to 1-star were: 0%, 10.84%, 31.03%, 55.36%, and 50.00%, respectively; and that among the review ratings that included the keyword 'bug report' in the feedback, the percentages of ratings from 5-star to 1-star were: 0%, 0%, 22.41%, 33.93%, and 46.38%, respectively. We can see that for the keyword 'shortcoming', there was a huge increase from 31% 3-star ratings to 50.00% 1-star ratings and similarly, for the keyword 'bug report', there was a big jump from 22.41% 3-star ratings to 46.38% 1-star ratings. As the data showed, 3-star was basically the cut-off in users' app ratings, as the majority of user reviews related to 'shortcoming' and 'bug report' was accounted for in 3-star and below reviews. Therefore, from the perspective of development teams, user review analysis that focuses on 3-star and below reviews is relatively cost-effective in app optimisation.

Appbot is a website exclusively designed to help development teams further understand user reviews. Appbot calculates the average star rating, provides rankings of reviews based on the most frequently appearing words, and combines star ratings with text to inform development teams whether there is any need for imminent correction while serving as correction support to development teams for the next version release of the app. However, from the perspective of development teams, information that only presents flaws in the app is not sufficient for developers to quickly identify the source of and reasons for the problem, since development teams still need to spend a lot of time identifying the exact problem area in the complex programming before they can further resolve the problem.

The discussion in the introduction section shows that user favorability can be promoted through the creation of a good review ecosystem, achieving a high download rate and an increase in profits. However, most of the current analytic tools used in user reviews focus on user emotions, frequently used words and sentences, or custom searches for specific words or meanings as a basis for analysis; a tool that can help development teams clearly identify the specific problem area and the version with ongoing problems is still missing. Therefore, development teams need to spend a lot of time analysing the huge volume of reviews in order to pinpoint the function pain point before they can report to engineers for repair.

Therefore, the goal of this study is to identify user pain points from a huge volume of messy consumer reviews. Combined with the system architecture of the app, the system function areas identified as pain points were analysed and presented in a visualization chart format. A preliminary model was then created to provide development teams with queries for fast judgment, serving as support for decision-making in upgrade proposals.

This paper is organized as follows. In Section II, we present the literature review. Section III introduces the method and the content analysis study. Section IV reports on the results and summarizes the related work.

II. LITERATURE REVIEW

As a new genre of word-of-moth information, online consumer product feedback is an emerging market phenomenon that is playing a more significant role in consumers' purchase decisions. Online user feedback is information left by users based on their personal experiences and can therefore be regarded as a novel type of communication tool that helps consumers identify the most appropriate products [3]. According to [4], [13], user feedback is like electronic word-of-mouth (eWOM) marketing, and WOM marketing is widely recognised as a very influential communication method. Prior to making a purchase, consumers tend to refer to online feedback systems. Therefore, from the perspective of providers of goods and services, online feedback and feedback volume directly impacts the sales volume of products and services. Furthermore, user reviews and evaluations will form an ecosystem; that is, bad ecosystems will slowly affect the sales volume of products or sales and gradually deteriorate into an even worse ecosystem, creating a huge roadblock during product promotion and sale. Therefore, developers must pay attention to the trend in user reviews at all times. When reviews are found to be forming a bad cycle, timely changes must be made to products and services to prevent a bad ecosystem from forming. On the contrary, a good ecosystem will continue increasing the sales volume intangibly, resulting in a positive multiplying effect in sales; good mass effect will create widespread benefits to development teams.

Platform service providers are the medium between developers and users. Nowadays, all major software and publishing platforms such as the Apple App Store and the Google Play Store have provided a user reviews section on the bottom of each product page that also shows the average rating of the product, providing consumers with easy access to other users' tips and comments on their personal experiences. Before downloading an app (especially for apps that are not free), app users can easily check the ratings of the respective app, hence cutting down the cost of time spent searching. In addition, since reviews are made by users who are also consumers of the same product, their reviews are considered more credible than the information provided by developers due to conflicts of interests. Ante [1] pointed out that majority of consumers look up user reviews and ratings before making a purchase. Because of this, the consumer's first impressions become the basis for consumption. For developers, platform service providers not only can bring in high subscription volume and browsing volume but can also save development teams time on product promotion. Online user reviews also facilitate development teams to release faster updates on products and services.

Vasa et al. [13] argued that although the user review is a new concept in the app industry, user reviews have been regarded as a business strategy in other industries for many years. Negative reviews allow developers to focus on specific areas that need to be corrected. Therefore, development teams can prioritise updates based on the urgency expressed in the feedback, which will result in better subsequent user reviews. According to [14], [16], in the hotel industry, making appropriate analysis of reviews will generate business opportunities. These two studies found that prioritising updates on design or service process that most consumers felt inappropriate makes consumers feel valued by the business, thereby increasing the probability that consumers will make repurchases or leave better reviews in the future, both of which are beneficial to the service provider.

According to [12], user reviews are a form of value co-creation. [2] additionally found that product evaluation provided by consumers are perceived by fellow consumers as more trustworthy than information provided by sales personnel. One of the reasons why most consumers trust consumer reviews was put forward in [3]: that consumer reviews are based on personal usage experiences, leading to the creation of a unique type of product information that can help consumers identify products that they really need. Therefore, online user review systems provide a venue for consumers to share their opinions and experiences about products. On the other hand, such venues also provide valuable information resources to potential buyers, facilitating effective and rational purchase decisions. Users' word-of-mouth is more convincing than traditional media [4].

From the perspective of sellers, [6] indicated that subsequent to service failure, the majority of service providers will take remedial measures to improve consumer experience, hoping to change consumers' negative word-of-mouth into positive word-of-mouth. In terms of development, user's negative feedback related to system errors are often valuable information that can be collected for analysis and upgrades, as well as the promotion of satisfaction intensity in related products and services. [5] also pointed out from research results that user reviews are similar to users' needs, ideas, or ways of improvement that provide positive inputs to development personnel.

From the perspective of users, the majority of designs in product promotion are focused on the strengths of products, with shortcomings left off. However, user reviews are the opposite: consumers will take a neutral stance when making comments, pointing out both the strengths and shortcomings of the product. This is in essence a type of promotion that is co-created by a group of consumers, and is therefore of more reference value and is important information for decision-making by new consumers.

From the perspective of developers, launching new versions and functionalities to maintain user freshness is important, but user reviews will directly impact customer retention rate such that excessive negative reviews will be a threat to product promotion and sales, and therefore should not be neglected. Thus, how to strike a balance between retention rate and freshness intensity is a serious challenge to development teams.

III. METHODS

Based on the literature review, this study put forward two areas of improvement that should be addressed in user review analysis: 1. The volume of user reviews was too huge making efficient classification impossible; 2. It was impossible to pinpoint problem areas from user reviews. In light of these two areas, this study adopted a system structure and information visualization to simultaneously resolve the above two problems. Taking advantage of information visualization characteristics, complex data would be converted into images that development team members could understand, and related problems could then be quickly clarified.

Thus, this study was divided into four stages: 1. User review data collection; 2. Data arrangement and analysis; 3. Visualization of analysed results; and 4. Heuristic evaluation, as explained in Figure 1.

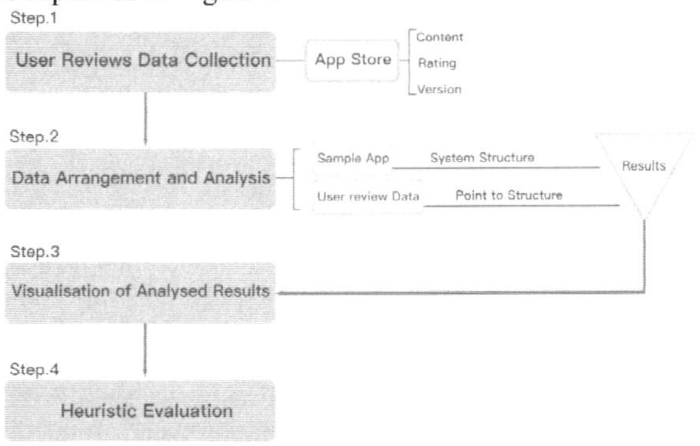

Figure 1. Study Flowchart

Sample App Selection

The two appropriate sample apps selected for examination (due to the fact that the maximum number of user reviews iTunes allows for scraping is 500, app selection criteria in this study was having more than 500 reviews) in this study were Walkr (Figure 2) and OPUS: Rocket of Whispers (Figure 3) after obtaining agreements from the two related development teams to provide assistance. The following is a brief introduction of the two development teams and the respective apps they have developed.

Walkr

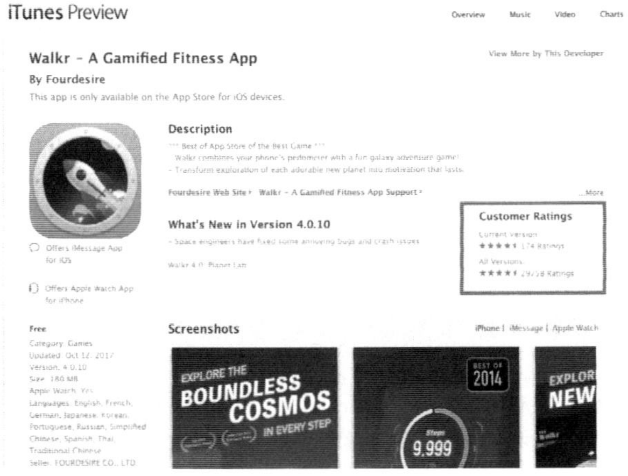

Figure 2. Walkr (captured on 13th October 2017), data source:iTunes

Walkr (Figure 2) is a game app developed by Fourdesire in Taiwan that was released in August 2014 with nearly 30,000 user reviews on versions released in the United States.

OPUS: Rocket of Whispers

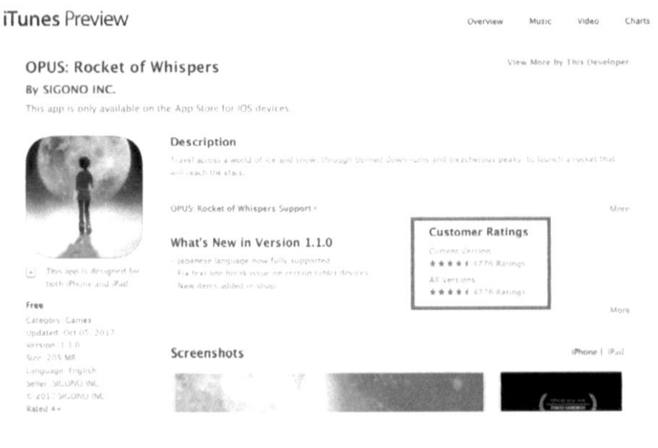

Figure 3. OPUS: Rocket of Whispers (captured on 13th October 2017), data source:iTunes

OPUS: Rocket of Whispers was a game app developed by Sigono in Taiwan that was released on 14th September 2017. Its user reviews in Taiwan reached 4,000 immediately after release.

The following steps and pictures are presented using Walkr as an example.

Step 1. User Review data collection

Since it was time-consuming and error-prone to manually enter reviews, Python programming was employed because of its simple logic, fast download speed, and ability to handle massive data. The development team only needed to enter the review download addresses that Apple iTunes allowed to open and define the data needed, and they could then be quickly extracted. The reviews were from the Apple iTunes stores in United States and Taiwan to ensure languages used in post-hoc comparison were English and Chinese only. The following five types of data were also scraped: review date (Date), review title (Title), review content (Content), Rating (Rate), and version (Version). However, due to the fact that the maximum number of user reviews Apple iTunes allowed for scraping in each app was 500, this study ranked the data based on the feature 'Most Helpful'. Users mark that they agree or disagree with other users' reviews, and the system would rank the reviews based on number of users that agreed to determine the 'Most Helpful' feature. That is, the more users who agreed with a review, the higher the review would be ranked. This ranking mechanism could eliminate invalid reviews to a certain extent, alleviating the burden in subsequent data arrangement. For each app, 500 user reviews would be scraped as raw data, which were then directly exported to Excel, as shown in Figure 4.

date	title	content	rate	version
2015-03-05'	Not Happy with	You really should allow us to j	1	1.3.6
2017-07-13'	Need to update w	Can't play as after the July upd	1	4.0.0
2016-08-30'	Crashes all the ti	This app used to be great, cute	1	2.2.3
2017-07-13'	Update: New ver	Updated review: I was really lc	1	4.0.0
2017-07-13'	Great walking ap	Another Update: Unfortunately	1	4.0.1
2017-07-14'	Support Needed	I have to edit my original 5star	1	4.0.1
2016-02-29'	Really like it, but	This game encourages you to w	2	2.1.7
2016-03-10'	I hate the ads	The game is fun, save a few litt	2	2.1.7
2016-01-07'	A fun, yet tediou	It would be nice if there was m	2	2.1.5

Figure 4. Partial map of Walkr's raw review data

Step 2. Data Arrangement and Analysis

This stage involved raw data arrangement and mapping of the app framework. Raw data were sorted based on Rate and reviews that were 3-stars and below with emojis or garbled reviews were eliminated; only raw data refreshed with text arrangement were retained.

Secondly, the app structure was drawn using mind mapping, and all clickable buttons in the app were drawn from left to right according to the page flowchart (Figure 5). Lastly, Python programming was employed using the text search function to search for the function areas mentioned in the reviews, that is, all the reviews that mentioned a certain function were included in the mind map (Figure 6 is a magnified version of the area enclosed in red in Figure 5). Orange text represents 3-star reviews and red text represents 1-star and 2-star reviews.

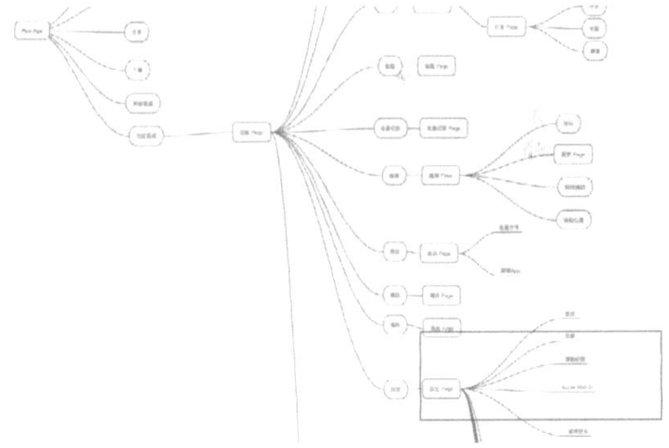

Figure 5. Partial system structure of Walkr(1)

Figure 6. Partial system structure of Walkr(2)

Step 3. Visualization of analysed results

App structure is often large, and although problems are mostly concentrated in certain areas, with reviews included, too much data and too big a page will not only make it difficult to spot the problematic function area, but also make the review text section impossible to read. Therefore, in the visualization design stage, the functions mentioned in user reviews were first sorted out in the structure using a version timeline to sort on the timeline axis that could on the one hand enhance readability, and on the other hand allow the development team to gain a clear understanding of whether the functional problem in the version was ongoing or coincidental, and facilitate decisions on update priorities. Figure 8 is a visualization chart.

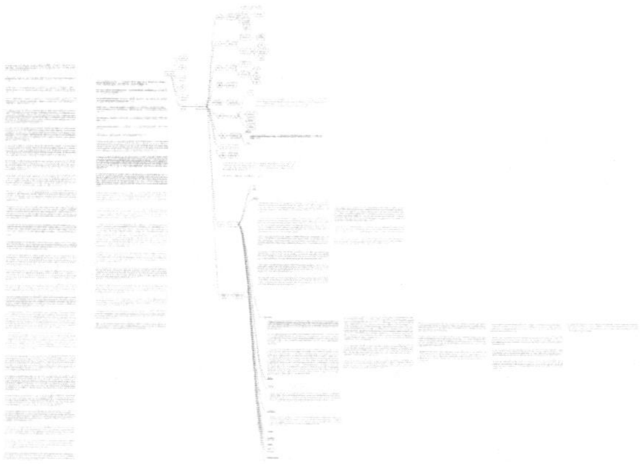

Figure 7. Partial system structure of Walkr(3)

Figure 8 is a visualization chart showing the user reviews analyzed by Walkr and it is composed of six block areas that allowed the development team members to easily understand and analyze the results. The meanings represented by the six block areas are presented in the following accordingly.

1) App name

2) Icon: orange circle represents 3-star user reviews and red circle represents 1- and 2-star reviews.

3) Problematic functional structure (viewed together with block area 4): the functional structure mentioned in user reviews in the system structure in Figure 7. For example, activity tracking was mentioned by users in Figure 6 and, therefore, activity tracking was included in this block area to be viewed in conjunction with the version timeline.

4) Version Timeline (viewed in conjunction with block area 3): version that users reported problematic in the related function. For example, under activity tracking in Figure 6, there were 9 users reporting a problem in the following 8 versions: 1.3.3, 1.3.5, 1.3.6, 2.0.1, 2.0.2, 2.1.8, 2.1.10, and 2.1.13, all of which were 3-star ratings and were therefore denoted by orange circles. According to the activity tracking in Figure 8, the order was sorted according to versions. Among them, version 2.02 appeared twice and was therefore denoted with "x2" on top.

5) Sentiment Analysis: the higher the number, the more negative the user sentiment is. Red represents 1- and 2-star user ratings; orange represents 3-star user ratings.

6) Raw Data: the number of user reviews searched are noted here; the number of 3-star, 2-star, and 1-star reviews are also given; grey represents the number of 4- and 5-star user reviews.

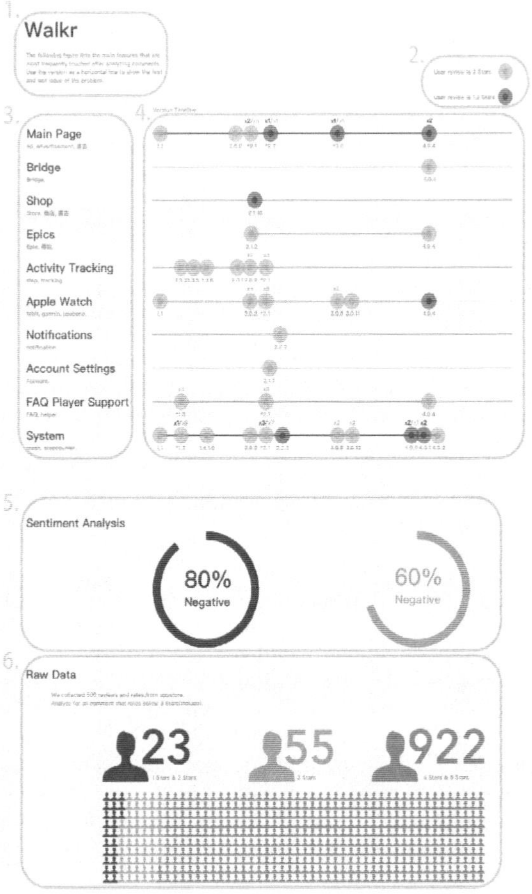

Figure 8. Partial system structure of Walkr(3)

Method

Taking the epic function in Figure 8 as an example: when users reported problems in version 2.1.2, which were also reported in version 4.04, it could be deduced that such functional problems might likely be coincidental and perhaps had to do with hardware problems in users' mobile phones. In that case, developers could choose to repair functions that were mentioned more frequently in reviews. For example, for the function of Apple Watch (The sixth item in block 3 of Figure 8) that users have repeatedly mentioned about system failure from version 1.1 to version 4.0.4, development teams could intercept the programming codes directly to test and repair the related area shown on the picture.

As for system function (The last item in block 3 of Figure 8), there were significantly more orange circles (3-star) than red circles (1- and 2-star), indicating on the one hand that there was not an urgent need for system improvement. However, repairs targeted at maintenance purposes such as system logistics, interface design, and logo design would make the system more better and could closely follow users' needs. On the other hand, it can be seen (In block 4 of Figure 8) that the development team has actually made gradual system-related revisions as shown in the increase in spacing between version 3 and version 4, indicating that system stability and overall logistics design were gradually recognised by users resulting in lower probability of getting reviews of 3 stars (inclusive) and below. This could be viewed as a sign of the gradual maturity of the system.

Step 4. Heuristic Evaluation

This study adopted a heuristic evaluation for validation by sending the development team the system architecture and a design of the visualisation chart for review together with two questionnaires that they were asked to fill out as feedback. There were 7 true-false questions in Questionnaire I aiming at understanding whether the results of the present study were useful to development teams. There were four short-answer questions in Questionnaire II, the topics of which were focused on the following: methodology adopted by the development team in previous user review analysis, possible dilemmas development teams have encountered, and the development team's thoughts on the recommendations made in the present study. Below is a brief introduction of the background of the three experts invited to participate in the evaluation (as shown in Table 1) and the two questionnaires (Table 2 and Table 3) of questions listed with respective reasons for question design.

The questions were designed not only to help the researcher of this study obtain the development team's thoughts and recommendations on the results, but also (and equally importantly) to share the development team's practical experience in handling issues and bottlenecks in the past, the essential elements and application approaches needed for user review behaviour analysis, and the identification of context from feedback while helping the development team further understand the advantages and shortcomings of apps so that the development team can draw on the advantages for better performance in the future while making corrections to deficiencies for further improvement.

The three experts invited to take part in the heuristic evaluation were team members in charge of user behaviour studies. In Questionnaire I, all three experts raised the issue that the system architecture or functions seemed irrelevant to the overall system architecture. To address this issue, the following explanation was presented to the development team: the user review analysis approach provided in the present study was designed exclusively for internal use within the development team. Therefore, during architectural mapping, the development team could refer to the files of the original system architecture design and edit the design accordingly until reaching full integration without leaving any deviation. Regarding mapping function keywords, the way the present study named and understood the keywords might be different than that of the development team. However, if the system functions chart was created by the development team, not only could the team focus on new functions for independent analysis, but common function issues could also be identified for further investigation, resulting in a higher level of accuracy. The experts also mentioned that they hoped to have more detailed user reviews.

TABLE I. LIST OF EXPERTS

Expert	Position	Years of Experience	Affiliation
A	Sales	3.5 years	Fourdesire
B	Sales	4 years	Fourdesire
C	Product Manager	8 years	Sigono

TABLE II. QUESTIONNAIRE I.

No	Reason for question design	Question
1	To understand the background and experience of the team member.	What is your position in the development team? How many years of related experience do you have?
2	To understand whether the developer agrees with the importance of user reviews.	As a study of user behaviour, do you think that User Review analysis will help improve development projects?
3	To understand whether negative reviews have a higher priority for consideration of handling and if duration is an important basis.	Did the ratings of 1-, 2-, and 3-star help the development team quickly adjust the priority list of issues to be handled?
4		Was information related to the problematic version and the duration of problem an important indicator to the development team?
5	To understand whether the present study can effectively help alleviate the developer's burden in analysing user reviews.	The present study combined user reviews with system function architecture. Did this approach enhance the development team's precision in identifying and handling the problem areas?
6		To continue with the above, did the problems located in the function area that was identified in user reviews (such as the area enclosed in red shown in the figure below) help shorten the time needed for the development team in system optimisation?
7	To understand whether the results of the present study are accurate.	According to the development team's past experiences, were the problematic functions listed in the visualisation chart of the present study accurate? (Here accuracy is defined as: 1. whether the system functions pointed

No	Reason for question design	Question
1	To understand the background and experience of the team member.	What is your position in the development team? How many years of related experience do you have?
		out in user reviews were accurate, and 2. whether the function actually existed in user feedback.

This was due to the fact that iTunes' limit on the number of user review downloads allowed for each app was 500, so the present study could not provide more to the team. The general public is not allowed to obtain all user reviews for any single app. However, the app's developer is allowed to download every single review. Therefore, if developers are to take charge of data scraping from different versions, especially scraping 1-star reviews, a certain degree of improved operationality is guaranteed, meaning that results will be more accurate.

TABLE III. QUESTIONNAIRE II.

No	Reason for question design	Question
1	To understand the benefits the development team has gained from the results of the present study.	What do you think is the most helpful feature in the areas of updating and optimisation provided in the case study of the present study?
2	To understand the past issues encountered by the development team and to try to resolve them using the results of the present study.	What are the most common issues or bottlenecks the development team has encountered in previous versions?
3	To understand the important features that the development team will pay attention to when studying user reviews.	How did your development team handle user reviews in the past?
4	To understand the expert's suggestions to the results of the present study.	Is there anything else or any particular item the development team would like to further understand that has not been discussed in the results?
5	Q&A	Lastly, if there are still any questions or interest in the topic of this study, you are welcome to leave message here with your contact information. We will reply as soon as possible.

Feedback from the three experts on analysis made in the present study is arranged and presented as follows:

1) After the new version release of a function, the follow-up evaluation should be conducted on user reviews related to this function.

2) Add more enrichment to the visualisation chart.

3) In terms of user reviews of higher ratings, in the case of Walkr, which had relatively fewer 1- to 3-star reviews, analysing 4- and 5-star reviews may help find out what functions users like and why.

4) The suggested approach was able to expedite the identification of problem areas and versions.

5) Visualisation design facilitated understanding of the severity of issues and the frequency of occurrence.

6) To understand whether issues were resolved by version iteration.

7) System architecture and function names did not fit the overall system.

8) The number of reviews was not enough, and the flexibility of the visualisation chart was limited.

Lastly, the questionnaires that were returned showed that after eliminating the programming bugs that needed repair, the development team did not know how to focus on the issues raised in user reviews, nor did they know how to set up a priority list of issues to be corrected. In other words, team members did not have a dedicated set of analytical tools that allowed them to handle the large volume of user reviews from various sources, and they had not set a priority list of issues to be corrected.

IV. CONCLUSIONS

As seen from the analysis in the present study, user reviews are a key factor in judging whether there is gradual growth in an app. If there are enough user reviews, taking a comprehensive view on user reviews helps developers understand whether an app is on the right track for growth. Visualisation charts also provide development teams easy understanding in user review distribution and direction, reducing the search time for identifying issues while quickly understanding the real needs of users.

It is found from the two case studies that if an app only has a few negative reviews, if user reviews are classified into directional (clearly pointing out the area in system function or architecture) system architecture review and non-directional (mostly focusing on narrative of user experience) user review, few directional user reviews mean that the app currently does not have any issues in structural functions. The majority of users are satisfied with the system functions and have therefore switched focus to expressing ideas and suggestions to the system, hoping that the development team can follow the direction of the reviews in updating. At this time, the development team can follow the original plan to announce the new release of functions to increase user freshness. On the contrary, having more directional than non-directional user reviews means that users think that there is problem in the system function. Ignoring users' requests at this time will result in user churn. Thus, the development team must fix the problem as soon as possible, rather than releasing new functions, to calm down angry users and alleviate user churn.

The greatest challenge encountered in the course of this study was in heuristic review because this study is still at the model design stage; it needs verification and evaluation from an outstanding and experienced development team in the industry to help perfect the design process of the research results. In addition, business secrets may be involved in the research process, which most developers cannot provide for assistance in evaluation. At the same time, core members of the development team were not easy to get in touch with; emails sent to development companies were often declined by the support team, resulting in a challenge in seeking experts to participate in the heuristic evaluation.

REFERENCES

[1] S. E. Ante, Amazon: Turning consumer opinions into gold. Business Week, 15, 2009.

[2] B. Bickart and R. M. Schindler, "Internet forums as influential sources of consumer information, " Journal of interactive marketing, vol. 15, no. 3, pp. 31-40, 2001.

[3] Y. Chen, and J. Xie, "Online consumer review: Word- of-mouth as a new element of marketing communication mix," *Management science*, vol. *54*, no. 3, pp. 477-491, 2008.

[4] D. Godes, and D. Mayzlin, "Using online conversations to study word-of-mouth communication," *Marketing science*, vol. *23,* no. 4, pp. 545-560, 2004.

[5] E. Guzman, and W. Maalej, "How do users like this feature? a fine grained sentiment analysis of app reviews," 2014 IEEE 22nd International Requirements Engineering Conference (RE), Karlskrona, 2014, pp. 153-162, doi: 10.1109/RE.2014.6912257.

[6] C. W. Hart, J. L. Heskett, and W. E. Jr. Sasser, "The profitable art of service recovery," *Harvard Business Review, vol. 68*, no. 4, pp. 148–156, 1990.

[7] M. Hu, and B. Liu, "Mining and summarizing customer reviews," Proc. 10th ACM SIGKDD international conference on Knowledge discovery and data mining (KDD '04), ACM, New York, NY, USA, 2004, pp. 168-177, doi: 10.1145/1014052.1014073.

[8] C. Iacob, and R. Harrison, "Retrieving and analyzing mobile apps feature requests from online reviews," 2013 10th Working Conference on Mining Software Repositories (MSR). IEEE Press, 2013, pp. 41-44, doi: 10.1109/MSR.2013.6624001.

[9] X. Meng, and H. Wang, "Mining user reviews: from specification to summarization," In Proceedings of the ACL-IJCNLP 2009 Conference Short Papers, pp. 177-180, 2009.

[10] D. Pagano, and W. Maalej, "User feedback in the appstore: An empirical study," 2013 21st IEEE International Requirements Engineering Conference (RE), Rio de Janeiro, 2013, pp. 125-134, doi: 10.1109/RE.2013.6636712.

[11] G. Somprasertsri, and P. Lalitrojwong, (2010). "Mining Feature-Opinion in Online Customer Reviews for Opinion Summarization," *J.UCS*, vol. *16,* no. 6, pp. 938-955, 2010.

[12] F. T. C. Tan, and R. Vasa, "Toward a social media usage policy," Proc. ACIS 2011, pp. 84-89.

[13] R. Vasa, L. Hoon, K. Mouzakis, and A. Noguchi, "A preliminary analysis of mobile app user reviews," Proc. 24th Australian Computer- Human Interaction Conference (OzCHI '12), ACM, New York, NY, USA, 2012, pp. 241-244, doi: 10.1145/2414536.2414577.

[14] I. E. Vermeulen, and D. Seegers, "Tried and tested: The impact of online hotel reviews on consumer consideration," Tourism management, vol. 30, no. 1, pp. 123-127, 2009.

[15] P. M. Vu, T. T. Nguyen, H. V. Pham, and T. T. Nguyen, "Mining user opinions in mobile app reviews: A keyword-based approach (t), " 2015 30th IEEE/ACM International Conference on Automated Software Engineering (ASE), Lincoln, NE, 2015, pp. 749-759, doi: 10.1109/ASE.2015.85

[16] Q. Ye, R. Law, and B. Gu, "The impact of online user reviews on hotel room sales, " International Journal of Hospitality Management, vol. 28, no. 1, pp. 180-182, 2009.

[17] C. H. Yin, "網路口碑對線上應用程式的購買意圖之影響-以 Apple App Store 為例" [The Influence of eWOM on purchase Intention of Online Applications: An Empirical Study of Apple App Store], 2011, URL: http://hdl.handle.net/11296/t9tju5.

Moving with Style: Classifying Human and Robot Movement at Home

Trenton Schulz, Jo Herstad, Jim Torresen
University of Oslo
Postbox 1072 Blindern
0316 Oslo, Norway
Email: [trentonw|johe|jimtoer]@ifi.uio.no

***Abstract*—A robot moving in the home is a new experience for most people. Classifying the different ways that humans and robots move together can help in designing interactions. In this paper, we first put robots' movements into two categories: global—where a robot changes position in the home—or local—where a robot's position does not change, but parts of it move. We also look at the idea of animation and how it can give a robot style. Building on these definitions, we present four movement conditions to classify movement between a human and robot at home. Using familiarity, we can recognize some of these conditions from other interactions we have. Using animation, we can give the robot a style that can make the robot's movement more familiar and easier to understand. We close the paper with possible ways of using this classification system for future research.**

***Keywords*–human-robot interaction; animation; style; movement; familiarity; home**

I. INTRODUCTION

The "elderly wave" is an issue that many western countries are examining [1]. The number of people that will be retiring and needing care will be much larger than the people entering the workforce for these jobs. Consequently, some countries and areas have set goals that more elderly should live independently at home longer. One way of addressing this issue is to turn to *welfare technology* that can assist the elderly [2]. One example is using the Internet of Things and smart home sensors for reporting and helping elderly complete tasks [3][4]. Another example is using these sensors to provide someone with a warning when things go wrong, such as an elderly person falling [5]. But all these sensors in the house may transform it from a home to a place where elderly may feel they are under surveillance with no privacy and little control over their life.

Robots may be an alternative for helping out at home. Robots can be mobile and customized for handling different kinds of tasks. A robot may give the person a chance of feeling in control and a feeling of privacy. For example, an elderly person could tell the robot to leave the room. Robots cannot replace a human in every context, but it can provide support for issues when a person cannot be present or help contact a person. Robots may help in ways that would otherwise require another human to always be present, and have diverse knowledge. For example, robots can collect data and use algorithms to give early warnings about issues (e.g., falling down, low blood pressure, or suffering from poor nutrition).

Robots have been making their way into the home. Domestic robots cut the lawn and vacuum, but other robots have been around to provide entertainment (the robot dog Aibo [6]) or stress relief (the Paro seal [7]). We are working to create a robot that stays with the elderly at home and serves as a safety alarm and perform other services that the elderly want. The aim is to improve quality of life of the elderly at home. It is an opportunity for collaboration between the robot, the elderly at home, and the assisted living help.

Unlike other types of technology at home that is either stationary or wearable, robots can move around and possibly perform tasks on their own. This raises several questions: How can we make the robot familiar? How do robots' movement affect our interaction with them? Are there better ways for this movement to happen? We wish to examine these questions. We will begin by trying to define animation, movement, and style (Section II). Next, we propose a framework for classifying movements between a person and a robot (Section III). Then, we will look at how familiarity can help make this robot motion familiar, and we will present how style created through animation can help in this familiarity (Section IV). Finally, we will look at some limitations with this framework and ideas for future work (Section V) before concluding the article (Section VI).

II. BACKGROUND: MOVEMENT, ANIMATION, AND STYLE

First, we will define animation, movement, and style for this paper. We will also look at some projects that have involved robots and animation.

The physical idea of movement (or motion) is a change in position over time that can work for some types of robot movement we will call this *global movement* (Figure 1a). If we were to imagine the robot in a house, global movement would mean the robot moves in a room or moves to another room. Let us define another type of motion where parts of the robot move, but its global position does not change (Figure 1b). This is *local movement*. Returning to our imaginary robot at home above: its local movement would be moving parts on its body (for example, rotating its body or moving an appendage on its body) that do not move the complete robot in the room. There is one situation left: *no movement*. That is, when a robot standing still and not moving any parts of the body. To keep the classification system simple, let us assume that no movement is a special case of local movement. Of course, local movement and global movement can be combined.

There are many ways a robot's movement can be accomplished. The robot can move at a constant speed, it can speed up as it starts out and slow down, or it can back up to get a running start and can abruptly stop when it gets to the destination. We can think of these approaches as *animating* the robot. Normally, we associate *animation* with cartoons and film, where one combines frames together to create movement on screens, but the *American Heritage Dictionary* also defines animation as, "the act, process, or result of imparting life, interest, spirit, motion, or activity" [8].

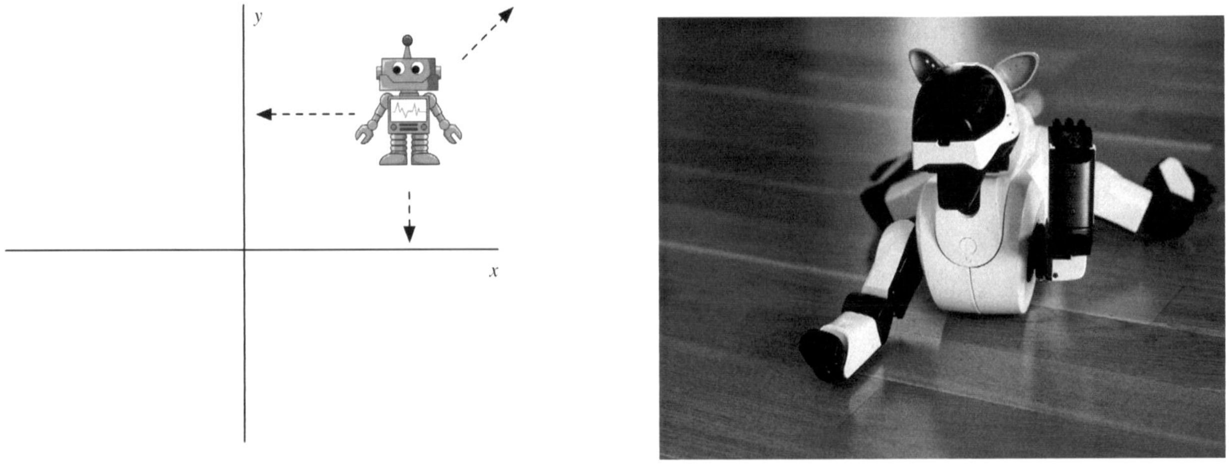

(a) (b)

Figure 1. Examples of global and local movement: in global movement (a), the robot moves in a two-dimensional plane; the Aibo laying down and waving (b) is an example of local robot movement.

Another way we can think of animating robots is *moving with style*. With *style*, we are using Gallaher's definition: "the way in which a behavior is performed" [9, p. 133]. Gallaher pointed out that style can also be thought of as *expressive movement*. Gallaher was looking at people's style, but this concept has been successfully applied to robots [10].

How does animation make the robot move with style? Animation gives the robot an interesting way of moving. This animated motion can make the robot seem likes it has a personality. The motion can also help the robot to better communicate what it is planning to do (the robot's intention for lack of a better term).

Are there any design principles or guidelines for adding this style? Looking at the history of animation on film, Thomas and Johnston [11] documented twelve principles of animation that animators at Disney used to create good animations. These principles include: (*a*) *squash and stretch*—an animated object squashes and stretches its form, but never truly loses its recognizable shape; (*b*) *anticipated action*—an object needs to prepare itself before performing an action; (*c*) *follow through and overlapping action*—actions are not done in isolation, characters move seamlessly between them; (*d*) *arcs*—limbs move in arcs, not straight up-down, left-right motions; (*e*) *secondary action*—the object's main action causes other secondary actions to occur at the same time; and (*f*) *exaggeration*—over-emphasizing an action helps people understand a characters feelings.

Adopting principles of animation from film can help in making robots animated. Breazeal [12] references them when working on the Kismet robot. Van Breemen [13] tried to apply these principles in the facial expressions of the iCat [14]. His reason for doing this was to make the robot's behavior more natural and less machine-like. This would make the robot easier to accept and have easier interactions.

As mentioned above, animation can make things "look alive" or give them *animacy*. This may also give us some feelings about them. Several experiments have been run where a person works with an animated robot for a while, but then is asked to "kill" it by, for example, destroying it with a hammer or turning off its power to erase its memory [15]–[17].

There are several examples of using animation to communicate a robot's intention. Takayama, Dooley, and Ju [18] showed how the animation principles can make it easier for a human to understand and predict what a robot is doing. Gielniak and Thomaz [19] found that creating anticipation for motion (i.e., one of the twelve principles of animation from above) made it easier for people to predict what the robot was going to do. In a later study, Gielniak and Thomaz [20] experimented with exaggerating movement for a robot to tell stories. People that saw the exaggerated movements remembered those parts of the story better. These movements need not be big or elaborate. For example, in a nod to the animation principle of secondary action, a study with elderly people ran by Louie, McColl, and Nejat [21] found that the participants enjoyed the "facial expressions and different tones of voice" [21, p. 148]. Finally, Baraka, Rosenthal, and Veloso [22] made the intentions of a robot moving around independently more understandably by adding animated lights to make the robot's state more visible.

III. Classifying Human and Robot Movement

Human-computer interaction (HCI) has a tradition of studying the use, design, and evaluating ways interfaces and interactions are taking place in different contexts between humans and stationary computers in workplace settings, public places, and home settings. Mobile computing raised the importance of the context of use and interaction to researchers' attention. This lead to the research area of *context aware computing* [23]. Ubiquitous and ambient computing raise the idea of computers in the home, but hidden from view and not moving.

The conditions for the interaction taking place between humans and computers in a stationary and mobile situation are similar; there is a stable spatial arrangement between the people and computers. In both situations, humans and computers are interacting in the same place, with a stationary relationship in-between the human and the computer.

The spatial conditions change when robots enter the scene. We may be used to moving things outside our home like automobiles, buses, boats and trams. We are all living in a shared world where we are used to other people moving around at home and in public places. Yet in a home setting, we are not familiar or used to *things* moving around except when moving into a place, (e.g., renovating, or moving out of a place). Furniture is moved, and there is movement of things by residents and guests in the home, but very few things move *on their own*.

In the home context, we can classify this movement: (*a*) Things that we move around: furniture, peripherals, clothes, machines like vacuum cleaners or furniture on wheels. (*b*) Things moving themselves: domestic robots (robot vacuum cleaners and robot lawn mowers) and our safety alarm robots. If we examine the spatial arrangement for movement between one human and one robot and classify the movement as *local* and *global* from Section II, we get the following four conditions (Table I):

1) Human moves locally and the robot moves locally,
2) Human moves locally and the robot moves globally,
3) Human moves globally and the robot moves locally, and
4) Human moving globally and the robot moving globally.

TABLE I. MOVEMENT CONDITIONS FOR HUMANS AND ROBOTS

Condition	Human	Robot
1	Local	Local
2	Local	Global
3	Global	Local
4	Global	Global

This framework for classification also gives a way to compare the human-robot movement with other objects. In Condition 1 and Condition 3, when the robot is moving locally (including being completely still as per Section II), the human is either moving locally or globally. This is similar to conditions for interacting with stationary computers. We can see Condition 1 when a person watches TV, and we can see Condition 3 when a person approaches a switch or walks towards a remote control.

The other conditions are more unusual in the home before robots. For example, Condition 2 happens when toys are moving. But Condition 4 does not have good analogs other than perhaps chasing a moving toy. These other conditions also indicate something that is unfamiliar. Gibson and Ingold [24] find we are indeed familiar with movement, and they work out the importance of movement on perception. But what we are not used to is being around things that move—and not being controlled or steered by other people! What can we do to make this situation more familiar?

IV. FAMILIARITY AND MOVING ROBOTS AT HOME

To make robots moving at home more familiar, we need to examine what familiarity is. Once we have an idea what familiarity is, we can look at how we can make a robot's movement familiar. We can also see how animation and style can help in making these situations familiar.

A. Familiarity

Familiarity plays a role in how people interact and use things and objects. The common sense meaning of familiarity is trivial. The familiar is often what we are comfortable and safe with, be it situations, technologies, relationships, activities or other people. We are often unfamiliar with is things we do not engage with, have no skills with or understanding of, or are foreign to us.

These three concepts; involvement, understanding and unity of user-world are, according to Turner and Walle [25], ideas that we can apply to get a grip on familiarity. Turner and Walle stated that familiarity unfolds over time. Hence, familiarity points to activities of daily living where we are engaged and skillful people going about our everyday lives. When breakdowns or interruptions happens, i.e., something is faulty, missing or in our way for us to proceed, the separation between people and their world is taking place, and equipment and activities become visible as objects for our analysis [26]. However, this is not the primordial way of being in the world.

Van de Walle, Turner, and Davenport claimed, "What is observable are the outcomes: easiness, confidence, success, performance, which are all manifestations or signs of familiarity," [27, p. 467]. This shows that familiarity is subjective; it can be described by observing activities or asked questions in interviews. One way of investigating possible ways of using robots in the home is to learn from what we already are familiar with of movement. Harrigan and Rosenthal [28] provided an introduction into non-verbal human behavior, including *proxemics*. Hall [29] observed that human-social spatial distances vary by degree of familiarity between the people interacting and the number of people interacting. Hall later provided a framework that identifies the main social spatial zones by interaction and situations. He estimated these distances visually in terms of arms lengths, close contact and threat/flight distances—and researchers have since assigned precise numerical values.

B. Making a robot's movement more familiar

For all people, movement is a phenomenon that they are familiar with. Moving within a place such as a home are examples of the movement that we all experience in our everyday life. We are familiar with seeing other people move. We are familiar with seeing things move (for example, in the house). We move about in concert with things such as phones, watches, and footwear. There is nothing extraordinary with this familiarity of movement of things and other people.

By focusing on familiarity of movement, we build on people's preexisting involvement, understanding and relationship with the everyday world. We know how to move along bicycles, automobiles, trains, trucks, metro cars as large objects that move about. Even though we do not see the driver of a metro car, we are familiar with the movement that unfolds. In our homes, we are familiar with other people, and perhaps animals, moving about the house. We are also familiar with moving things around in our homes by ourselves, or by other people. Moving a chair closer to the fireplace, or carrying wood to the stove are two examples that we are familiar with. If not done by ourselves, it is at least something that we have seen in pictures or on film.

Walters, Dautenhahn, Te Boekhorst, *et al.* [30] have used human-human proxemics for investigating interaction with robots. Yet this is all based upon a model of distances and proxemics that has human-human movement as its base. Another possibility may be to use human-thing distances and proxemics as the starting point. This would be grounded in our familiarity with movement of things.

If we think of familiar movement where an object moves with us, we can find some examples: (*a*) navigating traffic, with cars, bicycle and public transport material, (*b*) walking with a rolling suitcase, (*c*) operating a wheelchair, (*d*) operating a walking stick, and (*e*) operating a walker. We are all familiar with these movements, but there is no field of literature to find out more about these types of movement. Yet the concept of familiarity helps us find these examples.

C. Making a robot more familiar by giving it style

In Section II, we posited that an animated robot moves with style. Several of the robots from Section II do not move from their location, but the way they move their parts makes them appear more friendly and easier to relate to. Animation also makes it possible to experiment with different kinds of interaction depending on the animation style.

To jump back to HCI and graphical user interfaces, programmers can move items across the screen in many ways, but animating can help people understand what is going on when they are using a program. There is a different mood or tone when a window minimizes by shrinking down to a small area on the screen versus simply scaling the window. Just as animated graphical user interface elements help explain what is going on, the way a robot moves can be helpful in explaining what is going on in an interaction with a robot. Naturally, there are limitations—for example, robots must obey the laws of physics and some types of motion put extra strain on the robot [31]—but we can give a robot its own style by animating it.

Animation can be present in all conditions in Section III. For example, in Condition 1, the robot does not move globally, but its local movement can still be animated by moving parts of its body. This animation can give the robot a style, add some personality, and give the effect of presence for the robot [32]. For example, if the person is asking a question or the robot is providing feedback, animation can provide feedback to the person about the robot's state and other relevant information. This does not have to be complex; a part of the robot rotating can suffice, or lights blinking to indicate the robot is listening. A simple rotation that follows the person can help keep the interaction going in Condition 3.

Condition 2 can build on top of the animation from Condition 1. Here, the animation of parts of the robot's body can be combined with its global movement. For example, if the person asks for some privacy, the robot can start moving away. This can give the person a sense of what the robot is going to do. Animation could also affect how fast the robot moves, combining animations could make a robot "appear" angry, sad, surprised, or happy.

Since these two conditions can build on top of each other, animation can also help with the *transition* between them. This can offer the human a cue to the robot's intention (i.e., it is about to move or about to stop as Gielniak and Thomaz [19] researched). From the robot's side, it can also try to determine the human's cue to get information if it too should start or stop.

Condition 4 is still unfamiliar for most of us in indoor settings. But animating the robot's movements can give it a style to make it seem like this condition is more familiar. The way the robot moves can imitate another person or an animal. These imitations can remind us of other situations where we and something else move, and this can make a robot and human moving at the same time more familiar.

Looking at proxemics, animation can aid in building a rapport between the robot and the human. Mumm and Mutlu [33] discuss how a rapport is necessary for people to be willing to get (physically) close to a robot or answer personal questions. Mumm and Mutlu also point out that until a rapport is established, certain actions that signal a good rapport (like maintaining eye contact) should be avoided. Obaid, Sandoval, Złotowski, *et al.* [34] found different distances for an approaching robot based on the posture of the human (sitting or standing).

A framework for looking at movement gives us a way to animate this movement and give it style. The way these movements are animated may influence how willing someone is to interact with it. As Saerbeck and Bartneck [35] found when looking at how people experienced motion of robots, the speed and way a robot moved caused people to describe the personality or mood of the robot. Building on this work, Noordzij, Schmettow, and Lorijn [36] found people associated negative and positive emotion to a simple robot simply by adjusting how it accelerated. On the other hand, if a robot moves too slow, people may assume that the robot can never get anything done and simply will not interact with it. If we desire interaction with a robot that moves, we need to make it an inviting experience.

Finally, familiarity does not have to just be in the *form* of the robot. A challenge we can find from Hoffman and Ju [37] is that robots that resemble something we are familiar with (e.g., an animal or human) may bring expectations that are difficult to achieve with current technology. Instead, a robot moving expressively can be used for clues to interaction. These movements follow physical properties in the world that people are already familiar with and give them a starting point for their interaction.

V. Future Work

There are limitations with this classification as it only looks at a specific case of one human and one robot, and we can explore different directions of movement as well. Yet, even at its simple level, it gives us many questions we can investigate: how can the robot move to bring trust and assurance when the person is working with the robot? What activities can a robot do that are not available when a technology is stationary or only handheld? What conditions are necessary so that people and robots can work together? How are these interactions affected by the animation, proximity, automation, control, and delegation? We can also examine the transition between the different classifications.

Moving with style can be helpful. But different people prefer different styles, and some style may work well in some situations than others. Finding styles that are compatible with the robot, the people, and the situation will be a challenge.

Returning to the issue of having a robot at home with the elderly. Another issue to look at is how the animation can be tested. Many of the animation studies that we cited in Section II were run in lab situations. This works well for testing items in a controlled environment, but robots at home need to work in more chaotic environments. Testing the animations out in a home environment may be necessary to see if the animation is helpful for the elderly.

Though we looked at movement conditions, an issue not examined here is control. From our discussions in gathering requirements from the elderly, people have different opinions about a robot moving at home when they have control of its movement versus it moving on its own. There is also a question about what control means in a home situation with the elderly. In Section I, we highlighted the idea of the elderly asking the robot to leave, but are there points when the robot should stay? Can it easily be called back?

As Chanseau, Lohan, and Aylett [38] found, people who wanted a feeling of control also wanted robots to be more autonomous. The size of the robot and a person's anxiety towards robots also influences proxemics. These issues are important when introducing a robot—especially moving robots—in the home of the elderly. Introducing a robot that can detect falls benefits no one if it moves around the home and becomes an obstacle to stumble over in everyday life. Then, it is a fall *creator* for the elderly instead of a *detector*.

Finally, this classification focused on a single robot and a single person at home. But there are many questions one could explore to expand or apply this in other areas. Are there other situations outside of home where this classification applies as well? What happens when you add more "moving parts" like other people and robots? Does animating a robot work in all situations? What about animating robots that have limited movement? These are all questions to explore in future research.

VI. Conclusion

We have defined animation, movement, familiarity, and style. Using these definitions, we have looked at movement of robots in the home and classified the movement in relation to humans and their movements. We have found parallels with other types of movement in the home and ways that having a robot moving in the home may be unfamiliar to someone. We have also suggested animating the robot will make it move with style. This style can give the robot a personality and make the robot more familiar to people living at home.

We have started our investigation with the elderly by running focus groups and discussing the issues of robots at home and how a robot's appearance and movement affects them. The information and the elderly's opinions have been helpful, and they seem interested in what things robots can do. We will be presenting this in future work and are integrating their feedback into our future activities. We hope our classification of movement and incorporating animation can help in this.

Acknowledgments

This work is partly supported by the Research Council of Norway as a part of the Multimodal Elderly Care Systems (MECS) project, under grant agreement 247697. Thanks also to Tone Bratteteig, Hanne Cecilie Geirbo, Guri Verne, and Diana Saplacan for comments and suggestions.

References

[1] G. Hagemann. (2015). Babyboom og eldrebølge, [Online]. Available from: http://www.norgeshistorie.no/oljealder-og-overflod/hus-og-hjem/1915-babyboom-og-eldrebolge.html [retrieved: 2018-01-17].

[2] D. C. Søndergård, "Future Challenges and the Role of Welfare Technology," Nordic Center for Welfare and Social Issues, Stockholm, Sweden, 2014.

[3] T. Schulz, K. S. Fuglerud, H. Arfwedson, and M. Busch, "A Case Study for Universal Design in the Internet of Things," in *Universal Design 2014: Three Days of Creativity and Diversity*, H. Caltenco, P.-O. Hedvall, A. Larsson, K. Rassmus-Gröhn, and B. Rydeman, Eds., IOS Press, 2014, pp. 45–54, ISBN: 978-1-61499-403-9.

[4] T. Halbach and T. Schulz, "MobileSage – A Prototype Based Case Study for Delivering Context-Aware, Accessible, and Personalized On-Demand Help Content," *International Journal of Advances in Intelligent Systems*, vol. 7, pp. 267–278, 1 & 2 2014, ISSN: 1942-2679.

[5] S. Kido, T. Miyasaka, T. Tanaka, T. Shimizu, and T. Saga, "Fall detection in toilet rooms using thermal imaging sensors," in *2009 IEEE/SICE International Symposium on System Integration (SII)*, 2009, pp. 83–88. doi: 10.1109/SI.2009.5384550.

[6] T. Makimoto and T. T. Doi, "Chip technologies for Entertainment Robots - present and future," in *Digest. International Electron Devices Meeting,*, 2002, pp. 9–16. doi: 10.1109/IEDM.2002.1175768.

[7] K. Wada, T. Shibata, T. Saito, and K. Tanie, "Psychological and social effects of robot assisted activity to elderly people who stay at a health service facility for the aged," in *2003 IEEE International Conference on Robotics and Automation (Cat. No.03CH37422)*, IEEE, 2003, 3996–4001 vol.3, ISBN: 0-7803-7736-2.

[8] *Animation*, in *American Heritage Dictionary of the English Language*, 5th, Houghton Mifflin Harcourt Publishing Company, 2011.

[9] P. E. Gallaher, "Individual differences in nonverbal behavior: Dimensions of style.," *Journal of personality and social psychology*, vol. 63, no. 1, p. 133, 1992.

[10] J. E. Young, T. Igarashi, E. Sharlin, D. Sakamoto, and J. Allen, "Design and Evaluation Techniques for Authoring Interactive and Stylistic Behaviors," *ACM Trans. Interact. Intell. Syst.*, vol. 3, no. 4, 23:1–23:36, 2014, ISSN: 2160-6455. doi: 10.1145/2499671.

[11] F. Thomas and O. Johnston, *The Illusion of Life: Disney Animation*, 1st Hyperion ed. New York: Hyperion, 1995, 575 pp., ISBN: 978-0-7868-6070-8.

[12] C. Breazeal, *Designing Sociable Robots*, ser. Intelligent Robotics and Autonomous Agents. Boston, Massachusetts, USA.: MIT Press, 2002, ISBN: 978-0-262-02510-2.

[13] A. J. N. van Breemen, "Bringing robots to life: Applying principles of animation to robots," in *Proceedings of Shapping Human-Robot Interaction Workshop Held at CHI 2004*, Citeseer, 2004, pp. 143–144.

[14] A. van Breemen, X. Yan, and B. Meerbeek, "iCat: An Animated User-interface Robot with Personality," in *Proceedings of the Fourth International Joint Conference on Autonomous Agents and Multiagent Systems*, ser. AAMAS '05, New York, NY, USA: ACM, 2005, pp. 143–144, ISBN: 978-1-59593-093-4. doi: 10.1145/1082473.1082823.

[15] C. Bartneck, M. Verbunt, O. Mubin, and A. Al Mahmud, "To Kill a Mockingbird Robot," in *2007 2nd ACM/IEEE International Conference on Human-Robot Interaction (HRI)*, 2007, pp. 81–87. doi: 10.1145/1228716.1228728.

[16] C. Bartneck, M. van der Hoek, O. Mubin, and A. Al Mahmud, ""Daisy, daisy, give me your answer do!" switching off a

robot," in *2007 2nd ACM/IEEE International Conference on Human-Robot Interaction (HRI)*, 2007, pp. 217–222.

[17] C. Bartneck, T. Kanda, O. Mubin, and A. Al Mahmud, "The perception of animacy and intelligence based on a robot's embodiment," in *2007 7th IEEE-RAS International Conference on Humanoid Robots (Humanoids 07)*, IEEE, 2007, pp. 300–305, ISBN: 978-1-4244-1861-9.

[18] L. Takayama, D. Dooley, and W. Ju, "Expressing Thought: Improving Robot Readability with Animation Principles," in *Proceedings of the 6th International Conference on Human-Robot Interaction*, ser. HRI '11, New York, NY, USA: ACM, 2011, pp. 69–76, ISBN: 978-1-4503-0561-7. doi: 10.1145/1957656.1957674.

[19] M. J. Gielniak and A. L. Thomaz, "Generating anticipation in robot motion," in *2011 RO-MAN*, 2011, pp. 449–454. doi: 10.1109/ROMAN.2011.6005255.

[20] ——, "Enhancing Interaction Through Exaggerated Motion Synthesis," in *Proceedings of the Seventh Annual ACM/IEEE International Conference on Human-Robot Interaction*, ser. HRI '12, New York, NY, USA: ACM, 2012, pp. 375–382, ISBN: 978-1-4503-1063-5. doi: 10 . 1145 / 2157689.2157813.

[21] W.-Y. G. Louie, D. McColl, and G. Nejat, "Acceptance and Attitudes Toward a Human-like Socially Assistive Robot by Older Adults," *Assistive Technology*, vol. 26, no. 3, pp. 140–150, 2014, ISSN: 1040-0435. doi: 10.1080/10400435.2013.869703.

[22] K. Baraka, S. Rosenthal, and M. Veloso, "Enhancing human understanding of a mobile robot's state and actions using expressive lights," in *2016 25th IEEE International Symposium on Robot and Human Interactive Communication (RO-MAN)*, 2016, pp. 652–657. doi: 10.1109/ROMAN.2016.7745187.

[23] P. Agre, "Changing places: Contexts of awareness in computing," *Human Computer Interaction*, vol. 16, pp. 177–192, 2-3 2001.

[24] K. R. Gibson and T. Ingold, *Tools, Language and Cognition in Human Evolution*. Cambridge University Press, 1994, 504 pp., ISBN: 978-0-521-48541-8.

[25] P. Turner and G. van de Walle, "Familiarity as a basis for universal design," *Gerontechnology*, vol. 5, no. 3, pp. 150–159, 2006, ISSN: 1569-111X. doi: 10.4017/gt.2006.05.03.004.00.

[26] T. Winograd and F. Flores, *Understanding Computers and Cognition: A New Foundation for Design*. Intellect Books, 1986, 236 pp., ISBN: 978-0-89391-050-1.

[27] G. Van de Walle, P. Turner, and E. Davenport, "A study of familiarity," in *Human-Computer Interaction-INTERACT*, vol. 3, 2003, pp. 463–70.

[28] J. Harrigan and R. Rosenthal, *New Handbook of Methods in Nonverbal Behavior Research*. Oxford University Press, 2008.

[29] E. T. Hall, *The Hidden Dimension*, 1st. New York, NY, US: Doubleday & Co, 1966, vol. xii, 201 pp.

[30] M. L. Walters, K. Dautenhahn, R. Te Boekhorst, *et al.*, "An empirical framework for human-robot proxemics," in *Procs of New Frontiers in Human-Robot Interaction*, Edinburgh, Scotland, 2009.

[31] M. J. Gielniak, C. K. Liu, and A. L. Thomaz, "Secondary action in robot motion," in *19th International Symposium in Robot and Human Interactive Communication*, 2010, pp. 310–315. doi: 10.1109/ROMAN.2010.5598730.

[32] W. A. Bainbridge, J. Hart, E. S. Kim, and B. Scassellati, "The effect of presence on human-robot interaction," in *RO-MAN 2008 - The 17th IEEE International Symposium on Robot and Human Interactive Communication*, 2008, pp. 701–706. doi: 10.1109/ROMAN.2008.4600749.

[33] J. Mumm and B. Mutlu, "Human-robot Proxemics: Physical and Psychological Distancing in Human-robot Interaction," in *Proceedings of the 6th International Conference on Human-Robot Interaction*, ser. HRI '11, New York, NY, USA: ACM, 2011, pp. 331–338, ISBN: 978-1-4503-0561-7. doi: 10.1145/1957656.1957786.

[34] M. Obaid, E. B. Sandoval, J. Złotowski, *et al.*, "Stop! That is close enough. How body postures influence human-robot proximity," in *2016 25th IEEE International Symposium on Robot and Human Interactive Communication (RO-MAN)*, 2016, pp. 354–361. doi: 10.1109/ROMAN.2016.7745155.

[35] M. Saerbeck and C. Bartneck, "Perception of Affect Elicited by Robot Motion," in *Proceedings of the 5th ACM/IEEE International Conference on Human-Robot Interaction*, ser. HRI '10, Piscataway, NJ, USA: IEEE Press, 2010, pp. 53–60, ISBN: 978-1-4244-4893-7.

[36] M. L. Noordzij, M. Schmettow, and M. R. Lorijn, "Is an Accelerating Robot Perceived As Energetic or As Gaining in Speed?" In *Proceedings of the 2014 ACM/IEEE International Conference on Human-Robot Interaction*, ser. HRI '14, New York, NY, USA: ACM, 2014, pp. 258–259, ISBN: 978-1-4503-2658-2. doi: 10.1145/2559636.2559793.

[37] G. Hoffman and W. Ju, "Designing Robots With Movement in Mind," *Journal of Human-Robot Interaction*, vol. 3, no. 1, pp. 89–122, 2014, ISSN: 2163-0364. doi: 10.5898/JHRI.3.1.Hoffman.

[38] A. Chanseau, K. S. Lohan, and R. Aylett, "How motor speed of a robot face can influence the "older" user's perception of facial expression?" In *2015 24th IEEE International Symposium on Robot and Human Interactive Communication (RO-MAN)*, 2015, pp. 468–473. doi: 10.1109/ROMAN.2015.7333596.

Detection and Classification of RBCs and WBCs in Urine Analysis with Deep Network

Xingguo Zhang, Guoyue Chen, Kazuki Saruta and Yuki Terata
Faculty of Systems Science and Technology
Akita Prefectural University
Akita, Japan
e-mail: {xingguozhang, chen, saruta, terata}@akita-pu.ac.jp

***Abstract*—Urinary sediment examination is used to evaluate the possible urinary tract diseases of patients. Currently, numerous approaches are applied to automatically detect Red Blood Cells (RBCs) and White Blood Cells (WBCs) from urinary sediment images. However, it is still a challenging task due to the cellular heterogeneity. Deep learning approaches have been shown to produce encouraging results on image detection in various tasks. In this paper, we investigate issues involving Faster Regions with Convolutional Neural Network (Faster R-CNN) for the construction of an end-to-end urine analysis system. We propose an effective baseline for RBCs and WBCs detection on urinary sediment images by using a pre-train Faster R-CNN model. We evaluate our urine analysis system on a large dataset of urinary sediment images which consist of more than 6,000 annotated RBCs and WBCs images. Our results show competitive accuracy and acceptable run time. Prospectively, the proposed methods could provide support to pathology practice in terms of quantitative analysis of tissue constituents in whole-slide images, and it could potentially lead to a better understanding of urinary tract diseases. Code and dataset will be made publicly available.**

Keywords- Urinary Sediment; RBC; WBC; Faster R-CNN; Applications in Medicine.

I. INTRODUCTION

Currently, urinary sediment microscopy plays an important role in the clinical diagnosis of urinary tract diseases [1][2]. It is possible to diagnose a patient's disease by identifying the type and amount of sediment in the urine specimen which is effective on early detection and disease control. The development of the Automatic Urinalysis System has been attractive to scholars over the past few years.

The higher clinical value of sediment in the urine mainly includes RBCs and WBCs. The qualitative and quantitative analysis of RBCs and WBCs in urine sediment can not only be helpful in detecting the disease but also help to explore various options for urethral diseases treatment.

Several solutions for urinary sediment microscopy using computer vision methodology have been proposed by different studies [3][4]. However, it is still a challenging task due to the cellular heterogeneity.

In 2005, nephrologists began to report concerns about the frequent discrepancies in some reported results of urine sediment microscopy [5][6]. For instance, the diagnostic accuracy rates of acute kidney injury based on reports by medical technologists and nephrologists were <25% and 69–92%, respectively [5]. These differences could be caused by the number of dysmorphic red blood cells identified, which tend to be underestimated by image processing technologists. In addition, dysmorphic RBCs were often misclassified as WBCs, besides, the reports issued by medical laboratory technologists overlooked the description of dysmorphic RBCs.

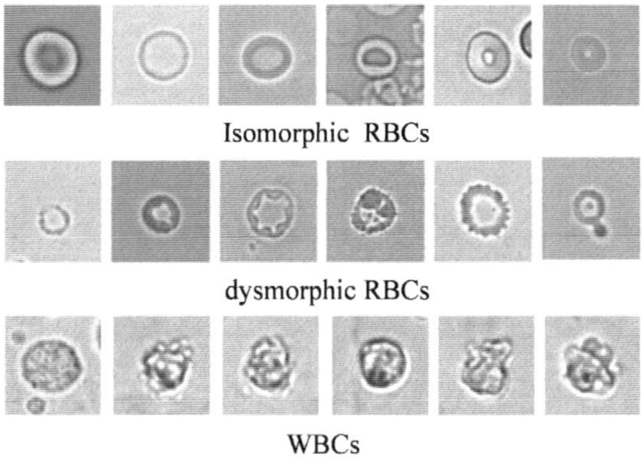

Figure 1. Isomorphic red blood cells (RBCs), dysmorphic RBCs and write blood cells (WBCs).

One way to explore these cell types is to use morphological clues in local neighborhoods to develop automated cellular recognition via image analysis, which can then be deployed for sophisticated tissue morphometry.

There are several factors that impede automatic detection and classification of RBCs and WBCs. On one hand, the inferior image quality may arise due to autofocus failure during the digitization of slide. On the other hand, complex tissue architecture, clutter of nuclei, and diversity of nuclear morphology pose a challenging problem.

Particularly, in case of the large numbers of dysmorphic RBCs appearing at urinary sediment, the detection accuracy is significantly declined, due to the dysmorphic RBCs is very similar to the WBCs in terms of cellular morphology (Figure 1). Dysmorphic RBCs are usually transformed by the red blood cells being squeezed through the walls of the blood vessels, causing the damage of cell wall. Furthermore, such cases are not rare. Therefore, we need an effective approach to distinguish the variety of objects from urine sediment, especially isomorphic RBCs, dysmorphic RBCs and WBCs.

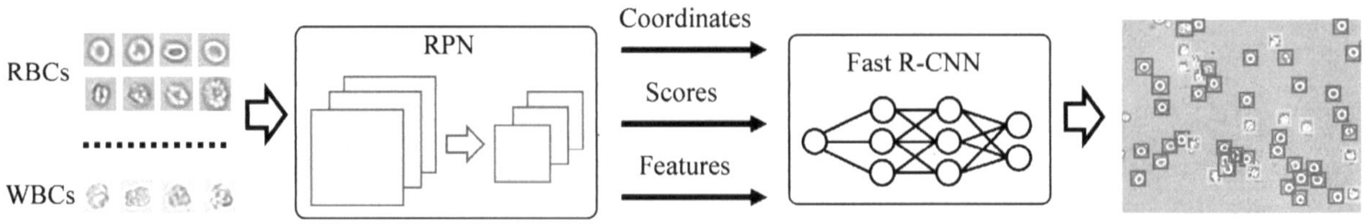

Figure 2. Our urinary sediment detection pipeline.

Faster R-CNN [14] is a particularly successful method for general object detection. It consists of two components: region proposal and estimate object candidates, which is generally considered to be more effective for smaller objects detection. However, there are few studies on the use of Faster R-CNN for urinary sediment detection.

In this paper, we would investigate issues involved Faster R-CNN for construction of end-to-end urine analysis system. In addition, we would propose an effective baseline for RBCs and WBCs detection on urinary sediment images by using a pre-train Faster R-CNN model. In here, we expect both isomorphic RBC and dysmorphic RBC to be detected as RBC.

The rest of the paper is organized as follows: Section 2 introduces the related works. Section 3 presents the pipeline that we used for detecting RBCs and WBCs. Section 4 is devoted to experimental evaluation, whereas conclusions are drawn in Section 5.

II. Related Work

Cell and nucleus classification have been applied to diverse histopathology related applications. Most existing methods for cells detection share similar computation pipelines: thresholding followed by morphological operations, region growing, level sets, k-means, and graph-cuts.

Cosatto et al. [7] proposed the detection of cell nuclei using the difference of Gaussian (DoG) followed by Hough transform to find radially symmetrical shapes. Vink et al. [8] employed AdaBoost classifier to train two detectors, one used pixel-based features and the other merged the results of two detectors to detect the nuclei in immunohistochemistry stained breast tissue images on the base of Haar-like features. Dalle et al. [9] and Cosatto et al. [7] used shape, texture and size of nuclei for nuclear pleomorphism grading in breast cancer images.

Recently, the prevalent success of deep learning approach in computer vision, such as Regions with Convolutional Neural Network (R-CNN) [10], Region Proposal Network & Binary Forest (RPN_BF) [11] and Spatially Constrained Convolutional Neural Network (SC-CNN) [12] have shown good performance on a large number of histopathological image datasets. The R-CNN method [10] trains CNNs end-to-end to classify the proposal regions into object categories or background. Fast R-CNN [13] enables end-to-end detector training on shared convolutional features and shows compelling accuracy and speed. In [11], an RPN_BF approach has been proposed an RPN that generates candidate boxes, convolutional feature maps, and a Boosted Forest that classifies these proposals using these convolutional features. Korsuk et al. [12] proposed a SC-CNN classifier to detect colon cancer cells.

III. Convolutional Neural Network

CNN is one of the basic theories for deep learning, therefore we briefly recap such network.

A CNN f is a composition of a sequence of L functions or layers $(f_1, \ldots, f_L)$ that maps an input vector x to an output vector y, i.e.,

$$\begin{aligned} Y &= f(x; w_1, \ldots, w_L) \\ &= f_L(\cdot\,;\, w_L) \circ f_{L-1}(\cdot\,;\, w_{L-1}) \circ \ldots \\ &\quad \circ f_2(\cdot\,;\, w_2) \circ f_1(\cdot\,;\, w_1) \end{aligned} \tag{1}$$

where w_L is the weight and bias vector for the l the layer fl. Conventionally, f_L is defined to perform one of the following operations: a) convolution with a bank of filters; b) spatial pooling; and c) non-linear activation. Given a set of N training data $\{(x^i, y^i)\}_{i=1}^N$, we can estimate the vectors $w_1, \ldots, w_L$ by solving the optimization problem

$$\operatorname{argmin}_{w_1,\ldots,w_L} \frac{1}{N} \sum_{i=1}^N l(f(x^i; w_1, \ldots, w_L), y^i) \tag{2}$$

where l is an appropriately defined loss function. Numerical optimization of (2) is often performed via backpropagation and stochastic gradient descent methods.

IV. Rbc and Wbc Detection Based on Faster R-cnn

In this section, we describe our RBCs and WBCs detection pipeline for urinary sediment images by Faster R-CNN [14].

Faster R-CNN consists of two components, as shown in Figure 2: an RPN that generates candidate boxes as well as convolutional feature maps, and a Fast R-CNN used for object detection. RPN is used to compute candidate bounding boxes, scores, and convolutional feature maps. The candidate boxes are fed into Fast R-CNN for further classification, using the features pooled from the convolutional feature maps computed by RPN. Finally, non-maximum suppression (NMS) is used to merge the similar results and get the output. In here, we use a urinary sediment image dataset to train the RPN and Fast R-CNN network.

A. RPN network

The RPN network shares full-image convolutional features with the detection network, thus enabling nearly cost-free region proposals. An RPN is a fully convolutional network that simultaneously predicts object bounds and objectness scores at each position. The RPN is trained end-to-end to generate high-quality region proposals, which are used by Fast R-CNN for detection.

We fixed the aspect ratio of anchors (Region Proposal Boxes) [14] as 1:1 (width / height). This is because that we need a square box to mark the positions of the cells. This is unlike the original RPN [14] for detect general object that has anchors of multiple aspect ratios. In order to detect multi-scale RBCs and WBCs, we use anchors of 3 different scales, starting from 20 pixels length of square box side with a scaling stride = 1.2.

Following [14], we adopt the VGG-16 net [15] pre-trained on the ImageNet dataset [16] to initialize the network parameters. The RPN is built on top of the Conv5_3 layer, which is followed by an intermediate 3×3 convolutional layer and two sibling 1×1 convolutional layers for classification and bounding box regression (more details in [14]). The output layer of the RPN net provides confidence scores and regression coordinate of the predicted boxes, which can be used as the input for Fast R-CNN network.

B. Fast R-CNN network

For the detection process, we adopt Fast R-CNN network as mentioned at [14]. To speed up the process, [14] developed a technique that allows for sharing convolutional layers between the two networks, rather than learning two separate networks. For the convenience of the reader, we briefly recap such approach.

A 4-step training algorithm has been adopted to learn shared features via alternating optimization. In the 1st step, the RPN network has been train. And this network is initialized with an ImageNet pre-trained model and fine-tuned end-to-end for the region proposal task. In the 2nd step, they train a separate detection network by Fast R-CNN using the proposals generated by the 1st step. In the 3rd step, they use the detector network to initialize RPN training, but fix the shared convolutional layers and only fine-tune the layers unique to RPN. Finally, keeping the shared convolutional layers fixed, and fine-tune the unique layers of Fast R-CNN. As such, both networks share the same convolutional layers and form the Faster R-CNN network. In this solution, the RPN and Fast R-CNN networks are merged into one network during training.

C. Implementation Details

For RPN and Fast R-CNN training, an anchor is considered as a positive example if it has an Intersection-over-Union (IoU) ratio greater than 0.7 with one ground truth box, and otherwise consider as negative. For Fast R-CNN training, we construct the training set by selecting the top-ranked 100 proposals of each image by RPN network. At test process, we only use the top 300 proposals in an image, which are classified by the Fast R-CNN. We adopt NMS to output the detect results.

V. EXPERIMENT AND RESULTS

In this section, we describe our experimental setup details and the results.

A. The dataset

This study involves electron microscope image. We collected urine samples from 100 patients, and through urine centrifuge to obtain urine sediment. It was then magnified by an electron microscope 400 times and photographed with a digital camera. All images have a common size of 1280 × 1024 pixels.

Manual annotations of nuclei were conducted mostly by an experienced pathologist and partly by a graduate student under supervision of and validation by the same pathologist. A total number of 5,215 RBCs and 4,828 WBCs were marked. Figure 3 shows some examples of the urinary sediment images in the dataset. We selected 3,000 random images as the training samples. The test samples also included 2,000 images selected from the rest of the dataset.

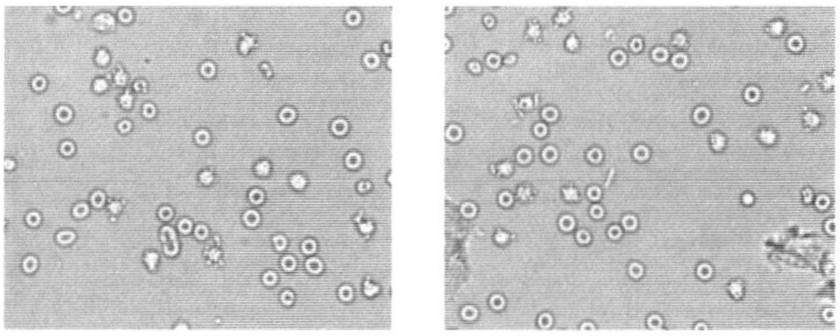

Figure 3. Example images of urinary sediment images dataset used in this experiment.

B. Evaluation metrics

The objective of this experiment is to detect all RBCs and WBCs in an image by locating their positions, and obtain their class labels. In particular, the performance of an algorithm is evaluated in terms of the tradeoff between precision, Recall, and F1 score.

First, a detected bounding box and a ground truth bounding box (GT) are considered a true positive (TP) if the area covered by their intersection ≥ 70%. A GT that does not have a match is considered a False Negative (FN), or a Miss. A detected bounding box that does not have a matching GT is considered as a False Positive (FP). The F1 score (also F-score or F-measure) is a measure of a test's accuracy. It considers both the precision p and the recall r of the test to compute the score: p is the number of correct positive results divided by the number of all positive results, and r is the number of correct positive results divided by the number of positive results that should have been returned. Here, we use F1 score to quantitatively assess the detection performance. The F1 score is computed by the following equation:

$$F_1 = 2 \cdot \frac{precision \cdot recall}{precision + recall} \tag{3}$$

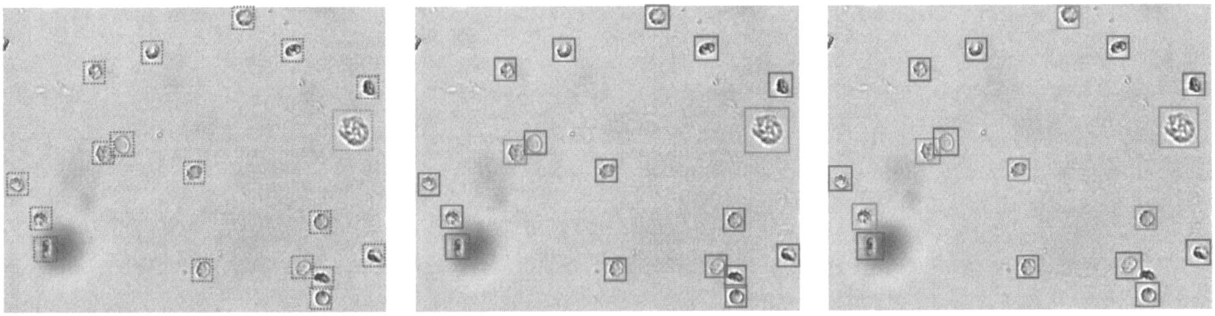
(a) (b) (c)

Figure 4. Qualitative results for RBCs and WBCs detection in urine images. (a) Ground truth image. (b) Detection results of our approach. (c) Detection results of RPN_BF.

C. Comparative Results

In this section, our final detectors were evaluated with other state-of-the-art methods using our urinary sediment dataset.

Figure 4 and Table 1 report the performance on detection and classification for our dataset. Figure 4 are qualitative results for RBCs and WBCs detection in urine images. (a) Ground truth image. RBCs are shown as red dashed Box, WBCs are shown as green dashed box. (b) Detection results of our approach. (c) Detection results of RPN_BF. Here, detected as RBCs are shown as red box, and detected as WBCs are shown as green box. It can be seen that our detector show better performance.

TABLE I. COMPARATIVE RESULT FOR RBCS AND WBCS DETECTION

Method	Weighted Average F1 score
Our	**0.914**
RPN_BF	0.862
HOG	0.688

From the results of the images it can be seen that our detector is competitive in terms of the detection quality with respect to RPN_BF and provides significant improvement over HOG+SVM.

In addition, we have observed the shapes of isomorphic RBCs can change in response to the osmolarity of urine. The isomorphic RBCs swell to spheres in urine with a low specific gravity, and they shrink to the shape of a spiked disk or a spiked sphere in urine with a high specific gravity.

The presence of dysmorphic RBCs leads to the difficulty of distinguishing, which may seriously affects the accuracy of the urinary sediment microscopy system. Therefore, a precise count of dysmorphic RBCs is very important for evaluating glomerular bleeding before renal biopsy.

We profiled the execution of our system on a desktop architecture which features a 2.4GHz Intel i7 CPU, a NVIDIA GTX1080 GPU and 32GB of RAM. The system requires, on average, 96ms to process a frame at a resolution of 1280×1080 pixels. It can be consider as an acceptable running time.

VI. CONCLUSION

In this paper, we investigate issues involving Faster R-CNN for construction of end-to-end urine analysis system. We proposed an effective baseline for RBCs and WBCs detection on urinary sediment images, using a pre-train Faster R-CNN model. Isomorphic, dysmorphic RBCs and WBCs were successfully identified. We comprehensively evaluate this method, the experiment results presenting competitive accuracy and acceptable speed.

Prospectively, the proposed methods could benefit the pathology practice in terms of quantitative analysis of tissue constituents in whole-slide images, and could potentially lead to a better understanding of urinary tract diseases.

However, this study only focused on type 2 cells in urinary sediment, our current results will require additional studies using a wider spectrum of cells and sediment, for examples, Epithelial Cells, Bacteria, Yeast and Parasites. In future work, more theoretical and experimental studies will be conducted to analyze the performance.

REFERENCES

[1] M. A. Perazella, "The Urine Sediment as a Biomarker of Kidney Disease," American Journal of Kidney Diseases, vol. 66, pp. 748–755, 2015.

[2] J. A. Simerville, W. C. Maxted, and J. J. Pahira, "Urinalysis: a comprehensive review," American family physician, vol. 71, pp. 1153–1162, 2005.

[3] M. Yasuda, "Japanese guideline for clinical research of antimicrobial agents on urogenital infections," Journal of Infection and Chemotherapy, vol. 17, pp. 579–594, 2011.

[4] R. Davis, et al. "Diagnosis, evaluation and follow-up of asymptomatic microhematuria (AMH) in adults," ,Journal of Urology, vol, 188, pp. 2473–2481, 2012.

[5] J. J. Tsai, J. Y. Yeun, V. A. Kumar, and B. R. Don, "Comparison and interpretation of urinalysis performed by a nephrologist versus a hospital-based clinical laboratory," American journal of kidney diseases, vol, 46, pp. 820–829, 2005.

[6] M. Kanbay, B. Kasapoglu, and M. A. Perazella, "Acute tubular necrosis and prerenal acute kidney injury: utility of urine microscopy in their evaluation a systematic review," Int. Urol. Nephrol., vol. 42, pp. 425–433, 2010.

[7] E. Cosatto, M. Miller, H. P. Graf, and J. S. Meyer, "Grading nuclear pleomorphism on histological micrographs," Int. Conf. Pattern Recognition, pp. 1–4, 2008.

[8] J. P. Vink, M. Van Leeuwen, C. Van Deurzen, and G. De Haan, "Efficient nucleus detector in histopathology images," Journal of microscopy, vol.249, no. 2, pp. 124–135, 2013.

[9] J. R. Dalle, H. Li, C. H. Huang, and W. K. Leow, "Nuclear Pleomorphism Scoring by Selective Cell Nuclei Detection," IEEE Winter Conf. on Applications of Computer Vision, pp. 1–6, 2009.

[10] R. Girshick, J. Donahue, T. Darrell, U. C. Berkeley, J. Malik, "R-CNN: Region-based Convolutional Neural Networks," Computer Vision and Pattern Recognition, pp. 2–9, 2014.

[11] L. Zhang, L. Lin, X. Liang, K. He, "Is Faster R-CNN Doing Well for Pedestrian Detection?" European Conference on Computer Vision, pp. 1–15, 2016.

[12] K. Sirinukunwattana, S.E.A. Raza, Y.W Tsang, I.A. Cree, D.R.J. Snead, N.M. Rajpoot," Locality Sensitive Deep Learning for Detection and Classification of Nuclei in Routine Colon Cancer Histology Images," IEEE Transactions on Medical Imaging, pp. 1196–1206, 2016.

[13] R. Girshick, "Fast R-CNN: Fast Region-based Convolutional Networks for object detection," IEEE International Conference on Computer Vision, pp. 1440–1448, 2016.

[14] S. Ren, K. He, R. Girshick, J. Sun, "Faster R-CNN: Towards Real-Time Object Detection with Region Proposal Networks," Advances in neural information processing systems, pp. 91–99, 2015.

[15] L. C. Chen, G. Papandreou, I. Kokkinos, K. Murphy, A. L. Yuille, "Semantic Image Segmentation with Deep Convolutional Nets and Fully Connected CRFs," International Conference on Learning Representations , pp. 1–14, 2016.

[16] O. Russakovsky, et al. "ImageNet Large Scale Visual Recognition Challenge," International Journal of Computer Vision, vol. 115, pp. 211–252, 2015.

Line-Drawing Presentation Strategies with an Active-Wheel Mouse

Yoshihiko Nomura, Yoshiaki Kashino, Tokuhiro Sugiura
Graduate School of Engineering
Mie University
Tsu, Japan
e-mail: {nomura, y-kashino, sugiura}@mach.mie-u.ac.jp

***Abstract*— The objective of this study is to develop a presentation method of line-drawings by using a finger-tactile interface, i.e., an *"active-wheel mouse,"* which can present slippages to users via the user's fingertip skin. The interface embodies an active wheel being rotatable in any direction, with any speed and for any duration of time. Through the slippage stimuli, the interface can present stroke motions with any direction, velocity and length to users. In this paper, we proposed two kinds of presentation strategies, called an *"after-recognition go strategy"* and a *"while-perceiving go strategy"* for some line-drawings being connected with several line-segments, and their perceptual performance was examined. The former employed an off-line, open loop scheme, and the latter does an on-line closed loop control scheme. By evaluating lengths and directions of subjects' reproduced line-segments, a feasibility of the interface and the presentation methods were confirmed.**

Keywords-fingerpad; tactile sensation; slippage; interface.

I. INTRODUCTION

Human beings get a large amount of information via vision from the surroundings. Therefore, once we lose our vision, we shall suffer inconveniences in daily life. Many assistive devices were developed as an alternative. Visually impaired persons utilize sensations other than the vision such as skin-sensations and proprioceptive sensations. For examples, some handy-and-portable devices were proposed for character presentation and walking route guidance [1]-[4]. They can present motion information by using tactors, and, yet, there are some tasks to be solved: ① the number of physical properties to be presented was restricted in such a way that only motion direction can be presented, ② the working area was also restricted to several millimeters.

The objective of this study is to develop an operational strategy by utilizing our developed tactile-device, i.e., an Active-Wheel Mouse (AWM) [5][6]."

The remainder of the paper is structured as follows. The hardware and software of the system employed in this work are explained in Sections II and III, respectively. That is, Section II outlines our developed AWM, and Section III introduces two line-drawing-stroke presenting strategies to be compared in this paper: one is an after-recognition go strategy (ARG-S), and the other a while-perceiving go strategy (WPG-S). Next, two stages of experiments follow the system descriptions. Practically, in Section IV, perceptual characteristics of simple patterns of 1-, 2-, and 3-strokes are presented as a basic study, and, in Section V, those for complicated patterns of 5-strokes are presented as an example of practical applications. The paper closes with a conclusion and remarks for further developments.

II. ACTIVE-WHEEL MOUSE, A FINGER-TACTILE INTERFACE

A. *Apparatus*

In our previous work [5][6], we have developed an AWM: a specific mouse interface, at the front of which a finger-tactile interface is attached as shown in Figure 1. The finger-tactile interface can rotate a wheel around the wheel central axis in any horizontal direction by two stepping motors (M15SP-2N and M25SP-6NK (Mitsumi Electric Co., LTD., Tokyo, Japan) (see Figure 1.). The former rotates the wheel, and the latter swivels the wheel rotating part. The rotation and the swivel result in slippage velocity and direction, respectively. Here, the velocity together with the time duration decide the slippage lengths. The diameter and thickness of the wheel are 20 mm and 6 mm, respectively (see Figure 1. (b)). Particularly, it is noted that raised dots are formed on the wheel peripheral surface to enhance slippage perceptual performance [7][8]: as for the raised dots, the height is 0.5 mm, and the diameter of the bottom circle is 1.7 mm. The dot interval was decided as 10.5 mm so that the dots appear one by one on the fingerpad to make the slippage perception easier [5][6].

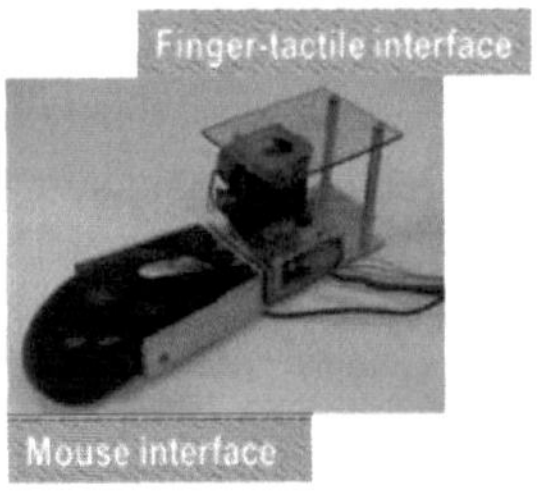

(a) Finger-tactile interface is attached to a mouse interface: it constitutes an active-wheel mouse.

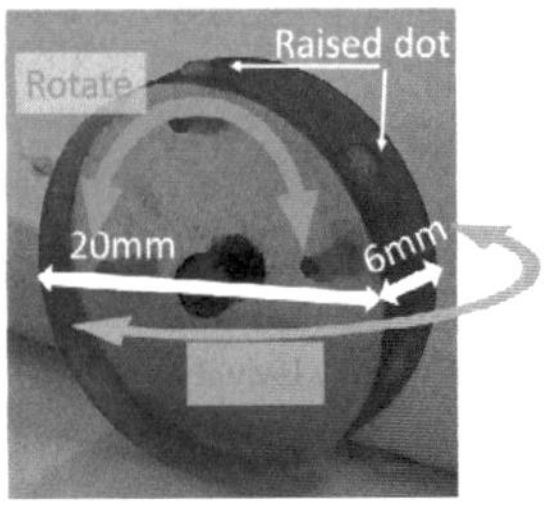

(b) Raised dots formed on a wheel peripheral surface.

Figure 1. Active-wheel mouse.

While holding the mouse body, touching their finger-pad on the rotating wheel peripheral surface from above, users can accept slippage stimulus (see Figure 2.).

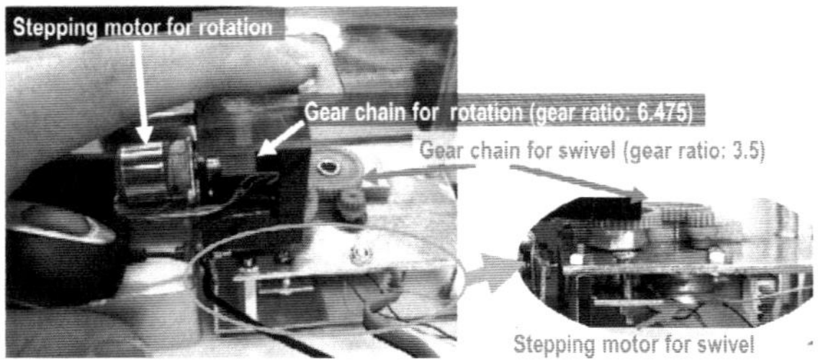

Figure 2. Side view of the finger-tactile interface.

Here, note that the circumference of the wheel is circular, and the shape of the slippage is physically not a straight line, but an arc. However, it is not easy for us to perceive the arc-shaped slippages. Therefore, users are instructed not to perceive the slippage as arc segment, but as straight line segments.

III. LINE-DRAWING-STROKE PRESENTING STRATEGIES

Two control schemes were applied: one control scheme is off-line and the other is on-line. In terms of the former, we introduced a line-drawing-stroke presenting strategy, i.e., "After-Recognition Go Strategy", and, in terms of the latter, "While-Perceiving Go Strategy." The strategies will be explained in the following.

A. *After-Recognition Go Strategy*

In this section, a presenting strategy for line-drawing-strokes, that is, the after-recognition go strategy, is explained. The strategy is carried out in the following procedure.

[Step 1] A subject holds the mouse in his right hand. Then, he touches his index-fingerpad on the wheel from above.

[Step 2] Finger-tactile interface swivels the rotating unit in a given direction. Next, it rotates the wheel with a given velocity and angle (see Figure 3. ①) .

[Step 3] While accepting the slippage stimulus, the subject recognize the stimulus as a straight line motion. (See Figure 3. ②.)

[Step 4] The subject drags AWM so as to reproduce his recognized motion (see Figure 3. ③).

[Step 5] The subject memorizes the drag motion as a stroke (see Figure 3. ④).

[Step 6] Just after memorizing stroke, the subject sends a signal by pressing a button in the left hand.

[Step 7] Return to [Step 2] till all the strokes are memorized.

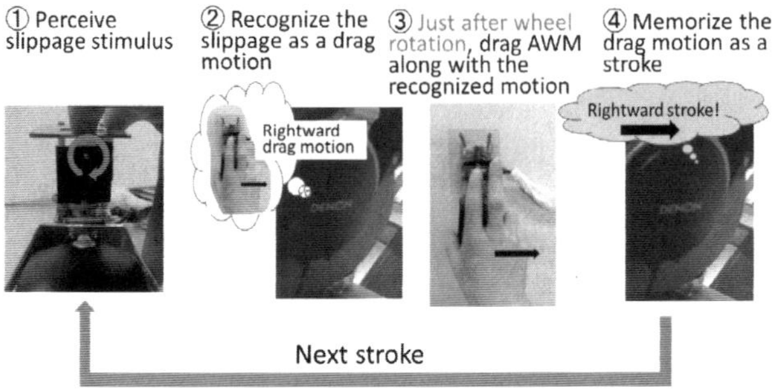

Figure 3. "*After-Recognition Go strategy*" for line-drawing-stroke teaching & learning.

B. *While-Perceiving Go Strategy*

In this section, the second presenting strategy for line-drawing-strokes, that is, the while-perceiving go strategy, is explained.

[Step 1] A subject holds the mouth in his right hand. Then, he touches his index-fingerpad on the wheel.

[Step 2] As shown in Figure 4. , the finger-tactile interface swivels in a specific direction. At a time, the wheel rotates with another specific velocity under a positional feedback control scheme: as shown in Figure 4. the direction is given by the positional difference vector between the present position and a sub-goal of a desired stroke. The velocity is given by the desired velocity at the proximal point on a desired trajectory.

[Step 3] While accepting the slippage stimulus, the subject recognizes the stimulus as a straight line motion, and drags AWM along with the recognized motion (see Figure 5. ① and ②).

[Step 4] The subject memorizes the drag motion as a stroke (see Figure 5. ③).

[Step 5] Just after memorizing stroke, the subject sends a signal by pressing a button in his left hand.

[Step 6] Return to [Step 2] till all the strokes are presented.

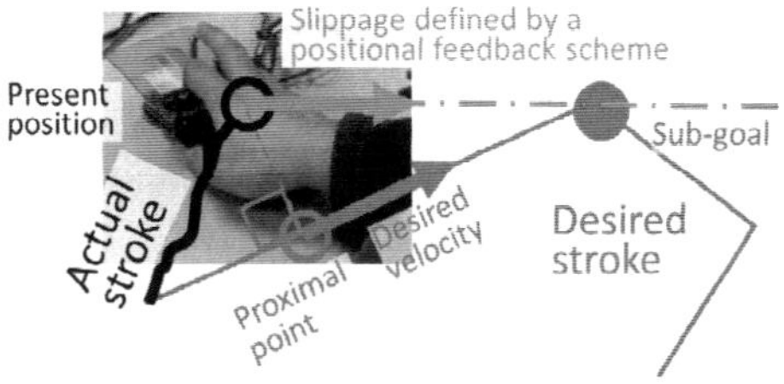

Figure 4. Explanation of a positional feedback scheme employed in "*While-Perceiving Go Strategy* " as a stroke presentation method. The slippage velocity is given as the desired velocity at the proximal point on a desired trajectory.

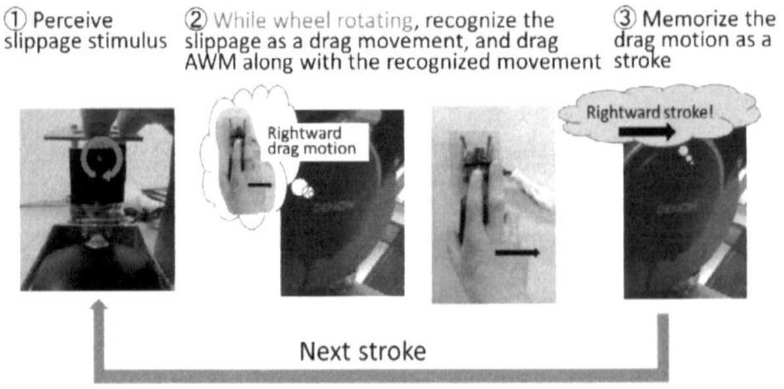

Figure 5. "*While-Perceiving Go Strategy* " for stroke presentation. The step ② in this figure can be regarded as an on-line integration of the steps ② and ③ in Figure 4, i.e., the "*After-Recognition Go Strategy.*"

Here, note that the point of the strategy is in a position feedback control scheme as explained in [Step 2].

IV. Basic Experiment

A. *Experimental Method*

1) Experimental Conditions: In order to confirm a potential of the "after-recognition go" method as a drawing presentation, a line-drawing-stroke presenting experiment was carried out.

Five healthy right handed males in their 20s (22~24, 22.6 (mean) ± 0.9 (SD)) participated in the experiment. The stroke drawings from single to three strokes were presented as shown in Figure 6. All the strokes were of the uniform motion, i.e., constant-velocity straight line motion. The factors and the factor levels are shown in TABLE I. In the experiment, the levels for each of the presentation-mode factor and the stroke-number factor were given by a pseudo-random order.

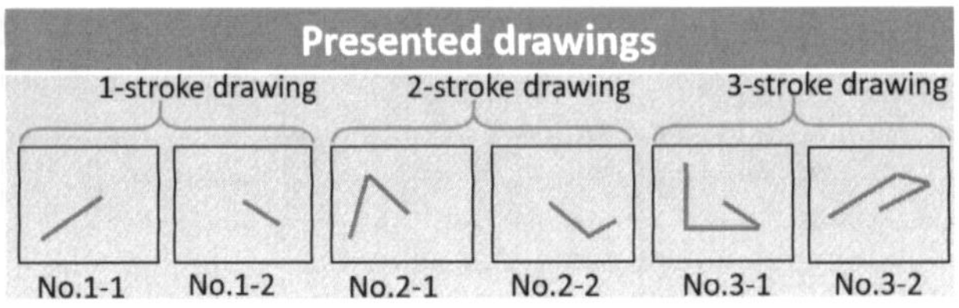

Figure 6. Presented drawings used for a stroke learning experiment.

TABLE I. Factors and Factor Levels in Basic Experiment.

Factor	Level
Subject	5 males
Presentation strategy	While-perceiving go, After-recognition go
Presented stroke pattern	6 stroke patterns in total: 2 patterns for each of 1-stroke, 2-strokes, and 3-strokes
Length	Randomly chosen between 50 - 150 mm
Speed	Randomly chosen between 12 - 50 mm/s
Direction	Randomly chosen between 0 - 359 deg.

2) Procedures: The experiment was carried out by the following procedures (see Figure 7.).

[Step 1] For each of the presentation strategies, ARG-S or WPG-S as described in Section III, subjects repeat accepting slippages until they finish recognizing whole drawing trajectories.

[Step 2] They repeat accepting slippages until they finish recognizing the whole velocity variation.

[Step 3] They reproduce the memorized stroke trajectory by using AWM, while the system records the mouse movements.

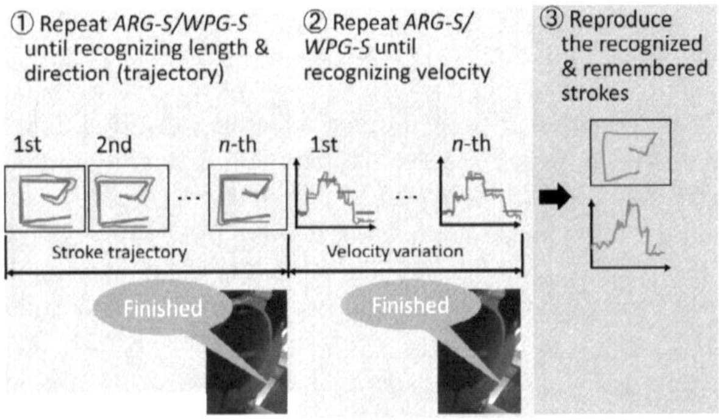

Figure 7. Experimental procedures.

3) Evaluation Values: We obtained secants from actual strokes where the word "secant" represents the line segment connected from start to end point. Next, we defined evaluation values by the differences of the lengths as well as the angles between the secants of the actual strokes and the desired strokes for each of the strokes (see Figure 8.). That is,

$$\Delta l = l_{secant} - l_{desired} \quad (1)$$

$$\Delta\theta = \theta_{secant} - \theta_{desired} \quad (2)$$

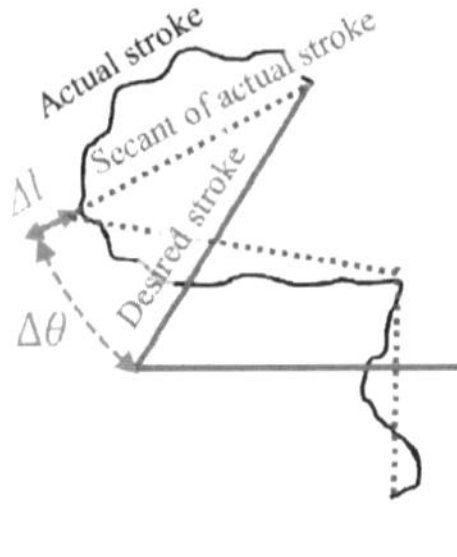

Figure 8. Evaluation values: the differences of lengths and angles between the secants of actual trajectory and the desired trajectory.

In addition to these, a velocity difference of v_{mean} from $v_{desired}$ was also employed as an evaluation value:

$$\Delta v = v_{mean} - v_{desired} \quad (3)$$

where v_{mean} is the mean velocity of the time-varying actual velocity, and $v_{desired}$ is the desired velocity.

B. *Experimental Results*

As with some three-stroke drawings, experimental results of the ARG-S are shown in Figure 9. Trajectories and velocities are shown in (a) and (b), respectively.

For the errors of the lengths and angles of the reproduced trajectories, as well as the velocities, means and standard deviations were calculated and shown in Figure 10. (a), (b), and (c), respectively. In addition to that, the means and standard deviations of the per-stroke time duration, i.e., the elapsed time, for the recognizing and memorizing steps, [Step 2] and [Step 3], in Section IV A 2) are shown in Figure 10. (d). Comparing the two presentation strategies, i.e., the ARG-S and WPG-S, we found the following results.

1) A result of t-test on population means of the errors: There was no significant difference between the ARG-S and the WPG-S with respect to the reproduced lengths, angles, and velocities (see Figure 10. (a), (b), and (c), respectively.) On the other hand, as shown in Figure 10. (d), the ARG-S was superior to the WPG-S by a significant level of 1 % with respect to the per-stroke time duration: a test statistic t of 2.70 > a critical value $T^{29,28}{}_{0.01}$ of 2.00 where $T^{29,28}{}_{0.01}$ represents $T^{DOF1,DOF2}{}_{significant\ level}$.

2) A result of F-test on variance ratios of the errors: the ARG-S was inferior to the WPG-S by a significant level of 0.1 % with respect to the reproduced lengths and angles: a test statistic F of 2.94 > a critical value $F^{59,58}{}_{0.001}$of 2.40 with respect to the reproduced lengths; a test statistic F of 3.03 > a critical value $F^{59,58}{}_{0.001}$ of 2.40 with respect to the reproduced angles where $F^{59,58}{}_{0.001}$ represents $F^{DOF1,DOF2}{}_{significant\ level}$. Yet, there was no significant difference between them with respect to the reproduced velocities. On the other hand, the ARG-S was, vice versa, superior to the WPG-S by a significant level of 0.1 % with respect to the per-stroke time duration: a test statistic F of 5.57 > a critical value $F^{29,28}{}_{0.001}$ of 3.34.

3) Subjects' report: In addition, all the subjects reported that, especially near sub-goals, they felt much more exhausted in the WPG-S than in the APG-S. They suggest humans are not able to catch up with the closed-loop feedback-control scheme: for achieving the closed-loop feedback-control, it is necessary to respond in a short period of time, but humans cannot respond so.

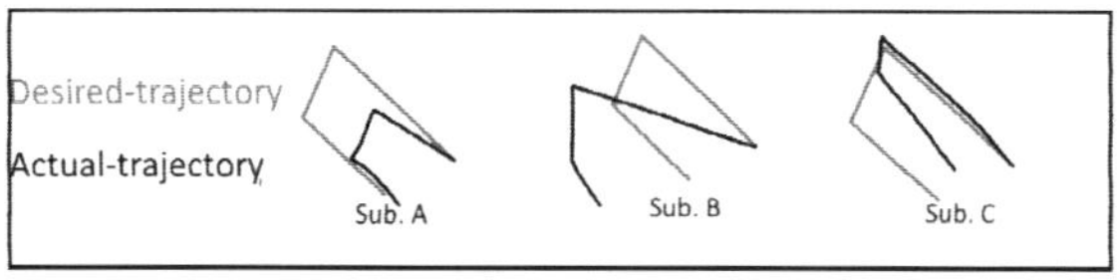

(a) Recognized trajectory.

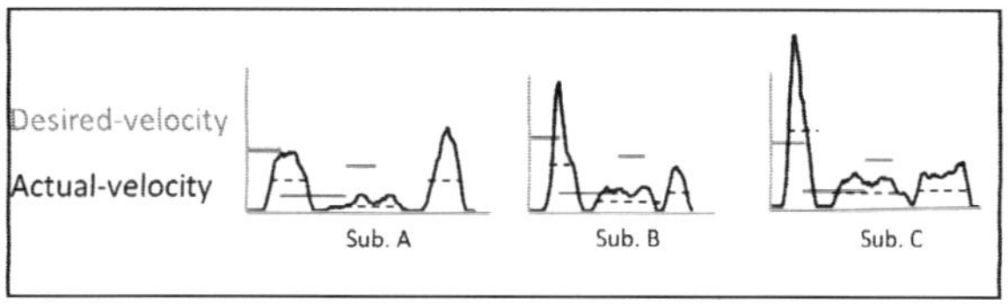

(b) Recognized velocity variation.

Figure 9. Some examples of the recognition with three-stroke drawings.

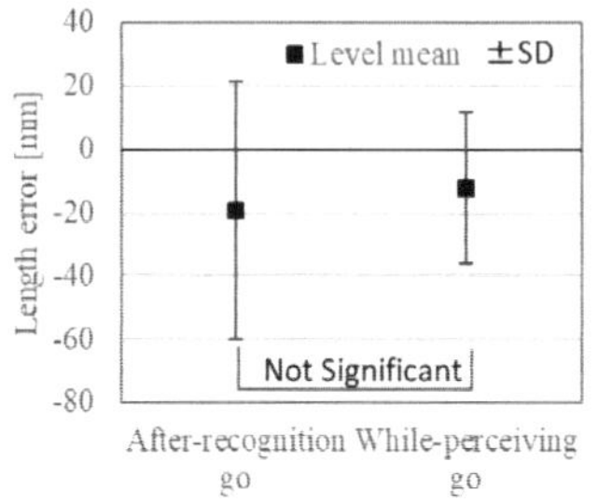

(a) Lengths.

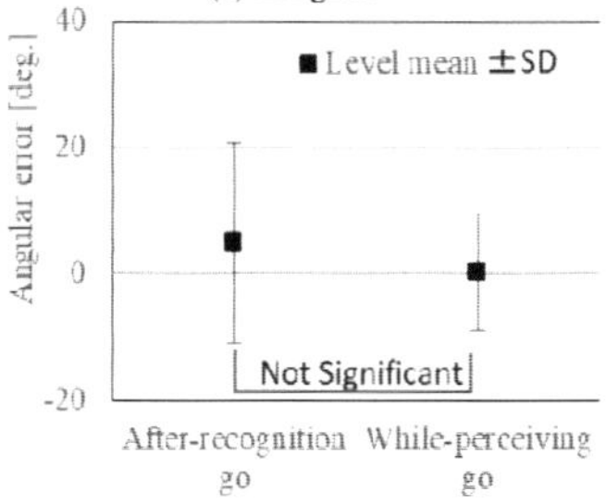

(b) Angles.

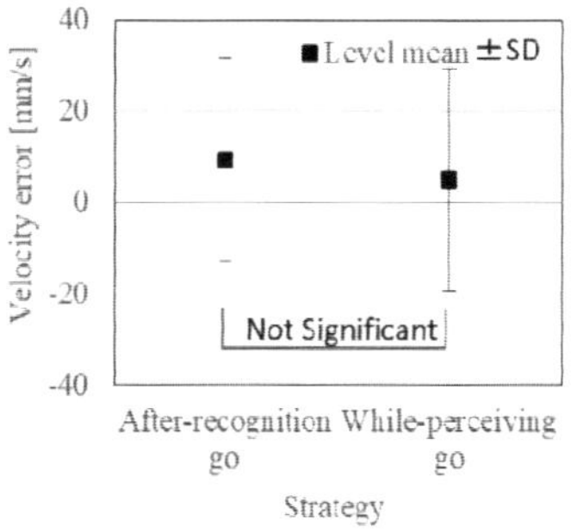

(c) Velocity

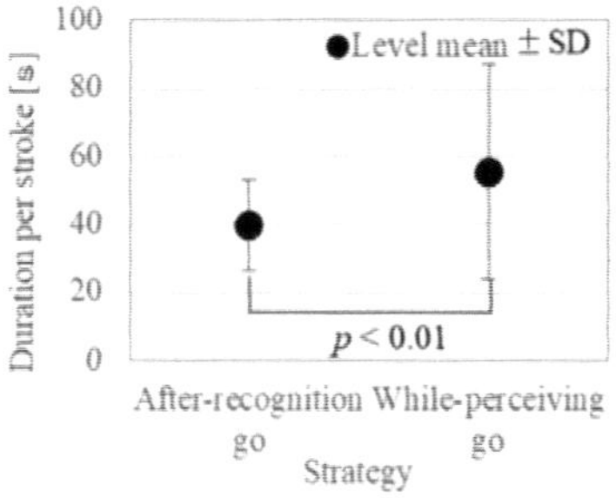

(d) Time duration per stroke.

Figure 10. Root mean squared errors with respect to the recognized length, angles, and velocities for multi-stroke drawings.

The errors of the lengths, angles, and velocities showed little differences between the two strategies, but the time duration showed significant differences. Therefore, the time duration was considered to carry more significant weight than the errors of the lengths, angles, and velocities. As a result, the ARG-S, whose time duration had the advantages in terms of population means and variances, was recommended for further studies.

V. PRACTICAL EXPERIMENT

A. Experimental Method

1) Experimental Conditions and Procedures: We carried out a practical experiment in order to confirm the effectiveness of the above-selected stroke-presention strategy, i.e., the ARG-S. In the practical experiment, the number of strokes was increased to five. The experimental conditions are shown in TABLE II.

TABLE II. FACTORS AND FACTOR LEVELS IN PRACTICAL EXPERIMENT.

Factor	Level
Subject	3 males (around age 23)
Presentation strategy	After-recognition go strategy
Presented stroke pattern	2 patterns of 5-strokes
Length	Randomly chosen between 10 - 150 mm
Speed	Randomly chosen between 12.5 - 70 mm/s
Direction	Randomly chosen between 0 - 359 deg.

The procedures were almost the same as those in Section IV.A.2) except that each of the strokes was presented only once, and no repetition was allowed. In addition, the presented lengths were individually adjusted to each of the subjects to cancel the foreshortening effect of perceived lengths as shown in Figure 10.

B. Experimental Results

Experimental results are shown in Figure 11. In this figure, presented drawing patterns are shown in the leftmost cells, and the perceived drawing patters are in the other cells.

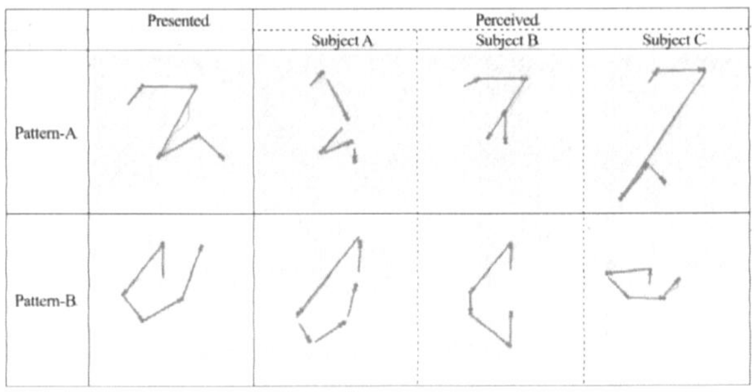

Figure 11. Experimental results of multi-stroke line drawing perception by using the active-wheel mouse.

Although it leaves much to be improved, the perceived drawing patterns capture the essential features of such complicated patterns. It shows a potential of the proposed finger tactile interface and the stroke presentation strategy.

VI. CONCLUSION AND FUTURE WORK

Two multiple-stroke presenting strategies using a tactile interface, i.e., AWM were presented: one is an after-recognition go strategy, and the other is a while-perceiving go strategy. As a result of multiple-stroke recognition experiments, the following conclusions were confirmed.

Although the after-recognition go strategy was inferior to the while-perceiving go strategy in terms of the variance ratios of the errors with respect to the lengths and angles, the after-recognition go strategy was, vice versa, superior to the while-perceiving go strategy in terms of the time duration from the viewpoints of population means and variance ratios. In addition to that, all the subjects reported that they were much more exhausted in the while-perceiving go strategy than in the after-recognition go strategy. As a result, it can be said that the while-perceiving go strategy that does employ a closed-loop on-line positional feedback scheme does not work well, while the after-recognition go strategy that employs an open-loop control scheme does work better.

In the future, accuracy and efficiency need to be improved. Although it is difficult, further extension of applicable scope, such as curved strokes and accelerated strokes is expected.

ACKNOWLEDGMENTS

This work was partly supported by KAKENHI (Grant-in-Aid for Challenging Exploratory Research 15H02929 from Japan Society for the Promotion of Science (JSPS)

REFERENCES

[1] N. Tsuda, N. Kato, and Y. Nomura, "Instruction of arm motion for calligraphy using vibrotactile stimulations," 2011 IEEE/ASME International Conference in Advanced Intelligent Mechatronics (AIM), pp. 677-682, 2011.

[2] A. Causo, S. H. Yeo, and I. M. Chen, "Vibrotactile motors on stationary arm as directional feedback to correct arm posture," 2012 IEEE/ASME International Conference in Advanced Intelligent Mechatronics (AIM), pp. 202-207, 2012.

[3] S. L. Norman, A. J. Doxon, B. T. Gleeson, and W. R. Provancher, "Planar hand motion guidance using fingertip skin-stretch feedback," IEEE Transactions on Haptics, vol. 7, no. 2, pp. 121-130, 2014.

[4] A. Ion, E. J. Wang, and P. Baudisch, "Skin drag displays: dragging a physical tactor across the user's skin produces a stronger tactile stimulus than vibrotactile," Proceedings of the 33rd Annual ACM Conference on Human Factors in Computing Systems, pp. 2501-2504, 2015.

[5] Y. Nomura and S. Oike, "Active-wheel mouse for human-computer interface: slippage-perception characteristics on fingerpad," Proceedings of 10th International Conference, UAHCI 2016, Part of HCI International 2016, part II, pp. 54-61, 2016.

[6] Y. Nomura, Y. Kashino, and S. Oike, "Proposal of active-wheel-based finger-tactile interface and its slippage-presenting functions," Transactions of the JSME, vol. 83, no. 852, pp. 1-17, 2017 (in Japanese)

[7] Y. Nomura and K. Iwabu, "Length perceptual characteristics on raised-dot slippages," Human-Computer Interfaces and Interactivity: Emergent Research and Applications, IGI Global, pp. 286-308, 2014.

[8] Y. Nomura and H. Kato, "Raised-dot slippage perception on fingerpad using active wheel device," Recent Advances on Using Virtual Reality Technologies for Rehabilitation, Nova Science Publishers, Inc. New York, pp. 165-172, 2015.

Depth Perception for Virtual Object Displayed in Optical See-Through HMD

Kazutake Uehira
Kanagawa Institute of Technology
Atsugi, Japan
e-mail: uehira@nw.kanagawa-it.ac.jp

Masahiro Suzuki
Tokiwa University
Mito, Japan
e-mail: masuzuki@tokiwa.ac.jp

***Abstract*— This paper presents depth perception for virtual objects displayed with an optical see-through type head-mounted display (HMD) when there is a real object in front of it. In the real world, we cannot see the object behind another object. However, in augmented reality using an optical see-through type HMD, it is seen overlapping the object in front of it. We researched depth perception for a virtual object for this case. Perception of the depth of a virtual object in such a situation is very important to enable development of a technique of interaction with a virtual object. From the subjective test performed, we found that human vision could perceive the depth of a virtual object for the above case although there were significant differences between individuals, especially in short distances from the user.**

Keywords- HMD; optical see-through; virtual object; depth perception.

I. INTRODUCTION

Research into augmented reality (AR), in which virtual objects in a real world assist our activities, has recently become popular. ARs that enable users to interact with a virtual object are attracting attention [1][2]. In many studies on AR, a head-mounted display (HMD) has been used. There are two types of HMD; video see-through and optical see-through. The former does not show the real world directly to the user, but shows it captured by the camera, and virtual objects are rendered in the captured image by image processing. On the other hand, when using an optical see-through type, a user can see the real world directly and virtual objects are superimposed in the real world; therefore, user can see their actual hands directly. This is very important when a user interacts with a virtual object using their hands because it is natural for users interacting with virtual objects directly with their actual hands instead of using virtual hand. From this point of view, the optical see-through type HMD is more suitable. However, a problem with this type occurs in that when a virtual object is superimposed behind a real world object, it becomes translucent instead of being naturally obscured. This unnaturalness may affect a user's depth perception of the virtual object. It is important to accurately obtain the depth of a virtual object that a user perceives for natural interaction. In this study, we evaluated the effect of the semi-transparency of virtual objects on depth perception.

II. DEPTH PERCEPTION FOR INTERACTION

Figure 1 outlines the importance of the system acquiring perceived depth for users. If the depth obtained by the system and that perceived by the user are different as shown in Figure 1, the system cannot react with the virtual object when the user sees that his or her hand touched it. This prevents smooth interaction between user's hand and virtual object.

Figure 2 outlines the problem of the optical see-through type HMD. Figure 2 (a) shows that from the side, the virtual object is located farther than the user's hand as the user reaches towards it. Figure 2 (b) shows the view from a user's point of view and the subsequent problem of the optical see-through type HMD. In the real world, when an object is positioned behind another object, it cannot be seen due to occlusion by the front object. However, the virtual object is seen in a translucent state although it is located farther than the user's hand.

The main factor for the depth perception of an object at a short distance in human vision is binocular disparity; however, occlusion is also used as a cue of the depth. In the

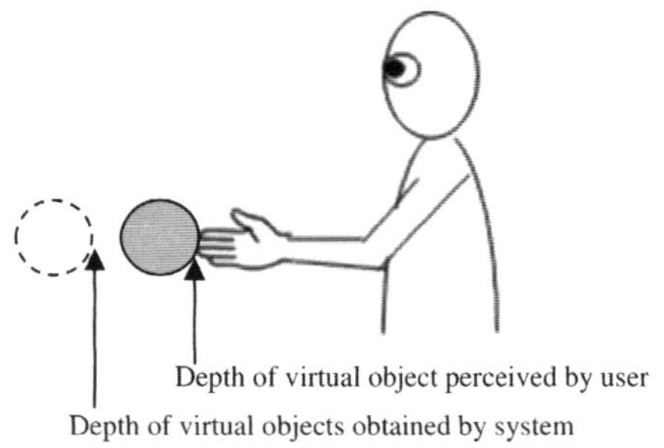

Figure 1. Interaction with virtual object using actual hand.

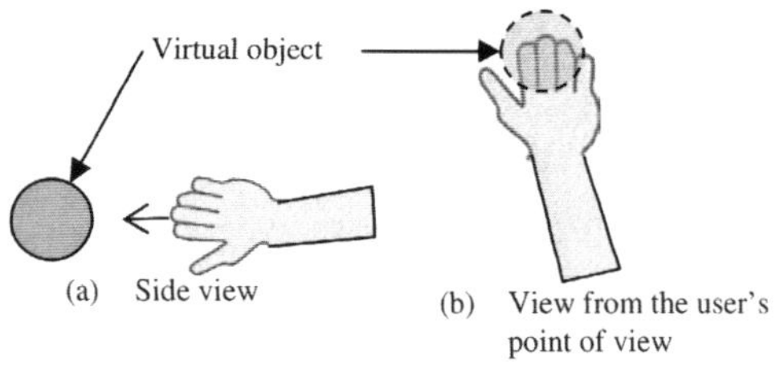

Figure 2. Problem of optical see-through type HMD.

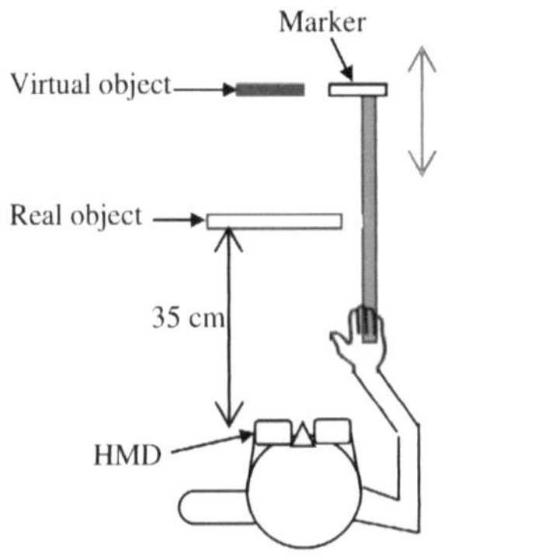

Figure 3. Layout in the subjective test.

real world, the depth perceived from binocular disparity and occlusion is almost the same, however, in the case shown in Figure 2, these two depths contradict each other. Binocular disparity is expected to be the dominant factor of depth perception; however, the absence of full occlusion by a hand has a possibility of affecting depth perception. In this study, we conducted a subjective test about the depth perception for the case shown in Figure 2.

III. Subjective Test

Figure 3 shows the layout of the subjective test. We used an HMD with two 1280×720 pixel OLED displays for both eyes, which provides the equivalent of an 80 inch display 5 m ahead by magnifying optics.

Virtual objects were square white patterns. The pattern size was 11 cm on the virtual screen 5 m ahead, therefore if it is seen, for example, 1 m ahead; it will be perceived as a square of about 2 cm in size. We set the brightness of the pattern to a grayscale value of 127, of which the maximum is 255. The virtual object is displayed within a distance range of 40 to 80 cm, which is the range where people can manipulate things directly with their own hands. A real object that is white was placed 35 cm from the observer's eye position. Although the virtual object is located behind it, it overlaps the real object.

Five subjects, all with normal eyesight and could see stereoscopically, moved a thin plate-shaped marker using their right hand and stopped it at a position just beside the virtual object to indicate the depth of the virtual object perceived by the subject. For reference, we conducted the same test without the real object.

IV. Results and Discussion

Figure 4 shows the results of the subjective test. In both cases where there was an actual object or not, the perceived depth of the virtual object increased as the depth set based on binocular disparity increased. However, the differences of data between subjects were significant in the case where there was an actual object, particularly at a short distance. This is considered to be due to the instability of the depth perception of the virtual object due to the existence of the

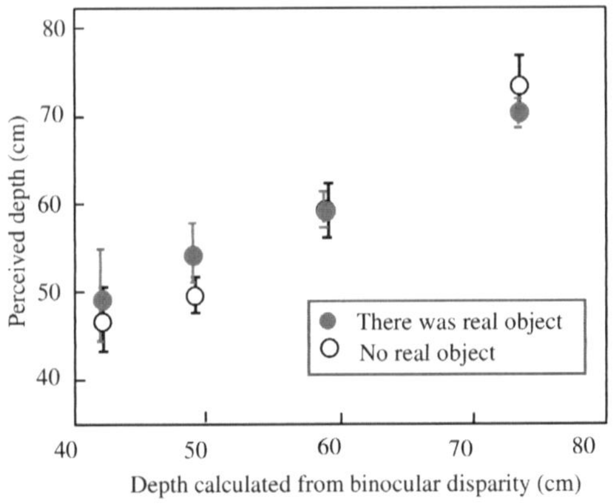

Figure 4. Result of subjective test

real object. Furthermore, the reason that this difference increases at a short distance seems to be due to the large binocular disparity at a short distance.

The result in this study shows that some technique that reduces the influence of the real object for this purpose is needed.

V. Conclusion and Future Work

We researched depth perception for virtual objects displayed in an optical see-through type HMD when there is a real object in front of the virtual object. We clarified from the subjective test that perceived depth of the virtual object changed depending on binocular disparity. However, the depth perception in human vision became varied under the influence of real objects existing in front of it, and the difference between individuals was significant.

In the future, we need to reduce the influence of the real object. To achieve this, we will try to develop a technique that can display only a part of the virtual object that is not obscured by a real object. This will improve the depth perception of a virtual object because it is the same in the real world.

Acknowlegement

This work was supported partly by JSPS KAKENHI Grant Number 15K00289 and partly by MEXT-Supported Program for the Strategic Research Foundation at Private Universities

References

[1] J. Tedjokusumo, S.Z. Zhou, and S.F. Winkler Immersive Multiplayer Games With Tangible and Physical Interaction. IEEE Transactions on Systems Man and Cybernetics Part A-Systems and Humans, vol. 40, no. 1, pp. 147–157, 2010.

[2] K. Kim, D. Maloney, G. Bruder, J. N. Bailenson, and G. F. Welch, The effects of virtual human's spatial and behavioral coherencewith physical objects on social presence in AR, Computer Animation and Virtual World, vol. 28, pp. 3-4, 2017.

Classifying Daily Activities regardless of Wearable Motion Sensor Orientation

Aras Yurtman and Billur Barshan

Department of Electrical and Electronics Engineering
Bilkent University, 06800 Ankara, Turkey
Email: {yurtman, billur}@ee.bilkent.edu.tr

***Abstract*—Most studies on wearable sensing assume that each sensor is correctly placed on the body, fixed to a pre-determined position at a pre-determined orientation. This is not practical and feasible in many applications where elderly, disabled, or injured people need to place the sensor units on their own, especially for wireless and small sensor units. It is a considerable improvement to make wearable systems robust against the placement orientations of the sensors, and further, to allow the sensors to be placed at any orientation. For this purpose, we propose a transformation based on Singular Value Decomposition (SVD) that removes the absolute orientation information from the sensor data. We apply this transformation in the pre-processing stage of the standard human activity recognition scheme using multiple publicly available datasets, classifiers, and cross-validation techniques, and achieve an average accuracy that is only 7.56 % lower than the reference approach with fixed sensor orientations. The most common method that is an alternative to the proposed transformation is taking the Euclidean norm of 3D data vectors, which obtains 13.50 % lower accuracy than the reference approach. We show that randomly oriented sensors cause a reduction of 21.21 % in the activity recognition accuracy when no transformation is applied for orientation invariance; hence, the standard system cannot handle incorrectly oriented sensors. On the other hand, the proposed approach allows users to place the sensor units at any orientation on their body with an acceptable reduction in the accuracy, outperforming the common Euclidean norm approach.**

***Keywords*–Human activity recognition; Wearable sensing; Orientation-invariant sensing; Motion sensors; Singular value decomposition.**

I. INTRODUCTION

The exceptional development of mobile devices and their sensing capabilities have enabled them to seamlessly obtain information about people's activities and behaviors. Human activity recognition finds application in the human-computer interaction, healthcare, surveillance, military, and entertainment domains [1]. There are mainly two approaches in activity recognition: wearable sensing and computer vision. As a result of increased computational power and reduced size and weight of mobile devices, wearable sensing has become applicable to various scenarios in a less obtrusive manner, whereas the vision-based approach requires external cameras that reduce the mobility of the subject and raise privacy concerns [2].

In wearable sensing applications including human activity recognition, it is often assumed that each wearable device that contains sensors is placed at a pre-determined position on the body at a pre-determined orientation. Wearable devices have reduced in size and gained wireless communication capabilities; hence, they have become more likely to be incorrectly placed on the body. For instance, smart phones can be carried in a pocket at different orientations, and it is obtrusive to require the user to place his/her phone in his/her pocket always at a fixed orientation. Moreover, in some applications, these sensors are used by elderly, disabled, injured people, or children who may have difficulty in determining the orientation of the sensors for correct placement. However, while there are many studies on activity recognition using wearable motion sensors, only a small fraction of them considers incorrectly orientated sensors [3].

Inertial sensors (accelerometers and gyroscopes) and magnetometers are the common types of wearable motion sensors. Each sensor is typically tri-axial, acquiring data on three mutually perpendicular axes that are part of the device. When the sensor is placed at the same position at a different orientation, the acquired data have a representation in a new, rotated coordinate frame. Wearable systems that assume correct sensor placement are not robust against this change in general. We propose a transformation that removes the dependency of the data on the sensor axes while keeping most of the information content of the data. In this approach, the transformed data are invariant to the orientation at which the sensors are placed on the body, which enables the users to place the sensor units at any orientation at the pre-determined positions.

The rest of this paper is organized as follows: We summarize the related work in Section II. The proposed method for orientation invariance is described in Section III. Section IV includes the description of the datasets, the activity recognition scheme, and the experimental results. In Section V, the proposed method is discussed comparatively with the existing approaches. We state our conclusions and directions for future work in Section VI.

II. RELATED WORK

The most common and the simplest approach in the literature to achieve robustness to incorrectly oriented sensors is to take the Euclidean norm (that is, the magnitude) of the 3D vectors acquired by tri-axial sensors. The Euclidean norm of the acquired vectors does not depend on the orientation of the sensor. References [4]–[7] use the magnitude in classification, whereas [1][8][9] append the magnitude to the tri-axial sensor data as a fourth axis.

The second approach assumes that the gravity component is dominant over the linear acceleration component in the acceleration vectors during daily activities, and estimates this direction by averaging the accelerometer data [10]–[13]. Then, the tri-axial vectors are decomposed into vertical and horizontal components [10]–[12]. Reference [13] additionally calculates the forward-backward direction of the body as the principal axis that is perpendicular to the vertical axis.

In our earlier work [14], we proposed two alternative transformations to remove the information regarding absolute sensor orientation without making any assumptions about the sensor configurations or usage scenario. The first transformation extracts geometrical features from tri-axial sensor data, whereas the second projects the sensor data onto three principal axes in each time segment. Both transformations are shown to significantly improve the activity recognition accuracy when the sensors are randomly oriented. Reference [15] applies Principal Component Analysis (PCA) to the tri-axial data to remove the information related to absolute sensor orientation.

Another approach is to estimate the sensor orientation relative to the Earth frame, based on accelerometer, gyroscope, and magnetometer data [16]. Then, the sensor readings can be represented in the fixed Earth frame, independent of the sensor orientation.

Reference [17] classifies the orientation of the sensor unit among four pre-determined orientations based on the acquired data while the unit is moving and rotates the sensor data accordingly. Reference [18] assumes that incorrect placement of a sensor unit only affects the class means in the feature space, which may not be always true, and compensates for this by using the expectation-maximization algorithm. In [19], orientation invariance is achieved based on calibration postures that the subjects need to perform after placing the sensor units. Reference [20] develops a robust classification methodology against corruption in some portion of the data to handle incorrect placement of some of the sensor units.

III. PROPOSED TRANSFORMATION FOR ORIENTATION INVARIANCE

The tri-axial sensor data are originally acquired in the sensor coordinate frame in terms of the x, y, z axes that depend on the orientation at which the sensor is fixed on the body. To achieve orientation invariance, we apply SVD to the data to represent them in terms of the principal axes.

The sensor data acquired in a time segment can be represented as a matrix

$$\mathbf{A} = [\mathbf{a}_1 \ \mathbf{a}_2 \ \cdots \ \mathbf{a}_N] \tag{1}$$

where $\mathbf{a}_i = [a_{ix} \ a_{iy} \ a_{iz}]^\mathsf{T}$ $(i = 1, \ldots, N)$ is the acquired data vector in 3D space at time sample i. We decompose $\mathbf{A}$ into three matrices by SVD as

$$\mathbf{A} = \mathbf{U}\boldsymbol{\Sigma}\mathbf{V}^\mathsf{T} \tag{2}$$

In the compact form, $\boldsymbol{\Sigma}$ is a 3×3 diagonal matrix containing the singular values of $\mathbf{A}$. The 3×3 and $3 \times N$ matrices $\mathbf{U}$ and $\mathbf{V}$ contain the left and right singular vectors in their columns, respectively. Since $\mathbf{A}$ consists of real numbers, $\mathbf{U}$ and $\mathbf{V}$ have orthonormal columns and satisfy $\mathbf{U}\mathbf{U}^\mathsf{T} = \mathbf{U}^\mathsf{T}\mathbf{U} = \mathbf{I}_{3\times3}$ and $\mathbf{V}^\mathsf{T}\mathbf{V} = \mathbf{I}_{N\times N}$.

Placing the sensor unit at a different orientation is equivalent to applying the same rotation to all the data vectors in 3D space, provided that the sensor unit is rigidly attached to the body. Here, we assume that the sensor unit moves together with the body part it is placed on, regardless of the orientation at which it is fixed on the body. This assumption is implicitly made in almost all studies on orientation invariance because otherwise the sensor unit would rotate independently of the body and would not be able to capture substantial information about the body motion.

A different orientation of the sensor causes each of the acquired data vectors $\mathbf{a}_i$ to be rotated by the same (unknown) rotation matrix $\mathbf{R}$ as $\tilde{\mathbf{a}}_i = \mathbf{R}\mathbf{a}_i$, which can be represented as the matrix product $\tilde{\mathbf{A}} = \mathbf{R}\mathbf{A}$. Using (2), the rotated data matrix can be expressed as

$$\tilde{\mathbf{A}} = \mathbf{R}\left(\mathbf{U}\boldsymbol{\Sigma}\mathbf{V}^\mathsf{T}\right) = (\mathbf{R}\mathbf{U})\,\boldsymbol{\Sigma}\mathbf{V}^\mathsf{T} = \tilde{\mathbf{U}}\boldsymbol{\Sigma}\mathbf{V}^\mathsf{T} \tag{3}$$

The last term corresponds to the SVD of $\tilde{\mathbf{A}}$ with a new left singular matrix, $\tilde{\mathbf{U}} = \mathbf{R}\mathbf{U}$, because the SVD representation is unique (up to the signs of the principal vectors [21]) and $\tilde{\mathbf{U}}$ is also an orthonormal matrix that satisfies the properties

$$\begin{aligned} \tilde{\mathbf{U}}\tilde{\mathbf{U}}^\mathsf{T} &= (\mathbf{R}\mathbf{U})(\mathbf{R}\mathbf{U})^\mathsf{T} = \mathbf{R}\mathbf{U}\mathbf{U}^\mathsf{T}\mathbf{R}^\mathsf{T} = \mathbf{R}\mathbf{R}^\mathsf{T} = \mathbf{I}_{3\times3} \\ \tilde{\mathbf{U}}^\mathsf{T}\tilde{\mathbf{U}} &= (\mathbf{R}\mathbf{U})^\mathsf{T}(\mathbf{R}\mathbf{U}) = \mathbf{U}^\mathsf{T}\mathbf{R}^\mathsf{T}\mathbf{R}\mathbf{U} = \mathbf{U}^\mathsf{T}\mathbf{U} = \mathbf{I}_{3\times3} \end{aligned} \tag{4}$$

where the $\mathbf{R}$ matrix is orthonormal: $\mathbf{R}^\mathsf{T}\mathbf{R} = \mathbf{R}\mathbf{R}^\mathsf{T} = \mathbf{I}_{3\times3}$.

We observe from (2) and (3) that the matrices $\boldsymbol{\Sigma}$ and $\mathbf{V}$ remain the same when $\mathbf{A}$ is rotated. Hence, the matrix product

$$\mathbf{B} \triangleq \boldsymbol{\Sigma}\mathbf{V}^\mathsf{T} \tag{5}$$

is taken as the transformed data that are invariant to the orientation at which the sensor is placed on the body.

This transformation is indeed equivalent to a rotation by $\mathbf{U}^\mathsf{T}$ (which may be left or right handed) because $\mathbf{U}^\mathsf{T}\mathbf{A} = \mathbf{U}^\mathsf{T}\mathbf{U}\boldsymbol{\Sigma}\mathbf{V}^\mathsf{T} = \boldsymbol{\Sigma}\mathbf{V}^\mathsf{T} = \mathbf{B}$. In this way, the data, which are originally in terms of the x, y, z axes of the sensor frame, are represented in terms of three orthogonal principal axes $\mathbf{u}_1$, $\mathbf{u}_2$, $\mathbf{u}_3$ that are the columns of $\mathbf{U}$.

If a sensor unit contains multiple types of tri-axial sensors such as an accelerometer and a gyroscope, a joint transformation can be calculated for all the sensors because they are exposed to the same rotation. To calculate a joint SVD, the $\mathbf{A}$ matrices acquired from multiple sensors can be concatenated horizontally. To transform the data, each data matrix is pre-multiplied by the transpose of the left singular matrix $\mathbf{U}$ of the joint SVD.

The original sensor data $\mathbf{A}$, the randomly rotated data $\tilde{\mathbf{A}}$, and the transformed data $\mathbf{B}$ are plotted in Figure 1 for the walking activity performed by subject 1 in dataset D_4. Note that $\mathbf{B}$ can be obtained by applying the proposed transformation to either $\mathbf{A}$ or $\tilde{\mathbf{A}}$. We observe that the periodic nature of the walking activity is preserved in the transformed signal.

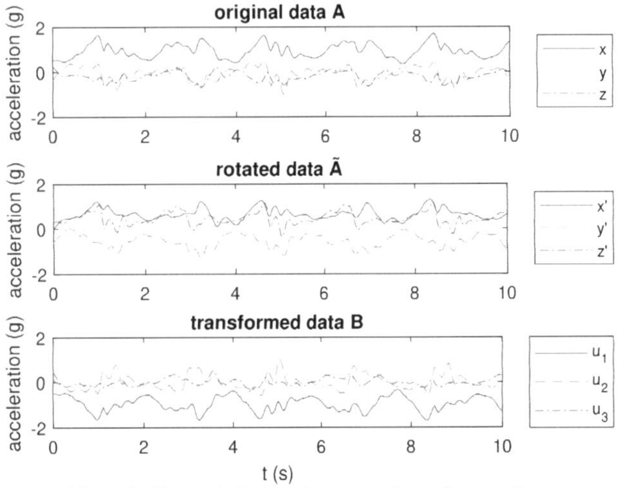

Figure 1. The original, rotated, and transformed sensor data.

TABLE I. ATTRIBUTES OF THE FIVE DATASETS.

dataset	D_1 [22]	D_2 [23]	D_3 [24]	D_4 [25]	D_5 [26]
no. of subjects	8	4	30	14	15
no. of activities	19	5	6	12	7
activities (*: stationary activity)	(1*) sitting, (2*) standing, (3*,4*) lying on back and on right side, (5,6) ascending and descending stairs, (7) standing still in an elevator, (8) moving around in an elevator, (9) walking in a parking lot, (10,11) walking on a treadmill in flat and 15° inclined positions at a speed of 4 km/h, (12) running on a treadmill at a speed of 8 km/h, (13) exercising on a stepper, (14) exercising on a cross trainer, (15,16) cycling on an exercise bike in horizontal and vertical positions, (17) rowing, (18) jumping, (19) playing basketball	(1) sitting down, (2) standing up, (3*) standing, (4) walking, (5*) sitting	(1) walking, (2) ascending stairs, (3) descending stairs, (4*) sitting, (5*) standing, (6*) lying	(1) walking, (2,3) walking left and right, (4,5) ascending and descending stairs, (6) running forward, (7) jumping, (8*) sitting, (9*) standing, (10*) sleeping, (11,12) ascending and descending in an elevator	(1*) working at a computer, (2) standing up–walking–ascending/descending stairs, (3*) standing, (4) walking, (5) ascending/descending stairs, (6) walking and talking with someone, (7*) talking while standing
no. of units	5	4	1	1	1
no. of axes per unit	9	3	6	6	3
unit positions	torso, right and left arm, right and left leg	waist, left thigh, right ankle, right upper arm	waist	front right hip	chest
sensor types	accelerometer, gyroscope, magnetometer	accelerometer	accelerometer, gyroscope	accelerometer, gyroscope	accelerometer
dataset duration (hr)	13	8	7	7	10
sampling rate (Hz)	25	8	50	100	52
no. of time segments	9,120	4,130	10,299	5,353	7,345
segment duration (s)	5	5	2.56	5	5
no. of features (with no transformation)	1,170	276	234	156	78

IV. Experimental Methodology and Results

To assess the performance of the proposed method, we apply the standard activity recognition scheme on multiple datasets, classifiers, and cross-validation techniques.

A. Datasets

We use five publicly available datasets, which have different sensor configurations and have been acquired by different research groups [22]–[26]. Brief information about the datasets is provided in Table I.

B. Pre-Processing

The time-domain data are divided into segments of fixed duration (see Table I). Then, we apply one of the following pre-processing methods:

- **REF (Reference):** No transformation is applied.
- **ROT (Random Rotation):** The tri-axial data acquired from each sensor unit in each time segment are rotated by a different random rotation matrix generated from independently and uniformly distributed roll, pitch, and yaw angles [27] in the interval $[0, 2\pi)$.
- **NORM (Euclidean Norm):** The Euclidean norm of each 3D data vector is taken. This is an existing approach for orientation invariance [4]–[7] and included for comparison.
- **SVDT (SVD-based Transformation):** We apply the proposed transformation defined in Section III to each sensor unit in each time segment separately. This method is robust against placing each sensor unit at a different orientation in each time segment.

C. Classification

After transforming the time-domain data, the following statistical features are extracted from each axis of each time segment: minimum, maximum, mean, variance, skewness, kurtosis, the coefficients of the autocorrelation sequence for the lag values of $5, 10, \ldots, 50$ samples, and the five largest Discrete Fourier Transform (DFT) peaks (that are at least 11 samples apart) with the corresponding frequencies. Fewer autocorrelation coefficients and DFT peaks can be used in some datasets if there are not sufficiently many time samples in a segment. The number of features extracted from a single time segment of the untransformed data is provided in the last row of Table I for each dataset.

The features are normalized to the interval $[0, 1]$ for each subject in each dataset. Then, PCA is used to reduce the number of features to 30.

Classification is performed by four state-of-the-art classifiers (see [28] for further information):

- **Bayesian Decision Making (BDM):** A multi-variate Gaussian distribution is fitted to the training feature vectors of each class. For a test feature vector, the class that has the highest class-conditional probability is selected.
- **k-Nearest Neighbor (k-NN):** The training phase consists of the storage of the training vectors with their true labels. A test vector is assigned the most common class label among the k training vectors that are closest to it in terms of the Euclidean distance. A suitable value of k is selected as 7.
- **Support Vector Machines (SVM):** The features are mapped to a higher-dimensional space by using the Gaussian Radial Basis Function (RBF). A binary classifier is trained for each distinct class pair to divide the feature space into two regions by a hyperplane that maximizes the margin. The classification relies on the decision of the most confident classifier. The RBF and penalty parameters are optimized as $\gamma = 0.2$ and $C = 40$, respectively, by a two-level grid search [14].
- **Artificial Neural Networks (ANN):** Three layers of neurons with a sigmoid output function are used. The number of neurons in the input and output layers are 30 and as many as the number of classes, respectively. The number of neurons in the intermediate layer is selected as the nearest integer to the average of the optimistic and pessimistic cases [14]. Coefficients of the linear combinations are randomly initialized in $[0, 0.2]$ and determined by the back-propagation algorithm with an adaptive stopping criterion [14] and a learning rate of 0.3. In classification, the test vector is fed to the input and the class corresponding to the maximum output is selected.

Two cross-validation techniques are used to assess the accuracy: P-fold (with $P = 10$) randomly divides the feature vectors into P partitions and tests each partition by a classifier trained by the feature vectors in the remaining partitions. Leave-1-subject-Out (L1O) considers each subject's data as a partition and follows the same approach as P-fold. L1O is more challenging and generalizable than P-fold because the training and test vectors belong to different subjects in L1O.

D. Results

The accuracies for all the classifiers, pre-processing approaches, and datasets are shown in the bar chart in Figure 2. A stick centered at the tip of each bar indicates plus/minus one standard deviation in the accuracy over the cross-validation iterations. Figures 2(a)–(c) show the results for all the activities, stationary activities, and non-stationary activities, respectively. (Stationary activities are denoted by an asterisk (*) in Table I.) Figure 3 shows the accuracy values averaged over the four classifiers and the five datasets for each approach and cross-validation technique separately for the the whole activity set, stationary, and non-stationary activities.

As observed from Figures 2 and 3, the highest accuracy is obtained by using the REF approach where the orientations of the sensor units are fixed and no transformation is applied to the data. The accuracy considerably drops in the ROT approach where the acquired data are rotated randomly to simulate the placement of the sensor units at random orientations and no transformation is applied for orientation invariance. This shows that the standard activity recognition scheme is not robust against incorrectly oriented sensors. Among the two types of transformations for orientation invariance, the proposed approach SVDT performs significantly better than the widely used approach NORM on the average. This is especially observed for datasets D_1 and D_4 and for non-stationary activities.

V. Discussion

We consider different approaches at the pre-processing stage to observe the effects of incorrectly oriented sensors and the transformations for orientation invariance, unlike most of the existing studies. The sensor units are correctly placed on the body in all the datasets that we use, and we synthetically rotate the signals to simulate randomly oriented sensors. This enables us to use the same data in both approaches so that we can fairly compare them. If a new dataset were recorded for randomly rotated sensors, it would have a different level of difficulty in activity recognition because of the variations that occur in the data. These variations can be observed from the standard deviations over the cross-validation iterations in Figure 2. Reference [29] investigates the variations in the activity data within and between subjects in detail.

When we apply the existing or the proposed transformation to the sensor data, we mathematically ensure that the transformed data are not affected by the orientations at which the sensors are fixed to the body. In other words, the same data can be obtained by transforming the original and randomly rotated data (up to the signs of the axes in SVDT). Therefore, we do not need to record a new dataset with different sensor orientations to observe the effects of the orientation-invariant transformations on the activity recognition accuracy.

In the ROT approach, we rotate the tri-axial sensor data separately for each sensor unit in each time segment. Hence, the training and test sets contain data corresponding to different sensor orientations. This is advantageous for the system because in the training phase, the classifiers may adapt to the variation in the data by relying on (the linear combinations of) the features that are more robust against the changes in sensor orientations. Keeping the training data unchanged and rotating only the test data may result in a higher accuracy compared to the method we use.

In Section III, we allow the user to initially place the sensors on his/her body at any orientation, but we assume that the sensor rotates together with the body part on which it is placed; that is, the sensor is rigidly attached to the body. This assumption is required even for the simplest approach, NORM, because otherwise the motion sensors would record different signals when they rotate freely independent of the body movements. In particular, the gravity vector acquired by the accelerometer, the angular rate detected by the gyroscope, and the magnetic field of the Earth measured by the magnetometer would be all unrelated to the body motion in this case.

A sudden change in the orientation of the sensor with respect to the body corrupts the signals for a short time interval. If the data are transformed by the NORM approach, the same, short time interval will be corrupted in the transformed data. If the proposed transformation SVDT is applied, different principal vectors will be obtained, and the whole transformed data will be affected. Since we transform each time segment separately, only the corresponding segment(s) will be affected, which corresponds to a short time interval because the segments have a duration of at most 5 seconds.

There is an important advantage of the method we propose over most of the existing approaches: Our method only requires a transformation to be added at the pre-processing stage, without a need to modify the rest of the activity recognition system. The input and output of the transformation are both tri-axial and of the same form. The transformation does not change the physical units of the acquired data and their dimensionality; hence, does not require any modifications in the following steps in the activity recognition paradigm.

VI. Conclusions and Future Work

In wearable sensing, it is mostly assumed that the sensors are placed on the body at fixed orientations, which is not feasible in many applications such as monitoring of the elderly or children. We show that incorrectly oriented wearable sensors significantly decrease the activity recognition accuracy, which is consistently valid for multiple datasets, classifiers, and cross-validation tests. We propose an SVD-based transformation to represent the tri-axial data in terms of three principal axes to remove the information of absolute sensor orientation. In most cases, this method significantly increases the accuracy when the sensors are placed at random orientations, providing an accuracy close to the reference approach with fixed sensor orientations in some cases. Our approach achieves a better overall accuracy than the conventional Euclidean norm method and can be integrated into most of the existing systems without much effort.

As future work, the proposed method can be applied to other applications of wearable sensing, such as fall detection [30] and physical therapy [31], and extended to handle the incorrect positions of the sensor units in addition to incorrect orientations.

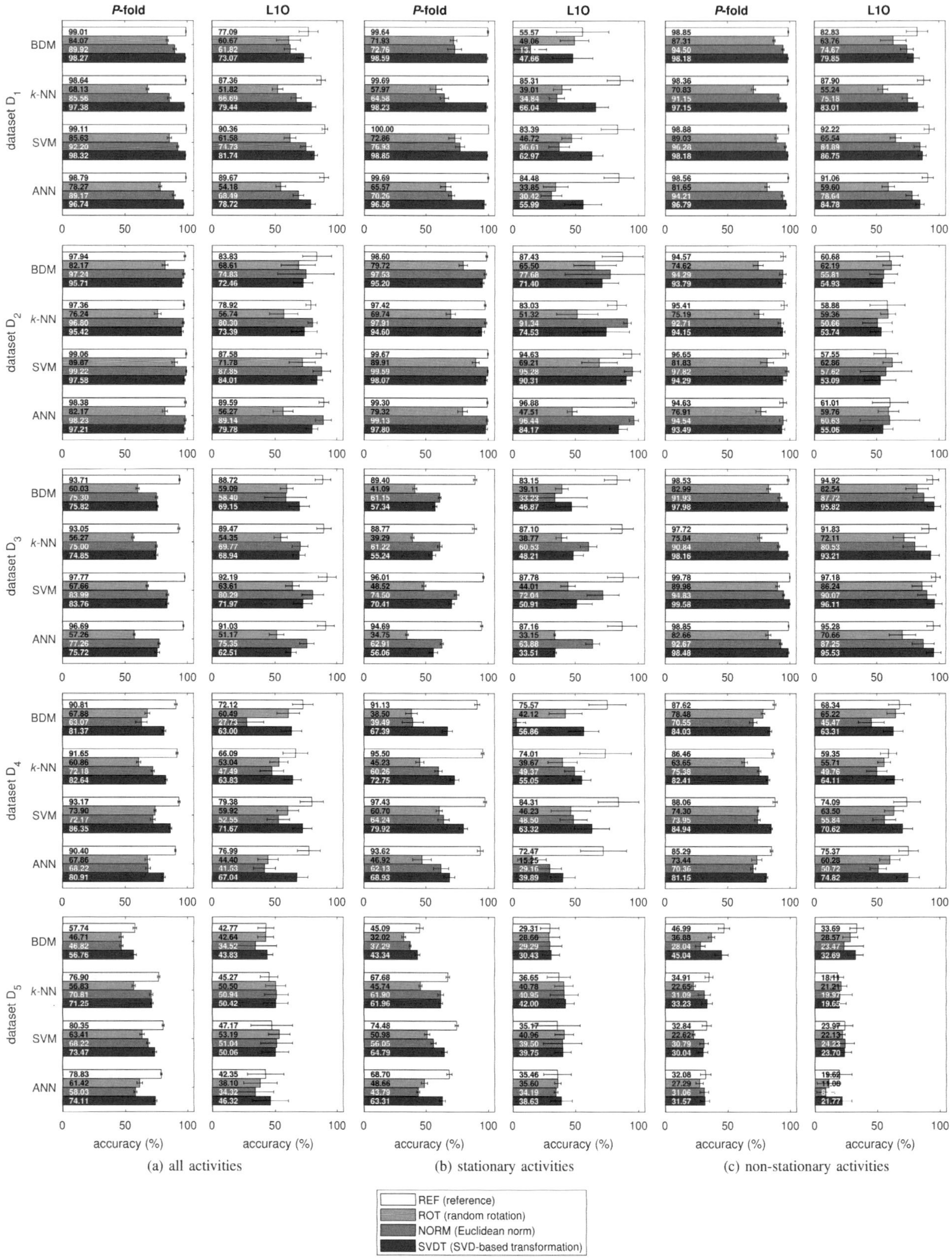

Figure 2. Activity recognition accuracy of each classifier for each pre-processing approach for each dataset. The horizontal stick centered at the tip of each bar indicates plus/minus one standard deviation in the accuracy over the cross-validation iterations.

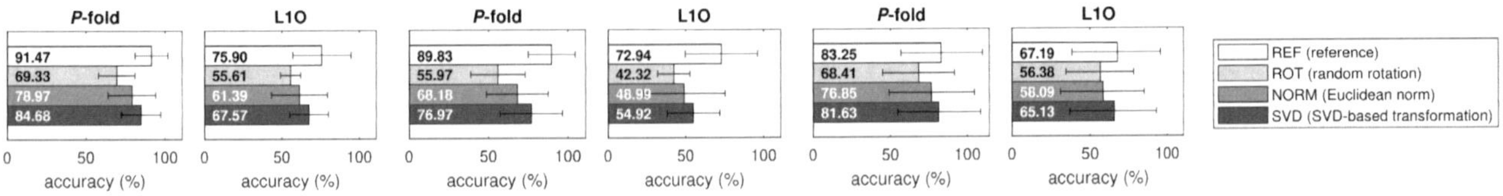

(a) all activities (b) stationary activities (c) non-stationary activities

Figure 3. Activity recognition accuracy averaged over the classifiers and the datasets for each pre-processing approach. The horizontal stick centered at the tip of each bar indicates plus/minus one standard deviation in the accuracy over the classifiers and the datasets.

REFERENCES

[1] M. Shoaib, S. Bosch, Ö. D. İncel, H. Scholten, and J. M. Havinga, "Fusion of smartphone motion sensors for physical activity recognition," *Sensors*, vol. 14, no. 6, pp. 10146–10176, June 2014.

[2] O. D. Lara and M. A. Labrador, "A survey on human activity recognition using wearable sensors," *IEEE Communications Surveys and Tutorials*, vol. 15, no. 3, pp. 1192–1209, Third Quarter, 2013.

[3] J. Morales and D. Akopian, "Physical activity recognition by smartphones, a survey," *Biocybernetics and Biomedical Engineering*, vol. 37, no. 3, pp. 388–400, May 2017.

[4] K. Kunze and P. Lukowicz, "Sensor placement variations in wearable activity recognition," *IEEE Pervasive Computing*, vol. 13, no. 4, pp. 32–41, October–December 2014.

[5] S. Bhattacharya, P. Nurmi, N. Hammerla, and T. Plötz, "Using unlabeled data in a sparse-coding framework for human activity recognition," *Pervasive and Mobile Computing*, vol. 15, pp. 242–262, December 2014.

[6] S. Reddy *et al.*, "Using mobile phones to determine transportation modes," *ACM Transactions on Sensor Networks*, vol. 6, no. 2, article no. 13, February 2010.

[7] P. Siirtola and J. Röning, "Recognizing human activities user-independently on smartphones based on accelerometer data," *International Journal of Interactive Multimedia and Artificial Intelligence: Special Issue on Distributed Computing and Artificial Intelligence*, vol. 1, no. 5, pp. 38–45, June 2012.

[8] L. Sun, D. Zhang, B. Li, B. Guo, and S. Li, "Activity recognition on an accelerometer embedded mobile phone with varying positions and orientations," *Proceedings of the 7th International Conference on Ubiquitous Intelligence and Computing*, 26–29 October 2010, Xi'an, China, *Lecture Notes in Computer Science*, vol. 6406, no. 1, pp. 548–562, Springer, Berlin, Heidelberg, Germany, 2010.

[9] M. Janidarmian, A. R. Fekr, K. Radecka, and Z. Zilic, "A comprehensive analysis on wearable acceleration sensors in human activity recognition," *Sensors*, vol. 17, no. 3, article no. 529, March 2017.

[10] Y. Yang, "Toward physical activity diary: motion recognition using simple acceleration features with mobile phones," *Proceedings of the 1st International Workshop on Interactive Multimedia for Consumer Electronics*, pp. 1–10, 23 October 2009, Beijing, China.

[11] H. Lu *et al.*, "The Jigsaw continuous sensing engine for mobile phone applications," *Proceedings of the 8th ACM Conference on Embedded Networked Sensor Systems*, pp. 71–84, 3–5 November 2010, Zürich, Switzerland.

[12] N. Wang, S. J. Redmond, E. Ambikairajah, B. G. Celler, and N. H. Lovell, "Can triaxial accelerometry accurately recognize inclined walking terrains?" *IEEE Transactions on Biomedical Engineering*, vol. 57, no. 10, pp. 2506–2516, October 2010.

[13] A. Henpraserttae, S. Thiemjarus, and S. Marukatat, "Accurate activity recognition using a mobile phone regardless of device orientation and location," *Proceedings of the International Conference on Body Sensor Networks*, pp. 41–46, 23–25 May 2011, Dallas, TX, U.S.A.

[14] A. Yurtman and B. Barshan, "Activity recognition invariant to sensor orientation with wearable motion sensors," *Sensors*, vol. 17, no. 8, article no. 1838, August 2017.

[15] J. Morales, D. Akopian, and S. Agaian, "Human activity recognition by smartphones regardless of device orientation," *Proceedings of SPIE-IS&T Electronic Imaging: Photonics: Mobile Devices and Multimedia: Enabling Technologies, Algorithms, and Applications*, R. Creutzburg and D. Akopian (eds.), SPIE vol. 9030, pp. 90300I-1–90300I-12, 18 February 2014, San Francisco, CA, U.S.A.

[16] Y. E. Ustev, Ö. D. İncel, and C. Ersoy, "User, device and orientation independent human activity recognition on mobile phones: challenges and a proposal," *Proceedings of the ACM Conference on Pervasive and Ubiquitous Computing*, pp. 1427–1436, 8–12 September 2013, Zürich, Switzerland.

[17] S. Thiemjarus, "A device-orientation independent method for activity recognition," *Proceedings of the International Conference on Body Sensor Networks*, pp. 19–23, 7–9 June 2010, Biopolis, Singapore.

[18] R. Chavarriaga, H. Bayati, and J. del R. Millán, "Unsupervised adaptation for acceleration-based activity recognition: robustness to sensor displacement and rotation," *Personal and Ubiquitous Computing*, vol. 17, no. 3, pp. 479–490, June 2011.

[19] M. Jiang, H. Shang, Z. Wang, H. Li, and Y. Wang, "A method to deal with installation errors of wearable accelerometers for human activity recognition," *Physiological Measurement*, vol. 32, no. 3, pp. 347–358, February 2011.

[20] O. Banos, M. A. Toth, M. Damas, H. Pomares, and I. Rojas, "Dealing with the effects of sensor displacement in wearable activity recognition," *Sensors*, vol. 14, no. 6, pp. 9995–10023, June 2014.

[21] L. De Lathauwer, B. De Moor, and J. Vandewalle, "A multilinear singular value decomposition," *SIAM Journal on Matrix Analysis and Applications*, vol. 21, no. 4, pp. 1253–1278, April 2000.

[22] K. Altun and B. Barshan, "Daily and Sports Activities Dataset," *UCI Machine Learning Repository*, University of California, Irvine, School of Information and Computer Sciences, 2013. Available from: http://archive.ics.uci.edu/ml/datasets/Daily+and+Sports+Activities, retrieved: January 2018.

[23] W. Ugulino *et al.*, "Wearable Computing: Classification of Body Postures and Movements (PUC-Rio) Data Set," *UCI Machine Learning Repository*, University of California, Irvine, School of Information and Computer Sciences, 2013. Available from: https://archive.ics.uci.edu/ml/datasets/Wearable+Computing%3A+Classification+of+Body+Postures+and+Movements+(PUC-Rio), retrieved: January 2018.

[24] J. L. Reyes-Ortiz, D. Anguita, A. Ghio, L. Oneto, and X. Parra, "Human Activity Recognition Using Smartphones Data Set," *UCI Machine Learning Repository*, University of California, Irvine, School of Information and Computer Sciences, 2012. Available from: https://archive.ics.uci.edu/ml/datasets/Human+Activity+Recognition+Using+Smartphones, retrieved: January 2018.

[25] M. Zhang and A. A. Sawchuk, "USC-HAD: a daily activity dataset for ubiquitous activity recognition using wearable sensors," *ACM International Conference on Ubiquitous Computing Workshop on Situation, Activity, and Goal Awareness*, pp. 1036–1043, 5–8 September 2012, Pittsburgh, PA, U.S.A.

[26] P. Casale, O. Pujol, and P. Redeva, "Human activity recognition from accelerometer data using a wearable device," *Proceedings of the Iberian Conference on Pattern Recognition and Image Analysis*, 8–10 June 2011, Gran Canaria, Spain, *Pattern Recognition and Image Analysis, Lecture Notes in Computer Science*, vol. 6669, pp. 289–296, Springer, Berlin, Heidelberg, Germany, 2011.

[27] B. Kastner, *Space Mathematics: Math Problems Based on Space Science*, Dover Books on Aeronautical Engineering, Courier Corporation, Washington, D.C., WA, U.S.A., 2013.

[28] R. O. Duda, P. E. Hart, and D. G. Stork, *Pattern Classification*, John Wiley & Sons, New York, NY, U.S.A., 2000.

[29] A. Yurtman and B. Barshan, "Investigating inter-subject and inter-activity variations in activity recognition using wearable motion sensors," *The Computer Journal*, vol. 59, no. 9, pp. 1345-1362, September 2016.

[30] A. T. Özdemir and B. Barshan, "Detecting falls with wearable sensors using machine learning techniques," *Sensors*, vol. 14, no. 6, pp. 10691–10708, June 2014.

[31] A. Yurtman and B. Barshan, "Automated evaluation of physical therapy exercises using multi-template dynamic time warping on wearable sensor signals," *Computer Methods and Programs in Biomedicine*, vol. 117, no. 2, pp. 189–207, November 2014.

Extended Method to Alternate the Estimation of Global Purposes and Local Objectives in Multiple Human-Agent Interaction

Yoshimasa Ohmoto*, Takashi Suyama* and Toyoaki Nishida*
*Department of Intelligence Science
and Technology
Graduate School of Informatics
Kyoto University
Kyoto, Japan
Email: ohmoto@i.kyoto-u.ac.jp, suyama@ii.ist.i.kyoto-u.ac.jp, nishida@i.kyoto-u.ac.jp

Abstract—**We are interested in how to realize the natural interaction between human and agent in a virtual world the same way the human-human interaction occurs in real-world. The differences between virtual experiences and real-world experiences highlight the fact that the former are not equivalent to the latter. We focused on the mental stances to establish the social relationships between humans and agents. The purpose of this study was to investigate whether the extended method to alternate the estimation of local objectives and global purposes using a network-connected two-layer model in multiple human-agent interaction (eAEGL model) could induce the intentional stance in human participants. We conducted an experiment to evaluate the effect of the proposed method using two types of agents: an agent that implemented eAEGL model and a simple goal-oriented agent. The results suggest that the participants who interacted with the eAEGL agent considered the agent to be an interaction partner and they positively involved the agent in their virtual world experiences.**

Keywords*–*Multi-modal interaction; human-agent interaction; multi-user interaction; intentional stance.

I. Introduction

Many people use information technologies and devices to perform their everyday tasks. Virtual reality (VR) techniques and devices are developing rapidly and virtual reality technology will be widely applied to training games that are used in education, medical services, wellness, and fitness [1]. People can acquire various skills through game playing [2] or through games used for physical rehabilitation [3]. Additionally, software developers evaluate the user interface during the game usage [4]. In these applications, virtual agents are used as interaction partners, such as an instructor for the training, a rival character for giving motivation, or a crowd simulating a situation.

However, the differences between virtual experiences and real-world experiences highlight the fact that the former are not equivalent to the latter. For example, the character agents in the virtual world are not usually regarded as familiar friends but, more prosaically, as multi-modal interfaces that provide useful information. In such cases, once the user has learned the rules of social interaction in the virtual world, he or she may not be able to probe the true nature of those rules. As a result, the user either obeys the rules blindly or finds them impossible to follow. Therefore, we should consider how to establish the social relationships between humans and agents.

In previous studies [6][7], we focused on the mental stances that people took when interacting with their interaction partner using three categories: physical stance, design stance, and intentional stance [8]. The interaction partner can be both a human and an agent. We considered the intentional stance and the design stance as follows. The intentional stance is a mental state in which people assume unobservable inner state parameters for the interaction partner's behaviour estimation. Examples of the unobservable inner state parameters are a behaviour model, emotional aspects, and decision-making strategies of the interaction partner. Therefore, people who assume the intentional stance pay attention to various interaction parameters because they do not accurately identify the parameters that are important to obtain acceptable results in the interaction. The design stance is a mental state in which people believe they can estimate the interaction partner's behaviour by the observable interaction parameters. Therefore, people who assume the design stance pay attention to only the observable parameters that are clearly related to the interaction. The main difference between the intentional stance and the design stance is that people expect and accept that the results of the interaction are different when they provide the same interaction behaviour to their interaction partner.

In our previous studies [7][9], we proposed a method to alternately propagate estimates of human's objectives of the subordinate tasks (local objectives) and human's purposes of the entire task (global purposes) during a collaboration task through humna-agent interaction, using a network-connected two-layer model of emphasizing factors. An agent implementing this method estimates the human ' s local objectives from his/her behaviour, and the human ' s global purposes from the time series patterns of the local objectives. We believe that this method, which could provide consistency and coordination between local objectives and global purposes, could be useful to enhance factors that induce and maintain the intentional stance. For smooth interaction, it is important to understand the meta-rules to maintain the consistency and coordination, and the meta-rules are composed of some heuristics. By using this method, participants spontaneously speculate on the meta-rules through the interaction and pay attention to the unobservable inner state of the agent.

Recently, we applied the alternating estimation of human mental states in one-to-one human-agent interaction in a previous study [7]. However, multiple users often join a virtual world simulation and interact with an agent in different situations. Therefore, we should consider how to estimate and integrate the alternating estimations of multiple human mental states for an agent's decision making in human-agent interaction.

In the present study, we extended the method to alternate the estimation of participants' local objectives and global purposes using a network-connected two-layer model in one-to-one human-agent interaction to multiple human-agent interaction. We separately described the local objectives in local tasks and global purposes for the entire task for each human. Then, the agent decides which global purpose of the human is similar or conflicts with the agent's global purpose. Subsequently, the agent provides a goal-oriented behaviour related to the global purposes, to support the local objectives in the local tasks.

This paper is organized as follows: In Section 2, we briefly introduce the related works. Section 3 provides an outline of the proposed method. Section 4 contains a description of our experiment that compared experimental and control groups, and presents our results. In Section 5, we discuss the achievements of this research and some future work. We present our conclusion in Section 6.

II. Related work

The typical way to speculate about a human's intentions within human-agent interaction is human-agent communication through a dialogue. Kitamura et al. [10], for example, developed a system that matches users' queries with search targets by communicating with users throughout the interview. Most of the research considered that people had reliable demands and needs and they tried to uncover them. However, especially in collaborative tasks, people's demands and needs are ambiguous and they are interactively changed through the tasks in many cases. In human-human interaction, we do not think that we can precisely speculate people's intentions only through a dialogue.

Agents that collaboratively perform various tasks have been proposed in many studies, such as subordinate support agents when people perform tasks on their own initiative and automated attentive agents which automatically perform tasks in line with a human's wishes [11]. We assumed that the intentional stance was partially induced in the participants in the collaborative task because, if not, the engagement for the collaboration would have been low and they might have failed in the collaboration.

Some mutually directable methods and concepts affect task performance [12][13]. Mixed-initiative, for example, refers to a flexible interaction strategy wherein each agent can contribute to the task it does best. Furthermore, in general, the agents' roles are not determined in advance, but are opportunistically negotiated between them as the problem is being solved. In many cases, they merely provide a division of roles among interaction members; therefore, the consistency and coordination for performing the task are still managed by the main person.

Dindo et al. [14] proposed that humans use the intentional stance as a learning bias that sidesteps the (difficult) structure learning problem and bootstraps the acquisition of generative models for others' actions. They provided an example of how structure initialization can help in the learning of new parts of the model. In the example, they connected the action layer and intention layer by networks and identified the user's intentions from the sequence of the actions. This revealed that the network-connected layered model is effective for estimating the intentions of humans. They considered the intentional stance as a template of the structure generating the observed behaviour. In contrast, we consider the intentional stance itself as being an important factor to determine interaction behaviours.

Shirouzu et al. [15] investigated how collaboration leads to abstract and flexible problem solving. The results indicated that two factors, namely, individuals' activeness in choosing and confirming the initial strategies and the frequent role exchange between task-doing and monitoring in collaborative situations, interact in collaboration to generate various solutions differing in the degree of abstraction. These solutions are then reflected upon by the participants to lead them to abstraction. This shows that the observer's mental factors influence his/her evaluation of an observation target. In addition, in multiple human-agent interaction, a participant has an interaction-doing role whereas another has a monitoring role. Therefore, we should consider that the development of the human-agent relationships is different from that of one-to-one human-agent interaction.

III. Method to alternate estimation by representing global and local goal-oriented behaviour

Some methods induce the intentional stance, such as an agent resembling a human or an animal in appearance [16][17]. These methods mainly focus on inducing the intentional stance at the first impression. However, if the activities among the participants, including the agent, were not mutually influenced by them each other in collaborative long-term interaction, the participants would regard even human-human interactions as 'mechanical' because these interactions make people believe that they can estimate the interaction partner's behaviour by the observable interaction parameters.

In previous studies, we proposed a method to alternate estimation of local objectives and global purposes in a decision-making situation [9] and applied the method to a collaborative task for inducing and maintaining the intentional stance [7]. We called this Alternate Estimation by representing Global and Local goal-oriented behaviour (AEGL). AEGL separately describes an interaction partner's local objectives in local tasks and global purposes of the entire task. The agent implementing the method estimates the interaction partner's local objectives and global purposes based on the interaction responses. After the estimation, the agent updates its own local objectives depending on the estimated partner's global purposes. We expected that the interaction partner also estimates the agent's global purposes from its behaviour for the local tasks in one-to-one interaction. However, multiple users often join a collaboration task and interact with an agent in different situations. In addition, when the agent interacts with multiple users, the agent needs to prioritize the order of the interaction with the users and consider the user's global purposes. In this study, we extended the method used to alternate the estimation of local objectives and global purposes by a network-connected two-layer model in one-to-one human-agent interaction to multiple human-agent interaction. We called this extended method as eAEGL. Figure 1 shows the outline of this process.

The main difference between the eAEGL in this study and the AEGL in the previous work is to estimate the purposes of multiple interaction partners and then to evaluate the effect of agent's interaction behavior towards each interaction partner based on the degree of influence on agent's purpose. The eAEGL had lists of local objectives and global purposes, and

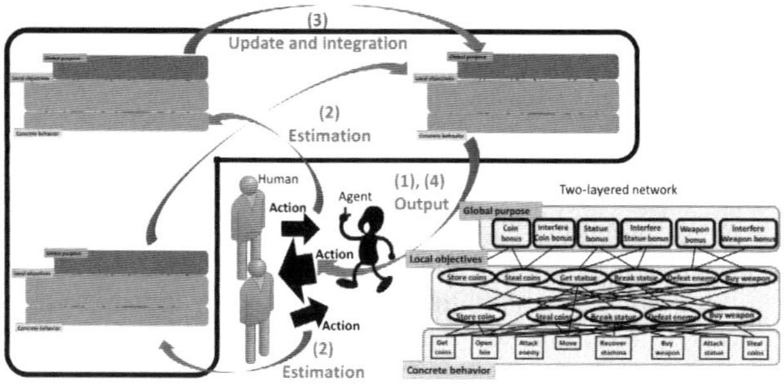

Figure 1. Outline of the alternating estimation process.

the relational networks for each user and its own depending on the task. The parameters of the network nodes were updated in a correspondent interaction behaviour of each user that included verbal and nonverbal responses. Subsequently, the parameters of the local objective nodes or global purpose nodes were speculated based on the parameters of the network-connected nodes. Based on the speculated parameters of global purpose nodes, eAEGL evaluated whether the user was collaborative or competitive, and how strongly influenced was the user's purpose on the agent's global purpose. This is an extended point. We briefly explain the interaction process below.

First, an agent with eAEGL determines its local objective based on weighted global purposes and provides appropriate behaviour to achieve the local objective. Subsequently, the agent estimates the local objectives of each user based on the behaviour and responses. From the estimation, the agent updates the weights of estimated global purposes of each user. Based on the updated global purposes, the agent evaluates whether each user is collaborative or competitive, and how strongly the user's purpose influences the agent's global purpose. The strength of the influence is the priority of the user. The agent calculates the cost when intervening with the higher priority user. If the cost is lower than a certain level, the agent increases the weights of the agent's global purpose related to the intervention. Finally, all parameters of the global purposes of each user and the agent are updated and integrated, then the agent modifies and determines its local objective based on the parameters.

The agent's representation to provide the goal-oriented behaviour for inducing and maintaining the intentional stance is different depending on whether the user is collaborative or competitive. When the user is collaborative, the agent tries to support the user's local objectives if possible, but the agent represents its global purposes through the local objective activities. When the user is competitive, the agent tries to interfere with the user's local objectives. The interference itself is a representation of the agent's global purposes. The agent's behaviour is modified through the interaction like a trial-and-error process. By repeatedly conducting the processes, the agent can represent the goals of the agent's activities towards the multiple users.

IV. EXPERIMENT

We conducted an experiment to investigate the effects of the proposed method on a user's impressions of the agent. In the experiment, participants played a "triangular field game" as a task. In this game, three players, an agent and two participants, competed for scores obtained in multiple ways. The participants could obtain scores regardless of other players and interfere with other players. The task and the relationships between the global purposes and the local objectives are more complex than those in the previous study. One of the reasons why we used the competitive task was that the participants usually ignored an agent's behaviour when multiple human players participated in a collaborative task. It was very hard to induce the participants' active interaction towards an agent when participants ignored the agent in a collaborative task.

In the task, we used two types of agents: an 'eAEGL agent' that provided interaction behaviour to the participants based on the eAEGL and a 'goal-oriented agent' that performed goal-oriented actions which took the game states of all participants into account, such as game scores and the positions in the game field. Both agents represented their goal to induce the intentional stance. The eAEGL agent controlled the representations based on the participants' inner state, such as collaborative or competitive. The goal-oriented agent prioritized its own global purposes. For example, in a situation in which a human participant interferes with an agent's purpose and another human participant very effectively obtain scores, the goal-oriented agent tries to confront with the interfering participants, but the eAEGL agent evaluates the effect of each participant's behavior and sometimes tries to interfere with the participant obtaining scores.

The reason we did not adopt the AEGL agent in our previous research was that, when the AEGL agent interacted with multiple participants, the agent's behaviour often changed owing to the influence of the participant who interacted immediately before. This means that it became rather difficult to estimate the agent's intentionality from its goal-oriented behaviour. We assumed that if the extended alternating estimation could influence the mental stance of the participants more than providing basic goal-oriented behaviour, the eAEGL agent could induce and maintain the intentional stance.

Both agents were controlled by the experimenter manually based on the predefined rules (Wizard of Oz). But, the behaviour planning of the agents were automatically determined based on the corresponding method; the eAEGL agent used the method to alternate estimation by representing global and local goal-oriented behaviour and the goal-oriented agent used the method to plan its own goal depending on the game states and situations. Each agent provided its next local objective and the experimenter controlled each agent based on the predefined rules. The expressions of the multimodal behaviour by the agents were also automatically produced.

To evaluate this, we analysed how frequently the participants spontaneously interfered with the agent's behaviour. Although the players competed for scores in the task, the players could not get scores by interfering with other players. Therefore, if the participants considered that the agent was not an interaction partner to perform the task excitingly, it would be more efficient to get a high score by not interfering with the other players. We assumed that, when the participants had an intentional stance toward the agent, they tried to interfere with the agent. In addition, we asked the participants to complete a questionnaire after the experiment.

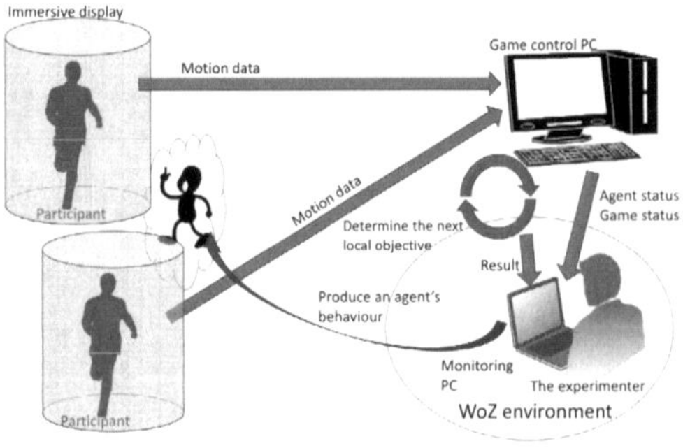

Figure 2. The experimental environment.

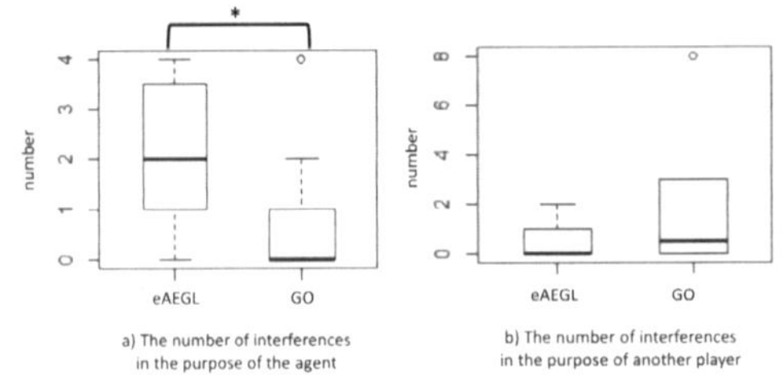

Figure 3. Results of the number of interferences in the purpose of other players.

A. Task

An agent and two participants joined a triangular field game in which three players competed for scores obtained in multiple ways. In the game, each player had their own field in which each player stored treasures. The fields were placed in a triangular form. At the centre of the triangle, there was a neutral field where three resources existed: gold coins, artistic statues and weapons. When the players stored the resources in their own fields, they obtained a score. Each player could use the resources to get bonus scores, but the player needed to spend considerable resources and time. While the player spent time to get a bonus score, other players could interfere with the process to get a bonus score. The winner was the player with the highest score. One game session lasted for 20 min.

The agent's primary global purpose was to gather bonus scores. First, the agent tried to store statues. After the agent stored enough statues to get a bonus score, he immediately spent them to get the score. The agent evaluated the state of the game including other players' scores and the bonus process of other players at regular intervals. The goal-oriented agent selected a most efficient way to get scores or to keep the score different from the other players. The eAEGL agent estimates the global purposes of each participant and the priority. If the cost when interacting with the higher priority participant was low enough, the agent tried to interact with the participant. When the participant was collaborative (e.g., when the participant tried to interfere with another participant with whom the agent also tried to interfere), the agent tries to support the participant's local objectives. When the participant was competitive, the agent tries to interfere with the participant's local objectives.

B. Experimental setting

The experimental setting is shown in Figure 2. We used an Immersive Collaborative Interaction Environment (ICIE) [18] and Unity3D [19] to construct the virtual environment and the two agents. ICIE uses a cylindrical immersive display that is composed of eight portrait orientation liquid-crystal-displays (LCD) with a 65-inch screen size, arranged in an octagonal shape. In this environment, participants could look around in the virtual space with a low cognitive load, as in the real world. A participant's virtual avatar could be controlled by a game pad.

C. Procedure

The interactive agent who joined the game was randomly selected. First, the participants were instructed regarding the experimental procedures. The experimenter provided the following instructions about the agent: 'The agent can recognize simple words. The agent has basic knowledge about the task. The agent changes its behaviour and strategies depending on your behaviour'. After the instructions were provided, the experimenter started the game. The participants first performed a practice session and then performed two game sessions. Each game session lasted for 20 min, with a 5-min rest interval between sessions. In the rest interval and at the end of the task, the participant completed questionnaires.

Eighteen Japanese college students (14 men and 4 women) participated in the experiment. They were undergraduate students aged 18 to 24 years (an average of 21.1 years). All of them interacted with one of the agents for approximately 40 min. Ten participants (8 men and 2 women) interacted with the goal-oriented agent (the 'GO group') and the rest interacted with the eAEGL agent (the 'eAEGL group').

D. Analysis of the number of interferences in the purpose of other players

We counted the number of the interferences in the bonus process of other players. The players could not get scores by interfering with other players. Therefore, it is more efficient to get a high score by not interfering with the other players. If the participants considered that the agent was an interaction partner who would make the task exciting, they tried to interact with the agent by interfering in the bonus process.

We compared the results from the eAEGL group with those from the GO group. These results are shown in Figure 3. A Mann-Whitney U test showed that the number of interferences with the agent in the eAEGL group was significantly more than that in the GO group ($Z = -2.03$, $p = 0.047$). On the other hand, there was no significant difference between the number of interferences with another participant in the eAEGL group than that in the GO group ($Z = 0.835$, $p = 0.41$). This result suggests that eAEGL was successful in inducing the intentional stance in multi-user interaction.

E. Analysis of the questionnaires

The purpose of this analysis was to investigate how the proposed method tested in the present study influenced the participants' subjective impressions. The participants rated the impressions of the agent on a seven-point scale, presented as ticks on a black line without numbers. The Q1 and Q2 were rated after the end of each session. The Q3 and Q4 were rated

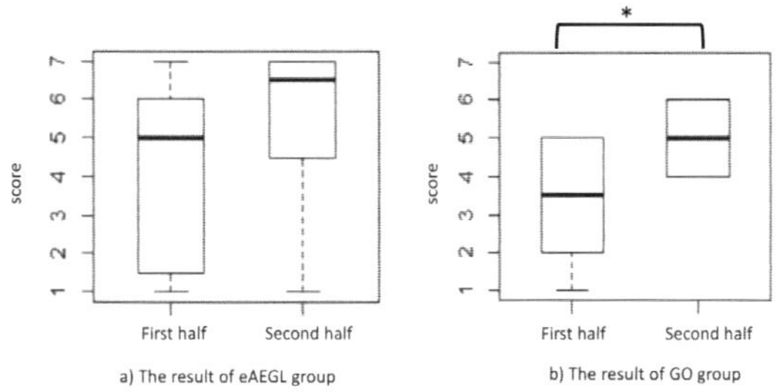

Figure 4. Q1: How carefully did the agent consider your intentions?

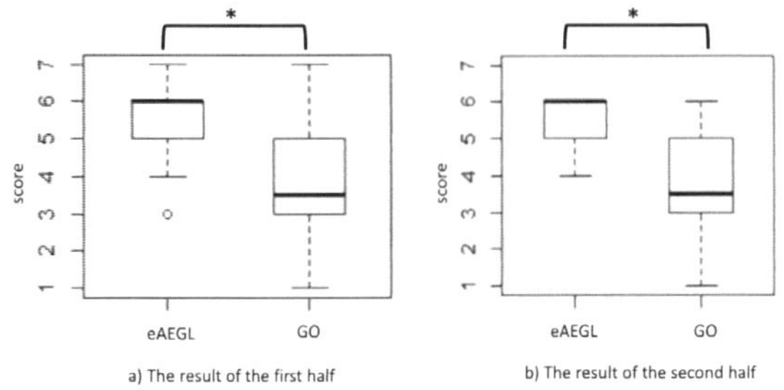

Figure 5. Q2: How strongly do you think that the agent considered its strategies based on players' intentions?

after the end of the experiment. We post-coded these scores from 1 to 7. We performed the Mann-Whitney U tests on the questionnaire data.

1) Q1: How carefully did the agent consider your intentions?: The eAEGL agent estimated the global purposes of each participant and the estimations were reflected on the changes of the agent's global purpose. The GO agent evaluated the states of the game including the results of the participants' behaviour and the results were reflected on the changes of the agent's global purpose. Therefore, the participants' intentions were more quickly reflected on the global purpose of the eAEGL agent than that of the GO agent. This question was asked to confirm whether the difference influenced the participants' feeling. This question was rated after the end of each session. The results have been shown in Figure 4. In the first and second sessions, there are no significant differences (first: $Z = -0.808$, $p = 0.44$; second: $Z = -1.40$, $p = 0.18$). On the other hand, we performed the Wilcoxon signed-rank test between the responses regarding the first and second half. Although there was no significant difference in the eAEGL group ($Z=-1.56$, $p=0.16$), the score for the second session was significantly higher than that for the first session in the GO group ($Z = -2.38$, $p = 0.023$). This indicates that the participants in the eAEGL group could quickly understand that the participants' intentions were reflected on the global purpose of the agent. The participants in the GO group firstly needed to understand the game structures and the strategies for identifying the relationships between the results of the participants' behaviour and the changes of the agent's behaviour.

2) Q2: How strongly do you think that the agent considered its strategies based on players' intentions?: Although both agents changed their global purposes and their behaviour depending on the participants' behaviour, there is a difference in the causal relationship between the global purpose of the agent and the intentions of the participant. This question was asked to confirm whether the participants were aware of the rules to determine the agent's strategies. This question was rated after the end of each session. The results are shown in Figure 5. In both the first and second sessions, the score for the eAEGL group was significantly higher than that for the GO group (first: $Z = -2.13$, $p = 0.030$; second: $Z = -2.40$, $p = 0.015$). In addition, there are no obvious differences between the first session and the second session. This indicates that the participants were aware of the effect of the influence of factors that determined the agent's behaviour early in the task.

3) Q3: How strongly do you want to play the game with the agent again?: This question was asked to confirm whether

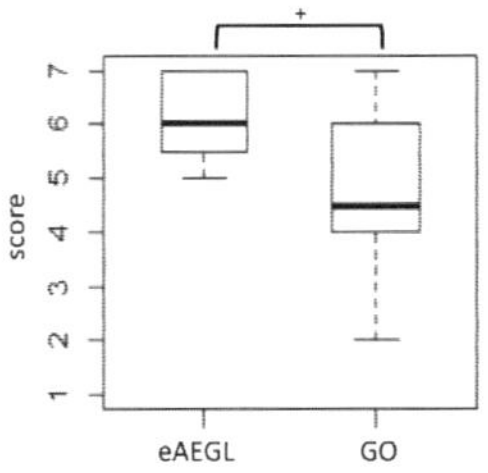

Figure 6. Q3: How strongly do you want to play the game with the agent again?

the agent's behaviour based on the eAEGL influenced the subjective feeling of the participants. The result is shown in Figure 6. There was a marginally significant difference between the groups ($Z = -1.96$, $p = 0.058$), which suggests that the participants preferred the eAEGL agent.

4) Q4: How actively did you involve this task?: This question was asked to confirm whether the agent's behaviour based on the eAEGL influenced the evaluation of the whole of the task. The result is shown in Figure 7. The score for the eAEGL group was significantly higher than that for the GO group ($Z = -2.12$, $p = 0.042$). The human-agent interaction which was not needed to efficiently achieve the task goal influenced the positive impression about the whole of the task.

V. DISCUSSION

The main contribution of this study is that the eAEGL model is useful to induce the intentional stance of the participant in complex multiple human-agent interaction. An analysis of the number of interferences in the purposes of other players helped us confirm that the eAEGL group spontaneously interacted with the agent to perform the task excitingly. In addition, in Q3 and Q4 of the questionnaires, the scores for the eAEGL group were relatively high. From these results, we suggest that the participants who interacted with the eAEGL agent considered that the agent was an interaction partner (i.e., the participants took the intentional stance) and they positively involved the agent in their virtual world experiences. The suggestion is in agreement with our previous research [7], and it can be said that we can extend the method to alternate the estimation of local objectives and global purposes in one-to-one human-agent interaction to multiple human-agent interaction.

The Q1 and Q2 of the questionnaires were similar but the results were different. The Q1 asked the impression of the agent's attitude towards the participant. The Q2 asked the

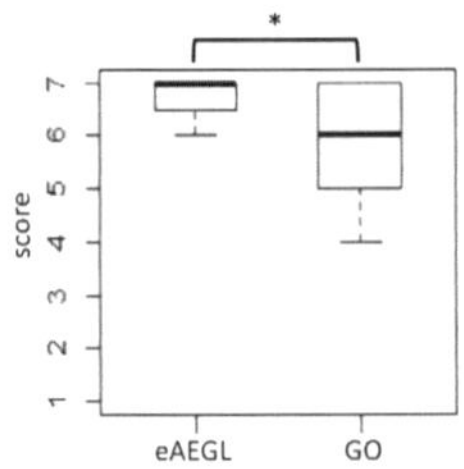

Figure 7. Q4: How actively did you involve this task?

impression of the agent's attitude towards all participants. In this study, we applied the eAEGL to multiple-user interaction, so that a participant could observe the interaction between another participant and the agent. We expect that the observation is important to estimate the agent's behaviour model. Multi-user interaction requires a complex decision-making process to estimate multiple participants' intentions and decide their actions. By providing the opportunity to observe interactions made by others, there is an advantage that it becomes easier to estimate the behaviour model of the agent relatively. Although it becomes easier to estimate the behavioural model of the agent, we should be careful that participants are more likely to take a design stance. It is important to continuously and mutually change the inner state, such as through eAEGL, in natural long-term interactions.

In this study, we could confirm that the agent could induce active interaction from the participants. This is one of the limitations in our previous study. In addition, we could apply the eAEGL to relatively long-term interactions. On the other hand, we had to hand-code the two-layered relational networks depending on the task. In the future, we will apply the machine learning techniques to reconstruct the relational networks through the human-agent interaction.

VI. Conclusion

The purpose of this study was to investigate whether the extended method to alternate the estimation of local objectives and global purposes using a network-connected two-layer model in multiple human-agent interaction could induce the intentional stance in human participants. To evaluate the method, we implemented two types of agents: an eAEGL agent (that mutually estimates and changes global purposes based on the priority and relationship with each participant), and a goal-oriented agent (that performed goal-oriented actions which took the game states of all participants into account). We conducted an experiment to evaluate the effect of the proposed method. The results suggest that the participants who interacted with the eAEGL agent considered the agent to be an interaction partner and they positively involved the agent in their virtual world experiences. In future work, we will attempt to update the relational two-layer network, which is determined by the agent's basic strategies and behaviour, during the human-agent interaction.

Acknowledgment

This research is supported by Grant-in-Aid for Young Scientists (B) (KAKENHI No. 16K21113), and Grant-in-Aid for Scientific Research on Innovative Areas (KAKENHI No. 26118002) from the Ministry of Education, Culture, Sports, Science and Technology of Japan.

References

[1] A. V. S. Mokka, J. Heinilä, and P. Välkkynen, "Fitness computer game with a bodily user interface," in Proceedings of the second international conference on Entertainment computing., 2003, pp. 1–3.

[2] M. Graafland, J. Schraagen, and M. Schijven, "Systematic review of serious games for medical education and surgical skills training," vol. 99, no. 10, 2012, pp. 1322–1330.

[3] P. Rego, P. M. Moreira, and L. P. Reis, "Serious games for rehabilitation: A survey and a classification towards a taxonomy," in Proceedings of the 5th Iberian Conference on Information Systems and Technologies (CISTI)., 2010, pp. 1–6.

[4] K. Collins, K. Kanev, and B. Kapralos, "Using games as a method of evaluation of usability and user experience in human-computer interaction design," in Proceedings of the 13th International Conference on Humans and Computers. University of Aizu Press, 2010, pp. 5–10.

[5] Y. Maeda, K. Anezaki, and Y. Takeuchi, "An agentbased model for simulating the group dynamics involved in excluding a minority," in Proc. 1st World Congress on Social Simulation, vol. 1, 2006, pp. 79–86.

[6] Y. Ohmoto, S. Takashi, and T. Nishida, "Effect on the mental stance of an agent's encouraging behavior in a virtual exercise game," in COGNITIVE 2016: The Eighth International Conference on Advanced Cognitive Technologies and Applications. IARIA, 2016, pp. 10–15.

[7] Y. Ohmoto, T. Suyama, and T. Nishida, "A method to alternate the estimation of global purposes and local objectives to induce and maintain the intentional stance," in Proceedings of the Fourth International Conference on Human Agent Interaction. ACM, 2016, pp. 379–385.

[8] D. C. Dennett, The intentional stance. MIT press, 1989.

[9] Y. Ohmoto, A. Matsumoto, and T. Nishida, "The effect of alternating propagation of local objective and global purpose by a network-connected two-layer model of emphasizing factors," 2015, pp. 246–251.

[10] M. Kitamura et al., "Design and development of dialogue system for laddering search service," IEICE technical report. Natural language understanding and models of communication, Tech. Rep., 2008.

[11] B. Shneiderman and P. Maes, "Direct manipulation vs. interface agents," interactions, vol. 4, no. 6, 1997, pp. 42–61.

[12] J. Allen, C. I. Guinn, and E. Horvtz, "Mixed-initiative interaction," Intelligent Systems and their Applications, IEEE, vol. 14, no. 5, 1999, pp. 14–23.

[13] G. Klein, D. D. Woods, J. M. Bradshaw, R. R. Hoffman, and P. J. Feltovich, "Ten challenges for making automation a" team player" in joint human-agent activity," IEEE Intelligent Systems, vol. 19, no. 6, 2004, pp. 91–95.

[14] H. Dindo, F. Donnarumma, F. Chersi, and G. Pezzulo, "The intentional stance as structure learning: a computational perspective on mindreading," Biological cybernetics, vol. 109, no. 4-5, 2015, pp. 453–467.

[15] H. Shirouzu, N. Miyake, and H. Masukawa, "Cognitively active externalization for situated reflection," Cognitive science, vol. 26, no. 4, 2002, pp. 469–501.

[16] B. Friedman, P. H. Kahn Jr, and J. Hagman, "Hardware companions?: What online aibo discussion forums reveal about the human-robotic relationship," in Proceedings of the SIGCHI conference on Human factors in computing systems. ACM, 2003, pp. 273–280.

[17] W. H. Dittrich and S. E. Lea, "Visual perception of intentional motion," PERCEPTION-LONDON-, vol. 23, 1994, pp. 253–253.

[18] T. Nishida, A. Nakazawa, Y. Ohmoto, and Y. Mohammad, Conversational Informatics: A Data-Intensive Approach with Emphasis on Nonverbal Communication. Springer, 2014.

[19] "Unity," http://unity3d.com/ (2017/12/01).

Picking Assistance System with MS-KINECT and Projection Mapping

Yuki Takehara, Yoshitoshi Murata
Faculty of Software and Information Science
Iwate Prefectural University
Takizawa, Japan
e-mail: g031m104@s.iwate-pu.ac.jp, y-murata@iwate-pu.ac.jp

Takamichi Yoshikawa
Aioi Systems Co., Ltd
Ota-ku, Tokyo, Japan
e-mail: yoshikawa@hello-aioi.com

Abstract—**Industry 4.0 is a well-regarded concept for automation in manufacturing. However, a shortage of high-skilled workers has necessitated realistic solutions for establishing high productivity and quality. We propose an information and communications technology (ICT) picking assistance system to lower human errors for high quality. In this system, MS-KINECT detects whether a hand is inserted into the correct cell of a shelf to pick items and whether a hand is inserted into the correct box in a cart to put items in. The miss-detection rate for wrong operation in the picking process is very low in an experimental evaluation, and we expect it to be very close to zero in a near future. We determine that the proposed picking error detection function would be useful for business. However, we must improve the delivery detection accuracy because of its higher detection error rate in an experimental evaluation. In this system, projection mapping technologies are used to indicate which cell items should be picked from, instead of using a lamp. The indicating system which uses a projector lowers the introduction cost than existing one when compared to the existing system using a lamp. We clarified that gray sandpaper is one of the best materials to serve as a tag for MS-KINECT to recognize indicated colors and digits.**

Keywords-Smart factory; Industry 4.0; picking; KINECT; projection mapping.

I. INTRODUCTION

The German government's Industry 4.0 (ID4) initiative *Industrie 4.0* has revolutionized Germany's manufacturing industry [1], with goods in "smart factories" being moved, picked, and delivered automatically [2]. ID4 technologies are useful for establishing high productivity and quality in light of a shortage of high-skilled workers. If the latest manufacturing robotics and custom assembly lines were introduced in model factories for ID4, products would be automatically conveyed and assembled, and there would be fewer workers. However, it is impossible for most existing factories to replace all of their manufacturing lines with more advanced ones. Realistic solutions for establishing high productivity and quality in light of a shortage of high-skilled workers are as follows:

(1) Developing and introducing information and communications technology (ICT) systems to assist a low-skill worker to be close to a high-skill worker and lower the human error.
(2) Replacing workers with robotics step by step.

In this paper, we propose an ICT picking assistance system to lower human errors in the picking process. The picking process is when a worker picks items, such as assembly parts out of numbered cells on shelves and puts them into boxes. For example, in an automobile assembly factory, a worker takes different parts from cells of a shelf and puts them into assortment boxes corresponding to production orders. The parts in each cell are the same, and different items are stored in different cells. Assortment boxes are carried to workers on an assembly line. If a worker picks parts from an incorrect cell and the parts are subsequently assembled into a product, it would take too much time to detect the incorrect parts and exchange them with correct ones. In the worst case, an automobile assembled with incorrect parts could be shipped. These processes in which such mistakes can occur are widely used, not only in assembly factories, but also at delivery centers.

Even though picking operations are monotonous, completely preventing mistakes is difficult because workers are human. Therefore, there are several kinds of picking assistance systems for decreasing incorrect pickings. Aioi Systems Co. Ltd. to which one of co-authors belongs provides the digital picking system "L-PICK," which indicates the cells of a shelf and the number of items to pick from those cells by lighting a lamp mounted on each cell [3]. However, since L-PICK does not have a function that detects incorrect picking, completely preventing it is impossible. Many companies request Aioi Systems Co. Ltd. to develop and provide the picking error detection system to lower recovery cost. Hence, we developed an operation error detection system for the picking process with MS-KINECT [4]. In this system, two sets of MS-KINECT v1 [5] trace a hand wearing a colored glove from diagonally backward and monitor whether the hand is inserted into a cell. Since this system uses a color tracing function to measure the position of a hand, it cannot be applied to a food material delivery service because of differences in food color.

This time, we developed a new picking assistance system for the picking process. It uses a set of MS-KINECT v2 mounted on the top of a shelf. Since our partner Aioi Systems Co. Ltd. has developed a new cell lighting technology that uses a projector [3], we used it in our new system. Our system recognizes the position of a cell lit by a projector and the number presented on a tag, detects the position of a cell into which a hand is inserted, counts the number of times a hand has been inserted into the cell, and compares them with recognized ones. In addition to picking functions, we have developed delivery functions. Our delivery assistance function detects whether a hand that has items is inserted into the correct delivery box.

The miss-detection rate for wrong operation in the picking process is very low in an experimental evaluation, and we expect it to be very close to zero in a near future. We determine that the proposed picking error detection function would be useful for business. However, we must improve the delivery detection accuracy because of its higher detection error rate in an experimental evaluation.

After introducing related work in Section II, detection methods for incorrect operations are introduced in Section III. Detection technologies in which MS-KINECT are used are introduced in Section IV. Experiments and results are described in Section V. Conclusions and future work are described in Section VI.

II. RELATED WORK

Human beings have excellent abilities. Workers in an automobile assembly factory can use their sense of vision and touch to detect subtle depressions or distortions that a computer system cannot. On the other hand, human beings sometimes make mistakes. Several kinds of assistance systems that decrease the number of mistakes have therefore been developed. Existing picking assistance systems are introduced in this section.

A picking assistance system has some of the following four functions:

(1) Indicating a cell of a shelf from which an item should be picked and the number of items that should be picked from that cell.

(2) Detecting whether a worker has picked the correct number of items from the correct cell.

(3) Indicating the box or cell of a tray in which picked items should be stored.

(4) Detecting whether a worker has put items in the correct box or cell of a tray.

There are several kinds of system for indicating cells. Aioi Systems Co. Ltd. provides the digital picking system "L-PICK," which indicates cells of a shelf and the number of items to pick from those cells by lighting a lamp mounted on each cell [3]. There are several systems in which a Head-Up Display (HUD) and augmented reality technology are used to assist picking operations. Schwerdtfeger used a semi-transparent HUD and augmented reality technology enabling a worker to see an arrow or frame displayed in front of a cell of a shelf [6]. Baumann used a single-eye HUD, and a worker recognized a cell from which he or she would pick up items with guidance displayed on a mirror of the HUD [7][8]. Guocompared the HUD, cart-mounted display (CMD), Light, and Paper Pick List as picking assistance systems [9]. This system also provided the delivery assistance function. They concluded that the pick-by-HUD and pick-by-CMD were superior by all metrics than the current pick-by-paper and pick-by-light systems, but the differences between the HUD and CMD were not significant and did not show that a HUD was better than a CMD. However, experimental results should be different in other experimental conditions. In practical situations, the number of cells (in that paper they were called bins) is usually less than 12, and a worker can see a lighted lamp at a glance. And multiple lamps are not lighted simultaneously; a single lamp is lighted for each occurrence where an item is picked up. Therefore, the practical error rates and task times recorded in this study would produce better results than those in that study. Furthermore, it is not certain whether a worker should have a palm-size PC and wear a HUD for extended periods. In our research, most workers would not like to carry a barcode reader.

As described above, systems indicating a cell by a lamp have been used in business. Likewise, indicating systems using an HUD have been developed in research.

We consider a picking and delivery error detection method in the next section.

III. PICKING AND DELIVERY ERROR DETECTION METHODS

In this section, prospective methods for detecting whether items are picked from the correct cell and delivered to the correct box are introduced and evaluated. This time, in addition to detecting when items are picked from a cell, these methods determine when a hand is inserted into a cell, when a tag, such as the barcode attached to a cell is read, and when a picked item is dropped, and a new item is picked. The following are the prospective methods:

(1) Reading a **barcode** attached on a cell with a barcode reader.
(2) Reading a **passive Radio Frequency (RF)-ID** set on a cell with a RF-ID reader.
(3) Reading an **active RF-ID** set on a cell with a RF-ID reader.
(4) Detecting change of weight with a **load sensor**.
(5) Detecting when a hand and/or arm is inserted into the correct cell with a **photoelectric sensor**.
(6) Detecting when a hand and/or arm is inserted into the correct cell with a **3D camera,** such as MS-KINECT.

The above methods are narrowed down by the following evaluation criteria:

(1) Additional cost to introduce a detection function.
(2) Additional operations for a worker.
(3) Detection accuracy.

An evaluation of the picking error detection methods is shown in Table I. As for barcodes, the cost of attaching a barcode to each cell is cheap, and barcode readers are not expensive. However, carrying a barcode reader and scanning barcodes are cumbersome for workers.

Passive RF-ID presents the same difficulties as barcodes. In addition to having to carry a RF-ID reader, the weak signal strength of passive RF-ID requires positioning the reader in close proximity to a RF-ID tag.

As for active RF-ID, despite having to carry the reader, it does not need to be positioned in close proximity to a RF-ID tag because the signal strength is strong. However, because of their strong signal strength, active RF-ID readers sometimes read RF-ID tags placed in other cells.

As for load sensors, their detection accuracy is high. However, they are usually expensive, and each sensor must be wired to a PC. Introduction costs are therefore high. The same holds true for photoelectric sensors.

3D cameras using MS-KINECT usually cost a few hundred dollars. While introduction costs would be high under our proposed system because one MS-KINECT set would be required per shelf, our system alleviates the need for workers to carry a reader, and the detection accuracy is high. We have determined that 3D cameras would be the best method overall for our picking assistance system.

The following three prospective methods are considered for delivery:

(1) Detecting change of weight with a **load sensor**.
(2) Detecting whether a hand is inserted into the correct box with a **photoelectric sensor**.
(3) Detecting whether a hand is inserted into the correct box with a **3D camera,** such as MS-KINECT.

The evaluation criteria for delivery is the same as those for picking. The evaluations for the above three methods are the same as those in Table I. We think a method using a 3D camera is the best for delivery when its accuracy is high.

TABLE I. EVALUATION OF PICKING ERROR DETECTION METHODS

Method	A. Cost	A. Operation	Accuracy
Barcode	Low	Big	Middle
Passive RF-ID	Middle	Big	Low
Active RF-ID	Middle	Little	Middle
Load	High	Little	High
Photoelectric	High	Little	Middle
3D camera	Low	Little	This paper

IV. DETECTION TECHNOLOGY

In this section, a detection technology by which a worker picks items from a cell, delivers them to a box, and a reading technology that detects the number on a tag lit by a projector are introduced.

A. *Detection technology for picking items from the correct cell*

As described in the previous section, a technology that detects whether a worker picks items from an indicated cell is needed. Since detecting whether a worker is picking items from a cell is difficult, we decided to focus on detecting when a hand is inserted into a cell and counting the number of times a hand is inserted into an indicated cell instead of detecting and counting hands picking items from an indicated cell. The motion monitoring function in MS-KINECT is popularly used to estimate position of joints on the body. However, the MS-KINECT must be set in front of the body between 0.5 – 5 m. It is impossible to set the MS-KINECT in front of a worker in a factory or delivery center. Therefore, Open-CV color tracing technologies [10] were used to trace hands in our previous system. And, since two MS-KINECT sets were needed for each shelf, the system was not economical. Therefore, we decided not to use the color tracing technology and opted to detect a hand inserted into a cell using a MS-KINECT set.

From past experiments we have determined that the best mount position for a MS-KINECT to detect whether a hand enters a cell is just above the surface of a shelf aperture. The MS-KINECT 3D camera searches for a hand and arm just over the surface of a shelf aperture as shown in Fig. 1. The MS-KINECT must be set at a position in which its 3D camera can observe the entire shelf aperture. This system detects whether a hand is inserted by changing the depth in front of a cell. When a hand and/or arm is inserted into a cell, the depth in such a view is changed from L_f to L_h. A change in depth L_h corresponds to the length between the MS-KINECT and the hand and/or arm. Its position is within the cell aperture in which the hand and/or arm is inserted.

The coordinates of the four corners of each cell are pre-set before estimating the cell number. In Fig. 1, the coordinates of 16 corners are pre-set. The number of the cell in which a hand is inserted is estimated by comparison between a coordinate of the detected hand and the coordinates of four corners for each cell ⓝ.

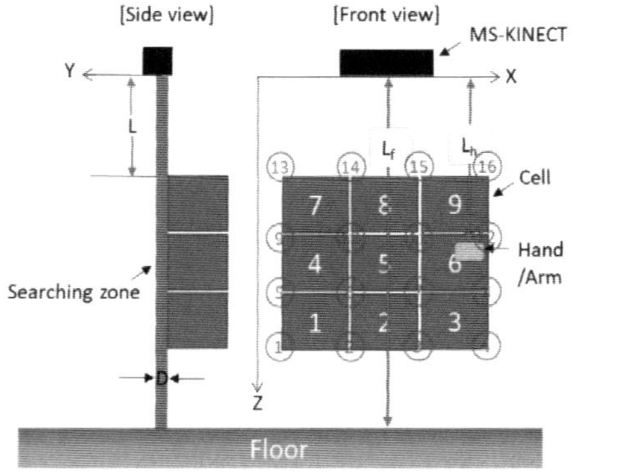

Figure 1. Mounting position of MS-KINECT and searching zone

B. *Lighting a tag and number*

Since our partner AIOI System Co. Ltd. has developed the new lighting method into which the projection mapping technology is used to indicate a picking cell, our experimental system uses this projection mapping technology. A very short focal projector mounted near the MS-KINECT lights a tag attached to a cell and projects a digit on it to indicate the cell and the number of items to be removed as shown in Fig. 2.

A computer knows which tag of a cell is lit, so there is no need for it to detect which tag is lit with the MS-KINECT. In this case, the MS-KINECT is connected to a computer. However, we plan to develop a picking robot that picks items up and puts them into an indicated box in the near future. Since the robot must detect which tag is lit and read a digit on it, we developed a technology that realizes the above functions with the MS- KINECT. In this system, the font used for digits is a seven-segment font as shown on the right side of Fig. 2. Our system recognizes which kind of number is presented by detecting which segments are white.

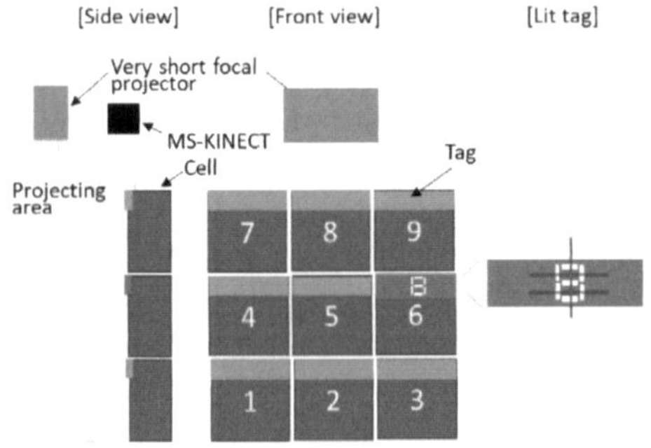

Figure 2. Layout of projector and cells

C. *Detection technology for delivering items*

We imagine a delivery cart as shown in Fig. 3. A MS-KINECT is mounted to search the surface of a mass of boxes. The search zone is just above the mass of boxes. When a hand/arm or item is inserted into a box, the PC on this cart detects whether a hand/arm or item is inserted into the box by the change in depth.

The number of the box that a hand is inserted into is estimated to compare it with a coordinate of the detected hand and the coordinates of four corners for each box, the same as for a cell in Section IV-A.

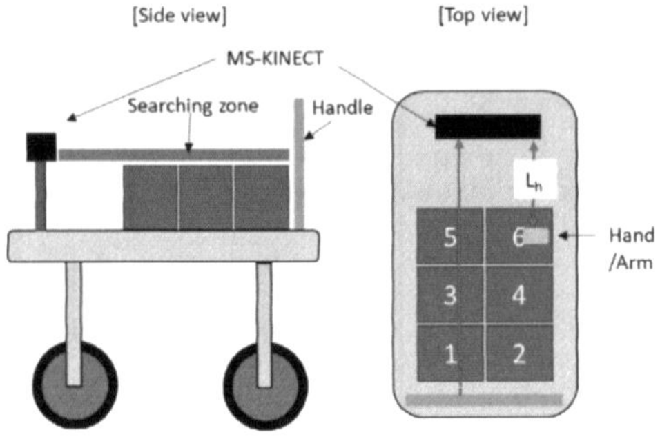

Figure 3. Image of delivery cart

V. EXPERIMENT

We developed an experimental shelf as shown in Fig. 4. An MS-KINECT is mounted 65.5 cm away from the shelf. The shelf consists of 3 x 3 cells. The size of the shelf is 67.5 x 64.5 cm, and the size of each cell is 22.5 x 21.5 cm. The length between the floor and the bottom of the shelf is 98 cm. We measured the error rates for detecting a hand inserted into a cell and whether the MS-KINECT can recognize a lit tag and the number on it using the experimental shelf.

Before estimation, the coordinates of the corners of each cell are pre-set using the pre-set windows shown in Fig. 5. The corner number is selected with the corner number button. The coordinates of each corner are entered by clicking a corner or inputting digits. The red grid of the shelf aperture is generated by clicking the grid button.

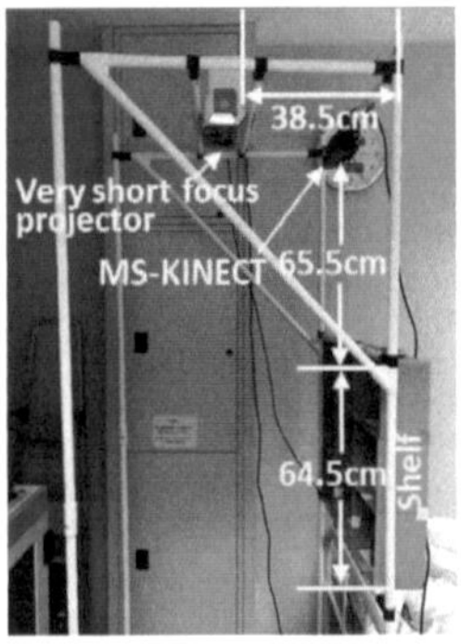

Figure 4. Experimental shelf

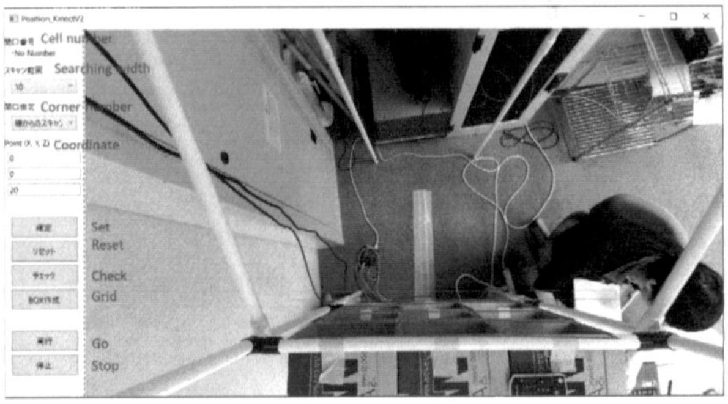

Figure 5. Pre-set window

A. *Detection error rate for picking operation*

The detection error rate for picking operation would change depending on the width D of the searching zone, the searching period, the cell position, and the threshold width to detect a hand and/or arm. We measured the detection error rate under conditions in which the width D of the searching zone is 1 cm / 3cm / 5 cm / 10 cm, the searching period is 500 msec. / 1000 msec., and the threshold width for detecting a hand and/or arm is 1 cm. Beer cans were used as picking items. The number of participants was ten. Each participant picks an item from each cell five times. The average detection error rates of every cell vs. the width of searching zone D are 1 cm / 3cm / 5 cm / 10 cm as shown in Fig. 6. The parameter of this figure is the searching period. The detection error rate in 500 msec. is lower than that in 1000 msec. in each the searching width D. The average error rate for each cell in which the searching period is 500 msec. is shown in Table II. The error rate increases in accordance with an increase in width D. This is because a participant tends to insert his/her hand into a cell through the searching zone in front of other cells.

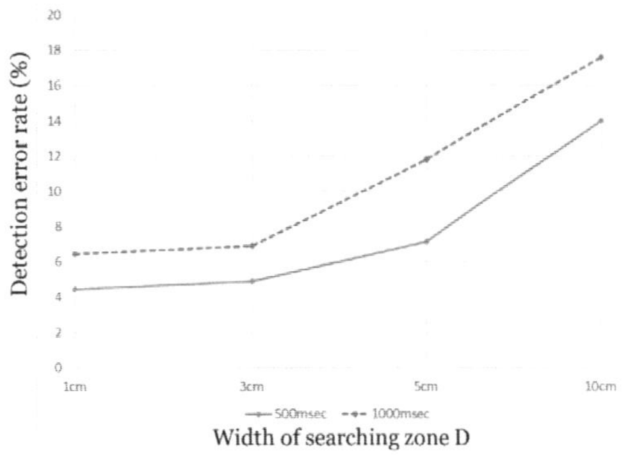

Figure 6. Average detection error rates for every cell

TABLE II. AVERAGE DETECTION ERROR RATES (%) FOR EACH CELL

Cell #	1cm	3cm	5cm	10cm
1	2	0	0	4
2	4	4	4	6
3	4	6	4	0
4	4	0	0	1
5	6	6	2	8
6	2	8	14	20
7	6	0	10	24
8	4	16	10	28
9	8	4	20	26

The most serious problem in the picking error detection system is that the system recognizes wrong operations to be fair. We measured the miss-detection rate for wrong operation. In this experiment, a correct cell is No. 5. The number of participants is ten. Each participant picks an item from cells around the No. 5 cell five times. The detection rate for wrong operations to be wrong, detection rate for wrong operation to be fair and practical detected wrong operations are shown in Table III. Average detection rate for wrong operations to be wrong is 95.7 %. And, the proposed system did not recognize wrong operations to be fair, completely detected wrong operations.

TABLE III. MISS-DETECTION RATE FOR WRONG OPERATIONS

Cell #	Detection Rate (%)	No. 5 cell D. Rate (%)	Detected errors
1	98	0	1-6
2	98	0	2-3
3	96	0	3-6, 6
4	98	0	1-4
5			
6	96	0	6-9, 3-6
7	94	0	(4-7) x 3
8	96	0	(5-8) x 2
9	90	0	(6-9) x 5

However, the system recognized that a participant picked an item from the No. 6 cell, even though he picked it from the No. 3 cell. The reason of this error detection is that the system detects an item in front and within 1 cm from the No. 6 cell after picking from the No. 3 cell. We think this miss-detection rate is low, but not enough. This reason would cause the detection for wrong operation to be fair. We plan to constitute a few cm non-detection area around each cell, and guard time not to detect after detecting an item to be picked from a cell. We think these constitutions would lower the detection rate for wrong operation to be fair exceedingly close to zero.

B. Recognition of a lit tag and the number on it

We noticed that the color through the video camera of the MS-KINECT was very different from the color we recognized and that the color through the video camera of the MS-KINECT changed in accordance with the color and luster of a tag. Example colors on a sheet of white paper, black paper, and gray sandpaper are shown in Fig. 7. The differences between the colors as displayed on a smartphone and those as displayed on the MS-KINECT are shown in Fig. 8. The colors displayed on a smartphone are almost equal to those seen with the naked eye. We selected red, green, and blue as the colors projected on a tag. The color characteristics of the MS- KINECT are very different from those of a smartphone. As a result, gray sandpaper is the best material for representing original colors. Our system can read every number perfectly on a red, green, or blue background. When implementing systems for clients, these three colors are usable.

Figure 7. Colors on tags as displayed on video camera of MS-KINECT

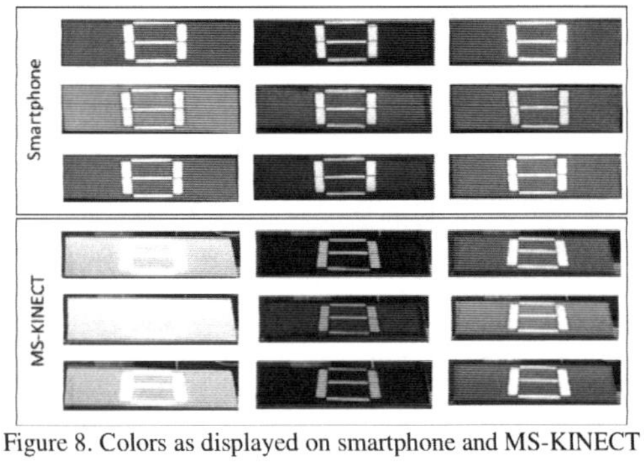

Figure 8. Colors as displayed on smartphone and MS-KINECT

C. Delivery error rate

We measured the delivery error rate using six boxes on a table as shown in Fig. 9 instead of using a delivery cart. The MS-KINECT is placed on another table. It was placed 60 cm from the top of the boxes. From the results of Experiment A, we decided that the searching period is 500 msec. and that the width of the search zone is 1 cm.

Since we noticed that our system easily detected multiple boxes, we constituted a 5 cm wide non-detection area on boxes that are on the near side of a worker, as shown in Fig. 9. When the depth far from the boxes was not fixed, the detection accuracy was poor and unstable. We set the screen low to fix the maximum depth from the MS-KINECT. The average error rate for each box is shown in Table IV. The number of participants was five, the same as in the picking experiment. Each participant puts an item into each box five times. Overall, the error rate, especially the double count rate, is high.

In some cases, a worker might throw an item into a box, so we also measured the delivery error rate when items were thrown into a box. However, our system could not detect a thrown item because the searching period of 500 msec. was longer than the necessary period for detecting an item.

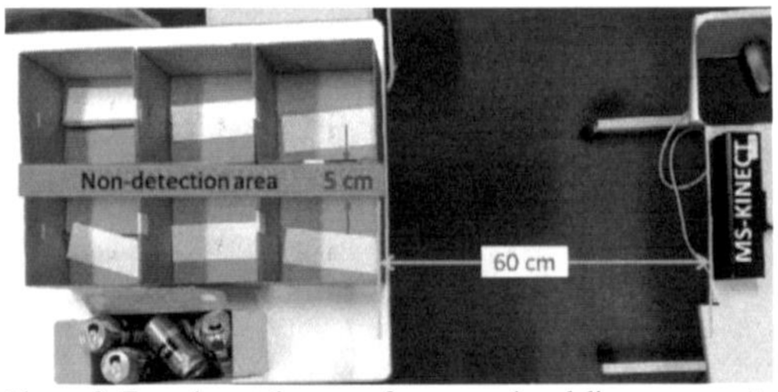

Figure 9. Experimental system for measuring delivery error rate

TABLE IV. AVERAGE DELIVERY ERROR RATES (%) FOR EACH BOX

Box number	No-detection	Double count	Total
1	0	12	12
2	0	8	8
3	8	20	28
4	4	0	4
5	24	4	28
6	0	12	12

VI. CONCLUSION AND FUTURE WORK

A realistic solution for establishing high productivity and quality for the picking process in light of a shortage of high-skilled workers is to introduce a picking assistance system that detects incorrect operations by workers. We introduced a picking and delivery assistance system in which an MS-KINECT detects whether a hand is inserted into the correct cell of a shelf to pick items and whether a hand is inserted into the correct box on a cart to put items in.

The miss-detection rate for wrong operation is very low in this system, and it is possible to be exceedingly close to zero in a near future. We determine that the proposed picking error detection function would be useful for business. The other hand, we must improve the delivery detection accuracy. We try to adopt the MS-KINECT motion monitoring function to estimate the position of hand.

ACKNOWLEDGEMNT

Thanks to Kazuhiro Yoshida for help in performing this research. This project is partially supported with the competitive research funding by Iwate Prefectural University.

REFERENCES

[1] Industrie 4.0; http://www.bmwi.de/Redaktion/EN/Dossier/industrie-40.html, [retrieved: February, 2018].

[2] What is a smart factory? ; http://www.bmwi.de/Redaktion/EN/FAQ/Industrie-4-0/faq-industrie-4-0-03.html, [retrieved: February, 2018].

[3] AIOI SYSTEMS Co., LTD Digital Picking System Products Introduction; https://www.hello-aioi.com/en/product/product-list/, [retrieved: February, 2018].

[4] Y. Uda, K. Yoshida, and Y. Murata, "Operation Error Detection System in Picking Processes by Camera Depth Sensors," IPSJ, Transaction of Consumer Device and Service, Vol.6 No.1, pp. 1-12, 2016, [written in Japanese].

[5] Meet Kinect for Windows; https://developer.microsoft.com/en-us/windows/kinect, [retrieved: February, 2018].

[6] B. Schwerdtfeger, and G. Klinker, "Supporting order picking with augmented reality," Proceedings of 7th IEEE/ACM International Symposium on Mixed and Augmented Reality, pp. 91–94, 2008.

[7] H. Iben, H. Baumann, C. Ruthenbeck, and T. Klug, "Visual based picking supported by context awareness: Comparing picking performance using paper-based lists versus list presented on a head mounted display with contextual support," Proceedings of 11th International Conference on Multimodal Interfaces, pp. 281–288, 2009.

[8] H. Baumann, T. Starner, H. Iben, and P. Zschaler, "Evaluation of graphical user-interfaces for order picking using head-mounted displays," Proceedings of 13th International Conference on Multimodal Interfaces, pp. 377–384, 2011.

[9] A. Guo et al., "A comparison of order picking assisted by head-up display (HUD), cart-mounted display (CMD), light, and paper pick list, "Proceedings of 2014 ACM International Symposium on Wearable Computers, pp. 71–78, 2014.

[10] Open-CV; https://opencv.org/, [retrieved: February, 2018].

User Centered Design of a Knowledge Management System for Production Workers

Gianni Campatelli, Sandro Mehic
Department of Industrial Engineering
University of Firenze
Firenze, Italy
e-mail: gianni.campatelli@unifi.it, sandro.mehic@unifi.it

***Abstract*—This paper depicts a knowledge management system developed by the authors as a service to be used by workers of the production sector. The service has been developed within the framework of FACTS4WORKERS project, which aims to provide software, hardware and organizational strategies to improve the workers satisfaction. The approach to collect the workers requirements is based on the creation of artifacts able to support a smarter and easier communication with the end users. The solution presented in this paper is a Knowledge Management System developed to cope with the specific requirements of manufacturing workers. It aims to provide a real-time decision support to the workers and create a collaborative and inclusive work environment. The solution has been tested in a real production environment by the project partners.**

Knowledge Management System; Workers Satisfaction; Smart Services.

I. Introduction

One of the challenges that the European Community must cope with in the next years is the low attractiveness of jobs in the manufacturing sector. As highlighted in the Factory of the Future agenda [1], the reduced interest on younger generations for manufacturing jobs constitutes an obstacle for the re-industrialization of many European regions. In the last years, European Community has promoted many calls for proposal for the development of solutions to increase the satisfaction of workers in the manufacturing areas, creating new approaches and tools to empower and reskill the workers. One of the funded initiatives is the FACTS4WORKERS project, whose outcomes are briefly presented in this paper.

The general picture is that young people are not excited by the idea of working in a manufacturing plant since the perception of this job is connected to "old fashion" activities that are mainly focused on dirty-hands tasks without the use of modern communication tools, common in everyday life.

Many strategies have been proposed to tackle this issue. **Figure 1** shows a priority list of the possible actions, developed by the World Economic Forum [2]. Among these, the most important is the reskilling of the operators. This is not a trivial task since the operators that must be reskilled come from very different demographic, expertise, educational, and skill background. The challenge is to develop a smart approach that could be adopted proficiently by most of the actual workforce and that could generate interest and motivation for its continuous use.

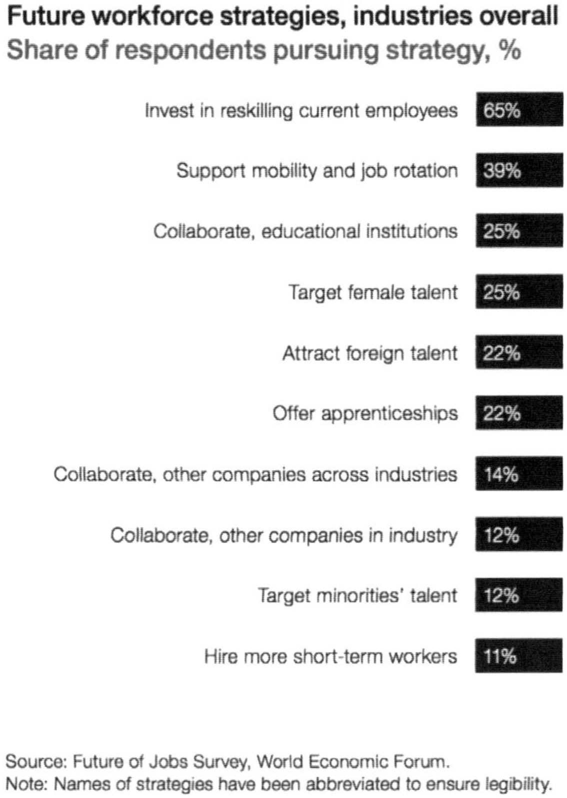

Figure 1. Future strategies for manufacturing workers

Many companies are looking to invest in operator reskilling while trying to keep low the costs, like the time required and the impact on the organizational structure of the workforce, especially in the Small and Medium Enterprises (SMEs). The most common approach is to develop a vertical solution based on the very specific requirements of a company, creating a reskilling path that is only partially reusable in other contexts. In all cases, the starting point should be an analysis of the reasons that led the company to implement a reskilling plan. The analysis starts with the evaluation of the role of the manufacturing workers. This has tremendously changed in the last decades: continuous automation of manufacturing processes has reduced their manual efforts, whereas managing the increasing complexity of the production system requires them to acquire higher skills. The Web has been one of the main sources of inspiration for new tools that enable the sharing of information and ideas; applications such as Wikipedia and Facebook created a new "social" environment where people could exchange information using new approaches. Nowadays, users do not only consume, but actively produce information and engage with the information produced by others in a collaborative way. This creates new possibilities and challenges for the industrial sector. Whereas younger workers "expect" to be able to work with recent technologies, older workers must not be left behind by creating a "digital divide" [3]. A growing number of studies has shown how social and mobile technologies can help capture and process social information [4]–[7].

When facing problems, especially of a technical nature, in their daily life most people use social environments to look for a solution. Some examples include repairing a broken household appliance, consulting information about the use of electronic devices, etc. The challenge of the developed service is to transfer this approach to the shop floor, enabling a smarter and faster problem-solving attitude of the workers and creating a more motivating and supporting social environment. A usability study of the online training approach highlights how the perception of new and innovative tasks could increase the satisfaction of the users [8]. Hence, production workers, often involved in manual work, could benefit from this innovative industrial social environment.

To meet this goal, the creation of a social environment within a manufacturing plant is required, supported by a highly usable platform and infrastructure, that will adopt smart services to enable the exchange of information among peers. The system will be composed of a Web front-end, able to run on a smart device, and a number of services that provide communication service and access to consult, generate and modify a knowledge database.

The rest of the paper is structured as follows. In Section II, the architecture of the developed solution is presented, while Section III depicts the approach used for the collection of worker requirements. Section IV describes the features of the developed Knowledge Management System, while Section V concludes this work.

II. FACTS4WORKERS PROJECT AND INDUSTRIAL CHALLENGES

This activity has been developed within the larger frame of FACTS4WORKERS project, whose aim is to create a smarter and a more satisfying working environment for manufacturing operators. The developed tool, able to support the knowledge sharing among workers and sustain the development of a collaborative environment, is only one of the industrial challenges defined by the project. These are summarized in **Figure 2** and briefly described in the following list:

- Industrial Challenge 1: Provide a personalized and augmented reality (AR) tools for the workers through which they can get immediate, context aware and hands free access to information on the shop-floor.
- Industrial Challenge 2: Provide a worker-centric knowledge management system through which the users can capture and access the knowledge shared by the rest of the coworkers, with main focus on the shop-floor level flows instead of office centered functionality.
- Industrial Challenge 3: Self-learning manufacturing workplaces are established through linking heterogeneous information sources from the worker's environment and beyond, and extracting patterns of successful production, transferring the result as decision-relevant knowledge to the worker.
- Industrial Challenge 4: The use of generated knowledge through knowledge management system and insight provided by the self-learning manufacturing workplace for an in-situ mobile learning to instruct and support operators during production.

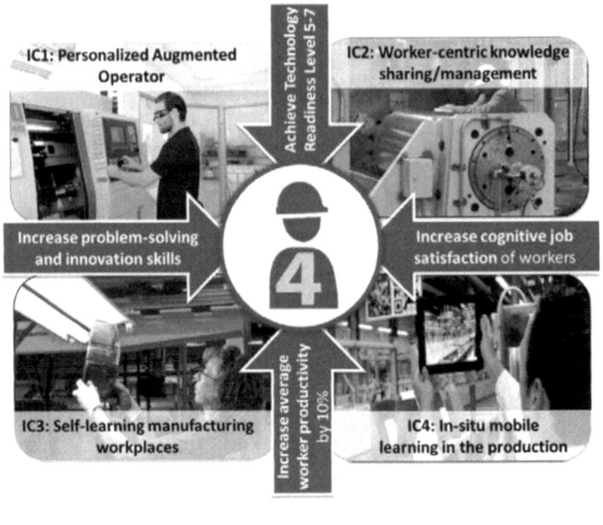

Figure 2. Industrial Challenges of F4W project

The objective of the developed tool is to support the workers in all the Industrial Challenges with different approaches.

Industrial Challenge 1: The augmented operator will profit from a social platform especially for the possibility to define specific "channels" for the information posting. One operator could decide to be updated about all the content created by a specific operator, that has more experience with the manufacturing process or is usually well trained in problem solving. Moreover, the data fed to the operator could be studied and analyzed thanks to the support of the other workers that "animate" the social platform and, in the past, have carried out similar task or have verified a similar behavior in the collected data.

Industrial Challenge 2: the second challenge is about the knowledge management and sharing. Here the developed service has the aim to enable the sharing among the peers of the knowledge about defect solving. In this case the class "defect" must be considered in a broader sense: a defect could be any issue that the production worker has to solve in order to have the production running smoothly. The database of the service stores all the encountered defects and the solutions adopted by the operators. The descriptive information will be augmented with multimedia content, such as video and audio tracks that show and further improve the provided solution. Additionally, social interactions will be captured in the form of comments and ratings, that again can include multimedia content to integrate the knowledge content for further use. The success rate of each solution will be calculated based on the feedback of the operators in order to allow the selection of the best solution available based on the evidence of the validity of the approach and the social comments received.

Industrial Challenge 3: the third challenge is related to self-learning; in this case the social exchange of data will enable the training of the operator directly thanks to the access to the data created by the other users. The availability of comments, video and other media created by expert workers will enable a self-learning of the operators. This will allow an easier organization of the workforce at the different machines in the shop-floor, incrementing the mobility of the workers in the plant and empowering them into the use of a larger number of machines/stations.

Industrial Challenge 4: the last industrial challenge wants to deal with in-situ learning, for which the operator needs to access a lot of different documents and multimedia contents. In this case is crucial to have a system able to motivate the production of media contents able to populate a training platform. The social service backbone is going to support the development of a repository of peer-to-peer process information. This information will be highly usable by the workers because produced by his peers. It is expected that the material will be produced by workers for workers, characterized by a very focused problem-solving attitude and a functional language and representation approach. Moreover, the content rating and the associated success rate of the solutions will allow the workers to select quickly the most interesting material to use, avoid time-consuming search and the reading of a lot of less-useful material.

After the definition of the objective of the service, an analysis of "off-the-shelf" solutions has been performed, highlighting the need to develop something smarter and more focused on the specific case. In order to have a tailored solution for the project objectives, many interviews have been carried out with manufacturing workers, implementing a user centered approach.

III. User Centered Approach to Design the Service

The knowledge management system could be a powerful tool to be deployed in an industrial environment, but some barriers could limit its successful introduction on the shopfloor. For this reason, a user centered approach has been designed and adopted in order to define the architecture of the optimal solution, keeping always the workers within the loop. Many authors, like Kukko [9], report that some barriers must be overcomed to have an effective sharing system, that otherwise lead to a knowledge mismanagement, responsible for unsatisfactory performance. These are mainly related to the users acceptance of the solution and a correct definition of the rules for managing the knowledge. However, supporting the knowledge sharing is one of the main drivers for continuous improvement actions [10]; it is one of the most useful approaches to cope with fast changing environment and context.

To design the architecture of a solution that could effectively support the workers and have a high degree of acceptability, it is crucial to fully understand the daily tasks and main issues that a worker must face. The approach used to collect such needs is based on widely known standards, like ISO9241-210, and human-centered design of interactive systems and Design Research's process model approach [11]. Both approaches are based on the assumption that complex problems [12] cannot be solved in a straightforward way but needs usually many iterations.

The used approach is based on the development of an initial context-of-use analysis that evolves in the definition of application scenarios. These scenarios have been developed by the researchers of the projects and later validated with the operators. An interesting solution developed by Heinrich & Richter [13] is the use of comics to contextualize the developed scenario and facilitate the communication with the workers, keeping the information level to its core and using a simple and context aware language. After the definition of the scenarios, the software developers elaborated a preliminary solution to cope with the challenge, providing mock-ups for its evaluation by the workers. Based on their feedback, the final release of the software has been deployed on the shop floor. During the whole process, the users are kept in the center of the definition process, with the aim to develop a user-centered application.

IV. Developed Knowledge Management System

The Knowledge Management System developed allows the workers to share their experiences and knowledge. The system supports a worker in case of a defect - general definition for a problem in the production area - and provides the support to deploy a corrective action. The study of different industrial organization, carried out within the framework of FACTS4WORKERS project has highlighted how the knowledge required to support the worker's activity could be described in the form defect->solution. This is a result exploited by many authors, like Vera et al. [14], that recognized how the knowledge required in a production environment is usually in the form problem/defect-> solution, since most of the cases that require a direct operation of the workers are related to the events' occurrence. Hence, the required knowledge is the causal relation between an event (defect) and a possible corrective actions (solution). This is not a univocal link since multiple solutions could be adopted to solve the same problem. To cope with this issue a solution ranking concept has been introduced, where the ranking is a measurement of the effectiveness of the suggested approach to resolve the events' occurance. General solution (e.g., "clean the device") could be applicable to a large variety of defects but have a poor effectiveness in some cases. The solution ranking allows the use of the same solutions based on their context effectiveness. The ranking is measured thanks to the worker's feedback on the adopted solutions. As the amount of the workers' feedback increases over time through the use of the system, the ranking functionality becomes more rapresentative of the best solutions for the frequently encountered defects.

The knowledge is initially generated by the users in term of new solutions that are able to solve a specific problem. After a training period in which the database is populated by the workers, following use of the system will enable the worker to receive a suggestion by the system about how to solve a specific issue, with the indications and suggestions of workers that have dealt with the same issue previously. In case of no solution for a defect, the system will use a semantic search engine to guess the best solution for the specific case looking for similar problems or offer the possibility to register a new solution. The algorithm uses natural language processing approach in order to extract information from the defect and solutions definitions, as stated by the operators in its own language – usually without a structured definition. Moreover, the Artificial Intelligence of the system will keep track of the acquired experience of the workers and suggest if the operator has enough experience with the application of a specific solution and, if necessary, will call a supervisor (Team Leader) to support the implementation of the suggested solution. The basic scheme of the solution is reported in **Figure 3**.

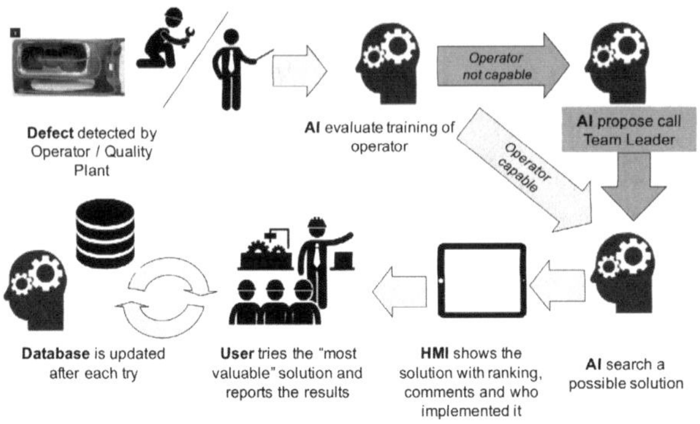

Figure 3. Scheme of how AI manage the workers generated knowledge

Moreover, the knowledge is filtered considering the worker profile. Profiling is fundamental to provide the correct/adequate information to a specific worker. The basic idea is that some information is not useful, or sometimes misleading, for people that do not have enough training to correctly understand them or are not authorized to deploy the corrective action. An example could be a complex maintenance operation. In general, the most skilled machine operators have some experience in maintenance operations. Based on the action required, the system recognizes if the operator is able to carry out a specific maintenance operation autonomously and provide all the needed instruction to him, otherwise another skilled operator is called in order to solve the problem as soon as possible.

The knowledge is generated by the workers thanks to a visual approach; it allows them to use actual and high usability technologies to insert the linked information (defect->solution) into the database. Since the information will be retrieved by a semantic search engine, it will be possible to use free text and multimedia file (pictures and videos) to describe both the problem and the solution. A mock-up that explains the user interface for generating knowledge is reported in **Figure 4**. Comment with text and other multimedia (video) could be later added. The AI will be able to select the optimal solution based on ranking. An example of interface is reported in **Figure 5**. The ranking of the solution is calculated by the system using the feedback of the workers after the application of a specific solution. This is a measure of the success of a specific solution to solve a problem and could be used to suggest the best solution to a worker to deal with a problem.

The developed system has been installed on-premise in different working environments, thanks to the availability of FACTS4WORKERS project partners. After a period of use, the feedback of the workers has been collected. All workers involved in the test of the prototype declared their satisfaction about the functionality and potential support that the KMS could provide. During this preliminary evaluation, we received feedback about the organization of the content on the HMI. This led to a reorganization of the information, to avoid reporting data with low interest for the workers and, in general, avoid distractions or low value added steps in the software application. Some appreciated features are the low intrusiveness of the system and its user friendly interface, since it requires very low IT expertise to be operated. The expected results for this implementation is not the reduction of defect rate but an increased capability of the workers to solve autonomously the problems/defects that could arise during their daily tasks, with positive effects in production rate (reduced down time of the production machines) and increased autonomy of the workers that lead to their empowerment and satisfaction. A more detailed presentation of the developed service is reported in [15]. An important characteristic of this service is the applicability of the solution in a large variety of production contexts. During FACTS4WORKERS project, the service has been deployed and tested in different companies, with business ranging from the assembly to the production of plastic and metal parts. In every case only minor adjustments of the front-end have been carried out, to comply with the different requests of the workers in terms of available data.

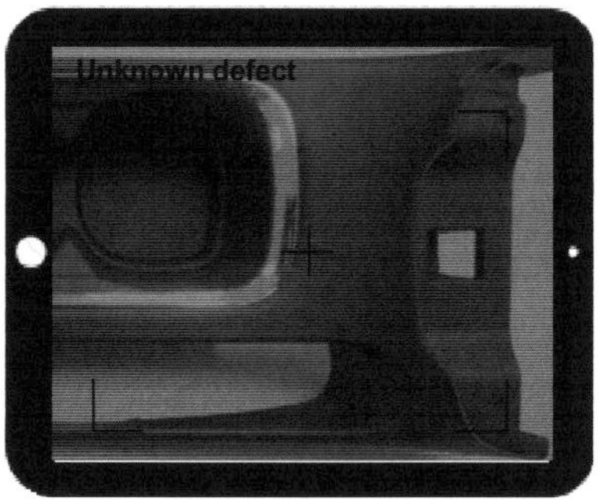

Figure 4. Mock-up for the user generated information

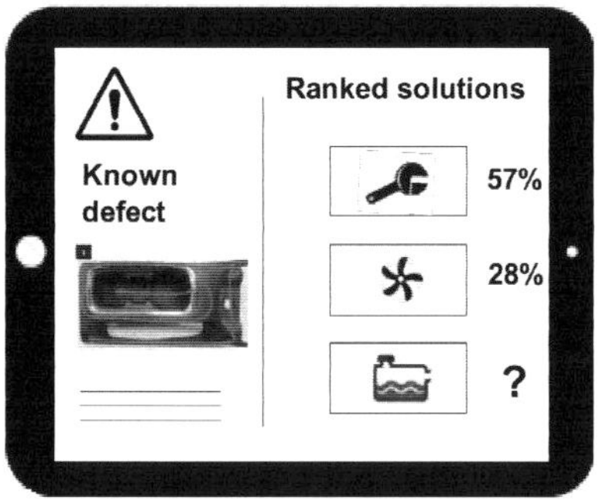

Figure 5. AI suggests the feasible solution with ranking

V. CONCLUSIONS

The knowledge management and sharing system proposed in this paper has been designed using a structured approach that enabled the smart evaluation of the workers requirements, allowing a faster and more user centered design of the service. The developed service has been installed on premises by many industrial partners, allowing a testing and validation phase of the effectiveness of the approach. The formalization of the knowledge has been carried out by the definition of a casual relation among defects and solutions, integrating in the system the tools to search and rate all the content introduced in the service database. At the end of the test phase, the developed service has been fine-tuned and the feedback form the workers have been very positive. In most of the cases, the proposed solution enabled the workers to solve the problem and promoted the culture of exchanging data and knowledge among peers, creating a more collaborative working environment.

ACKNOWLEDGEMENTS

This research was developed within the FACTS4WORKERS project, founded from the European Community's Horizon 2020 Research and Innovation Programme (H2020-FoF-04-2014) under grant agreement n. 636778.

REFERENCES

[1] EFFRA, "Factories of the Future: Multi-annual roadmap for the contractual PPP under Horizon 2020," 2014.

[2] World Economic Forum, Accelerating Workforce Reskilling for the Fourth Industrial Revolution An Agenda for Leaders to Shape the Future of Education, Gender and Work. 2017.

[3] J. B. Pick and T. Nishida, "Digital divides in the world and its regions: A spatial and multivariate analysis of technological utilization," Technol. Forecast. Soc. Change, vol. 91, pp. 1–17, Feb. 2015.

[4] A. Majchrzak, C. Wagner, and D. Yates, "The Impact Of Shaping On Knowledge Reuse For Organizational Improvement With Wikis," MIS Q., vol. 37, no. 2, pp. 455–469, 2013.

[5] G. Von Krogh, "How does social software change knowledge management? Toward a strategic research agenda," J. Strateg. Inf. Syst., vol. 21, no. 2, pp. 154–164, 2012.

[6] S. Faraj, S. L. Jarvenpaa, and a. Majchrzak, "Knowledge Collaboration in Online Communities," Organ. Sci., vol. 22, no. 5, pp. 1224–1239, 2011.

[7] E. M. Jennex, S. Smolnik, and D. Croasdell, "Knowledge management success in practice," in 47th Hawaii International Conference on System Sciences, HICSS 2014, 2014, pp. 3615–3624.

[8] A. M. F. Yousef, M. A. Chatti, U. Schroeder, and M. Wosnitza, "A usability evaluation of a blended MOOC environment: An experimental case study," Int. Rev. Res. Open Distrib. Learn., vol. 16, no. 2, 2015.

[9] M. Kukko, "Knowledge Sharing Barriers of Acquisitioned Growth: A Case Study from a Software Company," Int. J. Eng. Bus. Manag., vol. 5, no. 1, p. 1, 2013.

[10] H. J. Quesada-Pineda and J. Madrigal, "Sustaining continuous improvement: A longitudinal and regional study," Int. J. Eng. Bus. Manag., vol. 5, no. 1, p. 1, 2013.

[11] K. Peffers, T. Tuunanen, Rothenberger A. Marcus, and S. Chatterjee, "A design science research methodology for information systems," J. Manag. Inf. Syst., vol. 24, no. 3, pp. 45–77, 2007.

[12] J. Pries-Heje and R. Baskerville, "the Design Theory Nexus.," MIS Q., vol. 32, no. 4, pp. 731–755, 2008.

[13] P. Heinrich and A. Richter, "Captured and structured practices of workers and contexts of organizations - Project Report - FACTS4WORKERS: Worker-Centric Workplaces in Smart Factories," 2015.

[14] A. Vera-Baquero, R. Colomo-Palacios, and O. Molloy, "Real-time business activity monitoring and analysis of process performance on big-data domains," Telemat. Informatics, vol. 33, no. 3, pp. 793–807, Aug. 2016.

[15] G. Campatelli, A. Richter, and A. Stocker, "A collaborative knowledge management approach to empower manufacturing workers," Int. J. Knowl. Manag., vol. 12, no. 4, pp. 37–50, 2016.

Activity Recognition With Multiple Wearable Sensors for Industrial Applications

Adrien Malaisé, Pauline Maurice, Francis Colas, François Charpillet and Serena Ivaldi

Inria, Villers-lès-Nancy, F-54600, France
Université de Lorraine, Loria, UMR 7503, Vandoeuvre-lès-Nancy, F-54506, France
CNRS, Loria, UMR 7503, Vandoeuvre-lès-Nancy, F-54506, France
Email: firstname.surname@inria.fr

Abstract—**In this paper, we address the problem of recognizing the current activity performed by a human operator, providing an information useful for automatic ergonomic evaluation for industrial applications. While the majority of research in activity recognition relies on cameras observing the human, here we explore the use of wearable sensors, which are more suitable in industrial environments. We use a wearable motion tracking suit and a sensorized glove. We describe our approach for activity recognition with a probabilistic model based on Hidden Markov Models, applied to the problem of recognizing elementary activities during a pick-and-place task inspired by a manufacturing scenario. We show that our model is able to correctly recognize the activities with 96% of precision if both sensors are used.**

Keywords–Activity recognition; Hidden Markov Model; Wearable sensors.

I. INTRODUCTION

In developed countries, work-related musculoskeletal disorders (MSDs) are a major health issue. MSDs affect almost 50 % of industrial workers and represent an important cost for companies [1]. In order to reduce the prevalence of work-related MSDs, the ergonomics of the workplace needs to be evaluated and improved. Standards ergonomic assessment methods rely on pen-and-paper worksheets filled by experts, such as the commonly used European Assembly Worksheet (EAWS) [2][3]. Some digital human modeling software provide automatic filling of these ergonomic worksheets [4], but this cannot be done directly from raw data (video, motion capture, *etc.*) because the scoring system depends on the activity that is being performed (*e.g.*, walking, bending, carrying an object). The software user has first to manually identify the different types of movements occurring in the task. Therefore, there exists no tool to inform a worker in real-time whether s/he is performing a task in an ergonomic way or not. Yet, such an evaluation could help reducing the risk of MSDs. This is one of the objectives of the European AnDy project [5].

The first step towards a fully automatic ergonomic assessment is to automatically identify the different activities within an industrial task. To address this problem, this paper proposes a method based on wearable sensors and Hidden Markov Model (HMM). We focus our activity recognition on a pick-and-place task inspired by a manufacturing scenario. The whole-body motions of the operator are recorded with inertial sensors embedded in a suit. Though motion-capture based activity recognition using HMM already exists [6][7], the recognition rate is not yet perfect and could be improved. This can be an issue for industrial applications. Therefore,

a.

b.

Figure 1. Wearable sensors used in the experiment: (a) XSens MVN suit [16]; (b) e-glove from Emphasis Telematics.

we propose to complement the motion capture system with a glove embedding force sensors to detect hand contacts with the manipulated objects. This paper focuses on evaluating the benefit of using the contact information for the recognition performance with HMM-based models.

The paper is organized as follows: Section II presents state-of-the-art activity recognition methods based either on external sensors or on wearable sensors. Section III describes the proposed HMM-based recognition method and presents the experimental test-bed. The results of the comparison with *vs.* without contact information are presented in Section IV and discussed in Section V.

II. RELATED WORK

A. Motion capture based activity recognition

Human activity recognition methods can exploit external or exteroceptive sensors and wearable sensors [6][8][9].

Most external sensors approaches use vision-based systems, such as RGB-D cameras or optical motion capture systems. RGB-D cameras, such as Microsoft Kinect, require

Figure 2. Examples of activities extracted from the MVN Studio software. A: WAIT, B: REACH, C: CARRY, D: PLACE, E: WALK.

image processing to extract motion features. Conversely, in optical motion capture, the 3D trajectories of markers placed on the user are directly retrieved. A major problem of vision-based systems is that the user must always be in the camera's field of view, which limits the applicability in complex spaces. Occlusion of markers is another issue for robust motion detection, especially in cluttered environments.

To avoid these issues that are frequent in industrial conditions, wearable sensors can be used. Such sensors are then directly attached to the user, and no external sensor is needed. Inertial sensors placed on the limbs and torso of the user are the most commonly used [10] [11].

B. Algorithms for activity recognition

Classification algorithms have been widely used to recognize human daily activities, such as walking, sitting or lying [12][10]. Using three inertial sensors placed on the chest, right thigh and left ankle, Attal et al. [10] compared the k-Nearest Neighbor (k-NN), Support Vector Machines (SVM), and HMM algorithms for both supervised and unsupervised learning. They showed that with supervised learning k-NN gives the best performance, whereas with unsupervised learning HMM performs best. They showed that main advantage of using HMM was that the model took the temporal aspect into account. Dubois and Charpillet [12] showed that HMM can efficiently discriminate falls from other daily life activities. Mandery et al. [13] used HMM to identify the best performing sets of features for dimensionality reduction of motion capture data. They showed that a small subset of features was sufficient to perform accurate recognition. Interestingly, the velocity of the whole-body center of mass was always included in the relevant features.

All the aforementioned studies only used motion capture data. Conversely, Wächter and Asfour [14] used optical devices to track not only humans but also objects motions. The distance between the human and tracked objects was used to detect contact and pre-segment the data before the recognition step. Coupeté et al. [15] addressed the problem of real-time activity recognition in an industrial environment using HMM and object-related information. They used depth-cameras to capture human motion and inertial sensors to track tools manipulated by the worker. They showed that the tool-related information improved the classification performance from 80% to 94%.

III. METHOD

A. Experimental protocol

1) Material: We used two wearable systems: the MVN Link suit from Xsens [16] (Figure 1a) and the e-glove from Emphasis Telematics [17] (Figure 1b). The XSens MVN suit was used to capture the whole-body human motion with 17 wireless inertial sensors embedded in a lycra suit. The suit information was combined with a glove containing force sensors on the fingertips of thumb, index and middle fingers and on the palm. However, in this paper, we used only the palm force information to detect contacts.

The sample rates of the MVN suit and the glove are 240 Hz and 100 Hz, respectively. To synchronize the data, both systems used the same wireless network during data collection, and each recorded sample was associated to an absolute time-stamps value.

2) Task description: To evaluate our method, we designed a pick-and-place task of a 6 kg bar, inspired by packaging tasks on assembly lines in manufacturing industry.

One male participant performed 8 sequences of the task, with each sequence consisting of 6 to 8 pick-and-place. Each sequence started and ended in the same neutral pose. The bar was initially placed at a height of 45 cm on a 100×50 cm flat support. The participant was instructed to take the bar with both hands, carry it to the other side of the support, place the bar there and return to the initial position to perform the next iteration. Each sequence lasted around one minute. In order to add variability in the data, the participant was instructed to change the position of his hands on the bar, and to follow two different paths when going to and coming from the bar final position.

We defined seven states/activities (Figure 2):

- WAIT: standing still
- REACH: bending forward, without the bar
- PICK: standing up straight while holding the bar
- CARRY: walking while carrying the bar in the hands
- PLACE: bending forwards with the bar in the hands
- RELEASE: standing up straight with empty hands
- WALK: walking without holding the bar

B. Activity recognition algorithm

1) Hidden Markov Model: We use HMM-based supervised learning to recognize the activities with the `hmmlearn` [18] library in Python. The model is defined by N states representing the activities, such as WALK or PLACE (all activities are presented in Section III-A2), with $S = \{s_1, s_2, ..., s_N\}$ being the set of possible states. Each recorded sequence $k \in [1, K = 8]$ is represented by a series of discrete states $Q^k = \{q_0^k, q_1^k, ..., q_t^k, ...q_T^k\}$ and a series of T observations $X^k = \{x_1^k, ..., x_t^k, ..., x_T^k\}$ corresponding to motion capture and glove data. For each instant, the goal is to infer the current hidden state, such as $q_t^k = s_i$.

Three parameters $\{\Pi, A, B\}$ represent the model. $\Pi = \{\pi_1, \pi_2, ..., \pi_N\}$ denotes the initial state probabilities and is learned from the training set. For each state, π_i is equal

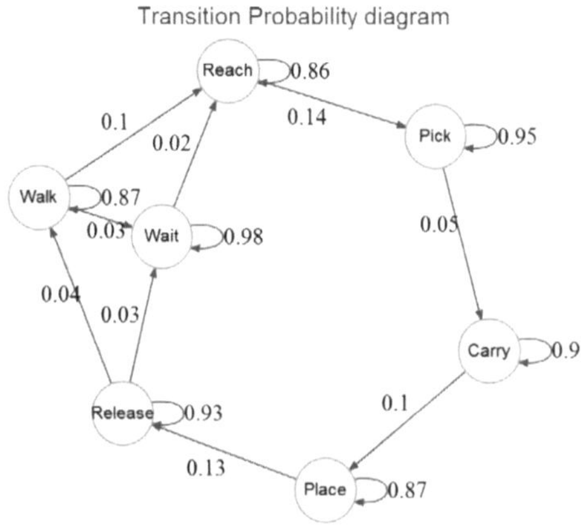

Figure 3. Probability transition diagram. The graph is not fully connected because some transitions are impossible. For instance, to PLACE an object, it first needs to be PICKED.

to the frequency of appearance of this state at the start of a sequence as in (1). $A = \{a_{ij}\}$ is the transition matrix probability, where a_{ij} is equal to the frequency of s_i following s_j in the training set (2) The transition matrix can also be represented by a probability transition diagram (Figure 3). $B = \{b_1, ..., b_N\}$ represents the emission distribution that models the observation (3). For each state, the emission b_i is computed as a multivariate Gaussian $\mathcal{N}(X, \mu_i, \Sigma_i)$ with μ_i and Σ_i the mean vector and the covariance matrix of the Gaussian variable, respectively. μ_i and Σ_i are learned from the observations X related to the state s_i in the training set.

$$\pi_i = p(q_0 = s_i) = \frac{\sum_{k=1}^{K-1} q_0^k = s_i}{K}, i \in [1, N] \quad (1)$$

$$a_{ij} = \frac{\sum_{k=1}^{K-1} \sum_{t=1}^{T} (q_t^k = s_j).(q_{t-1}^k = s_i)}{\sum_{k=1}^{K-1} \sum_{t=1}^{T} (q_{t-1}^k = s_i)}, i, j \in [1, N] \quad (2)$$

$$b_i = p(X|q_t = s_i) = \mathcal{N}(\mu_i, \sigma_i^2), i \in [1, N] \quad (3)$$

In this paper, we used $N = 7$, while T is different for each recorded sequence, from 444 samples for the shortest sequence to 715 samples for the longest one.

2) Normalization: As the data (observations) have different units (*e.g.*, Cartesian position, velocity, contact information), they need to be normalized. $\widetilde{x_t}$ is the vector containing the data x_t normalized within the range [-1,1]:

$$\widetilde{x_t} = 2.\frac{x_t - x_{min}}{x_{max} - x_{min}} - 1 \quad (4)$$

where x_{min} and x_{max} are constants computed from the data in the training set.

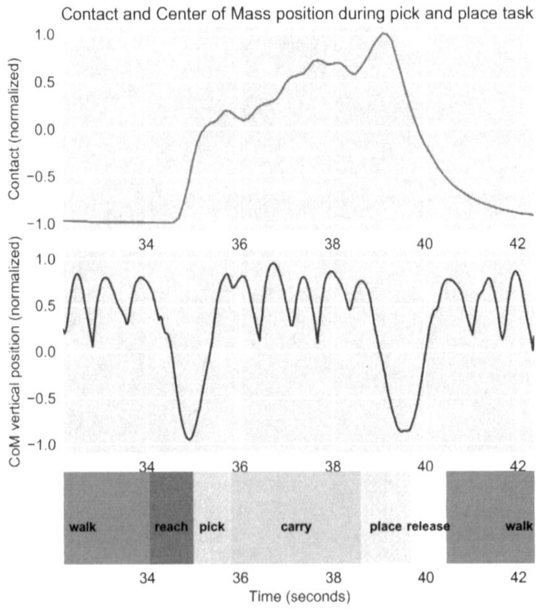

Figure 4. Example of normalized data used to train the model. Top: Time-series of the contact information from the e-glove; Middle: Time-series of the center of mass vertical position; Bottom: Manually labeled activities.

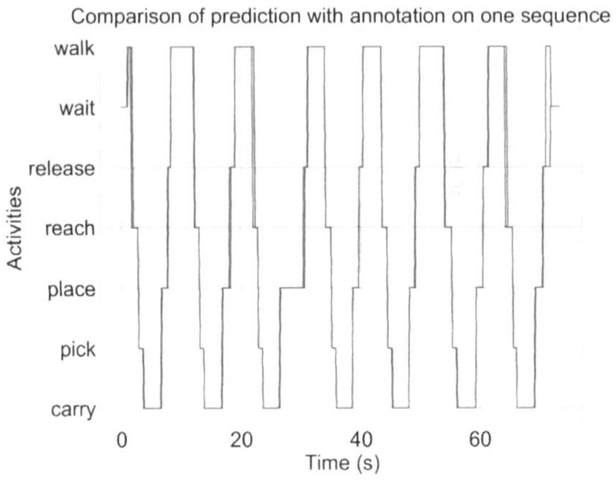

Figure 5. Comparison of manually annotated activities (red) and predicted activities (green).

3) Sliding window: In order to decrease the computational complexity and to reduce noise in the data, a sliding window filter is applied to the recorded motion capture and glove data. For each time window, the observation vector contains the average values of the data across this window. A 60 samples window is used, with an overlap of 30 samples between each window. As the frequency of the MVN Link system is 240 Hz, a window is 250 ms long. Given the 30 frames overlap, there is a new observation every 125 ms. This rate is sufficient since each activity lasts more than one second.

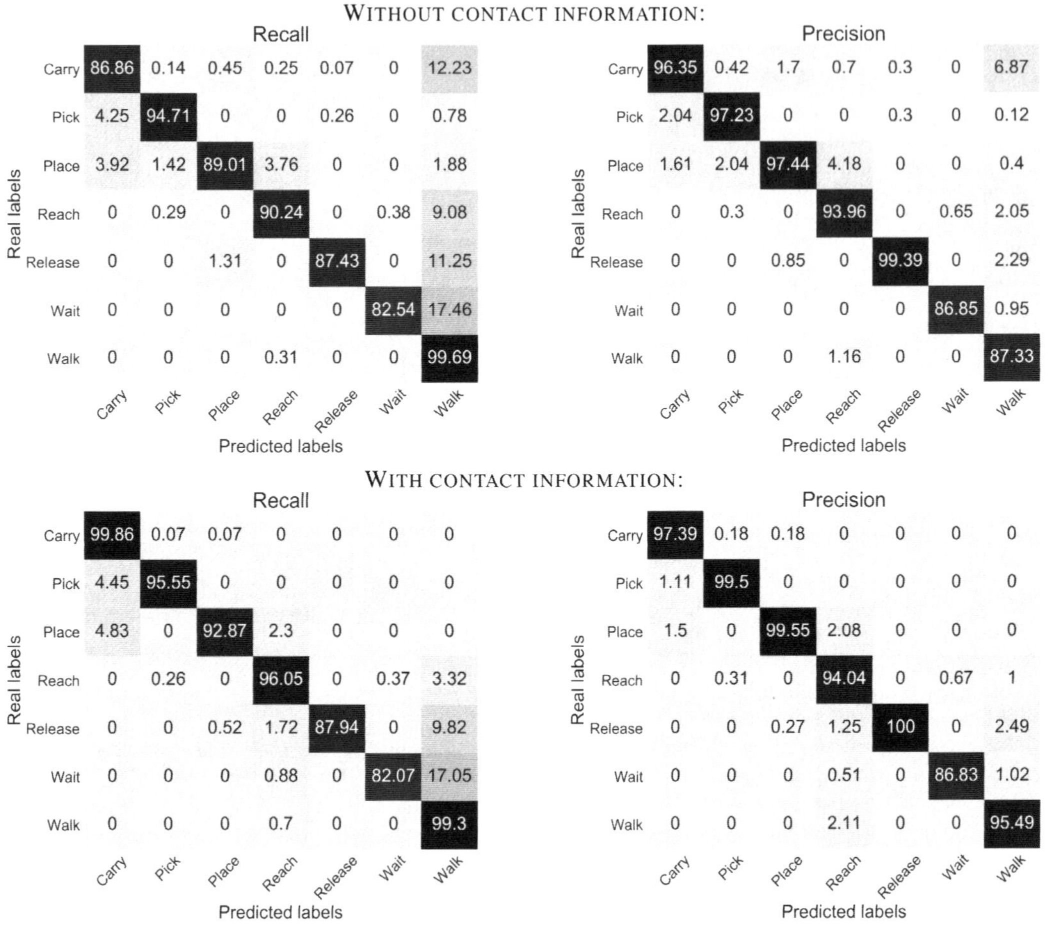

Figure 6. Recall and Precision scores for each state without (top) and with (bottom) contact information.

4) Data annotation: Given that we used supervised learning, the recorded sequences were manually segmented and annotated with the start and end of the different activities by using the Anvil annotation software [19]. .

C. Features selection

Based on the results of [13] and our pilot tests, we include the following motion-related features in the observation X: the vertical position of the center of mass, the 3D velocity of the center of mass, and the 3D velocity of both hands. The contact information is the normal force on the palm. Therefore, the observation vector x_t at each instant t is $x_t \in R^{10}$ without the contact information, and $x_t \in R^{11}$ with it.

D. Data analysis

1) Evaluation: The model is evaluated with cross-validation on the dataset consisting of $K = 8$ recorded sequences. At each iteration, the database is split between the training set that contains $K - 1$ sequences and the test set that contains 1 sequence. The training set is used to learn the parameters of the model, while the test set is used for the evaluation.

2) Metrics: In order to evaluate the advantage of adding the contact information, the recognition performances with and without contact information are compared on the same sequences. The model is evaluated with the Recall score, Precision score and F1-score (harmonic mean of *precision* and *recall*) as in (5 - 7):

$$\text{Recall}_i = \frac{\text{Number of samples correctly classified as class i}}{\text{Number of samples that belong to the class i}} \quad (5)$$

$$\text{Precision}_i = \frac{\text{Number of samples correctly classified as class i}}{\text{Number of samples classified as class i}} \quad (6)$$

$$\text{F1-score}_i = 2.\frac{\text{Precision}_i.\text{Recall}_i}{\text{Precision}_i + \text{Recall}_i} \quad (7)$$

For each metric, an average score is computed on all the iterations of the cross-validation.

IV. RESULTS

A. First insight

Some patterns are observable when the data of the vertical position of the center of mass and contact information are compared to the annotated activities (Figure 4). When the participant performs the activities WALK, REACH and RELEASE,

TABLE I. RECOGNITION PERFORMANCE (%) WITH AND WITHOUT CONTACT INFORMATION (LEFT AND MIDDLE COLUMNS), AND PERFORMANCE COMPARISON WITH WILCOXON TEST (RIGHT COLUMN).

	No contact	Contact	*p-value*
Recall	90.07	93.38	0.06
Precision	94.08	96.12	0.16
F1-score	91.99	94.71	0.05

the contact information data are equal to the minimum possible value. Whereas during PICK, CARRY and PLACE activities, the contact data have positive values. We can also identify when the user bends forwards and stands up straight by looking at the center of mass position. During the WALK and CARRY states, there are oscillations around a value of 0.5.

B. Margin of error

Most activities are correctly identified (Figure 5), but the transition between two states does not always happen at the exact same frame on the real and the predicted case. This kind of error is not relevant, as our future application does not require a 125 ms accuracy. Therefore, the performance scores are computed with a margin of error of one 125 ms time window before and after each observation. The classification is considered correct if the predicted state at time t corresponds to the annotated state at either time $t-1$, t, or $t+1$.

C. Overall results

The performance for each score with and without glove is presented in Table I. For each score, the contact information improves the results. The results are compared with a Wilcoxon signed-rank test and we found a significant difference for the F1-score (*p-value* $= 0.05$).

D. Performance for each activity

Figure 6 presents the precision and recall scores for each states. There is mainly a confusion between the RELEASE and WALK activities. This is mainly due to the fact that at the end of each sequence, the subject returns to a neutral position with a little step after placing the last bar. In the annotation, it was labeled RELEASE then WAIT without WALK transition, but the step was classified by the model as *walking* (this error can also be seen in Figure 5).

Figure 7 presents a comparison of the scores for each state for both conditions. We computed a Wilcoxon signed-rank test on the measure performance of *recall*, *precision* and *F1-score*. For most of the measures, there is no significant difference with or without the use of the contact information. We found a significant difference with the F1-score of PICK task, the precision score of PLACE activity, the recall score of REACH task and the precision and F1-score of WALK activity. However, when the contact information is added, there is an improvement of the performances for the recognition of each activity and a reduction of the uncertainty.

Overall, our results show that using both kinetics information and contact information is beneficial for activity recognition with our HMM-based model.

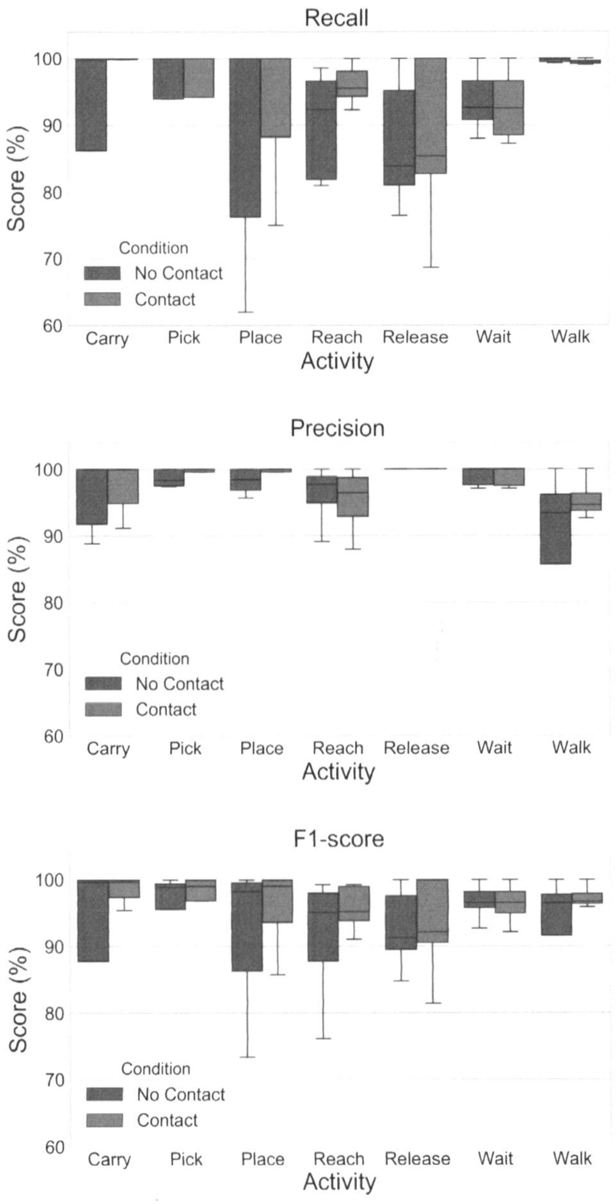

Figure 7. Classification performance with and without contact information for each activity: Recall score (top), Precision score (middle), and F1-score (bottom).

V. CONCLUSION

This paper presents a contextual use of Hidden Markov Model for activity recognition, applied to a pick-and-place task. We evaluate the benefit of using the hand-object contact information in addition to kinetics information to improve the classification performance. The overall performance is better by about 3 % when the contact information is added. The contact information could also increase the robustness of the recognition in case of data loss. For instance, if data corresponding to the PICK activity is unavailable, WALK and CARRY can easily be confused when the recognition is based on motion features only. With the contact information, the differentiation becomes trivial.

Nevertheless, the dataset we used consists of a single task. In order to test if the usefulness of the contact information can be generalized, future work includes collecting a dataset with more tasks and more variability in the tasks and related activities. Finally, the automation of the recognition process could be increased by adding an automatic selection of relevant features among all the available ones.

ACKNOWLEDGEMENTS

This work was supported by the European Union's Horizon 2020 Research and Innovation Programme under Grant Agreement No. 731540 (project AnDy). The authors wish to thank Lars Fritzsche and Emphasis Telematics SA (Dr. Giorgos Papapanagiotakis, Dr. Michalis Miatidis, Panos Stogiannos, Giannis Kantaris, Dimitris Potiriadis) for their support with the e-glove.

REFERENCES

[1] E. Schneider, X. Irastorza, M. Bakhuys Roozeboom, and I. Houtman, "Osh in figures: occupational safety and health in the transport sector-an overview," 2010.

[2] G. Li and P. Buckle, "Current techniques for assessing physical exposure to work-related musculoskeletal risks, with emphasis on posture-based methods," *Ergonomics*, vol. 42, no. 5, pp. 674–695, 1999.

[3] K. Schaub, G. Caragnano, B. Britzke, and R. Bruder, "The European Assembly Worksheet," *Theoretical Issues in Ergonomics Science*, vol. 14, no. 6, pp. 616–639, 2013.

[4] T. Bossomaier, A. G. Bruzzone, A. Cimino, F. Longo, and G. Mirabelli, "Scientific approaches for the industrial workstations ergonomic design: A review." in *ECMS*, 2010, pp. 189–199.

[5] S. Ivaldi, L. Fritzsche, J. Babic, F. Stulp, M. Damsgaard, B. Graimann, G. Bellusci, and F. Nori, "Anticipatory models of human movements and dynamics: the roadmap of the andy project," in *Proc. International Conf. on Digital Human Models (DHM)*, 2017.

[6] O. D. Lara and M. A. Labrador, "A Survey on Human Activity Recognition using Wearable Sensors," *IEEE Communications Surveys & Tutorials*, vol. 15, no. 3, 2013.

[7] H. Junker, O. Amft, P. Lukowicz, and G. Tröster, "Gesture spotting with body-worn inertial sensors to detect user activities," *Pattern Recognition*, vol. 41, no. 6, pp. 2010–2024, Jun. 2008. [Online]. Available: http://www.sciencedirect.com/science/article/pii/S0031320307005110

[8] J. K. Aggarwal and L. Xia, "Human activity recognition from 3D data: A review," *Pattern Recognition Letters*, vol. 48, no. Supplement C, pp. 70–80, Oct. 2014. [Online]. Available: http://www.sciencedirect.com/science/article/pii/S0167865514001299

[9] L. Lo Presti and M. La Cascia, "3D skeleton-based human action classification: A survey," *Pattern Recognition*, vol. 53, no. Supplement C, pp. 130–147, May 2016. [Online]. Available: http://www.sciencedirect.com/science/article/pii/S0031320315004392

[10] F. Attal, S. Mohammed, M. Dedabrishvili, F. Chamroukhi, L. Oukhellou, and Y. Amirat, "Physical human activity recognition using wearable sensors," *Sensors*, vol. 15, no. 12, pp. 31 314–31 338, 2015.

[11] A. Y. Yang, S. Iyengar, P. Kuryloski, and R. Jafari, "Distributed segmentation and classification of human actions using a wearable motion sensor network," in *Computer Vision and Pattern Recognition Workshops, 2008. CVPRW'08. IEEE Computer Society Conference on.* IEEE, 2008, pp. 1–8.

[12] A. Dubois and F. Charpillet, "Human activities recognition with RGB-Depth camera using HMM," in *Engineering in Medicine and Biology Society (EMBC), 2013 35th Annual International Conference of the IEEE.* IEEE, 2013, pp. 4666–4669.

[13] C. Mandery, M. Plappert, J. Borras, and T. Asfour, "Dimensionality reduction for whole-body human motion recognition," in *Information Fusion (FUSION), 2016 19th International Conference on.* IEEE, 2016, pp. 355–362.

[14] M. Wächter and T. Asfour, "Hierarchical segmentation of manipulation actions based on object relations and motion characteristics," in *Advanced Robotics (ICAR), 2015 International Conference on.* IEEE, 2015, pp. 549–556. [Online]. Available: http://ieeexplore.ieee.org/abstract/document/7251510/

[15] E. Coupeté, F. Moutarde, S. Manitsaris, and O. Hugues, "Recognition of Technical Gestures for Human-Robot Collaboration in Factories," in *The Ninth International Conference on Advances in Computer-Human Interactions*, 2016.

[16] D. Roetenberg, H. Luinge, and P. Slycke, "Xsens MVN: full 6DOF human motion tracking using miniature inertial sensors," *Xsens Motion Technologies BV, Tech. Rep*, 2009.

[17] "e-glove | Emphasis Telematics," URL: http://www.emphasisnet.gr/e-glove/ [accessed: 2018-01-30].

[18] "hmmlearn 0.2.1 documentation," URL: http://hmmlearn.readthedocs.io/ [accessed: 2018-01-30].

[19] M. Kipp, L. F. von Hollen, M. C. Hrstka, and F. Zamponi, "Single-person and multi-party 3d visualizations for nonverbal communication analysis." in *LREC*, 2014, pp. 3393–3397.

Orientation and Mobility Skills Consideration for Visually Impaired Persons Based on Brain Activity

Hiroaki Inoue
Tokyo University of Science, SUWA
Faculty of Engineering
Chino-city, Japan
e-mail: hiroaki-inoue@rs.tus.ac.jp

Masaya Hori, Yusuke Kobayashi, Takuya Kiryu
Tokyo University of Science, SUWA
Engineering, management graduate course
Chino-city, Japan
e-mail: {gh17612, gh17608, gh17605}@ed.tus.ac.jp

Yoshikazu Seki
National Institute of Advanced Industrial Science and Technology (AIST)
Human Informatics Research Institute
Tsukuba-city, Japan
e-mail: yoshikazu-seki@aist.go.jp

Shunji Shimizu
Tokyo University of Science, SUWA
Jichi Medical University
Department of computer media engineering
Psychiatric Course
Chino-city, Japan
e-mail: shun@rs.tus.ac.jp

Abstract- **Visually impaired persons recognize their surrounding by using a white cane or a guide dog while they walk. This skill called "Orientation and Mobility" is difficult to learn. The training of the "Orientation and Mobility Skills" is performed at the school for visually impaired persons. However, the evaluation of this skill is limited to subjective evaluation by teacher. We have proposed that a quantitative evaluation of the "Orientation and Mobility Skills" should be required. In this paper, we tried to execute the quantitative evaluation of the "Orientation and Mobility Skills" using brain activity measurements. In this experiment, brain activity was measured when subjects are walking in the corridor alone or with a helper guide. Experimental subjects were sighted persons whose visual information was blocked during walking. The blood flow of prefrontal cortex was increased as the movement distance of the subject increased when subjects walked alone. From this result, it can be considered that the feeling of fear and the attention relayed to "Orientation and Mobility Skills" could be measured quantitatively by measuring human brain activities.**

Keywords-NIRS; Visually impaired person; Brain activity.

I. INTRODUCTION

A visually impaired person recognizes the surroundings using a white cane and/or a guide dog while walking. It is very important to hear the environmental sounds for recognition of their own position and surrounding situations in details. This means, visually impaired people need "Orientation and Mobility Skills" [1][2] to recognize the surrounding situation by using sound information [3][4]. "Orientation and Mobility Skills" are necessary to move in an unfamiliar place. The training to gain "Orientation and Mobility Skills" is carried out at the school for visually impaired. However, the evaluation of the education received is a subjective method by teachers belonging to the school for visually impaired person. It is difficult for the teacher to understand everything the student recognizes even if a student is able to successfully walk a very difficult path. There is also a method of estimating the stress state during exercise from HF / LF. However, HF / LF is affected by heart rate variability due to exercise [5]. Therefore, we have proposed that quantitative evaluation of the "Orientation and Mobility Skills" should be required.

Near-infrared spectroscopy (NIRS) is easier to be used to measure brain activity compared to other measurement methods of brain activity such as Positron Emission Tomography (PET) and functional Magnetic Resonance Imaging (fMRI). In these other brain activities measuring methods, the subject's posture needs to be fixed in a supine position. Obviously, brain activity measurement during walking is impossible with these devices. NIRS can measure brain activity while subjects exercise. However, NIRS measurement data is influenced by noise of various factors. For example, there are noises due to heartbeat and body movement. It is also difficult to separate multiple information stimuli into individual elements. In this paper, we measured the brain activity data for the quantitative evaluation of the "Orientation and Mobility Skills".

In Section II, we describe the experimental method conducted in this paper. In Section III, we describe brain activity data obtained by these experiments. In Section IV, we describe the relationship between brain activity data and the stimulation by experimental tasks. In Section V, we present the summary of this paper and future works.

II. EXPERIMENTAL METHOD

The three experiments performed in this paper are described below.

A) Measurement of brain activity when walking alone in the corridor without visual information.

In this experiment, the brain activity when subjects walked alone was measured. The walking distance was approximately 20m. The subjects had their visual information blocked by the eye mask. The resting time for stabilizing the brain activity of the subjects was set before and after walking. This resting time was more than 10 seconds. The experimental place was the corridor where subjects walk on a daily basis. These experiments were performed with no other pedestrians. Subjects were 6 males who were sighted persons. The average age of them is 23.6 years old (SD = 0.47).

The experimental task setting was set as shown in the upper part of Figure 3. All subjects of the experiment walked on the same corridor. The subjects were instructed to walk at a constant speed as much as possible. Subjects were orally instructed the timing to start walking and stop walking. The measurement equipment of brain activity used for the experiment is "Pocket NIRS", which was produced by DynaSense Inc. in Japan (Figure 2). This NIRS device is lightweight and could measure brain activity in two channels in the prefrontal cortex. Measurement can be performed at a sampling rate of 100 Hz.

B) Measurement of brain activity when subjects walk with helper guide in the corridor.

In the above experiment, subjects walked alone in the corridor. In this experiment, the subjects walked with the pedestrians who simulated the guide helper. The experiment method was the same as the previous experiment. The experimental method is shown in the lower part of Figure 3. Subjects were the same persons as the A) experiment.

C) *Measurement of brain activity when walking in a wide space with visual blocking.*

The environment of this experiment is different from the A) and B) experiments. This experiment was performed in a gymnasium. A large space like gymnasium has different acoustic characteristics from the corridor. Auditory information is important for visually impaired persons to perceive the surrounding environment. Visually impaired persons also use their echoes and environmental sounds to recognize their position and situation. Such ability is referred to as obstacle perception. In the corridor, subject's footsteps sound from corridor floor reach the ear of the subject in a short time. Thus, there is a possibility that the existence of the wall could be recognized from the echo sound. In the gymnasium, it takes longer time for subject's footsteps from gymnasium floor to reach the subjects. On account of not making the subject conscious with the floor, we conducted this experiment in the gymnasium. The method of this experiment was the same as the previous two experiments. Subjects were the same persons as the A) and B) experiments.

III. EXPERIMENTAL RESULTS

A) Measurement of brain activity when walking alone in the corridor without visual information.

Figure 4 shows an example of brain activity data when one subject walked alone. The red line shows the change in oxygenated hemoglobin. The blue line shows the change in deoxygenated hemoglobin. As a result of this experiment, the cerebral blood flow did not increase when the subject started walking according to the instructions. When the movement distance of the subject increased to some extent, a

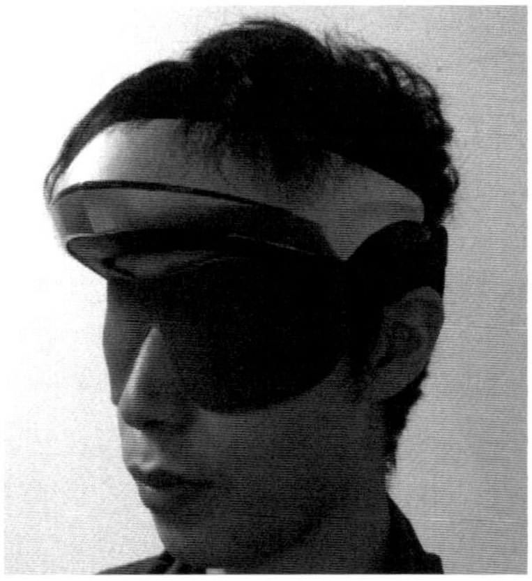

Figure 1. NIRS and eye mask which were wear when these experiments.

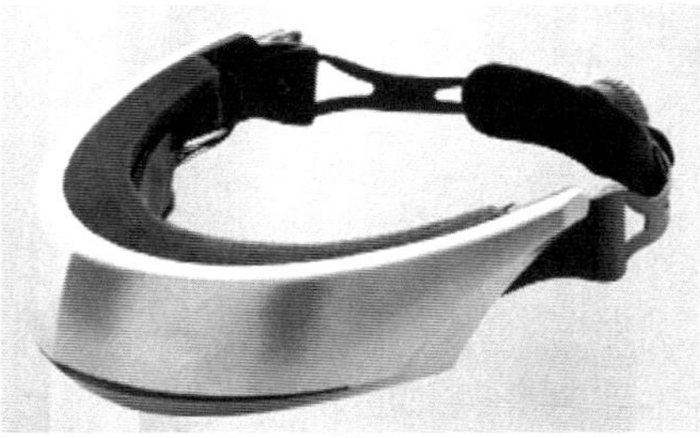

Figure 2. NIRS used in these experiments.

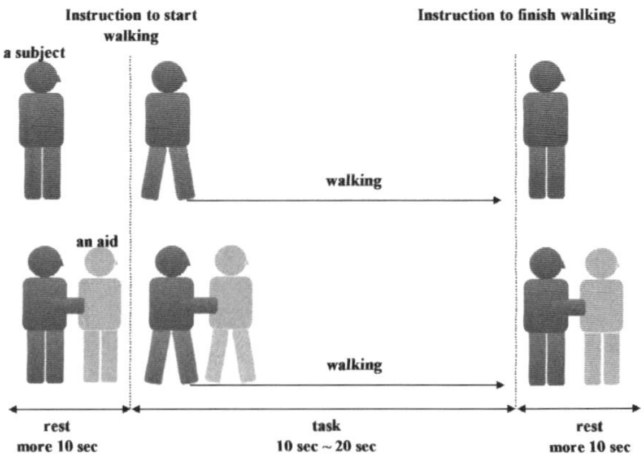

Figure 3. Flow of experiments

large increase in oxygenated hemoglobin could be confirmed on right and left prefrontal cortex. After subjects were instructed to stop walking, the blood flow on right and left prefrontal cortex gradually decreased. This tendency was seen from most subjects.

B) Measurement of brain activity when subjects walk with a helper guide in the corridor.

Figure 5 shows the brain activity result of the subjects when walking with a pedestrian who simulated a guide helper. In this experiment, the subject's cerebral blood flow decreased slightly after the onset of the gait task. Even when the migration distance increased, the concentration of oxygenated hemoglobin in the blood did not increase greatly. In an oral survey after the experiment, subjects said that they were able to concentrate on walking without feeling uneasy in this experiment.

C) *Measurement of brain activity when walking in a wide space with visual blocking.*

Figure 6 shows the measurement results when walking alone. Figure 7 shows the result of brain activity when accompanied by a pedestrian simulating a helper guide. An increase of blood flow on the prefrontal cortex was seen when the subject received instructions to walk. However, an increase in oxygenated hemoglobin that continued was not confirmed during walking. When subjects walk with a helper guide, there was no change in oxygenated hemoglobin similar to the previous experiment in the corridors.

IV. DISCUSSION

In these experiments, measuring brain activity was performed when subjects walked with a helper guide and when subjects walked alone. When subjects walked alone, it could be considered that subjects were in the state of mental strain. When subjects walked with a pedestrian who simulated a helper guide, subjects could rely on a pedestrian for safety confirmation and were able to walk by concentrating on walking. When subjects walked alone, most subject's oxygenated hemoglobin on prefrontal cortex did not show an increase after instruction to start walking. As subject's walking distance increased, most subject's oxygenated hemoglobin on prefrontal cortex was increased. Such a change in oxygenated hemoglobin is considered that subjects are strongly conscious of the possibility of collision with the wall or other obstacles. When subjects stopped walking, the oxygenated hemoglobin in prefrontal cortex decreased gradually.

In the case of accompanying the pedestrian who

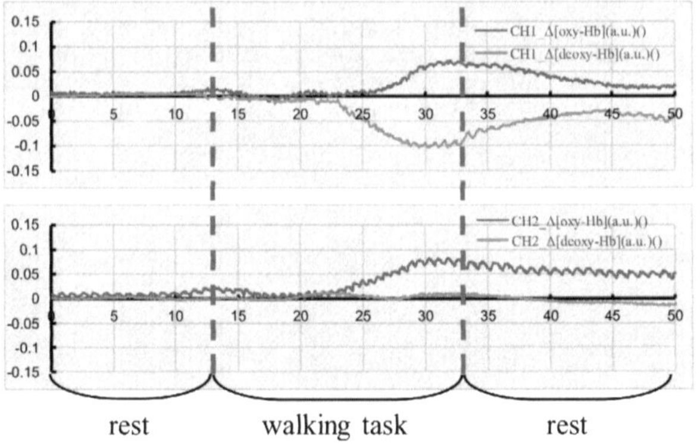

Figure 4. Measurement result of brain activity when the subject walked alone.

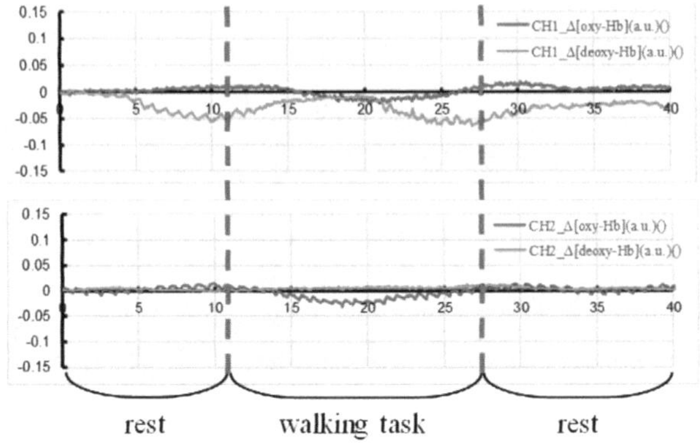

Figure 5. Measurement results of brain activity when subjects walked with guide helper.

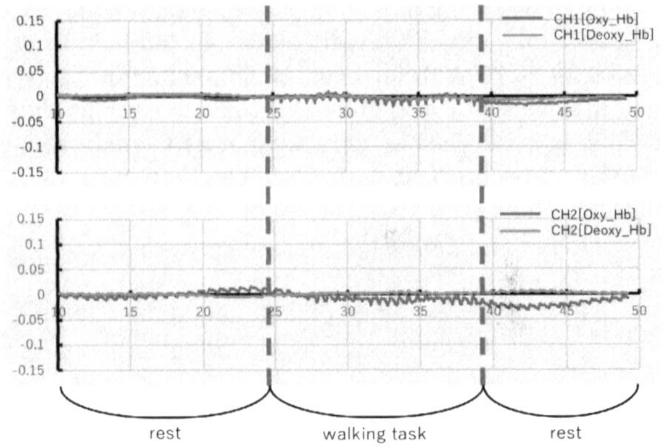

Figure 6. Measurement result of brain activity when the subject walked alone.

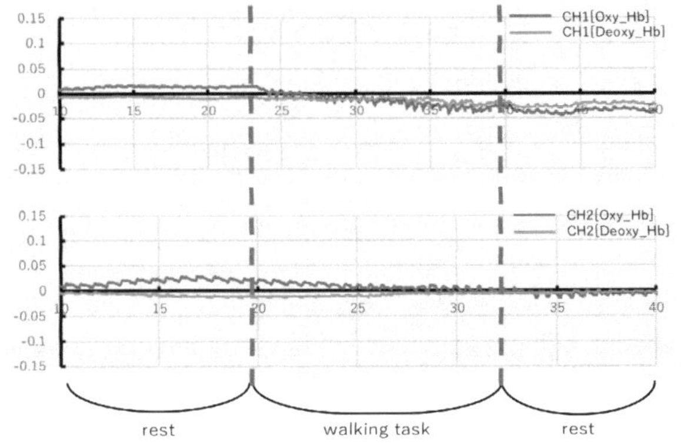

Figure 7. Measurement result of brain activity when the subject walked alone.

simulated with helper guide, an increase of oxygenated hemoglobin in prefrontal cortex as compared with the case of walking alone could not be confirmed. Oxygenated hemoglobin in the prefrontal cortex of the subjects decreased slightly during walking.

In addition, when subjects walked alone in the large space such as a gymnasium, no increase in oxygenated hemoglobin was observed with increased walking distance. Therefore, it is considered that the subject was able to walk without being conscious of a collision with a wall or an obstacle.

V. CONCLUSION

NIRS devices can measure brain activity easily without restraining the subject compared to other brain activity measuring devices. However, the obtained brain activity data may contain many noises originating from body movements and heartbeats. In the experiment conducted in this paper, the subjects were instructed to keep the walking speed as constant as possible. As the result, only heartbeat noise could be confirmed. This noise was sufficiently smaller than the brain activity data. Previous studies have not observed a large change in oxygenated hemoglobin during slow walking as well [6].

It is thought that brain activities data which were measured in these experiments include subjects' consciousness of collision with walls and obstacles. We think that there is a possibility to quantitatively measure if visually impaired persons correctly process the information and walk without feeling uneasy.

In the future work, we think that it is necessary to increase the number of subjects and types of experimental tasks. The place we used for experiments in this paper was a facility frequently used by subjects. As a psychological element, it is an experimental task that does not include brand new environment or interest.

REFERENCES

[1] Luigi F. Cuturi, Elena Aggius-Vella, Claudio Campus, Alberto Parmiggiani, Monica Gori, "From science to technology: Orientation and mobility in blind children and adults, " Neuroscience & Biobehavioral Reviews, Vol. 71, Pages 240-251, Dec 2016.

[2] Orly Lahav, David W. Schloerb, Mandayam A. Srinivasan, "Rehabilitation program integrating virtual environment to improve orientation and mobility skills for people who are blind," Computers & Education, Vol.80, pp. 1-14, Jan 2015.

[3] Y. Seki, T. Sato, "A training system of orientation and mobility for blind people using acoustic virtual reality," IEEE Trans. Neural Syst. Rehabil. Eng., Feb, vol. 19, no1, pp. 95-104, 2011.

[4] J. Bluaert, "Spatial Hearing," Oct, MIT Press published, 1996.

[5] A. Pichon, C. Bisschop, M. Roulaud, A. Denjean, "Spectral analysis of heart rate variability during exercise in trained subjects," Medicine & Science in Sports & Exercise, Oct, vol. 36, pp. 1702-1708, 2004.

[6] Mitsuo Suzuki, Ichiro Miyai, Takeshi Ono, Ichiro Oda, Ikuo Konishi, Takanori Kochiyama and Kisou Kubotaa, "Prefrontal and premotor cortices are involved in adapting walking and running speed on the treadmill:an optical imaging study," NeuroImage vol 23, pp. 1020-1026, 2004.

International Academy, Research,
and Industry Association (IARIA)
412 Derby Way
Wilmington, DE 19810

ISBN 978-1-5108-6171-8

CURRAN ASSOCIATES INC.
proceedings.com

Global Symposium on Leadership and Project Management 2025

Online
21-22 August 2025